# Lecture Notes in Computer Scie

*Commenced Publication in 1973*
Founding and Former Series Editors:
Gerhard Goos, Juris Hartmanis, and Jan van Leeuwen

Jan L. Camenisch   Christian S. Collberg
Neil F. Johnson   Phil Sallee (Eds.)

# Information Hiding

8th International Workshop, IH 2006
Alexandria, VA, USA, July 10-12, 2006
Revised Selcted Papers

 Springer

Volume Editors

Jan L. Camenisch
IBM Research
CH-8803 Rüschlikon, Switzerland
E-mail: jca@zurich.ibm.com

Christian S. Collberg
The University of Arizona
Tucson, AZ 85721, USA
E-mail: collberg@cs.arizona.edu

Neil F. Johnson
Johnson & Johnson Technology Consultants
Vienna, VA 22183, USA
E-mail: nfi@jjtc.com
and
Booz Allen Hamilton
B-8042, 8283 Greensboro Drive, MCLean
VA 22102, USA
E-mail: Johnson_neil@bah.com

Phil Sallee
Booz Allen Hamilton
B-8042, 8283 Greensboro Drive, MCLean
VA 22102, USA
E-mail: sallee_phil@bah.com

Library of Congress Control Number: 2007935081

CR Subject Classification (1998): E.3, K.6.5, K.4.1, K.5.1, D.4.6, E.4, C.2, H.4.3, H.3, H.5.1

LNCS Sublibrary: SL 4 – Security and Cryptology

ISSN        0302-9743
ISBN-10     3-540-74123-2 Springer Berlin Heidelberg New York
ISBN-13     978-3-540-74123-7 Springer Berlin Heidelberg New York

Springer is a part of Springer Science+Business Media

springer.com

© Springer-Verlag Berlin Heidelberg 2007
Printed in Germany

Typesetting: Camera-ready by author, data conversion by Scientific Publishing Services, Chennai, India
Printed on acid-free paper      SPIN: 12104833      06/3180      5 4 3 2 1 0

# Preface

These proceedings contain the 25 papers that were accepted for presentation at the Eighth Information Hiding Conference, held July 10–12, 2006 in Old Town Alexandria, Virginia. The papers were selected by the Program Committee from more than 70 submissions on the basis of their novelty, originality, and scientific merit. We are grateful to all authors who submitted their work for consideration. The papers were divided into ten sessions [Watermarking, Information Hiding and Networking, Data Hiding in Unusual Content (2 sessions), Fundamentals, Software Protection, Steganalysis, Steganography (2 sessions), and Subliminal Channels], showing the breadth of research in the field. This year was an important one in the history of the IHW: "Workshop" was dropped from the name to show that the field has matured and that the conference has become the premier venue for the dissemination of new results.

The conference employed a double-blind reviewing process. Each paper was examined by at least three reviewers. Papers submitted by Program Committee members were held to a higher standard. We relied on the advice of outside colleagues and would like to extend our thanks for their contribution to the paper selection process and their dedication to excellence in research.

We thank our sponsors Booz Allen Hamilton and Johnson & Johnson Technology Consultants for their financial and logistic support, including local arrangements, printing the pre-proceedings, and organizing the registration. The walking tour of Old Town Alexandria organized by Ira Moskowitz and the dessert cruise on board the Miss Christin were enjoyable highlights of the social program and we thank the organizers! Roger Zimmermann helped to run the submission server and without the help of Björn Assmann you would not be holding these proceedings in your hands. Thank you guys!

Finally, we wish to thank the many researchers who have contributed to extending the state of the art for information hiding research and hope these proceedings will be helpful for future developments.

January 2007

Jan Camenisch
Christian Collberg
Neil F. Johnson
Phil Sallee

# Organization

## Program Committee

Ross J. Anderson (University of Cambridge, UK)
Mauro Barni (Università di Siena, Italy)
Jack Brassil (HP Laboratories, USA)
Jan Camenisch (IBM Zurich Research Laboratory, Switzerland)
Christian Collberg (University of Arizona, USA)
Ee-Chien Chang (National University of Singapore, Singapore)
Ingemar J. Cox (University College London, UK)
Jessica Fridrich (SUNY Binghamton, USA)
Neil F. Johnson (Booz Allen Hamilton and JJTC, USA)
John McHugh (SEI/CERT, USA)
Ira S. Moskowitz (Naval Research Laboratory, USA)
Stefan Katzenbeisser (Philips Research, The Netherlands)
Darko Kirovski (Microsoft Research, USA)
Richard C. Owens (University of Toronto, Canada)
Andreas Pfitzmann (Dresden University of Technology, Germany)
Phil Sallee (Booz Allen Hamilton, USA)
Michiel van der Veen (Philips Research, The Netherlands)

## External Reviewers

Farid Ahmed
Richard Bergmair
Mike Bergmann
Rainer Boehme
Roberto Caldelli
Mehmet Celik
Massimiliano Corsini
Scott Craver
Alessia De Rosa
Shan He
Susan Hohenberger

Andrew Ker
Johannes Kinder
Patty Lafferty
Aweke Lemma
Keye Martin
Ginger Myles
Alessandro Piva
Mila dalla Preda
Victor Raskin
Antje Schneidewind
Franz Schneidewind

Dagmar Schönfeld
Ashwin Swaminathan
Morton Swimmer
James Troupe
Dan Wallach
Andreas Westfeld
Greg Zaverucha
Min Wu

# Table of Contents

## Hamiltonian Mechanics

## Video Watermarking by Using Geometic Warping Without Visible Artifacts

# Natural Watermarking: A Secure Spread Spectrum Technique for WOA

Patrick Bas[1,2] and François Cayre[2]

[1] CIS / Helsinki University of Technology
P.O. Box 5400
FI-02015 HUT FINLAND
[2] LIS/INPG
961, rue de la Houille Blanche BP 46
F-38042 St. Martin d'Hères Cedex, France

**Abstract.** This paper presents a spread spectrum (SS) watermarking technique that is secure against carriers estimation in a Watermark Only Attack framework. After reviewing the sufficient conditions to design secure algorithms for watermarking and steganography, we present a setup based on Blind Source Separation (BSS) theory to assess the lack of security of classical SS techniques such as classical SS or ISS. We motivate a new SS watermarking algorithm called Natural Watermarking (NW) where the estimation of the secret carriers is impossible and which achieves perfect secrecy thanks to unchanged Gaussian distributions of the secret carriers. The theoretical evaluation of the NW security is carried out and the case of multi-bit embedding is addressed. Finally, a robust extension of NW is presented and the properties of NW and Robust-NW are both practically verified.

## 1 Introduction

*Robustness*, *capacity* and *imperceptibility* have always been considered, since the very beginning of watermarking, as the main three constraints to respect in order to build a valuable watermarking scheme. Recently the watermarking community has thrown light on the problem of *security* which appears also to be a fundamental constraint to respect in order to guaranty the usability of a watermarking technology. Several authors [1][2][3] showed that some information about the secret key may leak from several observations of watermarked pieces of content. Using this information, it may be possible to estimate the secret key, and then to destroy the security of the considered scheme by removing, copying or altering the embedded messages. Several studies address also the security of practical watermarking techniques for digital images [4][5].

In this paper, we tackle the problem of security for the well-known class of spread spectrum (SS) watermarking schemes. In this case, the secret key which practically is the seed of a random generator, corresponds to the set of secret carriers that is used to convey the information. It is important to note that an attacker does not need the seed used to initialiaze the random number generator: the secret carriers are good enough to attack the watermark. We propose a

J. Camenisch et al. (Eds.): IH 2006, LNCS 4437, pp. 1–14, 2007.

watermarking scheme that is secure (e.g. it does not offer information leakage of the secret key) for the class of Watermark Only Attacks (WOA). This class of attacks, proposed by [1], considers an attack that is based on the observation of watermarked contents, watermarked with the same key but conveying different messages. We named the proposed scheme *natural spread spectrum watermarking* because embedding is achieved without altering the natural distribution of each secret carrier before and after embedding. As shown in the paper, this characteristic enables to achieve perfect secrecy. Moreover, when embedding several bits, we show that if each carrier is embedded in the contents with an amplitude following a Gaussian distribution, it is impossible to individually estimate the carriers.

The rest of the paper is divided into five sections. First, the security of classical SS techniques for WOA are analysed as a Blind Source Separation (BSS) problem: in section 2 we show that the characterisation of the distributions of each carrier for the observed contents enables to estimate the different carriers. Section 3 presents the constraints, principles and characteristics of Natural Watermarking (NW). The embedding, decoding and distortion related to NW are presented and the link with the Scalar Costa's Scheme, another scheme preserving perfect secrecy, is outlined. An extension of NW to increase the robustness is presented in section 4, the implications in term of security are also mentioned. Section 5 presents a comparison between the estimations of the secret carriers for different SS watermarking schemes including NW. We show that for NW it is impossible to estimate the carriers. For Robust-NW only the estimation of the watermark subspace is possible. Finally section 6 concludes this paper and presents open research lines for future works.

## 2    Assessing the Security of Spread-Spectrum Techniques Using BSS Techniques

### 2.1    Notations

Vectors are denoted in bold face ($\mathbf{v}$) and coefficients of vectors with parenthesis ($\mathbf{v}(i)$ is the coefficient number $i$ in vector $\mathbf{v}$). Matrices are denoted in capital bold face and are generally composed of several realizations of vectors of the same name, column-wise: the columns of $\mathbf{V}$ are several realizations $\mathbf{v}_1 \ldots \mathbf{v}_N$ of a "template" vector $\mathbf{v}$.

Let us denote $\mathbf{x}$ the host vector of $N_v$ coefficients into which we want to hide a binary message vector $\mathbf{m}$ of $N_c$ bits. The resulting watermarked vector is denoted $\mathbf{y}$. To this aim, we use $\mathbf{u}_i$ orthogonal carriers, $1 \leq i \leq N_c$. The decoded message is denoted $\hat{\mathbf{m}}$. It is to be estimated from $\mathbf{y}'$, a potentially degraded version of $\mathbf{y}$. Let us further denote $z_{\mathbf{v},\mathbf{u}_i}$ the correlation between a vector $\mathbf{v}$ and a carrier $\mathbf{u}_i$:

$$z_{\mathbf{v},\mathbf{u}_i} = <\mathbf{v}|\mathbf{u}_i> = \frac{1}{N_v} \sum_{k=1}^{N_v} \mathbf{v}(k)\mathbf{u}_i(k) \tag{1}$$

## 2.2 Information Theoretical Constraints for Perfect Secrecy

Perfect secrecy has different meanings according to the domain of application. For steganography, perfect secrecy means the impossibility to distinguish between an original content ($\mathbf{x}$) and a stego content ($\mathbf{y}$). Cachin studied the necessary conditions to obtain a secure steganographic scheme and claims that a scheme is secure if the Kullback-Leibler divergence $D_{KL}$ between the distributions $P_{\mathbf{x}}$ and $P_{\mathbf{y}}$ of $\mathbf{x}$ and $\mathbf{y}$ is null. The quantity $D_{KL}$ is defined by:

$$D_{KL}(P_{\mathbf{x}}||P_{\mathbf{y}}) = \sum_i P_{\mathbf{x}}(i) \log \frac{P_{\mathbf{x}}(i)}{P_{\mathbf{y}}(i)} \tag{2}$$

which means that perfect secrecy may be achieved if and only if the distributions of $\mathbf{x}$ and $\mathbf{y}$ are identical. A practical implementation of a steganographic scheme satisfying the perfect secrecy constraint has been proposed in [6].

For robust watermarking, the problem does not concern a possible distinction between the original and the watermarked content: it is not important to know wether a content is watermarked or not, but is it important not to disclose the secret carriers based on observations of pieces of watermarked contents. The concept of information leakage in the context of robust watermarking has been proposed in [1] and developed in [2][3]. The notion of information leakage stems from the definition of the mutual information between $N_o$ watermarked contents $\mathbf{Y}$ and the secret carriers $\mathbf{U}$ (where the $\mathbf{u}_i$ are the columns of $\mathbf{U}$ and the $N_o$ observed $\mathbf{y}$ are the columns of $\mathbf{Y}$):

$$I(\mathbf{U}, \mathbf{Y}) = H(\mathbf{Y}) - H(\mathbf{Y}|\mathbf{U}) = H(\mathbf{U}) - H(\mathbf{U}|\mathbf{Y}) \tag{3}$$

then a watermarking scheme is secure if the mutual information between $\mathbf{U}$ and $\mathbf{Y}$ is null: in this case there is no information leakage.

## 2.3 Spread Spectrum Carriers Estimation

As mentioned previously, a SS watermarking scheme is secure if it is impossible to estimate the secret carriers using observed signals. On the contrary, if a given technique enables to estimate the secret carriers $\mathbf{u}_i$ based only on the observations of $\mathbf{y}$, then the security of the watermarking scheme is greatly reduced. Such a tool can be provided using BSS theory. The goal of BSS is to decompose the observations as a mixture of signals having special statistical properties.

For example, a Principal Component Analysis decomposes observations into orthogonal components according to their variances, and an Independent Component Analysis decomposes the observations into independent signals. Making connections between BSS and SS watermarking is straightforward. A noteworthy property of the class of spread spectrum watermarking schemes is the fact that the embedding part of a SS scheme can be formulated exactly as a blind source separation problem:

$$\mathbf{Y} = \mathbf{X} + \mathbf{U}\mathbf{S_m}. \tag{4}$$

In this equation, the matrix $\mathbf{U}$ is an $N_v \times N_c$ matrix called the mixing matrix (in a BSS framework) and which represents in our case the different carriers $\mathbf{u}_i$ column-wise. The matrix $\mathbf{S_m}$ denotes the different sources that have to be extracted and represents the modulation signal for each carrier that is a function of the embedded message $\mathbf{m}$. The matrix $\mathbf{X}$ represents the host signals (column-wise) and shall be considered as noise in a BSS framework. The goal of BSS is to estimate the matrices $\mathbf{U}$ (the secret carriers) and $\mathbf{S_m}$ according to the observation matrix $\mathbf{Y}$.

In the case of WOA, this decomposition is possible thanks to the fact that each message is embedded independently from another one. It is consequently possible to use Independent Component Analysis techniques to break the security of many spread spectrum watermarking schemes.

The principle of ICA techniques is to find directions in the observed data space whose projections give singular distributions [7]. Based on the fact that the sum of independent variables tends to a Gaussian law, independent components are defined as the most "non-gaussian" components. Moreover, if the watermark components have a different variance than the host data, principal component analysis can be used to perform a reduction of dimension that makes the search of independent components easier.

We now focus on the estimation process of the secret carriers for two popular SS schemes (classical SS and ISS). The ability to estimate their secret carriers is presented.

**Classical Spread Spectrum Watermarking.** In the case of classical SS, the embedding is given for each vector by:

$$\mathbf{y} = \mathbf{x} + \sum_{i=1}^{N_c} \mathbf{b}(i)\mathbf{u}_i \tag{5}$$

where $\mathbf{b} \in \{-1; +1\}^{N_c}$ is the BPSK modulation of the embedded message $\mathbf{m}$.

**Improved Spread Spectrum Watermarking (ISS).** ISS was proposed in [8], it can be considered an informed-embedding variation of classical SS. The embedding is given in this case by:

$$\mathbf{y} = \mathbf{x} + \sum_{i=1}^{N_c} (\alpha \mathbf{b}(i) - \lambda \frac{z_{\mathbf{x},\mathbf{u}_i}}{||\mathbf{u}_i||})\mathbf{u}_i \tag{6}$$

where $\alpha$ and $\lambda$ are respectively calculated to respect the targeted distortion and to achieve the most little error probability after addition of white Gaussian noise.

Eq. 5 and Eq. 6 can be easily transposed in the multidimensional case to obtain a formulation similar to Eq. 4: the matrix $\mathbf{U}$ still contains the carriers and the matrix $\mathbf{S_m}$ contains the modulation signals for each carrier.

To assess the security of a SS-based technique, we have decided to adopt the following methodology which is generally used in BSS benchmarks:

1. We generate $N_o$ observa tions of watermarked contents and generate the matrix of observations $\mathbf{Y}$.
2. We whiten the observed signals using principal component analysis. To reduce the searching time, a reduction of dimension is therefore performed. If we consider that the host signal is generated from an i.i.d. process, the subspace containing the watermark generated by $N_c$ carriers will be included into a $N_c$-dimensional space of different variance [9]. We consequently select the subspace generated by eigenvectors presenting singular (lower or higher) eigenvalues.
3. We run the FastICA algorithm [10] on this subspace to estimate the independent components and the independent basis vectors (e.g. the secret carriers).
4. We compute the normalized correlation $c$ between each original and estimated carriers. A value of $c$ close to 1 means that the estimation of the component is accurate. An estimation close to 0 means that the estimation is erroneous. If $N_c = 2$, we evaluate the estimation accuracy by plotting a 2D constellation of points of coordinates $(c_1; c_2)$. A successful estimation will then provide a point close to one of the four cardinal points $(0, 1)$, $(0, -1)$, $(1, 0)$, $(-1, 0)$[1].

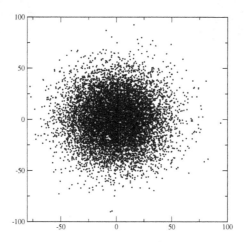

**Fig. 1.** Joint distributions of two carriers for original contents. $N_o = 10000$, $N_v = 512$, $\sigma_{\mathbf{x}}^2 = 1$.

We have depicted the empirical joint distributions of two carriers in the observed watermarked signals (see Fig. 2) and applied our estimation setup for $N_c = 2$ secret carriers (see Fig. 3). In both cases the host vectors are Gaussian

---

[1] We use $N_c = 2$ for illustration purposes, hiding more bits would require to use the Hungarian method [11] to assign original and estimated carriers prior to the computation of the normalized correlation $c$.

i.i.d. signals of law $\mathcal{N}(0,1)$ and two carriers where used during the embedding. The Watermark to Content Ratio (WCR) was fixed in both case to $-21dB$. For each SS scheme, the joint distribution of the carriers in the observed content is the sum of four bi-dimensional Gaussian distributions. Note that the variance of each distribution is less important for ISS embedding than for SS because of the embedding optimization performed by ISS. Note also that the global variance of the distribution for SS is more important than for ISS. For each distribution, the directions of the two carriers (horizontal and vertical axis) are easily identifiable by the ICA algorithm.

Additionally we see that the Cachin criterion which considers the distributions of original and watermarked contents is not fulfilled for this two schemes. Fig. 1 depicts the distribution of the two same carriers for original contents. This distribution is rather different than the distributions after SS watermarking.

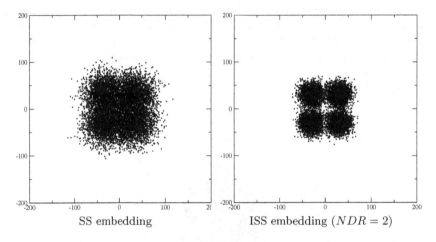

SS embedding                    ISS embedding ($NDR = 2$)

**Fig. 2.** Joint distributions of two carriers for SS and ISS schemes. For both schemes $N_o = 10000$, $WCR = -21dB$ and $N_v = 512$, $\sigma_{\mathbf{x}}^2 = 1$.

Fig. 3 depicts the normalized correlation between the original and estimated carriers for 100 trials considering every 1000 watermarked vectors. We can notice that the estimations are globally more accurate for SS than for ISS. In this case, this is mainly due to the fact that the variance of the embedding for ISS is lower than for SS and consequently the estimation of the subspace relative to the watermark is less accurate in the second case.

## 3   Natural Spread Spectrum Watermarking

In this section, we show how to build a SS-based watermarking scheme in such a way that the identification of the watermarking subspace spanned by the secret carriers is impossible.

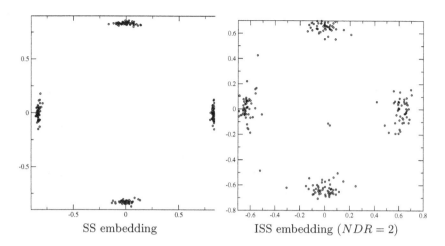

SS embedding                    ISS embedding ($NDR = 2$)

**Fig. 3.** Normalized correlations between the two estimated carriers and the real ones. For both schemes $N_o = 1000$, $WCR = -21dB$ and $N_v = 512$.

## 3.1  Embedding and Decoding

If we consider a carrier $\mathbf{u}_i$ such that its coefficients follows a Gaussian model ($\mathbf{u}_i \sim \mathcal{N}(0, \sigma_{\mathbf{u}_i}^2)$), and host signals $\mathbf{x} \sim \mathcal{N}(0, \sigma_{\mathbf{x}}^2)$ then the random variable $z_{\mathbf{x},\mathbf{u}_i}$ follows a Gaussian law of parameters $z_{\mathbf{x},\mathbf{u}_i} \sim \mathcal{N}(0, \sigma_{\mathbf{u}_i}^2 \sigma_{\mathbf{x}}^2)$. Note that this property is true because of the Central limit theorem as far as $N_v$ is important. Moreover, this property is still valid if $\mathbf{x}$ does not follow a Gaussian model. The goal of NW is to design the embedding in such a way that the distribution of $z_{\mathbf{x},\mathbf{u}_i}$ before and after embedding will remain identical. Moreover, as it is shown at the end of this section, the fact that each carrier follows a Gaussian distribution prevents the estimation of the different carriers and guarantees the security of the scheme.

The decoding rule remains the same than for usual SS schemes:

$$\hat{\mathbf{m}}(i) = 1 \text{ if } z_{\mathbf{y}',\mathbf{u}_i} > 0 \tag{7}$$

$$\hat{\mathbf{m}}(i) = 0 \text{ if } z_{\mathbf{y}',\mathbf{u}_i} < 0 \tag{8}$$

The watermarked vector $\mathbf{y}$ is:

$$\mathbf{y} = \mathbf{x} + \mathbf{w} \tag{9}$$

where the watermark signal $\mathbf{w}$ is computed as follows:

$$\mathbf{w} = -\sum_{i=1}^{N_c} \left(1 + (-1)^{\mathbf{m}(i)} \text{sign}(z_{\mathbf{x},\mathbf{u}_i})\right) \frac{z_{\mathbf{x},\mathbf{u}_i}}{\|\mathbf{u}_i\|^2} \mathbf{u}_i \tag{10}$$

which means that the watermark $\mathbf{w}_i$ associated to each carrier $\mathbf{u}_i$ follows this simple embedding rule:

$$\mathbf{w}_i = 0 \text{ if } \mathbf{m}(i) = 1 \; ; \; z_{\mathbf{x},\mathbf{u}_i} > 0 \tag{11}$$

$$\text{or } \mathbf{m}(i) = -1 \text{ ; } z_{\mathbf{x},\mathbf{u}_i} < 0 \qquad (12)$$

$$\mathbf{w}_i = -2\frac{z_{\mathbf{x},\mathbf{u}_i}}{\|\mathbf{u}_i\|^2}\mathbf{u}_i \text{ if } \mathbf{m}(i) = 1 \text{ ; } z_{\mathbf{x},\mathbf{u}_i} < 0 \qquad (13)$$

$$\text{or } \mathbf{m}(i) = -1 \text{ ; } z_{\mathbf{x},\mathbf{u}_i} > 0 \qquad (14)$$

Eq. 10 states that $\mathbf{x}$ is symetrically modified iff $\text{sign}(z_{\mathbf{x},\mathbf{u}_i}) \neq (-1)^{\mathbf{m}(i)}$. This embedding rule is depicted on Fig. 4.

Note that the embedding rule used for NW is quite similar to the rule used for ISS. In both cases, each carrier $\mathbf{u}_i$ is modulated according to the correlation $z_{\mathbf{x},\mathbf{u}_i}$. For ISS, $z_{\mathbf{x},\mathbf{u}_i}$ is used to increase the distance between the different codewords and increase the robustness. For NW, $z_{\mathbf{x},\mathbf{u}_i}$ is used to not modify the natural distribution of the carriers and consequently to increase the security.

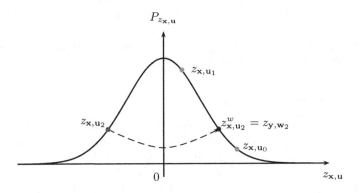

**Fig. 4.** Natural watermarking for $\mathbf{m} = \{1,1,1\}$ ($N_c = 3$). Only the third bit calls for a model-based symmetry.

## 3.2 Distortion

Distortion is usually expressed by means of the WCR (Watermark to Content Ratio), in dB. Under the assumption that, on average, one bit out of two calls for a symmetry, we are able to compute the MSE.

The pdf of the watermark (on each sample) is the following:

$$\text{if } x < 0 \ f(x) \sim \mathcal{N}(0, 4\sigma_x^2\sigma_u^2/N_v) \qquad (15)$$

$$\text{if } x \geq 0 \ f(x) = \delta(x)/2 \qquad (16)$$

Then:

$$\sigma_W^2 = \frac{2\sigma_x^2\sigma_u^2}{N_v} \qquad (17)$$

and the Watermark-to-Content-Ratio is expressed as follows:

$$WCR = 10\log\sigma_W^2/\sigma_x^2 = 10\log\frac{2\sigma_u^2}{N_v} \qquad (18)$$

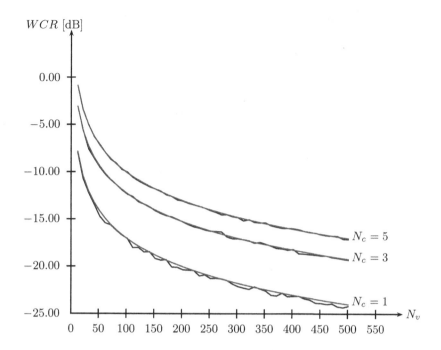

**Fig. 5.** Comparison between theoretical and practical $WCR$

We shall stay with this last approximation, since Fig. 5 shows no difference between this theoretical approximation and the practical measurements.

If targeting a classical $WCR = -20dB$, Eq. 18 leads to the trivial relation $N_v = 200N_c$ if we set $\mathbf{u} \sim \mathcal{N}(0,1)$ and $\mathbf{x} \sim \mathcal{N}(0,1)$.

### 3.3    Theoretical Evaluation of the Security of Natural Watermarking

The goal of this section is to show that NW enables to have no information leakage in the case of a WOA setup. We first compute the mutual information for a scheme using only one carrier $\mathbf{u}$ ($N_c = 1$: therefore the message $m$ is a scalar binary value).

We consider the case $z_{\mathbf{x},\mathbf{u}} > 0$ but the equations are similar if $z_{\mathbf{x},\mathbf{u}} < 0$. The embedding formula can be expressed as:

$$\text{If } m = 1 \text{ then } \mathbf{y} = \mathbf{x} \tag{19}$$

$$\text{If } m = 0 \text{ then } \mathbf{y} = \mathbf{x} - 2\frac{\mathbf{u}\mathbf{u}^\top}{N_v}\mathbf{x}. \tag{20}$$

By construction, $\mathbf{y}$ can also be modelled as an i.i.d. Gaussian process: $\mathbf{y} \sim \mathcal{N}(0,1)$. Then:

$$H(\mathbf{y}) = H(\mathbf{x}) = \frac{N_v}{2}\log(2\pi e). \tag{21}$$

We recall that the mutual information between one observation $\mathbf{y}$ and a secret carrier $\mathbf{u}$ is given by:

$$I(\mathbf{y}; \mathbf{u}) = H(\mathbf{y}) - H(\mathbf{y}|\mathbf{u}). \tag{22}$$

Because the pdfs $f_{\mathbf{y}|\mathbf{u}, m=1}(x)$ and $f_{\mathbf{y}|\mathbf{u}, m=0}(x)$ are disjoint, and supposing that $\Pr[m = 1] = \Pr[m = 0] = 1/2$, the conditional $H(\mathbf{y}|\mathbf{u})$ is given by:

$$H(\mathbf{y}|\mathbf{u}) = \frac{1}{2}(H(\mathbf{y}|\mathbf{u}, m = 1) + H(\mathbf{y}|\mathbf{u}, m = 0)) + \log(2). \tag{23}$$

Using Eq.19, Eq.20 and the definition of differential entropy, it is easy to show that $H(\mathbf{y}|\mathbf{u}, m = 1) = H(\mathbf{x}) - \log 2$ and $H(\mathbf{y}|\mathbf{u}, m = 0) = H(\mathbf{x} - 2\mathbf{u}\mathbf{u}^\top\mathbf{x}/N_v) - \log 2$.

We obtain then the following expression of conditional entropy for NW:

$$H(\mathbf{y}|\mathbf{u}) = \frac{1}{2}H(\mathbf{x}) + \frac{1}{2}H(\mathbf{x} - 2\frac{\mathbf{u}\mathbf{u}^\top}{N_v}\mathbf{x}) \tag{24}$$

where

$$H(\mathbf{x} - 2\frac{\mathbf{u}\mathbf{u}^\top}{N_v}\mathbf{x}) = H((\mathbf{I} - 2\frac{\mathbf{u}\mathbf{u}^\top}{N_v})\mathbf{x}) = H(\mathbf{x}) + \ln|\det(\mathbf{I} - 2\frac{\mathbf{u}\mathbf{u}^\top}{N_v})|. \tag{25}$$

Because $||\mathbf{u}||^2 = N_v$, the matrix $\mathbf{I} - 2\mathbf{u}\mathbf{u}^\top/N_v$ is an elementary reflection which corresponds to an orthogonal matrix:

$$(\mathbf{I} - 2\frac{\mathbf{u}\mathbf{u}^\top}{N_v})(\mathbf{I} - 2\frac{\mathbf{u}\mathbf{u}^\top}{N_v})^\top = \mathbf{I} - 4\frac{\mathbf{u}\mathbf{u}^\top}{N_v^2} + 4\frac{\mathbf{u}\mathbf{u}^\top\mathbf{u}\mathbf{u}^\top}{N_v^4} = \mathbf{I}$$

since $\mathbf{u}^\top\mathbf{u}/N_v^2 = 1$. Consequently $|\det(\mathbf{I} - 2\mathbf{u}\mathbf{u}^\top/N_v)| = 1$ and we obtain:

$$H(\mathbf{y}|\mathbf{u}, m = -1) = H(\mathbf{x}) \tag{26}$$

and:

$$I(\mathbf{y}; \mathbf{u}) = H(\mathbf{y}) - H(\mathbf{x}) = H(\mathbf{x}) - H(\mathbf{x}) = 0. \tag{27}$$

If we now consider $N_o$ observations, and because $\mathbf{x}_1, ..., \mathbf{x}_{N_o}$ are independent random vectors, then due to Eq.19 and Eq.20, $\mathbf{y}_1, ..., \mathbf{y}_{N_o}$ and $\mathbf{y}_1|\mathbf{u}, ..., \mathbf{y}_{N_o}|\mathbf{u}$ are also independent vectors. Consequently we have the following properties:

$$H(\mathbf{y}_{N_o}|\mathbf{y}_{N_o-1}, ..., \mathbf{y}_1) = H(\mathbf{y}) \tag{28}$$

$$H(\mathbf{y}_1, .., \mathbf{y}_{N_o}) = N_o H(\mathbf{y}) = N_o H(\mathbf{x}) \tag{29}$$

$$H(\mathbf{y}_1, .., \mathbf{y}_{N_o}|\mathbf{u}) = N_o H(\mathbf{y}|\mathbf{u}) = N_o H(\mathbf{x}) \tag{30}$$

and finally using Eq. 29 and Eq. 30:

$$I(\mathbf{Y}; \mathbf{U}) = N_o H(\mathbf{X}) - N_o H(\mathbf{X}) = 0 \tag{31}$$

Note that having a mutual information between the secret key and the observed content being null has already been found for another watermarking scheme. In [3], authors show that for the Scalar Costa's Scheme [12] and an embedding parameter $\alpha = \frac{1}{2}$, there is no information leakage too. Such a similar result is not surprising because in both cases, the distributions of $\mathbf{x}$ and $\mathbf{y}$ are the same.

Note also that natural watermarking also theoretically satisfies to the steganographic definition of security recalled in section 2.2. Because the distributions of $\mathbf{x}$ and $\mathbf{y}$ are the same, $D_{KL}(P_{\mathbf{x}}||P_{\mathbf{y}}) = 0$.

### 3.4 Multi-bits Embedding

When $N_c > 1$ carriers are used, the security of the scheme can be seen as a problem of blind source separation: is it possible to separate a mixture of independent Gaussian variables with equal variance ?

ICA theory claims that it is impossible to perform such a separation because the joint distribution of such a mixture is rotationally symmetric [7]. Here, it is not possible for an BSS technique to find singular directions observing NW-watermarked vectors as it was possible with classical SS or ISS. Fig 6 illustrates the joint distribution of two original carriers obtained after Natural Watermarking. The distribution cannot be used to find the direction of the carriers.

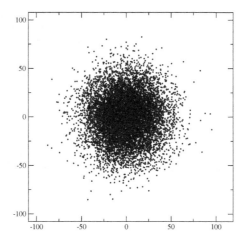

**Fig. 6.** Joint distributions of two carriers for NW. $N_o = 10000$, $WCR = -21dB$, $N_v = 512$, $\sigma_{\mathbf{x}}^2 = 1$. The direction of the original carriers (horizontal and vertical axis) can not be estimated on a multivariate Gaussian distribution.

## 4   Toward Robust Natural Watermarking

One solution to increase the robustness of the NW scheme is to increase the variance of the Gaussian distribution associated with each carrier. We can modify the embedding rule of NW (cf. Eq. 10) in such a way that the distribution of each carriers will still remain Gaussian, but will have a standard deviation proportional to a scale factor $s$. This modification enables to increase the average distance between codewords coding different symbols but also to increase the embedding distortion. The new modulation for Robust-NW is then given by:

$$\mathbf{w} = -\sum_{i=1}^{N_c} \left(1 + s(-1)^{\mathbf{m}(i)} \operatorname{sign}(z_{\mathbf{x},\mathbf{u}_i})\right) \frac{z_{\mathbf{x},\mathbf{u}_i}}{\|\mathbf{u}_i\|^2} \mathbf{u}_i \tag{32}$$

and the distribution of the correlation $z_{\mathbf{x},\mathbf{u}_i}$ of one carrier $\mathbf{u}_i$ now follows the model $z_{\mathbf{x},\mathbf{u}_i} \sim \mathcal{N}(0, s^2 \sigma_{\mathbf{u}_i}^2 \sigma_{\mathbf{x}}^2)$. If $s = 1$, the embedding rule corresponds to NW, if $s > 1$, the robustness is increased and this leads to Robust-NW. The expression of the $WCR$ becomes:

$$WCR = 10 \log \frac{(s^2 + 1)\sigma_u^2}{N_v} \tag{33}$$

Using Robust-NW leads also to another important consequence. Because distributions of carriers are now distinct from distributions of other components of watermarked contents, it is then possible to estimate the subspace related to the watermark using, for example, principal component analysis (PCA). But, if $N_c > 1$, it is still not possible to estimate each carrier separately. Consequently the attacker can remove the watermark by zeroing all the projections on every carriers but still he has no access to the hidden message itself: he cannot copy it to another content or modify the embedded message because he does not know the values of $z_{\mathbf{x},\mathbf{u}_i}$. Consequently the very security of the system is still preserved[2].

As a remark, we have also to point out that, even if this implementation enables to obtain robustness on one hand, on the other hand the degradation of the host signal become rather significant. For example, if $\sigma_n^2 = \sigma_{\mathbf{x}}^2 = 1$ (which is equivalent to a $NDR = 1$ for ISS) and $N_v = 512$, for a same $BER = 12\%$ for both schemes, then the distortion is far more important for NW than for ISS ($WCR = -15dB$ for NW and $WCR = -21dB$ for ISS). For comparison, in the case of NW with $WCR = -21dB$, we have $BER = 25\%$.

## 5   Results

The aim of this section is to assess the theoretical properties of NW and Robust-NW. We have used the estimation setup proposed in section 2.3 for classical SS and ISS considering the same parameters ($N_c = 2$, $N_o = 1000$). The distortion for NW remains the same ($WCR = -21dB$) but is different for Robust-NW ($WCR = -14dB$, $s = 3$). Normalized correlations between the two estimated and original carriers are depicted on Fig. 7 for 100 different trials. For NW (left

---

[2] One may argue that the whole private subspace is already an important information about the secret. We would like to emphasise however that Robust-NW is proved to deliver better security since it explicitly does not allow for estimation of the carriers.

plot), the estimation of the secret carriers is unsuccessful because every point is very close to the origin for each trial. The right plot, obtained for Robust-NW, illustrates the fact that in this case the watermark subspace is estimated (the distance between each point and the origin is close to 1), but that the estimation of the two carriers is not possible because each trial leads to a point which is randomly chosen on the unitary circle.

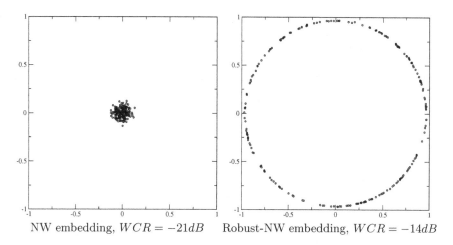

NW embedding, $WCR = -21dB$    Robust-NW embedding, $WCR = -14dB$

**Fig. 7.** Normalized correlations between the two estimated carriers and the original ones. For both schemes: $N_o = 1000$ and $N_v = 512$.

# 6   Conclusions and Future Works

This paper has presented a solution to obtain a secure spread spectrum watermarking scheme called Natural Spread Spectrum Watermarking for WOA. The security is guaranteed by two important properties:

- The distribution of each secret carrier is the same for the marked and original contents. From this property stems the fact that the mutual information between the secret carrier and the observed contents is null (condition of perfect secrecy for watermarking). Additionally, the embedding satisfies also the condition of secrecy for steganography. Note however that this first property is not true for Robust-NW ($s > 1$).
- The watermark subspace is equivalent to a mixture of Gaussian components having the same variance. BSS theory demonstrates that it is impossible to estimate each component (carrier) in this particular case.

We have also proposed a extension of NW to increase the robustness called Robust-NW which increases the variance of distributions of each carrier while preserving a multivariate Gaussian distribution. However, the compromises done to obtain a secure watermarking scheme have to balanced with the relative weak robustness of NW in comparison with SS or ISS. Our future works will concentrate on this point to discover if such a compromise is mandatory or if it is possible to obtain a more robust extension of NW. Anyway, Natural Watermarking should already be considered a secure alternative for fragile watermarking applications.

We would like also to propose a practical implementation of NW for real-life contents such as images or sounds. This will enable to evaluate specifically the perceptual distortion of the proposed system.

## Acknowledgements

The work described in this paper has been supported (in part) by the European Commission through the IST Programme under Contract IST-2002-507932 ECRYPT and the National French projects ACI-SI Fabriano and RIAM Estivale.

## References

1. Cayre, F., Fontaine, C., Furon, T.: Watermarking security part I: Theory. In: Proceedings of SPIE, Security, Steganography and Watermarking of Multimedia Contents VII, vol. 5681, San Jose, USA (2005)
2. Comesaña, P., Pérez-Freire, L., Pérez-González, F.: Fundamentals of data hiding security and their application to spread-spectrum analysis. In: 7th Information Hiding Workshop, IH05, Barcelona, Spain. LNCS, Springer, Heidelberg (2005)
3. Pérez-Freire, L., Comesaña, P., Pérez-González, F.: Information-theoretic analysis of security in side-informed data hiding. In: 7th Information Hiding Workshop, IH05, Barcelona, Spain. LNCS, Springer, Heidelberg (2005)
4. Bas, P., Hurri, J.: Security of dm quantization watermarking scheme: a practical study for digital images. In: International Workshop on Digital Watermarking, Sienna, Italy. LNCS, Springer Verlag, Berlin, Germany (2005)
5. Cayre, F., Fontaine, C., Furon, T.: Watermarking security part II: Practice. In: Proceedings of SPIE, Security, Steganography and Watermarking of Multimedia Contents VII, vol. 5681, San Jose, USA (2005)
6. Sallee.: Model-based steganography. In: International Workshop on Digital Watermarking (IWDW). LNCS, vol. 2, Springer, Heidelberg (2003)
7. Hyvärinen, A., Karhunen, J., Oja, E.: Independent Component Analysis. John Wiley & Sons, New York, NY (2001)
8. Malvar, Florencio.: Improved spread spectrum: A new modulation technique for robust watermarking. IEEE Transactions on Signal Processing, vol. 51 (2003)
9. Doërr, G.J., Dugelay, J.L.: Danger of low-dimensional watermarking subspaces. In: ICASSP 2004. 29th IEEE International Conference on Acoustics, Speech, and Signal Processing, pp. 17–21. Montreal, Canada (2004)
10. Hyvärinen, A.: Fast and robust fixed-point algorithms for independent component analysis. IEEE Transactions on Neural Networks 10(3), 626–634 (1999)
11. Kuhn, H.W.: The Hungarian method of solving the assignment problem. Naval Res. Logistics Quart. 2, 83–97 (1955)
12. Eggers, J.J., Buml, R., Tzschoppe, R., Girod, B.: Scalar costa scheme for information embedding. IEEE Trans. on Signal Processing 51(4), 1003–1019 (2003)

# An Improved Asymmetric Watermarking System Using Matrix Embedding

Scott Craver

Department of Electrical and Computer Engineering
Binghamton University

**Abstract.** In the asymmetric watermarking problem, we wish to embed a signal in a piece of multimedia and later prove that we have done so, but without revealing information that can be used by an adversary to remove the signal later.

There have been several published solutions to this problem, which suffer from the twin problems of size and time complexity. We provide a protocol similar to the one described in [5], but with substantial improvements in time and space. Our protocol is non-interactive, and each exchange of information between the prover and verifier involves a smaller payload of data. The algorithm uses a form of matrix embedding with pseudo-random Gaussian matrices. Aside from an improvement in efficiency, it possesses other practical advantages over previous protocols.

## 1 Introduction

Asymmetric watermarking refers to the problem of embedding a signal, and proving that it has been embedded, without actually revealing it or otherwise revealing information allowing an attacker to damage the hidden data. Several protocols for accomplishing this have been published, by placing detection within the framework of a zero-knowledge protocol [5,4,1] or by creating statistical artefacts which can be exhibited without revealing the signal [10].

Some of these systems suffer from inversion attack vulnerabilities: the attacker can simply pick a signal that correlates with the image, and prove asymmetrically that he knows it [6]. Because the prover is no longer allowed to reveal the watermark, verifying that it is a valid watermark becomes difficult. Those which are not vulnerable still have high space and time complexity, due to interactive protocols in which amounts of data comparable to the multimedia data itself are exchanged repeatedly.

In this paper we outline an asymmetric embedding method using pseudo-random Gaussian matrix embedding. A key $K$ is used to generate a pseudo-random matrix $G[K]_{M \times N}$. Given a data vector $x_{N \times 1}$ extracted from the multimedia object, we tune in to one "channel" of the data by computing the product $y = G[K]x$. Embedding consists of determining the watermark signal $w$ such that $\hat{y} = G[K](x + w)$ is the message we want to transmit. In practice we will embed multiple messages in multiple channels using multiple keys $K_i$ by solving one system of linear equations.

J. Camenisch et al. (Eds.): IH 2006, LNCS 4437, pp. 15–25, 2007.

The asymmetric part uses the inversion attack principle described in [5] and [4]. There, the authors embed a few watermarks in an image and use inversion attacks to generate a large number of counterfeit ones. All of the watermarks are detectable in the test image, and a zero-knowledge proof is used to show that at least one watermark is real. An attacker who wants to render the real watermarks undetectable can attempt to damage a large number of the counterfeit marks; but since these counterfeit marks *are the image's content,* this amounts to damaging the image significantly.

In our algorithm, we embed a few watermarks using specific keys $K_i$, and supply a prover with a large number of extra random keys. Extracting a signal using most of these keys will result in channel noise, which serves the same role as the counterfeit watermarks of the previous protocol.

## 1.1   Why This New Method Is an Improvement

There are several factors that make this new system an improvement over the previous protocol. First, in this new protocol Alice only needs to provide Bob with a list of generating keys, not a list of watermarks themselves. In [5], the watermarks are as large as the watermarked data vector $X$, and hundreds must be provided as part of the proof. Owing to the construction of that secret watermark vector, Alice cannot provide the PRNG seed that generates the watermarks— doing so would reveal crucial information about how the watermarks are created, revealing which are real and which are fake. In our algorithm, Alice can provide Bob with a list of embedding keys which generate the watermarks. This results in a considerable size reduction in representing the watermark data. Instead of providing a bundle of watermarks $M$ times the size of the "image," we can provide a bundle of keys $M$ times some small size, such as 56 bits. The keys do not even need to be large enough to prevent brute force, because they are not kept secret. They are simply pseudo-random seeds.

Second, our verification protocol is non-interactive. This is not a trivial form of non-interactive protocol in which the same data payload is sent all at once; rather, we provide a single-step protocol whose payload is comparable to a single step of the interactive one. This provides a substantial reduction in protocol traffic.

Another advantage of our system is that Alice does not need to fix the number of counterfeit watermarks in advance. The protocol in [5] requires the image to be divided into shares in advance, that all counterfeit watermarks are constructed at the same time as the new watermarks are added. In our protocol, Alice need not perform any inversion attacks during embedding; she can invent as many false watermarks as she wants during verification.

A final advantage of our system is that the image data size is not strictly bound to the payload size. In other words, the cryptographic objects we embed do not have to be too large or too small owing to the size or nature of the data.

In [1], watermark vector elements are blinded by using them as exponents, for example $B_i = a^{w_i} \pmod{p}$. Cryptographic protocols have certain requirements for the bit-sizes of this data; a watermark vector element $w_i$ needs to have sufficiently many bits in order for this kind of commitment to be secure. To be completely secure, $w_i$ should be uniformly distributed over $\mathbb{Z}_{p-1}$. Natural data needs to be carefully shaped to meet the requirements of the protocol.

Meanwhile in [5], the data objects are of length comparable to the image vector $x$. If we have a very large watermark vector relative to the bitstring we want to embed, we lose embedding efficiency, and allow an attacker to target those particular components of the vector in which our payload is stored. In our algorithm, the matrix $G[K]$ reduces the data vector to whatever size is appropriate for embedding. This allows the data size to be as large as we want.

The main disadvantage of our system is the amount of cover data needed. The embedding strength of the watermark depends on the number of bits embedded and the vector size. This means that for an appropriate embedding strength, the number of coefficients used for embedding may be on the order of $10^4$ or $10^5$. While this seems large, consider that the features we use for embedding should contain as much of the image's content as possible.

## 2    Asymmetric Watermarking with a Selection Channel

The concept of a *selection channel* is described by Anderson and Petitcolas in [2]. It consists of a method of selecting a "location" in a media object for embedding data, indexed by a parameter such as a secret key. This general approach to data hiding provides security through the multiplicity of choices available to both the embedder and the attacker. An attack must target many different locations in order to damage the hidden data, analogous to a pirate digging up half an island to find a treasure chest without a map.

For a chosen algorithm, we will denote $X(\omega)$ as the message extracted from the media object $X$ using the selection channel parameter $\omega$.

For asymmetric watermarking, we employ the following technique:

1. Alice chooses a large prime $p$ and element $g \in \mathbb{Z}/p\mathbb{Z}$ of high order.
2. Alice chooses an appropriate selection channel algorithm.
3. For various channel parameters $\omega_i$, Alice embeds integers $X(\omega_i) = H_i = g^{h_i}$ (mod $p$). This is embedding by replacement. The values $h_i$ are random seeds which constitute the secret watermark information.
4. Alice distributes the resulting media object $X$.

Mathematical objects used in cryptography are usually fragile, and can not be trusted to survive an attack. Thus we employ a proof that uses the image after embedding as a "digital negative." We can prove facts about the negative, while also showing that it corresponds closely to the suspect pirate image.

1. Bob is caught distributing a modified object $Y$.
2. Alice presents $X$, her selection channel algorithm, $p$ and $g$, and a large set of random parameters $\{\omega_k\}$ of which some of her real embedding parameters $\{\omega_i\}$ are a subset.

3. For each parameter, Bob extracts messages $X(\omega_k)$ and $Y(\omega_k)$, and tests for correlation on each pair.
4. Bob records the subset of parameters $\{\omega_k\}$ for which a correlation was found between $X(\omega)$ and $Y(\omega)$. With hope, there will be an $\omega_k$ for which the message $X(\omega_k)$ is one of Alice's embedded integers.
5. Alice proves that she knows the discrete logarithm for at least one unspecified message.

That last step can be performed in zero-knowledge with a large number of transmissions as described in [5]. We have a more efficient algorithm for verification, described below. A key point, however, is that detection and verification are separated. This postponement of watermark verification permits this general approach of watermarking using inversion attacks. To Bob, every parameter $\omega_k$ potentially points to a watermark, and a minority of them actually are. If Bob cannot distinguish between real watermarks and random channel noise, then a careful verification protocol can prove the existence of a watermark without locating it.

In summary: Alice uses a selection channel to "tune in" to various parts of the image $X$. She embeds messages in those parts. Later, when a suspect image $Y$ appears, Alice provides a long list of channels, and Bob can "tune in" to the same channel of both images and verify that the data in those channels match. It is then up to Alice to prove using a protocol that at least one channel of $X$ contains not noise but a carefully constructed message.

## 3  Embedding with Pseudo-random Gaussian Matrices

This technique is inspired by the matrix embedding codes of Fridrich and Soukal [8]. In their protocol, they employ a general procedure of transforming a bit string into a message using matrix arithmetic over $\mathbb{Z}/2\mathbb{Z}$. We can employ similar techniques; however, the field $\mathbb{Z}/2\mathbb{Z}$ does not possess topological properties which are necessary for robustness. We use matrices over $\mathbb{R}$ instead, whose components are $N(0, \sigma^2)$ Gaussian.

### 3.1  The Matrix Embedding Framework

Suppose we have extracted a real data vector $x_{N \times 1}$ from a media object, which we want to watermark. To be specific we want to add a vector $w_{N \times 1}$, whose power is a fraction $\alpha$ of the original: $\sum w_i^2 = \alpha \sum x_i^2$. We will see that the vector dimension $N$ and $\alpha$ are tied together by the number of bits we want to embed, so that $N$ must be large. On the other hand there are only so many features we can extract from some media, such as images. In practice, the dimension $N$ of the vector will be on the order of $10^4$ or $10^5$.

Next, we have a set of messages $\{m_i\}$ of equal length. In practice, 4096 bits is a fair datagram length. We want to embed cryptographic objects which we can use in a zero-knowledge proof or other asymmetric protocol. The way our architecture works, the embedding does not have to be robust, which is helpful because the objects we embed are inherently sensitive to single bit errors.

Next, *we will encode each message* $\{m_i\}$ *as a vector* $y_{M \times 1}$ *of double-precision reals*. The value must be chosen to follow a Gaussian distribution, which we achieve by companding. Each double-precision real holds a 52-bit mantissa, but we cannot embed 52 datagram bits bits per real owing to arithmetic errors which occur when this vector is operated upon. In experiments, we have been able to rely on 32 bits per mantissa, with more if we want to code our data appropriately. This represents a 4096-bit datagram as a 128-element vector.

We now have a set of vectors $\{y_i\}$ of dimension $M$, and a message vector $x$ of dimension $N$. For each vector $y_i$ we pick a secret key $K_i$ and use it as a seed to generate a pseudo-random Gaussian matrix $G[K_i]_{M \times N}$. Each row of $G[K_i]$ is a vector of *i.i.d.* $N(0, \sigma^2)$ Gaussian variables. This is our selection channel algorithm: the matrix product $z[K_i]_{M \times 1} = G[K_i]x$ is the message extracted from the data vector. For selected keys $K_i$, we want to set $z[K_i] = y_i$, so that our message is "located" in that channel.

Finally, for embedding purposes, we will combine all of the datagram vectors $\{y_i\}$ into a single vector $y_{DM \times 1}$, where $D$ is the number of datagrams. Our gaussian matrices similarly combine into a matrix $G_{DM \times N}$, and the product of our embedding should be $Gx = y$. To be exact, $y = [y_1^T | y_2^T | \cdots | y_D^T]^T$ and, $G = [G[K_1]^T | G[K_2]^T | \cdots | G[K_D]^T]^T$.

During the watermark *verification* phase, we will need to treat each $G[K_i]$ separately; for embedding, it is best to treat all the message data as a single vector, and all of the Gaussian matrices as a single matrix $G$.

Table 3.1 summarizes the notation thus far.

| Symbol | meaning |
|---|---|
| $x_{N \times 1}$ | The data vector extracted from the multimedia, of dimension $N$ |
| $w_{N \times 1}$ | The signal vector we will ultimately add to $x$ |
| $\alpha$ | The power ratio $\sum w_i^2 / \sum x_i^2$ |
| $\{m_i\}_{i=1}^{D}$ | Message datagrams |
| $\{y_i\}_{i=1}^{D}$ | Message datagrams encoded as double-precision reals |
| $\{K_i\}_{i=1}^{D}$ | Message embedding keys |
| $\{G[K_i]_{M \times N}\}_{i=1}^{D}$ | Pseudo-random Gaussian matrices derived from keys |
| $z[K]_{M \times 1} = G[K]x$ | Message extracted from $x$ using key $K$ |
| $G_{DM \times N}$ | All Pseudo-random matrices concatenated into single matrix |
| $y_{DM \times 1}$ | All datagram vectors concatenated into single vector |

**Fig. 1.** The notation used in this section

## 3.2 Embedding

Embedding is actually very simple. We want to choose vector $w$ so that $G(x + w) = y$, or $Gw = (y - Gx)$. With $DM \ll N$ this is an underdetermined system, and since each row is a vector of *i.i.d.* Gaussians, $GG^T$ is a $DM \times DM$ matrix that is invertible with very high probability.

To embed, we construct our watermark vector as a weighted sum of columns from $G^T$: only components within the span of these vectors will have any useful embedding effect. The solution is the vector

$$w = G^T (GG^T)^{-1}(y - Gx)$$

which will place all of our datagrams $\{y_k\}$ into their respective channels.

Note that this is really embedding by replacement. True, we are *adding* a vector $w$ to the data vector $x$, and we will detect later via correlation; however, within the scope of our selection channel algorithm, we have caused whatever signal was present in $z[K_i]$ to be completely replaced with $y_i$.

### 3.3    Encoding of Datagram Vectors

The datagram vectors should be chosen so that they statistically resemble channel noise. Thankfully this is easy, because each element of the channel noise vector $z[K_i]$ is the dot product of $x$ with a distinct vector of *i.i.d.* $N(0, \sigma^2)$ Gaussians. Hence the noise vector elements are *i.i.d.* $N(0, (\sum x_i^2)\sigma^2)$.

This means that each vector element of $y$ must also be chosen to be an *i.i.d.* $N(0, (\sum x_i^2)\sigma^2)$ Gaussian variable. To encode our data packets this way we compand, scaling each n-bit parcel to a value $v \in [0, 1]$ and computing $\Phi^{-1}(v)$ where $\Phi(x) = 0.5(1 + erf(x/\sqrt{2}))$.

### 3.4    What Is the Watermark Strength?

The reader has probably noticed that something is missing from the embedding procedure: *any parameter to control the watermark power*. The watermark is completely determined from the data vector $x$, the specific bit strings $m_i$, and their keys which generate the matrix $G$. There is no opportunity to scale this vector to make it strong or weak.

In fact, the relative strength of the watermark is determined by the dimension parameters $M$ and $N$, and the number of datagrams $D$ we wish to embed. In turn, $M$ and $D$ derive from the number of bits we want to embed—almost! The dimensionality of these vectors effects the overall arithmetic error in the embedding process, which in turn restricts the number of bits that can be embedded per coefficient. This factor can be ignored for the time being, however, as we determine the embedding strength as a function of $DM$ and $N$.

For the equation we need to solve, $w = G^T(GG^T)^{-1}(y - Gx)$, the vector $(y - Gx)$ will contain elements that are $N(0, 2(\sum x_i^2)\sigma^2)$. The total vector power will have an expected value of $2DM(\sum x_i^2)\sigma^2$.

Meanwhile, the pseudo-random matrix $GG^T$ will have diagonal elements with a mean of $N\sigma^2$, and non-diagonal elements with a mean of 0. Thus we should expect the intermediate vector $p_{DM \times 1} = (GG^T)^{-1}(y - Gx)$ to have a power of $\sum p_i^2 = 2MD(\sum x_i^2)/N^2\sigma^2)$. Finally, the watermark $w = Gp$ will have elements that are $N(0, 2MD(\sum x_i^2)/N^2)$. Its power will be $\sum_i w_i^2 = \frac{2MD}{N} \sum x_i^2$.

In other words, the fraction $\alpha$ will be $2MD/N$. For example, if we have an $M = 128$ and $D = 5$, and we want an $\alpha = 0.04$, then we need $N = 1280 \times 25 = 32000$. For small data objects, extracting 32000 elements to watermark may be a challenge. Remember, however, that the goal is to choose a vector which represents as much of the image's content as possible.

To summarize, we control the weakness of the added watermark through the length of the data vectors we extract from the media, and the bitrate we want to achieve. The bad news is that we generally need a long data vector for embedding, which is easy for audio or video, but difficult for images. The good news is that we can make the impact of the watermark arbitrarily weak by increasing the dimension $N$.

### 3.5 Detection and Robustness

In the detection phase, Bob takes an individual block $G[K_i]$ and computes $G[K_i]x$ on Alice's image, and $G[K_i]\hat{x}$ on his own copy. In the naive case in which $\hat{x} = x + \epsilon_{N \times 1}$, then $G[K_i]\epsilon$ will be a vector of $N(0, \sigma^2 \sum \epsilon_i^2)$. This versus $G[K_i]x$, a vector whose elements are $N(0, \sigma^2 \sum x_i^2)$. The signal-to-noise ratio in the transformed domain is the same as in the real domain. This is confirmed by observation, as described in section 5.

## 4   Verification Protocol

If we wish, we can use the zero-knowledge protocol described in [5]. In this protocol, all messages $m_k$ are sent from Alice to Bob in a blinded format, and on a coin flip Alice either reveals the discrete logarithm of one of these blinded messages, or reveals the blinding algorithm.

Instead, we use an asymmetric algorithm that is not strictly zero-knowledge. This uses public-key encryption using the El Gamal cipher [11].

1. Alice provides Bob with a large number of selection channel parameters $\{\omega_i\}$. A few of them point to real messages.
2. Bob extracts the messages $m_i = X(\omega_i)$, after verifying that they are indeed detectable in his own image $Y$.
3. Bob uses a pseudo-random seed $s$ to generate a set of encryption parameters $\{r_i\}$. He also chooses an arbitrary challenge message $M$.
4. For each $m_i$, Bob uses El Gamal to compute the ciphertext $C_i, R_i =$ Encrypt$(M, s)$

$$C_i = \{M|s\} \cdot X_i^{r_i} \pmod p, R_i = g^{r_i} \pmod p$$

5. Bob sends all pairs $\{C_i, R_i\}$ to Alice.
6. For one index $i$ for which Alice knows the discrete log of $X_i$, Alice computes $\{M|s\} = C_i \cdot R_i^{-h_i} \pmod p$.
7. Alice then uses the PRNG seed $s$ to compute all other parameters $\{r_i\}$ and decrypts all of Bob's messages. She can now verify that the messages are identical, and contain no tracing information.
8. Alice sends Bob $M$, or a hash $h(M)$.

The penultimate step ensures that Bob is not placing distinct information in each message to determine which one Alice is decrypting. This requires the PRNG hash for generating Bob's nonces to be sent with each encrypted message.

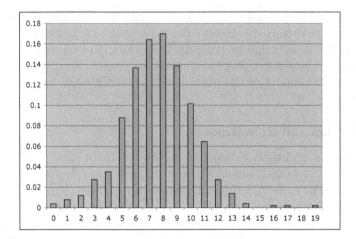

**Fig. 2.** Number of mantissa bits lost during embedding. There are 52 mantissa bits in a double-precision floating point number.

**Fig. 3.** Peppers image before and after embedding

The payload size of this protocol is still large. It requires a one-time transmission of $2BM$, where B is the size of a message (on the order of thousands of bits), and $M$ is the number of parameters $\{\omega_k\}$ originally sent by Alice. All other transmissions are smaller: Alice initially sends M parameters, which can be smaller than a discrete exponential, and ultimately sends one hash value, which is smaller than a discrete exponential.

In contrast, the protocol in [5] required an initial transmission of $M$ shares (not the parameters that generated them, but the messages themselves) followed by an interactive protocol of $t$ trials. In each protocol step Alice sends $M$ messages, and with probability $\frac{1}{2}$ sends a discrete logarithm of one message (in the other case Alice must send the $M$ blinding factors, but if they are securely generated from an PRNG seed she could simply send that). This produces a payload size of $(t+1)BM + tB$. The number of interactive trials $t$ is the log base 2 of the cheater's success rate. A reasonable value for $t$ would be between 10 and 30. Thus this protocol is more size efficient by a decimal order of magnitude.

In terms of time efficiency, the above protocol requires $M$ encryptions and $M$ decryptions, or $2M$ discrete exponentials. The algorithm in [5] requires $tM$ discrete exponentials for Alice, and an expected $t(M/2+1)$ discrete exponentials by Bob. Hence, $t(3M/2 + 1)$ operations are needed for the old protocol, giving us a work reduction of approximately $3t/4$.

## 5   Implementation

We implemented the embedding algorithm for computer images with varying values of $DM$ and $N$. Figure 3 illustrates additive embedding in full-frame DCT

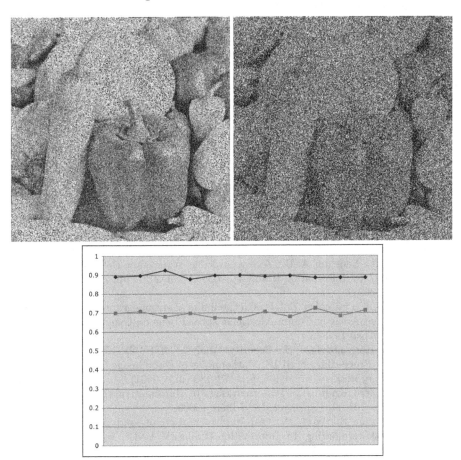

**Fig. 4.** Severely damaged images. Left, channel noise is 0.25 the signal power. Right, channel noise is same as signal power. Below, normalized correlation of random selection channels in the noisy images.

coefficients with $N = 160000$ and $DM = 256$. The expected embedding power is $\alpha = 0.0032$; in experiments the actual value ranged from 0.0029 to 0.0034.

Figure 2 shows the bit errors resulting from the entire process of encoding, embedding, extraction and decoding. Our simple encoding scheme places 32 bits in each coefficient, which survive the process. More sophisticated coding can exploit the remaining bits.

In figure 4 we see the result of a simple attack on the data vector $x$. Here, a noise vector $e$ of $1/4$ the signal variance is added to the data vector. From our previous analysis, we expect the correlation within each channel to be the same as the overall correlation between $x$ and $x + e$. Hence we expect a normalized correlation of 0.89, which we observe. Figure 4 also shows the results for more severe degradation in which the signal and noise are of equal variance.

## 6 Conclusions

In this paper we have outlined a matrix embedding method for asymmetric watermarking. This utilizes the technique of Craver, Liu and Wolf to hide a collection of watermarks among a list of false watermarks, and later prove that at least one watermark is legitimate.

Our method uses a selection channel in which watermark keys, rather than watermarks themselves, can be transmitted to the verifier—a huge size improvement over the algorithm in [5]. The prover can provide as many false watermarks as she wants, or change them from detection to detection, whereas in [5] the number of false watermarks is fixed at embedding. Finally, a one-step protocol is used rather than an interactive zero-knowledge protocol, which reduces the amount of data exchanged as well as compute time by a decimal order of magnitude.

## References

1. Adelsbach, A., Sadeghi, A.-R.: Zero-Knowledge Watermark Detection and Proof of Ownership. In: Information Hiding IV. LNCS, vol. 2137, pp. 273–288. Springer, Heidelberg (2001)
2. Anderson, R.J., Petitcolas, F.A.P.: On the limits of steganography. In: IEEE Journal of Selected Areas in Communications, special issue on Copyright and Privacy Protection (April 1998)
3. Craver, S., Katzenbeisser, S.: Security Analysis of Public-Key Watermarking Schemes. In: Proceedings of SPIE, Mathematics of Data/Image Coding, Compression and Encryption IV, vol. 4475, pp. 172–182 (July 2001)
4. Craver, S.: Zero Knowledge Watermarking. In: Information Hiding III. LNCS, vol. 1768, pp. 101–116. Springer, Heidelberg (2000)
5. Craver, S., Liu, B., Wolf, W.: An Implementation of, and Attacks on, Zero-Knowledge Watermarking. In: Information Hiding IV. LNCS, vol. 3200, pp. 1–12. Springer, Heidelberg (2004)
6. Craver, S.: The Return of Ambiguity Attacks. In: Proceedings of SPIE, Security and Watermarking of Multimedia Contents IV, pp. 252–259 (January 2002)
7. Cox, I., Miller, M., Bloom, J.: Digital Watermarking. Morgan Kaufmann, San Francisco (2002)

8. Fridrich, J., Soukal, D.: Matrix embedding for large payloads. In: Proceedings of SPIE, Security and Watermarking of Multimedia Contents VIII, pp. 6072–68 (January 2006)
9. Hartung, F.H., Su, J.K., Girod, B.: Spread spectrum watermarking: malicious attacks and counterattacks. In: Proceedings of SPIE, pp. 147–158, San Jose, CA (February 1999)
10. Hartung, F.H., Girod, B.: Fast Public-Key Watermarking of Compressed Video. In: Proceedings of IEEE International Conference on Speech and Signal Processing (1997)
11. Schneier, B.: Applied Cryptograpy: Protocols, Algorithms, and Source Code in C, 2nd edn. John Wiley and Sons, New York (1996)
12. Viega, J., Girouard, Z., Messier, M.: Secure Programming Cookbook. O'Reilly (2003)

# A Cryptographic Method
# for Secure Watermark Detection

Michael Malkin[1] and Ton Kalker[2]

[1] Stanford University,
Stanford, CA, USA
mikeym@cs.stanford.edu
[2] Hewlett-Packard Laboratories
Palo Alto, CA, USA
ton.kalker@hp.com

**Abstract.** We present a semi-public key implementation of quantization index modulation (QIM) watermarking called Secure QIM (SQIM). Given a signal, a watermark detector can learn the presence of an SQIM watermark without learning anything anything else from the detection process. The watermark detector first transforms the signal with a secret transform, unknown to the detector, and then quantizes the transform coefficients with secret quantizers, also unknown to the detector. This is done with the use of homomorphic cryptosystems, where calculations are performed in an encrypted domain. A low-power, trusted, secure module is used at the end of the process and reveals only if the signal was watermarked or not. Even after repeated watermark detections, no more information is revealed than the watermarked status of the signals. The methods we present are for watermark systems with quantizers of stepsize 2.

## 1 Introduction

When watermarking occurs for the purposes of digital rights management (DRM), watermark embedding is performed in a trusted environment, while watermark detection is performed "in the wild". That is, the watermark detector is assumed to be a trusted party, but it is generally operating in a hostile environment where the end-user would like to circumvent the DRM. One way to keep the watermarking secret and functionality out of the hands of hostile parties is to embed it in a physically secure device, such as a smartcard, which can be operated in a black-box manner. However, such devices generally have very low computing capacity, and will be unable to perform watermark detection very quickly on their own. Our strategy, also proposed in other papers, is to have the watermark detector work in an encrypted domain and use a trusted secure device, called the *secure module*, to finish the detection process.

Secure QIM (SQIM) uses public and private keys much like public key cryptosystems such as RSA. The private key is used by the watermark embedder to generate watermarks while the public key is used by the watermark detector to

J. Camenisch et al. (Eds.): IH 2006, LNCS 4437, pp. 26–41, 2007.

perform watermark detection in an encrypted domain. Finally, the secure module uses the private key to decrypt the results produced by the watermark detector. The secure module must be initialized by communication with the watermark embedder to receive the private key information. In a sense, this system is not truly asymmetric but rather semi-asymmetric, since the aid of a trusted third party (the secure module) is required.

Our first goal is to ensure that the act of detecting a watermark reveals as little information as possible to the watermark detector. Because the secure module is low-power and low-bandwidth, our second goal is to ensure that the watermark detector takes on as much of the computational burden as is possible, and transmits a few bits to the secure module as possible. Two cryptosystems are used to allow the watermark detector to perform the necessary calculations without learning any information about the watermarking secrets. These systems are *homomorphic*, meaning that an operation performed on ciphertexts corresponds to another operation performed on plaintexts. For example, in the Paillier cryptosystem (see Section 3.1), if $E(\cdot)$ is the encryption function, then $E(x)E(y) = E(x + y)$. The homomorphic properties of these cryptosystems are what make it possible for the watermark detector to run the algorithm without learning anything.

However, even though the watermark detector gains no extra knowledge through the detection process, knowledge of the presence or absence of watermarks is sufficient to mount *oracle attacks* (see Cox and Linnartz [5], Venturini [18], and Li and Chang [14], for example). The purpose of these attacks is to find the boundary separating watermarked signals from non-watermarked signals, and use this boundary to learn the watermarking secret. Such attacks are much more powerful than attacks on the cryptosystems presented in this paper, and are possible whenever a watermark detector can test signals for watermarks.

One defense against oracle attacks is to increase the time required for watermark detection, effectively limiting the speed of the "oracle" (See Venturini [18]). This would not be possible with a fully assymetric watermarking scheme, since the speed of such a watermark detector would be limited only by the speed of the machine that is running it. A trusted secure module could have a built-in delay, or a limit on the number of watermark detections per minute, and could thereby help to slow the rate of convergence of oracle attacks.

On the other hand, the use of a secure module introduces side channel attacks, for example timing attacks (see Kocher [10], and Brumley and Boneh [2]), and power attacks (see Kocher et al. [12]). In these attacks, the secure module is monitored externally to guess at the operations occurring internally. An implementation of SQIM would have to take side channel attacks into account, but a detailed discussion of these attacks is beyond the scope of this paper.

Quantization Index Modulation (QIM), developed by Chen and Wornell [4], embeds a watermark into an signal by manipulating the signal so that transform coefficients are quantized in a specific manner. A watermark detector transforms a signal and checks to see if the transform coefficients are appropriately quantized. There are two phases to securely detecting a QIM watermark. First a *hidden transform* is performed on the signal, and second the transform coefficients are quantized via *hidden quantization*. After hidden quantization the secure module counts the number of watermarked transform coefficients and reveals whether a threshold of the coefficients were watermarked. The method presented in the paper only works for quantizers with stepsize 2.

Attempts have been made at completely asymmetric watermarking schemes (see Eggers et al. [6] and Hachez and Quisquater [7]), but these have generally not been completely successful. Another specific method of performing asymmetric watermarking involves multi-round zero knowledge proofs (see Adelsbach and Sadeghi [1], for example). Kalker [8] introduced the idea of using a secure module to enable semi-public key watermarking, using a variant of the Paillier cryptosystem to perform secure spread spectrum watermarking. In comparison with the spread spectrum scheme, a SQIM scheme must implement a nonlinear operation in an encrypted domain, namely quantization. For more discussion of secure watermarking and the SQIM system, see Malkin [11].

Section 2 outlines the QIM watermarking scheme. Section 3 reviews homomorphic cryptography and introduces the two cryptosystems used in this paper. Section 4 discusses how to perform a hidden transform, while Section 5 discusses how to perform hidden quantization. Section 6 presents the full Secure QIM system. Finally, in Section 7 we discuss the efficiency of SQIM and in Section 8 we prove that SQIM is zero knowledge and that it is secure.

## 2   QIM

We consider a simple variant of QIM with dithered scalar quantizers. Our purpose is not to improve the watermarking aspects of QIM, but to ensure that watermark detection is secure. Therefore, watermark embedding is not changed at all, and watermark detection is changed only in that all calculations are performed in a secure manner. We will discuss watermark detection first, and then explain how a watermark is embedded into a signal. We are only concerned with whether or not a signal was watermarked, so we do not use the watermark to embed data into a signal.

To detect a watermark in a signal, the signal is first transformed with a secret, random linear transform, for example a DCT or wavelet transform. For every transform coefficient $t_i$, there are two secret quantizers, $Q_0^i$ and $Q_1^i$. If $t_i$ is closer to a quantization point on $Q_0^i$, then it corresponds to 0, otherwise it corresponds to 1. In this way, each transform coefficient is assigned a value. If a threshold of transform coefficients have the correct, watermarked value, then the signal is considered to be watermarked. If not, the signal is considered not watermarked.

Embedding a watermark into a signal involves changing the signal so that the correct values are obtained after quantizing the transform coefficients. The most straightforward approach is to transform the signal, quantize the transform coefficients, and perform the inverse transform. Other embedding schemes, such as distortion-compensated QIM [4], may also be used.

# 3 Homomorphic Cryptosystems

We use two cryptosystems, the Paillier cryptosystem and the Goldwasser-Micali cryptosystem, both of which are *probabilistic public-key* cryptosystems. They are public key in that a public key is used to encrypt plaintext, while a private key is needed to decrypt a ciphertext, and the two keys are computationally not easily derived from each other. They are probabilistic in the sense that the same plaintext is represented by a large number of ciphertexts. This is important when the range of possible plaintexts is small. For example, when encrypting 0 or 1, a non-probabilistic cryptosystem can produce only 2 possible ciphertexts, whereas a probabilistic cryptosystem can produce many different ciphertexts.

This last property is especially important in the current application. For example, if samples were in the range $[0, ..., 255]$, then there would be only 256 possible encryptions of the samples. This would make it much easier to break the system by looking at the transcripts of many watermark detections. Even relabelling the sample values would not solve the problem; there would be 256! possible relabellings, but statistical analysis could be used to easily find the correct one. With probabilistic cryptosystems, the values would be effectively *blinded*, so that this essentially brute-force searching attack would not be possible.

Both of these cryptosystems share another important property: they are homomorphic. This means that a mathematical operation performed on ciphertexts corresponds to a mathematical operation performed on plaintexts. For example, if $E(\cdot)$ corresponds to encryption in the Paillier cryptosystem, then we can write the homomorphism of the Paillier cryptosystem as

$$E(a_1)E(a_2) = E(a_1 + a_2).$$

Homomorphic cryptosystems enable the watermark detector to perform calculations without explicitly knowing what is being calculated or finding out the results of the calculation. For example, given $\alpha = E(a)$, but not knowing the value of $a$, we could compute the encryption of $7a + 3$ as

$$\alpha^7 E(3) = E(7a + 3).$$

Furthermore, with the right public values, it would be possible for us to compute, in the encrypted domain, any polynomial function of a given public input. For example, say $\alpha_1 = E(a_1)$, $\alpha_2 = E(a_2)$, and $\alpha_3 = E(a_3)$ were public, and we were asked to compute $a_1 x^2 + a_2 x + a_3$ in the encrypted domain. We could do this as

$$\alpha_1^{(x^2)} \alpha_2^x \alpha_3 = E(a_1 x^2 + a_2 x + a_3).$$

We would know the encryption of the polynomial, but have no knowledge of the actual value.    -

## 3.1 Paillier Cryptosystem

The Paillier cryptosystem is homomorphic, with multiplication of ciphertexts corresponding to the addition of the plaintexts. Furthermore, exponentiation of a ciphertext corresponds to multiplication of the plaintext. We present a very brief summary of the system. See Paillier [13] for more details.

Let $N = pq$, where $p$ and $q$ are primes. Choose $g \in \mathbb{Z}_{N^2}^*$ such that the order of $g$ is divisible by $N$. Any such $g$ is of the form $g \equiv (1 + N)^a b^N \bmod N^2$ for a pair $(a, b)$, where $a \in \mathbb{Z}_N$ and $b \in Z_N^*$. Note that $(1 + N)^a \equiv 1 + aN \bmod N^2$, so $g \equiv (1 + aN)b^N \bmod N^2$. Let $\lambda = \mathrm{lcm}(p - 1, q - 1)$. The public key is $(g, N)$, the private key is $\lambda$. For message $m$ and blinding factor $r \in \mathbb{Z}_N^*$, Paillier encryption is defined as

$$E_P(m, r; g, N) = g^m r^N \bmod N^2.$$

Note the equalities:

$$E_P(m_1, r_1; g, N) \cdot E_P(m_1, r_1; g, N) = E_P(m_1 + m_2, r_1 r_2; g, N),$$

$$E_P(m, r; g, N)^k = E_P(mk, r^k; g, N).$$

In the Paillier cryptosystem, decryption is more complicated than encryption. First note that for any $x \in \mathbb{Z}_{N^2}^*$,

$$x^\lambda \equiv 1 \,(\bmod\ N),$$
$$x^{N\lambda} \equiv 1 \,(\bmod\ N^2).$$

Given $c = E_P(m, r; g, N) = g^m r^N \bmod N^2$, we can see that

$$\begin{aligned} c^\lambda &\equiv g^{m\lambda} r^{N\lambda} \\ &\equiv (1 + N)^{am\lambda} b^{\lambda N m} \\ &\equiv 1 + am\lambda N \,(\bmod\ N^2). \end{aligned}$$

Note also that $g^\lambda \equiv [(1 + N)^a b^N]^\lambda \equiv 1 + a\lambda N \,(\bmod\ N^2)$. Therefore,

$$\frac{(c^\lambda \bmod\ N^2) - 1}{N} = a\lambda m \quad \text{and} \quad \frac{(g^\lambda \bmod\ N^2) - 1}{N} = a\lambda$$

To simplify, let $f_N(x) = \frac{(x \bmod\ N^2) - 1}{N}$. Then we decrypt by computing

$$m = D_P(c; g, \lambda, N) = \frac{f_N(c^\lambda)}{f_N(g^\lambda)} \bmod N.$$

Optimizations are discussed by Catalano et al. [3], Damgård and Jurik [15], and Kalker [8].

## 3.2   Goldwasser-Micali Cryptosystem

The Goldwasser-Micali cryptosystem was developed in 1984 by Goldwasser and Micali [16]. It encrypts a single bit of information and is homomorphic in that multiplying ciphertexts corresponds to finding the XOR of the plaintexts. This cryptosystem is based on *quadratic residues*. A number is a quadratic residue modulo an odd prime $p$ if it is the square of some number modulo $p$.

**Definition 1 (Legendre symbol).** *The Legendre symbol is defined as*

$$\left(\frac{x}{p}\right) = \begin{cases} 0 & \text{if } x \equiv 0 \pmod{p} \\ 1 & \text{if } x \text{ is a quadratic residue modulo } p \\ -1 & \text{if } x \text{ is a quadratic non-residue modulo } p \end{cases}$$

By Euler's criterion[17], we compute $\left(\frac{x}{p}\right) = x^{\frac{p-1}{2}} \pmod{p}$.

In the case of a composite modulus, the *Jacobi symbol* is used instead of the Legendre symbol.

**Definition 2 (Jacobi symbol).** *For $N = pq$, where $p$ and $q$ are odd primes, the Jacobi symbol is*

$$\left(\frac{x}{N}\right) = \begin{cases} 0 & \text{if } \gcd(x, N) > 1 \\ 1 & \text{if } \left(\frac{x}{p}\right) = \left(\frac{x}{q}\right) \\ -1 & \text{if } \left(\frac{x}{p}\right) = -\left(\frac{x}{q}\right) \end{cases}$$

**Definition 3 (QR).** *Let $QR(N)$ be the set of all quadratic residues modulo $N$.*

**Lemma 1.** $x$ *is a quadratic residue modulo $N$ iff $\left(\frac{x}{p}\right) = \left(\frac{x}{q}\right) = 1$. If $x$ is a quadratic residue modulo $N^2$ then it is a quadratic residue modulo $N$.*

*Proof.* If $x \in QR(N)$ then $x = y^2 + kN = y^2 + kpq$ for some $y, k$, so $x \equiv y^2 \pmod{p}$ and $x \bmod p \in QR(p)$. The same holds for $q$, so $\left(\frac{x}{p}\right) = \left(\frac{x}{q}\right) = 1$. Given $x$ such that $\left(\frac{x}{p}\right) = \left(\frac{x}{q}\right) = 1$, we know that there exist $a$ and $b$ such that $a^2 \equiv x \pmod{p}$ and $b^2 \equiv x \pmod{q}$. By the Chinese Remainder Theorem [9], there exists a $y$ such that $y \equiv a \pmod{p}$ and $y \equiv b \pmod{q}$. Since, $y^2 \equiv x \pmod{p}$ and $y^2 \equiv x \pmod{q}$, we know that $y^2 \equiv x \pmod{N}$, and therefore $x \in QR(N)$. If $x \in QR(N^2)$ then $x = y^2 + kN^2$ for some $y, k$, so $x \bmod N \in QR(N)$. $\square$

**Definition 4 (Q̃R).** $x$ *is a* pseudosquare *modulo $N$ if $\left(\frac{x}{p}\right) = \left(\frac{x}{q}\right) = -1$. Define $\tilde{Q}R(N)$ to be the set of pseudosquares modulo $N$.*

It is easy to calculate Jacobi symbols, even if the factors of $N$ are unknown (see Koblitz [9]). However, if the factorization of $N$ is unknown, it is not always easy to determine quadratic residuosity. For any $x \in QR(N) \cup \tilde{Q}R(N)$, $\left(\frac{x}{N}\right) = 1$, but determining if $x \in QR(N)$ is a classical hard problem in cryptography and is assumed to be impossible without factoring $N$. If $p$ and $q$ are known, it is easy to determine if such an $x$ is a quadratic residue by computing $\left(\frac{x}{p}\right) = x^{\frac{p-1}{2}} \pmod{p}$ as above.

**The Goldwasser-Micali Cryptosystem.** Let $N = pq$, where $p$ and $q$ are safe primes. Choose $g \in \tilde{Q}R(N)$. $N$ and $g$ are public while the factorization of $N$ is private. Encryption takes as input a single bit $b$ and a random blinding factor $r \in \mathbb{Z}_N^*$. The Goldwasser-Micali cryptosystem is defined as

$$E_{GM}(b, r; g, N) = g^b r^2 \bmod N.$$

Decryption is defined as

$$D_{GM}(x; p, q) = \begin{cases} 0 \text{ if } x \in QR(N) \\ 1 \text{ if } x \in \tilde{Q}R(N) \end{cases}$$

If the factorization of $N$ is known, decryption can easily be done by computing $\left(\frac{x}{p}\right) = x^{(p-1)/2} \bmod p$. Otherwise decryption is not possible, since it requires distinguishing members of $QR(N)$ from members of $\tilde{Q}R(N)$ (see Section 3.2).

This system is homomorphic in that multiplying ciphertexts is equivalent to XORing plaintexts. Note the following equalities:

$$E_{GM}(b_1, r_1; g, N) \cdot E_{GM}(b_2, r_2; g, N) \equiv g^{b_1 + b_2} (r_1 r_2)^2 \pmod{N}.$$

$$\equiv E_{GM}(b_1 \oplus b_2, r_1 r_2; g, N) \pmod{N}.$$

The last equality holds because only the least bit of $b_1 + b_2$ matters, and $\oplus$ is equivalent to modulo 2 addition.

# 4    Phase I: Hidden Transform

The first phase of Secure QIM is a hidden linear transform. This means that the watermark detector takes the sample values from the signal and performs a transform on the sample values without learning the transform or the resulting transform coefficients.

Using the Paillier cryptosystem, we know how to perform addition and multiplication in the plaintext domain by performing the corresponding operations of multiplication and exponentiation in the ciphertext domain. Let a signal consist of $m$ samples, $\boldsymbol{y} = (y_1, ..., y_m)^T$. The random transform takes $\boldsymbol{y}$ as input and produces $n$ transform coefficients, $\boldsymbol{t} = (t_1, ..., t_n)^T$. Let the watermark embedder choose an orthogonal transform $\boldsymbol{S} = \{s_{ij}\}$, for $i = 1...n$ and $j = 1...m$, and let $\boldsymbol{s}_i$ be row $i$ of the transform. Note that $\boldsymbol{t} = \boldsymbol{S}\boldsymbol{y}$ and $t_i = \boldsymbol{s}_i \cdot \boldsymbol{y}$.

The watermark detector is not allowed to know any of the values of $\boldsymbol{S}$, nor any of the values of $\boldsymbol{t}$. This is achieved by performing all the calculations in the Paillier encrypted domain. First, the watermark embedder chooses $N = pq$, where $p$ and $q$ are primes, and chooses a random $g \in \mathbb{Z}_{N^2}^*$ such that the order of $g$ is divisible by $N$. Next, for $i \in [1, n], j \in [1, m]$, it generates random $\beta_{ij} \in \mathbb{Z}_N^*$. The public key consists of encryptions of the transform matrix $\boldsymbol{V} = \{v_{ij}\}$ where $v_{ij} = E_P(s_{ij}, \beta_{ij}; g, N)$.

The watermark detector wants to find $c = (c_1, ..., c_m)$, the hidden transform coefficients. It does so by computing

$$c_i = \prod_j (v_{ij})^{y_j} \bmod N^2.$$

For later convenience in notation, define $w_i = \prod_{j=1}^m \beta_{ij}^{y_j}$. Then by the homomorphic properties of the Paillier cryptosystem, we have

$$c_i = \prod_j v_{ij}^{y_j} \bmod N^2 = \prod_j E_P(s_{ij}, \beta_{ij}; g, N)^{y_j} \bmod N^2$$

$$= \prod_j E_P(s_{ij} y_j, \beta_{ij}^{y_j}; g, N) \bmod N^2 = E_P(\sum_j s_{ij} y_j, \prod_j \beta_{ij}^{y_j}; g, N)$$

$$= E_P(s_i \cdot y, w_i; g, N) = E_P(t_i, w_i; g, N).$$

## 5  Phase II: Hidden Quantization

This section will present a simplified version of the hidden quantization scheme, uncoupled from the hidden transform, for a clearer presentation. The full version will be presented in Section 6.

The watermark embedder chooses $N = pq$, where $p$ and $q$ are safe primes, and $g \in \tilde{Q}R(N)$. It also chooses private quantization values $q = (q_1, ..., q_n)$ where each $q_i \in \{0, 1\}$, and blinding values $\gamma = (\gamma_1, ..., \gamma_n)$ where each $\gamma_i \in \mathbb{Z}_N^*$, and calculates $k = (k_1, ..., k_n)$, $k_i = E_{GM}(q_i, \gamma_i; g, N)$. It publishes $g$, $N$, and $k$, and reveals the value of $p$ to the secure module.

The watermark detector knows the public values $g$, $N$, and $k$. Assume in this section that it has $n$ unencrypted transform coefficients, $t = (t_1, ..., t_n)$. If the signal is watermarked, these coefficients will each quantized so that $t_i \equiv q_i \pmod 2$, but for any given coefficient, the watermark detector does not know the correct quantization value. The key point to notice is that if the signal is watermarked, $t_i \oplus q_i \equiv 0 \pmod 2$.

First, the watermark detector chooses $\alpha = (\alpha_1, ..., \alpha_n)$, with $\alpha_i \in \mathbb{Z}_N^*$, and encrypts the transform coefficients,

$$c_i = E_{GM}(t_i \bmod 2, \alpha_i; g, N).$$

Then it computes

$$
\begin{aligned}
f_i &= c_i k_i \\
&= E_{GM}(t_i \bmod 2, \alpha_i; g, N) E_{GM}(q_i, \gamma_i; g, N) \\
&= E((t_i \bmod 2) \oplus q_i, r_i; g, N).
\end{aligned}
$$

Note that $f_i$ is a Goldwasser-Micali encryption of 0 if $t_i$ is watermarked, 1 otherwise.

The secure module has a threshold function, $T(n)$. It is given as input $f_1, ..., f_n$, decrypts each $f_i$, sums the values, and announces that the data is watermarked if

$$\sum_{i=1}^{n} D_{\mathrm{GM}}(f_i; p, q) \leq T(n).$$

# 6   Secure QIM

This section presents the full system, in which the watermark detector performs a hidden transform on the input data and then quantizes the transform coefficients while still in the encrypted domain. It is a combination of the systems from Sections 4 and 5 with a careful choice of $g$ and the blinding factors so that the ciphertexts of the hidden transform can be used for hidden quantization. In Sections 6.1, 6.2, and 6.3, we discuss the basic SQIM scheme, and in Section 6.4 we present modifications that prevent abuse by a malicious adversary.

## 6.1   Initialization

The watermark embedder chooses $N = pq$, where $p$ and $q$ are safe primes. Recall that for such $N$, $\lambda = \mathrm{LCM}(p - 1, q - 1)$. $g \in \mathbb{Z}_{N^2}^*$ is chosen so that $g \bmod N \in \tilde{\mathrm{QR}}(N)$ and the order of $g$, denoted $\mathrm{ORD}(g)$, is $kN$, where $k | \lambda$. All such $g$ can be generated as follows. Choose $a \in Z_N^*$, so $\mathrm{GCD}(a, N) = 1$, and $b \in \tilde{\mathrm{QR}}(N)$. Let $g = (1 + N)^a b^N \bmod N^2$. Because $(1 + N)^a \equiv 1 + aN \bmod N$, we can write

$$g = (1 + aN)b^N \bmod N^2.$$

*Claim.* $g \bmod N \in \tilde{\mathrm{QR}}(N)$ and $\mathrm{ORD}(g) = kN$.

*Proof.* Notice that $g \equiv b^N \pmod{N}$. Since $N$ is odd, $b^N \bmod N \in \tilde{\mathrm{QR}}(N)$, so $g \bmod N \in \tilde{\mathrm{QR}}(N)$. Because $\mathrm{ORD}(1 + N) = N$ and $\mathrm{GCD}(a, N) = 1$, $\mathrm{ORD}(1 + N)^a = N$. Let $k = \mathrm{ORD}(b^N)$. Since $b^N \in Z_N^*$, $k | \phi(N)$, and since $N$ and $\phi(N)$ share no factors, $\mathrm{GCD}(k, N) = 1$. Therefore, $\mathrm{ORD}(g) = \mathrm{ORD}(1 + N)\mathrm{ORD}(b^N) = kN$.                                                                                              □

## 6.2   Watermark Embedding

The watermark embedder chooses an orthogonal transform $S = \{s_{ij}\}$, for $i = 1...n$ and $j = 1...m$. Let $s_i$ be row $i$ of the transform. The embedder also chooses $q = (q_1, ..., q_n)$, with each $q_i \in \{0, 1\}$. It takes as input the signal $x = (x_1, ..., x_m)$ and produces a watermarked signal $y = (y_1, ..., y_n)$ such that for all $i$, $s_i \cdot y \equiv q_i \pmod{2}$.

For $i \in [1, n], j \in [1, m]$, $\beta_{ij}$ is chosen such that $\beta_{ij} \in \mathrm{QR}(N)$. For $i \in [1, n]$, $\gamma_i$ is chosen so that $\gamma_i \in \mathrm{QR}(N)$. Let $V = \{v_{ij}\}$ where $v_{ij} = E_P(s_{ij}, \beta_{ij}; g, N)$, and $k = (k_1, ..., k_n)$ where $k_i = E_{\mathrm{GM}}(q_i, \gamma_i; g, N)$. The public watermarking key consists of $N$, $V$, and $k$.

## 6.3   Watermark Detection

First, the watermark detector finds the encrypted transform coefficients $c = (c_1, ..., c_m)$. Recall that $t_i = s_i \cdot y$. Let $w_i = \prod_{j=1}^m \beta_{ij}^{y_j}$. Then

$$c_i = \prod_j v_{ij}^{y_j} \bmod N^2 = E_P(t_i, w_i; g, N) = g^{t_i} w_i^N \bmod N^2.$$

At this point we change from looking at ciphertexts modulo $N^2$ and begin looking at them modulo $N$. This is done so that the ciphertexts will be compatible with the Goldwasser-Micali cryptosystem.

We will now show that if $t_i \bmod 2 = 0$, then $c_i \bmod N \in QR(N)$, otherwise $c_i \bmod N \in \tilde{Q}R(N)$. Since each $\beta_{ij} \in QR(N)$, then $w_i \in QR(N)$ and therefore $(w_i)^N \bmod N \in QR(N)$. If $t_i \bmod 2 = 0$, then $g^{t_i} \bmod N \in QR(N)$. Otherwise, since $g \bmod N \in \tilde{Q}R(N)$, $g^{t_i} \bmod N \in \tilde{Q}R(N)$. Therefore, if $t_i \bmod 2 = 0$ then $c_i \in QR(N)$ otherwise, $c_i \in \tilde{Q}R(N)$. In both cases $\left(\frac{c_i}{N}\right) = 1$. Therefore,

$$c_i \bmod N = E_{GM}(t_i \bmod 2, w_i^N g^{2\lfloor \frac{t_i}{2} \rfloor}; g, N).$$

Now we begin hidden quantization. Let $f_i = c_i k_i \bmod N$ and $z_i = w_i^N g^{2\lfloor \frac{t_i}{2} \rfloor}$.

$$f_i = c_i k_i \bmod N = E_{GM}(t_i \bmod 2, z_i; g, N) E_{GM}(q_i, \gamma_i; g, N) \bmod N$$

$$= E_{GM}((t_i \bmod 2) \oplus q_i, \gamma_i z_i; g, N).$$

So, $D_{GM}(f_i; p, q) = (t_i \bmod 2) \oplus q_i$, which is 0 if $t_i$ was correctly quantized, 1 otherwise.

The secure module is given as input $f_1, ..., f_n$ and knows a threshold function $T(n)$. It decrypts each $f_i$, sums the values, and announces that the data is watermarked if

$$\sum_{i=1}^n D_{GM}(f_i; p, q) \leq T(n).$$

## 6.4   Verification

It is possible for a malicious watermark detector to abuse the secure module. For example, if a watermark detector has a Goldwasser-Micali ciphertext $y = E_{GM}(x, r; g, N)$ but does not know $x$, it can set the input to the secure module to be $n$ copies of $y$. If the secure module says "watermarked", then the detector knows $x = 0$, otherwise it knows that $x = 1$. The watermark detector can trick the secure module into functioning as a Goldwasser-Micali decryption oracle.

To prevent this sort of abuse, we force the watermark detector to prove that each query to the secure module is valid in that is comes from an honest execution of the SQIM algorithm. If the a query is not proved to be valid, the secure module refuses to respond.

There are two steps to prove validity. First the detector proves *legitimacy*, the fact that the inputs to the secure module are the result of homomorphic operations on ciphertexts from existing public watermarking keys. This prevents the detector from inventing new ciphertexts to use as input to the secure module, as in the example above. Next the detector proves *wholeness*, which prevents mixing and matching attacks. This prevents the watermark detector from mixing parts of multiple transform matrices, and forces it to calculate all transform coefficients with the same signal.

We now describe the modifications to the Secure QIM scheme that are necessary to prove legitimacy and wholeness. Section 8.1 describes how the modifications prove these properties.

**Legitimacy.** Each public watermarking key must now include two encryptions of the transform matrix: $V = \{v_{ij}\}$, $v_{ij} = E_P(s_{ij}, \beta_{ij}; g, N)$; and $W = \{w_{ij}\}$, $w_{ij} = E_P(s_{ij}, \beta_{ij}; h, N)$; where $h$ is formed as $g$ is in Section 6.1, but $h \neq g$. The watermark detector uses $V$ to compute $c = \{c_i\}$ as in Section 6.3, and likewise uses $W$ to compute $c' = \{c'_i\}$. Note that the decryptions of $c_i$ and $c'_i$ are equal, but the ciphertexts that were used to generate $c_i$ were encrypted with $g$, while those that were used to generate $c'_i$ were encrypted with $h$.

Queries to the secure module now consist of $n$ 4-tuples: $(c_i, c'_i, k_i, f_i)$. The secure module checks that for all $i$,

$$D_P(c_i; g, \lambda, N) = D_P(c'_i; h, \lambda, N), \tag{1}$$

then checks that

$$f_i = c_i k_i \bmod N. \tag{2}$$

If either of these conditions do not hold for any $i$, then $f_i$ is not legitimate and the secure module does not respond to the query.

**Wholeness.** The wholeness constructions make use of a public hash function, $H(\cdot)$. Any hash function will do as long as it is collision-resistant. This means that it is difficult to find any pairs $(x, y)$ where $x \neq y$ but $H(x) = H(y)$.

During initialization, the watermark embedder chooses a random $\theta = \{\theta_1, ..., \theta_n\}$ where $\theta_i \in Z_N^*$. It includes in the watermarking public key $\sigma = E_P(H(\theta), \rho_0; g, N)$ as well as $\Theta = \{\Theta_1, ..., \Theta_n\}$, where $\Theta_i = E_P(\theta_i, \rho_i; g, N)$ and the $\rho_i$ are random blinding factors. It also includes $\Delta = E_P(H(\theta, k), \tau; g, N)$, with blinding factor $\tau$. Note that the hash in $\Delta$ includes $k$, not $q$.

In Section 6.2, the hidden transform was chosen as $S = \{s_{ij}\}$, for $i = 1...n$ and $j = 1...m$. We now add an extra row, $s_0$, to the top of the matrix $S$. $s_0$ is formed as a random linear combination of the all the other rows, $s_i$:

$$s_0 = \sum_{i=1}^{n} \theta_i s_i.$$

Letting $k_0 = 0$ and $f_0 = 0$, we can say that the 4-tuple corresponding to $s_0$ is $(c_0, c'_0, k_0, f_0)$.

When the secure module receives a query, it is first given $\sigma$, $\Theta$, and $\Delta$. It decrypts $\sigma$ and $\Theta$ and checks if $D_P(\sigma; g, \lambda, N) = H(\theta_1, ..., \theta_n)$. If not, $\theta$ is corrupt and the secure module refuses to respond. Next it checks if that $D_P(\Delta; g, \lambda, N) = H(\theta_1, ..., \theta_n, k_1, ..., k_n)$. If not, $k$ is corrupt and the secure module refuses to respond. Finally, it checks if

$$D_P(c_0; g, \lambda, N) = \sum_{i=1}^{n} \theta_i D_P(c_i; g, \lambda, N). \tag{3}$$

If equation 3 does not hold, the transform was corrupt and the secure module does not respond.

# 7  Efficiency

In this section we will compare the efficiency of standard QIM with that of Secure QIM. Note that in both cases, the secure module starts off knowing the Paillier and Goldwasser-Micali private keys, but does not know any transform matrices or quantization values. In standard QIM, performed with a random transform on a secure module, the secure module is given a signal, an encrypted transform matrix, and encrypted quantization values, and performs QIM watermark detection by itself.

In our analysis we are concerned with the communication and computation required of the secure module. Let signals be of length $m$ and let there be $n$ transform coefficients. Samples of the signal are k-bit numbers and encryptions modulo $N$ have $\ell = \log_2 N$ bits.

**Communication.** In standard QIM, the secure module can receive all the information in an efficiently encrypted form. As such, we will calculate the number of bits that would be required unencrypted, and will assume that encryption adds negligible overhead. The secure module receives the signal ($mk$ bits), the encrypted transform matrix ($mnk$ bits), and the encrypted quantization values ($n$ bits), for a total of $mnk + mk + n$ bits. The $mnk$ term will dominate.

In SQIM, each number is encrypted individually modulo $N$ or $N^2$. The secure module receives $(n + 1)$ 4-tuples of $6\ell$ bits ($6(n + 1)\ell$ bits), $\sigma$ ($2\ell$ bits), $\Theta$ ($2n\ell$ bits), and $\Delta$ ($2\ell$ bits), for a total of $8n\ell + 10\ell$. The $8n\ell$ term dominates.

In comparison, standard QIM requires $\frac{m}{8}\frac{k}{\ell}$ times more bits than SQIM. Since $m$ is the number of samples in the signal, this is a very large difference. For example, consider a signal of $m = 10^5$ samples, with $k = 24$, $n = 25$, and $\ell = 1024$. Then SQIM requires 26.3 kilobytes while standard QIM requires 7.4 megabytes. At a rate of 9600 bits per second, it would take 22.4 seconds to complete the SQIM data transfer, whereas it would take 1.8 hours for the standard QIM data transfer.

**Computation.** The computational costs are harder to compute and more dependent on specific implementation. We estimate the cost of standard QIM as the cost of performing the transform. Assuming straightforward matrix multiplication, this will have a running time of $O(nmk^2)$. We estimate the cost of SQIM based on the total number of decryptions. There are approximately $5n$ decryptions, which results in a running time of $O(n\ell^3)$. $\ell^3$ very large, but $\ell$ is fixed based on security needs. $k$ is generally in a small range, say 8 to 24 bits. So, the relative performance is highly dependent on the number of samples in the signal. With a small number of samples, standard QIM will be faster, while with a very large number of samples SQIM will be faster.

## 8   Security

Given the security of the Goldwasser-Micali and Paillier cryptosystems, our system is secure and zero knowledge. Length limitations prevent detailed proofs, so we offer proof sketches instead. More detailed proofs appear in Malkin [11].

### 8.1   Proof of Verification

The proof of zero knowledge rests upon the fact that invalid queries to the secure module will be rejected. Now we sketch proofs of this fact, taking our notation from Sections 6.2 and 6.3.

**Legitimacy.** Recall that equation 1 requires that

$$D_P(c_i; g, \lambda, N) = D_P(c_i'; h, \lambda, N).$$

It is impossible for a watermark detector to produce $c$ and $c'$ such that this equation holds, other than by generating them homomorphically from hidden transform values.

Assume that algorithm $\mathcal{A}$ can produce $c$ and $c'$ that satisfy equation 1. By definition of Paillier decryption, that is equivalent to saying

$$c = g^m r_1^N \bmod N^2 \tag{4}$$

$$c' = h^m r_2^N \bmod N^2 \tag{5}$$

for some $m$ and some blinding factors $r_1$ and $r_2$. Note however, that $\mathcal{A}$ doesn't know $g$ or $h$. This means that equations 4 and 5 must simultaneously be true for all possible pairs $(g, h)$ (perhaps with a different $m$ per pair). This is not possible, so $\mathcal{A}$ can not exist. Note that this proof can also be extended to work when the algorithm $\mathcal{A}$ is probabilistic.

The only access to $g$ and $h$ that the detector has is through the encrypted values in the public watermarking key, so all $c$ and $c'$ are the result of homomorphic operations on such values.

Equation 2 ($f_i = c_i k_i \bmod N$) guarantees that the $f_i$ were generated by performing hidden quantization on $c_i$ with the supplied $k_i$. This means that hidden quantization was legitimately performed on a legitimate hidden transform.

**Wholeness.** The watermark detector can not mix and match $\Theta_i$ from different public watermarking keys, because $\sigma$ would not match $\Theta$ and the collision resistance of $H$ prevents the detector from constructing a match. Likewise, all the $k_i$ must come from the same $\mathbf{k}$ or $\Delta$ won't match. Furthermore, $\Theta$ and $\mathbf{k}$ must come from the same public watermarking key, or $\Delta$ won't match.

In any watermark detection, all the $v_{ij}$ must come from the same $\mathbf{V}$, and that $\mathbf{V}$ is the one associated with $\Theta$. If a watermark detector mixes and matches coefficients from different $\mathbf{V}$ it can not fulfill equation 3:

$$D_P(c_0; g, \lambda, N) = \sum_{i=1}^{n} \theta_i D_P(c_i; g, \lambda, N).$$

Encrypting both sides of equation 3, we see

$$c_0 = \prod_{i=1}^{n} c_i{}^{\theta_i} = \prod_{i=1}^{n} \Theta_i{}^{D_P(c_i; g, \lambda, N)}.$$

A mix-and-match attack would have to generate $c_0$, but neither of these equalities can be formed homomorphically. An algorithm $\mathcal{A}$ that can generate $c_0$ without knowing these decryptions can be used to compute the computational Diffie-Hellman problem: given $g^a$ and $g^b$, compute $g^{ab}$. This is assumed to be impossible, so $\mathcal{A}$ can't exist.

We showed that for a given $\Theta$ there is only one possible $\mathbf{k}$ that will be accepted, and also for a given $\Theta$ there is only one possible $\mathbf{V}$ that will be accepted, and that no mixing and matching is possible

## 8.2   Proof of Zero Knowledge

By definition, SQIM is zero knowledge if the watermark detector can simulate what it sees during watermark detections. This is easy if the detector is honest.

The detector has a watermarking public key, is given (or chooses) a signal $s$, and receives a bit $b$ from the secure module, so its view is $v = (s, b)$. $s$ is chosen from a distribution $D$ that includes whether or not $s$ is watermarked. To simulate this view, first choose a transform matrix and quantization values, then choose a signal $s'$ according to D. Since the transform matrix and quantization values are known, it is easy to see if $s'$ is watermarked. Let $b' = 1$ if $s'$ is watermarked, $b' = 0$ otherwise, and let the view of the simulation be $v' = (s', b')$. $v$ and $v'$ are identically distributed, so SQIM is honest-detector zero knowledge.

The verification system ensures that the view of a dishonest watermark detector is the same as that of an honest watermark detector because dishonest queries are ignored. Therefore, SQIM is zero knowledge from the perspective of the watermark detector.

Note that there are no zero knowledge proofs here. The secure module is trusted, so it does not have to prove that its calculations are correct.

## 8.3   Proof of Security

In both the Paillier and Goldwasser-Micali cryptosystems, any properly-formed $N$ with large-enough factors is secure. The security of the Paillier cryptosystem is independent of the choice of $g$, and any $g$ such that $g \bmod N \in \tilde{\text{QR}}(N)$ is secure for the Goldwasser-Micali cryptosystem. Therefore, even though we choose $g$ in a unique manner, it is still secure.

The security of Paillier encryption depends on the blinding factors, which we also choose in a unique manner. Since the blinding factors in standard Paillier encryption are chosen at random from $Z_N^*$, choosing them from a subset of non-negligible size does not introduce security problems; if it did, then choosing them at random from $Z_N^*$ would have a non-negligible chance of encountering the same problems. A problem would exist if the subset were small enough to make a brute-force search possible, but $|\text{QR}(N)| = \frac{1}{4}|\mathbb{Z}_N^*|$, so this is not a concern. Therefore, our choice of blinding factors is secure.

The only public watermarking values are either Paillier ciphertexts or Goldwasser-Micali ciphertexts which are acted upon homomorphically. Since $N$, $g$, and the blinding factors are chosen securely, these ciphertexts are as secure as the Paillier and Goldwasser-Micali cryptosystems, respectively.

The only area where the security of SQIM does not derive immediately from the Paillier and Goldwasser-Micali cryptosystems is when Paillier ciphertexts are taken modulo $N$ and converted into Goldwasser-Micali ciphertexts. However, this is still provably secure. Consider these ciphertexts to belong to a new, hybrid cryptosystem. The essence of the proof is that any algorithm that has an advantage in decrypting these hybrid ciphertexts can be shown to have an advantage decrypting Goldwasser-Micali ciphertexts. Since we assume the security of the Goldwasser-Micali cryptosystem, no such algorithm can exist, and the hybrid cryptosystem is secure.

## 9   Conclusion

We have presented a Secure QIM system, one in which most of the work of watermark detection can be performed in the open without any information about the private key being leaked. A secure module, such as a smartcard, is used to perform the final portion of watermark detection, revealing only if the signal is watermarked and no other information about the watermark. Our hidden transform utilizes the Paillier cryptosystem, while our hidden quantization uses the Goldwasser-Micali cryptosystem, and a robust verification system is used to force all watermark detectors to honestly follow the SQIM algorithm.

The novelty of SQIM lies in the coupling of two cryptosystems to implement a semi-private key QIM, and in the verification system which prevents watermark detectors from cheating. Furthermore, our system is provably secure, assuming the security of the Paillier and Goldwasser-Micali cryptosystems.

# References

1. Adelsbach, A., Sadeghi, A.: Zero-knowledge watermark detection and proof of ownership. In: Information Hiding Workshop (2000)
2. Brumley, D., Boneh, D.: Remote timing attacks are practical. In: 12th USENIX Security Symposium (2003)
3. Catalano, D., Gennaro, R., Howgrave-Graham, N., Nguyen, P.Q.: Paillier's cryptosystem revisited. In: CCS '01: Proceedings of the 8th ACM conference on Computer and Communications Security, pp. 206–214. ACM Press, New York, NY, USA (2001)
4. Chen, B., Wornell, G.W.: Quantization index modulation: A class of provably good methods for digital watermarking and information embedding. IEEE Trans. on Information Theory 47(4), 1423–1443 (2001)
5. Cox, I.J., Linnartz, J.-P.M.G.: Public watermarks and resistance to tampering. In: International Conference on Image Processing (ICIP'97), pp. 26–29 (1997)
6. Eggers, J., Su, J., Girod, B.: Asymmetric watermarking schemes (2000)
7. Hachez, G., Quisquater, J.-J.: Which directions for asymmetric watermarking. In: XI European Signal Processing Conference (2002)
8. Kalker, T.: Secure watermark detection. In: Allerton Conference (2005)
9. Koblitz, N.: A Course in Number Theory and Cryptography. Springer, Heidelberg (1994)
10. Kocher, P.: Timing attacks on implementations of diffie-hellman, rsa, dss, and other systems. In: Crypto (1996)
11. Malkin, M.: Cryptographic Methods in Multimedia Identification and Authentication. PhD thesis, Stanford University (2006)
   http://theory.stanford.edu/~mikeym/papers/malkin-thesis.pdf
12. Jaffe, J., Kocher, P., Jun, B.: Differential power analysis: Leaking secrets. In: Crypto, Springer, Heidelberg (1999)
13. Paillier, P.: Public-key cryptosystems based on composite degree residuosity classes. In: Proceedings of Eurocrypt '99, vol. 1592, pp. 223–238. Springer, Heidelberg (1999)
14. Chang, E.C., Li, Q.: Security of public watermarking schemes for binary sequences. In: Information Hiding Workshop (2002)
15. Damgård, I., Jurik, M.: A generalisation, a simplification and some applications of paillier's probabilistic public-key system. In: Proc. of Public Key Cryptography (2001)
16. Micali, S., Goldwasser, s.: Probabilistic encryption. Journal of Computer and Systems Science 28, 270–299 (1984)
17. Stinson, D.: Cryptography: Theory and Practice. CRC Press, Boca Raton, FL (1995)
18. Venturini, I.: Counteracting oracle attacks. In: Proceedings of the 2004 Workshop on Multimedia and Security, pp. 187–192. ACM Press, New York (2004)

# Steganographic Communication in Ordered Channels

R.C. Chakinala[1,*], A. Kumarasubramanian[1,*], R. Manokaran[1,*],
G. Noubir[1,**], C. Pandu Rangan[2,***], and R. Sundaram[1,*,†]

[1] Northeastern University, Boston, MA
ravich,abishe,rajsekar,noubir,koods@ccs.neu.edu
[2] Indian Institute of Technology - Madras, Chennai
rangan@iitm.ernet.in

**Abstract.** In this paper we focus on estimating the amount of information that can be embedded in the sequencing of packets in ordered channels. Ordered channels, e.g. TCP, rely on sequence numbers to recover
from packet loss and packet reordering. We propose a formal model for
transmitting information by packet-reordering. We present natural and
well-motivated channel models and jamming models including the $k$-
distance permuter, the $k$-buffer permuter and the $k$-stack permuter. We
define the natural information-theoretic (continuous) game between the
channel processes (max-min) and the jamming process (min-max) and
prove the existence of a Nash equilibrium for the mutual information rate.
We study the zero-error (discrete) equivalent and provide error-correcting
codes with optimal performance for the distance-bounded model, along
with efficient encoding and decoding algorithms. One outcome of our
work is that we extend and complete D. H. Lehmer's attempt to characterize the number of distance bounded permutations by providing the
asymptotically optimal bound - this also tightly bounds the first eigen-
value of a related state transition matrix [1].

## 1 Introduction

In this paper we model and prove the existence of a novel covert channel in any
ordered channel. We define a *ordered* channel as one in which the basic units of
communication (eg. packets in network channels) are linearly ordered. A common

---

* Greatly appreciate financial and moral support from Mr. Madhav Anand, bene-
factor of Northeastern University, and founder and president of International Integrated Inc. (NASDAQ:ICUB).
** The research of this author was in part supported by NSF Career Award CNS-
0448330.
*** The author would like to thank Microsoft Research, India for their generous
support.
† The research of this author was in part supported by a grant from the DARPA
NMS program.

example of an ordered channel is the TCP communication channel which uses the *sequence number* field to order the packets. The crux of our hiding scheme is to re-order the packets, and thus sending information. Thus, the scheme involved coding by permuting the packets in the channel.

Communication in covert channels is usually modeled using five players namely, Alice, stego-Alice, Jammer, stego-Bob, Bob, in the order of access to a basic unit of communication (eg. packet). Alice and Bob are the legitimate senders using the ordered channel. stego-Alice and stego-Bob are the players involved in extracting a covert channel. stego-Alice works by permuting the packets sent by Alice and thus trying to communicate with stego-Bob. We use the notion of a Jammer to encapsulate the effects of attempts to intercept such covert channels. The Jammer works by permuting the packets, after they are sent by stego-Alice and before received by stego-Bob[1].

The capacity of the channel is measured by the information rate [2] of the channel. Since the channel is covert, stego-Alice should not inordinately permute the packets. Similarly, giving the Jammer, complete permuting power would render any stego-Alice useless[2]. Hence, we assign permuting power to the stego-Alice and the Jammer. Also, stego-Alice and Jammer are usually implemented in hardware and the permuting powers come up due to restricting the hardware complexity.

We formalize a variety of natural models of permuting power for the stego-Alice and the Jammer. We consider two distinct ways of analyzing the capacity of the channel. In the *continuous* case, we formulate the channel as a zero-sum game played by the stego-Alice and the Jammer where the stego-Alice tries to maximize the capacity of the channel. We prove the existence of a nash equilibrium for any given power (strategy space) of the stego-Alice and the Jammer. On the other hand, we have the *discrete* case, where we provide concrete encoding and decoding algorithms, parametrized on the stego-Alice and Jammer power, to communicate. We obtain tight bounds on the capacity of the covert channel were possible.

The rest of the paper is organized as follows. The following section talks about the related works. In section III, we formalize the channel model and introduce the various models to restrict the stego players and the jammers. In Section IV we analyze the general channel capacity as a two player game and prove that a Nash equilibrium exists. We set the stage for the following sections by characterizing the zero-error capacity of the channel. Section V is an analysis of restricted permutations, and in particular distance restricted permutations. In section VI, VII we prove bounds on zero-error the channel capacity in the models that we introduce and provide polynomial time encoding and decoding schemes.

---

[1] The concept of Jammer also encapsulates the inherent errors (eg. re-ordering of packets due to routing) that exist in the ordered channel.

[2] As we prove, for many natural models, the stego-Alice needs more power than the Jammer to effectively communicate.

## 2    Related Work

Considering the set of codewords to be a set of permutations for traditional channels has been studied in theory [3]. However, in our model channel errors are permutations, rather than symbol errors. In [4], asymptotically good error-correcting codes for correcting transposition, insertion and deletion errors have been designed. However their codebook is not restricted to only permutations. To the best of our knowledge considering only permutations as both codewords and errors is novel and also well suited for the covert TCP channel that we consider.

A partial characterization of "$k$-distance" permutations[Sec.3] have been done in the past [1]. Lehmer gives explicit ways to derive the number of permutations satisfying this condition for small values of $k$ (1, 2 and 3).For every $k$, the number of "$k$-distance" permutations of length $n$ equals to $O(\mu_k^n)$. In course of our work, we obtain tight asymptotic bounds on the value of $\mu_k$.

Our work is in part a logical extension to the reordering scheme proposed in [5]. We analyze the reordering channel in a suitably defined mathematical model and provide bounds on the channel capacities. The scheme proposed in [5] has the following defects. Firstly, the encoding and decoding algorithm are not optimal and are not polynomial time. We have very simple polynomial time encoding and decoding schemes which asymptotically achieve the maximum channel capacity. Further, there is no characterization of the capacity, nor any model describing it.

## 3    Preliminaries

### 3.1    The Steganographic Channel

We consider as the underlying host channel one where Alice communicates with Bob using a stream of *ordered* packets. Since we are interested in hiding additional information into the channel by reordering the packets, the fundamental operations performed by the stego players are permutations. The stego players are assumed to know the total ordering among the packets and decide beforehand on the block length $n$ and number the packets in order from the set $\{1, 2, \ldots, n-1, n\}$. Let $S_n$ denote the symmetric group of $n$ elements and $e$ its identity element. Assume Alice sends the packets to Bob in the natural order $e = (1 \ldots n)$. Denote by $\pi = (\pi(1), \ldots \pi(n))$ a permutation where the $i$th element is $\pi(i)$. A code, in this scenario, is $\mathcal{C} \subseteq S_n$ whose rate we define to be $\frac{\log_2(|\mathcal{C}|)}{n}$. We define the following models of permuters to restrict the permutations possible for the stego players and the jammer.

### 3.2    Distance Bounded Permuters

In any ordered communication channel, the latency of the channel is increased if the packets are reordered. For a covert communication with a bound on the maximum latency in receiving a packet at the actual receiver we define the following permuter.

**Definition 1.** *A k-distance permuter is one in which the permutation $\pi$ of the input is such that $|i - \pi(i)| \le k, \forall i \in \{1, \ldots, n\}$.*

### 3.3  Buffer Bounded Permuters

**Definition 2.** *A k-buffer permuter uses a random access buffer of size k elements. There are two operations that a k-buffer permuter can perform.*

1. **put:** *The k-buffer permuter removes one element from the input stream and places it in the buffer. This operation can be performed iff the buffer is not full.*
2. **remove:** *The permuter removes one element from the buffer and places it in the output stream. This operation can be performed iff the buffer is not empty.*

Define a *k-buffer permutation* to be a permutation realizable by a valid sequence of *put*'s and *remove*'s a *k*-buffer permuter. We note that the only possible 1-buffer permutation is the identity permutation *e*. Let $B_n^{(k)}$ denote the number of different *k*-buffer permutations of *n* elements. Note that unlike *k*-distance permuters, *k*-buffer permuters are not reversible; there exists a permutation $\pi$ that is a *k*-buffer permutation such that $\pi^{-1}$ is *not* a *k*-buffer permutation.

### 3.4  Restrictions on the Nature of the Buffer

**Definition 3.** *A k-stack permuter is a k-buffer permuter where the buffer accessible to the k-buffer permuter is not a random access buffer but a stack.*

## 4  A Game Theoretic Approach

In this section, we study the covert communication as a information-theoretic game. We define the strategies of the "players" as follows. Let *S* denote the set of all permutations to which the sender can permute *e*. Let *T* denote the set of all permutations to which the adversary can permute any element of *S*. Consider the directed graph $G(V, E)$, where $V = S \cup T$. A directed edge $(p \to q) \in E$ iff the adversary can permute $p \in S$ to $q \in T$.

To communicate, the sender selects a probability distribution over *S* and does source coding [2] to transmit information. The adversary selects, for each vertex in *S* a probability over the set of neighbours[3] in *G* to reduce the information rate. Extending the distribution chosen by the sender to the whole of *V* (by assigning zero probability mass on the vertices that the sender cannot "reach"),

---

[3] Typically, an adversary is allowed to leave the permutation sent by the sender as it is, leading to self loops in the graph *G*.

we have a probability distribution $X$ over $V$. The adversary chooses the conditional probability $p(y|x)$ of the permutation $x$ being transformed into $y$ for every edge $(x \rightarrow y)$ in $E$. Extending the conditional probabilities to all pairs of vertices, we have a distribution $Y$ over $V$, representing the probability of the final permutation (after both sender and adversary have made their "move"). Then, the information rate is given by,

$$I(X;Y) = H(X) - H(X|Y)$$

where, $H(X)$ and $H(X|Y)$ are the entropy functions.

This naturally leads to a zero-sum game [6] with objective function $I(X;Y)$ where the strategies of the players are as defined above. Suppose $U$ and $V$ denote the set of all strategies of the sender and the adversary of choosing a distribution and a conditional "transition" probabilities respectively, we have the following theorem that proves the existence of a saddle point.

**Theorem 1.** *The game as defined above satisfies the min-max equation*

$$\min_{v \in V} \max_{u \in U} I(X;Y) = \max_{u \in U} \min_{v \in V} I(X;Y)$$

Any pair of strategies that achieves this value of the game is said to be "optimal" to each other. In particular, the above theorem also proves the existence of a *Nash equilibrium*. Hence there exists optimal strategies for the sender and the adversary such that no player has anything to gain by changing his own strategy.

## 4.1   Characterization of Nash Equilibrium

The structure of the graph could help in obtaining the value of the game. The following lemmas are useful in determining the value of the graph. The proofs of the lemmas are omitted due to lack of space.

**Lemma 1.** *If there exist two vertices $x_1$ and $x_2$ such that there is an edge $(x_1 \rightarrow y)$ iff $(x_2 \rightarrow y)$, then, there is an optimal strategy set where the sender assigns $p(x_2) = 0$*

Similarly, we have the following lemma for the edge player. The proof of the lemma is very much along the lines of the above proof and hence omitted.

**Lemma 2.** *Suppose there exists two vertices $y_1$ and $y_2$ such that $(x \rightarrow y_1)$ iff $(x \rightarrow y_2)$, then there is an optimal strategy set where the adversary assigns $p(y_2|x) = 0 \forall x$.*

For the purpose of constructing error-correcting codes, we need to find the largest set of symbols in $S$ such that the adversary cannot "confuse" two symbols by permuting the them to the *same* element. Thus, for the general graph game, we have the following theorem.

**Lemma 3. (Confusion Graph Lemma.)** *Given the directed graph $G$, with adjacency matrix $A$, defined as in 4. Let $H$ denote the underlying undirected graph with adjacency matrix $A + AA^T$. This graph contains an edge between every pair of elements that can be confused and hence the largest independent set of subgraph of $H$ induced by the vertices of $S$ gives the set of symbols over which an optimal error-correcting code can be constructed.*

# 5   Restricted Permutations

Note: Due to space constraints, we use the symbol $\gg$ to denote proofs are found in the appendix section of the extended version [7].

The information theoretic results show the existence of a game theoretic equilibrium. However the zero-error model, when one would like to decode exactly to the correct code word, is also important in the practical sense. Below we show for several noise models what the zero-error capacity is and provide codes to communicate in this situation.

$k$-distance permutations accurately capture the real world constraints of memory and latency. In this section we study in detail the properties of $k$-distance permutations. The nature of permutations of $n$ elements, given for each element $i$ a set of possible positions it can move to have been extensively studied [1], [8], [9]. We reproduce some relevant parts for the sake of completeness.

For $k = 1$, observe that $P_n^{(1)} = F_{n+1}$ the $(n+1)$-th Fibonacci number. Finding the recurrence for $P_n^{(k)}$ is in general difficult. So is computing it as a function of $n$ and $k$. [1] provides a computational method to evaluate $P_n^{(k)}$. However the method has exponential complexity in $k$. Further they leave the exact asymptotics open. We briefly outline the method below.

Consider an intermediate position in the construction of any permutation of length $n$ obeying the $k$-distance property. Let this be denoted as $(\pi(1), \ldots, \pi(h-1))$. Suppose also that $h$ is much larger than $k$; we have to decide on the value of $\pi(h)$ depending on the values of $(\pi(h-1)-(h-1), \ldots, \pi(h-k)-(h-1))$, which we call a state. The state contains information as to the relative displacement of each of the previous $k$ elements, using which we could determine the set of values that $\pi(h)$ can take. Upon choosing a feasible $\pi(h)$, we move to a new state, $(\pi(h) - h, \ldots, \pi(h - k + 1) - h)$. Construct a directed graph with vertices as all possible states, a directed arc between states $a$ and $b$ iff state $b$ is reachable from $a$ via a feasible extension of the permutation terminating with the state $a$. Let the adjacency matrix of this graph be denoted by $A$. The number of ways of extending a partially built permutation $\pi(1 \ldots h)$ to $\pi(1 \ldots h + i)$, is the number of directed paths of length $i$ in the graph, starting with the state $(\pi(h) - h, \pi(h-1) - h, \ldots, \pi(h-k+1) - h)$, and ending at the state $(\pi(h+i) - h - i, \ldots, \pi(h+i-k+1) - h - i)$, which is the corresponding entry in $A^i$. The growth of this entry is of the order of $\mu_k^i$, where $\mu_k$ is the largest eigenvalue of the matrix $A$. Hence, $\lim_{n \to \infty} \frac{P_n^{(k)}}{\mu_k^n} = 1$ where $\mu_k$ is the eigenvalue of the state matrix $A$ corresponding to $k$-distance permutations.

As an illustration, consider the simple case of 1-distance permutations. The state information consists of just $(\pi(h) - h)$, and thus the set of states $V = \{(0), (-1), (1)\}$, since an object $h$ cannot move more than one place away from its initial position. From the restrictions of 1-distance permutations, the state transition matrix is seen to be $\begin{pmatrix} 1 & 0 & 1 \\ 1 & 0 & 1 \\ 0 & 1 & 0 \end{pmatrix}$ Evaluating the largest eigen-value of this matrix we find that its equal to $\mu_1 = \frac{1+\sqrt{5}}{2}$, and thus the number of 1-distance permutations goes as $\left(\frac{1+\sqrt{5}}{2}\right)^n$, as expected. During the course of our work, by having provided an upper bound and lower bound for the values of $P_n^{(k)}$, we also have provided bounds on the value of the eigen-value of this state transition matrix.

# 6  Bounds

We begin with a lemma on the $k$-buffer model.

**Lemma 4.** $B_n^{(k)} = k^{n-k} k!$ if $n > k$ and $B_n^{(k)} = n!$ if $n \leq k$.                ≫

## 6.1  Upper Bound

Any $k$-distance permutation can be trivially obtained as an output of $k + 1$-buffer. Thus a trivial upper bound for the number of $k$-distance permutations is $B_n^{(k+1)}$. We provide a tighter upper bound using Bregman's theorem as follows.

**Lemma 5.** For $n > k$, $P_n^{(k)} \leq ((2k+1)!)^{n/(2k+1)}$                ≫

**Corollary 1.** $\lim_{k \to \infty} \mu_k \leq \frac{2k+1}{e} + o(1)$, by the Stirling's approximation.

## 6.2  Lower Bound

A naive lower bound for $P_n^{(k)}$ that is also constructive in yielding an encoding scheme when the Stego players are $k$-distance permuters is as follows.

**Lemma 6.** $P_n^{(k)} > (k+1)!^{n/(k+1)}$ if $n > k+1$ and $P_n^{(k)} = k!$ if $n \leq k+1$. ≫

In the absence of a jammer the stego player could encode information as $k$-distance permutation using the above lemma since it is simple to index the set of permutations $S_{k+1}$ [10], it is also straightforward to extend this indexing scheme to $(S_{k+1})^{\frac{n}{k+1}}$. Thus given a single index from $\{0, \ldots, (k+1)!^{n/(k+1)} - 1\}$, one can output the corresponding $k$-distance permutation.

## 6.3  A Limiting Bound on $\mu_k$

**Lemma 7.** $\lim_{k \to \infty} \mu_k \geq \frac{2k+1}{e} + o(1)$.

*Proof.* Define permutations, $p$, where $|i - p(i)| \mod n \leq k$ as $k$-circular permutations. Let $C_n^{(k)}$ be the number of such permutations. From [1], using Van der Warden's theorem on permanents of doubly stochastic matrices [11], $\lim_{n \to \infty} (C_n^{(k)})^{\frac{1}{n}} \geq \frac{2k+1}{e}$.

Also, $\lim_{n \to \infty} (\frac{P_n^{(k)}}{C_n^{(k)}})^{\frac{1}{n}} = 1$, hence $\lim_{k \to \infty} \mu_k \geq \frac{2k+1}{e}$.

We provide a mapping from every circular permutation to some set of linear permutations. Consider any circularly permuted, $k$-distance permutations $p = (p_1, \ldots, p_n)$. Let there be $y$ elements in $p_1, \ldots, p_k$ that are from the set $\{n - k + 1, n-k+2, \ldots, n\}$ and $x$ elements in $p_{n-k+1}, \ldots, p_n$ from the set $\{1, \ldots, k\}$. These elements make this circular permutation not a linear order permutation. Move the elements in $p_1, \ldots, p_k$ which belong to $\{n-k+1, n-k+2, \ldots, n\}$, to the end of the permutation in that order. Similarly move the elements in $p_{n-k+1}, \ldots, p_n$ from the set $\{1, \ldots, k\}$ to the front of the permutation in that order. It is easy to see that we have moved each object only closer to its initial position and thus the property that it is a $k$-distance permutation is satisfied. The total number of such circular permutations which can map to a linear permutation is seen to be $\sum_{x,s} {}^k P_x {}^k P_s \leq (k!e)^2$. Since this is a constant factor independent of $n$, $\lim_{n \to \infty} (\frac{P_n^{(k)}}{C_n^{(k)}})^{\frac{1}{n}} = ((e(k)!)^2)^{\frac{1}{n}} = 1$, and hence the theorem follows.

**Theorem 2.** $\lim_{Lim_k --> \infty} \frac{\mu_k}{\frac{2k+1}{e}} = 1.$

*Proof.* Follows from lemma 7, lemma 1.

# 7  Encoding and Decoding Schemes

In this section, we provide error correcting codes for different stego sender and jammer powers. For each of the models defined in 3 we provide error correcting codes and bounds when possible.

## 7.1  Error Free Channel

We first consider the case where the channel is error-free. We provide codes, encoding and decoding algorithms. The maximum information capacity of the channel is just the logarithm of the number of different symbols that can be transmitted across in the absence of any error. Thus we would like to aim for encoding schemes where given an index between 0 and the maximum possible number of different symbols, we want the encoder the output a symbol.

**Buffer bounded permuters.** An algorithm to encode any index between 0 and $B_n^{(k)}$ into a $k$-buffer permutation is as follows.

**Encode any $0 \leq x < B_n^{(k)}$ into a $k$-buffer permutation using $n$ elements**

---

```
 1: while n > 1 do
 2:     Fill the k-buffer with as many elements from the input as possible (min(n, k)).
 3:     Sort the k-buffer.
 4:     for i = 1 to k do
 5:         if x < iB_{n-1}^{(k)} then
 6:             Output the i-th element of the sorted buffer.
 7:             x ← x − (i − 1)B_{n-1}^{(k)}
 8:             n ← n − 1
 9:             break
10:         end if
11:     end for
12: end while
13: Output the last packet left. {n = 1 here.}
```

The above algorithm is a direct modification of the counting procedure 4. The decoding procedure is to reconstruct the entire encoding algorithm's working by looking at the values of the output symbol one after another.

**Buffer bounded stack permuters.** Consider a steganographer who is $k$-buffer bounded stack permuter. This is typically the ideal model for a high-speed memory restricted device. Stacks are immensely fast to implement on hardware and thus provide great practical advantage. The number of permutations achievable by a $k$-buffer stack permuter is a generalization of the $n$-th Catalan number. The $n$-th Catalan number $C_n$ is the number of well bracketed expressions of say, $'('$ and $')'$, of length $2n$ and also the number of different possible output permutation of an $n$-buffer (or when $k > n$) [12]. A generalization of the Catalan number is $_kC_n$ which counts the number of bracketed expressions of maximum depth $k$, or in other words, the number of permutations output by a $k$-buffer stack permuter.

A recurrence for the generalized Catalan number is

$$_kC_n = \sum_{i=0}^{n-1} {_{k-1}C_i} \cdot {_kC_{n-1-i}}$$

The recurrence can be used to construct an index/encoding for the $k$-buffer stack permuter as follows. Note that a table of values, $_kC_n$ can be constructed in time $O(n^2k)$ using a dynamic programming approach. Assume that the values are available tabulated. We constructed a well-balanced bracketing of length $2n$ with maximum depth $k$. Clearly this can be translated into $k$-buffer stack permutation by interpreting the opening braces, $'('$ as a push into the buffer and the closing brace $')'$ as a pop from the buffer. Consider the following recursive algorithm,

**Given $0 \leq x < {}_kC_n$, output a well-bracketed expression of length $2n$ and maximum depth $k$**

---

Encode$(n, k, x)$

---

1: sum $\leftarrow 0$
2: **if** $n$ equals 0 **then**
3:     **return** { Output the NULL string (nothing)}
4: **end if**
5: **if** $k$ equals 1. **then**
6:     Output $n$ pairs ().
7: **end if**
8: **for** $i = 0$ to $n - 1$ **do**
9:     **if** $x < \text{sum} + {}_{k-1}C_i \cdot {}_kC_{n-1-i}$ **then**
10:       $x \leftarrow x - \text{sum}$
11:       $y = x \div {}_{k-1}C_i$ {The floor function}
12:       $z = x \mod {}_{k-1}C_i$
13:       Output $'('$
14:       Encode(i, k-1, z)
15:       Output $')'$
16:       Encode(n-1-i, k, y)
17:       **return**
18:     **else**
19:       sum $\leftarrow \text{sum} + {}_{k-1}C_i \cdot {}_kC_{n-1-i}$
20:     **end if**
21: **end for**

The above algorithm is just an implementation of two ideas. First, similar to the general $k$-buffer permutations, we use the recurrence relation to try and encode. Second, if $X, Y$ are two sets, then to output an element of $X \times Y$ given any integer $0 \leq z < |X||Y|$, the easiest way is to output the $(z \div |Y|)$-th element from $X$ and $(z \mod |Y|)$-th element from $Y$. Using this fact, we have constructed an algorithm to encode into the set of all $k$-buffer stack permutations. A decoder can again simulate the actions of the encoder as it can simulate the $k$-buffer stack, and get a well balanced parenthesis expression and invert it to get the corresponding index according to the above algorithm.

**Distance bounded permuters.** Similar to the idea for buffer bounded permuters, the outputs of a 1-distance permuter can easily be indexed [13]. However the problem is no longer trivial when considering values of $k \geq 2$. One way around is to convert the proof 6.2 into an encoding scheme in a straight forward manner using the fact that permutations can be indexed. This technique however results in under utilization of the channel capacity. More precisely, since we have an upper bound on the rate of the channel as $\log\left(\frac{2k+1}{e}\right)$, using this simple scheme, we achieve a rate of $\frac{\log((k+1)!^{\frac{n}{k+1}})}{n} \simeq \log\left(\frac{k+1}{e}\right)$, asymptotically reaching the best bound.

## 7.2   Channel with Adversarial Errors

In this section we consider channels with error or a jammer who tries to disrupt the stego communication. Under different models of jammer and steganographer capabilities, we discuss the possibility of error free communication and develop codes.

**Buffer bounded permuters.** $k$-buffer permutations are not reversible, and so it is not obvious as to whether stego players do need more "power" than the jammer. We show below that indeed the stego players do need more power.

**Theorem 3.** *Let* $p = (p_1, p_2, \ldots, p_n)$, $q = (q_1, q_2, \ldots, q_n)$ *be any two permutations obtained from the output of a $k$-buffer with input $e$. Then there exists another permutation $r = (r_1, r_2, \ldots, r_n)$ such that $r$ can be obtained as the output when $p$ and $q$ are passed through two separate $k$-buffers.*

*Proof.* Consider the following figure which is self explanatory. Without loss of generality, assume that both the buffers are full. If not one could always move the packets in from the input stream as long as both the buffers are filled. We

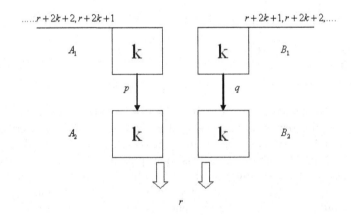

prove the theorem using mathematical induction. Let the number of packets be $n$. We prove inductively on $n$ as follows.

1. **Base case.** True for $n < 2k$. Clear true for $n <= k$.
2. **Inductive case 1.** Consider the theorem true for $n-1 \geq k$ and $n-1 < 2k-1$. Assume that $A_2$ and $B_2$ are both filled. If not, we can move elements into them from $A_1$ and $B_1$. $|A_2 \cup B_2| = n = |A_2| + |B_2|$ - $|A_2 \cap B_2|$.
   $n = k + k - |A_2 \cap B_2|$. Since $n < 2k$, there is at least one element in $A_2 \cap B_2$, which can be output. Renumbering the packets now from 1 to $n - 1$, gives a proof by the inductive hypothesis for $n - 1$ elements.

3. **Inductive case 2.** From case 1, the theorem is true up till $n = 2k - 1$. If $n \geq 2k$, assume that all the buffers are filled. The last element to be filled was filled into $A_1$ and $B_1$ respectively. Thus $A_2 \cup B_2 < 2k$ and hence once again, they have an element in common. Output this element and renumber the packets thus reducing the problem to the case of $n - 1$ elements. By induction, the theorem is true for all $n$.

This rules out the possibility of an error-correcting code when both Stego-Alice and the Jammer use the same "power" of the jammer. Although the zero-error capacity for this case is 0, the mutual information rate $I(X; Y)$ is non-zero for this case.

## 7.3   Distance Bounded Permuters

Since inverse of $k$-distance permutations are $k$-distance permutations, we cannot transfer any information (in the adversarial model) when the sender is only as much capable as the jammer. Hence assume that the steganographic sender can send $k+t$-distance permutations and the jammer is allowed to use only $k$-distance permutations as errors. In this section we assume that $n$, the block length and $k$ are sufficiently large quantities that the stirling's approximation is valid.

**Lemma 8.** *Sphere packing bound Note that the following definition of a distance between two permutations, $p = (p_1, \ldots, p_n), q = (q_1, \ldots, q_n)$ as $d(a, b) = \max(|i - j| | p_i = q_j, 0 \leq i < n, 0 \leq j < n)$, is metric space on the set of all permutations. There are various definitions of metric spaces on permutation [14]. Our definition is motivated by the fact that $k$-distance permutations are nothing but those permutations $p$, with $d(p, e) \leq k$.*

*Suppose the jammer is a $k$-distance permuter and the sender is a $k+t$-distance permuter, $t > 0$. Then, if the sender chooses a set of codewords $C$, from each code word, draw spherical balls of radius $k$. These balls must be disjoint. If each ball of radius $k$, contains $N_k$ elements of this space, Hence we have,*

$$|C| N_k \leq N_{k+t}$$
$$\log(|C|) + \log N_k \leq \log N_{k+t}$$
$$\log(|C|) \leq log N_{k+t} - \log N_k$$

Note that $N_k$ is nothing but the number of different $k$ distance permutations, which asymptotically tends to $(\frac{2k+1}{e})^n$. Using this, we get

$$log N_{k+t} - \log N_k \leq n \log \frac{2k + 2t + 1}{2k + 1}$$

Consider the following lower bound which is also converted into an encoding scheme.

**Lemma 9.** *For each value of $r = \llcorner(k+t)/(2k)\lrcorner, r > 1$, consider for any permutation $p = (p_1, \ldots, p_n)$, the elements $(p_i, p_{i+2k}, \ldots), i < 2k$, the relative order of none of these elements can be changed by a $k$-distance permuter since each element is at least $2k$ away from the rest. Suppose thus, one chooses to permute only these elements $(p_i, p_{i+2k}, \ldots$ using any $r$-distance permutation on them (note that the sender is capable of doing this from the defn. of $r$), then the maximum amount of information transfer possible is atleast equal to, when $r$ is large, $\log\left((\frac{2r+1}{e})^{\frac{n}{2k}}\right)^{2k}$. (The block length of each $r$ distance subsequence is $\frac{n}{2k}$ and there are $2k$ such subsequences.*

$$\log\left(|C|\right) \geq n\log\left(\frac{2r+1}{e}\right)$$

$$\log\left(|C|\right) \geq n\log\left(\frac{(2(k+t)/2k+1)}{e}\right)$$

We thus acheive a rate asymptotically equal to the upper bound even in the presence of error. To convert this result into a practical coding scheme, one needs an efficient encoding coding scheme for the case of $r$-distance permutations in the absence of error.

We now prove that on the minimum block length required to transfer information across a $k$-distance jammer is $2k+1$. The code length requirement is irrespective of the sender's power. Thus even if the sender could send any permutation involving $2k$ elements, the adversary would still be able to perform $k$-distance operation on the two permutations to coalesce them to the same permutation. We infer that if at all any information transfer has to be made by the sender then $n \geq 2k+1$.

**Lemma 10.** *Any permutation in $S_{2k}$ is reachable from the identity permutation using at the most two $k$-distance operations.*

*Proof.* From any permutation $\pi \in S_{2k}$, we can sort the first $k$ elements and the second $k$ elements parallelly in one $k$-distance move. Any element $x \leq k$ in the second block will be within $k$ distance from its position in the identity permutation. Similarly, any element $x > k$ in the first block will be within $k$ distance from its position in the identity permutation. Another $k$-distance operation will take this permutation to the identity permutation. Since the $k$-distance operations are reversible, the lemma follows.

We now focus on providing error correcting codes. When there is no adversary, a sender with 1-distance is capable of $F_{n+1}$ number of permutations of $S_n$ [1]. We briefly explain a code that achieves the limit by describing a function from $\{0, 1, \ldots F_{n+1} - 1\}$ to the set of all 1-distance permutations on $n$ elements. Any number in the domain can be encoded in the Fibonacci numbering system [15], represented by a binary tuple of length $n - 1$ with no consecutive ones. The required permutation is obtained by composing the permutations $\pi_i = (i, i+1)$ for every 1 in the $i$th position. We note that since no two consecutive binary digits in the tuple are 1, the $\pi_i$s do not overlap and thus can be composed in any order.

Next, we show that when the sender is capable of just $k + 1$ distance and the channel has a $k$-distance jammer, with a block length of $n \geq 2k + 1$, we can send $\Theta(n)$, bits of information.

If the sender is $k$-distance and the adversary is $k - 1$-distance, there are two permutations in $S_{2k-1}$ such that, the sender can permute the identity to any of them using only $k$-distance but the adversary cannot reduce both to the same permutation using $k - 1$ distance.

**Lemma 11.** *The permutation $(k + 1, \ldots 2k - 1, k, 1, \ldots k - 1)$ and the identity permutation $(1, \ldots 2k - 1)$ cannot be both reduced to the same permutation by a $k - 1$ distance operation.*

*Proof.* Suppose that there exists such a permutation $\pi$. Then $\pi(1) = k$, as only $k$ can reach the first position from both the above permutations. Similarly $\pi(2k - 1) = k$. Hence, $\pi$ is no longer a permutation.

Further, in the identity permutation, $(1 \ldots 2k - 1)$, only the first $k$ elements need to be fixed. Thus for a block of size $n$, we can either fix the first $k$ elements and encode the rest $n - k$ elements or apply the permutation $(k + 1, \ldots 2k - 1, k, 1, \ldots k - 1)$ and recursively encode the rest $n - 2k + 1$ elements. Thus we obtain the recurrence $P_n = P_{n-k} + P_{n-2k+1}$ for the size of the code of block size $n$.

The decoding strategy involves looking at the first element of the encoded permutation $p_1 = \pi(1)$. If $p_1 < k$, we can deduce that the first $k$ elements were fixed and thus scratch out all numbers from $1 \ldots k$, substitute $x - k$ for $x$ and recursively decode the resultant string. If $p_1 > k$, we can deduce that the first $2k - 1$ elements were permuted and hence scratch them out and, substitute $x - 2k + 1$ for $x$ and add $P_{n-k}$ to the result of recursively decoding the resultant string.

## 8   Practical Results on TCP

Any communication protocol which requires packet sequence numbers can be used for steganography using our algorithms. We consider the TCP for our simulation because it is the most prevalent protocol in the Internet today. Also it is interesting to look at the interplay between TCP and our algorithms especially considering the fact that excessive packet reordering affects TCP congestion control adversely. For our purposes we use the 32-bit *Sequence Number* field in the TCP packet header. Alternatively one could also use the *Sequence Number* [5] field of the *Authentication Header* and *Encapsulating Security Payload* in the IPSec.

We performed simulations using *ns-2.28 Network Simulator* to study the behaviour of TCP under packet re-orderings. Our simulations are based on the TCP Tahoe variant. We used the BRITE topology generator for generating a

50 node 2-level hierarchical network topology which was created based on the Waxman's probability model. In this model, the probability of interconnecting two nodes $u, v$ is given by

$$P(u, v) = \alpha e^{-d/\beta L}$$

where $0 < \alpha, \beta \leq 1$, $d$ is the Euclidean distance from node $u$ to $v$, and $L$ is the maximum distance between any two nodes.

We chose $\alpha = 0.15, \beta = 0.2$. From the resulting topology, 25 pairs of nodes were chosen and TCP flows were started by choosing one node as a sink and the other as the source. An ftp agent was started on each of the TCP sources. Keeping this as the minimum network traffic, we performed 200 simulations choosing a pair of nodes $s_i$ and $d_i$ for $i \in \{1, 2, 3...200\}$, each time with $s_i$ as the source node and $d_i$ as the destination node. The experiment was conducted for 200 such pairs of nodes and the ratio of new throughput to the actual channel throughput (without reordering) was computed for each value of $k \in \{1, 2, 3\}$.

From the histograms thus obtained, we observe that the throughput obtained using k-distance permutations is greater than 91% for more than 68%,60% and 30% of the source-destination pairs, for $k = 1,2$ and 3 respectively. The corresponding average stego-information rates are 8.21bps, 11.42bps and 3.54bps. Even here, we observe that a $2 - distance$ scheme performs better than the $1 - distance$ in terms of stego-information rate, though the ratio $t_r$ gets affected.

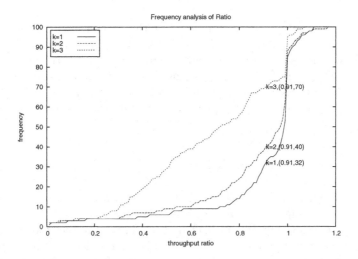

**Fig. 1.** Cumulative Relative Frequency of $t_r$

## 9   Conclusion

We formalize various models for packet re-ordering channels. We analyze the channel as information-theoretic game and prove the existence of Nash equilibrium. Motivated by ordered channels, eg. TCP, we introduce a new distance metric on permutations and provide error correcting codes in this metric and prove combinatorial bounds. Our codes asymptotically reach the upper bound. We simulated in detail the effects of our covert channel in various topologies and found a good correlation between the theoretical and simulated results. Being a preliminary work, this paper opens up a lot of research in this direction.

# References

1. Lehmer, D.H.: Permutations with strongly restricted displacements. In: Erdös, P., Renyi, A., Sós, V. (eds.) Combinatorial theory and its applications II, pp. 755–770 (1970)
2. Shannon, C., Weaver, W.: The Mathematical Theory of Communication. University of Illinois Press, Urbana, Illinois (1949)
3. Blake, I.F.: Permutation codes for discrete channels (corresp.). IEEE Trans. Inform. Theory 20, 138–140 (1974)
4. Schulman, L.J., Zuckerman, D.: Asymptotically good codes correcting insertions, deletions, and transpositions. IEEE Trans. Inform. Theory 45(7), 2552–2557 (1999)
5. Ahsan, K., Kundur, D.: Practical data hiding in TCP/IP (2002) [Online]. Available `http://citeseer.ist.psu.edu/ahsan02practical.html`
6. Karlin, S.: Mathematical Methods and Theory in Games, Programming and Economics.Dover, TODO year, vol. 2, ch. Some chapter TODO
7. Steganographic communication in ordered channels (2006) [Online]. Available `http://abishekk.googlepages.com/stego.pdf`
8. Mendelsohn, N.S.: Permutations with confined displacements. Canadian Math. Bulletin 4, 29–38 (1961)
9. ——, The asymptotic series for a certain class of permutation problems. Candian Jour. Math. B., 8, 234–244 (1956)
10. Campbell, W.H.: Indexing permutations. J. Comput. Small Coll. 19(3), 296–300 (2004)
11. Egorychev, G.: The solution of Van der Waerden's problem for permanents. Advances in math 42, 299–305 (1981)
12. Knuth, D.E.: Fundamental Algorithms. In: The Art of Computer Programming, 2nd edn. vol. 1(1.2), pp. 10–119. Addison-Wesley, Reading, Massachusetts (1973)
13. Diaconis, P., Graham, R., Holmes, S.P.: Statistical problems involving permutations with restricted positions. Festschrift in Honor of William van Zwet (1999) [Online]. Available: `http://www-stat.stanford.edu/~susan/papers/perm8.ps`
14. Deza, M., Huang, T.: Metrics on permutations, a survey. Journal of combinatorics, Information and System Sciences (1998) [Online]. Available: `http://www.liga.ens.fr/~deza/papers/voldpapers/huang/huangperm.pdf`
15. Zeckendorf, E.: Representation des nombres naturels par une somme de nombres de fibonacci ou de nombres de lucas. Bull. Soc. Roy. Sci. Liege 41, 179–182 (1972)

# Analyzing Network-Aware Active Wardens in IPv6

Grzegorz Lewandowski, Norka B. Lucena, and Steve J. Chapin

Systems Assurance Institute
Syracuse University
Syracuse, NY 13244, USA
grlewand@syr.edu, {norka,chapin}@ecs.syr.edu

**Abstract.** A crucial security practice is the elimination of network covert channels. Recent research in IPv6 discovered that there exist, at least, 22 different covert channels, suggesting the use of advanced active wardens as an appropriate countermeasure. The described covert channels are particularly harmful not only because of their potential to facilitate deployment of other attacks but also because of the increasing adoption of the protocol without a parallel deployment of corrective technology. We present a pioneer implementation of *network-aware* active wardens that eliminates the covert channels exploiting the *Routing Header* and the hop limit field as well as the well-known *Short TTL* Attack. Network-aware active wardens take advantage of network-topology information to detect and defeat covert protocol behavior. We show, by analyzing their performance over a controlled network environment, that the wardens eliminate a significant percentage of the covert channels and exploits with minimal impact over the end-to-end communications (approximately 3% increase in the packet roundtrip time).

**Keywords:** covert channels, evasion attacks, active wardens, stateless, stateful, network-aware, traffic analysis, traffic normalizers, active mappers.

## 1 Introduction

Although as of today publicly-accessible Internet addresses are primarily IPv4, the adoption of the Internet Protocol version 6 (IPv6)[1] is becoming imminent. For example, news from the IPv6 Task Force [1] report significant progress in both deployment and policy regarding networks using IPv6 technology in various continents [2,3]. IPv6 summits and other events present applications and services that will drive commercial implementations of IPv6 [4,5,6,7]. The U.S. government established that all federal agencies must deploy IPv6 by June 2008 [8], without disregarding the challenge of the Department of Defense (DoD) of monitoring operational IPv6 networks for unauthorized IPv6 traffic [9]. That global embracement of IPv6 calls for closer examination of its security risks, especially of those which are not so obvious nor possibly overcome by IPv4 security technologies.

Lucena, et al. [10] presents a comprehensive examination of covert channels in IPv6. It analyses 22 different network storage channels at the IP level, classifying them by

---

[1] IPv6 is also referred as the Next Generation Internet Protocol or IPng.

J. Camenisch et al. (Eds.): IH 2006, LNCS 4437, pp. 58–77, 2007.

type of header. To defeat the identified channels, it defines three types of active wardens: stateless, stateful, and network-aware, which differ in complexity and ability to block some types of covert channels. A *stateless* active warden normalizes IPv6 traffic according to a protocol specification, without remembering anything about the packet that have already passed by. A *stateful* active warden records and recalls previous packet behaviors to discover a conceivably larger spectrum of hidden channels. A *network-aware* active warden is a stateful active warden with knowledge of network topology. The description of those active wardens is only conceptual. Until now, there has not been discussion of how one can implement network-aware wardens.

The IPv6 covert channels appear to be subtle types of aggression, when comparing to well-known buffer overflow attacks, for example. However, they are as harmful, especially under the presence of sophisticated adversaries[2]. It is feasible for an attacker to secretly transmit information into or out of a compromised machine residing on a secure network through the use of covert channels. For example, hacker Alice, after installing a key stroke logger and obtaining users' credentials, retrieves stolen information employing a covert channel. Alternatively, after installing a backdoor program, cracker Bob sends commands via a covert channel. Understanding that the use of IPv6 covert channels might be particularly damaging when an attacker utilizes them with the purpose of maintaining long-term control over a compromised machine, we present and evaluate an implementation of *network-aware* active wardens.

In this study, we consider two of the channels described in [10] and a well-known aggression in IPv4 [11,12,13,14]: the Routing Header covert channel, the Hop Limit channel, and the Short TTL Attack, respectively. The first two covert channels exemplify secret communication mechanisms of high and low bandwidth, respectively. The last one defines a relevant crossover point between the two versions of the IP protocol. The *Routing Header covert channel* takes advantage of the IPv6 source routing functionality to transfer data in a way that violates system security policies. The *Hop Limit channel* achieves a similar goal by manipulating the hop limit field of the IPv6 header. The *Short TTL* Attack allows an attacker to mask malicious communications or another attack from a Network Intrusion Detection System (NIDS). For a more detailed description of these attacks, please see Appendix A.

To prove that network-aware active wardens constitute an appropriate countermeasure against the selected IPv6 covert channels, we measure their effectiveness within a controlled network environment, by estimating a percentage of extermination per case and by measuring the increase over the roundtrip time of end-to-end traffic flows. We aim to defeat the selected channels, while causing roundtrip times increments no higher than 5%.

The remainder of this document is organized as follows. Section 2 compiles previous work on network covert channels in both IPv4 and IPv6, summarizing existing countermeasures. Section 3 specifies the design and implementation of the network-aware active wardens, presents results of performance tests set up on a controlled network, and discusses the implication of the obtained outcomes. Finally, Section 4 draws conclusions and suggests future directions of research related with the topic.

---

[2] The more secure nature of IPv6 in relation to IPv4 demands even more knowledgeable foes.

## 2  Related Work

Research in network covert channels [15] comprises the study of both network- and transport-layer protocols, such as IP, TCP, ICMP, and application-layer protocols, such as HTTP. It is not surprising to observe that the majority of the literature relates to network storage channels [10,16,17,18,19,20,21,22,23,24] rather than network timing channels [15,25,26,27,28]. Timing channels are presumably less attractive because of their synchronization issues and their low bandwidth in comparison to storage channels. However, it is somewhat peculiar that given the increasing use of IPv6, most of the research still concerns IPv4.

The most effective defensive mechanisms against network storage channels for IPv4 are protocol scrubbers [13], traffic normalizers [11], and active wardens [29,30,31,32]. Protocol scrubbers and traffic normalizers focus on eliminating ambiguities found in the traffic stream, carefully crafted with the purpose of evading network intrusion detection systems. *Ambiguous* network packets are those that could have different interpretations at endpoints depending on the implementation of the protocol stack. Covert channels are certainly a form of ambiguous traffic. Handley and Paxson [11] describes IP, UDP, TCP, and ICMP normalizations based on protocol semantics, highlighting the importance of preserving the end-to-end protocol semantics. In the same order of ideas, active wardens, as presented by Fisk et al. [32], are network services resembling a firewall that modify all traffic under the assumption that it is carrying steganographic content. Active wardens defeat steganography by making semantics-preserving alterations to packet headers (e.g. zeroing the padding bits in a TCP packet). These techniques, although effective for most IPv4 covert channels, do not record any state or gather network topology information.

Among the approaches and technologies that gather topology information with the purpose of detecting undesired traffic on the network are active mappers [14], NetFlow [33], network monitors such as Ntop [34], and certain implementations of the Simple Network Management Protocol (SNMP) [35], such as IBM Tivoli NetView [36], HP OpenView Network Node Manager [37], Marconi ForeView, and Sun Solstice Site Manager [38]. Shankar and Paxson [14] proposes an alternative approach to traffic normalizers [11] called *active mappers* that minimizes the performance penalties caused by packet reassembling. Active mapping involves building profiles of the network topology and the TCP/IP policies of hosts to help NIDSs disambiguate the interpretation of network traffic. The mappers gather topology information *actively*, sending specially crafted probing messages to each host on the network. Ntop, from www.ntop.org, is a traffic measurement and monitoring system with an embedded NIDS that gathers certain information about network topology and host relationships [34]. Ntop learns about topology based on network flows, so it actually depends on the existence of those flows: there is no knowledge without flow. Therefore, the view of the topology drawn by Ntop might be incomplete in certain situations (for example, when flows traveling to adjacent subnets do not pass by the system). NetFlow version 9, supporting IPv6, provides several services being the most important flow recording. It also provides information about traffic routing. The commercial SNMP products provide an understanding of the physical network topology through different information gathering mechanisms.

Network-aware active wardens are not exactly traffic normalizers nor active mappers, but an innovative technology that comprises some of the best features of both. Active mapping is meant to work in conjunction with NIDSs, assisting them in resolving network ambiguity. In consequence, they do not eliminate the ambiguities. They aid NIDSs to alert network administrators of unwanted protocol behavior with more precision (than without the mappers). Active wardens, with knowledge of the network topology, defeat covert channels based on network ambiguities without significant overhead, actually alleviating the workload of a NIDS positioned after the warden.

## 3  Network-Aware Active Wardens

As originally defined in Lucena, et al. [10], *network-aware* active wardens are the most sophisticated type of wardens. A network-aware active warden can not only reinforce protocol syntax and semantics preservation (both passively or actively), but also perform address verification using topology information about the surrounding networks. The following subsections explain the design of our implementation of a network-aware active warden, list assumptions made, and analyze performance measurements. To simplify the discussion, from this point on, a network-aware active warden will be referred simply as warden, active warden, or just Wendy.

### 3.1  Overview and Rationale

**Objectives.** The main purpose of an active warden is to the break covert channel communication or to remove the cover traffic masking an attack from a NIDS, as in the Short TTL scenario. In the former case, the goal is to disable the covert channel without affecting the legitimate usage of the exploited header. That is, only packets carrying covert data in their headers should be modified, preserving the protocol semantics[3]. In the latter case, the purpose is to remove the "mask" so the ulterior attack becomes visible to a NIDS. The warden itself does not perform the detection, but eliminates the evasion.

**Assumption 1.** *The warden always attempts not to break the overt communication taking place through a suspicious flow.*

A secondary, but no less important, goal of a network-aware active warden is to take advantage of network topology information to properly defeat the covert channels. As detailed in Section 2, there exist multiple ways for a warden to gather such information: scanning network administrators' topology tables, sending probing messages to individual hosts on the network [14], and using network-monitoring tools [33,34] or particular applications implementing SNMP [36,37,38].

**Assumption 2.** *The warden already possesses the topology information of the guarded network, previously acquired through complementary technologies.*

---

[3] When preserving header functionality is not a concern, the covert channels can be defeated by simply disabling specific header support on a given network.

**Location.** The Internet comprises a collection of autonomous systems. An *autonomous system*[4] (AS) is a subset of routers that make up an internetwork and exchange information through a common routing protocol [39]. An *autonomous system border router* (ASBR) exchanges information between two ASs, maintaining separate topological databases for each. The location of the warden within the network topology, formed by those ASs, significantly affects her ability to detect covert communication.

There are two prevailing locations where to place the warden, depending on the network architecture Wendy wants to protect. A warden who sits on or near an ASBR (see Figure 1) is a *border* warden. A warden who sits on or near an internal router is a *link* warden. Border wardens aim to block covert communication channels established between an interior host and a point outside the local autonomous system (regardless of which participant originates the inter-AS channel). Link wardens disable intra-AS channels.

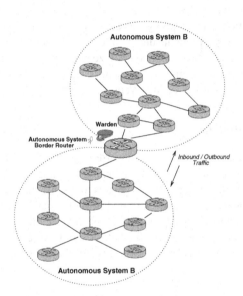

**Fig. 1.** Border Warden

Consequently, the location within the network topology determines the type of information the warden has available as well as the actions she can take. If Wendy is a link-level warden, she has information about all the nodes of the subnet. However, all that information is useful only to local or internal traffic verification. On the other hand, if Wendy is a border warden, she can observe inbound and outbound AS traffic, which is presumably more susceptible to attack.

**Assumption 3.** *Wendy is a border warden.*

---

[4] In the Internet protocol context, autonomous systems are called *routing domains*.

## 3.2   Attack Model

The implemented active warden relies on several assumptions about the adversary's capabilities. Those assumptions agree with the ones presented in [10], and generally are not stronger.

The opponents behave *actively* [30]. They have both the resources and skills to alter packets in transit, by either modifying values of protocol fields or by injecting an entire field, a header, or a crafted packet.

**Assumption 4.** *Adversaries can modify network packets traveling between nodes.*

As it is for the wardens, the location within the protected AS is relevant for the attackers.

**Assumption 5.** *Adversary Alice is located within the protected AS. Adversary Bob is located outside of Alice's network.*

Following Shannon's maxim "the enemy knows the system" [40], it is possible that Alice knows about both the existence and the location of the warden. In addition, if Alice learns about Wendy, she can also learn about the topology of the network under her attack.

**Assumption 6.** *Adversaries may or may not have knowledge of the existence of the warden and her location.*

Adversaries who do not know about the wardens are said to be *blind*.


## 3.3   Covert Channel Defense

This subsection describes the countermeasures taken by the implemented warden to eliminate the *Routing Header* covert channel, the *Hop Limit* channel, and the *Short TTL* Attack. Relevant details about the operation of these channels appear in Appendix A.

**Eliminating the Routing Header Covert Channels.**   To defeat the covert channels in the Routing Header, an active warden has to perform several checks on the protocol semantics and behavior. We identify for different ones. The first check is somewhat simpler than the remainder four being based exclusively on the IPv6 specifications [41,42] and the address spacc allocation document [43].

- **Hop Address Check.** This check relies on the fact that only *aggregatable global unicast* addresses are meaningful within a packet's Routing Header [41]. *Multicast* addresses are explicitly forbidden, plus *local* addresses (both *unique-local* and *link-local*) are not supposed to cross site the boundary of the protected AS. Hence, the border warden should not observe any of the last two address types.

   In addition, "a routing header is not examined or processed until it reaches the node identified in the `destination address` field" [41], giving Alice and Bob enough opportunities through intermediate hosts of interpreting the covert message. Our implementation of active warden performs a more aggressive check, verifying at the border router that all addresses contained in the Routing Header are, in fact, *aggregatable global unicast* addresses.

*Aggregatable global unicast* addresses begin with the bit pattern 001. Assuming that the covert messages follow a uniform random distribution, there is one in eight chance of beginning with the bits 001. Therefore, a *blind* attacker will have, at least, 87.5% chance of being caught when injecting messages crafted as addresses in a Routing Header (see Appendix B for details).

For the following checks, it is important to distinguish between incoming and outgoing traffic. *Incoming* traffic refers to packets whose source address is outside the AS and whose destination address belongs to the AS. *Outgoing* traffic, contrarily, has a source address within the AS and a destination address outside the AS. The direction in which the traffic flows determines what types of checks are needed. Table 1 summarizes the corresponding required checks. Because the analysis of both directions is symmetric, we discuss only the case of outgoing traffic.

**Table 1.** Topology Checks Required Depending on the *Segments Left* Field Value (*Visited* or *Not Visited*) for Both Incoming and Outgoing Traffic

|  | Router Address Check | IP Range Check |
|---|---|---|
| Addresses Marked as *Visited* | *outgoing* | *incoming* |
| Addresses *Not Visited* | *incoming* | *outgoing* |

- **Router Address Check.** For outgoing packets whose Routing Header addresses are marked as *visited*, Wendy verifies whether or not they are valid inside the protected AS. In addition, because only routers perform packet forwarding, those addresses must correspond to routers. Therefore, if already-visited addresses in the Routing Header of an outgoing packet do not belong to addresses of internal AS routers, she concludes that a covert channel exists.
- **IP Range Check.** Alternatively, if the addresses in the Routing Header of an outgoing packet are marked as *not visited*, the warden inspects if they fall within the range of addresses assigned to the AS. If so, it means that the packet will eventually come back to the system. Appropriately, Wendy will also suspect that a covert communication is taking place. This check is a more elaborate version of the address-based ingress/egress filtering performed by some firewalls.
- **Tandem Check.** It is possible to circumvent the last two checks by crafting an outgoing packet whose Routing Header addresses are marked as *not visited* and do not match the IP range of the AS. The converse deception also holds for incoming packets. However, if there are active wardens positioned near both the origin and the destination of the covert communication, an attacker cannot easily generate covert packets without being detected. For example, an attacker Alice wants to transmit a covert message from A to B in the scenario of Figure 2. To be able to deceive the active warden sitting on A's border router, she will have to mark all the fake addresses as *not visited* while making them different from any address within A's IP address range. However, when a packet formatted in such manner arrives to

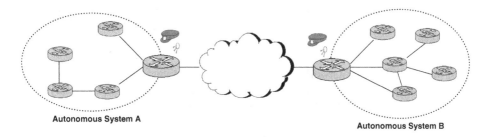

Autonomous System A

Autonomous System B

**Fig. 2.** Example of Tandem Wardens Performing Topology Checks

B, the active warden residing in B's border router will perform the usual verification. The only way then for the attacker be able to bypass that second warden is to have knowledge about B's router addresses. While not impossible that particular situation requires additional effort from the adversary. That is, even when Alice possesses knowledge of B's topology, she can only conceal messages that mimic actual router addresses within B's routing domain, not just any arbitrary data. The only option left for the adversary then is to manipulate the order of legitimate router addresses in the header to convey a message. That channel however has low bandwidth in comparison to the original channel, specifically, $128/log_2(r)$ times lower, where $r$ stands for the number of router within the AS (refer to Appendix B for bandwidth calculations).

Once Wendy identifies the presence of a covert channel, she proceeds to eliminate it. The trivial way of eliminating any channel is to simply drop the suspicious packet. That action might, in most cases, break the overt communication. As stated in assumption 1, Wendy will always prefer less disruptive methods. A more appropriate solution is to strip the covert message from a packet and allow it to proceed normally. Whether the warden can actually modify the Routing Header or not depends on whether the packet is IPSec protected or not[5]. For the purposes of this study, the IPv6 traffic is not IPSec protected.

**Eliminating the Hop Limit Covert Channels.** The Hop Limit covert channel makes use of a `hop limit` field in IPv6 packet headers to transmit covert messages. The detection of this channel is troublesome because the value of the hop count can vary naturally as an effect of packets traveling different routes. A trivial attempt to break the channel is for the warden to reset the hop limit value in all packets in transit to an arbitrary value. That however can be potentially damaging as it prevents the `hop limit` field from its intended purpose, to avoid packets traveling indefinitely and

---

[5] Under IPSec, the modification of a packet header might result in failure of the integrity check, causing the packet to be discarded. It is important to note that if an attacker intercepts and modifies a legitimate packet without having access to the IPSec security context, that packet will be analogously dropped. If the adversary does know the security context and protects the covert message under the IPSec integrity check, the overt communication may not be legitimate third-party traffic and may be discarded anyway.

hence saturating the network in the case of a routing cycle. If a warden chooses to reset the field to a *small* value, it lowers the risk of encountering a cycle, but increases the probability that legitimate packets will expire on their way to the destination without reaching it.

On the other hand, a network-aware active warden applies her knowledge to manipulate the hop limit field in a safer manner. For incoming packets, Wendy can infer the minimum hop limit value which is sufficient to prevent the packets from expiring before their intended destination. If the initial hop limit value is enough to reach the destination, the warden resets it to the inferred value. If it is not large enough, the warden takes similar actions to the ones stated in the Short TTL Attack. In both cases, Wendy defeats the channel 100% of the times, when occurring on inbound traffic. For outgoing packets, the warden is not always able to make similar premises about the minimum hop limit value. However, when the covert communication involves two ASs (e.g., Alice resides in AS A and Bob in AS B), each of them protected by a warden as in Figure 2, it is plausible to disable the covert communication. Symmetrically, the traffic seen by one of the wardens as outgoing will, in fact, be incoming from the standpoint of the other warden. To completely, eliminate the channel when happening in outbound traffic, Wendy might reset the hop limit value as done by IPv4 traffic normalizers [11] for the TTL value, but at the risk of incurring the same drawbacks.

**Eliminating the Short TTL Attack.** The Short TTL Attack utilizes packets with a small hop limit value to mask another attack from being detected by a network intrusion detection system. The active warden is not concerned with detecting the covert attack, but with removing the cover traffic so that an existing network intrusion detection system is able to detect the attack.

Handley and Paxson [11] proposes to prevent the exploit through the use of a traffic normalizer that either drops packets with a short TTL or restores the TTL value to a number that would guarantee packet delivery. The first solution is not actually implemented by the normalizer because of the lack of a topology gathering mechanism. Nevertheless, Shankar and Paxson [14] did carry out the suggested approach with a successful outcome. As discussed in the previous case, resetting the TTL value in IPv4 or the hop limit value in IPv6 without any knowledge of the network topology compromises the interconnected system. Our implementation of Wendy overcomes those difficulties with her network topology knowledge, defeating the Short TTL evasion 100% of the times.

To illustrate the concept, Figure 3 shows an example of how the warden helps defeat a Short TTL attack. An adversary targeting host **X** might conceal the attack by masking the traffic with a hop limit value expiring at router **C**. If the only defense is a NIDS located before **C**, the malicious traffic might circumvent it. However, if active warden Wendy works in combination with a NIDS, she is able to detect that the packets will not reach the final destination **X** and drop them before they pass by the NIDS. In the presented scenario, Wendy should discard all packets addressed to **D** if their hop limit value is smaller than 2.

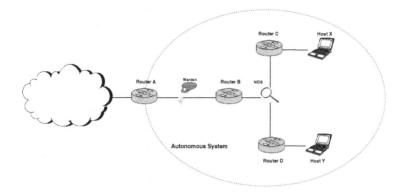

**Fig. 3.** Active Warden and NIDS Positioning

## 3.4 Prototype Implementation

We implemented our prototype of a network-aware active warden as a kernel module in a Linux router, running Fedora Core 4, kernel version 2.6.14. The prototype uses the *netfilter hooks* library to intercept and examine network traffic. The same machine also runs a firewall in permissive mode. Because the firewall operates in that mode without enforcing any complex rules, the impact of the active warden on the network performance tends to be more visible. Our Wendy acts as a border warden, as shown in Figure 4.

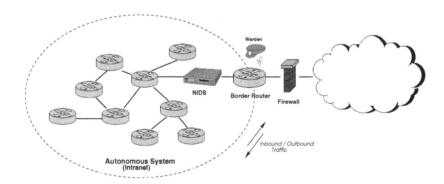

**Fig. 4.** Location of the Active Warden with respect to the guarded AS. Wendy renders useless the possible covert channels and evasions contained in the traffic that already bypassed the firewall before it is checked by the NIDS.

In addition, the prototype runs within a controlled network environment, which allows Wendy to have a preconfigured knowledge about the network topology. To ensure constant access times, the topology knowledge is stored in a hashtable that maps node addresses to hop distances.

The controlled network environment consists of a router connected to two subnets. One simulates the protected AS (Intranet) through a number of IPv6 addresses, varying from 10 to 1000. The second one mimics the outside world (Internet).

### 3.5   Results

We evaluated the effectiveness of the implemented warden computing the average roundtrip times for different packet sizes, different lengths of Routing Header, and different Intranet sizes, performing 10 measurements each time.

Figure 5 exhibits average roundtrip times for packets of 64-byte length and of 4096-byte length traveling between end points, with and without the warden siting on the border router. The obtained values for 64-byte packet were $0.3029ms \pm 0.0004ms$ (without warden) and $0.3136ms \pm 0.0002ms$ (with the warden). The difference found between the averages represents a 3.3% increase of the roundtrip time. Similarly, for 4096-byte packets the average times were $1.8939ms \pm 0.0006ms$ (without the warden) and $1.9037ms \pm 0.0003ms$ (with the warden). There was only a 0.5% increase in the average times of the larger packets.

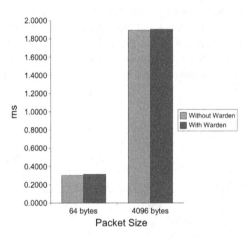

**Fig. 5.** Average Roundtrip Times of Packets of Sizes 64 and 4096 Bytes

Figure 6 shows average roundtrip times of packets carrying no Routing Header or Routing Header with 1 and 16 addresses. When the packets did not have a Routing Header the average roundtrip times were $0.250ms \pm 0.001ms$ (without the warden) and $0.257ms \pm 0.002ms$ (with the warden), exhibiting a total increase of 2.8%. Analogously, with a 1-hop Routing Header the average roundtrip times varied from $0.268ms \pm 0.002ms$ (without the warden) to $0.277ms \pm 0.002ms$ (with the warden), where the increment is 3.3%. For a 16-hope Routing Header, the achieved values were $0.382ms \pm 0.002ms$ (without the warden) and $0.389ms \pm 0.003ms$ (with the warden), being the case with minimum increase: 1.8%.

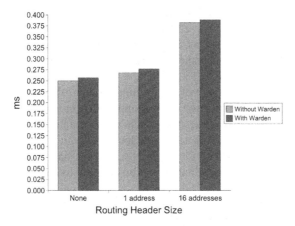

**Fig. 6.** Average Roundtrip Times of Packets with No Routing Header and Routing Headers containing 1 and 16 addresses

Figure 7 displays the differences in average roundtrip times when the packets traverse networks composed of 10 and 1000 hosts. As observed graphically, there was no difference at all in the average times obtained for the two network sizes. Precisely, the average times recorded were $0.303ms \pm 0.001ms$ (without the warden) and $0.313ms \pm 0.001ms$ (with the warden).

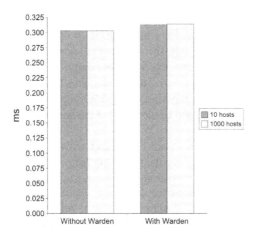

**Fig. 7.** Average Roundtrip Times of Packets Traversing Networks of 10 and 1000 Hosts

### 3.6   Discussion

Analyzing the test results presented in Subsection 3.5, we observe the following:

1. The relative delay introduced by our active warden decreases as the packet size grows. This is presumably caused by the fact that the border router works harder when distributing larger packets, while the warden's load of scanning the Routing Header stays the same. Hence, the absolute overhead remains constant, causing the relative overhead to shrink.
2. Both the presence and the size of the Routing Header affects the warden's performance. This is trivially explained by the Routing Header normalizations performed by the warden, which require scanning each of the contained addresses.
3. The size of simulated network topology does not influence the warden's performance. This is not a surprising outcome because the data structures used by the warden to store topology information exhibit constant lookup times.

We initially envisioned to produce a network-aware active warden that completely defeated the selected covert channels, without increasing packet roundtrip times in more than 5%. As detailed in Subsection 3.3, we found that it is virtually impossible to eliminate some of them under our attacker model. However, the percentages of elimination estimated for each case are significant, especially considering that several of them are close to 100% and that, even when the attacker can circumvent our warden, the bandwidth of the secret communication drops dramatically. On the other hand, regarding the overhead caused by the warden in the packet roundtrip time, the results indicate that we reached our goal. All tests showed increases in the average roundtrip times of approximately 3%, being 3.3% the highest.

When comparing our implementation of network-aware active wardens to IPv4 technologies that deal with network ambiguities [11,14], the prototyped warden presents both differences and similarities. Wendy behaves as a traffic normalizer because she also performs active protocol semantics reinforcement. Moreover, she resembles an active mapper when using network topology information to disambiguate traffic. However, our active warden differs in the way she obtains the knowledge about the topology. In addition, the prototype implementation does not compromise significantly the performance of packets traveling end-to-end. That occurs, presumably, for two reasons: a) the use of more precise methods of handling network ambiguities (when comparing to the ones in traditional normalizer), and b) the fact that the warden does not perform packet reassembling.

Finally, considering future directions of research as well as possible improvements in the warden evaluation, we identify the following factors:

- While a controlled network environment was useful for gathering initial results, this environment obviously did not provide large volume of traffic. It is necessary to repeat the tests over a real-world network and compare the results.
- Our warden defeated only two of the 22 covert channels described in [10]. It is critical to extend the warden implementation in such way that can block the rest of the channels.
- Our covert channel countermeasures may be compromised by attacker who knows the system by, for example, taking control of the warden or by launching a denial-of-service attack. It is critical to examine the robustness of the warden in future implementations.

# 4  Conclusions

In this study we designed and implemented a version of *network-aware* active wardens [10] to defeat the *Routing Header* covert channel, the *Hop Limit* covert channel, and the *Short TTL* attack. The warden not only normalized the protocol semantics, but also utilized network topology information to effectively defeat the covert channels and exploits. It proved to render useless instances of covert communication occurring within a controlled network environment, while causing a penalty in the packet roundtrips of only approximately 3%.

Based on our initial results, we believe that *network-aware* active wardens are a promising technology that represents a step forward in the elimination of new security threats in IPv6 such as recently discovered covert channels. We also hope that our work generate discussion regarding other adequate countermeasures and feasible fixes to the protocol.

# References

1. The IPv6 Portal. Retrieved on June 22, 2005 from the World Wide Web: http://www.ist-ipv6.org/ (2005)
2. Press Trust of India: TRAI wants govt to kickstart shift to ipv6 through e-gov. http://www.hindustantimes.com/news/181_1578124,00020020.htm (2005)
3. ChinaView: China, EU to build wide-band network. Retrieved on January 12, 2006 from the World Wide Web: http://news.xinhuanet.com/english/2006-01/12/content_4045153.htm (2006)
4. United States IPv6 Summit. Retrieved on November 05, 2005 from the World Wide Web: www.usipv6.com/ (2005)
5. Global Summit IPv6. Retrieved on May 17, 2005 from the World Wide Web: http://www.ipv6-es.com/05/in/i-intro.php (2005)
6. IPv6 Forum Korea. Retrieved on October 13, 2005 from the World Wide Web: http://www.ipv6.or.kr/ (2005)
7. Luxembourg IPv6 Summit 2005. Retrieved on June 22, 2005 from the World Wide Web: http://wiki.uni.lu/ipv6/Luxembourg+IPv6+Summit+2005.html (2005)
8. Evans, K.S.: Memorandum for the chief information officers, M-05-22. http://www.whitehouse.gov/omb/memoranda/fy2005/m05-22.pdf (2005)
9. United States Government Accountability Office: Internet protocol version 6: Federal agencies need to plan for transition and manage security risks. Technical Report GAO-05-471 (2005) http://www.gao.gov/new.items/d05471.pdf.
10. Lucena, N.B., Lewandowski, G., Chapin, S.J.: Covert channels in IPv6. In: Proceedings of the $5^{th}$ Workshop on Privacy Enhancing Technologies, Dubrovnik (Cavtat), Croatia (2005)
11. Handley, M., Paxson, V.: Network intrusion detection: Evasion, traffic normalization, and end-to-end protocol semantics. In: Proceedings of the $10^{th}$ USENIX Security Symposium, Washington, DC, USA, USENIX Association (2001)
12. horizon<jmcdonal@unf.edu>: Defeating sniffers and intrusion detection systems. Phrack Magazine Volume 8, Issue 54 (1998) Retrieved on May 13, 2005 from the World Wide Web: http://www.phrack.org/phrack/54/P54-10.
13. Malan, G.R., Watson, D., Jahanian, F., Howell, P.: Transport and application protocol scrubbing. In: Proceedings of the IEEE INFOCOM 2002 Conference, Tel-Aviv, Israel (2000) 1381–1390

14. Shankar, U., Paxson, V.: Active mapping: Resisting NIDS evasion without altering traffic. In: Proceedings of the 2003 IEEE Symposium on Security and Privacy, Washington, DC, USA, IEEE Computer Society (2003) 44–61

15. Cabuk, S., Brodley, C.E., Shields, C.: IP covert timing channels: Design and detection. In: Proceedings of the $11^{th}$ ACM Conference on Computer and Communications Security, Washington DC, USA, ACM Press (2004) 178–187

16. Handel, T., Sandford, M.: Hiding data in the OSI network model. In Anderson, R., ed.: Information Hiding: Proceedings of the First International Workshop, Cambridge, U.K., Springer (1996) 23–38

17. Abad, C.: IP checksum covert channels and selected hash collision. Retrieved on January 3, 2005 from the World Wide Web: http://gray-world.net/cn/papers/ipccc.pdf (2001)

18. Bauer, M.: New covert channels in HTTP - adding unwitting web browsers to anonymity sets. In Samarati, P., Syverson, P., eds.: Proceedings of the 2003 ACM Workshop on Privacy in the Electronic Society, Washington, DC, USA, ACM Press (2003) 72–78 ISBN 1-58113-776-1.

19. daemon9 (route@infonexus.com): Loki2 (the implementation). Phrack Magazine, 51, article 6 (1997) Retrieved on August 27, 2002 from the World Wide Web: http://www.phrack.org/show.php?p=51&a=6.

20. daemon9 (route@infonexus.com), alhambra (alhambra@infornexus.com): Project loki. Phrack Magazine, 49, article 6 (1996) Retrieved on August 27, 2002 from the World Wide Web: http://www.phrack.org/show.php?p=49&a=6.

21. Dunigan, T.: Internet steganography. Technical report, Oak Ridge National Laboratory (Contract No. DE-AC05-96OR22464), Oak Ridge, Tennessee (1998) [ORNL/TM-limited distribution].

22. Giffin, J., Greenstadt, R., Litwack, P., Tibbetts, R.: Covert messaging through TCP timestamps. In: Second Workshop on Privacy Enhancing Technologies. Volume 2482 of Lectures Notes in Computer Science., San Francisco, CA, USA, Springer-Verlag Heidelberg (2003) 194–208

23. Ka0ticSH: Diggin em walls (part 3) - advanced/other techniques for bypassing firewalls. New Order (2002) Retrieved on August 28, 2002 from the World Wide Web: http://neworder.box.sk/newsread.php?newsid=3957.

24. Rowland, C.H.: Covert channels in the TCP/IP protocol suite. Psionics Technologies (1996) Retrieved on November 13, 2004 from the World Wide Web: http://www.firstmonday.dk/issues/issue2_5/rowland/.

25. Ahsan, K.: Covert channel analysis and data hiding in TCP/IP. Master's thesis, University of Toronto (2002)

26. Ahsan, K., Kundur, D.: Practical data hiding in TCP/IP. In: Proceedings of the ACM Workshop on Multimedia Security at ACM Multimedia. (2002)

27. Servetto, S.D., Vetterli, M.: Codes for the fold-sum channel. In: Proceedings of th $35^{35}$ Annual Conference on Information Science and Systems (CISS), Baltimore, MD, USA (2001)

28. Servetto, S.D., Vetterli, M.: Communication using phantoms: Covert channels in the Internet. In: Proceedings of the IEEE International Symposium on Information Theory (ISIT), Washington, DC, USA (2001)

29. Anderson, R.: Stretching the limits of steganography. In Anderson, R., ed.: Information Hiding: Proceedings of the First International Workshop, Cambridge, U.K., Springer (1996) 39–48

30. Anderson, R.J., Petitcolas, F.A.: On the limits of steganography. In: IEEE Journal of Selected Areas in Communications: Special Issue on Copyright and Privacy Protection. (1998) 474–481

31. Craver, S.: On public-key steganography in the presence of an active warden. In Aucsmith, D., ed.: Information Hiding: Proceedings of the Second International Workshop, Portland, Oregon, U.S.A., Springer (1998) 355–368
32. Fisk, G., Fisk, M., Papadopoulos, C., Neil, J.: Eliminating steganography in Internet traffic with active wardens. In Oostveen, J., ed.: Information Hiding: Preproceedings of the Fifth International Workshop, Noordwijkerhout, The Netherlands, Springer (2002) 29–46
33. Cisco: Cisco IOS NetFlow. Retrieved on November 17, 2005 from the World Wide Web: http://www.cisco.com/en/US/products/ps6601/products_ios_protocol_group_home.html (2005)
34. Deri, L., Suin, S.: Improving network security using Ntop. In: Third International Workshop on the Recent Adcances in Intrusion Detection, RAID 2000, Toulouse, France (2000)
35. Case, J., Fedor, M., Schoffstall, M., Davin, J.: A simple network management protocol (SNMP). Retrieved on January 13, 2005 from the World Wide Web: http://www.ietf.org/rfc/rfc1157.txt (1990) RFC 1157.
36. IBM: Tivoli NetView. Retrieved on November 17, 2005 from the World Wide Web: http://www-306.ibm.com/software/tivoli/products/netview/ (2005)
37. HP: Network node manager advanced edition. Retrieved on November 17, 2005 from the World Wide Web: http://www.managementsoftware.hp.com/products/nnm/index.html (2005)
38. Sun: Solstice site manager. Retrieved on November 17, 2005 from the World Wide Web: http://www.sun.com/software/solstice/sm/index.xml (2005)
39. Doyle, J.: Routing TCP/IP. Volume I. Cisco Press, Indianapolis, IN 46240 (1998)
40. Shannon, C.E.: Communication theory of secrecy systems. Technical report (1949)
41. Deering, S., Hinden, R.: Internet protocol, version 6 (IPv6) specification. Retrieved on October 08, 2004 from the World Wide Web: http://www.ietf.org/rfc/rfc2460.txt?number=2460 (1998) RFC 2460.
42. Hinde, R., Deering, S.: IP version 6 addressing architecture. Retrieved on October 08, 2004 from the World Wide Web: http://www.ietf.org/rfc/rfc2373.txt?number=2373 (1998) RFC 2373.
43. (IANA), I.A.N.A.: Internet Protocol version 6 address space. Retrieved on October 29, 2005 from the World Wide Web: http://www.iana.org/assignments/ipv6-address-space (2005)
44. (IANA), I.A.N.A.: IP version 6 parameters. Retrieved on October 28, 2004 from the World Wide Web: http://www.iana.org/assignments/ipv6-parameters (2004)

# A    Covert Channels of Communication and Exploits

The description as well as the associated adversary model summarized in Subsections A.1 and A.2 correspond to the one presented in [10]. The *hop limit* exploit characterized in Subsection A.3 reassembles the Short TTL Attack for IPv4 reported by several authors [11,12,13,14].

### A.1    Routing Header Covert Channels

The *Routing Extension Header* contains a list of intermediate routers a packet in transit should visit on the way to its destination. As the packet moves through the network, routers mark their addresses as "visited" and send the packet on to the next address in the list. The IPv6 Parameters document [44] enumerates three different types of routing, but only one of them, *Type 0*, is fully described in the specification [41]. Figure 8 shows

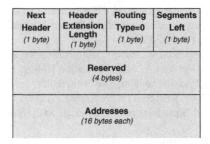

**Fig. 8.** Format of the Routing Header

**Table 2.** Identified Covert Storage Channels in the Routing Header

| ID | Field | Covert Channel | Bandwidth |
|----|-------|----------------|-----------|
| $\alpha$ | *Routing Type: 0 - Reserved* | Hide data in unused bits | 4 bytes/packet |
| $\beta$ | *Routing Type: 0* | Set one or more false addresses[6] | Up to 2048 bytes/packet |

the format of the routing header when routing type is 0. Table 2 summarizes plausible covert channels exploiting such format.

$\alpha$ There exists a *reserved* field in the routing header structure when the *routing type* is 0. Alice can hide 4 bytes of covert data per packet using this channel.

$\beta$ When the *routing type* is 0, Alice can fabricate "addresses" out of arbitrary data meaningful to Bob[7]. She appends the covert data and sets the `segments left` field accordingly. In most cases, she would like to prevent any node from attempting to process the fake addresses. Setting the segments left value to 0 will make the addresses to appear visited. Contrarily, a non zero value will indicate that such addresses need to be visited. Figures 9 and 10 display two different types of embedding in the routing header when the routing is 0:

- one where Alice chooses to create a completely new header to send Bob 48 bytes of covert information, and
- another one where she uses an already existing header to embed a covert message of 32 bytes.

Based on the maximum extension header payload length, Alice can potentially insert up 2048 bytes. Therefore, she will be extending the entire IPv6 packet by the same amount of bytes.

### A.2   Hop Limit Covert Channel

The `hop limit` of the IPv6 header shown in Figure 11 indicates the number of hops a packet can still traverse before being destroyed. It is analogous to the TTL field in

---

[6] This covert channel, when authentication is used, requires recalculating or circumventing the ICV.

[7] In this situation, Bob does not need to be at the final destination of the packet. He only needs to observe the packet somewhere along the communication path.

**Fig. 9.** $\beta$ **Covert Channel in the Routing Extension Header,** when Alice creates fake addresses in a packet that did not originally a routing extension header

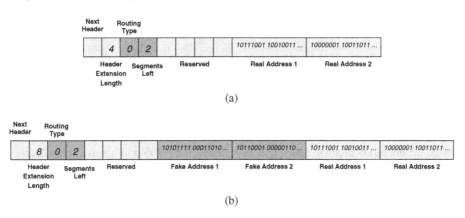

(a)

(b)

**Fig. 10.** $\beta$ **Covert Channel in the Routing Extension Header,** when Alice inserts fake addresses in a packet already containing a routing extension header. (a) Original routing extension header, (b) Routing header after Alice inserts the covert data.

IPv4, however the TTL refers to the number of seconds remaining not the number of hops.

The *hop limit* channel[8] involves a crafted manipulation of its value. Alice send an initial hop limit value, $h$, and modifies the hop limit value of subsequent packets. Bob interprets the covert message by checking the variations in the hop limit values of packets traversing his location. One scheme has Alice signaling a 0 by decreasing the hop count from the prior packet, and a 1 by increasing the hop count relative to the prior packet. A drawback of this channel is that packets do not necessarily travel the same route, so the number of intermediate hops may vary, introducing noise. To overcome this, Alice can choose a $\delta$ that is greater than the expected noise, and use hop counts less than $h - \delta$ signal a 0, and hop counts greater than $h + \delta$ to signal a 1. Bob then compares the received hop count to $h$ to deduce the bit. The bandwidth of this channel is limited. Alice needs to modify $n$ packets to send $n - 1$ bits of information.

### A.3 Short TTL Exploit

In the IPv4 context, an attacker can manipulate the packet's TTL field to mask another attack from a network intrusion detection system (NIDS) [11,12,13,14]. An appropriately

---

[8] This channel is called channel $\epsilon$ in [10].

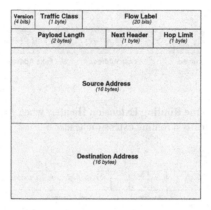

**Fig. 11.** IPv6 Header Format

set TTL value causes a packet to expire before it reaches its destination but after it has passed by any NIDS along the way. In consequence, the NIDS will see a different traffic pattern than the destination host will and might be unable to detect an ongoing attack. A similar mechanism can be applied to IPv6 traffic by exploiting the `hop limit` field in the IPv6 header (recall Figure 11).

## B    Rationale of the Percentages of Covert Channel Elimination

### B.1    Routing Header Covert Channel

**Case: Blind Adversary.** Because *aggregatable global unicast* addresses must use the prefix 001, there is one in eight chance $(1/8)$ that a *blind* adversary will select a fake address that follows such pattern. Let $P_{Interception}$ be the probability of the active warden interception the adversary's covert communication,

$$P_{Interception} = 1 - \frac{1}{8} \tag{1}$$

In addition, every fake address the *blind* attacker wishes to inject to convey cover messages have to begin with the same pattern. Therefore, the odds of blocking a bogus address are higher with the next one inserted. That is,

$$P_{Interception} = 1 - \frac{1}{8^n} \tag{2}$$

where $n$ is the number of injected addresses.

**Case: Warden-Aware Adversary.** A *warden-aware* adversary that attempt to circumvent the actions taken by an active warden has a unique alternative to manipulate the order of legitimate router addresses in the Routing Header.

Let $C_{Bandwidth}$ be the channel bandwidth measured in bits per packet, $n$ be the number of addresses present in a Routing Header. The bandwidth of a Routing Header covert channel based on the order of the contained addresses is given by the equation,

$$C_{Bandwidth} = 128 * n \qquad (3)$$

considering that each address has a length of 16 octets (128 bits).

However, if the attacker is forced to use only real router addresses, such bandwidth also depends on the number of routers, $r$, within the protected AS. That is,

$$C_{Bandwidth} = log_2(r^n) = n * log_2(r) \qquad (4)$$

The ratio between 3 and 4,

$$\frac{128}{log_2(r)} \qquad (5)$$

represents bandwidth loss the adversary will suffer when her actions are limited by the active warden.

# Video Watermarking by Using Geometric Warping Without Visible Artifacts

Dima Pröfrock, Mathias Schlauweg, and Erika Müller

Institute of Communications Engineering,
University of Rostock,
Rostock 18119, Germany,
{dima.proefrock, mathias.schlauweg, erika.mueller}@uni-rostock.de

**Abstract.** Our paper proposes an enhanced video watermarking approach. The fundamental idea is to use geometric warping for watermarks with high predictable robustness to lossy compression. We explain the basic watermarking approach which uses a block based statistic (Normed Centre of Gravity - NCG) to describe the geometric structure of blocks. The NCG also is used to choose robust blocks. To embed the watermark information the chosen blocks are changed by geometric warping. To extract the watermark, the original video is not necessary. The NCG is used to detect the watermarked blocks and compute the embedded watermark bit. In some cases, the independent geometric warping of blocks which contain the same object results in visible artifacts. We propose to link blocks in space and time to block groups. In contrast to the basic approach, the blocks of one block group can be warped in dependence on each other. Thus, the visible artifacts are prevented.

## 1   Introduction

Current information technologies are based more and more on digital multimedia data. The use of digital data instead of analogue data offers many advantages. A lot of digital data can be produced in a very short time and it becomes more and more trivial to edit and finish the data. As opposed to analogue data, digital data can be endlessly copied without any loss of quality. However, the technologies to manipulate and copy data are often used in an illegal manner.Hence, there is a growing importance of applications such as data authentication, copyright and data hiding. Digital watermarking offers contributions in these fields. It describes techniques to embed additional information, the watermark, into digital data [1].Transparency, robustness and capacity are some important and application dependent properties of watermarking. Especially in the case of video watermarking, watermarks with high robustness to lossy compression are required. Generally, videos are compressed with lower data rates as single images. Hence, image watermarking techniques can not be automatically used for video watermarking.

There are watermarking approaches that solve the problem by embedding the watermark into the compressed domain during or after the encoding process

J. Camenisch et al. (Eds.): IH 2006, LNCS 4437, pp. 78–92, 2007.

(e.g., [2], [3]). This method has the advantage that the watermarking process is not influenced by the compression. However, the watermarks are generally not robust to a transcoding of the video. This paper presents a watermark approach in the uncompressed domain. The uncompressed video is watermarked and can be compressed with different compression algorithms and data rates. The watermark is robust to the compression.

Generally, the watermark is embedded into the irrelevant information of video data to be invisible. This results in problems because compression algorithms try to remove irrelevant information. In [4], we propose a basic watermarking approach which embeds the watermark in the relevant information of videos but in an imperceptible manner. This approach is based on geometric warping of blocks. Because common compression algorithms are PSNR (Peak Signal to Noise Ratio)-optimized, they try to maintain the geometric structure. With this approach a high robustness to the new H.264/AVC compression standard can be achieved. At present, the new H.264/AVC standard, developed for a broad range of applications, provides the highest coding performance [5], [6]. Because this, especially a H.264/AVC compression is suitable to verify the robustness of this new watermarking approach. However, in some cases the basic watermarking process described in [4] results in visible artifacts. We propose a method to prevent these artifacts and improve the video quality.

In this paper, we present an improvement of a basic watermarking approach. Firstly, the fundamental idea of watermarking by geometric warping is described. Afterwards, the principle of the basic approach is explained. Therefore, a statistic to describe the object borders in blocks is introduced. We propose a method to choose robust blocks for watermarking and to detect watermarked blocks even after lossy compression. The enhanced embedding process is explained. The next section describes the way to reduce the artifacts of the basic approach. The several subsections contain information about the reasons for the artifacts, the approach to prevent them, an algorithm to realize the approach as well as results and analyzes of the basic approach enhancement.

## 2   Watermarking by Geometric Warping

Commonly, the watermark is embedded in the perceptual invisible part of the video. The compression algorithms try to remove the perceptual invisible part of the video. Generally, both systems use the PSNR to measure the perceptual quality degradation. Because this, both systems use the same definition for relevant video data. This implies a contradiction. We can not embed a watermark in video parts which are removed during the compression process. We can solve this problem as shown in Figure 1.

The optimal way to embed the watermark with robustness to lossy compression is to embed the watermark in the relevant part of video data. Because common compression algorithms are PSNR-optimized, the relevance is defined by the PSNR. We propose in [4] to change the geometric structure

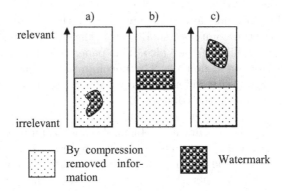

Fig. 1. Watermark embedding by using gaps of the compression algorithm a), defined embedding strength b) or by using the relevant video information c)

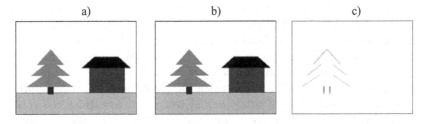

Fig. 2. Original image a), by geometric warping changed image b) and difference image c). The geometric warping process moved the tree by some pixel to the left side.

of the video to embed the watermark. Because the PSNR-optimization, compression algorithms try to maintain the geometric structure. At the same time, the geometric embedding process can be imperceptible. For example see Figure 2. The PSNR between both images is 27.7 dB. However, the difference is imperceptible.

## 3    The Basic Approach

### 3.1    The Normed Centre of Gravity (NCG)

To realize the geometric warping process, we introduce in [4] a new statistic, the Normed Centre of Gravity (NCG). The NCG is similar to the gravity centre of one block. However, it is independent from the block borders and every gray-value of the pixel has the same influence to the NCG. The NCG is computed in the following way.

First, the mean values of the rows and columns of the block are computed. The results are two vectors $\underline{m}_x$ and $\underline{m}_y$. The vector $\underline{m}_x$ is used to compute the x-coordinate of the NCG, the vector $\underline{m}_y$ is used to compute the y-coordinate.

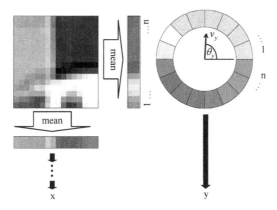

**Fig. 3.** Computing scheme for the NCG x,y-coordinates

Therefore, the two vectors of mean values are arranged in two circles. Now, the two-dimensional vector $\underline{v}_k$ ($k = $ x or y) is computed.

$$\underline{v}_k = \begin{pmatrix} \sum\limits_{i=1}^{n} \underline{m}_k(i) \cdot \cos\left(\dfrac{\pi}{n} + \left((i-1) \cdot \left(\dfrac{2 \cdot \pi}{n}\right)\right)\right) \\ \sum\limits_{i=1}^{n} \underline{m}_k(i) \cdot \sin\left(\dfrac{\pi}{n} + \left((i-1) \cdot \left(\dfrac{2 \cdot \pi}{n}\right)\right)\right) \end{pmatrix} \tag{1}$$

For each vector, the vector angles $\Theta_x$, $\Theta_y$ and the vector lengths $L_x$, $L_y$ are computed. The vector angles are used to compute the x,y-coordinates of the NCG.

$$x = \frac{n \cdot \Theta_x}{2 \cdot \pi} \qquad y = \frac{n \cdot \Theta_y}{2 \cdot \pi} \tag{2}$$

### 3.2 Choosing and Detecting Robust Blocks

To embed a watermark bit, robust blocks are chosen. Robust blocks are blocks with a high $L = \sqrt{L_x^2 + L_y^2}$. The spatial position of object borders inside these blocks is very robust to lossy compression. To choose robust blocks a threshold is used (see [4]). For example, blocks with $L > 430$ are robust to H.264/AVC compression with very low data rates. However, $L$ is slightly influenced by compression. Hence, it is a problem to find the correct blocks for watermark extraction after compression. To solve this problem we create a gap as shown in figure 4 b). In this example, blocks with $330 < L_{original} <= 430$ are changed so that $L_{new} = 330$ and blocks with $430 < L_{original} < 530$ are changed so that $L_{new} = 530$. This gap is sufficient for a correct detection of blocks even after compression with low data rates.

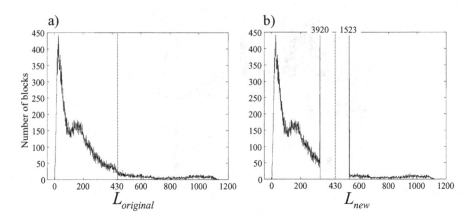

**Fig. 4.** Creating a gap in Video "Bus" for correct detection of robust and non-robust blocks around the threshold 430 with a) original distribution of $L$ and b) distribution after creating a gap

### 3.3 Enhanced Embedding Process

In [4], we use a QIM approach [7] and quantize the NCG x,y-coordinates of robust blocks. Therefore we can distinguish 3 cases. There are blocks with robust x-coordinates (high $L_x$), robust y-coordinates (high $L_y$) and blocks with robust x,y-coorinates (high $L_x$ and $L_y$). We use a hard decision to embed the watermark bit. In dependence on these cases we quantize the x-, y- or y,x-coordinates. To extract the bit we have to know which coordinate was used for embedding. However, after lossy compression $L_x$ and $L_y$ are slightly changed. Hence, the decision for the quantized coordinate can fail at the extraction process.

To solve this problem we don't use the NCG x,y-coordinate directly to embed the bit. The x,y-coordinates are mapped to an adaptive quantization lattice that is defined by $L_x$, $L_y$ and the variable *quant*. *quant* is inversely proportional to the quantization step size and defines the embedding strength. Mapping the x,y-coordinates to the adaptive quantization lattice is described by equation 6 and yields the value s. The different robustness of the NCG x- and y-coordinate is considered in equation 4. The influence of lossy compression to $L_x$ and $L_y$ is reduced by using equation 3. Equation 5 enables a linear mapping of the x,y-coordinates which is independent of block borders.

$$f_f(a,b) = \frac{(e^{\frac{1.8 \cdot a}{1200}})}{1 + (1 - |\frac{a-b}{1200}|) \cdot (e^{\frac{1.8 \cdot a}{1200}} - e^{1.8})} \tag{3}$$

$$f_x(L_x, L_y), f_y(L_x, L_y) = \begin{cases} L_x \leq L_y \rightarrow & \begin{array}{l} f_x = f_f(L_x, L_y) \cdot \frac{L_x}{L_x + L_y} \\ f_y = 1 - f_x \end{array} \\ L_x > L_y \rightarrow & \begin{array}{l} f_y = f_f(L_y, L_x) \cdot \frac{L_y}{L_x + L_y} \\ f_x = 1 - f_y \end{array} \end{cases} \tag{4}$$

$$tria(a,q) = \begin{cases} modulo(a, \frac{16}{q}) \leq \frac{8}{q} \rightarrow tria = \frac{modulo(a, \frac{16}{q}) \cdot q}{16} \\ modulo(a, \frac{16}{q}) > \frac{8}{q} \rightarrow tria = \frac{16 - modulo(a, \frac{16}{q}) \cdot q}{16} \end{cases} \tag{5}$$

$$s(x,y) = f_x(L_x, L_y) \cdot tria(x, quant) + f_y(L_x, L_y) \cdot tria(y, quant) \tag{6}$$

The used quantization lattice is self-adapting on each block (see Figure 5 II). The quantization lattice consists of periodically arranged minima ($s = 0$) and maxima ($s = 1$). To embed a watermark bit we don't quantize the NCG x,y-coordinates but we move the x,y-coordinates on the quantization lattice to the next minimum (to embed a watermark bit '0') or maximum (to embed a watermark bit '1'). For example see Figure 5. In column II the quantization lattice of blocks of column I with the original NCG x,y-coordinates (marked with a cross) can be seen. The blocks of column I are changed by geometric warping to embed a watermark bit '0' (column III). The result can be seen in

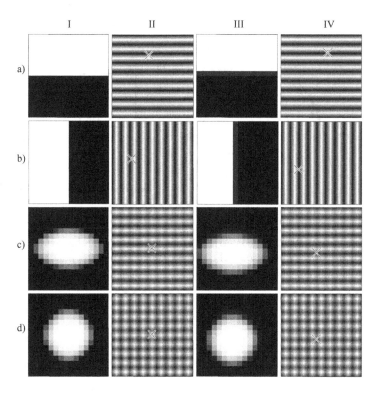

**Fig. 5.** Enhanced embedding process with a) robust y-coordinate, b) robust x-coordinate, c) robust y-, slightly robust x-coordinate and d) robust x,y-coordinate. Column I shows the original blocks, column II shows the quantization lattice with NCG x,y-coordinates, column III shows watermarked blocks and column IV shows the new quantization lattice of watermarked blocks with new NCG x,y-coordinates.

Figure 5 column IV. The NCG x,y-coordinates are at the minima (black areas represent the minima, white areas the maxima ) on the quantization lattice. To extract the embedded bit, the original block is not required. Only the NCG x,y-coordinates have to be mapped to the quantization lattice of the changed block. The use of equation 6 delivers a value between 0 and 1. The watermark bit '0' is extracted if $0 \leq s < 0.5$, the watermark bit '1' is extracted if $0.5 \leq s \leq 1$.

### 3.4   Achievable Robustness

Because the PSNR-optimization, we assume that the position of object borders is very robust to lossy compression. The position of object borders is described by the NCG and mapped to an adaptive quantization lattice yielding the value s. The strength of the object border is described by the $L$. Higher $L$ yields a stronger object border. Figure 6 shows the robustness of the embedded watermark information bits to H.264/AVC compression. Different $L$ and a block size of 16x16 pixels are used. The embedding process changes the position of the object borders by maximal 0.5 pixels.

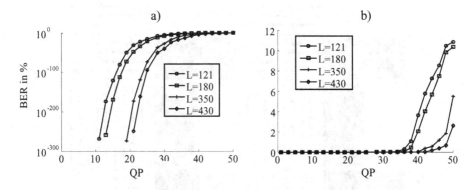

**Fig. 6.** Bit error rate (BER) of geometric warping based watermarking with logarithmic and linear BER axes. $QP$ represents the H.264/AVC quantization parameter. A higher $QP$ yields a lower compression data rate.

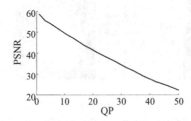

**Fig. 7.** Reduced quality of the reference video "Bus" caused by lossy H.264/AVC compression

The relationship between the H.264/AVC quantization parameter $QP$ and the resulting PSNR of the compressed video is shown in figure 7.

As shown in figure 6, the robustness of geometric warping based watermarking to lossy compression is very high even on a strong lossy compression quality distortion. At the same time, the capacity is relatively high (see figures 8 and 16).

### 3.5   Results of the Basic Approach

The approach is tested by embedding watermarks in standard videos "Bus", "Horse", "Horse2", "Waterfall" and "Foreman". The video resolution is 352x288 pixels. The embedding strength is $quant = 16$ with a block size of 16x16. This is equivalent to a quantization of NCG x,y-coordinates with a quantization step size of one. The watermark is embedded with different robustness to H.264/AVC compression. A higher $QP$ yields lower data rates and reduces the watermark capacity if we use the same embedding strength to embed the watermark. The capacity depends on the required robustness of the watermark and the video content. The watermark is embedded with robustness to H.264/AVC compression with $QP_{max}$ between 26 and 40. Figure 8 shows the results. As expected, the capacity of videos without distinct objects, such as "Waterfall", is lower than in videos with distinct objects, such as "Bus".

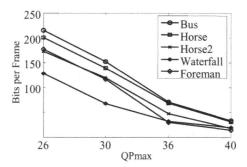

**Fig. 8.** Capacity in Bits per Frame. The embedding strength is $quant = 16$. The watermarks are embedded with robustness to different H.264/AVC compression. $QP_{max}$ defines the highest $QP$ at which the watermark can be extracted.

The watermark results in visible artifacts as shown in Figure 9 b) and c). However, the watermark is imperceptible if viewers don't compare pixels but see the video as a whole. The frame in Figure 9 a) contains 22 watermarked blocks. For example, the wooden bole in the bottom right corner contains six of them. But, without comparing the original pixels with the changed pixels nobody is able to notice these blocks.

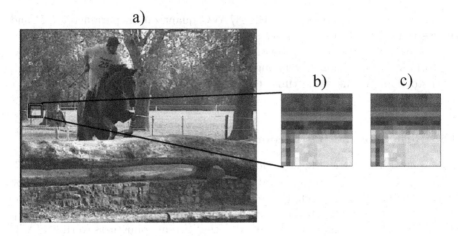

**Fig. 9.** Watermarked frame of "Horse" a), original block b) and watermarked block c)

## 4   Block-Linking for Improved Quality

### 4.1   Artifacts of the Basic Approach

The embedded watermark is imperceptible and robust to lossy compression with low data rates. However, in some cases visible artifacts can be found after the watermarking process. There are two kinds of artifacts. If one edge passes several robust blocks which are changed by geometric warping to embed the watermark, visible steps on the edge are produced. Hence, steps on long edges in single frames are the first type of artifacts (see Figure 10). The second type of artifacts can appear, if several blocks in succeeding frames with the same block position are changed by geometric warping. Even if there are no visible differences between the original and the watermarked single frames, there are visible flicker-effects if the video is played.

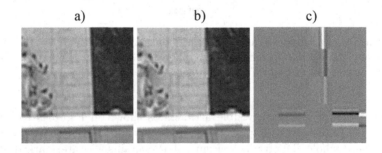

**Fig. 10.** Part of "Bus" a) original, b) watermarked with visible artifacts and c) difference image

## 4.2    Prevent Artifacts by Block Linking

The artifacts are the result of the independent warping of the blocks. To solve this problem, we propose to link blocks which contain the same object to block groups. Now, the warping process of one block in one block group can consider the warping process of the other blocks of the same group. In this way, the artifacts can be prevented.

**Linking Process.** To prevent artifacts and flicker-effects, we have to consider the video as a 3D-space. Two dimensions in space (coordinates x, y) and one dimension in time (frame number, coordinate t). The linking process uses neighboring robust blocks. It is probably that neighboring blocks contain the same object. Hence, robust blocks which are neighbors in spatial as well as in temporal position are linked to block groups. Figure 11 shows some block groups of the first 10 frames of the video "Bus". It can happen that one block group contains more than one object. However, this is not a disadvantage for preventing artifacts.

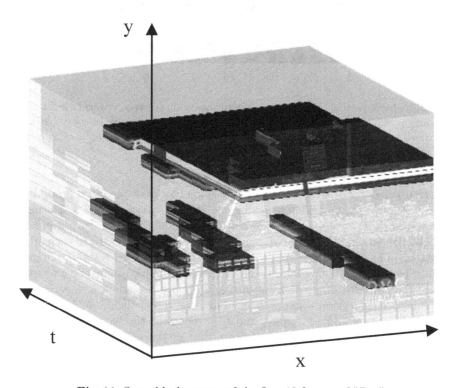

**Fig. 11.** Some block groups of the first 10 frames of "Bus"

**Principle of Preventing Artifacts.** To prevent the artifacts, we do not embed a watermark bit in every block of one block group. We define a minimum spatial and temporal distance $d$ between blocks which will be watermarked. The blocks of one block group which are not chosen for watermarking are used to create a smooth transition between the watermarked blocks. For example see Figure 12. Figure 12 shows one black and one white object which are divided into 7 blocks. Embedding a watermark by geometric warping in each block inducts visible artifacts (Figure 12 b). The artifacts are reduced by choosing only the block 1, 4 and 7 for watermarking (Figure 8 c) and using the blocks 2, 3, 5 and 6 to create a smooth transition between the watermarked blocks (Figure 12 d).

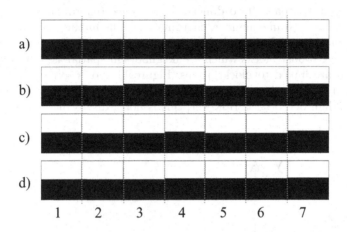

**Fig. 12.** Reducing artifacts by using a smooth transition between watermarked blocks. Therefore is exhibited a) blocks without watermark, b) watermark in every block, c) watermark in block 1, 4, 7 and d) watermark in block 1, 4, 7 by using block 2, 3, 5, 6 for smooth transitions.

**Algorithm for Choosing Blocks.** Only some blocks of one block group have to be chosen for watermarking to realize the principle outlined in 3.3. To enable the watermark detection, this process has to be unambiguous. To prevent the artifacts, the chosen blocks should maintain a minimum distance $d$ to each other. Investigation has shown that small-sized block groups can use a small minimum distance to prevent artifacts. However, bigger-sized block groups have to use a higher minimum distance to prevent artifacts. Hence, we adapt $d$ in each block group for each dimension whereas $d_x$, $d_y$ and $d_t$ represent the minimum distance for each dimension and $x_{size}$, $y_{size}$ and $t_{size}$ represent the block group size for each dimension. Investigations have shown that distance $d > 0.5$ is suitable to prevent the artifacts.

$$d_i = \lfloor log(d \cdot (i_{size} - 1) + 1) + 0.5 \rfloor \qquad (i = x, y \text{ or } t) \qquad (7)$$

To achieve a maximal watermark capacity, as much as possible blocks of the block group have to be chosen for watermarking. Hence, the following algorithm has to find a maximum number of blocks in a block group which have a minimum distance to each other. We realize it in the following way:

1. The block group is chosen. Block groups have arbitrary forms which depend on video content. For example see Figure 13 a.
2. For each dimension x, y and t of the block group a minimum distance $d_x$, $d_y$ and $d_t$ is computed (equation 7).
3. For each block, the numbers of blocks inside an ellipsoid are counted (Figure 13 a,b). The semi-axes of the ellipsoids are defined by $d_x$, $d_y$ and $d_t$. The center of the current ellipsoid is defined by the current block. For better illustration Figure 13 shows the principle only for a 2D block group.
4. The blocks with the least neighbors are chosen for watermarking (Figure 13 c). Are more than one chosen blocks inside an ellipsoid, only one of them (the first) is used for watermarking (Figure 13 d,e). This process is unambiguous.
5. The chosen blocks and all blocks within the ellipsoids around the chosen blocks will not be considered in the next steps.
6. The steps 3-4 are repeated until all blocks are chosen for watermarking or have a distance lower than the minimum to a chosen block (Figure 13 d-f).

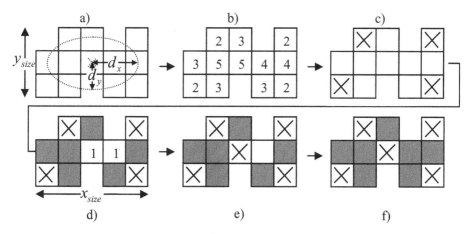

**Fig. 13.** Example for choosing blocks for watermarking with a minimum distance in one block group with a) block group and ellipsoid, b) counted neighbors, c) first chosen blocks, d) counted remaining blocks, e) chosen blocks of the second iteration and f) all chosen blocks

**Smooth Transition between Watermarked Blocks.** The chosen blocks are used for watermarking. The watermarking bits '0'/'1' are embedded by moving the NCG x,y-coordinates on the quantization lattice to minima/maxima. This is done by geometric warping. The warping strength differs from block to block. Only the chosen blocks have to be warped. However, to reduce the visible effect of the geometric warping process, the other blocks of the block group also will be warped (Figure 14). The warping strength of these blocks depends on the warping strength of the watermarked blocks. It is computed by using a simple Gaussian filter. Thus, a smooth transition between watermarked blocks is achieved.

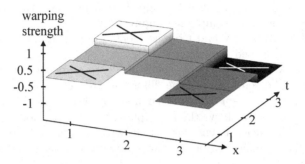

**Fig. 14.** A simplified example of warping strength in one block group. The watermarked blocks are labeled with a cross.

### 4.3 Results of the Linking Process

Linking blocks to block groups, choosing blocks with a minimum distance, watermarking them and using the other blocks for a smooth transition prevents the described artifacts. It can be clearly seen by comparing Figure 10 with Figure 15. The visible artifacts in single frames as well as the flicker-effects in succeeding frames are prevented.

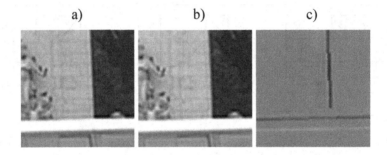

**Fig. 15.** Part of "Bus" a) original, b) watermarked without visible artifacts and c) difference image

There is one disadvantage of this method. Without block linking, all robust blocks are used for watermarking. With block linking, only some blocks of a block group are used for watermarking. This results in a lower watermark capacity. Hence, with the block linking method and a minimum distance $d > 0$ we can not embed the same number of bits as without block linking. The capacity depends not only on the minimum distance $d$ and the number of robust blocks. It also depends on the size and form of the block groups which depends on the video content. It can be seen clearly in Figure 8 and Figure 16. To test our approach, we embed watermarks in standard test videos "Bus", "Horse", "Horse2", "Waterfall" and "Foreman". The test conditions are the same as in

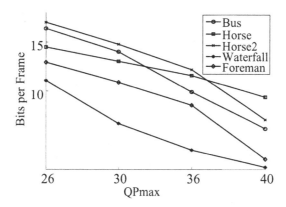

**Fig. 16.** Capacity in Bits per frame with block linking and a minimum distance of 0.5

section 3.5. Figure 8 shows the capacity by using all robust blocks. Figure 16 shows the capacity by using block linking and a minimum distance of 0.5.

Though "Bus" contains more robust blocks than "Horse2", the capacity with block linking is lower because "Bus" contains bigger block groups than "Horse2". As we said above (see 4.2), it is possible that one block group contain more than one object. However, several small block groups can contain more watermark bits (without visible artifacts) as one big block group. Hence, the watermark capacity can be increased in future works by changing the block linking method.

## 5  Conclusions

This paper presents an enhanced watermarking approach. The fundamental idea of using geometric warping for watermarks is explained. The basic watermarking approach is introduced. It uses a block based statistic (NCG) to describe the geometric structure of blocks. The NCG is also used to choose only robust blocks for watermarking. To detect robust blocks even after lossy compression we propose to change some blocks in a preprocessing step. The watermark information bits are embedded by moving the NCG x,y-coordinates on a block dependent quantization lattice. This is done by geometric warping of the block. The watermark is robust to lossy compression. The watermark capacity is analyzed. In some cases, the independent geometric warping of blocks which contain the same object results in visible artifacts. Especially on long edges, visible steps can appear. Additionally, flicker-effects in succeeding frames can be observed. In this paper we propose to link blocks in space and time to block groups. As opposed to the basic approach, the blocks of one block group can be warped in dependence on each other. Thus, the visible artifacts are prevented by our enhancement. However, the block linking approach reduces the watermark capacity. The capacity is analyzed and compared with the capacity of the basic approach.

# References

1. Cox, J., Miller, M.: The First 50 Years of Electronic Watermarking. EURASIP J. of Applied Signal Processing, vol. 2002, pp. 162–132 (2002)
2. Qui, G., Marziliano, P., Ho, A.T.S., He, D., Sun, Q.: A hybrid watermarking scheme for H.264/AVC video. In: Proc. of the ICPR vol. 4, pp. 865–868 (2004)
3. Pröfrock, D., Richter, H., Schlauweg, M., Müller, E.: H.264/AVC video authentication using skipped macroblocks for an erasable watermark. In: Proc. of Visual Communications and Image Processing - VCIP, vol. 5960 (2005)
4. Pröfrock, H., Schlauweg, M., Müller, E.: A New Uncompressed-Domain Video Watermarking Approach Robust to H.264/AVC Compression. In: Proc. of Signal Processing, Pattern Recognition and Applications - SPPRA (2006)
5. Wiegand, T., Sullivan, G.J., Bjontegaard, G., Luthra, A.: Overview of the H.264/AVC Video Coding Standard. IEEE Transactions 13, 560–576 (2003)
6. Draft ITU-T recommendation and final draft international standard of joint video specification (ITU-T Rec. H.264/ISO/IEC 14486-10 AVC, in Joint Video Team (JVT) of ISO/IEC MPEG and ITU-T VCEG, JVT-G050 (2003)
7. Chen, B., Wornell, G.W.: Quantization index modulation methods for digital watermarking and information embedding of multimedia. Journal of VLSI Signal Processing 27, 7–33 (2003)

# Time-Scale Invariant Audio Watermarking Based on the Statistical Features in Time Domain

Shijun Xiang[1,2], Jiwu Huang[1,2], Rui Yang[1,2]

[1] School of Information Science and Technology,
Sun Yat-sen University, Guangzhou 510275, China
[2] Guangdong Key Laboratory of Information Security Technology,
Guangzhou 510275, China
isshjw@mail.sysu.edu.cn

**Abstract.** In audio watermarking, the robustness to desynchronization attacks such as TSM (Time-Scale Modification) operations, is still an open issue. In this paper, both mathematical proof and experimental testing show that the histogram shape (represented as the relative relation in the number of samples among three different histogram bins) and the audio mean are two robust features to the TSM attacks. Accordingly, a multi-bit robust audio watermarking algorithm based on the two statistical features is proposed by modifying the histogram. The audio histogram with equal-sized bins is extracted from a selected amplitude range referred to the audio mean, and then the relative relations in the number of samples among groups of three neighboring bins are designed to carry the watermark by reassigning the number of samples in the bins. The watermarked audio signal is perceptibly similar to the original one. Simulation results demonstrated that the hidden message is very robust to the TSM, cropping, and a variety of other distortions in Stirmark Benchmark for Audio.

## 1 Introduction

Audio watermarking [1][2] plays an important role in ownership protection. According to IFPI (International Federation of the Phonographic Industry) [3], STEP2000 [4] and SDMI (Secure Digital Music Initiative) [5], audio watermarking should be robust to temporal scaling of ±10% and be able to resist most common signal processing manipulations and attacks, such as random cropping, MP3 compression, resampling and etc.

Among the various problems to be solved in audio watermarking, the robustness against desynchronization distortions such as TSM and random cropping, is the most challenging one for previous watermarking schemes yet. Desynchronization attacks that cause displacement between encoder and decoder are difficult for a watermark to survive. In [6], the synchronization code was introduced aiming at conquering cropping attacks. However, the synchronization code is very vulnerable to TSM. For example, a small amount of scaling (i.e.,

J. Camenisch et al. (Eds.): IH 2006, LNCS 4437, pp. 93–108, 2007.
© Springer-Verlag Berlin Heidelberg 2007

±1%) will be able to cause the watermark extraction failed. TSM is a common audio processing manipulation in a variety of software tools, such as CoolEditPro V2.1. Under TSM operations, even with the scaling amount of ±10%, the auditory quality of audio is still rather perfect since HAS (Human Auditory System) is not sensitive to TSM. This makes TSM to be a serious attack operation in audio watermarking. Generally, there are mainly two modes of TSM operations, *pitch-invariant* scaling and *resample* scaling. The pitch-invariant mode preserves audio pitch, while the resample mode keeps pitch and tempo neither by modifying playback speed.

Few algorithms can effectively resist the TSM. In the existing literature, several algorithms have been proposed aiming at solving this problem by using exhaustive search [7], synchronization pattern [6][8], invariant watermark [9][10], implicit synchronization [11], informed detection [12]. In [7], the authors applied the detection engine to search the watermark for resynchronization by performing multiple correlation tests. One possible problem for multiple correlation tests is the false alarm. In [9], the authors proposed a time-scale invariant watermarking embedding strategy by changing the length of the intervals between two successive peaks of the smoothed waveform. The watermark detection highly depends on the selection of the threshold. In [10], the authors presented an audio watermarking method by using music content analysis. The watermark is embedded into the edges of audio signals by using FFT (Fast Fourier Transform) technique. The watermark is robust to ±9% pitch-invariant TSM but vulnerable to resample stretching mode, which will change the edges in the signal. The watermarking methods based on the peak points may suffer from the attack of removing the peaks. In [12], side information is exploited to improve the searching of the watermark aiming at solving playback speed modifications. One weakness of this scheme is that the detection procedure is not blind. On the basis of [8], Tachibana [13] further improved the watermark performance against random time stretching from ±4% up to ±8% by using multiple pseudo-random arrays. This method is time consuming.

The above mentioned approaches share the problems that the watermark performance is difficult to satisfy the requirements of IFPI or STEP2000 (stretching of ±10%), and, the watermarking schemes usually focus on one type of desynchronization attacks, such as pitch-invariant TSM mode [10], resample TSM mode or playback speed modifications [12], and cropping [6]. In this paper, we propose a multi-bit audio watermarking algorithm based on the audio statistical features described by the histogram specification, concentrating on combating the desynchronization problem caused by time-scale modifications. Histogram-based watermarking strategy was first introduced for image watermarking in [14]. By using the robustness of image color histogram to rotations and geometric transformations, the authors in [15] proposed a general method for watermarking color histogram of image. The 1-bit watermarking scheme is very robust to image geometric distortions. The basic idea in our algorithm is that the TSM operations with the resample and pitch-variant stretching modes may be represented as an approximately temporal linear scaling operation in practice, verified by extensive testing. Theoretically, it has been proven that the number of samples in the audio histogram bin is linear to temporal linear scaling, and the audio mean is invariant to such attack. In experimental testing, it is observed that the number of samples in the bins is almost linear to the TSM attacks, and the audio mean is rather robust to this kind of scaling attacks. As a conclusion, the audio mean and the relative relations in the number of samples among different bins are taken as two robust features to the TSM. As a robust feature to TSM, the audio mean is exploited to compute the histogram with equal-sized bins from a selected amplitude range so that the watermark is robust to amplitude scaling. The use of three successive bins as a group is designed to embed one bit of information by reassigning the number of samples in the three bins. In the extraction, the synchronization code is introduced for searching of the watermark. The original audio is not required. The experimental results show that the proposed watermarking strategy is very robust to the TSM attacks. In our testing, even though the TSM of $\pm 30\%$ with pitch-invariant or resample modes, the extracted watermark is still at a very low error rate. Additionally, we analyze the performance of the proposed watermarking algorithm and report the experimental results regarding the quality evaluation of the watermarked audio, the watermark robustness against common signal processing operations regarding Stirmark Benchmark for Audio [16].

In the next section, we describe the effects of the TSM on the number of samples in the bins based on both the theoretical analysis and experimental method. This is followed by a description of a general framework for our proposed watermarking embedding and detecting strategy. We then analyze the watermark performance and test the watermark robustness on desynchronization distortions, as well as some common signal processing and some common attacks in Stirmark Benchmark for Audio. Finally, we draw the conclusions.

## 2    Invariant Features to TSM

Via both theoretical analysis and extensive experiments, it has been found that the number of samples in the histogram bins is linear to temporal linear scaling, and approximately linear to TSM operations with pitch-invariant and resample modes. It implies that the relative relation in the number of samples among different bins is approximately invariant to the TSM operations. It is also noted that the audio mean is very robust to the TSM operations.

A *histogram* is often used to describe the data distribution. The most common form of the audio histogram is obtained by splitting the range of the sample value into equal-sized bins. Then for each bin, the number of samples from the audio that fall into each bin is counted. The style of histogram may be described by

$$H = \{h(i)|i = 1, \cdots, L\},\tag{1}$$

where $H$ is a vector denoting the volume-level histogram of audio signal $F = \{f(i)|i = 1, ..., N\}$, and $h(i), h(i) \geq 0$ denotes the number of samples in the $i^{th}$

bin and satisfy $\sum_{i=1}^{L} h(i) = N$. Suppose that the resolution of a signed audio signal is $R$ bits, the number of bins $L$ can be calculated as

$$L = \begin{cases} 2^R/M & \text{if } \ Mod(2^R/M) = 0 \\ \lfloor 2^R/M \rfloor + 1 & \text{other,} \end{cases} \tag{2}$$

where $M$ is the size of bins, $h(i)$ includes all samples the range of sample value from $-2^{R-1} + (i-1) \cdot M$ to $-2^{R-1} + i \cdot M - 1$, and $\lfloor \cdot \rfloor$ is the floor function.

## 2.1  Theoretical Proof

In order to better describe the relationship between the audio histogram and the temporal linear scaling, we rewrite the audio histogram described in Equation (1) with the continuous form, denoted by

$$F(t) = \begin{cases} f_1(t) & \text{if } \ t \in T_1 \\ f_2(t) & \text{if } \ t \in T_2 \\ \vdots & \vdots \\ f_L(t) & \text{if } \ t \in T_L, \end{cases} \tag{3}$$

where $F(t)$ is the corresponding continuous version of the discrete signal $F$. $T_i \mid i = 1, \ldots, L$ is a set of time pieces corresponding to $f_i(t)$. In time piece $T_i$, $f_i(t)$ will fall into the bin $h(i)$.

Consider temporal linear scaling of the signal $F(t)$ through a factor $\alpha$. If $F(t)$ is denoted by Equation (3), the corresponding scaled version is formulated as

$$F'(t) = F(t/\alpha) = \begin{cases} f_1(t/\alpha) & \text{if } \ t \in \alpha \cdot T_1 \\ f_2(t/\alpha) & \text{if } \ t \in \alpha \cdot T_2 \\ \vdots & \vdots \\ f_L(t/\alpha) & \text{if } \ t \in \alpha \cdot T_L, \end{cases} \tag{4}$$

Equation (4) indicates that the scaling on $F(t)$ is equivalent to the scaling on its sub-functions $\{f_i(t)\}$.

Furthermore, consider the mean of $F(t)$ before and after scaling. If the scaled mean are denoted by $\bar{A}'$, the relationship between the original mean $\bar{A}$ and $\bar{A}'$ is

$$\begin{aligned} \bar{A}' &= \frac{1}{T'} \int_{t=0}^{T'} |F'(t)| dt = \frac{1}{\alpha T} \int_{t=0}^{\alpha T} |F'(t)| dt \\ &= \frac{1}{\alpha T} \int_{t=0}^{\alpha T} |F(t/\alpha)| dt = \frac{1}{T} \int_{t=0}^{\alpha T} |F(t/\alpha)| d(t/\alpha) \\ &= \frac{1}{T} \int_{t_1=0}^{T} |F(t_1)| dt_1 = \bar{A} \end{aligned} \tag{5}$$

Equation (5) indicates the modified mean value is invariant to linear scaling.

In the discrete case, Equations (1), (3) and (4) imply that after temporal linear scaling with a factor $\alpha$, the number of samples in each bin, $h(i)$, theoretically goes to $\alpha \cdot h(i)$. Note that if $\alpha$ is not an integer, the interpolation processing will occur among neighboring bins, possibly resulting in a few samples added or lost for different bins. As a result, the number of samples among different bins is approximately linear to temporal linear scaling. From Equation (5), it is noted that for a continuous signal, its mean is an invariant feature to temporal linear scaling. In the discrete case, it implies that the mean of digital signal is approximately invariant to temporal linear scaling.

In the following experimental testing, it is noted that the TSM may be represented as an approximately temporal linear scaling operation. As a result, the audio mean is rather robust to the TSM, and the relative relations in the number of samples among different bins is almost invariant to the TSM.

## 2.2    Experimental Testing

Pitch-invariant and resample are two different kinds of stretching modes, which will modify the length of an audio signal in time domain. The pitch-invariant TSM mode preserves the audio pitch. Differently, the resample TSM mode scales the audio by playing audio with a higher or lower speed. This processing preserves the pitch and the tempo neither. For example, audio phase change in DA/AD processing via soundcards may be represented as a resample scaling mode [17]. Based on the knowledge above, the resample stretching mode may be taken as a temporal linear scaling processing, mathematically no effect on the relative relations in the number of samples among different bins. The pitch-invariant stretching mode may be considered as an approximately temporal linear scaling operation. Hence, it is expected that the relative relationships in the number of samples among different bins is approximately invariant or robust to the TSM, which is demonstrated by conducting the following extensive testing.

We choose a clip from our test data set, drum music denoted as *drum.wav* (16-bit signed mono audio file sampled at 44.1 kHz with the length of 25s), to test the effects of the TSM.

The histograms are extracted from *drum.wav* and all correspondingly scaled versions with the equal-sized bins. The bin width $(M)$ is 500. The number of bins $(L)$ is calculated as 132 by using Equation (2). Fig. 1 shows that under $\pm30\%$ scaling with the resample and pitch-invariant modes, the histogram shape remains almost unchanged. It implies that the relative relations in the number of samples among different bins is rather stable under the TSM. Fig. 2 and Fig. 3 show the effects of the TSM with the two stretching modes on those bins satisfying $h(k) >> L$ under the scaling amount of 70% and 130%, respectively. Fig. 4 shows the average amplitude values of original audio and its scaled versions under TSM of 70%~130% with pitch-invariant and resample modes. As to other kinds of audio, such as pop music, piano music and speech, the simulation results are similar.

In Fig. 2 and Fig. 3, the left sub-plots are the estimated scaling factors by using the bins of the original and scaled files, formulated as

$$\alpha_k = \frac{h'(k)}{h(k)} \approx \alpha \quad \text{for } h(k) \gg L \tag{6}$$

where $\alpha_k$ denote the estimated scaling factor in the $k^{th}$ bin, $h'(k)$ is the scaled version of $h(k)$, where $h(k) \gg L$, i.e., the number of samples in each bin is

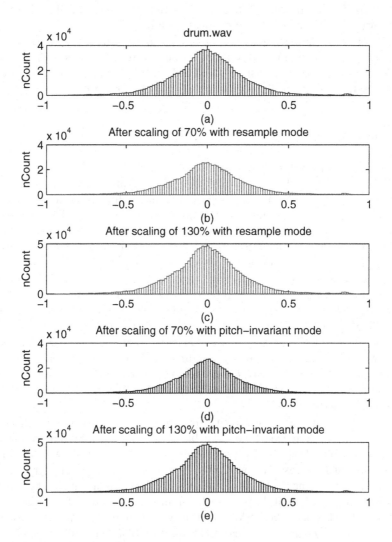

**Fig. 1.** The audio histograms under the TSM attacks, five sub-plots: (a) original, (b) under 70% scaling with resample mode, (c) under scaling of 130% with resample mode, (d) after scaling of 70% with pitch-invariant mode, and (e) after scaling of 130% with pitch-invariant mode

considerably larger than the number of bins. And, the right sub-plots in Fig. 2 and Fig. 3, demonstrate the effects of the TSM with different scaling amount on the relative relations in the number of samples among three neighboring bins calculated and denoted by $\beta_k$,

$$\beta_k = \frac{2 \cdot h(k)}{h(k+1) + h(k-1)} \quad \text{for } h(k) \gg L \tag{7}$$

The scaled audio files are obtained by using the CoolEditPro V2.1. Based on extensive testing with different audio signals, we have the following observations:

i. Pitch-invariant and resample TSM operations may be considered approximately linear scaling operations for those bins satisfying $h(k) \gg L$. Even though the TSM of 70% and 130%, the linear relation is approximately logical. It means that the relative relation in the number of samples among these bins is almost invariant to such scaling attacks. It is noted that $\beta_k$ is from 0.9 to 1.1. As to other bins, 0~40 and 90~132 not listed in Fig. 2 and Fig. 3, $\alpha_k$ is away from $\alpha$ since these bins hold less samples. As a result, $\beta_k$ is far away from 1.

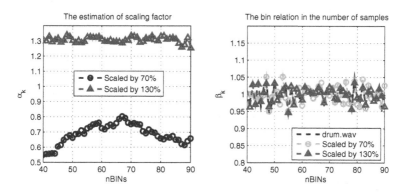

**Fig. 2.** The plots for the TSM attacks of 70% and 130% with the pitch-invariant mode

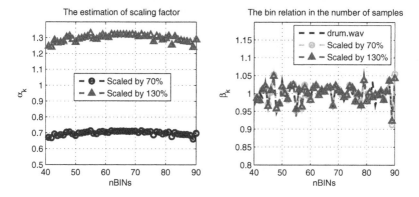

**Fig. 3.** The plots for the TSM attacks of 70% and 130% with the resample mode

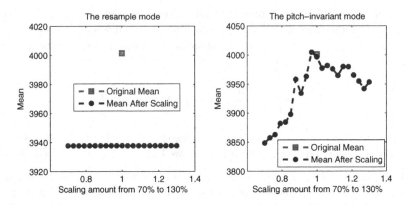

**Fig. 4.** The mean curves of the example audio and the scaled ones under the TSM of 70% ∼ 130% with resample (left) and pitch-invariant (right) stretching modes, respectively. It is noted that from the scaling amount of 70% to 130% with the step size of 3%, the audio means under the resample mode keep stable but somewhat less than original one, but have different results for the pitch-invariant TSM of different scaling amount. The error ratios of mean are between ±5%.

ii. The mean of the audio is robust enough to the TSM, also fulfilling the analysis in Equation (5). Under 70%∼130% TSM, the error ratio of mean is between ±5% according to the extensive testing.

As a conclusion, if we embed the watermark into those bins satisfying the condition $h(k) \gg L$ by applying two invariant representations (the audio mean and the relative relation among different bins), it is expected that the watermark will be very robust to TSM attacks.

## 3   Proposed Watermarking Algorithm

In this section, a multi-bit watermark aiming at solving the TSM manipulations is proposed. The watermark insertion and recovery are described by the histogram specification. The robustness of the audio mean and the relative relation in the number of samples among different bins to the TSM attacks presented in the previous section are used in the design. The mean invariance property is used to select the amplitude range to embed bits so that the watermark can resist amplitude scaling attack and avoid exhaustive search. In the extraction, a synchronization code is exploited to eliminate the effect of TSM on the audio mean.

### 3.1   Embedding Strategy

The basic idea of the proposed embedding strategy is to extract the histogram from a selected amplitude range. Divide the bins into many groups, each group

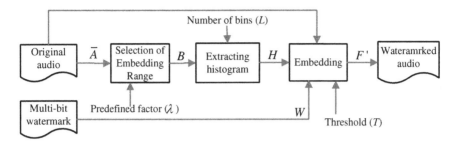

**Fig. 5.** Watermark embedding framework

including three consecutive bins. For each group, one bit is embedded by reassigning the number of samples in the three bins. The watermarked audio is obtained by modifying the original audio according to the watermarking rule. The embedding model is shown in Fig. 5.

The detail embedding process is described as follows. Suppose that there is a binary sequence $W = \{w_i \mid i = 1, \cdots, L_w\}$ to be hidden into a digital audio $F = \{f(i) \mid i = 1, \cdots, N\}$. The modified mean value of the audio, denoted by $\bar{A}$, is calculated as

$$\bar{A} = \frac{1}{N} \sum_{i=1}^{N} |f(i)| \tag{8}$$

Select the amplitude range $B = [-\lambda\bar{A}, \lambda\bar{A}]$ from $F$ to extract the histogram $H = \{h(i) \mid i = 1, \cdots, L\}$, where $L \geq 3L_w$, to embed all watermark bits. $\lambda$ is a selected positive number for satisfying $h(i) \gg L$. $\lambda \in [2.0, 2.5]$ is a suggested range so that the histogram bins extracted can hold enough samples. This observation is achieved based on the extensive testing on different kinds of audio signals.

Suppose that three consecutive bins, denoted by BIN_1, BIN_2 and BIN_3, their samples in the number are $a$, $b$ and $c$, respectively. We apply the following watermarking rules to embed one bit of information, described as

$$\begin{cases} 2b/(a+c) \geq T & \text{if } w(i) = 1 \\ (a+c)/2b \geq T & \text{if } w(i) = 0, \end{cases} \tag{9}$$

where $T$ is a selected threshold used to control the watermark robustness performance and the embedding distortion. Referred to Section 2.2, $T$ should be not less than 1.1 in order to effectively resist the TSM.

If the embedded bit $w(i)$ is $'1'$ and $2b/(a+c) \geq T$, no operation is needed. Otherwise, the number of samples in three neighboring bins, $a$, $b$ and $c$, will be adjusted until satisfying $2b'/(a'+c') \geq T$, referred to Equation (9). In case of embedding the bit $'0'$, the procedure is similar. The rules applied to modify $a$, $b$ and $c$ as $a'$, $b'$ and $c'$ are referred to Equations (10), (11), (12) and (13).

If the embedded bit $w(i)$ is $'1'$ and $2b/(a+c) < T$, some selected samples from BIN_1 and BIN_3 in the number denoted by $I_1$ and $I_3$, will be modified to BIN_2, achieving $2b'/(a'+c') \geq T$. The modification rule is described as Equation (10).

$$\begin{cases} f_1'(i) = f_1(i) + M, & 1 \leq i \leq I_1 \\ f_3'(i) = f_3(i) - M, & 1 \leq i \leq I_3, \end{cases} \quad (10)$$

where $f_1(i)$ and $f_3(i)$ denote the $i^{th}$ modified sample in BIN_1 and BIN_3, $f_1'(i)$ and $f_3'(i)$ are the modified version of $f_1(i)$ and $f_3(i)$. $M$ is the bin width. Obviously, the modified samples move to BIN_2. $I_1$ and $I_3$ are computed by using the following equation,

$$I_1 = I \cdot a/(a+c), \quad I_3 = I \cdot c/(a+c), \quad I \geq [T(a+c) - 2b]/(2+T) \quad (11)$$

If the embedded bit $w(i)$ is $'0'$ and $(a+c)/2b < T$, $I_1$ and $I_3$, some selected samples from BIN_2 will be modified to BIN_1 and BIN_3, respectively, achieving $(a'+c')/2b' \geq T$. The rule is described as Equation (12).

$$\begin{cases} f_2'(i) = f_2(i) - M, & 1 \leq i \leq I_1 \\ f_2'(j) = f_2(j) + M, & 1 \leq j \leq I_3 \end{cases} \quad (12)$$

where $f_2(i)$ denotes the $i^{th}$ modified sample in BIN_2, $f_2'(i)$ and $f_2'(j)$ are the corresponding modified version of $f_2(i)$ and $f_2(j)$. $I_1$ and $I_3$ are computed by

$$I_1 = I \cdot a/(a+c), \quad I_3 = I \cdot c/(a+c), \quad I \geq [2Tb - (a+c)]/(1+2T) \quad (13)$$

About the proofs of Equations (11) and (13), please refer to Appendix.

This process is repeated to embed all watermark bits. In our proposed embedding strategy, the watermark is embedded by directly modifying the values of some selected samples from the original audio. Hence the embedding process includes the reconstruction of watermarked audio, which is denoted by $F' = \{f'(i) \mid i = 1, \cdots, N'\}$.

## 3.2   Watermark Extraction

Consider the effects of the TSM on the audio mean may cause the watermark detection failed, a predefined searching space denoted by $[\bar{A}''(1 - \triangle_1), \bar{A}''(1 + \triangle_2)]$ is designed for resynchronization. Here, $\bar{A}''$ denotes the mean of the watermarked audio $F'' = \{f''(i) \mid i = 1, \cdots, N''\}$, which has undergone some desynchronization attacks, such as TSM operations with different stretching modes. Based on our previous experimental analysis in Section 2.2, $\triangle_1$ and $\triangle_2$, the down and up searching error ratios of mean, are suggested not less than 5%. We use a PN (Pseudo-random Noise) sequence as a synchronization code, $\{Syn(i)\}$, followed by the hidden multi-bit watermark, $\{Wmk(i)\}$, shown in Fig. 6. Only the watermark also provides the synchronization capability. The merit of part of payload as synchronization code can keep the watermark unknown for the detector.

Our goal is to get an estimate of hidden bits, $W'' = \{w_i'' \mid i = 1, \cdots, L_w\}$ by selecting an amplitude range from $F''$ at a low error rate. $W''$ is composed of

| Synchronization Code<br>{$Syn(i)$} | The hidden multi-bit information<br>{$Wmk(i)$} |
| --- | --- |

**Fig. 6.** Data structure of hidden bit stream [6]

{$Syn(i)$} and {$Wmk(i)$}. The histogram of $F''$ is extracted with $L$ bins as in the process of watermark embedding. Compute the number of samples in three consecutive bins and denoted by $a''$, $b''$ and $c''$. By comparing them, we can extract one bit of hidden information,

$$w_i'' = \begin{cases} 1 & \text{if} \quad 2b''/(a'' + c'') \geq 1 \\ 0 & \text{other} \end{cases} \tag{14}$$

The process is repeated until all hidden bits are extracted. Once the synchronization code {$Syn(i)$} is matched with the extracted synchronization bits {$Syn_1(i)$} or the searching process is finished, according to the best matching, we extract the hidden watermark following the synchronization bits, denoted by {$Wmk_1(i)$}. In the extraction, the parameters, $L_w$, $\lambda$ and {$Syn(i)$}, are beforehand known, so the detection process is blind.

## 4   Performance Analysis

In this section, we evaluate the performance of the proposed algorithm in terms of embedding capacity (payload), robustness on amplitude scaling, and computational cost of searching the watermark in the extraction. Suppose that the mean of an audio is $\bar{A}$ and the parameter $\lambda$ is applied to compute the embedded region. The embedding capacity $P$ of the proposed algorithm can be expressed as

$$P = 2\lambda \cdot \bar{A}/(M \cdot G) \tag{15}$$

where $M$ denotes the size of the bins, and $G$ is the number of the bins designed to embed one bit, not less than 2 and equal to 3 in our proposed watermarking scheme in order to reduce the watermark distortion.

In the case of amplitude scaling attack, though the selected range, $B$, is amplified, the number of the samples in each bin is unchanged since the histogram is extracted referred to audio mean. It is due to the fact that the sample values and their median are amplified correspondingly under amplitude scaling. Hence, the algorithm is immune to such attack.

In the extraction, an ideal searching step is related to $\lambda$, and designed as $S = 1/\lambda$ so that the selected amplitude range $B$ is added or reduced with a unit of sample-level at a time, such as from $\pm 10000$ to $\pm 9999$ or to $\pm 10001$. The maximum searching times is estimated as

$$O = \bar{A} \cdot (\triangle_1 + \triangle_2)/S = \lambda \cdot \bar{A} \cdot (\triangle_1 + \triangle_2) \tag{16}$$

Equation (16) shows that that the computational cost of searching for the watermark is related to the mean of audio, and the error ratios of mean caused by the TSM.

## 5    Experimental Results

The proposed algorithm is applied to a set of audio signals including pop, light, rock, piano, drum and electronic organ. The parameter $\lambda = 2.5$ is selected to extract the histogram with 181 bins. A clip (20s, mono, 16 bits/sample, 44.1 kHz and WAVE format) cut from the light music titled $'danube'$ is used as the example audio watermarked with 60 bits of information composed of a 20-bit synchronization sequence and the 40-bit watermark, with the embedding threshold $T = 1.5$. In the embedding, the probability of the watermarked samples their values added or reduced is approximately equivalent, hence the watermark hardly has the affection on the audio mean, which are 4001.3 and 4001.3 before and after embedding, respectively. In the extraction, we assign $\triangle_1 = \triangle_2 = 6\%$ for the watermark detection with the searching step size of $S = 1$. The relative relation in the number of samples among three neighboring bins is calculated by Equation (7) and plot in Fig. 7.

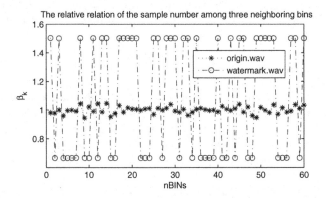

**Fig. 7.** The relative relation in the number of samples before and after watermarking

**Table 1.** Robustness Performance to Common Audio Processing Operations

| Attack Type | BER | Attack Type | BER |
|---|---|---|---|
| Normalize | 0 | Gaussian(35 dB) | 0 |
| MP3 (128 kbps) | 0 | MP3 (112 kbps) | 1/60 |
| Re-quantization $16 \rightarrow 32 \rightarrow 16$ (bit) | 0 | Resample $44.1 \rightarrow 16 \rightarrow 44.1$ (kHz) | 0 |
| Low pass (8 kHz) | 0 | Low pass (7 kHz) | 7/60 |
| Volume (10 $\sim$ 50%) | 0 | Volume (110 $\sim$ 150%) | 0 |

The SNR is 43.97 dB, with the ODG (Objective Difference Grade) of -1.31 implemented by EAQUAL 0.1.3 alpha [18] considered the HAS. The higher SNR is that only a small part of samples is modified for watermarking. The satisfied ODG value is due to the fact that those watermarked samples are modified with

**Table 2.** Robustness Performance to part of cropping and jittering attacks

| Attack Type | BER | Attack Type | BER |
|---|---|---|---|
| Cropping (10*20000) | 0 | Cropping (3s) | 0 |
| Jittering (1/500) | 0 | Jittering (1/1500) | 0 |
| Jittering (1/1000) | 0 | Jittering (1/2000) | 0 |

**Table 3.** Robustness Performance to two different TSM modes

| Pitch-Invariant TSM | BER | Resample TSM | BER |
|---|---|---|---|
| TSM -30% | 3/60 | TSM -30% | 0 |
| TSM -25% | 0 | TSM -25% | 0 |
| TSM -20% | 0 | TSM -20% | 0 |
| TSM -15% | 0 | TSM -15% | 0 |
| TSM -10% | 0 | TSM -10% | 0 |
| TSM -5% | 0 | TSM -5% | 0 |
| TSM +5% | 0 | TSM +5% | 0 |
| TSM +10% | 0 | TSM +10% | 0 |
| TSM +15% | 0 | TSM +15% | 0 |
| TSM +20% | 0 | TSM +20% | 0 |
| TSM +25% | 0 | TSM +25% | 0 |
| TSM +30% | 0 | TSM +30% | 0 |

a lower amplitude. A suggesting strategy to reduce the watermark distortion is to exclude the 91st bin (holding the zero-value samples) for watermarking.

We test the robustness of the proposed algorithm according to IFPI [3] with BER (Bit Error Rate). The audio editing and attacking tools adopted in our experiments are CoolEditPro V2.1, and Stirmark Benchmark for Audio V0.2. The test results under common audio signal processing, random cropping, time-scale modification and Stirmark for Audio are listed in Tables 1-4. From Table 1 we can see that our algorithm is robust enough to some common audio signal processing manipulations, such as, MP3 compression of 112 kbps, low pass of 8 kHz, etc.

Table 2 shows the strong robustness to random cropping. In our experiments, even 20000 samples cropped at each of ten randomly or randomly cropping one portion of the audio with the length of 3s, it does not make any affection to the extracted watermark. As for jittering attacks, an evenly performed random cropping, the algorithm also shows strong robustness. The reason is that the cropping attack in time domain, to some extent, may be viewed as an approximately temporal linear stretching operation because the cropped samples, usually, obey the approximate distribution in sample values as the original audio signal.

Random stretching includes the resample mode and pitch-invariant modes. The test results of a light music under TSM from -30% to +30% with two different stretching modes are tabulated in Table 3. The proposed algorithm shows strong robustness to this kind of attacks up to ±30% for pitch-invariant

**Table 4.** Robustness performance to some common attacks in StirMark for Audio

| Attack Type | BER | Attack Type | BER |
|---|---|---|---|
| AddBrumm_100 | 4/60 | AddNoise_100 | 0 |
| AddBrumm_1100 | Failed | AddNoise_300 | Failed |
| Compressor | 0 | ExtraStereo_30 | 0 |
| Amplify | 0 | ExtraStereo_50 | 0 |
| Exchange | 0 | ExtraStereo_70 | 0 |
| ZeroCross | 3/60 | Normalize | 0 |
| Stat2 | 0 | CutSample | 0 |
| Nothing | 0 | Smooth2 | 0 |
| Original | 0 | Smooth | 0 |
| FFT_RealReverse | 0 | FlipSample | 0 |

TSM and the resample TSM, far beyond the $\pm10\%$ requested by the IFPI and STEP2000, and it is higher than 9% in [10] and 8% in [13]. Referred to the analysis in Section 2, this is mainly due to the relative invariance of the number of samples in different bins and the robustness of the audio mean to such attacks.

Stirmark Benchmark for Audio is a common robustness evaluation tool for audio watermarking techniques. All listed operations are performed by using default parameters implemented in the system. From Table 4, it is found that the watermark shows stronger resistance to those common attacks. In the cases of failure ('*Failed*' means the BER is over 20%), the audio mean is changed severely or the audio quality is distorted largely.

Overall, our algorithm is robust to common desynchronization operations including the pitch-invariant and the resample scaling, random cropping and jittering attacks.

## 6   Conclusions

In this paper, we propose a multi-bit audio watermarking method based on the statistical features in time domain by the histogram shape insensitivity to TSM. The histogram shape is interpreted as the relative relation of different bins in population.

Via theoretical analysis and extensive experiments, we show the superiority of the proposed statistical features, the relative relations in the number of samples among different bins and the audio mean. The two features are very robust to the TSM. Accordingly, by applying the two investigated features combined with synchronization match technique, an audio watermarking scheme robust to the TSM is designed. Since only a small portion of audio samples are somewhat modified in the embedding, the watermark is inapparent and inaudible.

The extensive experimental works have shown that the proposed watermarking strategy has conquered those challenging desynchronization attacks, such as time scaling and random cropping. The watermark also achieves good robustness against some common signal processing operations, such as MP3 compression, additional noises, amplitude scaling attack, etc. This work is very useful due to its strong robustness to desynchronization attacks.

In further work, we will discuss the underlying robustness principle of the proposed watermarking scheme to cropping. The security of the watermark and how to combine the frequency transformation techniques to improve the watermark robustness are also two further considerations.

## Acknowledgments

Authors appreciate the support by NSFC (60325208,90604008), National 973 Program (2006CB303100), NSF of Guangdong (04205407). We also thank the anonymous reviewers for their constructive suggestions.

## References

1. Arnold, M.: Audio Watermarking: Features, Applications and Algorithms. In: Proc. of IEEE International Conference on Multimedia and Expo, New York, USA, vol. 2, pp. 1013–1016 (2000)
2. Swanson, M.D., Zhu, B., Tewfik, A.H.: Current State of the Art, Challenges and Future Directions for Audio Watermarking. In: Proc. of IEEE International Conference on Multimedia Computing and Systems, vol. 1, pp. 19–24 (1999)
3. Katzenbeisser, S., Petitcolas, F.A.P.(eds.): Information Hiding Techniques for Steganography and Digital Watermarking. Artech House, Inc. (2000)
4. International Evaluation Project for Digital Watermark Technology for Music (2000) In: http://www.jasrac.or.jp/watermark/ehoukoku.htm
5. SDMI Call For Proposals, Phase II (2000) In: http://www.sdmi.org/download/
6. Wu, S.Q., Huang, J.W., Huang, D., Shi, Y.Q.: Efficiently Self-Synchronized Audio Watermarking for Assured Audio Data Transmission. IEEE Trans. on Broadcasting 51, 69–76 (2005)
7. Kirovski, D., Malvar, H.: Robust Covert Communication over A Public Audio Channel Using Spread Spectrum. In: Proc. of Information Hiding Workshop, pp. 354–368 (2001)
8. Tachibana, R., Shimizu, S., Nakamura, T., Kobayashi, S.: An Audio Watermarking Method Robust against Time and Frequency Fluctuation. In: Proc. of SPIE International Conference on Security and Watermarking of Multimedia Contents III, vol. 4314, pp. 104–115 (2001)
9. Mansour, M., Tewfik, A.: Time-Scale Invariant Audio Data Embedding. In: Proc. of IEEE International Conference on Multimedia and Expo, pp. 76–79 (2001)
10. Li, W., Xue, X.Y., Lu, P.Z.: Robust Audio Watermarking Based on Rhythm Region Detection. Electronics Letters 41, 218–219 (2005)
11. Wu, C.P., Su, P.C., Kuo, C.-C.J.: Robust and Efficient Digital Audio Watermarking Using Audio Content Analysis. In: Proc. of SPIE International Conference on Security and Watermarking of Multimedia Contents II, vol. 3971, pp. 382–392 (2000)
12. Sylvain, B., Michiel, V.D.V., Aweke, L.: Informed Detection of Audio Watermark for Resolving Playback Speed Modifications. In: Proc. of the Multimedia and Security Workshop, pp. 117–123 (2004)

13. Tachibana, R.: Improving Audio Watermarking Robustness Using Stretched Patterns against Geometric Distortion. In: Proc. of IEEE International Conference on Multimedia, pp. 647–654 (2002)
14. Coltuc, D., Bolon, P.: Watermarking by Histogram Specification. In: Proc. of SPIE International Conference on Security and Watermarking of Multimedia Contents II, vol. 3657, pp. 252–263 (1999)
15. Roy, S., Chang, E.C.: Watermarking color histograms. In: Proc. of International Conference of Image Processing, vol. 4, pp. 2191–2194 (2004)
16. Steinebach, M., Petitcolas, F.A.P., Raynal, F., Dittmann, J., Fontaine, C., Seibel, S., Fates, N., Ferri, L.C.: StirMark Benchmark: Audio Watermarking Attacks. In: Proc. of International Conference on Information Technology: Coding and Computing, pp. 49–54 (2001)
17. Xiang, S.J., Huang, J.W.: Analysis of D/A and A/D Conversions in Quantization-Based Audio Watermarking. International Journal of Network Security 3, 230–238 (2006)
18. http://www.mp3-tech.org/programmer/sources/eaqual.tgz

## Appendix

When the embedding bit is $'1'$ and $2b/(a + c) < T$, we reassign the number of samples in three neighboring bins by modifying the values of those selected samples from BIN_1 and BIN_3 in the number denoted by $I_1$ and $I_3$ to satisfy $2b'/(a' + c') \geq T$. So $a' = a - I_1$, $c' = c - I_3$, $b' = b + I_1 + I_3$. Where $a', b', c'$ is the corresponding modified version of $a, b, c$. Without the loss of generality, let $I = I_1 + I_3$ and $a/c = I_1/I_3$ making that the modified samples in the number is proportionable to the number of samples in the bins. Referred to Equation (9), we have the following deduction,

$$2b'/(a' + c') \geq T \Longleftrightarrow 2(b + I_1 + I_3)/(a + c - I_1 - I_3) \geq T$$
$$\Longleftrightarrow (I_1 + I_3) \geq [T(a + c) - 2b]/(2 + T)$$
$$\Longleftrightarrow I \geq [T(a + c) - 2b]/(2 + T)$$

The proof of Equation (11) is finished.

Similarly, when the embedding bit is $'0'$ and $(a + c)/2b < T$, the values of those selected samples from BIN_2 are modified to make $I_1$ and $I_3$ samples to fall into BIN_1 and BIN_3, respectively, to satisfy $(a' + c')/2b' \geq T$. Let $a/c = I_1/I_3$, $I = I_1 + I_3$. Similarly, from the expressions $a' = a + I_1$, $c' = c + I_3$, $b' = b - I_1 - I_3$, we have

$$(a' + c')/2b' \geq T \Longleftrightarrow (a + c + I_1 + I_3) \geq 2T(b - I_1 - I_3)$$
$$\Longleftrightarrow (I_1 + I_3) \geq [2Tb - (a + c)]/(1 + 2T)$$
$$\Longleftrightarrow I \geq [2Tb - (a + c)]/(1 + 2T)$$

The proof of Equation (13) is finished.

# Content-Aware Steganography: About Lazy Prisoners and Narrow-Minded Wardens

Richard Bergmair[1] and Stefan Katzenbeisser[2]

[1] Computer Laboratory, University of Cambridge
[2] Institut für Informatik, Technische Universität München
{rbergmair,skatzenbeisser}@acm.org

**Abstract.** We introduce content-aware steganography as a new paradigm. As opposed to classic steganographic algorithms that only embed information in the syntactic representation of a datagram, content-aware steganography embeds secrets in the semantic interpretation which a human assigns to a datagram. In this paper, we outline two constructions for content-aware stegosystems, which employ, as a new kind of security primitive, problems that are easy for humans to solve, but difficult to automate. Such problems have been successfully used in the past to construct Human Interactive Proofs (HIPs), protocols capable of automatically distinguishing whether a communication partner is a human or a machine.

## 1 Content-Aware Steganography

In his 1984 landmark paper [23], Gustavus Simmons illustrated what is now widely known as the *prisoners' problem*: Two accomplices in a crime, Alice and Bob, are arrested in separate cells. They want to coordinate an escape plan, but their only means of communication is by way of messages conveyed for them by Wendy the warden. Should Alice and Bob try to exchange messages that are not completely open to Wendy, or ones that seem suspicious to her, they will be put into a high security prison no one has ever escaped from. Simmons' solution to the prisoners' problem is phrased in an interesting way: Alice and Bob "will have to deceive the warden by finding a way of communicating secretly in the exchanges, i.e. of establishing a 'subliminal channel' between them in full view of the warden, even though the messages themselves contain no secret (to the warden) information" [23]. In other words, Alice is trying to convey a particular piece of information which is represented as a single *datagram*. This datagram is available to both Wendy and Bob—but it contains different *information* to Wendy than to Bob.

Informally speaking, a subliminal channel is one that transmits datagrams that have at least two possible interpretations. Each datagram is intentionally given an obvious interpretation (the cover) that is innocuous to Wendy, and a non-obvious interpretation (the secret) that is suspicious to Wendy, and thus cannot be transmitted in plain sight. The security of the stegosystem usually relies on some assumption of an advantage that Bob has over Wendy, when it comes

J. Camenisch et al. (Eds.): IH 2006, LNCS 4437, pp. 109–123, 2007.

to the *interpretation* of the message: Bob can interpret the message with regard to its secret meaning, while Wendy can only interpret the message as the cover.

In the past, many stegosystems have been constructed, most of them using images, digital audio, or video as cover. Consider for example a simplistic LSB scheme for image-based steganography in which the cleartext message is written into the LSBs of an image without any further cryptographic concealment. The datagram has an obvious interpretation, which is visual perception by a human user of the pattern that appears on screen when it is opened in their favourite image viewer. It also has a non-obvious interpretation, which is to extract the LSBs and view their concatenation, say, in a hex-editor. Under the assumption that Alice constantly sends Bob bitmap images that Wendy is not willing to wade through with a hex-editor, this simplistic system might be attributed some kind of security. However, Wendy will probably try to *automatically* analyze all datagrams exchanged between Alice and Bob to gain knowledge of a subliminal channel. This notion of automaticity in steganalysis has probably received too little attention in the past, which is why we shall, in this paper, take the challenging point of view that a stego object should not be considered perfectly secure as long as its *semantics* are prone to *automatic interpretation by a machine*.

Due to recent progress in the field of steganalysis (see for example [17]), LSB substitution techniques must be considered completely insecure today. To understand why LSB steganography was compromised, it is important to bear in mind that a bitmap image is not just a sequence of bytes, but rather a representation for some specific semantic content. It could, for example, be a vector drawing consisting of uniformly colored geometric shapes. If a set of pixels can be identified as representing, say, an oval shape colored in a certain tone of blue, and half of these pixels deviate in their color by the LSB, this might give us some evidence of steganography taking place. A 24-bit bitmap might also be a photograph taken by a digital camera with a CCD that leaves noise with special characteristics in the images [20]. If these characteristics cannot be found in the LSBs of the image, then again we have gained evidence to suspect that steganography is taking place.

We believe the way in which LSB substitution has been compromised is stereotypical for how the steganography vs. steganalysis battle is usually fought, namely by steganalysis exploiting the false assumption made by steganography that a meaningful digital object can be specified *solely* in terms of syntactic properties. Stegosystems are usually broken by exploiting *semantic* inconsistencies introduced into the cover when hiding a secret. This is a limitation which is inherent with every steganographic system that takes a cover and applies modifications in order to obtain a stego object: an attacker that possesses a more accurate semantic cover model than the embedder can break the system easily. Thus, a security vulnerability is necessarily opened in any steganographic system whose participants are computers that employ state-of-the art cover models, as soon as the state of the art improves.

In this paper, we propose an alternative view of steganography, which takes semantic aspects into account and hides information in the *semantics* (rather than the syntactic representation) of a datagram sent over a channel. We call such systems *content-aware steganography*. At the heart of the paradigm lies the assumption that Wendy the warden is a *computer* (and not a human), while Alice and Bob are both humans. Given the massive increase in communication over the last years, this is an assumption which seems to be justified, as large-scale manual steganalysis is not possible.

A content-aware stegosystem chooses stego objects in such a way that both the human sender and receiver can easily assign a secret semantic interpretation to the transmitted datagrams, whereas for a computer (such as Wendy) it is inherently difficult to perform the same task. In extending the analogy of Alice and Bob, we may think of the prisoners as being "lazy" when sending or receiving subliminal messages: as humans they can trivially assign and infer a secret semantic interpretation to a stego object. (Thus, one can view content-aware stegosystems as implementing a special supraliminal channel [16]). On the other hand, the warden Wendy is "narrow-minded" in the sense that her inherent limitations as a data processing device do not allow her to infer the secret interpretations of stego datagrams. We have to stress at this point, that it is not the intention of the present contribution to compete with current notions of steganographic security, but rather to complement them by suggesting *content-awareness* as a new security property that should hold for a secure system in addition to the well-established ones.

Content-aware stegosystems are constructed in such a way that a successful steganalytic attack would require solving an Artificial Intelligence problem that can currently not be tackled with state-of-the-art algorithms. We will show that Human Interactive Proofs (HIPs), which were recently developed to distinguish humans from computers in security applications, readily lend themselves to the construction of such content-aware stegosystems.

The rest of the paper is organized in the following way. Section 2 gives a thorough explanation of the new steganographic paradigm we propose, motivating it from a principal and conceptual point of view and Section 3 gives a generic construction of a content-aware stegosystem which draws its security from a Human Interactive Proof. These two sections are embedded in this paper in such a way that the more technically minded reader may choose to skip them, but will still be able to follow the rest of this paper. Sections 4 and 5 introduce two practical content-aware stegosystems, one that hides steganographic content in audiovisual content and one that uses natural language texts as covers. Finally, Section 6 will review related work in light of the new paradigm.

## 2   On Data and Information

Traditionally, stego objects have been treated as meaningless objects, which is an assumption most probably stemming from cryptography: in the context of cryptography, access to a cryptogram leaves an eavesdropper without any knowledge. By virtue of its definition, a cryptogram does not carry any meaning beyond that which must be inferred by means of the decryption routine. A stego object however, which has to resemble an innocuous cover in every respect, does carry such meaning. A stego object can only be identified as innocuous or suspicious after it has been *interpreted and assigned meaning*, which extends the cryptologic picture into a semantic dimension as we move on from pure cryptography to steganography.

Turning back to our intuitive picture of steganography, the essence of the new paradigm is that we are dealing with *data* in the context of cryptography, as opposed to steganography, which deals with *information*. The distinction between data and information is based on the degree of understanding an observer has about a given observation. In particular, we shall call an observation a piece of data if we see it in a purely symbolic way, void of inherent meaning but capable of being processed to make sense.

Once we commit to this conception of data and information, it becomes apparent that the role of *understanding* as a means to elevate a given observation from data to information and knowledge is quite crucial. Ackoff [1] notes that understanding is by virtue of its nature a cognitive process. It can only be automated to the degree to which computers succeed in simulating this process. Thus, any claim attributing a human level of information-processing capability to a fully computerized system must be presupposing a hypothesis whose confirmation has resisted decades of research in Artificial Intelligence: that biological cognition is a computational process. Thus we feel driven to the point of view, that computers may not be regarded as directly operating on information as such in any way. Of course, the success of computerized systems in supporting human-controlled information processing systems is undisputed. Yet, this does not contradict the view that computers are essentially limited in their domain of operation to simple data since information processing may still happen implicitly in a computerized system within the brains of its human users.

These ideas about data and information have a strong impact on data and information processing in the context of cryptography and steganography: In the new paradigm we have in mind, a joint coding and encryption scheme lies at the core of every stegosystem. The purpose of this scheme is to provide security for the transmitted *data*; in addition, it performs appropriate coding for the communication channel which is used to transmit subliminal information. In the sequel, we will refer to this core solely as the cryptosystem. In an outer layer, a steganographic operation extends the cryptosystem by semantic aspects: its purpose is to let Alice transmit meaningful pieces of *information*. The stego layer thus controls the semantic interpretation of a datagram and provides resistance against automated steganalysis.

Figure 1 depicts this idea of content-aware steganography. The inner area of the figure represents the cryptosystem: The message input to the encryption routine is treated as a piece of data. The encryption routine translates this message into a cryptogram which is another piece of data; the routines for decryption and cryptanalytic attack basically invert this mapping. The encryption routine does not need to take into account any semantics, since it can always reinterpret its input as a random choice of one element from a finite message space, regardless

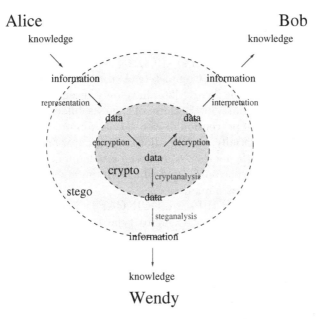

**Fig. 1.** Content-aware steganography

of whether this input is actually a representation for an image, a sound, or a text. The decryption routine and the cryptanalytic attack typically do not need to take into account any semantics either.

The outer area of the figure depicts the steganographic layer: The message that Alice actually wants to convey, is a piece of information. The act of representation degrades this information to data, so it can be run through the cryptosystem. The acts of interpretation or steganalysis, on the other hand *reassign meaning* to the data which is supposed to equal the original message, and therefore yield information again: the whole stegosystem essentially operates within the information domain. Clearly, the act of representation must take into account semantics, since Alice has exactly one piece of semantic content in mind when she represents it, and the acts of interpretation and steganalysis have to deal with semantics, since they have to reconstruct exactly that semantic content. The crucial requirement is that Wendy is unable (even after performing cryptanalytic attacks on the transmitted *data*) to correctly infer the secret semantics of the datagrams transmitted over the channel.

## 3   HIP: A New Security Primitive for a New Kind of Steganography

In this section, we propose a general construction for a content-aware stegosystem out of any Human Interactive Proof (HIP). Once we admit that Wendy is a computer and Bob is a human sitting in front of a computer, all we have to do is to make the solution to the problem of determining the secret interpretation of the stego object depend on the solution of a problem that only humans can solve correctly.

Human Interactive Proofs (HIPs) [19,31,25], better known under the more specific model of CAPTCHAs (Completely Automated Public Turing tests to tell Computers and Humans Apart) [26], have only recently gained attention in the computer security community because of their usefulness in the fight against worms and spam and the prevention of web-service abuse, denial-of-service, and dictionary attacks. Essentially, an HIP allows a computer program to determine whether it interacts with another computer or a human. HIPs are based on complex Artificial Intelligence problems which computers cannot solve with the same speed and accuracy as humans.

Currently the best-known HIPs are OCR CAPTCHAs that display heavily distorted text to a user and ask them to type the text into an input field. Typically, humans have no problem in performing this task while an automated solution requires solving the complex problem of optical character recognition, which is still unsolved for heavily distorted text. The underlying assumption of the OCR CAPTCHA is that once a communication partner solves this challenge correctly, one can safely assume that it is a human.

---

**for** $k := 1, \ldots, n$ **do**
    The tester constructs a test/solution pair $(t_k, s_k)$
        such that $t_k \in T$ and $s_k \in S$
    The tester sends the test $t_k$ to the testee
    The testee makes a choice $h_k$ for a solution of $t_k$
    The testee sends $h_k$ to the tester

    *// The tester checks if testee could be a computer*
    **if** $h_k \neq s_k$ **then**
        Do not draw any conclusions and stop
    **end**
Conclude that the testee is human

**Fig. 2.** $n$-round Human Interactive Proof

---

In general, a Human Interactive Proof involves a set of tests $T = \{t_1, t_2, \ldots\}$, a set of solutions $S = \{s_1, s_2, \ldots, s_{|S|}\}$, for $|S| \in \mathbb{N} \setminus \{0, 1\}$, and an algorithm that produces a random test/solution pair $(t, s)$ where $t \in T$ and $s \in S$; everyone who answers $s$ to $t$ is considered to be a human. In theory, for an HIP to be secure, $T$ must be countably infinite at least (otherwise there exists an algorithm that already contains the solutions to all problems hardcoded in the program file). In practice it is desirable that $|T|$ is as large as possible. We will assume that for each test $t \in T$ there is a set $C_t \subseteq S$ of candidate-solutions for $t$, which includes the correct solution $s$ to $t$ and a number of invalid solutions (thus, $|C_t| \geq 2$ for all tests $t$). Let $I_{C_t} : C_t \mapsto \{0, 1, \ldots, |C_t| - 1\}$ be a one-to-one mapping from the elements of a given set of candidate solutions to the smallest $|C_t|$ natural

---

**for** $k := 1, \ldots, n$ **do**

    Alice constructs a test/solution pair $(t_k, s_k)$

      such that $t_k \in T$ and $s_k \in S$

    Alice constructs a claim

      $c_k \leftarrow I_{C_{t_k}}^{-1}((I_{C_{t_k}}(s_k) + \overline{m}_k) \bmod |C_{t_k}|)$

    Alice sends the test/claim pair $\overline{e}_k = (t_k, c_k)$ to Bob

    Bob makes a choice $h_k$ for a solution of $t_k$

    Bob computes $\overline{m}'_k \leftarrow (I_{C_{t_k}}(c_k) - I_{C_{t_k}}(h_k)) \bmod |C_{t_k}|$

---

**Fig. 3.** Content-aware stegosystem

numbers. For the sake of simplicity, we assume that all tests $t \in T$ have the same number $b$ of candidate solutions, i.e. $|C_t| = b$ for all $C_t$.

Figure 2 shows how a Human Interactive Proof is performed. The tester enters a loop and constructs $n$ test instances $t_k$ together with respective solutions $s_k$. The tester shows the instances $t_k$ to the testee. The testee provides solutions $h_k$ for all instances; finally the testee is verified to be a human if they responded with the expected solutions in all $n$ rounds (i.e., $h_k = s_k$ for $k = 1, \ldots, n$).

A secure Human Interactive Proof can be used as central primitive to construct content-aware stegosystems. In particular, we make the assumption that *sending a test instance of an HIP over a channel is not per se suspicious*. This assumption, which must be verified for each instantiation of the general construction presented in this section, is a direct extension of the general assumption of classic steganography that sending, for instance, images or pieces of literary text does not itself raise the awareness of Wendy. In practice we could, for example, assume that Wendy generally tolerates English language text being exchanged between Alice and Bob. We can then set up a stegosystem on the basis of a text-domain HIP, such as the word-sense disambiguation HIP [6]. Alternatively we could assume that Wendy tolerates images being exchanged. We would then use an image HIP such as the famous OCR CAPTCHA [26] or image recognition CAPTCHAs [14]. Sections 4 and 5 will discuss these two concrete constructions.

The general construction of a content-aware stegosystem from an HIP is shown in Figure 3. Once Alice wants to send a piece of information $m$ to Bob, she fixes a datagram representation of $m$ as an integer sequence of length $n$ with elements between 0 and $b - 1$, i.e., $\overline{m} = \overline{m}_1 \overline{m}_2 ... \overline{m}_n$, where $\overline{m}_i \in \{0, 1, ..., b - 1\}$. One can think of $\overline{m}$ as the radix-$b$ expansion of a natural number smaller than $b^n$. Note that the construction can be straightforwardly generalized to the case of differing numbers of candidate-solutions $|C_t|$ by thinking of $\overline{m}$ as a mixed-radix expansion.

To send the message, Alice constructs $n$ test instances $t_k$ of the HIP together with corresponding solutions $s_k$. In addition, she constructs a *claim* which corresponds to a (possibly incorrect) solution to $t_k$, called $c_k$, computed as

$$c_k \leftarrow I_{C_{t_k}}^{-1}((I_{C_{t_k}}(s_k) + \overline{m}_k) \bmod |C_{t_k}|).$$

Thus, Alice uses the map $I_{C_{t_k}}$ to obtain the numerical representation of $s_k$ and adds $\overline{m}_k$ to it; subsequently, she uses the inverse mapping to map the result back to a candidate solution. Finally, Alice sends both $t_k$ and $c_k$ to Bob. One can think of that as Alice claiming $c_k$ to be the solution to $t_k$. If Bob is able to compute the correct solution to $t_k$ (i.e., solve the HIP), he can reconstruct the secret message $\overline{m}$ precisely and thus can gain an understanding of the information $m$ Alice sent.

**Claim 1.** (Decodability by humans) *Suppose that Bob is human and is thus able to solve all instances of the HIP correctly. After termination of the steganographic transmission, the message $\overline{m}' = \overline{m}'_1 \overline{m}'_2 ... \overline{m}'_n$ received by Bob will be equal to the original message $\overline{m}$ submitted by Alice.*

*Proof sketch:* Consider the stego transmission of the $k$-th symbol. Since Bob is human, he is able to choose $h_k$ in such a way that $h_k = s_k$ (otherwise he would fail to pass the HIP and thus not be considered human). Bob reconstructs the $k$-th message element by setting $\overline{m}'_k = (I_{C_{t_k}}(c_k) - I_{C_{t_k}}(h_k)) \bmod |C_{t_k}|$. Substituting $c_k$ and letting $s_k = h_k$ results in $\overline{m}'_k = (I_{C_{t_k}}(I_{C_{t_k}}^{-1}((I_{C_{t_k}}(s_k) + \overline{m}_k) \bmod |C_{t_k}|)) - I_{C_{t_k}}(s_k)) \bmod |C_{t_k}|$, yielding to $\overline{m}'_k = \overline{m}_k \bmod |C_{t_k}|$. Since $\overline{m}_k < |C_{t_k}|$, we have $\overline{m}'_k = \overline{m}_k$, which means that Bob has correctly decoded the message. □

We now argue that the steganalysis problem for Wendy is hard. As mentioned above, at this point we rely on the general assumption that Wendy will find the transmission of HIP instances, i.e. the tuples $(t_k, c_k)$ suspicious neither by themselves nor in the transmitted sequence; thus we assume the existence of an appropriate encoding function such that transmission of the coded tuples will be considered innocuous. This assumption must, of course, be verified in practice on a case-by-case basis. (In the subsequent sections we will outline two such encodings for a linguistic and an audiovisual HIP).

Wendy may apply cryptanalytic methods on the datagrams sent between Alice and Bob. These techniques may result in a "suspicion" $\overline{w}$, i.e., a datagram that she believes was exchanged covertly. However, due to our limited understanding of the underlying AI problem, Wendy, being a computer, will not be able to recover the sent datagram $\overline{m}$. The next claim asserts that if $\overline{m} = \overline{w}$, Wendy could pass the HIP, which contradicts the security of the HIP.

**Claim 2.** (Content-awareness) *Suppose that, after termination of the steganographic transmission, Wendy's suspicion $\overline{w}' = \overline{w}'_1 \overline{w}'_2 ... \overline{w}'_n$ will be equal to the original message $\overline{m}$ submitted by Alice. Then Wendy would pass the HIP on the instances submitted over the channel.*

*Proof sketch:* We assume that Wendy has managed to guess $\overline{w}_k$ in such a way that $\overline{w}_k = \overline{m}_k$. Wendy can use that message to obtain a solution $s'_k$ to the HIP instances $t_k$ by letting $s'_k = I_{C_{t_k}}^{-1}((I_{C_{t_k}}(c_k) - \overline{w}_k) \bmod |C_{t_k}|)$. To see that this is really a solution to the HIP, we can substitute $c_k$ and $\overline{m}_k = \overline{w}_k$ to obtain $s'_k = I_{C_{t_k}}^{-1}((I_{C_{t_k}}(I_{C_{t_k}}^{-1}((I_{C_{t_k}}(s_k) + \overline{m}_k) \bmod |C_{t_k}|)) - \overline{m}_k) \bmod |C_{t_k}|)$. This finally yields

$s'_k = I_{C_{t_k}}^{-1}(I_{C_{t_k}}(s_k) \bmod |C_{t_k}|)$ and thus $s'_k = s_k$. This means that Wendy can solve the HIP on those instances used to transmit the subliminal message.    □

## 4    An Audiovisual Content Recognition Stegosystem

In order to show how the generic construction can be applied to a particular domain, we will develop in this section a stegosystem based on an audiovisual content-recognition HIP, similar to the image recognition CAPTCHA in [14]. We will first describe this HIP, and subsequently show how to turn this HIP into a content aware stegosystem according to the general construction of Section 3.

The original setup of the recognition HIP is as follows: Alice has available a database of images and/or sound files labelled by a human according to its semantic content. Alice could, for instance, use her digital album, containing photos, images and videos from her holidays, all of which were carefully hand-labelled by her in order to more easily find them on her computer; a label could, for instance, be "Charlie and me visiting Alcatraz". We assume that this database is private to Alice. Alice could, for instance, add new content to her album at a faster rate than she "uses them up" by publishing the content or using it for a HIP.

The HIP operates in the following manner. The test instance of the HIP consists of a number of items from her media database, including labels, which can either be incorrect or correct. Alice generates a test/solution-pair $(t, s)$ by picking 8 media files from the database, and relabelling them to obtain a sequence

$$t = \langle (x_1, l_1), (x_2, l_2), ..., (x_8, l_8) \rangle,$$

where each $x_i$ is a multimedia file and $l_i$ is a label. One of the media files is correctly labeled with a label from Alice's private database, whereas all other labels are randomly picked (e.g., taken from different media items in the database). Alice presents the test instance $t$ to Wendy, who has to choose the index of the correctly labeled file. If she passes the test, she is considered human (the test can be repeated in order to increase the level of confidence).

This HIP can be converted into a content-aware stegosystem by using the general methodology outlined in Section 3. First we need a way to encode the test instances of the HIP in such a way that they are not, by themselves, suspicious. For this purpose, Alice could generate an e-mail with a body that reads like "Hello Bob! Here are the images of my last vacation, you wanted to see.", and a number of attachments containing image files named after their labels. She can easily write this message body herself, so this need not be automated.

The receiver Bob solves the HIP and thus is able to find the index of the attachment which is correctly labelled. The only remaining issue for Bob is to recover the secret message bit from the message index. This can be done quite easily. For instance Bob could order the media files alphabetically according to their label and let the index of the correctly labelled file represent three bits from the message. Since Alice is free in her choice about the labels she can easily choose them in a way that lets Bob recover the message she wants to transmit. However, Wendy cannot tell which of the images bears the correct label, since that would require her to *understand* the label, and *recognize* the content of the media-file.

This process can, of course, be iterated by sending more images (and arranging them in blocks of 8), which makes it possible to transmit messages that are longer than three bits. Additional unnecessary images could be used to conceal the length of the secret message.

## 5   A Linguistic Text Understanding Stegosystem

Recognition of audiovisual content is not the only AI-problem that lends itself to HIPs and consequently to content-aware steganography. In this section we will outline a content-aware stegosystem [5] that is based on a word-sense disambiguation HIP [6]. It can only be broken by an arbitrator who can understand the meaning of natural language text, which is an Artificial Intelligence problem that cannot be solved satisfactorily yet. Again, we start by outlining how Alice can use this problem to carry out an HIP to test whether Wendy is human, and then go on to extend the HIP to a stegosystem that enables her to pass on secret information to Bob if Wendy is a computer.

The HIP uses natural language sentences as test instances. Alice constructs a test-instance by writing down a sentence like

*The radio station didn't want to **send** the song.*

She designates one word within this sentence, which she looks up in a synonymy-dictionary like WordNet. This dictionary contains sets of words which can be used interchangeably in some context; note that these synonymy sets are not disjoint, as one word can have several different meanings depending on the context. For example, looking up the word *send* will give Alice information of the following form:

$$\text{syn}(send, c_1) = \{\,air,\ broadcast,\ send\,\}$$
$$\text{syn}(send, c_2) = \{\,send,\ ship,\ transport\,\}$$
$$\text{syn}(send, c_3) = \{\,mail,\ post,\ send\,\}$$

Depending on the linguistic context $c_s$ the word *send* is used in, it can be considered synonymous to a different set of words. Sometimes, *send* can be replaced by *broadcast* and sometimes by *post*. Since Alice is human and can fully understand the sentence, she can identify the context the word *send* is used in (in this example context $c_1$).

She now presents the sentence to Wendy, who has access to the synonymy set database, and asks her to choose the correct sense of the selected word from the database. If Wendy is a computer she will not know that a song can be aired or broadcast, but not shipped or transported by a radio station. Therefore all

Wendy can do here is to make a guess: If she could reliably choose the right set of replacements, she would have solved the problem of word-sense disambiguation, which has been of considerable interest to computational linguists ever since the first attempts at automatic machine translation were made in the 1950s. To this day, the performance of machines in word-sense disambiguation is nowhere near the performance of humans.

This HIP can be turned into a content-aware stegosystem in the following way. To transmit a secret message, Alice uses a natural language sentence as cover and selects one word (which is contained in at least two synonymy sets) in the sentence as before. The position of the word to be replaced is determined according to a key shared between Alice and Bob. The selected word is then replaced by a different word from an *incorrect* synonymy set; the replacement is selected according to the secret message. Alice could simply sort the elements of a synset in alphabetical order and assign the resulting indices as codewords. For example, by replacing the word *send* by words from the synonymy set $c_2$ we can encode one bit of information:

$$
\textit{The radio station didn't want to} \left\{ \begin{array}{ll} - & \textit{send} \\ 0 & \textit{ship} \\ 1 & \textit{\textbf{transport}} \end{array} \right\} \quad \textit{the song.}
$$

Since Bob is a human, he can easily spot the incorrect word in the sentence. By looking up the index of the word in the shared synonymy set database, the secret message can be recovered. However, Wendy will be unable to distinguish a correct sentence from a sentence carrying secret information, as this would require her to solve the problem of word-sense disambiguation.

Again, it should be easy to embed a sequence of such HIP test-instances into an innocuous cover. This will simply be a sequence of sentences, i.e. natural language text, that can hardly be considered suspicious in itself.

## 6   Related Work

So far we have introduced from a conceptual side the paradigm of content-aware steganography, and have presented two examples of what an actual stegosystem based on this paradigm could look like. In this section we will discuss some stegosystems developed in the past, and analyze them from the point of view of content-aware steganography. In particular, we shall be interested in linguistic stegosystems.

The most widely cited contribution to linguistic steganography is perhaps that of Peter Wayner, who studied the use of $n$-gram language models [27] and probabilistic context-free grammars [28] as statistic language models by which an arbitrator identifies messages as containing natural-language. The assumption is that such data will generally be accepted by the warden, and therefore the same language model can be used to generate innocent looking stego objects.

Although Wayner's work is an important theoretical contribution to the field, his techniques cannot be directly applied to mimic natural language, since neither

$n$-gram models nor probabilistic context-free languages can be specified that handle languages remotely comparable in complexity to natural languages such as English. Practical techniques will therefore generally have to trade off some encoding efficiency, for example by using an embedding scheme where only single words in an innocuous piece of text are replaced by synonyms. This is what the systems by Chapman et al. [10,11,9,13,12], Winstein [29,30], and Bolshakov et al. [7,8] do. These systems basically suffer from the problem of word-sense ambiguity. Therefore they will make some substitutions that a human would never make, and will never make some other substitutions that a human would make. Other systems for linguistic steganography proposed in the past include those by Atallah et al. [2,3,24,4], by Chiang et al. [15], Nakagawa et al. [21], and Niimi et al. [22].

Another interesting variant was put forward by Grothoff et al. [18]. They proposed a stegosystem that mimics the output of statistic machine translation systems under the assumption that the arbitrator accepts such text. If we admit such an assumption, then, in our opinion, such a system should not be considered linguistic steganography any more, since all the languages that play a role in the steganographic protocol are then artificial. On the other hand, one might want to question this assumption. In this case it is important to note that the steganographic encoder used is essentially a statistical machine translation system itself: It operates on text that is publicly available in some language. The encoder translates the text into another language, embedding a secret along the way. The assumption that such output from a statistical machine translator is acceptable to Wendy can be motivated only by assuming that Wendy is cooperative, in that she wants to permit such a translator to be used somewhere in the channel between Alice and Bob. However, Wendy may also want to prohibit such traffic, and require Alice to send the source-text, and Bob to run the translator. Similarly, Wendy might whitelist a number of translations resulting from widely used standard-software and prohibit other translations from being exchanged. In our opinion the assumption that Wendy accepts poorly translated text should therefore be dropped, and the system should be considered as a linguistic stegosystem instead. However, in this case the system becomes conceptually very similar to Wayner's original scheme, except that hidden Markov models are used as language models, rather than probabilistic context-free grammars.

If we turn back to Wayner's original framework, we can highlight a number of vulnerabilities that should become obvious, once a content-aware point of view is taken. The natural language text which is assumed by Wendy as innocuous is generated and interpreted by humans. However the stegosystem generates and interprets messages by means of, say, an $n$-gram model, although $n$-gram models are not necessary and not sufficient as generators for the natural language actually spoken by humans. They generate sentences a human would never produce, and will never generate some sentences that a human would produce. Both of these clues, if observed by the arbitrator a statistically significant number of times, can, in principle, be used to break the scheme, since every piece of text produced by the system comes from a well-known meta-model. The language model itself can be drawn from the meta-model by means of language learning techniques. $N$-grams can be learned by counting the occurrences of $n$-tuples of words (as done in code-breaking of substitution ciphers), Markov models can be learned by counting state-transitions in a finite-state automaton, and probabilistic context-free languages can be learned by counting rule applications in context-free derivations. It can be seen that these possible exploits display a universal pattern: as soon as a steganographic generator uses a computational language model to generate stego-objects, the model can be learned from data, and therefore the system can eventually be broken.

This supports the point of view that served as the conceptual point of departure in this paper: There are only two possible ways in which a linguistic stegosystem can be perfectly secure: (1) The system is content-unaware and therefore requires that Alice and Bob have a *perfect semantic model* that generates all and only the messages also generated by humans. However, this is hardly achievable. (2) The system is content-aware, and thereby turns the tables, so that it is now Wendy who must have access to a perfect semantic model during steganalysis. This can be done, as outlined before, by having humans take part in embedding and extracting the secret.

## 7  Conclusion

In this paper we have introduced the concept of content-aware steganography as a new paradigm of steganography, stemming from a shift in perspectives towards the objects of steganography. We pointed out that, in the predominant paradigm of steganography, the nature of these objects is that of data. We departed from the observation that systems relying on this paradigm are eventually broken on grounds of attacks that exploit the fact that the digital objects we encounter in everyday life are more than data—that they are meaningful and can be interpreted to give us information. This led us to abandon the point of view that steganographic objects can be characterized in terms of the data that represent them, and to take the new point of view that steganographic objects should be considered pieces of information as such.

To overcome the limitations of current steganographic systems, we introduced content-aware steganography, which hides secret messages in the semantic interpretation of a datagram. Finally, we introduced new content-aware steganographic algorithms that rely on Human Interactive Proofs as a security primitive: the steganalysis problem of the introduced schemes is directly related to a problem considered hard in Artificial Intelligence.

**Acknowledgements.** We would like to thank the anonymous reviewers for their suggestions on improving an earlier version of the paper. Richard Bergmair gratefully acknowledges financial support by an EPSRC studentship and a Cambridge European bursary and would like to thank the benefactors who made this possible.

# References

1. Ackoff, R.L.: From data to wisdom. Journal of Applied Systems Analysis 16, 3–9 (1989)
2. Atallah, M.J., Raskin, V., Crogan, M., Hempelmann, C., Kerschbaum, F., Mohamed, D., Naik, S.: Natural language watermarking: Design, analysis, and a proof-of-concept implementation. In: Moskowitz, I.S. (ed.) Information Hiding: Fourth International Workshop. LNCS, vol. 2137, pp. 185–199. Springer, Heidelberg (2001)
3. Mikhail J. Atallah, Victor Raskin, Christian F. Hempelmann, Mercan Topkara, Radu Sion, Umut Topkara, and Katrina E. Triezenberg. Natural language watermarking and tamperproofing. In Fabien A. P. Petitcolas, editor, *Information Hiding: Fifth International Workshop*, volume 2578 of *Lecture Notes in Computer Science*, pages 196–212. Springer (October 2002)
4. Bennett, K.: Linguistic steganography: Survey, analysis, and robustness concerns for hiding information in text (May 2004)
5. Bergmair, R.: Towards linguistic steganography: A systematic investigation of approaches, systems, and issues. final year project, April 2004 submitted in partial fulfillment of the degree requirements for B.Sc (Hons.) to the University of Derby (2004)
6. Bergmair, R., Katzenbeisser, S.: Towards human interactive proofs in the text-domain. In: Zhang, K., Zheng, Y. (eds.) ISC 2004. LNCS, vol. 3225, Springer, Heidelberg (2004)
7. Bolshakov, I.A.: A method of linguistic steganography based on collocationally-verified synonymy. In: Fridrich, J.J. (ed.) IH 2004. LNCS, vol. 3200, pp. 180–191. Springer, Heidelberg (2004)
8. Calvo, H., Bolshakov, I.A.: Using selectional preferences for extending a synonymous paraphrasing method in steganography. In: Sossa Azuela, J.H. (ed.) Avances en Ciencias de la Computacion e Ingenieria de Computo - CIC'2004: XIII Congreso Internacional de Computacion, pp. 231–242 (October 2004)
9. Chapman, M.: Hiding the hidden: A software system for concealing ciphertext as innocuous text. Master's thesis, University of Wisconsin-Milwaukee (1997)
10. Chapman, M., Davida, G.I.: Nicetext system official home page. http://www.nicetext.com
11. Chapman, M., Davida, G.I.: Hiding the hidden: A software system for concealing ciphertext in innocuous text. In: Han, Y., Quing, S. (eds.) ICICS 1997. LNCS, vol. 1334, pp. 11–14. Springer, Heidelberg (1997)
12. Chapman, M., Davida, G.I.: Plausible deniability using automated linguistic steganography. In: Davida, G., Frankel, Y. (eds.) InfraSec 2002. LNCS, vol. 2437, Springer, Heidelberg (2002)
13. Chapman, M., Davida, G.I., Rennhard, M.: A practical and effective approach to large-scale automated linguistic steganography. In: Davida, G.I., Frankel, Y. (eds.) ISC 2001. LNCS, vol. 2200, Springer, Heidelberg (2001)
14. Chew, M., Tygar, J.D.: Image recognition CAPTCHAs. In: Zhang, K., Zheng, Y. (eds.) ISC 2004. LNCS, vol. 3225, Springer, Heidelberg (2004)
15. Chiang, Y.-L., Chang, L.-P., Hsieh, W.-T., Chen, W.-C.: Natural language watermarking using semantic substitution for chinese text. In: Kalker, T., Cox, I.J., Ro, Y.M. (eds.) IWDW 2003. LNCS, vol. 2939, pp. 129–140. Springer, Heidelberg (2004)
16. Craver, S.: On public-key steganography in the presence of an active warden. In: Aucsmith, D. (ed.) IH 1998. LNCS, vol. 1525, pp. 355–368. Springer, Heidelberg (1998)

17. Fridrich, J., Goljan, M., Hogea, D., Soukal, D.: Quantitative steganalysis of digital images: estimating the secret message length. Multimedia Systems 9, 298–302 (2003)
18. Grothoff, C., Grothoff, K., Alkhutova, L., Stutsman, R., Atallah, M.: Translation-based steganography. In: Barni, M., Herrera-Joancomarti, J., Katzenbeisser, S., Pérez-González, F. (eds.) Information Hiding, 7th International Workshop (IH 2005), Barcelona, Spain. LNCS, vol. 3727, pp. 219–233. Springer, Heidelberg (2005)
19. Hopper, N.J., Blum, M.: Secure human identification protocols. In: Advances in Crypotology, Proceedings of Asiacrypt '01 (2001)
20. Nasir Memon Mehdi Kharrazi, Husrev T.Sencar. Blind source camera identification. In: Proceedings of the National Conference on Image Processing (ICIP '04) (2004)
21. Nakagawa, H., Sampei, K., Matsumoto, T., Kawaguchi, S., Makino, K., Murase, I.: Text information hiding with preserved meaning – a case for japanese documents. IPSJ Transaction 42(9), 2339–2350 (2001)
22. Niimi, M., Minewaki, S., Noda, H., Kawaguchi, E.: A framework of text-based steganography using sd-form semantics model. IPSJ Journal, 44(8) (August 2003)
23. Simmons, G.J.: The prisoners' problem and the subliminal channel. In: Advances in Cryptology, Proceedings of CRYPTO '83, pp. 51–67 (1984)
24. Topkara, M., Taskiran, C.M., Delp, E.J.: Natural language watermarking. In: Delp, E.J., Wong, P.W.(eds) Security, Steganography, and Watermarking of Multimedia Contents VII, vol. 5681 (January 2005)
25. von Ahn, L., Blum, M., Hopper, N.J., Langford, J.: HIPs. http://www.aladdin.cs.cmu.edu/hips/
26. von Ahn, L., Blum, M., Hopper, N.J., Langford, J.: CAPTCHA: using hard ai problems for security. In: Advances in Cryptology, Eurocrypt 2003. LNCS, vol. 2656, pp. 294–311. Springer, Heidelberg (2003)
27. Wayner, P.: Mimic functions. Cryptologia XVI/3, 193–214 (1992)
28. Wayner, P.: Strong theoretical steganography. Cryptologia XIX/3, 285–299 (1995)
29. Winstein, K.: Lexical steganography. http://alumni.imsa.edu/~keithw/tlex
30. Winstein, K.: Lexical steganography through adaptive modulation of the word choice hash. http://alumni.imsa.edu/~keithw/tlex/lsteg.ps
31. Xerox PARC. In: First Workshop on Human Interactive Proofs (January 2002)

# Noisy Timing Channels with Binary Inputs and Outputs*

Keye Martin and Ira S. Moskowitz

Center for High Assurance Computer Systems, Code 5540
Naval Research Laboratory
Washington, DC 20375
{kmartin,moskowitz}@itd.nrl.navy.mil

**Abstract.** We develop the algebraic theory of timed capacity for channels with binary inputs and outputs in the presence of noise, by obtaining a formula for capacity in terms of the unique solution of a nonlinear algebraic equation. We give provably correct numerical algorithms for solving this equation, specifically tailored toward calculating capacity. We use our results to establish that information theory has an inherent discontinuity in it: the function which assigns the unique capacity achieving distribution to the noise matrix of a binary channel has no continuous extension to the set of all noise matrices. Our results provide new formulae in the case of untimed binary channels as well. Our results are important in the study of real-world systems, such as the NRL Network Pump® system and traffic analysis in anonymity systems.

## 1  Introduction

A *timing channel* is a covert channel[1] [6] where the output symbols are distinct time values — information is passed only via the concept of time. In [14] simple timing channels (STCs) were analyzed. An STC is a noiseless covert timing channel. The fact that capacity (C) of STCs can be calculated from both a mutual information—expected time (asymptotic) and an algebraic approach was of course first done by Shannon and further analyzed in [14]. Up until this paper, with one exception, the capacity of *noisy* timing channels could only be studied via the mutual information—expected time approach. The exception to this was the analysis of the timed Z-channel in [12]. In [12] it was shown that the capacity of a timed Z-channel, which is the simplest version of a timing channel with noise, could be given as the base two logarithm of the root of a polynomial. Thus mimicking Shannon's results for STCs. This ability to view the capacity in an algebraic sense is extremely appealing.

Once an algebraic formulation of capacity is obtained, one has at their disposal a tool that can be used to study and learn about all channels, as opposed

---

* Research supported by the Naval Research Laboratory.
[1] Unless noted otherwise all channels in this paper are both discrete and memoryless (DMC) (which also implies stationary distributions).

to just a particular channel. For instance, in [14], the algebraic approach makes many capacity relations obvious that would normally be obfuscated by viewing the capacity as simply the maximum of the ratio of the mutual information (in bits per symbol) to the expected time (units of symbols per unit time). Another advantage to the algebraic formulation is that it allows one to develop algorithms for calculating timed capacity and to prove they are correct before implemented. Currently, practitioners who determine the threat posed by covert timing channels within high assurance devices do not usually perform capacity calculations because of the mathematical complications involved. So while our knowledge of timed capacity continues to advance, it is simply theory that practitioners do not benefit from. But since the algebraic approach yields provably correct algorithms for calculating timed capacity, we can develop software that will perform these calculations for them, greatly improving the current methods used to analyze covert channels in high assurance devices.

This paper shows how to algebraically derive the capacity of a noisy timing channel with two input symbols and two output symbols. We call these $(2, 2)$ *timing channels,* with the idea that they are in general noisy being implicitly understood. This is an important result in the hopeful path to attempting to show that Shannon's capacity results in general have an algebraic solution. Aside from the interesting mathematical flavor of our results, we motivate the study of $(2,2)$ timing channels with two open problems from the high assurance computing literature. The first example is from the NRL Network Pump® system, and the second example is from the area of anonymous communications.

## 2    The NRL Pump

In [5] the Network Pump was discussed as a solution to a secure, reliable, pragmatic, and robust method of sending messages up from several "Lows" to several "Highs". When a Low sends to a High, message acknowledgments, or ACKs, are required for reliability. Unfortunately ACKs can be used to send information from High to Low, which is against our wishes (Low can talk to High, but High should not be able to talk to Low if we desire security). Even if the ACKs are stripped down, the timing of the ACKs forms the basis of a covert timing channel from a High to a Low. The Network Pump moderates the timing of the ACKs to moderate (but not eliminate entirely) the covert channel threat, while at the same time not degrading system performance in an intolerable manner. In this paper we will only concern ourselves with one Low and one High, the non-network version of the Pump [4]. This serves us well, because both the network and non-network versions of the Pump use the same basic algorithm. We will use the term Pump from now on.

The Pump works as follows: Low sends a message to the Pump, the Pump stores that message in the Pump buffer, the Pump sends an ACK to Low, when Low receives the ACK it sends its next message to the Pump (handshake protocol). High removes a message from the Pump buffer and sends an ACK (different from the ACK to Low) to the Pump. High also uses a handshake protocol to send its next message. The effectiveness of the Pump is how it sends the ACK to Low. The Pump uses a moving average $\mu_m$ of the past $m$ High ACK times. From this moving average it calculates a random variable with mean $\mu_m$ (a modified—so that it does not have an infinite tail—exponential random variable with mean $\mu_m$). The Pump sends the ACK to Low based on a draw from this random variable (of course there are some processing time and time-out modifications also).

**Fig. 1.** The NRL Pump

In brief, the Pump minimizes the covert channel threat that is opened up by using ACKs (to not use ACKs is not considered a wise choice in most applications). That is, instead of a Pump, if one used a store and forward buffer between Low and High with only a handshake protocol, High, by slowing down could allow the buffer to fill, and then the High ACK times would become transparent to Low with virtually no noise. We refer to this as the Full Buffer Channel. The Pump prevents this by forcing the Low ACK rate to be slaved to the High ACK rate. Furthermore, since a moving average in conjunction with a random variable is used to determine the Low ACK rate, the ability for High to covertly signal Low is severely compromised. However, the threat is not totally eliminated. We refer to the threat that is left as the *residual channel*.

For example if High ACKs quickly for $100 \cdot m$ ACKS and then slowly for $100 \cdot m$ ACKs, this change in rate can signal a bit to Low. Bounds on the residual channel capacity are given in [5], and the authors of [5] stated that the Pump meets those bounds. However, no one has been able to give closed form results for the residual channel capacity (see also [13]). This paper gives results in an important case. It is not clear that the residual channel capacity will ever be solved in its generality, nor is it clear that it is necessary to do so. However, this paper does shed some light on the problem and should be used with the capacity bounds as given in [5]. Notice that, to avoid the issue of the residual channel capacity others have modified the Pump to make it change Low ACK rates in "quantum" jumps [18]. While this does make the capacity trivial to calculate, it is not clear that it is a better solution since the quantum Pump approach may degrade system performance too much. So rather than modify the Pump algorithm, we improve the residual channel capacity analysis.

### 2.1 Simplified Residual Channel Analysis

We simplify the behavior of High to two modes; a "slow" ACK rate, and a "fast" ACK rate. This serves well to motivate the study of (2,2) timing channels. Our concern is the ability for High to change the tempo at which it ACK messages from the Pump, and have this change reflected in the Low ACK time. There are two situations to consider. The first is when High goes from slow to fast, and the second is when High goes from fast to slow.

Consider that High is ACKing at a slow rate $r_s$ and then goes to a fast rate $r_f$. It takes many ACKs for this to be reflected in the Low ACK because of the moving average construction of the Pump algorithm (in addition the noise of the random variable further confuses the situation). However, if High has been ACKing at the slow rate, and if the moving average is $m$, and on the next ACK High speeds up, $\mu_m$ decreases from $r_s$ to $\frac{m-1}{m}r_s + \frac{1}{m}r_f$. Of course, the larger $m$ is, the less this effect, and these values are the mean for the exponential variable. However, let us assume for the sake of argument and for a worse case bounding argument, that the draw from the exponential random variable does not introduce noise and that the values $r_s$ and $\frac{m-1}{m}r_s + \frac{1}{m}r_f$ can be perfectly reflected in the Low ACK rate. Then we would have an STC with the two output symbols being $\frac{m-1}{m}r_s + \frac{1}{m}r_f$ and $r_s$. However, the draw from the random variable does introduce noise. The range of output values is quantized by the clock precision on the Low side. There are in fact many output symbols. Also, the distribution of the output symbols changes because of the moving average construction. Therefore, we see that the actual channel is a noisy timing channel with two input symbols (we assume that High is restricted to two behaviors — fast and slow) $\iota_f$ and $\iota_s$, with many output symbols. In this paper we restrict our analysis to the simplified case of two output symbols $o_f$ and $o_s$, representing a fast output and a slow output, respectively. Keeping in mind that output symbols are formed from a moving average we see that if the input is $\iota_f$ ($\iota_s$) then the output will most likely be $o_f$ ($o_s$). Thus we have a (2,2) timing channel, and there need be no assumption of symmetry in the probabilities, due to the simplifications made and the behavior of the exponential random variable. Thus the (2,2) timing channel serves us well as a model of Pump behavior via a covert channel analysis of the residual channel. Algebraic, closed form knowledge of (2,2) timing channel capacity lets one have a better understanding of the trade-offs between different system parameters involved in the Pump.

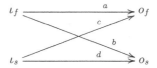

**Fig. 2.** Channel transition diagram

## 3   Anonymity

In this section we consider an example of a (2,2) timing channel that arises in anonymity and Mix theory.

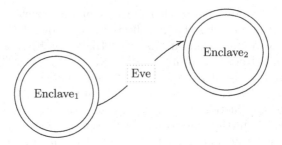

**Fig. 3.** Restricted Passive Adversary Model

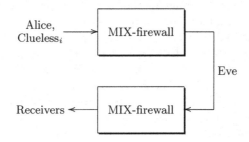

**Fig. 4.** MIX-firewalls with Restricted Passive Adversary

We will start by considering two types of simple Mixes: a threshold Mix and a timed Mix, and how a covert channel may exist in an anonymity system between a user Alice in a transmitting enclave and an eavesdropper Eve. In past papers covert channel analysis was only done for these two Mixes. In this paper we extend that analysis to more complex and realistic Mixes.

Consider a threshold Mix [19] of threshold $\theta \geq 2$. The Mix is the exit node of an enclave. Senders in the enclave send their messages to the Mix. The Mix has a buffer of size $\theta$ messages and as soon as the buffer is filled, the Mix fires. We assume that the eavesdropper Eve is monitoring the traffic leaving the Mix. The Mix is actually a Mix-firewall in that Eve does not have direct knowledge of what is happening behind the firewall, thus Eve is a restricted passive adversary (RPA) and that is why we refer to the Mix as a Mix-firewall. The Mix-firewall protects an enclave from prying eyes. In fact, we assume that we have two Mix-firewalls protecting the internal doings of two private enclaves, this is illustrated in Figure 3. The Mix on the receiving end is responsible for making sure messages get to their intended recipients and is not germane to our analysis. Eve can only count the number of messages passing from Enclave₁ to Enclave₂. We assume that in Enclave₁ there are benign users, referred to as Clueless$_i$ and a malicious user Alice who is attempting to covertly communicate with Eve by influencing the message count that Eve has as a result of Eve's traffic analysis. This is illustrated in Figure 4, and was the same model used in [16].

The other type Mix that has been previously analyzed from a covert channel standpoint is a timed Mix. The above description for a threshold Mix holds for a timed Mix with the exception that the Mix fires its messages off at specific time increments $t$, rather than when there are a certain number of messages in the Mix. It is an interesting but trivial fact that the covert channels in a threshold Mix are timing channels, and that the covert channels arising in a timed Mix are storage channels.

Real Mixes are more complicated than these simplistic threshold or timing Mixes. A building block for a Cottrel [19] Mix that arises in the Mixmaster remailer [11] system is a threshold and timed Mix [19, Sec. 3.4]. A threshold and timed Mix [19] has a threshold $n$ and a period $t$ such that the Mix fires every $t$ time units provided there are at least $n$ messages in the Mix buffer. With this design in mind, consider a malicious user Alice in Enclave$_1$ who is attempting to covertly communicate with the eavesdropper Eve via traffic analysis. For simplicity, we assume that only Eve has knowledge of when the Mix fires, ignoring the fact that Eve may know how many messages are leaving the Mix, provided there is no padding. Therefore the output alphabet for Eve is the time that the Mix fires. If Alice can send at most $m$ messages to the Mix in time interval $t$, but $m < n$, Alice cannot guarantee that the Mix will fire. If $m$ is close to $n$ and there are sufficiently many Clueless also sending messages, then there is a high probability that the Mix fires at time $t$, and a non-zero probability that the Mix fires at $2t$ or greater. Of course the value of $m$ and the number of Clueless, along with a probabilistic understanding of the Clueless behavior determine the actually probability of Eve receiving the symbol $t$ versus $2t$ or greater. For simplicity of our model however we assume that the values that Eve receives are either $t$ or $2t$. Now consider that Alice wishes to send the symbol $2t$ to Eve. Alice can do this by delaying or sending a small number of messages to the Mix buffer. Again though, the behavior of the Clueless can influence when the Mix fires. If the Clueless send $n$ messages to the Mix by time $t$, then the Mix will fire at time $t$ regardless of Alice's wishes. Therefore we see that we can model a simplification of the timing channel that exists in the threshold and timed Mix as a $(2, 2)$ timing channel also.

## 4   The $(2, 2)$ Timing Channel

Now we will mathematically analyze the $(2, 2)$ timing channel. The input symbols are the fast and slow inputs, $\{\iota_f, \iota_s\}$, and the output symbols are the fast and slow outputs, $\{o_f, o_s\}$. This means that if $o_f$ is received, the transmission took $t_1$ units of time; if $o_s$ is received, it took $t_2$ units of time. However, the channel matrix does not incorporate time, time is missing from it. The channel matrix simply represents the conditional probability relationships between the input and output symbols. That is $a = P(o_f|\iota_f), b = P(o_s|\iota_f), c = P(o_f|\iota_s), d = P(o_s|\iota_s)$. The input probabilities are represented by the random variable $X$, $P(X = i), i = 1, 2$, which we simplify to $x_i$ is such that $P(\iota_f) = x_1$ and $P(\iota_s) = x_2$. Similarly we have the random variable $Y$ such that $P(o_f) = y_1$ and $P(o_s) = y_2$. We see from the channel transition diagram in Fig. 2 that the channel matrix and probabilistic relations are given by

$$M = \begin{pmatrix} a & b \\ c & d \end{pmatrix}$$

We summarize the probabilities as follows

$$\bar{y} = \bar{x} \cdot \begin{pmatrix} a & b \\ c & d \end{pmatrix}$$

Letting $x = x_1$ and using the fact that $x_1 + x_2 = 1 = y_1 + y_2$ we have that $y_1 = (a - c)x + c$ and $y_2 = 1 - y_1$. To calculate the capacity[2] we want to maximize [23,12]

$$I_t = \ln 2 \left( \frac{H(Y) - H(Y|X)}{E(T)} \right)$$

over all possible distributions $(x_1, x_2)$. It is important to keep in mind that $I_t$ represents the mutual information in nats per unit time which is the ratio of the mutual information in bits per symbol $(H(Y) - H(Y|X))$ to the expected time ( $E(T)$ ) for a symbol to be output, with the ratio normalized by $\ln 2$. Since in our situation we can view $I_t$ as a function of one variable, the maximization problem reduces to maximizing the function $I_t : [0, 1] \to \mathbb{R}$ given by

$$I_t(x) = \frac{h_e\big(f(x)\big) - x h_e(a) - (1 - x) h_e(c)}{t_1 f(x) + (1 - f(x)) t_2}$$

where $h_e : [0, 1] \to \mathbb{R}$ is $h_e(x) = -x \ln x - (1 - x) \ln (1 - x)$ and $f : [0, 1] \to [0, 1] \subseteq \mathbb{R}$ is $f(x) = (a - c)x + c$. Notice that $a + b = c + d = 1$ so that our channel matrix is actually

$$M = \begin{pmatrix} a & 1 - a \\ c & 1 - c \end{pmatrix}$$

and $P(y_i) = P(t_i)$. Since [3] entropy $h_e(x)$ is *strictly concave*: that is for $x, x' \in [0, 1]$ and $p \in [0, 1]$, we have

$$h_e(px + (1 - p)x') \geq p h_e(x) + (1 - p) h_e(x')$$

with equality if and only if $p = 0$, $p = 1$ or $x = x'$.

**Lemma 1.** *The function $I_t$ achieves a maximum value, and that maximum value is assumed at a point in the interior of $[0, 1]$.*

---

[2] Capacity is usually expressed in bits per unit time. For ease of computation, we will often mutual information in terms of nats rather than bits. When we finally give the closed form expression for capacity we will consider it in bits per unit time. Of course, when we are maximizing mutual information w.r.t. unit time the only difference between nats and bits is a normalization constant of $1/\ln 2$. Also note that $(\ln 2)^{-1} h_e(x) := h(x)$. In addition log is the base two logarithm.

**Proof.** Since $[0, 1]$ is a compact set the continuous function $I_t$ always achieves a maximum on $[0, 1]$. If $a = c$, then $I_t \equiv 0$ (the choice of an input symbol does not influence the probability of the output symbol), and so $I_t$ assumes its maximum at a point in $(0, 1)$. Suppose now that $a \neq c$. By strict concavity of $h_e$,

$$I_t(x) > \frac{h_e(f(x)) - h_e(xa + (1-x)c)}{t_1 f(x) + (1 - f(x))t_2}$$

when $x \in (0, 1)$. Then $I_t(1/2) > 0$. However, $I_t(0) = 0 = I_t(1)$, so the maximum value of $I_t$ must be assumed at some point of $(0, 1)$.    □

**Observation:** In the proof of the last result, we implicitly established the following: $I_t \equiv 0$ iff $a = c$, and so a channel has positive capacity iff $a \neq c$. However, because $\det(M) = a - c$, this means that a $(2, 2)$ timing channel has positive capacity iff its noise matrix is invertible.

**Lemma 2.** *The equation $\dot{I}_t = 0$ has at least one solution in the interior of $[0, 1]$.*

**Proof.** The maximum of $I_t$ is assumed at a point in the interior of $[0, 1]$ and $I_t$ is differentiable.    □

**Theorem 1.** *If the noise matrix of a $(2, 2)$ timing channel is invertible, then there is a unique $x \in (0, 1)$ where $I_t$ assumes its maximum. This value of $x$ is the unique solution on $[0, 1]$ of the equation*

$$g(x) := e^{-K/\dot{f}}(f(x))^{t_2} - (1 - f(x))^{t_1} = 0 \tag{1}$$

*where $\varepsilon = t_2 - t_1$ and $K = (c\varepsilon - t_2)h_e(a) + (t_2 - a\varepsilon)h_e(c)$.*

**Proof.** Let
$$m(x) = h_e(f(x)) - x \cdot h_e(a) - (1 - x) \cdot h_e(c).$$

Notice that $t_1 f(x) + t_2(1 - f(x)) = t_2 - \varepsilon f(x)$. For the sake of readability, we write $\dot{I}_t(x)$ as $\dot{I}_t$, $f(x)$ as $f$, etc. Then since $\dot{I}_t = 0$,

$$(t_2 - \varepsilon f)\dot{m} - m(-\varepsilon \dot{f}) = 0$$

and
$$\dot{m} = (\ln(1 - f) - \ln(f))\dot{f} - h_e(a) + h_e(c)$$

Then $(t_2 - \varepsilon f)\dot{m}$ is equal to

$$t_2 \dot{f} \ln(1-f) - t_2 \dot{f} \ln(f) - t_2 h_e(a) + t_2 h_e(c) - \varepsilon f \dot{f} \ln(1-f) + \varepsilon f \dot{f} \ln(f) + \varepsilon f h_e(a) - \varepsilon f h_e(c)$$

and
$$m\varepsilon \dot{f} = -\varepsilon \dot{f} f \ln(f) - \varepsilon \dot{f}(1 - f) \ln(1 - f) - \varepsilon \dot{f} x h_e(a) - \varepsilon \dot{f} h_e(c) + x\varepsilon \dot{f} h_e(c)$$

When we add these expressions, the first term of $m\varepsilon\dot{f}$ cancels with the sixth term of $(t_2 - \varepsilon f)\dot{m}$, and the second term of $m\varepsilon\dot{f}$ added to the first and fifth terms of $(t_2 - \varepsilon f)\dot{m}$ reduces to $t_1\dot{f}\ln(1-f)$. Thus, our sum reduces to

$$\left(-t_2\dot{f}\ln(f) - t_2 h_e(a) + t_2 h_e(c) + \varepsilon f h_e(a) - \varepsilon f h_e(c)\right) +$$

$$\left(t_1\dot{f}\ln(1-f) - \varepsilon\dot{f}x h_e(a) - \varepsilon\dot{f}h_e(c) + x\varepsilon\dot{f}h_e(c)\right)$$

which simplifies to

$$\dot{f}\ln\left(\frac{(1-f)^{t_1}}{f^{t_2}}\right) + (c\varepsilon - t_2)h_e(a) + (t_2 - a\varepsilon)h_e(c)$$

Thus, solving $\dot{I}_t = 0$ is equivalent to finding a zero of $g(x)$ as defined in Eq. (1). We know such a zero exists by Lemma 2. Now suppose $g$ had two zeroes. Then its derivative would have to be zero at some point in between since $g(x)$ is smooth. But

$$\dot{g} = \dot{f}\left(e^{-K/\dot{f}}t_2(f(x))^{t_2-1} + t_1(1-f(x))^{t_1-1}\right)$$

is never zero since it is the product of $\dot{f} = a - c \neq 0$ and a positive number.    □

Notice that the uniqueness in the result above does not follow from the usual convexity/concavity arguments because $I_t$ is not known to be convex/concave.

**Theorem 2.** *Let* $x \in (0,1)$ *be the unique solution of Eq. 1 for a* $(2,2)$ *timing channel with an invertible noise matrix. Then its capacity, measured in bits per unit time, is*

$$\left(\frac{h(a)(c-1) + h(c)(1-a)}{a-c} - \log(f(x))\right) \cdot \frac{1}{t_1} \tag{2}$$

*or, equivalently*

$$\frac{1}{\ln(2)}\left(\frac{h_e(a)(c-1) + h_e(c)(1-a)}{a-c} - \ln(f(x))\right) \cdot \frac{1}{t_1} \tag{3}$$

**Proof.** Going backward from Eq. 1, we see that $x$ satisfies

$$-\frac{K}{t_1\dot{f}} + \frac{t_2}{t_1}\ln(f(x)) = \ln(1 - f(x)).$$

Substituting this into $I_t$, abbreviating $f(x)$ as $f$, we have

$$I_t(x) = \frac{-f\ln(f) - (1-f)\ln(1-f) - xh_e(a) - (1-x)h_e(c)}{t_1 f + (1-f)t_2}$$

$$= \frac{-f\ln(f) - (1-f)\left(-\frac{K}{t_1\dot{f}} + \frac{t_2}{t_1}\ln(f)\right) - xh_e(a) - (1-x)h_e(c)}{t_2 - \varepsilon f}$$

$$= \frac{-t_1\dot{f}f\ln(f) - (1-f)\left(-K + t_2\dot{f}\ln(f)\right) - t_1\dot{f}xh_e(a) - t_1\dot{f}\cdot(1-x)h_e(c)}{t_1\dot{f}\cdot(t_2 - \varepsilon f)}$$

Now using $\varepsilon + t_1 = t_2$, $(f - c) = \dot{f}x$, we get

$$I_t(x) = \frac{-t_1\dot{f}f\ln(f) - (1-f)\left(-K + (\varepsilon + t_1)\dot{f}\ln(f)\right) - t_1(f-c)h_e(a) - t_1(\dot{f} - (f-c))h_e(c)}{t_1\dot{f}\cdot(t_2 - \varepsilon f)}$$

$$= \frac{(1-f)K + \dot{f}\ln(f)(-t_1 f - (1-f)(\varepsilon + t_1)) - t_1(f-c)h_e(a) - t_1(a-f)h_e(c)}{t_1\dot{f}\cdot(t_2 - \varepsilon f)}$$

$$= \frac{(1-f)K + \dot{f}\ln(f)(\varepsilon f - t_2) - t_1(f-c)h_e(a) - t_1(a-f)h_e(c)}{t_1\dot{f}\cdot(t_2 - \varepsilon f)}$$

Now we focus on the expression $(1 - f)K - t_1(f - c)h_e(a) - t_1(a - f)h_e(c)$. It equals

$$h_e(a)((1-f)(c\varepsilon - t_2) - t_1(f-c)) + h_e(c)((1-f)(t_2 - a\varepsilon) - t_1(a-f))$$

which is

$$h_e(a)(c-1)(t_2 - \varepsilon f) + h_e(c)(1-a)(t_2 - \varepsilon f)$$

Putting everything together, we get

$$I_t(x) = \frac{(t_2 - \varepsilon f)\left(h_e(a)(c-1) + h_e(c)(1-a) - \dot{f}\ln(f)\right)}{t_1\dot{f}\cdot(t_2 - \varepsilon f)}$$

$$= \frac{h_e(a)(c-1) + h_e(c)(1-a)}{(a-c)t_1} - \frac{\ln(f)}{t_1}$$

Finally, because capacity is measured in bits, we convert our logarithms to base 2 by multiplying by $1/\ln(2)$.    $\square$

## 5    Trinomials

Shannon showed in his classic paper [20] that the capacity for a noiseless timing channel can be expressed as the log of the largest real zero of an associated characteristic polynomial with trivial coefficients. The only known work extending this to noisy timing channels has been given in [12]. This paper extends Shannon's polynomial approach to the general $(2, 2)$ timing channel. We shall discuss the timed Z-channel below in detail, but first we will show how to interpret our results in Eq. 1 as a trinomial, and then show how to re-express the capacity from Eq. 2.

Eq. 1 is almost in the correct form but we need to apply some tricks to it. Let $\alpha = e^{-K/\dot{f}}$, then we can rewrite Eq. 1 as

$$\alpha f^{t_2} - (1-f)^{t_1} = 0$$
$$\alpha f^{t_2} = (1-f)^{t_1}$$
$$\alpha^{1/t_1} f^{t_2/t_1} = 1 - f$$
$$\alpha^{1/t_1} f^{t_2/t_1} + f = 1$$

Now letting $\zeta = \alpha^{1/t_1}$ and $\gamma = f^{-1/t_1}$ we have

$$\zeta\gamma^{-t_2} + \gamma^{-t_1} = 1 \tag{4}$$

Recall we solve for the unique $x \in (0,1)$ such that $((a-c)x+c)^{-1/t_1}$ solves Eq. 4. Equivalently, $x = \frac{\gamma^{-t_1}-c}{a-c}$. The derivative of $R(\gamma) := \zeta\gamma^{-t_2} + \gamma^{-t_1} - 1$ with respect to $\gamma$ is negative, so if $R(\gamma)$ has a positive root, then it has a unique positive root. We know $R(\gamma)$ has a positive root because of the relationship of $x$ and $\gamma$, therefore its positive root is unique. Note that Shannon [20, p. 380] discusses the largest real root, when it could have been more precisely referred to as *the positive root* (which then must be the largest real root)[3].

Now let us manipulate Eq. 2 a bit. By using the elementary properties of logarithms and the fact that $f = (a-c)x+c$ we see that Eq. 2 can be rewritten as

$$C = \log\left\{ \left[ \left(a^a(1-a)^{1-a}\right)^{1-c} \left(c^c(1-c)^{1-c}\right)^{a-1} \right]^{1/t_1(a-c)} \cdot \gamma \right\} \tag{5}$$

or, equivalently

$$C = \log\left[ \left(a^a(1-a)^{1-a}\right)^{1-c} \left(c^c(1-c)^{1-c}\right)^{a-1} \right]^{1/t_1(a-c)} + \log\gamma \tag{6}$$

## 6   Algorithms for Calculating the Capacity

Given that the capacity calculation depends entirely on our ability to compute the solution of Eq. 1, we now consider methods for calculating it which are provably correct.

Eq. 1, $g(x) = 0$, is a nonlinear equation that in most cases has no closed form solution, meaning that its solution is not expressible by a formula consisting of elementary functions i.e. we must resort to the use of numerical methods to solve it. There is no single numerical method that we are aware of that can solve all equations with solutions. The ability of a program or software package to solve an equation depends on the numerical method it uses and whether the method suits the particular equation. To efficiently calculate capacity in a non

---

[3] Shannon considers for $n > 1$ the equation $X^{-t_1} + X^{-t_2} + \ldots X^{-t_n} = 1$. Let $f(X) = \left(\sum_{i=1}^n X^{-t_i}\right) - 1$, since $\lim_{X\to 0^+} f(X) = \infty$ and $\lim_{X\to\infty} f(X) = -1$ we see that $f(x)$ has a positive zero. Since $\frac{df(X)}{dX} = -\sum_{i=1}^n t_i X^{-(t_i+1)} < 0$ we see that there is only one positive zero. Therefore, when Shannon referred to the "largest real solution," a more precise statement would have been "the unique positive zero." In fact, since $f(1) > 0$, this unique positive zero is in fact greater than one (which is to be expected from our Thm. 2). Notice too that Shannon's desire to also use difference equations required the times $t_i > 0$ to be positive integers, whereas our results only require the times $t_i > 0$ to be positive reals.

ad hoc manner we require a numerical method that converges for all $(2, 2)$ timing channels. *Because we have taken an algebraic approach to the problem of timed capacity, we are in the position to obtain exactly that.*

One way to calculate the unique solution of equation (1), $g(x) = 0$ is to iterate the function

$$\phi(x) = x - \frac{h(x)}{M}$$

where the constant $M = t_2 e^{-K/\dot{f}} + t_1$ and $h(x) = e^{-K/\dot{f}} x^{t_2} - (1 - x)^{t_1}$. It is shown in [8] that this algorithm converges to the unique zero starting from *any* $x \in [0, 1]$. Another method we have developed is a bracketing method i.e. we start with an interval that contains the solution and each iteration reduces the length of the interval by at least fifty percent. What is notable about this method is that it is not the bisection method. In fact, it *outdoes* the bisection method at *every* iteration. Again, the importance of these methods is that they are provably correct in all cases. Without them, we could not be sure of which method to use, or which initial guess to begin with.

## 7   Special Cases

We will now show how our results apply to some well-known special cases.

### 7.1   The Noiseless Channel

Let us see what happens to Eq. 4 and Eq. 6 when the channel is noiseless, that is the channel matrix $M$ collapses to the identity matrix.

$$\iota_f \xrightarrow{\hspace{2cm} 1 \hspace{2cm}} o_f = t_1$$

$$\iota_s \xrightarrow{\hspace{2cm} 1 \hspace{2cm}} o_s = t_2$$

Since $\zeta = \alpha^{1/t_1} = \left(e^{-K/\dot{f}}\right)^{1/t_1}$, $K = -t_2 h_e(1) + t_1 h_e(0) = 0$, and $\dot{f}(x) = 1$ we see that Eq. 4 reduces to

$$\gamma^{-t_2} + \gamma^{-t_1} = 1$$

and the capacity is

$$C = \log \gamma$$

The above two equations of course are exactly what Shannon gave [20, p. 380].

## 7.2    The Timed Z-Channel

We start by showing that our results extend the results in [12], for the timed Z-channel. For the timed Z-channel we have $c = 0 < a$, so $K = -t_2 h_e(a)$, $f(x) = ax$, so Eq. 1 becomes

$$e^{\ln(a^a b^{b/a})^{t_2}} (ax)^{t_2} - (1 - ax)^{t_1} = 0$$

and we have

$$(a^a b^{b/a})^{t_2} (ax)^{t_2} - (1 - ax)^{t_1} = 0$$
$$(a^a b^{b/a})^{t_2} (ax)^{t_2} = (1 - ax)^{t_1}$$
$$(a^a b^{b/a})^{t_2/t_1} (ax)^{t_2/t_1} = 1 - ax$$
$$(a^a b^{b/a})^{t_2/t_1} (ax)^{t_2/t_1} + ax = 1$$

now letting $ax = \gamma^{-t_1}$, the above can be expressed

$$(a^a b^{b/a})^{t_2/t_1} \gamma^{-t_2} + \gamma^{-t_1} = 1$$

which is the same as [12, Eq. 1].

Now let us apply our capacity result as given above to the timed Z-Channel. By Thm. 2 we see that capacity is $\log(ab^{b/a})^{1/t_1} (ax)^{-1/t_1}$ which agrees with [12, Thm. 1]. Also note that [12, Thm. 1] emphasizes the uniqueness of positive $\gamma$ which is equivalent to the uniqueness of $x \in (0,1)$. Unfortunately the authors of [12] did not include the uniqueness proof, whereas we have proved it above in Thm. 1, provided that $a \neq c$ (which holds for the timed Z-channel).

## 7.3    Timed Binary Symmetric Channel

In the case of a timed *binary symmetric channel*, where the probability of a bit flip is $p$, we have $a = 1 - p = d$ and $b = p = c$, so Eq. 1 takes the form

$$u^{t_2} - (k - u)^{t_1} = 0$$

where $u = f(x)e^{h_e(p)}$ and $k = e^{h_e(p)}$. The capacity of this channel easily follows from Eq. 2

$$C = \frac{1}{t_1} \left[ -\log\left((1 - 2p)x + p\right) - h(p) \right] \tag{7}$$

## 7.4    The Untimed Case

We refer to the (2,2) timing channel where $t_1 = t_2$ as the untimed (2,2) channel.

**Untimed and $a = c$:** Since $a = c$ we cannot use our results. However, in this situation, the capacity is zero, since the receiver gains no information when it receives a symbol. A channel such as this is called a *useless* or *zero-capacity* channel [1].

**Untimed and $a \neq c$:** Since $\varepsilon = 0$, $K = t_2(h_e(c) - h_e(a))$, so Eq. 1 is now

$$e^{t_2(h_e(a)-h_e(c))/(a-c)}(f(x))^{t_2} - (1 - f(x))^{t_1} = 0$$

Taking logs of both sides and simplifying yields

$$\ln\left(\frac{1 - f(x)}{f(x)}\right) = \frac{h_e(a) - h_e(c)}{a - c}$$

which is the equation we have to solve to calculate the capacity in the untimed case. As one would expect, the dependence on time is eliminated when $\varepsilon = 0$ regardless of the value of $t_2 = t_1$. Now we let $\beta = \frac{h_e(a)-h_e(c)}{a-c}$, and exponentiating both sides gives us

$$f(x) = \frac{1}{1 + e^\beta}$$

which results in

$$x(a, c) = \frac{1}{a - c}\left(\frac{1}{1 + e^\beta} - c\right) \tag{8}$$

Up to a trivial manipulation this is the same simple closed form expression for $x$ for the untimed binary input binary output channel as reported by Silverman [21, Eq. 6]. Note, as in [21] it is trivial to show that $x(a, c) = 1 - x(c, a) = x(1 - a, 1 - c)$. Notice that $x$ is a function defined on the unit square with its diagonal removed. Using Eq. 8, Eq. 2 and the fact that $e^\beta = 2^{\left(\frac{h(a)-h(c)}{a-c}\right)}$, reveals that the capacity in units of bits per symbol (since $t_1 = t_2$) is (see [21, Eq. 5])

$$C(a, c) = \frac{h(a)(c - 1) + h(c)(1 - a)}{a - c} + \log\left(1 + 2^{\left(\frac{h(a)-h(c)}{a-c}\right)}\right) \tag{9}$$

To compare our capacity expression Eq. 9 with Ash's [1, Eq. 3.3.5], we first find the inverse of our channel matrix

$$M^{-1} = \frac{1}{ad - bc}\begin{pmatrix} d & -b \\ -c & a \end{pmatrix} = \frac{1}{a - c}\begin{pmatrix} 1 - c & a - 1 \\ -c & a \end{pmatrix}$$

We let $q_{ij}$ be the entry from the $i$th row and $j$th column of $M^{-1}$. Now, working backwards from Eq. 9 and letting $\Delta = a - c$ we have

$$
\begin{aligned}
C &= \log\left\{\left(2^{\frac{1}{\Delta}[h(a)(c-1)+h(c)(1-a)]}\right)\left(1 + 2^{\frac{1}{\Delta}[h(a)-h(c)]}\right)\right\} \\
&= \log\left\{\left(2^{\frac{1}{\Delta}[h(a)(c-1)+h(c)(1-a)]}\right) + \left(2^{\frac{1}{\Delta}[h(a)(c-1)+h(c)(1-a)]}\right)\left(2^{\frac{1}{\Delta}[h(a)-h(c)]}\right)\right\} \\
&= \log\left\{\left(2^{\frac{1}{\Delta}[h(a)(c-1)+h(c)(1-a)]}\right) + \left(2^{\frac{1}{\Delta}[ch(a)-ah(c)]}\right)\left(2^{\frac{1}{\Delta}[-h(a)+h(a)+h(c)-h(c)]}\right)\right\} \\
&= \log\left\{\left(2^{\frac{1}{\Delta}[h(a)(c-1)+h(c)(1-a)]}\right) + \left(2^{\frac{1}{\Delta}[ch(a)-ah(c)]}\right)\right\} \\
&= \log\sum_{j=1}^{2} 2^{-\left[\sum_{i=1}^{2} q_{ji}h(Y|X=i)\right]}
\end{aligned}
$$

which is a classic closed form result for capacity as given by Ash [1, Eq. 3.3.5] for a 2x2 channel matrix. Also note that one can easily show (as in [21]) that $C(1-a, 1-c) = C(a, c) = C(c, a)$.

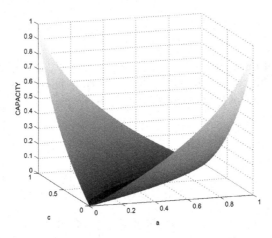

**Fig. 5.** Plot of Eq. 9: Capacity for the untimed (2,2) channel

**Untimed Capacity:** Using our results gives Fig. 5 which illustrates zero capacity along the diagonal and the symmetric nature of capacity. The fact that the capacity appears to be continuous is not accidental and will be discussed later in the paper. What is fascinating is that $x$, in both the timed and untimed cases, is not continuously extendible to the entire unit square. We will prove this later.

**Binary Symmetric Channel:** An untimed (2,2) channel is called a *binary symmetric channel* iff $a = 1 - p$ (equivalently $c = p$), so the channel matrix is

$$M = \begin{pmatrix} 1-p & p \\ p & 1-p \end{pmatrix}$$

The probability of a "bit flip" is thus $c$. (Since time is no longer a factor we use 1 and 2 to index the symbols rather that $f$ and $s$ as in the general (2,2) timing channel.) Applying Eq. 5 we obtain the well-known [1, Eq. 3.3.1] result that the

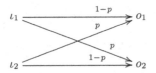

**Fig. 6.** Binary Symmetric Channel

capacity, in bits per symbol, for a binary symmetric channel is $1 - h(c)$ with the solution to Eq. 1 being $x = \frac{1}{2}$. Of course using $x = \frac{1}{2}$ along with $t_1 = t_2 = 1$ and Eq. 7, we also obtain this capacity result.

**Untimed Z-Channel:** Note that for the untimed Z-Channel we trivially obtain from Eq. 9 the result [24,22] that capacity is $\log\left(1 + (1-p)p^{\frac{p}{(1-p)}}\right)$ where $p$ is the probability of the noisy symbol being sent incorrectly.

## 8   The Discontinuous Nature of Capacity Achieving Distributions

In this section, we will use our algebraic characterization of capacity to prove an intriguing result for $(2,2)$ timing channels. Recall Eq. 1

$$e^{-K/\dot{f}}(f(x))^{t_2} - (1 - f(x))^{t_1} = 0$$

where $K = (c\varepsilon - t_2)h_e(a) + (t_2 - a\varepsilon)h_e(c)$ and $\varepsilon = t_2 - t_1$, and the formula for capacity Eq. 3:

$$C(a,c) = \frac{1}{\ln(2)} \cdot \left(\frac{h_e(a)(c-1) + h_e(c)(1-a)}{(a-c)} - \ln(f(x))\right) \cdot \frac{1}{t_1}$$

By solving for $x$ as a function of $a$ and $c$ we have,

$$x(a,c) = \frac{1}{a-c} \cdot \left(e^{\lambda(a,c)} - c\right), \tag{10}$$

where

$$\lambda(a,c) := \frac{h_e(a)(c-1) + h_e(c)(1-a)}{a-c} - C(a,c)\,t_1\ln 2$$

We see that the input distribution which achieves capacity varies continuously as a function of $a$ and $c$ on the set $\{(a,c) \in [0,1] \times [0,1] : a \neq c\}$. Note that $C(a,c)$ is a continuous function on the entire unit square (motivation for this can be seen in [16, sec. A.1] and [17, Thm. 8], whereas a proof is shown in [9]). We find the following theorem remarkable:

**Theorem 3.** *The function $x$ has no continuous extension to the entire unit square.*

Our goal in this section is to prove this new result. We will do so by showing that neither

$$\lim_{(a,c)\to(0^+,0^+)} x(a,c) \quad \text{nor} \quad \lim_{(a,c)\to(1^-,1^-)} x(a,c)$$

exists. Notice that the notation $(a,c) \to (0^+,0^+)$ means that we are free to approach the origin along any path provided we are within the unit square; the notation $(a,c) \to (1^-,1^-)$ says the same of $(1,1)$. The reason we excluded the exterior of the unit square from consideration presently is that $a$ and $c$ are probabilities in the noise matrix of a $(2,2)$ channel. We show that $\lim\limits_{(a,c)\to(0^+,0^+)} x(a,c)$ does not exist by showing that $\lim\limits_{a\to0^+} x(a,0) \neq \lim\limits_{c\to0^+} x(0,c)$ and we show that $\lim\limits_{(a,c)\to(1^-,1^-)} x(a,c)$ does not exists by showing that $\lim\limits_{c\to1^-} x(1,c) \neq \lim\limits_{a\to1^-} x(a,1)$. We calculate these limits by taking the unusual approach of viewing $x(a,c)$ as a function of $C(a,c)$. This we call an *implicit analysis*.

## 8.1  $a \to 0^+$, $c = 0$

This is Golomb's limit [2]. From Eq. 10 we have,

$$x(a,0) = (1-a)^{(1-a)/a} \cdot e^{-C(a,0)t_1 \ln 2.}$$

Now, because C is a continuous function of $(a,c) \in [0,1] \times [0,1]$, as $a \to 0^+$, $C(a,0) \to C(0,0) = 0$. Thus, $x(a,0)$ is the product of two functions which have limits as $a \to 0^+$, which means that $x$ has a limit as $a \to 0^+$. This limit is

$$\lim_{a\to0^+} x(a,0) = \lim_{a\to0^+} (1-a)^{(1-a)/a} \cdot \lim_{a\to0^+} e^{-C(a,0)t_1 \ln 2} = \lim_{a\to0^+} \frac{(1-a)^{1/a}}{1-a} \cdot 1 = \frac{1}{e} \cdot 1 = \frac{1}{e}$$

## 8.2  $a = 0$, $c \to 0^+$

From Eq. 10,

$$x(0,c) = 1 - \frac{(1-c)^{1/c}}{1-c} \cdot e^{-C(0,c)t_1 \ln 2}$$

As $c \to 0^+$, we obtain a limit of $1 - (1/e)$.

## 8.3  $a = 1$, $c \to 1^-$

This case bears a fundamental difference to the previous two. We not only use the expression for $x(a,c)$ but also the equation it satisfies. First, we know that $f(x) = (1-c)x + c$ and from Eq. 1, we have that

$$f(x) = \left((1-f(x))^{t_1} e^{K/(1-c)}\right)^{1/t_2}$$

Since $K = t_1 h_e(c)$, this tells us that

$$(1-c)x + c = \left((1-x)^{t_1} c^{(t_1 c)/(c-1)}\right)^{1/t_2}$$

Substituting this into the expression for capacity and solving for $x$ yields a new expression for $x(1,c)$,

$$x(1,c) = 1 - c^{c/(1-c)} \cdot e^{-C(1,c)t_2 \ln 2.}$$

If we now change variables from $c$ to $d = 1 - c$, we get

$$\lim_{c\to1^-} x(1,c) = \lim_{d\to0^+} x(1,1-d) = 1 - \lim_{d\to0^+} \frac{(1-d)^{1/d}}{(1-d)} \cdot 1 = 1 - \frac{1}{e}$$

## 8.4  $a \to 1^-$, $c = 1$

This proof follows the argument of the last. We know that $f(x) = (a-1)x + 1$ satisfies

$$f(x) = \left( e^{K/(a-1)}(1 - f(x))^{t_1} \right)^{1/t_2}$$

where $K = -t_1 h_e(a)$, so substituting this into the expression for capacity yields a new expression for $x(a, 1)$,

$$x(a, 1) = a^{a/(1-a)} \cdot e^{-C(a,1)t_2 \ln 2}$$

whose limit as $a \to 1^-$ is $1/e$.

## 8.5  The Extendability of $x(a, c)$

The first limit we considered was originally proved by Golomb in the untimed case and later extended to the timed case by Moskowitz et al. Note that Silverman [21] has noted the discontinuous behavior of $x$ for the untimed $(2,2)$ channel but his justification seems incomplete. The calculations we have just given in these four proofs unify both of these results. However, we have gone a step further here, having shown that neither Golomb's untimed limit nor Moskowitz's timed limit exists in the two dimensional sense: along one path to $(0,0)$ we obtain $1/e$, while along a different path to $(0,0)$ we obtain $1 - 1/e$, with similar behavior for $(1,1)$. This proves that the function $x$ is not extendible to a continuous function on the set of noise matrices: the largest set on which it can be continuous is $[0, 1] \times [0, 1] \setminus \{(0,0), (1,1)\}$. This is quite a perplexing result mathematically but it also teaches us something we did not previously know about timing channels.

Suppose that we have a timing channel with noise matrix $M$ and capacity achieving distribution $x$. If we vary $M$ ever so slightly in the sense of Euclidean distance, thereby obtaining a new channel with matrix $M_\varepsilon$, it would seem reasonable that the original distribution $x$ would be a good approximation to the capacity achieving distribution $x_\varepsilon$ for the new channel $M_\varepsilon$. It is exactly the fact that $x$ is not continuously extendible to the unit square which proves that this is not true! For instance, two positive capacity channels 1 and 2 can have noise matrices as close as one likes, and their capacity achieving distributions $x_1$ and $x_2$ can be at nearly a maximum distance i.e. $x_1 \approx (1/e, 1 - 1/e)$ versus $x_2 \approx (1 - 1/e, 1/e)$. Notice that this is the farthest apart two positive capacity achieving distributions for the untimed $(2,2)$ channel can be by the result of Majani and Rumsey[7]. We hope to find an alternate version of their proof using our results in future work. Our results are certainly consistent with theirs for the untimed $(2,2)$ channel. Even though the times in a general $(2,2)$ timing channel may assume any value, the limits $1/e$ and $1 - 1/e$ are recurring. It is as though they are fundamental constants in information theory whose exact significance is yet to be uncovered. The Majani and Rumsey results do not hold in general for $(2,2)$ timed channels as discussed for special cases in [12] and [15, Sec. 5].

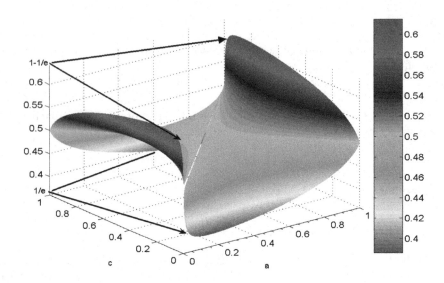

**Fig. 7.** Plot of Eq. 8: $x(a, c)$ for the untimed (2,2) channel

One question that remains concerns the continuous extendability to the interior of the diagonal. We have not proven that $x$ can be extended to a continuous function on $\{(a, c) : a = c \in (0, 1)\}$, but we do conjecture that this is the case, at which points we expect its value to be $x(a, c) = 1/2$. If this result were true, the diagonal would provide yet another path to $(0, 0)$ (and also to $(1, 1)$), with yet another distinct limit, in this case $1/2$.

Fig. 7 is a plot of $x(a, c)$ for the untimed (2,2) channel. It should be viewed in conjunction with Fig. 5 for a better appreciation. One can see the discontinuity that we have discussed at $(a, c) = (0, 0)$ or $(1, 1)$. Furthermore, we see that when the capacity is one, in other words, when $(a, c) = (1, 0)$ or $(0, 1)$, that $x(a, c) = 1/2$. We also see that the Majani and Rumsey limits illustrated along with the hypothesied behavior of $x = 1/2$ along the diagonal $\{(a, c) : a = c \in (0, 1)\}$.

Aside from teaching us these new things about timing channels, the 'implicit' arguments we have given in this section, precisely because they do not require that we have explicit expressions for either $x$ or $C(a, c)$, hold great promise for future work in analyzing the asymptotic behavior of channels in higher dimensions.

## 9    Conclusions and Future Work

We have given algebraic results concerning the capacity for (2,2) timing channels. Our results are directly applicable to the study of the residual channel in the Network Pump and to traffic analysis in anonymity systems. Our results show a direct relationship between the noise characteristics and the channel capacity. This can allow one to inject spurious noise into a high-assurance system in a judicious manner to lessen covert channel capacity, while at the same time not affecting system performance too much. This stands in contrast to padding message traffic to the maximum extent to remove a covert channel, or to making the moving average size too large in the Pump so as to be not responsive to system load.

Our paper is a first step in a plan we have to use the algebraic characteristics of the channel noise to lead us to sensible engineering solutions for problems which arise in the analysis of high assurance devices. For instance, our results will enable the development of a tool that will assist the practitioner in analyzing covert channels. Of particular note is the surprising result concerning the discontinuous nature of the capacity achieving distribution. This result tells us that channel coding based upon the noise matrix may behave in a 'chaotic' manner. This fact takes us very much by surprise. We plan to study the algebraic properties of channel matrices to determine whether there is an physical phenomena behind the appearance of $1/e$ in the asymptotic behavior of the capacity achieving distribution. We have started a study of algebraic information theory for untimed $(2, 2)$ channels in [10].

Please note that we plan to remove the restriction of binary inputs and binary outputs in future work. We have some preliminary results in this light.

## Acknowledgments

Dla naszych teściowych, and Dr. Gerard Allwein, for not being one of them. We also thank the reviewers for their helpful comments.

## References

1. Ash, R.B.: Information Theory. Dover (1965)
2. Golomb, S.: The limiting behavior of the Z-channel. IEEE/ Transactions on Information theory 26, 372 (1980)
3. Jones, G.A., Jones, J.M.: Information and Coding Theory. Springer, Heidelberg (2000)
4. Kang, M.H., Moskowitz, I.S.: A Pump for Rapid, Reliable, Secure Communication. In: 1st ACM Conference on Computer and Communications Security. ACM Press, New York (1994)
5. Kang, M.H., Moskowitz, I.S., Lee, D.C.: A Network Pump. IEEE Transactions on Software Engineering 22(5), 329–338 (1996)
6. Lampson, B.W.: A note on the confinement problem. Communications of the ACM 16(10), 613–615 (1973)
7. Majani, E.E., Rumsey, H.: Two results on binary input discrete memoryless channels. In: IEEE International Symposium on Information Theory, p. 104 (June 1991)
8. Martin, K.: NRL memorandum report: 5540–06-8945 (March 24, 2006)
9. Martin, K.: The simulation of covert timing channels (preprint 2006)
10. Martin, K., Moskowitz, I.S., Allwein, G.: Algebraic information theory for binary channels. In: Proc. 22nd Conference on the Mathematical Foundations of Programming Semantics. Electronic Notes in Theoretical Computer Science (2006)

11. Moeller, U., Cottrell, L., Palfrader, P., Sassaman, L.: Mixmaster protocol version 2. Internet-Draft (2003) `http://www.abditum.com/mixmaster-spec.txt`
12. Moskowitz, I.S., Greenwald, S., Kang, M.H.: An analysis of the timed Z-channel. IEEE Transactions on Information Theory 44(7), 3162–3168 (1998)
13. Moskowitz, I.S., Kang, M.H.: Discussion of a statistical channel. In: Proceedings 1994 IEEE-IMS Workshop on Information Theory and Statistics, Alexandria, VA, USA, p. 95. IEEE Computer Society Press, Los Alamitos (1994)
14. Moskowitz, I.S., Miller, A.R.: Simple timing channels. In: IEEE Computer Society Symposium on Research in Security and Privacy, pp. 56–64, Oakland, CA, (May 16-18, 1994)
15. Moskowitz, I.S., Newman, R.E.: Timing channels, anonymity, mixes, and spikes. In: Proc. Int. Conf. on Advances in Computer Science and Technology—ACST 2006 Puerto Vallerta, Mexico, 2006. IASTED (2006)
16. Moskowitz, I.S., Newman, R.E., Crepeau, D.P., Miller, A.R.: Covert channels and anonymizing networks. In: ACM WPES, pp. 79–88, Washington (October 2003)
17. Moskowitz, I.S., Newman, R.E., Crepeau, D.P., Miller, A.R.: A detailed mathematical analysis of a class of covert channels arising in certain anonymizing networks. Memorandum Report NRL/MRL/5540–03-8691, NRL (August 2003)
18. Ogurtsov, N., Orman, H., Schroeppel, R., O'Malley, S., Spatscheck, O.: Experimental results of covert channel limitation in one-way communication systems. In: Proc. IEEE 1997 Symposium on Network and Distributed System Security, pp. 2–15. IEEE, New York (1997)
19. Serjantov, A., Dingledine, R., Syverson, P.: From a trickle to a flood: Active attacks on several mix types. In: Petitcolas, F.A.P. (ed.) IH 2002. LNCS, vol. 2578, pp. 36–52. Springer, Heidelberg (2003)
20. Shannon, C.E.: A mathematical theory of communication. Bell Systems Technical Journal 27, 379–423, 623–656 (1948)
21. Silverman, R.A.: On binary channels and their cascades. IRE Transactions on Information Theory 1(3), 19–27 (1955)
22. Tallini, L.G., Al-Bassam, S., Bose, B.: On the capacity and codes for the Z-channel. In: Proc. ISIT 2002, pp. 422 (2002)
23. Verdú, S.: On channel capacity per unit cost. IEEE Transactions on Information Theory 36(5), 1019–1030 (1992)
24. Verdú, S.: Channel Capacity, Chapter 73.5. The Electrical Engineering Handbook, CRC Press (1997)

# A Computational Model for
# Watermark Robustness

André Adelsbach[1], Stefan Katzenbeisser[2], and Ahmad-Reza Sadeghi[3]

[1] Horst Görtz Institute for IT Security, Ruhr-Universität Bochum
andre.adelsbach@nds.rub.de
[2] Institut für Informatik, TU München
katzenbe@in.tum.de
[3] Horst Görtz Institute for IT Security, Ruhr-Universität Bochum
sadeghi@crypto.rub.de

**Abstract.** Multimedia security schemes often combine cryptographic schemes with information hiding techniques such as steganography or watermarking. Example applications are dispute resolving, proof of ownership, (asymmetric/anonymous) fingerprinting and zero-knowledge watermark detection. The need for formal security definitions of watermarking schemes is manifold, whereby the core need is to provide suitable abstractions to construct, analyse and prove the security of applications on top of watermarking schemes. Although there exist formal models and definitions for information-theoretic and computational security of cryptographic and steganographic schemes, they cannot simply be adapted to watermarking schemes due to the fundamental differences among these approaches. Moreover, the existing formal definitions for watermark security still suffer from conceptual deficiencies.

In this paper we make the first essential steps towards an appropriate formal definition of watermark robustness, the core security property of watermarking schemes: We point out and discuss the shortcomings of the existing proposals and present a formal framework and corresponding definitions that cover those subtle aspects not considered in the existing literature. Our definitions provide suitable abstractions that are compatible to cryptographic definitions allowing security proofs of composed schemes.

## 1  Motivation

Multimedia applications deploy various cryptographic and watermarking techniques to maintain security. Typical application scenarios are dispute resolving, proof of authorship and asymmetric and anonymous fingerprinting.

In this context, the security analysis and security proofs for the resulting composed schemes require a suitable formal framework and reasonable security definitions. Modern cryptography already uses established formal models and definitions for information-theoretic and computational security. Inspired by cryptographic methodology similar approaches have been proposed for

J. Camenisch et al. (Eds.): IH 2006, LNCS 4437, pp. 145–160, 2007.

steganography [1,2,3,4]. In contrast, less investigation has been done with this regard for watermarking schemes, and the existing approaches do not cover the subtle aspects essential for reasonable formal security definitions, analysis and abstraction of watermarking schemes.

The need for formal definitions of watermarking schemes, and their most notable properties, such as robustness, false-positive and false-negative probabilities, is manifold: first, one requires formal definitions as suitable abstractions to build, analyse and prove the security of applications on top of watermarking schemes. Second, one requires suitable formal definitions to prove the robustness of watermarking schemes. Furthermore, such definitions provide valuable guidance and basis in the development of provably robust watermarking schemes.

One should note that steganography, although likewise watermarking a means for information hiding, differs from watermarking with respect to various aspects. The most important difference concerns their requirements: In steganography there is a strong hiding requirement, stating that an adversary cannot even detect the *presence* of some stego-message in stego-data. In watermarking, however, one usually does want to prevent watermarks to be detectable by an adversary.[1] Instead, the challenging core property, distinguishing watermarking schemes from other cryptographic or data-hiding primitives, is the robustness property, which guarantees that a watermark cannot be removed without significantly distorting the stego-data and making it useless.[2] Due to the fundamental difference between steganography and digital watermarking, one cannot simply adapt recent definitions of steganographic security [3,4].

In this paper, we point out and discuss the shortcomings of the existing proposals for watermark security definitions as well as the subtle aspects/parameters that these proposals do not cover. In fact, our review shows that even the meaning of watermark security is still not well understood, mainly because many authors do not focus on the main, distinguishing security property of watermarking schemes, which cannot be achieved by applying complementary cryptographic measures: *robustness*. We propose formal (and intuitive) definitions for watermarking schemes, including robustness, that (i) incorporate these aspects/parameters and (ii) can be used as a suitable abstraction for security proofs of composed schemes in the context of various applications.

## 2    Related Work

In recent years, there has been a remarkable body of literature on definitions for robustness and security of watermarking schemes. Most of the existing proposals

---

[1] One may require watermarking schemes to provide an optional secrecy property, requiring that adversary cannot obtain any information about the concrete watermark embedded in the stego-data. This requirement is very different and much easier to achieve (e.g., by using standard encryption schemes) than the strong hiding property which is at heart of steganographic systems.

[2] Note, that we do not consider fragile watermarking schemes, because fragility can be achieved quite easily, using cryptographic primitives.

distinguish between the security and robustness of a watermark. In this context robustness concerns the amount of information on watermark that is revealed to an adversary, whereas the security often concerns the information revealed on secret embedding key. The corresponding definitions are based on information-theoretical or cryptographic methodologies.

Mittelholzer [2] proposed the first formal model, which defines *information-theoretic robustness* in terms of mutual information[3]: a robust watermarking scheme is defined to maximise the mutual information $I(WM; W''|K^{det})$ between the watermark $WM$ and the distorted stego-data $W''$, when given the detection key $K^{det}$. The maximum is defined over all allowed channels (adversaries), transforming watermarked data $W'$ into distorted data $W''$.

Kalker [5] introduced reasonable but informal definitions of watermark robustness and watermark security:[4] watermark robustness is defined as the property that the capacity of the watermarking channel degrades as a smooth function of the degradation of the stego-data. Security is defined as the inability of an adversary to remove[5], detect (or estimate), write or modify any bit of the watermark. The notion of "security" is very broad and, therefore, too strong for most applications of watermarking schemes.

Barni et al. [6] proposed a general security framework for watermarking systems, where they measure security by quantifying the information on the secret watermarking key that is leaked through stego-data the adversary can observe. The authors define security in terms of a two party game between a correct party and the adversary. The rules of the game determine the a-priori information given to the adversary and which he may use to win the game, i.e., break the respective security property of the watermarking scheme. In principle, this is a common approach in cryptography when defining security properties of cryptographic schemes. However, in [6] the authors distinguish between *fair* and *unfair* adversaries: according to the games' rules fair adversaries only use the a-priori information, whereas unfair adversaries try to gain secret information and take advantage of this knowledge. The distinction between fair and unfair adversaries is uncommon and restricts the adversary's strategies covered by the definitions and, thereby, weakens the definition significantly. For instance, the definition does not cover adversaries who exploit weaknesses of the watermarking scheme to get information about the watermarking key, although such adversaries are defined as fair in the framework of [6]. The authors argue that the leaked information will make it easier for an unfair adversary to attack the system's robustness (degrade the watermark channel) and, therefore, use it as a measure for the security of watermarking schemes. This intuition is likely to hold in most cases, but it is important to note that the converse does not hold, i.e., there are watermarking schemes with poor robustness, but which do not leak

---

[3] The mutual information $I(X;Y)$ between $X$ and $Y$ is defined as the reduction of entropy that $Y$ provides about $X$.

[4] Kalker models a watermarking scheme as a multiplexed communication system that multiplexes the original data channel and the watermark channel.

[5] Therefore, security, according to Kalker's definition, implies robustness.

any information on the secret watermarking key.[6] Hence, we conclude that the information leaked on the secret watermarking key is not a suitable measure for the robustness/security of the watermarking scheme. Furthermore, one cannot formally define and distinguish between fair and unfair adversaries.

Cayre et al. [7] focus on the security of watermarking schemes and do not consider security against application-level attacks, such as invertibility and copy-attacks. Although it is a good approach to narrow the definition to cover the essential, distinguishing properties of watermarking schemes only, the definition and measure of security chosen by the authors is too general: they measure the level of security of watermarking scheme in the number of observations (watermarked data) an adversary needs in order to estimate the secret watermarking key. Information leakage is measured using methods from information theory, such as Shannon's mutual information. More concretely, defining the adversary goal is a direct translation of Shannon's definition of security of encryption schemes. According to Cayre et al. [7] "the watermarking technique is perfectly secure if and only if no information about the secret key leaks from the observations". Intuitively, this informal definition seems to be reasonable, but not straightforward to define formally, such that it can be satisfied at all: assume the adversary has observed a triple $(W, WM, W')$, where the stego-data $W'$ results from embedding watermark $WM$ into the cover-data $W$, using the secret embedding key $K^{emb}$. Given these observations, the adversary has a reliable test to recognise the correct secret embedding key: the adversary can run through the whole key space and test for every candidate key, whether $W' \stackrel{?}{=} \texttt{Embed}(W, WM, K^{emb})$. This test allows the adversary to rule out most watermarking keys and, obviously, this observation leaks information on $K^{emb}$. The definition in [7] is mainly motivated by the intuition that "if a watermarking scheme does not provide perfect secrecy, then one would like to measure the information leakage about the key." However, defining watermarking security in terms of secrecy and information leakage about the key is not known to be necessary or sufficient for any meaningful security property of the watermarking scheme:[7] obviously it is *not sufficient* for robustness, because it does not rule out unkeyed non-robust watermarking schemes, e.g., a watermarking scheme that embeds the watermark by substituting all LSBs of an image.[8] Furthermore, this definition applies to applications where the same secret embedding key is used to embed several watermarks into different data: watermarking schemes insecure

---

[6] As an example consider a watermarking scheme, which uses the secret watermarking key as a one-time-pad to encrypt the watermark and embed it in the LSB of pixels identified by the remainder of the watermarking key. Obviously, this scheme does not leak any information about the watermarking key and the watermark, but can be easily removed by setting the LSB of any pixel to 0.

[7] It holds if there is an arguable equivalence between security and secrecy of the key, which holds for encryption schemes as considered by Shannon.

[8] Even the identity map would fulfil the perfect security definition, as it does not depend on a secret key (private communication with Nicholas Hopper, David Molnar and David Wagner).

according to this definition may nevertheless be secure in other applications, which use a fresh embedding key for every watermark.

Comesaña et al [8,9] closely follow the inadequate notion of security (information leakage) introduced in [6,7] as mentioned above. Their main achievement, compared to [7] is the definition of a new measure to quantify the leaked information and its application to spread spectrum watermarking.

Katzenbeisser [10] also follows this notion of security, suffering from the same problem, but proposes a computational definition of leaked information, which is inspired by computational security definitions for symmetric encryption schemes: the underlying model is a game between the adversary and the honest party (embedding oracle) where the adversary's goal of obtaining information about the key (winning the game) is modeled by his ability to distinguish whether given stego-data was more likely watermarked with one out of two keys, where the cover-data is chosen by the adversary and the actual embedding key is randomly chosen by the embedding oracle.

## 2.1   Summary and Discussion

We observe that in particular the definition of watermark security remains rather unclear. The main reason is that most researchers tried to define "watermark security" such that it captures any property that may be required by any conceivable application. As applications of watermarking schemes are manifold, posing different requirements on watermarking schemes, it is hard to come up with general definitions and even harder to come up with schemes that fulfil them.

Furthermore, it is more reasonable not to define one *low-granular* term, "watermark security", to comprise different *high-granular* requirements of different applications. High-granular requirements may be secrecy, integrity or authenticity of the watermark, dependency of the watermark on the cover-data (to prevent copy attacks), as well as robustness and collusion tolerance to name only the most important ones. Barely any application (if any at all) requires a single watermarking scheme to provide *all* these high-granular properties[9], beside the fact that it is a difficult, and unnecessary, task to design such watermarking scheme.

Moreover, *high-granular* properties required by certain applications can be attained using cryptographic building blocks on top of the watermarking scheme (layered approach): The secrecy[10] and authenticity/integrity of the watermark can be achieved by applying encryption respectively message authentication codes or digital signatures to the watermark before embedding it. Binding the watermark to the cover-data can be achieved by augmenting the watermark through appending a (robust/perceptual) hash of the cover data to the watermark and authenticating this augmented watermark.

---

[9] This can be compared to cryptographic hash functions. Some applications require hash functions to be collision-free, while some only require a hash-function to be one-way.

[10] This secrecy property should not be confused with the "steganographic hiding" property, which requires that not even the presence of the watermark can be detected.

We argue that a formal definition of a pure digital watermarking scheme should focus on its distinguishing features, which cannot be achieved by existing, well founded cryptographic primitives. As we argue in later sections these features are the capability of embedding additional information in data, the robustness property as well as detection/extraction errors. Nevertheless, for certain applications it makes sense to require that the watermarking scheme provides further security properties, which, as mentioned above, may be achieved by cryptographic means on the top of the watermarking scheme.

## 3   Basic Notations and Definitions

*Computation Model* We write algorithms $O \leftarrow \mathtt{Alg}(I)$ to denote running $\mathtt{Alg}$ on inputs $I$ and assigning the output to variable $O$. Optional inputs/outputs are set in squared brackets, i.e., in $\mathtt{Alg}(I_1, [I_2])$ the input of $I_2$ is optional. When we use the term *efficient* in the context of algorithms or computation we mean a Turing Machine with polynomial-time complexity.

*Probabilities and Negligible Functions.* We denote a probability function with **Prob**$[A :: B]$ where $A$ denotes the quantity for which the probability is computed and $B$ the (joint) random variable that induces the underlying probability space.

For example **Prob**$[pred(v_2) = \top :: v_1 \overset{R}{\leftarrow} \mathbb{Z}_n; v_2 \leftarrow \mathtt{Alg}(v_1)]$ means the probability that predicate *pred* holds on $v_2$, where the underlying probability space is induced by the random variable consisting of the random variables $v_1$, uniformly chosen from $\mathbb{Z}_n$, and $v_2$ which is the random value output by the algorithm $\mathtt{Alg}$ on input $v_1$. Furthermore, let $v$ be some arbitrary random variable or ensemble of random variables. Then, $[v]$ denotes the *support*, which is the set of all possible values $v$, i.e. those with non-zero probability.

A *negligible* function $\epsilon(x)$ is a function where the inverse of any polynomial is asymptotically an upper bound, i.e., $\forall d > 0 \; \exists x_0 \; \forall x > x_0 : \epsilon(x) < 1/x^d$. We denote this by $\epsilon(x) <_\infty 1/poly(x)$.

## 4   Formal Definition of Watermarking Schemes

### 4.1   Similarity

A suitable similarity function/predicate is a key aspect in the definition of watermarking schemes and the robustness property. Often, simple distortion metrics, such as the mean squared error (MSE) are used to define similarity. A suitable similarity measure has to consider the semantics and envisaged usage of data: for data such as software, a computational semantics is most suitable, whereas for data consumed by human beings a measure based on models of the human visual/audio system is most suitable (see e.g., Cox et al. [11]). However, the latter may be defined computational as well [12].

In the following we assume a suitable, polynomial-time computable *similarity function/predicate*, also referred to as *similarity test* $sim(W^\star, \hat{W})$, which given two data items $W^\star$ and $\hat{W}$ outputs $\top$ iff $W^\star$ can be considered sufficiently similar to (according to the usual, agreed semantics) and has been derived from $\hat{W}$. Note that $sim()$ does not need to be symmetric. We have chosen to encapsulate this crucial aspect in a single, general predicate, because it abstracts from the peculiarities of the data types and helps to come up with very clear definitions, based on which one can design and prove applications. In Section 6 we consider the necessary steps when using our definitions to build concrete watermarking schemes with provable robustness.

## 4.2    Systematics of Watermarking and Robustness Definitions

One has several degrees of freedom when formally defining watermarking schemes and the robustness property. We identified the following orthogonal parameters, which have to be considered carefully, because variation of these parameters leads to significantly different definitions. These parameters concern the type of watermarking scheme (detecting vs. extracting), error probabilities (false-positive and false-negative), all-quantified quantities [11], and adversary model. The latter distinguishes between computational and unconditional (information theoretical) adversaries, the a-priori knowledge of the adversary, active vs. passive adversaries and access to embedding or detection/extraction oracles. We consider these orthogonal parameters in the sequel. Based on the degrees of freedom caused by the variation of these parameters one can establish an *application independent systematic* of definitions for watermarking schemes, similar to the systematic for DL-based cryptographic assumptions introduced in [13]. We consider this as important future work, fertilising both the study of watermarking schemes in a more structured way and the exact specification of requirements of watermark-based applications. For application design one can choose the appropriate definition and watermarking scheme which best suits this application. The following definitions offer formal abstractions of watermarking schemes, which can be used to design and analyse a variety of protocols and applications. Furthermore, compared to previous definitions, our definitions comprise an explicit computational adversary model, including passive and active adversaries, as well as error probabilities of watermarking schemes. We first define the watermarking schemes and introduce error probabilities and robustness later.

**Definition 1 (Detecting Watermarking Scheme).** *Let $\mathcal{W}$ be the set of cover- and stego-data, let $\mathcal{WM} \subseteq \{0,1\}^+$ be the set of all possible watermarks, let $\mathcal{K}$ be the set of keys and let $par_{sec}^{wm}$ denote the security parameter of the watermarking scheme. A (detecting) watermarking scheme consists of three polynomial-time algorithms:*

---

[11] When defining properties (of watermarking schemes) it makes a fundamental difference, which items (cover-data, watermark, keys, stego-data) are all-quantified and which of them are assumed to be (randomly) chosen.

As a rule of thumb the more items are all-quantified, the stronger the resulting definition is.

- Key Generation Algorithm: *On input of the security parameters $par_{sec}^{wm}$, the probabilistic key generation algorithm* $\mathtt{GenKey}^{WM}(par_{sec}^{wm})$ *generates the matching keys* $(K^{emb}, K^{det})$ *required for watermark embedding and detection.*
- Embedding Algorithm: *On input of the cover-data $W$, the watermark $WM$ to be embedded and the embedding key $K^{emb}$, the probabilistic embedding algorithm* $\mathtt{Embed}(W, WM, K^{emb})$ *outputs the watermarked data (stego-data) $W'$, which is required to be perceptibly similar to the cover data $W$. We refer to this requirement as the* intactness property *or* imperceptibility property *and define it formally as:* $\forall W \in \mathcal{W}, \forall WM \in \mathcal{WM}, \forall (K^{emb}, K^{det}) \in [\mathtt{GenKey}^{WM}()]$:

$$W' \leftarrow \mathtt{Embed}(W, WM, K^{emb}) \implies sim(W', W) = \top \qquad (1)$$

- Detecting Algorithm: *On input of (possibly modified) stego-data $W''$, the watermark $WM$, the original cover-data $W$ (optional input), sometimes also referred to as* reference-data *in this context, and the detection key $K^{det}$, the probabilistic*[12] *detection algorithm* $\mathtt{Detect}(W'', WM, [W], K^{det})$ *outputs a Boolean value ind $\in \{\top, \bot\}$. Here, $\top$ indicates the presence and $\bot$ the absence of the watermark. The detecting watermarking scheme should fulfil a property, which is commonly referred to as the* effectiveness *of the watermarking scheme and which we define as follows:* $\forall W \in \mathcal{W}, \forall WM \in \mathcal{WM}, \forall (K^{emb}, K^{det}) \in [\mathtt{GenKey}^{WM}()]$ :

$$W' \leftarrow \mathtt{Embed}(W, WM, K^{emb}) \implies \mathtt{Detect}(W', WM, [W], K^{det}) = \top \quad (2)$$

The definition of extracting watermarking schemes is similar and has been omitted due to space limitations.

*Remark 1.* We refer to a watermarking scheme as being *symmetric* iff $K^{det} = K^{emb}$. In this case, we usually denote this key as $K^{wm}$ and refer to it as the *watermarking key*. *Blind* watermarking schemes do not require the cover-data $W$ as an input to $\mathtt{Detect}()$ or $\mathtt{Extract}()$ respectively. A blind watermarking scheme with $K^{det} \neq K^{emb}$ is called *asymmetric*.

*Remark 2.* Sometimes we require an algorithm that represents the sampling/ choice of a watermark $WM \in \mathcal{WM}$ by the application. We denote this sampling by $WM \leftarrow \mathtt{GenWM}(par_{sec}^{wm})$ and stress that $\mathtt{GenWM}()$ does not generate the watermark *signal*, but rather the encoded watermark message. Therefore, $\mathtt{GenWM}()$ is not part of the watermarking scheme, but rather a part of the application.

## 4.3   Error Probabilities of Watermarking Schemes

So far we did not allow the watermark detector/extractor to err, which is both a strong requirement and unrealistic in practice: As most practical watermarking schemes rely on statistical tests, their outputs inherently involve uncertainties and may be incorrect with a certain probability. Furthermore, for most applications a

---

[12] Although the majority of detection algorithms is not probabilistic we model detection as an probabilistic algorithm to make our definition as general as possible.

negligible error probability may be tolerated. For detecting watermarking schemes we distinguish two types of errors: *false-positive errors* and *false-negative errors*. Informally speaking, a false-positive error means that the detection algorithm indicates a watermark to be present, although it has actually not been embedded, whereas a false-negative error means that the detection algorithm indicates a watermark not to be present, although it actually has been embedded.

When using watermarking schemes as building blocks in protocols or other applications, these errors occur with certain probabilities, which result from the probability distribution of the watermark detector/extractor's inputs in that specific application environment. As these error probabilities are crucial to the performance of the overall applications or protocols, we will discuss them in more details and formalise them in the sequel. The formalisation will be exemplarily done for detecting watermarking schemes and we note that the definitions for extracting watermarking schemes are analogous.

**Definition 2 (False-Positives).** *We call an input tuple* $(W'', WM, W, K^{\text{wm}})$ *to the detection algorithm a* positive *iff* Detect$(W'', WM, W, K^{\text{wm}}) = \top$. *A false-positive is a tuple* $(W'', WM, W, K^{\text{wm}})$ *with:*

$$\text{Detect}(W'', WM, W, K^{\text{wm}}) = \top$$
$$\wedge \, \nexists W' : (W' \in [\text{Embed}(W, WM, K^{\text{wm}})] \wedge W'' \in \{\hat{W} | sim(\hat{W}, W')\})$$

We define the *positives set* of a watermarking scheme as the set of all input tuples $(W'', WM, W, K^{\text{wm}})$ yielding a positive detection result (*positive tuple*) $\mathcal{PS} := \{(W'', WM, W, K^{\text{wm}}) \mid \text{Detect}(W'', WM, W, K^{\text{wm}}) = \top\}$ and we define $\mathcal{FPS}$ as the set of all false-positives. Furthermore, we define the *positives rate* as the fraction of positive tuples to all such tuples $pr := |\mathcal{PS}|/|\mathcal{W} \times \mathcal{WM} \times \mathcal{W} \times \mathcal{K}|$ and, similarly, $fpr := |\mathcal{FPS}|/|\mathcal{W} \times \mathcal{WM} \times \mathcal{W} \times \mathcal{K}|$. Note that these rates are completely determined by the watermarking scheme and does not depend on the application context, in which the watermarking scheme is being used. In contrast, the *positives probability* and *false-positive probability* are not completely determined by the watermarking scheme, but additionally depend on the probability distribution of works, watermarks and watermarking keys (see [11]), *which itself depends on the context given by the application in which the watermarking scheme is being used.* In particular, the application's security requirements (or conversely the adversary's goals) and the underlying trust model play a central role in defining an adequate positives probability. Depending on the above aspects, one can distinguish several different types of positives probabilities. Here, we focus on *adversarial positives probabilities*: in most security applications, at least parts of the input tuple to Detect() can be computed freely by the adversary (without adhering to a pre-defined distribution), such that it triggers the detector and, in addition, fulfils a certain application dependent predicate side_condition.[13] We refer to these positive probabilities as *adversarial*

---

[13] In case of dispute resolving applications, the side-condition predicate may state that the false-positive watermark, computed by the adversary, is also detectable in the original work of the rightful author, thus leading to a deadlock.

*false-positives probabilities* and distinguish several adversarial false-positives probabilities, which vary depending on the a-priori information available to the adversary and the side-conditions the positives have to fulfil. Both strongly depend on the concrete application scenario, denoted as `application`, in which the watermarking scheme is used.

**Definition 3 (General Adversarial False-Positive Probability).** *Let $\mathcal{A}$ denote the adversary algorithm. We define the general adversarial positives probability $pp_{adv}(\mathcal{A})$ as follows:*

$Prob[(\texttt{Detect}(W', WM_\mathcal{A}, W_\mathcal{A}, K_\mathcal{A}^{wm}) = \top) \wedge$
$\texttt{side\_condition}((W, WM, K^{wm}, W'), (W_\mathcal{A}, WM_\mathcal{A}, K_\mathcal{A}^{wm}, W'_\mathcal{A})) ::$
$\quad (W, WM, K^{wm}, W') \leftarrow \texttt{application};$
$\quad (WM_\mathcal{A}, W_\mathcal{A}, K_\mathcal{A}^{wm}, W'_\mathcal{A}) \leftarrow \mathcal{A}([W], [WM], [K^{wm}], [W'], par_{sec}^{wm});]$

Note that, in contrast to the non-adversarial positives probabilities, the adversarial positives probabilities depend on the concrete adversary strategy (formalised by the algorithm $\mathcal{A}$), which the adversary employs to compute the positive tuple. Furthermore, one has several degrees of freedom regarding the a-priori information given to the adversary. We modelled this by defining the inputs to $\mathcal{A}$ as optional parameters. The adversarial false-positive probability has often been neglected in the design of security critical applications, such as dispute-resolving schemes and further copyright protection protocols, mostly because its impact on the security of the overall protocol has been underestimated.[14] It is obvious that in any application where the presence of watermarks serves as evidence, such as dispute resolving, authorship proofs or fingerprinting the false-positive probability becomes critical: the higher the false-positive probability is, the lower is the "conclusiveness" or "reliability" of a detected/extracted watermark as a piece of evidence. Finally, we want to note that it is difficult to actually determine these adversarial error probabilities or bound them from above for concrete watermarking schemes. Therefore, assumptions about upper bounds of these probabilities are very strong assumptions.

**Definition 4 (Negatives Rate).** *We define a negative as a tuple $(W'', WM, W, K^{wm})$, yielding a negative detection result, i.e., $\texttt{Detect}(W'', WM, W, K^{wm}) = \bot$. Furthermore, we define the negatives set of a watermarking scheme as the set of negative tuples $\mathcal{NS} := \{(W'', WM, W, K^{wm}) \mid \texttt{Detect}(W'', WM, W, K^{wm}) = \bot\}$ and we define the negatives rate as the fraction of negative tuples to all such tuples: $nr := |\mathcal{NS}|/|\mathcal{W} \times \mathcal{WM} \times \mathcal{W} \times \mathcal{K}| = 1 - pr$.*

More interesting is the definition of *false*-negatives, for which we require an appropriate notion of when an input tuple should actually be a positive tuple,

---

[14] In [11] (p. 30), Cox et al. state: "In the case of proof of ownership, the detector is used so rarely, that a probability of $10^{-6}$ should suffice to make false positives unheard of." Here, "probability" refers to random non-adversarial probability, which makes it quite easy for an adversary to compute false-positives, fulfilling certain side-conditions and, thereby, breaking the security of (see [14] for example.).

which itself *depends on the properties required from the watermarking scheme*: robust watermarking schemes require that the inputs of a run of the embedding algorithm $(W, WM, K^{\text{wm}})$ plus the stego-data, resulting from this run, *or any similar data, derived from the stego data,* is a positive. Following this view, a false-negative is always a breach of robustness.

**Definition 5 (False-Negatives and False-Negative Rate).** *For a robust watermarking scheme a* false-negative tuple *is a tuple* $(W'', WM, W, K^{\text{wm}})$ *with* $\text{Detect}(W'', WM, W, K^{\text{wm}}) = \bot$, *although* $W''$ *has been derived from watermarked data* $W' \leftarrow \text{Embed}(W, WM, K^{\text{wm}})$ *and* $sim(W'', W') = \top$ *holds, i.e., detection should be successful by the robustness property of the watermarking scheme.*

*Let* $\mathcal{FNS}$ *denote the set of all false-negatives. We define the* false-negative rate *as the fraction of false-negatives and the set of tuples that should trigger a perfectly robust detector according to our robustness definition:* $fnr := |\mathcal{FNS}|/|\mathcal{W} \times \mathcal{WM} \times \mathcal{W} \times \mathcal{K}|$.

Analogous to the discussion above, one can define *adversarial false-negative probabilities*, denoting the probability that an adversary can compute a false-negative tuple. Due to lack of space and its relation to the robustness definition we omit this definition here. In the following Section we formalise *"robust watermarking schemes"*, which can be seen as an extension of the effectiveness property to those data, which has been derived from the stego-data and is still sufficiently similar to it.

# 5 Computational Robustness Definitions

## 5.1 Robustness Against Passive Adversaries

Informally, the robustness property against passive adversaries states that a watermark should remain detectable, even if the stego-data has been (maliciously) modified. Clearly, detectability (or extractability) cannot be guaranteed for any modification[15]. Therefore, the correct informal characterisation of a *robust* watermarking scheme is that it can detect/extract the watermark even in a (maliciously) modified stego-data *as long as the stego-data is perceptibly similar to the cover-data.*

The robustness property is of great importance, especially in the context of copyright protection applications, because the detectability of embedded watermarks is crucial for the overall system security. Unfortunately, robustness is not well understood so far. Most researchers give informal characterisations of robustness or define it as resistance against an inherently incomplete list of known attacks [15,16,17]. Cox et al. [11] distinguish between *robustness* and *security* of watermarking schemes: they characterise "robustness" as the "the ability to detect the watermark after common signal processing operations", whereas they

---

[15] Consider for example a modification, which completely garbles the stego-data or transforms it to the constant bit-string $1^n$.

refer to "security" as the "ability to resist hostile attacks". As we address water-marks exclusively in the context of security critical applications, this distinction would be artificial and we define robustness to cover also the ability to resist hostile removal-attacks.

**Definition 6 (Symmetric Computational Robustness).** *We define a symmetric watermarking scheme to be* computationally robust, *iff*

$\forall WM \in \mathcal{WM}, \forall$ *probabilistic polynomial-time adversary* $\mathcal{A}$
$\boldsymbol{Prob}[\mathtt{Detect}(W'', WM, W, K^{\mathtt{wm}}) = \perp \quad \wedge \quad sim(W'', W') = \top ::$
$\quad W \leftarrow \mathcal{W};$
$\quad K^{\mathtt{wm}} \leftarrow \mathtt{GenKey}^{\mathtt{WM}}(par^{\mathtt{wm}}_{sec});$
$\quad W' \leftarrow \mathtt{Embed}(W, WM, K^{\mathtt{wm}});$
$\quad W'' \leftarrow \mathcal{A}(W', [WM], par^{\mathtt{wm}}_{sec});]$
$<_\infty 1/poly(par^{\mathtt{wm}}_{sec})$

Informally, this means that symmetric watermarking scheme is called robust, iff it is computationally infeasible for an adversary, given watermarked data $W'$ and the watermark $WM$, to produce perceptibly similar data $W''$, in which the same watermark $WM$ cannot be detected anymore.

When designing an application, one has to choose the correct robustness definition. Especially the input available to the adversary $\mathcal{A}$ depends on the context of the target application: In applications such as dispute resolving, it is reasonable to assume that the adversary does not know the watermark. However, in applications such as copy protection, there exists only a small set of possible watermarks (e.g., "copy permitted", "do not copy") and therefore, it is more realistic to assume that $\mathcal{A}$ gets $WM$ as an additional input. In general, the more inputs the robustness definition allows the adversary to use, the stronger it is (and the more difficult it is for a watermarking scheme to fulfil it). As a consequence, the following robustness definition for asymmetric watermarking schemes is even harder to achieve than that for symmetric schemes, because the adversary is granted access to the watermark and detection key as well[16].

**Definition 7 (Asymmetric Computational Robustness).** *An* asymmetric *watermarking scheme is called robust, iff*

$\forall WM \in \mathcal{WM}, \forall$ *probabilistic polynomial-time attacker* $\mathcal{A}$
$\boldsymbol{Prob}[\mathtt{Detect}(W'', WM, W, K^{\mathtt{det}}) = \perp \quad \wedge \quad sim(W'', W') = \top ::$
$\quad W \leftarrow \mathcal{W};$
$\quad (K^{\mathtt{emb}}, K^{\mathtt{det}}) \leftarrow \mathtt{GenKey}^{\mathtt{WM}}(par^{\mathtt{wm}}_{sec});$
$\quad W' \leftarrow \mathtt{Embed}(W, WM, K^{\mathtt{emb}});$
$\quad W'' \leftarrow \mathcal{A}(W', WM, K^{\mathtt{det}}, par^{\mathtt{wm}}_{sec});]$
$<_\infty 1/poly(par^{\mathtt{wm}}_{sec})$

The robustness definition for asymmetric schemes is very similar to that of symmetric schemes. The main difference is that the adversary additionally receives

---

[16] Amongst others, this provides the adversary with a detection oracle.

the public detection inputs (detection key and watermark). Alternatively, one may define robustness of asymmetric watermarking schemes by providing the adversary only with $W'$ and the public detection key. However, from the application's perspective, it does not make sense to make the detection key publicly available, without at the same time making the watermark publicly available. Therefore, we have chosen to provide the adversary with the watermark as well. Amongst others, this definition is suitable for copy control applications.

## 5.2   Robustness Against Active Adversaries

Early definitions of robustness and watermark security did not consider active adversaries, interacting with and, thereby, having indirect access to the embedder and detector, *including* the corresponding keys. As a matter of fact, these robustness definitions may be too weak for many applications of watermarking schemes.[17] Therefore, it is crucial to also consider robustness against active adversaries and have suitable definitions on-hand. Hence we desire to model adversaries that have access to the functionality of some public algorithm, initialised with some secret system parameter (e.g., the secret embedding or detection key), but without having direct access to this secret parameter. The common technique to model them is to provide adversaries access to oracle machines. The secret system parameter, used to initialise the oracle, is usually generated by the correct party according to the rules of the two party game underlying the respective computational security definition. Oracle machines can be restricted to answer a limited number of $t$, polynomially bounded in the security parameter, queries only. Such oracles are referred to as $t$-oracles. Actually, this "free" access to oracles is more than one would expect in most application settings, because there, the honest party, indirectly granting access to the embedder or detector, would usually not blindly apply it to any input data without some predefined verifications. [18] However, by modelling active attacks by granting *free* access to oracles, the definition becomes application independent and one is *on the safe side*, because this guarantees that one can design applications without implementing further checks to limit access to the oracle (e.g., copy-protection in CE devices).

   In analogy to the core algorithms of a watermarking scheme, i.e., the embedding and detection/extraction algorithm, we define two types of oracles, embedding oracles and detection/extraction oracles. Furthermore, one can distinguish

---

[17] Consider a dispute resolving scheme as an example (see [18] for an overview): here the author has to prove the presence of the watermark in the disputed work to a judge. As the disputed work usually has been generated by the adversary, the adversary has indirect, restricted access to the watermark detector, which, obviously, has to be modelled in the robustness definition.

[18] Consider watermark-based copy control as an example: the licensing authority might perform certain tests to make sure to embed a "copy freely" watermark only in reasonable looking data, such as to not compromise the security of the watermarking scheme, whereas the detector, embedded in a low-cost DVD recorder provides access to an unlimited detection oracle.

several kinds of embedding oracles according to the *secret information contained in the oracles* and *the form of queries answered by this oracle*. The most usual embedding oracles are discussed below:

1. **Embedding oracles with secret embedding key:** These embedding oracles are initialised with a secret watermark embedding key $K^{\text{emb}}$, as provided by the application/correct party in the security definition and answers $t$ queries of the form $(W_{\mathcal{A}}, WM_{\mathcal{A}})$. We denote such oracles, initialised with $K^{\text{emb}}$, as $\mathcal{O}^t_{\text{Embed}, K^{\text{emb}}}$. Given a query $(W_{\mathcal{A}}, WM_{\mathcal{A}})$ oracle $\mathcal{O}^t_{\text{Embed}, K^{\text{emb}}}$ replies with answer $W'_{\mathcal{A}} \leftarrow \text{Embed}(W_{\mathcal{A}}, WM_{\mathcal{A}}, K^{\text{emb}})$.

2. **Embedding oracles with secret embedding key and secret watermark:** Another type of embedding oracle, considered here, is initialised with a secret embedding key and a secret watermark and answers queries of the form $(W_{\mathcal{A}})$: given a query $(W_{\mathcal{A}})$ the embedding oracle $\mathcal{O}^t_{\text{Embed}, K^{\text{emb}}, WM}$ replies with answer $W'_{\mathcal{A}} \leftarrow \text{Embed}(W_{\mathcal{A}}, WM, K^{\text{emb}})$.

Similarly, one can define several types of detection/extraction oracles, depending on the secret oracle initialisation information and the form of queries answered by the detection oracle: the first type of detection oracle $\mathcal{O}^t_{\text{Detect}, K^{\text{det}}}$ is initialised with a secret detection key $K^{\text{det}}$ and answers queries of the form $(W'_{\mathcal{A}}, WM_{\mathcal{A}})$, whereas the second type $\mathcal{O}^t_{\text{Detect}, K^{\text{det}}, WM}$ is initialised with a fixed detection key $K^{\text{det}}$ *and a fixed secret watermark WM* and answers queries of the form $(W'_{\mathcal{A}})$. In asymmetric watermarking schemes, as defined above, the adversary is supposed to know the public detection key, which provides him with "unlimited access to an detection oracle". Therefore, to model active attacks against asymmetric watermarking schemes, one only has to consider embedding oracles. We denote an adversary, having oracle access to a set of oracles $\mathcal{O}_1, \ldots, \mathcal{O}_n$ as $\mathcal{A}^{\mathcal{O}_1, \ldots, \mathcal{O}_n}$. Finally, we define a symmetric watermarking scheme to be *computationally robust against active adversaries with access to an embedding and detection oracle*, iff

$$\forall WM \in \mathcal{WM}, \forall \text{ prob. polynomial-time attacker } \mathcal{A}$$
$$\textbf{Prob}[\text{Detect}(W'', WM, W, K^{\text{wm}}) = \perp \quad \wedge \quad sim(W'', W') = \top ::$$
$$\quad W \leftarrow \mathcal{W};$$
$$\quad K^{\text{wm}} \leftarrow \text{GenKey}^{\text{WM}}(par^{\text{wm}}_{sec});$$
$$\quad W' \leftarrow \text{Embed}(W, WM, K^{\text{wm}});$$
$$\quad W'' \leftarrow \mathcal{A}^{\mathcal{O}^t_{\text{Embed}, K^{\text{emb}}, WM}, \mathcal{O}^t_{\text{Detect}, K^{\text{det}}, WM}}(W', par^{\text{wm}}_{sec});]$$
$$<_\infty 1/poly(par^{\text{wm}}_{sec})$$

# 6   Conclusion and Cautionary Note

Formal definitions for security properties of watermarking schemes are crucial when proving the security of multimedia applications that combine cryptographic methods with watermarking. Existing literature on formal security definitions for watermarking is not extensive and still has conceptual shortcomings. In this paper, we discussed these shortcomings as well as the subtle aspects/parameters that existing proposals do not cover. We proposed a formal framework and definitions for watermarking schemes that incorporate these aspects/parameters and can be used as a suitable abstraction for security proofs of multimedia security schemes.

Finally, we stress that currently no watermarking scheme is known to fulfil the computational robustness definitions as defined above. Thus, the robustness assumption is a stronger assumption compared to standard number-theoretical assumptions in cryptography: Number-theoretical assumptions have shown their reasonability, since no efficient algorithms solving them have been found for a long period of time. In contrast, any watermarking scheme proposed so far and claimed to be robust fails to fulfil the computational robustness definition. This leaves us with a gap between our abstract model of robust watermarking schemes and the watermarking schemes available today. Nevertheless our formal definitions provide an appropriate abstraction (similar to the *marking assumption* in fingerprinting [19]) which can be used to design secure applications, such as dispute-resolving protocols.[19]

On the other hand, based on our work, provably robust watermarking schemes may be developed as follows: First, we have to define $sim()$ for the respective data type, which, based on the current understanding of the HVS, is a hard task for multimedia data. However, for data such as software, having a well-defined formal semantics, it seems to be feasible to come up with a suitable definition. Second, we have to choose a suitable computationally hard problem on the respective data type. For software, such problems are well-known for a long time [20] and also considered in the design of software obfuscation. Third, we have to define the watermarking scheme, such that embedding preserves similarity and such that an attacker, being able to break the scheme's robustness, can be used to efficiently and accurately solve a hard problem (proof by reduction).

# References

1. Cachin, C.: An information-theoretic model for steganography. In: Aucsmith, D. (ed.) IH 1998. LNCS, vol. 1525, pp. 306–318. Springer, Heidelberg (1998)
2. Mittelholzer, T.: An information-theoretic approach to steganography and watermarking. In: Pfitzmann, A. (ed.) IH 1999. LNCS, vol. 1768, pp. 1–16. Springer, Heidelberg (2000)
3. Hopper, N.J., Langford, J., von Ahn, L.: Provably secure steganography. In: Yung, M. (ed.) CRYPTO 2002. LNCS, vol. 2442, Springer, Heidelberg (2002)
4. Backes, M., Cachin, C.: Public-key steganography with active attacks. Report 2003/231, Cryptology ePrint Archive (2003)
5. Kalker, T.: Considerations on watermark security. In: IEEE International Workshop on Multimedia Signal Processing (MMSP'01) 2001, pp. 201–206 (2001)
6. Barni, M., Bartolini, F., Furon, T.: A general framework for robust watermarking security. Signal Processing, pp. 2069–2084 (2003)

---

[19] In fact, the marking assumption is even stronger than the robustness assumption, as it requires robustness against adversaries in possession of differently marked versions of the same cover-data.

7. Cayre, F., Fontaine, C., Furon, T.: Watermarking security, part one: theory. In: IS&T/SPIE International Symposium on Electronic Imaging 2005. In: Proceedings of the SPIE., SPIE (2005) pp.746–757. Security, Steganography, and Watermarking of Multimedia Contents VII (2005)
8. Comesaña, P., Pérez-Freire, L., Pérez-González, F.: An information-theoretic framework for assessing security in practical watermarking and data hiding scenarios. [21]
9. Comesaña, P., Pérez-Freire, L., Pérez-González, F.: Fundamentals of data-hiding security and their application to spread spectrum analysis. In: Barni, M. (ed.) IH 2005. LNCS, vol. 3727, pp. 146–160. Springer, Heidelberg (2005)
10. Katzenbeisser, S.: Computational security models for digital watermarks. [21]
11. Cox, I., Miller, M.L., Bloom, J.A.: Digital Watermarking. Morgan Kaufmann Publisher, San Francisco (2002)
12. Tran, N.: Hiding functions and computational security of image watermarking systems. In: 15th IEEE Computer Security Foundations Workshop, pp. 295–306. IEEE Computer Society Press, Los Alamitos (2002)
13. Sadeghi, A.R., Steiner, M.: Assumptions related to discrete logarithms: Why subtleties make a real difference. In: Pfitzmann, B. (ed.) EUROCRYPT 2001. LNCS, vol. 2045, pp. 243–260. Springer, Heidelberg (2001)
14. Adelsbach, A., Katzenbeisser, S., Sadeghi, A.R.: On the insecurity of non-invertible watermarking schemes for dispute resolving. In: Kalker, T., Cox, I., Ro, Y.M. (eds.) IWDW 2003. LNCS, vol. 2939, pp. 355–369. Springer, Heidelberg (2004)
15. Swanson, M.D., Kobayashi, M., Tewfik, A.H.: Multimedia data-embedding and watermarking technologies. In: Proceedings of the IEEE, vol. 86 (1998)
16. Katzenbeisser, S., Petitcolas, F.A.: Information Hiding: techniques for steganography and digital watermarking. Artech House Publishers (2000)
17. Hartung, F., Kutter, M.: Multimedia watermarking techniques. In: Proceedings of the IEEE, Special Issue on Identification and Protection of Multimedia Information, vol. 87, pp. 1079–1107 (1999)
18. Adelsbach, A., Sadeghi, A.R.: Advanced techniques for dispute resolving and authorship proofs on digital works. In: Proceedings of SPIE, Security and Watermarking of Multimedia Contents V, vol. 5020 (2003)
19. Boneh, D., Shaw, J.: Collusion-secure fingerprinting for digital data. In: Coppersmith, D. (ed.) CRYPTO 1995. LNCS, vol. 963, pp. 452–465. Springer, Heidelberg (1995)
20. Ausiello, G., Crescenzi, P., Gambosi, G., Kann, V., Marchetti-Spaccamela, A., Protasi, M.: Complexity and Approximation. Springer-Verlag, Berlin Germany (1999)
21. Piva, A. (ed.): In: 6th International Workshop on Image Analysis for Multimedia Interactive Services (WIAMIS 2005), Special Session on Media Security (2005)

# Hiding Information Hiding

Adam Young[1] and Moti Yung[2]

[1] Cryptovirology Labs
aly@cryptovirology.com
[2] RSA Labs and Columbia University
moti@cs.columbia.edu

**Abstract.** In this paper we introduce a new tool that hides whether or not an "encryption" algorithm actually performs encryption or not. We call this a computational questionable encryption scheme and show how it can be used to devise mobile agents that conceal whether they encrypt or delete data prior to data transmission. Such agents may be useful in the honest-but-curious setting in which the author of the agent wishes to keep confidential whether or not the agent collects and transmits data while in transit. Informally, a questionable encryption scheme adds a "fake" key generation algorithm to a PKCS. The key generation algorithms of a computational questionable encryption scheme produce a "public key" $y$ and a poly-sized witness $x$. Depending on which of the two key generation algorithms the user decides to use, $y$ is real or fake. When the cipher is supplied with a real $y$ then it produces decipherable ciphertexts and $x$ proves this. When the cipher is supplied with a fake $y$ then it produces *computationally* indecipherable ciphertexts (with respect to *everyone*) and $x$ proves this. We call the former a witness of encryption and the latter a witness of non-encryption. We formally define the notion of a computational questionable encryption scheme and present a construction for it based on the ElGamal cryptosystem. We prove the security based on the Decision Diffie-Hellman problem and a reasonable new intractability assumption in the random oracle model. Finally, we show how a computational questionable encryption scheme is related yet different from all-or-nothing disclosure of secrets and related notions.

## 1 Introduction

The theory of information hiding is broad in scope and encompasses everything from steganography, to subliminal channels in cryptosystems, to covert channels in operating systems. In this paper we expand the scope of information hiding even further by considering how to hide the true nature of a particular class of functions that execute in the *honest-but-curious* model. In this model, functions are executed by an agent (e.g., mobile agent) in an environment that can be trusted not to interfere with the operation of the function (i.e., trusted not to introduce faults) but that is curious and may seek to log and analyze the agent as it executes.

J. Camenisch et al. (Eds.): IH 2006, LNCS 4437, pp. 161–171, 2007.

In particular we present a new scheme that hides whether or not a function (that appears to be an asymmetric encryption function) actually encrypts plaintext or effectively deletes the plaintext. This is called a *questionable encryption* scheme and it can be used to make mobile agents more robust in the aforementioned threat model.

To motivate the introduction of this scheme, consider the following scenario. A mobile agent is found that passes a value that appears to be a public key to an asymmetric encryption function (e.g., in an OS API call). It also passes plaintext that is taken from the host system to the encryption function. The agent transmits the resulting ciphertext outside the host system. Without understanding the subtleties of public key cryptography it may be easy to jump to the conclusion that encryption is taking place and hence that sensitive information is being sent outside of the host computer system.

This assumption is inherently flawed since in some cases the requisite algebraic structure of the public key may be incorrect, or perhaps (e.g., in ElGamal [9]) the public key was sampled randomly without knowing the pre-image. An improperly generated public key can effectively *erase* plaintext data rather than encrypt it. This is one of the properties that a questionable encryption scheme provides.

Questionable encryptions enable a two pronged application. The user deploys numerous mobile agents, each with a unique "public key." Some of the agents contain a real public key and the rest contain a fake public key. Only the agents with the real public keys will transmit data that is gathered from the host system. The rest will effectively *delete* the plaintext prior to transmission although they will appear to asymmetrically encrypt data (deletion occurs since decryption is provably intractable in a *computational* questionable encryption scheme). The user later reveals witnesses of non-encryption at his or her discretion.

This application ensures that no particular agent (that has not had it's witness revealed) can be known for certain to actually transmit data outside the host. We argue that this provides a useful level of robustness in the honest-but-curious threat model for agents that collect and transmit data.

The contributions of this paper are the following:

1. We provide the first formal and complete definition of a *computational questionable encryption scheme*.
2. A construction is given based on ElGamal and we prove that it is secure based on the Decision Diffie-Hellman problem and a reasonable intractability assumption.
3. We show how questionable encryptions differ from all-or-nothing disclosure, $(1, 2)$-oblivious transfer, and deniable encryptions (we relate questionable encryptions to these primitives in Appendix A).
4. We describe an application of computational questionable encryptions that helps hide the true functionality of mobile agents that collect host data.

We implemented our computational questionable encryption scheme and describe how we did so in Section 6. We show that the portion of the implementation that needs to reside in the agent is *trivial* to implement using Windows Cryptographic API calls (built-in DLL calls).

## 2    Background

The notion of a questionable encryption scheme was informally presented in subsection 6.2.2 of [20]. However, no formal definitions were given and no proofs were provided. The work presents a heuristic computational questionable encryption scheme (based on equation 1) and a perfect questionable encryption scheme based on Goldwasser-Micali. However, the distinction was not made between *perfect* questionable encryptions and *computational* questionable encryptions.

The original computational questionable encryption heuristic is based on the problem of computing a triple $(x, y, s)$ satisfying,

$$g^x \bmod p = y = H(s) \text{ and } y \in G \tag{1}$$

Here $G$ is the group generated by $g$ and $H : \{0,1\}^* \to G$ is a random function. It is stated that $s$ is a large randomly chosen seed and the actual set from which $s$ is drawn is not specified. In this paper we present the formal definition of a computational questionable encryption scheme, present a construction with no ambiguities in the "seed," and prove that it is secure.

The first formal definition of a questionable encryption scheme was presented in [21]. This formally defined the notion of a *perfect* questionable encryption scheme. A perfect questionable encryption scheme is one in which indecipherability holds unconditionally while indistinguishability of real public keys vs. fake public keys relies on a computational intractability assumption. The construction utilizes the Paillier public key cryptosystem.

## 3    Definition

We now present the formal definition of a *computational* questionable encryption scheme. For review, the following definition is taken from [10].

**Definition 1.** $v$ *is negligible if for every constant* $c \geq 0$ *there exists an integer* $k_c$ *such that* $v(k) < \frac{1}{k^c}$ *for all* $k \geq k_c$.

Thus, $\nu$ is negligible in $k$ if it vanishes faster than any inverse polynomial in $k$.

Let $k$ be a security parameter. Define $G_0(\cdot)$ to be a probabilistic poly-time algorithm that on input $1^k$ outputs a pair of values $(x, y)$. Similarly, define $G_1(\cdot)$ to be a probabilistic poly-time algorithm that on input $1^k$ outputs a pair of values $(x, y)$. The generator $G_1$ outputs a private key $x$ and corresponding public key $y$ for the encryption algorithm $E$ and corresponding decryption algorithm $D$. Let $S_{1,k}$ denote the set of possible outputs of $G_1(1^k)$. Similarly, let $S_{0,k}$ denote the set of possible outputs of $G_0(1^k)$. Let $M$ be the message space for $E$. Let $c = E(m, y)$ denote the encryption of $m \in M$ under $y$ and let $m = D(c, x)$ denote the corresponding decryption operation.

We require that $(G_1, E, D)$ be a correct (and hence secure) public key cryptosystem. The security requirements for $(G_1, E, D)$ can be any well-accepted notion of security, e.g. semantic security against plaintext attacks [13], security against adaptive chosen ciphertext attacks, and so on. In the definition below, we require that semantic security against plaintext attacks holds (so this is our definition of **secure**). We show in Section 5 that our construction easily extends to provide chosen ciphertext security.

**Definition 2.** *Let $(F, G_0, G_1, E, D)$ be a public 5-tuple, let $(G_1, E, D)$ be a **secure** asymmetric cryptosystem, let $G_0$ be an efficient key generation algorithm, and let $F$ be an efficiently computable predicate. If the following properties hold,*

*(1) [indecipherability] if $(x, y) \in_R S_{0,k}$ is public then $E(\cdot, y)$ is semantically secure against plaintext attacks,*
    *and,*
*(2) [indistinguishability] the ensemble consisting of fake public keys $y$ that are generated according to $G_0(1^k)$ is unconditionally indistinguishable from the ensemble consisting of real public keys $y$ generated according to $G_1(1^k)$,*
    *and,*
*(3) [binding] it is intractable to find a 3-tuple $(x, x', y)$ such that $(x', y) \in S_{0,k}$ and $(x, y) \in S_{1,k}$,*
    *and,*
*(4) [verifiability] for all $(x, y) \in S_{0,k} \bigcup S_{1,k}$, $F(x, y) = b \Rightarrow (x, y) \in S_{b,k}$,*

*then $(F, G_0, G_1, E, D)$ is a **computational questionable encryption** scheme.*

Property (1) needs a bit of explanation. In our ElGamal instantiation, when $(x, y) \in S_{1,k}$, $x$ is the ElGamal private key and witness of encryption. Property (1) indicates that for $(x, y) \in S_{0,k}$ (i.e., $y$ is *fake*), encryption is secure *even if $x$ is public*. This is intentional since we want encryptions to be indecipherable by everyone in this case. We call it a computational questionable encryption scheme since indecipherability holds under an intractability assumption.

Properties 3 and 4 imply that it is intractable for a probabilistic polynomial time algorithm to find a $y$, a witness of encryption $x$ for $y$, and a witness of non-encryption $x'$ for $y$. In other words, these properties imply that it is hard to find $(x, x', y)$ such that $F(x, y) = 1$ and $F(x', y) = 0$. Therefore, the user that generates a single public key must "commit" to either a real or fake $y$.

Since $F$ and $y$ are public, a user who generates $(x, y)$ need only disclose $x$ to reveal his or her commitment. In other words, $x$ proves that the plaintext is effectively erased or that messages are securely encrypted, whichever is the case.

The indistinguishability requirement can be weakened. However, we have no need to weaken it in this paper. A satisfactory definition can be devised in which the ensemble for fake public keys is only polynomially indistinguishable from the ensemble corresponding to real public keys.

## 4    A Construction Based on ElGamal

We will now present a construction that is based on ElGamal. Let $p$ be a large prime and let $q$ be a large prime that divides $p - 1$ evenly. When $p$ is the safe prime $p = 2q + 1$ then the group parameter is $\mathfrak{p} = p$. When $p$ is of the form $p = aq + 1$ with $a > 2$ then the group parameter is $\mathfrak{p} = (p, q)$.

Let $k = |p|$ be a security parameter. Let $g$ be an element of $\mathbb{Z}_p^*$ that has order $q$. Therefore, $g$ generates the subgroup $G_q$ of $\mathbb{Z}_p^*$ having prime order $q$.

The parameters $(\mathfrak{p}, g)$ are public and are agreed upon by all. Everyone that participates in the use of the questionable encryption scheme must agree that $(\mathfrak{p}, g)$ provides a suitable setting for the DDH problem. This includes skeptical verifiers that employ the verification function $F$. For instance, $p$ and $q$ can be generated using the DSA parameter generation method in FIPS PUB 186-2. Alternatively, well-accepted pre-defined values for $(\mathfrak{p}, g)$ can be used, etc.

Let $T : \{0,1\}^* \rightarrow \{0,1\}^{|p|}$ be a random function. The function $T$ can be constructed using a random oracle. We define the random function $H$ that uses $T$ as follows.

$H(s)$:
1. set $i = 1$
2. format $i$ as a binary string $i_s$
3. compute $w = T(s \parallel i_s)$
4. if $(w \notin \mathbb{Z}_p^*)$ then set $i = i + 1$ and goto step 2
5. compute $t = w^{\frac{p-1}{q}} \bmod p$
6. if $(t = 1)$ then set $i = i + 1$ and goto step 2
7. output $t$ and halt

$G_0(1^k)$:
1. choose $x \in_R \mathbb{Z}_q^*$
2. format $p$ and $g$ as $|p|$-bit binary strings $p_s$ and $g_s$, respectively
3. compute $h = H(p_s \parallel g_s)$ and set $y = h^x \bmod p$
4. output $(x, y)$ and halt

$G_1(1^k)$:
1. choose $x \in_R \mathbb{Z}_q^*$
2. compute $y = g^x \bmod p$
3. output $(x, y)$ and halt

In ElGamal, as we define it, the message space is $G_q$. When $p$ is a safe prime there is an easy way to encode messages into the set of quadratic residues and later decode them. We need only shrink the actual message space to do this.

To encrypt based on ElGamal we select $t \in_R \mathbb{Z}_q^*$ and compute $(a, b) = (g^t, y^t m)$ for message $m \in G_q$. The public key is $y = g^x \bmod p$ and the private key is $x$. To decrypt we compute $m = ba^{-x} \bmod p$.

In the function $F$, we let $-1$ indicate failure. This value is not part of a predicate per se, since the expected output of $F$ is 0 or 1. However, the use of $-1$ reflects what should be in a proper implementation.

$F(x, y)$:
1. if $(x \notin \mathbb{Z}_q^*$ or $y \notin G_q)$ then output $-1$ and halt
2. if $y = g^x \bmod p$ then output 1 and halt

3. format $p$ and $g$ as $|p|$-bit binary strings $p_s$ and $g_s$, respectively
4. compute $h = H(p_s \parallel g_s)$
5. if $y = h^x \bmod p$ then output 0 and halt
6. output $-1$ and halt

Note that with negligible probability $H$ will end up returning a value $h$ that equals $g$. When this happens Property 3 of Definition 2 breaks down. To see this note that by choosing $x \in_R \mathbb{Z}_q^*$ and taking $x' = x$ it will be the case that $y = g^x = h^{x'}$. In this rare circumstance a predicate $F$ would be correct in outputting 0 or 1. Note that this failure occurs with a probability that is *negligible*. Furthermore, this failure is perfectly detectable. It is publicly verifiable whether or not $g = H(p_s \parallel g_s)$. Consequently it is trivial to rule out the occurrence of failure.

From the construction of $F$ it is easy to see that $F(x, y) = b \Rightarrow (x, y) \in S_{b,k}$. It follows that Property 4 of Definition 2 holds.

It is straightforward to adapt this approach to other discrete-logarithm based cryptosystems. For example, Cramer-Shoup can be used as a basis for computational questionable encryptions [7].

For certain applications questionable encryptions can be used in lieu of oblivious transfer. This has some benefits over certain oblivious transfer methods. We leave such applications open to investigation.

## 5   Security

First we review the Decision Diffie-Hellman problem (DDH). Let $\mathrm{IG}_0$ be an instance generator that on input $k$ (in unary) generates $(\mathfrak{p}, g)$. This pair of values is as defined in Section 4.

**Definition 3.** *A DDH algorithm $A_0$ for $(\mathfrak{p}, g)$ is a probabilistic polynomial time (in $k$) algorithm satisfying, for some fixed $\alpha > 0$ and sufficiently large $k$:*

$$|Pr[A_0(\mathfrak{p}, g, g^a, g^b, g^{ab}) = \text{``true''}] -$$
$$Pr[A_0(\mathfrak{p}, g, g^a, g^b, g^c) = \text{``true''}]| > \tfrac{1}{k^\alpha}$$

*The probability is over the random choice of $(\mathfrak{p}, g)$ according to the distribution induced by $\mathrm{IG}_0(k)$, the random choice of $a, b, c$ in $\mathbb{Z}_q^*$, and the bits used by $A_0$.*

The Decision Diffie-Hellman assumption is that no such $A_0$ exists.

It has been shown that an encryption scheme that is secure in the sense of message indistinguishability is semantically secure [13]. The other direction was proven in [16] and was also addressed by Goldreich [11,12].

Tsiounis and Yung showed that DDH is equivalent with the security in the sense of message indistinguishability of ElGamal. In the non-uniform model this is equivalent to semantic security. These results are summarized in the following theorems from [18].

**Theorem 1.** *If the ElGamal encryption scheme is not secure in the sense of indistinguishability, then there exists a probabilistic polynomial time Turing machine that solves DDH with overwhelming probability.*

**Theorem 2.** *If there exists an oracle $\mathcal{O}$ which solves the DDH problem with probability non-negligibly better than random guessing then the ElGamal encryption scheme is not secure in the sense of indistinguishability.*

Since $T$ is a random function it follows from the construction of $H$ that $h = g^{\alpha} = H(p_s \mid\mid g_s)$ for some $\alpha \in_R \mathbb{Z}_q^*$. So, $G_0$ outputs $(x', y)$ where $y = h^{x'} = g^{\alpha x'}$ mod $p$ and $x' \in_R \mathbb{Z}_q^*$. Taking $x = \alpha x'$ mod $q$ it follows that $(x, y)$ is a uniformly random ElGamal key pair (i.e., in accordance with the output of $G_1$). Message indistinguishability under $y$ when $\alpha x'$ is private immediately follows.

However, note that $x'$ *is public*. Since $\alpha$ is uniform in $\mathbb{Z}_q^*$ and is private it follows that $x = \alpha x'$ is private. We have therefore shown the following.

**Theorem 3.** *Let $(\mathfrak{p}, g, H(\cdot), x')$ be public where $x' \in_R \mathbb{Z}_q^*$ and define $y = H(p_s \mid\mid g_s)^{x'}$ mod $p$. If the DDH assumption holds then ElGamal encryption using the public key $(y, g, \mathfrak{p})$ is semantically secure against plaintext attacks.*

Theorem 3 implies that under the DDH assumption it is intractable for everyone to decrypt ciphertexts computed using the "fake" $y$. Theorem 3 proves that Property 1 of Definition 2 holds.

By definition, the fake public key $y$ equals $H(p_s \mid\mid g_s)^x$ mod $p$. By construction $H(p_s \mid\mid g_s)$ generates $G_q$. Since $x \in_R \mathbb{Z}_q^*$ it follows that the fake $y$ is uniform in $G_q$. Property 2 of Definition 2 therefore immediately follows.

**Assumption 1.** *Given $(\mathfrak{p}, g, H(\cdot))$ it is computationally intractable to find a pair $(x, x')$ satisfying $g^x = H(p_s \mid\mid g_s)^{x'}$ mod $p$.*

Property 3 of the definition of a computational questionable encryption scheme follows from Assumption 1. We have shown the following theorem.

**Theorem 4.** *If the DDH assumption holds and Assumption 1 holds then the 5-tuple $(F, G_0, G_1, E, D)$ is a computational questionable encryption scheme.*

Finally, we remark that it is straightforward to adapt this approach to build a computational questionable encryption scheme based on Cramer-Shoup [7]. We briefly sketch how to do so here. Cramer-Shoup utilizes two generators $g_1$ and $g_2$. Computational indecipherability is achieved via the use of the verifiably fake generators $h_1 = H(p_s \mid\mid g_{1,s} \mid\mid g_{2,s} \mid\mid 01)$, $h_2 = H(p_s \mid\mid g_{1,s} \mid\mid g_{2,s} \mid\mid 10)$, and $h_3 = H(p_s \mid\mid g_{1,s} \mid\mid g_{2,s} \mid\mid 11)$. Here the values $p_s$, $g_{1,s}$, and $g_{2,s}$ are $p$, $g_1$, and $g_2$, respectively, formatted as bit strings of length $|p|$-bits. The witness of non-encryption is a 3-tuple $(x_1, x_2, x_3) \in_R \mathbb{Z}_q^* \times \mathbb{Z}_q^* \times \mathbb{Z}_q^*$. The fake public key is $(g_1, g_2, c, d, h) = (g_1, g_2, h_1^{x_1}, h_2^{x_2}, h_3^{x_3})$. So, chosen ciphertext security can be achieved if needed.

An interesting aspect of questionable encryptions is the following. Cramer-Shoup is message-aware. So the receiver will not accept a message that the sender does not know. However, it is not *trapdoor-aware*. This could pose problems in practice since a questionable encryption scheme lets message recipients repudiate the receipt of plaintexts.

## 6    Implementation

We implemented the computational questionable encryption scheme. It is slightly modified since it uses Diffie-Hellman [8] instead of ElGamal. The encryption and decryption code uses the Microsoft DSS/DH Cryptographic Service Provider that is present on the Windows 2000 and Windows XP operating systems. The key generation code and the code for the function $F$ utilizes OpenSSL. The implementation uses a safe prime $p$ that is 1024-bits in length.

The Minimalist GNU for Windows (MinGW) development environment was employed to compile the experimental program. The encryption code that in theory would reside in a malware program is small and trivial to implement. This code makes the following Windows API calls to generate key material: CryptGenKey and CryptGenRandom. It also utilizes the following calls:

CryptAcquireContext, CryptExportKey, CryptImportKey, CryptEncrypt, CryptDestroyKey, and CryptSetKeyParam.

This shows that computational questionable encryptions are easy to utilize in MS Windows programs.

## 7    Application

An application of the questionable encryption scheme is as follows. An attacker decides to carry out a malware attack. He either generates a real public key or fake public key. The resulting public key $y$ is placed in a malware program that is then deployed. The polynomial-sized witness $x$ is kept secret.

The malware program collects private host data in a clandestine fashion and then questionably encrypts it. The resulting ciphertexts are then steganographically encoded into multimedia files (perhaps using *public key steganography*) and are then anonymously broadcast (e.g., using a mix network to conceal the location of the malware) for reconnaissance by the attacker.[1]

The attacker reads the covert broadcast like everyone else. If the public key is real then the attacker deciphers the broadcast (using a trial-and-error approach if a secure covert channel is in use). If the public key is real then only the attacker can decipher the broadcast because only the attacker knows the needed private decryption key. If the public key is fake then the attacker makes no attempt to decipher the broadcast since it is intractable to do so.

Suppose that the malware is fully reverse-engineered and analyzed. Suppose that core dumps are taken at every stage of its execution. Suppose that all

---

[1] Except for the questionable encryption stage, this attack is based on the notion of *Deniable Password Snatching* [19].

packets that it sends out are recorded. All of this information combined still does not prove that any information has been stolen whatsoever since the public key could be fake (the witness of encryption is needed).

This scenario has the logical consequence that it is intractable to prove or disprove the occurrence of data theft via malware that uses questionable encryptions. This is important since the specific charge of *theft* may be separate and distinct from unlawful computer access and/or use. However, the attack thus far described gives no rational explanation of why anyone would carry out such an attack using a *fake* public key.

The following more elaborate attack addresses this issue. A questionable encryption scheme is made available as an open-source package. Numerous attackers independently design and release malware that transmit plaintext through a questionable encryption filter. Some malware programs contain a real public key, others contain a fake public key.

On occasion a malware author anonymously publishes the witness of non-encryption $x$ for his or her malware program. Consider one such occasion. Suppose that the fake public key $y$ has been extracted from the malware and has been made public (for example, by a universally trusted antivirus firm). Using the predicate $F$, it is then publicly verifiable that $F(x, y) = 0$. This establishes precedent that *spoofing* is commonplace among malware that questionably encrypts data and then transmits the resulting "ciphertext." So, a malware writer that is accused of stealing data using a questionable encryption scheme can remain silent and leave open the possibility that the public key in the malware program is fake. The fallback is the historical use of fake public keys in malware.

A prosecutor that has insufficient evidence to prove that a malware program was used to steal data may resort to arguing that if the public key is flawed (i.e., fake) then it was stupidity rather than cupidity on the part of the accused that prevented the theft from succeeding. In other words, the accused may be charged with attempted theft. However, the widely adopted open-source questionable encryption package, public literature on the subject, and cases in which malware was retroactively proven to not steal data directly counters this argument; the accused may have only intended to spoof.

It is therefore perfectly logical for an attacker to use a questionable encryption scheme while having no intentions of stealing data. We also remark that large-scale coordinated malware attacks are a modern reality, in the form of so-called "botnets."

## 8    Conclusion

We presented a tool called a computational questionable encryption scheme that hides whether or not an asymmetric encryption function encrypts data or not. An instantiation was given based on ElGamal. The security was proven based on the Decision Diffie-Hellman problem and a reasonable intractability assumption. A spoofing application was shown that enables the user to cast doubt on whether or not an agent encrypts or effectively erases plaintext prior to transmission of the ciphertext. It was shown that computational questionable encryptions are related yet distinct from various forms of oblivious transfer.

**Acknowledgments.** We thank an anonymous IH '06 referee for pointing out the stupidity vs. cupidity line of reasoning in arguing intent to steal data. We also thank David W. Kravitz for helpful input regarding the selection of cryptographic parameters.

# References

1. Brassard, G., Crépeau, C., Robert, J.M.: All-or-nothing disclosure of secrets. In: Advances in Cryptology—Crypto '86, pp. 234–238 (1986)
2. Brassard, G., Crépeau, C., Robert, J.M.: Information Theoretic Reductions among Disclosure Problems. In: IEEE Symposium on Foundations of Computer Science, pp. 168–173 (1986)
3. Berger, R., Peralta, R., Tedrick, T.: A Provably Secure Oblivious Transfer Protocol. In: Advances in Cryptology—Eurocrypt '84, pp. 379–386 (1985)
4. Blum, M.: Three applications of the oblivious transfer: Part I: Coin flipping by telephone; Part II: How to exchange secrets; Part III: How to send certified electronic mail. UC Berkeley (1981)
5. Boneh, D.: The Decision Diffie-Hellman Problem. In: Proceedings of the Third Algorithmic Number Theory Symposium—ANTS, pp. 48–63 (1998)
6. Canetti, R., Dwork, C., Naor, M., Ostrovsky, R.: Deniable Encryption. In: Advances in Cryptology—Crypto '97, pp. 90–104 (1997)
7. Cramer, R., Shoup, V.: A practical public key cryptosystem provably secure against adaptive chosen ciphertext attack. In: Advances in Cryptology—Crypto '98, pp. 13–25 (1998)
8. Diffie, W., Hellman, M.: New Directions in Cryptography. IEEE Trans. on Info. Theory IT-22(6), 644–654 (1976)
9. El Gamal, T.: A Public Key Cryptosystem and a Signature Scheme Based on Discrete Logarithms. IEEE Trans. Info. Theory 31(4), 469–472 (1985)
10. Goldwasser, S., Bellare, M.: Lecture Notes on Cryptography. Manuscript (July 10, 1996)
11. Goldreich, O.: Foundations of Cryptography (1989) Class Notes. Available at `http://www.wisdom.weizmann.ac.il/people/homepages/oded/ln89.html`
12. Goldreich, O.: A uniform-complexity treatment of encryption and zero-knowledge. Journal of Cryptology 6(1), 21–53 (1993)
13. Goldwasser, S., Micali, S.: Probabilistic Encryption. Journal of Computer and System Sciences—JCSS 28(2), 270–299 (1984)
14. Kilian, J.: Founding cryptography on oblivious transfer. In: ACM Symposium on Theory of Computing—STOC, pp. 20–31 (1988)
15. Kilian, J.: Uses of randomness in algorithms and protocols. MIT Press, Cambridge (1990)
16. Micali, S., Rackoff, C., Sloan, B.: The notion of security for probabilistic cryptosystems. SIAM J. on Comput. 17(2), 412–426 (1988)
17. Rabin, M.: How to exchange secrets by oblivious transfer. Harvard Aiken Comp. Lab, TR-81 (1981)
18. Tsiounis, Y., Yung, M.: On the security of ElGamal-based encryption. In: Proc. Public Key Cryptography—PKC '98, pp. 117–134 (1998)

19. Young, A., Yung, M.: Deniable Password Snatching: On the Possibility of Evasive Electronic Espionage. IEEE Symp. on Sec. and Priv. 224–235 (1997)
20. Young, A., Yung, M.: Malicious Cryptography: Exposing Cryptovirology. John Wiley & Sons, Inc. England (2004)
21. Young, A., Yung, M.: Questionable Encryption and Its Applications. In: Proc. Int. Conf. on Cryptology in Malaysia—MyCrypt '05, pp. 210–221 (2005)

# A    Related Privacy Primitives

The use of witnesses in our scheme is different but related to the use of witnesses in deniable encryptions [6]. In our approach, Bob has a witness that the value is an encryption or non-encryption under an asymmetric encryption function. In a *deniable encryption*, Bob can show a witness for each possible interpretation of the cleartext. Another difference is in the operational setting. In a deniable encryption, Alice and Bob both know a secret key that enables Bob to identify the correct cleartext among the possible cleartext and deniability is a stronger requirement that enables the receiver to claim any message to an observer. Therefore, it requires specialized implementations as well as less efficient ones and it is basically a symmetric key encryption due to the shared key. In our scheme Alice only knows the public key of Bob as well as her own secret cleartexts.

(1,2)-oblivious transfer is covered in [4,17,3,14,15]. In (1,2)-oblivious transfer, Bob has no control over which of the messages he receives, but knows that he will receive one. A questionable encryption (q.e.) scheme implements a form of oblivious transfer wherein the message recipient has total control over whether or not the message is received. These variants are called all-or-nothing disclosure of secrets [1,2]. This is the same as in a computational questionable encryption, so a q.e. scheme can be viewed as a variation on all-or-nothing disclosure.

However, a major difference between the two notions is as follows. A computational q.e. scheme is a cipher that can be used repeatedly and independently to many snippets of data, not data defined in the scope of a single protocol as is the case with all-or-nothing disclosure. In a computational q.e. scheme the sender only needs to obtain the public key of the receiver once, and from then on messages (i.e., "ciphertexts") are sent in a one-way fashion from the sender to the receiver in an all-or-nothing disclosure. A computational q.e. scheme allows Bob to prove whether or not everything was received or nothing was received by revealing the associated witness.

# Reversible Watermarking of
# NURBS-Based CAD Models

Wolfgang Funk

Fraunhofer Institute for Computer Graphics Research IGD, Fraunhoferstr. 5,
64283 Darmstadt, Germany
wolfgang.funk@igd.fraunhofer.de
http://www.igd.fhg.de

**Abstract.** We present an algorithm for embedding robust reversible watermarks into CAD models that are represented by a collection of NURBS (Non Uniform Rational B-Spline) surface patches.

Changes to the geometry of the surface representation are introduced by moving one control point per surface patch. This approach provides robustness against converting the model into the mesh representation. The information needed to restore the original control point location is added to the knot vectors of the patch, thus enabling recovery of the original model from the watermarked NURBS representation.

We exploit the properties of the NURBS representation for preserving the continuity between adjacent patches. Continuity is the major criterion of designers for assessing the quality of surface models.

## 1 Introduction

The algorithm presented in this paper was designed to support a scenario that we refer to as *engineering scenario*. It deals with valuable 3D data that are created by highly skilled specialists in CAD-based production chains. Automobiles, ships, aircrafts and trains are examples for such models. Usually, a single digital master model is produced, which is the basis for tool creation and the reference for control measurements during production. In contrast to models designed for applications such as games or web sites with 3D support, high quality CAD surface models are represented as sets of parametric curves and surface patches, which are mathematically described by Non-Uniform Rational B-Splines (NURBS).

In general, the meaning of design information contained in a high quality CAD model is twofold: the functionality, i.e. the technical know-how and innovation represented by the model, and the aesthetic aspect of its shape. In the latter scenario, even slight modifications of the model may not be acceptable when the free form surface represented by the model must be reprocessed or is actually manufactured, e.g. by a milling machine. To cope with this restriction, the modification of the model introduced by the watermark must be reversible so that the master model can be restored.

J. Camenisch et al. (Eds.): IH 2006, LNCS 4437, pp. 172–187, 2007.

We present a watermarking scheme that preserves the important properties of the shape, in particular the continuity at the boundaries of surface patches. The watermark can be detected and reversed without reference to the original in the NURBS representation of the model. It can be verified in versions of the model that have been transformed into a polygonal mesh. The polygonization of NURBS surfaces is usually denoted as *tesselation*. Here, verification means that we can decide if a given watermark was embedded: this approach is often referred to as zero-bit or one-bit watermark in the literature; we prefer the term *one-bit watermark* in this paper. The security of our reversible watermarking scheme relies on knowledge about the locations of specific points that define the geometry of the NURBS surface, the *control points*, as well as the location of specific points in the parameter space of the surface, the *knots*.

The paper is organized as follows. In Sect. 2 we give a very short review of NURBS-based CAD models and the concept of trimmed surfaces. In Sect. 3 we state the problem and briefly describe the requirements of the engineering scenario. Section 4 reviews previous work on digital watermarking for models in parametric representation and puts our approach in context. Section 5 presents an overview of our watermarking scheme. Section 6 gives a detailed description of the embedding algorithm as well as the retrieval and reversal algorithm that operates on the NURBS representation. Section 7 details how we cope with preserving continuity between adjacent surface patches. In Sect. 8 we give a short description of verifying a watermark in tesselated versions of the model. Finally, we draw conclusions and look beyond the current status to questions not answered so far.

The algorithm presented in Sect. 6 operates on a single surface patch to embed or retrieve one information bit. In order to handle a complete watermark message, a framework for accessing and processing all patches of the model is required. A complete discussion of the framework is out of the scope of this paper, thus, in Sect. 7 we elaborate on the framework component that preserves continuity conditions. Some aspects of retrieving a complete watermark message are discussed in Sect. 8.

## 2  NURBS-Based CAD Models

In contrast to polygonal meshes, NURBS-based models are exact mathematical descriptions of the surface of objects. In general, a NURBS-based surface model is composed of NURBS curves and surface patches. Here we give a very short review of the definitions in the notation used by Piegl and Tiller [1].

A NURBS curve $\mathbf{C}(u)$ is a piecewise polynomial curve defined by control points $\{\mathbf{P}_i\}$ that form a control polygon, the weights $\{w_i\}$, and the $p$th degree B-Spline basis functions $\{N_{i,p}(u)\}$ defined on the nonperiodic and nonuniform *knot vector* $U = (u_0, ..., u_m)$. The knot vector represents the parameter values of the endpoints of the segments of the curve, the knots, and is a nondecreasing sequence of real numbers. A NURBS curve $\mathbf{C}(u)$ is given by

$$\mathbf{C}(u) = \frac{\sum_{i=0}^{n} N_{i,p}(u) w_i \mathbf{P}_i}{\sum_{i=0}^{n} N_{i,p}(u) w_i} \tag{1}$$

where $m = n + p + 1$. Each control point $\mathbf{P}_i$ is assigned a specific weight $w_i$.

A NURBS tensor product NURBS surface $\mathbf{S}(u,v)$ is defined by the bidi-rectional control point net $\{\mathbf{P}_{i,j}\}$, the corresponding weights $\{w_{i,j}\}$ and the nonrational B-spline basis functions $\{N_{i,p}(u)\}$ and $\{N_{j,q}(v)\}$ defined on the non-periodic and nonuniform knot vectors $U = (u_0, ..., u_r)$ and $V = (v_0, ..., v_s)$:

$$\mathbf{S}(u,v) = \frac{\sum_{i=0}^{n} \sum_{j=0}^{m} N_{i,p}(u) N_{j,q}(v) w_{i,j} \mathbf{P}_{i,j}}{\sum_{i=0}^{n} \sum_{j=0}^{m} N_{i,p}(u) N_{j,q}(v)} \tag{2}$$

where $r = n + p + 1$ and $s = m + q + 1$. Each control point $\mathbf{P}_{i,j}$ is assigned a specific weight $w_{i,j}$.

**Trimmed NURBS Surfaces.** Trimmed surface patches are used for more elab-orate models, e.g. for representing holes in patches or to blend surface patches that form a larger surface area. A trimmed surface patch consists of a tensor product NURBS surface and a set of ordered and oriented trimming NURBS curves that are defined in the parameter space of the surface patch. The curves exclude parts of the surface that are not considered for the shape of the object. In the following, both untrimmed and trimmed patches are simply referred to as "patches" if the discussion is valid for both. Otherwise, the "trimmed" and "untrimmed" property of patches is explicitly stated.

## 3    Requirements Analysis

Here we briefly summarize the workflow and properties of the scenario we had in mind when designing our reversible watermarking scheme.

*Model Creation.* The final digital model is the result of a complex and time-consuming construction and design process. The model may represent an auto-mobile or an airplane, but also consumer goods such as a household article. The final construction model (the master) is the basis for all production steps that follow, such as tool design and construction.

*Quality Preservation.* The watermark must preserve the design quality of the model. In particular, continuity conditions between adjacent patches of the model must not be changed.

*Delivery and Tracing.* The model, or parts of it, are delivered to divisions, suppliers or contractors as NURBS-based 3D data sets. Before delivery of the model, a watermark that identifies the point of delivery (an *active fingerprint*) is embedded into the model. If a copy of the model is traced outside of the permitted workflow, the watermark can be detected and the point of leakage can be identified.

*Model Representations.* The copy may be accessible in different representations. We cover the original NURBS representation and tesselated versions. The watermark should be detectable and reversible in the NURBS representation. Robustness of the watermark against translation and rotation of the model is required to be able to integrate the marked NURBS model into a more complex model[1]. For example, a part of a car can be modeled by one designer and then be merged with parts created by other designers. Watermark verification capabilities in 3D polygon meshes are required, as the tesselation of NURBS models is one of the most common processing operations.

## 4   Previous Work

Digital watermarks for 3D polygonal models have attracted more and more attention since the seminal work of Ohbuchi, Masuda and Aono [2]. They present fundamental algorithms for embedding information into 3D polygonal models that either manipulate the geometry or the connectivity of the model. Currently there are only few publications available that deal with digital watermarking and related techniques for models in parametric representation.

Ohbuchi, Masuda and Aono [3] present a watermarking algorithm that exactly preserves the geometric shape of the watermarked NURBS curve or surface, respectively. The basic idea behind their embedding scheme is that a NURBS curve or surface can be reparametrized without altering its geometric shape. The watermark itself is encoded as modification of coefficients of a rational linear function, which is used to reparametrize the curve or surface.

Fornaro and Sanna [4] introduce a marking scheme for Constructive Solid Geometry (CSG) models that is intended for model authentication purposes. The additional information consists of a hash value of parts of the model, which is encrypted with the private key of the provider of the model and is stored either as comment or as additional item in the CSG file. Even though the method is denoted as watermarking by its authors, it must be classified as a labeling method. The additional information can be easily separated from the original data, and the integration process depends on the file format that is used for storing the CSG data.

Ko et al. [5] describe a technique for estimating the similarity of two NURBS objects, based on 3 different test criteria. The first test relies on the Euclidian distance of the surfaces, whereas the second test compares the principal curvatures of the surfaces. The third test searches for generic umbilical points of both surfaces and compares the umbilics. The proposed features, such as principal directions and umbilics, provide a robust fingerprint of the NURBS data. The method of Ko et al. does not manipulate the original data and can be classified as a fingerprint algorithm for NURBS objects.

---

[1] In some cases, also robustness against uniform scaling may be required. However, CAD models are usually created according to strict specifications regarding dimensioning.

Nagahashi, Mitsuhashi and Mooroka [6] present a method for embedding digital watermarks into a Bézier polynomial patch by subdiving it into two patches. Their approach can be interpreted as a reparametrization of the patch and does preserve the shape of the patch; it shows properties similar to the method propsed by Ohbuchi, Masuda and Aono [3] for NURBS data. Moreover, it is easy to recover the original patch from the two subpatches. To overcome this particular weakness, the authors propose to change the boundary curves of the patch, so that the original patch can not be restored from the watermarked version. As pointed out by the authors, this can cause topological changes to the model, which may be not acceptable.

Some authors propose applying well-known watermarking methods from the image domain to projections of parameteric models and propagating the changes back into the original model to create a watermarked version of the original model. Lee, Cho and Lee [7] derive a so-called virtual model from the original NURBS model by setting all control points weights to a constant value. The virtual model is sampled at specific points in parameter space, and the coordinates in 3D space are interpreted as intensity values of 3 so-called virtual images (the $x$, $y$ and $z$ coordinate, respectively) at the sampled grid points in the $(u, v)$ parameter space. These images are watermarked using common methods for 2D intensity data and the changes are propagated back into the model. Mitrea, Zaharia and Prêteux [8] sample 3 virtual images directly from the control point coordinates. The virtual images undergo a Discrete Cosine Transform (DCT); a spread spectrum based watermark is embedded in the DCT domain and the changes are propagated back into the model.

Our approach differs from the watermarking algorithms for NURBS data published so far in important aspects. We change the shape of the model to enable watermark verification in tesselated versions of the model. The modifications introduced by our algorithm are reversible in the NURBS representation, such that the original shape can be perfectly restored if required in the application scenario. As the embedding stage of the algorithm works directly on the NURBS representation, we have immediate and mathematically exact control over the impact on the quality of the model and we can maintain the original continuity between patch boundaries.

## 5   Algorithm Overview

We study surface models that are composed of trimmed and untrimmed NURBS surface patches. Without loss of generality, many of the properties of the algorithm can be demonstrated with NURBS curves. We will use the term *embedding primitive* to refer either to a curve or a surface patch henceforth. The basic principle of our method is to change the geometry of an embedding primitive by moving one control point, and to encode the information to move the control point back to its original position within the same primitive. This is achieved without further changing the shape of the patch by inserting additional knots into the knot vectors.

The changes introduced by modifying a single control point will be also denoted as *robust feature*, whereas the changes to the knot vectors of the patch will be denoted as *semi-fragile feature*. In the context of this paper, a *feature* is defined as the combination of one robust feature and the corresponding semi-fragile feature. One feature encodes exactly one of two states, i.e. one bit of information, in a reversible way. From a different perspective, this approach can be seen as embedding the same watermark message twice into the model. First, a robust one-bit watermark is encoded by changing the geometry of a number of patches, next, a semi-fragile N-bit watermark is encoded by modifying the knot vectors of the same patches.

## 5.1 Embedding

The surface patches that build up the model are processed in a well-defined order. As there is no natural order of patches, an ordering scheme must be imposed on the model. We do not cover this issue here, but make the assumption that an appropriate scheme exists, which defines the sequence for accessing the patches[2]. After the ordering phase, each patch can be unambiguously identified and accessed by an index value.

In the second phase of the embedding procedure the algorithm checks each patch if it is suitable for watermark embedding[3]. Then it modifies the valid patches by moving control points and inserting new knots into the knot vectors.

The control point modifications lead to modifications of the geometry (the robust watermark), whereas the knot insertion step (the semi-fragile watermark) is used to invisibly[4] encode the information required to invert the control point modifications. Invalid patches are marked using a specific version of the knot insertion step, such that they can efficiently be identified during watermark retrieval. To restrict access to the embedded information, the selection of control points and parameter values for knot insertion can be based on pseudo-random numbers derived from a secret key (c.f. section 6.1).

## 5.2 Retrieval and Recovery of the Original

The retrieval procedure depends on the representation of the model to be analyzed. For the sake of simplicity this model will be denoted as *copy*, whereas the original model will be denoted as *original* henceforth. If the copy is available in NURBS representation, the blind detector for the semi-fragile watermark as detailed in section 6.2 can be applied. The information assembled by the blind detector can optionally be used to recover the original from the copy.

In the case of tesselated models we utilize a type of detector that was proposed by Bendens [10] and will be denoted as *model-verifier* henceforth. From known

---

[2] A straightforward implementation could sort the patches by the length of their bounding box diagonal.

[3] The identification of valid surface patches is discussed in detail in section 7.

[4] Knot insertion does not modify the geometry of curves and surfaces[9,1].

feature locations (the original control points in our case), rays are cast towards the expected modified surface and the intersection point is determined. The number of correct intersections is analyzed (see section 8 for details).

## 6   Core Algorithm

This section details the algorithm for embedding and detecting one feature[5] in a single NURBS surface patch and how the modifications can be reversed from the information contained in the copy. We introduce the algorithm step by step as "literate code" with some additional discussion where neccessary.

Without loss of generality, the principles of the surface modification methods that are presented in this section can be exemplified by curves. Thus, for sake of clarity, the basic properties of the algorithm will be demonstrated using a NURBS curve[6]. The figures presented in this section were exactly calculated based on a cubic NURBS curve defined by 7 control points and the knot vector $U = \{u_0, \ldots, u_{10}\} = \{0, 0, 0, 0, 0.5, 1, 1.5, 2, 2, 2, 2\}$. Here, all weights $\{w_i\}$ of the curve are set to 1. The curve endpoints interpolate the first and the last control point, respectively.

The *Control Point Shift (CPS)* method moves control points such that the embedding primitive is pulled towards or pushed away from the control point. The maximum amplitude of the shift occurs along the line defined by the original control point and the nearest point on the embedding primitive. The direction of the movement of the embedding primitive with respect to the control point encodes one bit.

### 6.1   Embedding

1. Check if the embedding primitive is suitable for feature embedding. Optionally preprocess it to ensure that continuity is preserved with respect to neighboring primitives in the model. The test and the preprocessing procedures are detailed in section 7. If the embedding primitive is classified as not suitable, mark it as invalid as detailed in step 6 below and finish processing of the primitive. Otherwise, a set of control points suitable for modification has been identified.

2. Select a control point $\mathbf{P}_k$ from the set of of suitable control points that have been identified in step 1.

3. Find the point $\mathbf{C}$ on the curve, which is closest to the selected control point $\mathbf{P}_k$. The line from $\mathbf{C}$ to $\mathbf{P}_k$ defines the direction of the control point shift. If the reference point $\mathbf{C}$ can not be determined, mark the primitive as invalid (see step 6) and finish processing.

4. Shift control point $\mathbf{P}_k$ along the line defined by $\mathbf{C}$ and $\mathbf{P}_k$ to its new location $\hat{\mathbf{P}}_k$. The control point shift is such that distance $d$ between $\mathbf{C}$ on the original and $\hat{\mathbf{C}}$ on the modified embedding primitive is achieved. The shift may be

---

[5] A feature is comprised of a robust feature and the corresponding semi-fragile feature.

[6] By "embedding primitive" we refer either to a curve or a surface patch.

either directed from the original reference point towards the original control point for a *pull* operation as in the example of figure 1, or away from the original control point for a *push* operation. Thus we have two possible states represented by the shift direction, which can be used to encode one bit of information. We will the denote the shift vector from the original control point to its new location as shift vector $\mathbf{S} = \hat{\mathbf{P}}_k - \mathbf{P}_k$ henceforth.

In case of a successful shifting operation, the robust feature embedding is completed and the algorithm proceeds with embedding the semi-fragile feature. If the shifting operation fails, mark the embedding primitive as invalid (see step 6) and finish processing. Successful embedding of the robust CPS feature is illustrated in Fig. 1. The original curve (solid line) has been modified (dotted line) such that the reference point $\mathbf{C}(\bar{u} = 0.527)$ on the curve has been shifted by the distance $d = 0.05$ units[7] towards the control point $\mathbf{P}_k$. This has been achieved by shifting $\mathbf{P}_k$ by $d_p = 0.084$ to $\hat{\mathbf{P}}_{\mathbf{k}}$.

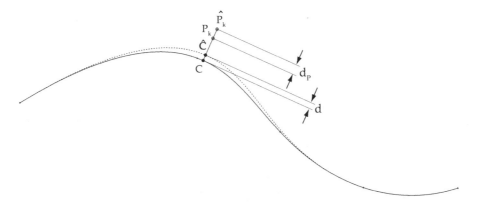

**Fig. 1.** CPS: Embedding a robust feature

5. The semi-fragile feature encodes the control point shift in the knots of the embedding primitive. The step discussed here is reiterated for each of the three components of the control point shift vector $\mathbf{S} = (S_x, S_y, S_z)$. For sake of clarity, we use only $S_x$ in the discussion[8].

Choose a knot span $[u_i, u_{i+1}]$ with the knot span length $L = u_{i+1} - u_i$ where to insert a new knot at $u$ that encodes $S_x$. For surfaces there are two knot vectors, thus the knot span may be selected from either of the two knot vectors of a patch.

Place a new knot into the chosen knot span such that subdiving the knot span by inserting a new knot encodes $S_x$. With

---

[7] By units we denote the internal measurement units of the model, e.g. millimeters or inches.

[8] A step, which is not detailed here, is that we set up a local coordinate system for the patch to be independent of rigid transforms and scaling. Such a coordinate system can be based, for example, on 3 corner points of the surface patch.

$$L_2 = |S_x| \quad \text{and} \quad \frac{L}{X} = L_1 + L_2$$

we get

$$L_2 = \frac{L}{X(1 + |S_x|)} \tag{3}$$

The scaling factor $X$ is selected from a predefined range that is a parameter of the algorithm. $X >= 2$ must hold, as a scaling factor $X < 2$ may result in $L_2 > 0.5 \cdot L$ and $L_2$ is required to fit into one half of the knot span, as discussed in the next paragraph.

As we encode $|S_x|$, an additonal criterium is introduced to encode the sign of $S_x$. The sign is mapped to knot insertion into the lower or upper half of the knot span[9]. Moreover, we have an additonal degree of freedom by inserting the knot either with respect to the lower or upper boundary of the selected half of the knot span.

Thus, depending on the sign of $S_x$ and the chosen reference (upper or lower boundary), a new knot is inserted at one of the following parameter values:

$$u = u_i + 0.5 \cdot L - L_2 \tag{4a}$$
$$u = u_i + L_2 \tag{4b}$$
$$u = u_i + 0.5 \cdot L + L_2 \tag{4c}$$
$$u = u_{i+1} - L_2 \tag{4d}$$

Figure 2 illustrates encoding of a semi-fragile feature for the modified curve from Fig. 1. To achieve $d = 0.05$ the original control point $P_2$ was shifted by $\mathbf{S} = (0.0344, 0.0770, 0)$.

- Knot span $[0.5, 1)$ was used to encode $S_x = 0.0344$. Scale factor $X = 3$ and the upper half of the knot span were selected for knot insertion. A knot is inserted at $u = 0.9111$.
- Knot span $[1, 1.5)$ was used to encode $S_y = 0.0770$. Scale factor $X = 2.5$ and the lower half of the knot span were selected for knot insertion. A knot is inserted at $u = 1.0642$.
- Knot span $[1.5, 2)$ was used to encode $S_z = 0$. With scale factor $X = 2$ the knot is inserted exactly at the middle of the knot span $u = 1.75$.

After embedding the 3 knots as descrived above, the semi-fragile feature has been successfully encoded and the embedding procedure is finished.

6. This step is only executed if one of the previous steps fails. With (3) and $X = 2$ and $S_x = 0$, we see that $L_2 = 0.5 \cdot L$ is possible for a shift vector with zero value components. Thus, an invalid embedding primitive is tagged by inserting an unique semi-fragile feature, which is represented by 3 knots inserted exactly at $u = u_i + 0.5 \cdot L$ into each of the 3 knots spans selected in step 5. This corresponds to a shift vector with all 3 components equal to zero (i.e. no control point shift at all).

---

[9] "Lower" and "upper" are used in the sense of lower and higher values of the parameter $u$.

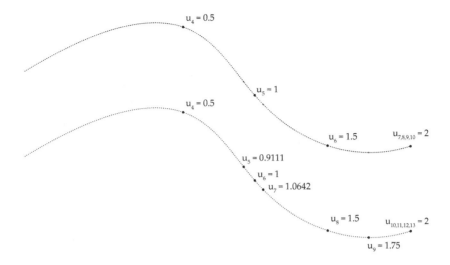

**Fig. 2.** Insertion of 3 knots with different scale factors $X$

**Security Considerations.** The steps for embedding one feature involve several selection processes that can be used to restrict access to the embedded information. The selection of the control point for encoding the robust feature as well as the knot spans for encoding the semi-fragile feature can be based on pseudo-randomly generated indices into the control polygon and the knot vector, respectively. For NURBS surfaces there is an additional degree of freedom in both cases, as we have a control net and two knot vectors (c.f. Sect. 2). The scaling factor used in the knot insertion step may be chosen pseudo-randomly from a predefined set of values.

In addition, there a several steps where we use mapping processes that can be scrambled based on a pseudo-random number: the actual state (i.e. bit value) that is represented by a specific direction of the control point shift; the choice of a specific half of the selected knot span for actually inserting an additional knot; and the reference value for measuring new knot span lengths, namely the upper or lower bound of the knot span. The number of possible combinations can be rather high for a typical NURBS surface patch. For a typical patch that has been preprocessed as detailed in Sect. 7, we get 64 valid control points and 441 valid knot spans for embedding. Thus the probability of selecting the correct 3 knots in correct order by randomly selecting 3 knot spans, and at the same time randomly selecting the correct control point, is extremely low.

## 6.2  Retrieval and Recovery of Original

The retrieval of the semi-fragile feature and the restoration of the original control point is essentially the inverse of the embedding procedure. First, the semi fragile feature is retrieved, thus decoding the watermark information. Next, the robust feature embedding can be reversed by restoring the orginal location of the control point, exploiting the information retrieved from the semi-fragile feature.

Retrieval of the semi-fragile feature and reversal of the embedding procedure requires the following sequence of steps. The control point and knot span selection process is the same as for the embedding procedure and is not reiterated here.

1. The step discussed here is reiterated for each of the three components of the control point shift vector $\mathbf{S} = (S_x, S_y, S_z)$. It is important that the knots are retrieved in reverse order of embedding, i.e. in the order $S_z, S_y, S_x$. For the sake of clarity we detail this step only for $S_z$.

   (a) Select parameter range $[u_i, u_{i+2})$ representing the original knot span length $L = u_{i+2} - u_i$. The knot that encodes $S_z$ has been inserted in this interval at $u_{i+1}$.

   (b) If $u_{i+1}$ is located exactly at $u = u_i + 0.5 \cdot L$, set $S_z = 0$ and finish processing of this component of $\mathbf{S}$.

   Then, with the appropriate expression from equation (4) we are able to calculate $L_2$ and from equation (3) we immediately get

$$S_z = \frac{L}{X \, L_2} - 1 \tag{5}$$

   Based on the mapping of the sign of $S_z$ to a particular half of the interval $[u_i, u_{i+2})$, decode the actual sign of $S_z$ from the location of $u_{i+1}$ within the interval.

   Remove the knot at $u_{i+1}$ before processing $Sy$. This is important, as during embedding this knot was not present when selecting the knot span used to encode $S_y$. Preserving the knot at $u_{i+1}$ would prevent finding the correct knot span for decoding $S_y$.

2. At this stage the control point shift vector $\mathbf{S}$, and consequently the watermark message bit encoded by the semi-fragile feature (push or pull), is known and the retrieval of the semi-fragile feature is completed. If $\mathbf{S} = (0, 0, 0)$, the embedding primitive is considered as invalid.

   The following step will only be necessary if the robust feature is to be reversed.

3. Remove the knot encoding $S_x$. This was not neccessary for decoding the control point shift vector. Next, restore the original control point location from $\mathbf{P_k} = \hat{\mathbf{P}}_k - \mathbf{S}$.

After running through the complete processing chain detailed above, the original geometry of the embedding primitive has been restored. If knot vector refinements (see Sec. 7) were neccessary to make the primitive suitable for embedding, these knots can be removed here. It must be emphasized that knot vector refinement in preprocessing steps did not change the geometry of the primitive; perfect restoration of the original geometry is independent from reversing knot refinement.

### 6.3 Robustness Considerations

Transformations of NURBS curves and surfaces are achieved by transforming the control points only [1], i.e. the knot vectors do not change. Correct decoding of the shift vector $\mathbf{S}$ is possible after translations, rotations and uniform scaling if we use a normalized local coordinate system for each patch. Thus the feature can be reversed in translated, rotated and uniformly scaled copies if the original NURBS representation is preserved.

It must be noted that watermark retrieval and reversal as described in the previous section depend on the integrity of the knot vectors and are not robust against knot insertion and knot refinement steps. Inserting additional knots or removing knots will prevent the algorithm from finding the correct combination of control point and knot triple for successful decoding and reversal. As we work with surface patches as embedding primitives, the algorithm is not robust against operations such as merging of patches. Nevertheless, watermark verification as described in section 8 is still possible after an additional tesselation step.

## 7    Preserving Continuity Between Patches

The concepts and theory of geometric and parametric continuity will not be reviewed here. Farin [11] discusses geometric continuity for surfaces, whereas Foley et al. [12] focus on geometric and parametric continuity for curves.

**Untrimmed Patches.** The impact of changes to a control point can be exactly specified by analyzing the knot vectors of the surface patch and the location of the control point within the control net of the patch. Modifying the control point $P_{i,j}$ with indices $i, j$ into the control net affects the surface only in the rectangular domain $[u_i, u_{i+p+1}) \times [v_j, v_{j+q+1})$ of the parameter plane [13,1], with the knot vectors $u$ and $v$, the surface degree $p$ in $u$, and the degree $q$ in $v$.

Thus, for each control point in the control net of the surface patch, it must be verified that the impact region does not touch the first and does not intersect[10] the last non-zero knot span of the patch. Otherwise, modifying the control point will impact the boundary curves and the control point will be classified as not suitable for embedding.

**Trimmed Patches.** For trimmed surface patches the impact region must not intersect or touch one of the trimming loops (intersection-test) and must be located inside the outer trimming loop (inside-test). Each trimming loop defined for the patch is approximated by a polygon. Subsequently, the rectangular impact region of each control point is subjected to the intersection- and inside-test with each of the polygonized trimming curves. The algorithm proposed by Piegl and Tiller [14] was used for polygonizing the trimming curves. It guarantees a defined maximum deviation of the polygon legs from the real trimming curve.

---

[10] The distinction between "touching" and "intersecting" is necessary, because the impact region is given by half-open intervals in $u$ and $v$.

Figure 3 shows the $(u, v)$ parameter plane of a trimmed surface patch with an inner and an outer trimming loop and the knot lines. In this case, the impact region of a suitable control point must be located within the black region of the parameter plane. All other knot spans will have an impact either on the outer or the inner trimming loop.

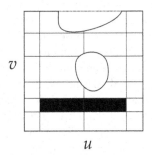

**Fig. 3.** Impact regions in the $(u, v)$ parameter plane

**Preprocessing of Invalid Patches.** If one of the aforementioned tests fails, the surface patch can be preprocessed such that it contains a set of control points suitable for embedding. As the impact region of a control point is determined by the knot vectors of the surface, knot insertion [9,1] is an appropriate tool for refining the knot vector and thus restricting the range of the impact region. To insert one new knot into a knot vector of a curve of degree $p$, we must calculate $p$ new control points and the total number of control points increases by one. It is important to note that knot insertion is equivalent to a change of the vector space basis, thus neither the geometry nor the parametrization of the curve is changed. Knot insertion for surface patches is performed by applying the technique for curves to the rows and columns of the control net of the patch.

To process an invalid patch, each non-zero knot span of both knot vectors is recursively subdivided into two knot spans of the same length. The recursion level is a parameter of the algorithm. A single recursion step will transform the $n \times m$ control net of the patch into a $2(n-1) \times 2(m-1)$ control net. After knot refinement, the validity check is reiterated.

## 8  Retrieval from Tesselated Models

The watermark verifier for tesselated versions of a copy depends on side information, namely, the coordinates of the original control points together with the particular bit of the watermark message encoded by each control point. By casting rays from the original control points directed along the control point shift, we determine the intersection points with the surface of the copy. If an intersection point within a given distance from the original control point can be found, we take the corresponding feature as detected.

If the number of detected features is interpreted as random variable, we can assign the detection result a probability that the copy has been randomly generated. The false positive probability for detecting $V$ or more features from a total of $N$ features is given by the cumulative binomial distribution $B(V, N, \mathsf{p})$ with probability $\mathsf{p} = 0.5$ for a random detection.

If the tesselated copy has undergone an affine transformation, preprocessing is necessary to align copy and original. This procedure is usually referred to as *registration* in computer vision or as *localization* in computer aided inspection and is a reseach topic in its own right. A simple yet efficient approach in the case of translations and rotations is based on expressing the original and the copy in the Euclidian coordinate system given by their principal components [15].

Various algorithms have been proposed for tesselating NURBS-based surface models. In particular for trimmed surfaces, tesselation is still a very active research topic and different methods generating meshes with different properties are available [16]. The impact of tesselation on the embedded watermark is different, depending on the tesselation algorithm. Some algorithms guarantee for a maximum Euclidian distance between the original and the generated mesh. We used an adaptive algorithm that specifies the maximum deviation in percent of the bounding box diagonal.

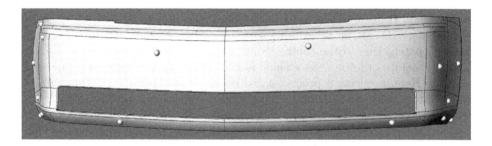

**Fig. 4.** Model with rendered patch boundaries and feature point locations indicated by spheres. Part of the car model courtesy of Jiro Katayama [17].

Figure 4 shows a part from a car model with rendered boundaries of the surface patches. The locations on the surface with maximum shift towards a control point (i.e. the reference points $\mathbf{C}$ from Sec. 6.1) are indicated by spheres. The control point shift was chosen as 0.03% of the measurement unit of the original model. For tesselation with 0.01% of the bounding box as tolerance, all 15 features could be verified, whereas verification failed in case of tesselation with 0.03% tolerance for the 2 features located in the long and small patches at the bottom of model. On one hand 15 features are not enough to be useful with the described detector, on the other hand the surface of the car model is composed of many parts. In a complete model we are able to embed a number of features that is large enough for the model verifier to yield a false positive probabilty small enough to be useful as decision criterium.

# 9   Conclusions

We presented a watermarking approach for high quality NURBS-based CAD models. In contrast to other robust schemes proposed up to now we work directy on the NURBS representation of the data. With our approach we have immediate control over the numerical quality of the model, such that the watermark can comply with a specific surface tolerance. The watermark embedding process can be reversed and we preserve continuity between patch boundaries, which is one of the most important properties of high quality industrial surface models. The watermarked NURBS model can be integrated into other models or scenes, as the boundaries of the model are not changed and the watermark can be retrieved and reversed in translated, rotated and scaled versions of the copy.

Our approach can be interpreted as embedding a robust one-bit watermark by changes of the geometry, and a semi-fragile N-bit watermark by modifying the knot vectors. The robust watermark can be verified in an informed detection process, while the semi-fragile watermark can be used both for blind detection and to recover the information for reversing the modifications introduced by the robust watermark.

So far we have tested the one-bit scheme only for robustness against tesselation of the copy. Additional modifications, such as mesh decimation, will be subject of future research. Currently the semi-fragile scheme is only robust against rigid transforms and uniform scaling. We will extend the robustness to general affine transforms by working with a local barycentric coordinate systems for each patch. Due to the control point and knot selection process, which relies on absolute ordering, the scheme is not robust against knot insertion and removal. Here, a selection process based on arc length parametrization will be investigated. Another topic to be considered in the near future is an in-depth analysis of the security of the algorithm.

Benchmarking the algorithm is one of our most important ongoing research tasks, thus detailed evaluation results will be presented in a follow-up study. In parallel to our benchmarking activities we are building up a database consisting of a diverse set of of high quality NURBS-based CAD models.

The most demanding application is the verificaton of the watermark in a two-dimensional version of the copy, i.e. from a rendered image. Currently we are working towards an image-verifier that compares a rendered copy against rendered versions of the model with known embedded watermark message and decides on the best match.

# References

1. Piegl, L., Tiller, W.: The NURBS Book. Springer-Verlag, Heidelberg, Germany (1997)
2. Ohbuchi, R., Masuada, H., Aono, M.: Watermarking Three-Dimensional Polygonal Models. ACM Multimedia 97, 261–272 (1997)

3. Ohbuchi, R., Masuda, H., Aono, M.: A Shape-Preserving Data Embedding Algorithm for NURBS Curves and Surfaces. In: Werner, R. (ed.) Proceedings of the 1999 International Conference on Computer Graphics, Canmore, Alberta, Canada, pp. 180–187. IEEE Press, Los Alamitos (1999)

4. Fornaro, C., Sanna, A.: Public key watermarking for authentication of CSG models. Computer Aided Design 32(12), 727–735 (2000)

5. Ko, K.H., Maekawa, T., Patrikalakis, N.M., Masuda, H., Wolter, F.E.: Shape Intrinsic Watermarks for Free-Form Objects. In: Proceedings of the 2004 NSF Design, Service and Manufacturing Grantees and Research Conference, Dallas, Texas (2004)

6. Nagahashi, H., Mitsuhashi, R., Morooka, K.: A method for watermarking to bézier polynomial surface models. Transactions of the Institute of Electronics, Information and Communication Engineers E87-D(1), 224–232 (2004)

7. Lee, J.J., Cho, N.I., Lee, S.U.: Watermarking for 3d nurbs graphic data. EURASIP Journal on Applied Signal Processing 14, 2142–2152 (2004)

8. Mitrea, M., Zaharia, T., Prêteux, F.: Spread spectrum robust watermarking for nurbs surfaces. WSEAS Transactions on Communications 3(2), 734–740 (2004)

9. Boehm, W.: Inserting new knots into B-spline curves. Computer-Aided Design 12(4), 199–201 (1980)

10. Benedens, O.: Robust Watermarking and Affine Registration of 3D Meshes. In: Petitcolas, F.A.P. (ed.) IH 2002. LNCS, vol. 2578, pp. 177–195. Springer, Heidelberg (2003)

11. Farin, G.: Curves and Surfaces for CAGD: a Practical Guide, 5th edn. Morgan Kaufmann, San Francisco, CA, USA (2002)

12. Foley, J., van Dam, A., Feiner, S.K., Hughes, J.F.: Computer Graphics: Principles and Practice. Addison-Wesley, Reading, MA, USA (1989)

13. Piegl, L.: Modifying the shape of rational B-splines. Part 2: surfaces. CAD 21(9), 509–518 (1989)

14. Piegl, L., Tiller, W.: Geometry-based triangulation of trimmed surfaces. CAD 30(1), 11–18 (1998)

15. Uccheddu, F., Corsini, M., Barni, M.: Wavelet-Based Blind Watermarking of 3D Models. In: Proceedings of the Multimedia and Security Workshop, Magdeburg, Germany, pp. 143–154. ACM, New York, NY, USA (2004)

16. Agoston, M.K.: Computer Graphics and Geometric Modeling: Implementation and Algorithms. Springer, London (2005)

17. Katayama, J.: Rhino 3D Modelling: Rhino Car Design School Data and Commentary. (Last accessed August 18, 2006)
http://www.rhino3d.co.jp/seminar/seminar_carstylinge.html

# A High-Capacity Data Hiding Method for Polygonal Meshes*

Hao-tian Wu and Yiu-ming Cheung

Department of Computer Science,
Hong Kong Baptist University, Hong Kong, China

**Abstract.** This paper presents a high-capacity data hiding method for 3D polygonal meshes. By slightly modifying the distance from a vertex to its traversed neighbors based on quantization, a watermark (i.e., a string of binary numbers) can be embedded into a polygonal mesh during a mesh traversal process. The impact of embedding can be tuned by appropriately choosing the quantization step. The embedded data is robust against those content-preserving manipulations, such as rotation, uniformly scaling and translation, as well as mantissa truncation of vertex coordinate to a certain degree, but sensitive to malicious manipulations. Therefore, it can be used for authentication and content annotation of polygonal meshes. Compared with the previous work, the capacity of the proposed method is relatively high, tending to 1 bit/vertex. Besides to define the embedding primitive over a neighborhood so as to achieve resistance to substitution attacks, the security is also improved by making it hard to estimate the quantization step from the modified distances. A secret key is used to order the process of mesh traversal so that it is even harder to construct a counterfeit mesh with the same watermark. The numerical results show the efficacy of the proposed method.

## 1 Introduction

With the development of digital modeling and visualization techniques for 3D objects, 3D models have been widely created and used for geometry representation, such as the cultural heritage recording like Digital Michelangelo Project [1], CAD models, and structural data of biological macromolecules [2]. As more and more 3D models appear, polygonal meshes in particular, how to hide information within them [3] has received much attention for a variety of purposes, ranging from copyright enforcement (e.g. [9,10]) to authentication (e.g. [4,6]). In this paper, we only discuss fragile watermarking of polygonal meshes, which is contrast to robust watermarking for the fragility of the embedded watermark. Compared with digital images, video and audio streams, there exists no grid for meshes, i.e., each vertex in a mesh is connected with variable neighboring vertices at different distances. This flexibility of mesh data makes it an attractive cover object for data hiding.

---

* This work was supported by a Faculty Research Grant of Hong Kong Baptist University with the Project Code: FRG/06-07/II-07.

J. Camenisch et al. (Eds.): IH 2006, LNCS 4437, pp. 188–200, 2007.

In the literature, quite a few watermarking methods (e.g.[4]-[18]) have been proposed to embed data into meshes. Depending on the applications, the requirements are different. For instance, one purpose of robust watermarking is to protect the copyright of digital works so that the embedded watermark is designed robust against outer processing while the original work can be used in the retrieval process [10]. In contrast, in fragile watermarking for authentication and integrity verification, the embedded data should be blindly retrieved and sensitive to illegal modifications [4], and high information rate is preferred. Nevertheless, there are some common requirements, such as security and fidelity. In [19], T. Kalker defined the security of robust watermarking as the inability of unauthorized users to remove, detect or change the watermark. A data hiding scheme is considered secure if there is little information leakage from the public domain. It should be assumed that the algorithms are publicly known and the attacker has sufficient computational capability so that some valuable information may be leaked from the observation of watermarked objects. Fidelity means that the embedded data is invisible (except the case that it is intentionally visible), i.e., the embedding process should not introduce noticeable distortion to the cover object. And it is often required that the introduced error can be numerically analyzed and bounded.

Only a few fragile watermarking algorithms (e.g.[4]-[8]) have been proposed for authentication of polygonal meshes. The first fragile watermarking of 3D objects is addressed by Yeo and Yeung in [4] for authentication and integrity protection by using a set of lookup tables (LUTs). If two values generated from the positions of a vertex and its traversed neighboring vertices are identical to each other, the vertex is considered as valid. Otherwise, its position will be perturbed until the two values match. Since the data embedded in [4] is sensitive to *R*otation, uniformly *S*caling and *T*ranslation transformations (denoted as RST hereinafter), its applications may be limited. By adapting the work in [4], Lin et al. proposed a fragile watermarking method in [5] to detect malicious attacks. They improve the mapping from vertex positions to location indices so that the embedded watermark is resistant to incidental data processing, such as vertex reordering, but RST transformations are still not allowed. Moreover, Benedens and Busch proposed the algorithm called Vertex Flood Algorithm (VFA) in [6] for mesh authentication. Basically, their algorithm modifies the vertices so that their distances to the centroid of a designated triangle encode the watermark bits. In this way, a certain amount of vertex coordinate truncation caused by format conversions, as well as RST transformations, can be allowed. As for a triangle mesh, the security of VFA relies on the selection of the start triangle since the vertex position can be modified without changing the distance from it to the centroid of the start triangle. Later, Cayre and Macq presented a steganographic scheme [7] for triangle meshes by treating a triangle as a two-state geometrical object. By choosing an appropriate Macro Embedding Procedure (MEP) order, a watermark can be imperceptibly embedded with robustness against RST transformations. The upper bound of capacity has been given in [7], but the optimal mesh traversal to reach it has not been addressed yet. Alternatively, in our previous work [8], a fragile watermark robust against RST transformations is embedded into polygonal meshes by quantizing the distances from the surface polygons to the mesh centroid. By choosing an appropriate quantization step, the embedded watermark can be made imperceptible and sensitive to illegal modifications. Although high information rate is required in fragile watermarking, the upper bound of capacity has not been reached in [8].

This paper presents a new data hiding method for polygonal meshes, in which the embedded data is designed to be robust against those content-preserving manipulations, such as RST manipulations and truncation of vertex coordinates to a certain degree, but sensitive to malicious manipulations. A new quantization method is employed to embed a watermark (i.e., a string of binary numbers) by slightly modifying the distance from a vertex to the centroid of its traversed neighbors. The impact of the embedding process, i.e., the difference between the original and watermarked meshes, can be tuned by choosing an appropriate quantization step. The capacity of the proposed method tends to 1 bit/vertex, which is higher than the former methods, such as 0.877 bit/vertex in [7]. It can be used for content annotation and authentication of polygonal meshes, or even secret message communication.

The rest of this paper is organized as follows. In the following section, the procedure of the data hiding method, including watermark embedding and retrieval, will be described in detail. The experimental results will be given and discussed in Section 3 by implementing the proposed method to authentication of polygonal meshes. Section 4 summarizes the paper and points out the future works.

## 2    A New Method to Hide Data Within Polygonal Meshes

Polygonal meshes are considered as the common representation of 3D shapes and it's easy to convert other types of 3D models into them. Despite the appearance attributes associated with 3D models, such as color, transparency and texture, there are two parts of information contained in the mesh data, i.e. the mesh geometry and topology. The mesh geometry can be represented by the set of vertex positions $V = \{v_1, \cdots, v_m\}$, which defines the shape of the mesh in $R^3$ given $m$ vertices in a mesh. The mesh topology, i.e., the connectivity between vertices, specifies the $n$ vertices $\{v_k^1, \cdots, v_k^n\}$ in the $k$-th polygon, as described by IndexedFaceSet in VRML [20] format. The proposed method is performed on polygonal meshes, consisting of embedding and retrieval processes, detailed as follows.

### 2.1    Data Embedding

Given a string of binary numbers $W = (w_i)_{i=1}^N$ with the length $N$, the task of embedding is hide the value of each bit $w_i$ into the mesh geometry. Since we aim to embed a watermark robust against RST transformations, the ratio between the distances in the cover mesh serves as a good candidate. In our method, the distance from a vertex to the centroid of its traversed neighbors is chosen as the embedding primitive so that the upper bound of capacity can be reached. If we choose the distance from a vertex to the centroid of all its neighbors as the embedding primitive and modify the distance to embed a binary number by adjusting its position, the positions of its neighboring vertices cannot be changed any more to preserve the embedded value. As a result, the capacity will drop since most of the vertex positions cannot be modified to embed binary numbers. Therefore, only the traversed vertices of each vertex are chosen to generate the embedding primitive so that high information rate is achieved.

The detailed process to embed a watermark $W = (w_i)_{i=1}^N$ is as follows: Initially, we use a secret key $K$ as the seed of pseudo-random generator to permute the face indices $F$ and vertex indices $I$, respectively. The process of mesh traversal is ordered by the permuted vertex indices $I'$ and face indices $F'$ as follows. Among those vertices in the polygon lastly indexed by $F'$, the one first indexed by $I'$ is traversed at first without adjusting its position since all of its neighboring vertices have not been traversed. Among the neighbors of the traversed vertices, the one first indexed by $I'$ will always be subsequently traversed. Suppose there is $m$ vertices in a polygonal mesh, there are $m-1$ embedding primitives because only the first traversed vertex has no traversed neighbor. For a newly traversed vertex $v_i$, $N_i$ neighboring vertices have been traversed and denoted as $(v_i^j)_{j=1}^{N_i}$. Then the centroid of the traversed neighbors can be calculated by

$$v_{ic} = \frac{1}{N_i} \sum_{j=1}^{N_i} v_i^j. \tag{1}$$

The distance $d_i$ from $v_{ic}$ to $v_i$ is chosen as the embedding primitive

$$d_i = \sqrt{(v_{icx} - v_{ix})^2 + (v_{icy} - v_{iy})^2 + (v_{icz} - v_{iz})^2}, \tag{2}$$

where $\{v_{icx}, v_{icy}, v_{icz}\}$ and $\{v_{ix}, v_{iy}, v_{iz}\}$ are the coordinates of $v_{ic}$ and $v_i$ in $R^3$, respectively. To embed a binary number $w_i$ by slightly changing $d_i$ with the quantization step $\Delta$, its corresponding integer quotient $Q_i$ and the remainder $R_i$ should be calculated by

$$\begin{cases} Q_i = \lfloor d_i/\Delta \rfloor \\ R_i = d_i \% \Delta \end{cases}, \tag{3}$$

and $d_i$ is modified by

$$d_i' = \begin{cases} d_i & \text{if } Q_i \% 2 = w_i \\ d_i + 2 \times (\Delta - R_i) & \text{if } Q_i \% 2 \neq w_i \ \& \ R_i \geq \frac{\Delta}{2} \\ d_i - 2 \times R_i & \text{if } Q_i \% 2 \neq w_i \ \& \ R_i < \frac{\Delta}{2} \end{cases} \tag{4}$$

so that $\lfloor d_i'/\Delta \rfloor \% 2 = w_i$. The error introduce by Eq.(4), i.e., the difference between the modified distance $d_j'$ and $d_i$, will not exceed the quantization step $\Delta$ so that the impact of embedding on the mesh content can be tuned with the quantization step $\Delta$. To allow slight change of $d'_j$, such as mantissa truncation due to the limited precision, a margin around the quantization grid is required. So Eq.(4) is slightly deformed by adding a parameter $\epsilon \in (0, \frac{\Delta}{2})$ through

$$
d'_i = \begin{cases} (Q_i + 1) \times \Delta - \epsilon & \text{if } Q_i\%2 = w_i \ \& \ \Delta - \epsilon < R_i \\ d_i & \text{if } Q_i\%2 = w_i \ \& \ \epsilon \le R_i \le \Delta - \epsilon \\ Q_i \times \Delta + \epsilon & \text{if } Q_i\%2 = w_i \ \& \ R_i < \epsilon \\ (Q_i + 1) \times \Delta + \epsilon & \text{if } Q_i\%2 \ne w_i \ \& \ \Delta - \epsilon < R_i \\ d_i + 2 \times (\Delta - R_i) & \text{if } Q_i\%2 \ne w_i \ \& \ \frac{\Delta}{2} \le R_i \le \Delta - \epsilon \\ d_i - 2 \times R_i & \text{if } Q_i\%2 \ne w_i \ \& \ \epsilon \le R_i < \frac{\Delta}{2} \\ Q_i \times \Delta - \epsilon & \text{if } Q_i\%2 \ne w_i \ \& \ R_i < \epsilon \end{cases} \tag{5}
$$

so that $d'_i\%\Delta \in (\epsilon, \Delta - \epsilon)$. As a result, the change of $d'_i$ within $(-\epsilon, \epsilon)$ can be allowed without changing the embedded value $w_i$. An appropriate value should be assigned to $\epsilon$ without disclosing the quantization step $\Delta$. If we choose the value of $\epsilon$ in proportional to $\Delta$, $\frac{\Delta}{6}$ for instance, the allowed range can be adjusted by appropriately choosing the quantization step $\Delta$. Consequently, the resulting $d'_i$ is used to adjust the position of $v_i$ by

$$
v'_i = v_{ic} + (v_i - v_{ic}) \times \frac{d'_i}{d_i}, \tag{6}
$$

where $v'_i$ is the adjusted vertex position. At each iteration, to embed one bit value, the position of the newly traversed vertex is adjusted to modulate the distance from it to the centroid of its traversed neighbors. So the number of the embedded bits is equal to the number of the adjusted vertices. Given $m$ vertices in the cover mesh, there will be $m - 1$ bit values embedded after the position of the last traversed vertex is adjusted so that the watermarked mesh is generated. After that, the position of mesh centroid is calculated by

$$
v_c = \frac{1}{m} \sum_{i=1}^{m} v'_i, \tag{7}
$$

and the distance from the last traversed vertex $v_l$ to the mesh centroid is calculated by

$$
D = \sqrt{(v_{lx} - v_{cx})^2 + (v_{ly} - v_{cy})^2 + (v_{lz} - v_{cz})^2}. \tag{8}
$$

The ratio $R$ between $D$ and $\Delta$ is obtained by

$$
R = D/\Delta, \tag{9}
$$

which will be used in the retrieval process to calculate the quantization step $\Delta$.

## 2.2   Message Retrieval

To retrieve the embedded data from the watermarked mesh, the quantization step $\Delta$ used in watermark embedding is required. To obtain $\Delta$, the distance

$D$ from the last traversed vertex to the mesh centroid is required, besides the parameter $R$. Since the mesh traversal is ordered by the permuted vertex indices $I'$ and face indices $F'$, the secret key $K$ is required to generate them. Therefore, the secret key $K$ and the parameter $R$ are used as the inputs of the retrieval process, besides the watermarked mesh.

The detailed process of watermark retrieval is as follows: At first, the vertex indices $I$ and face indices $F$ in the watermarked mesh are permuted by using $K$ as the seed of pseudo-random generator to generate $I'$ and $F'$, respectively. By performing the mesh traversal, the distance from a vertex to the centroid of its traversed neighbors can be calculated by using Eq.(1) and Eq.(2). If the watermarked mesh is intact, the obtained distances are those that have been modified in the embedding process, i.e., $\{d'_1, d'_2, \ldots, d'_{m-1}\}$, given $m$ vertices in the watermarked mesh. With the distance $D$ from the last traversed vertex $v_l$ to the mesh centroid calculated by Eq.(7) and the provided parameter $R$, the quantization step $\Delta$ is obtained by

$$\Delta = D/R. \tag{10}$$

With the obtained $\Delta$, the bit value $w'_i$ is extracted by

$$w'_i = \lfloor d'_i/\Delta \rfloor \%2. \tag{11}$$

The whole message string $W' = (w'_i)_{i=1}^{m-1}$ will be retrieved after the last bit is extracted from the last traversed vertex.

## 2.3 The Properties of the Embedded Data

Since the ratio between any two distances in a polygonal mesh is invariant to RST transformations, while the quantization step used in the retrieval process is proportional to the distance from the last traversed vertex to the mesh centroid, the ratio between the distance from a vertex to the centroid of its traversed neighbors and the quantization step remains the same after RST transformations, as well as the embedded watermark. After topological modifications that change the neighboring information between vertices, the mesh traversal in the retrieval process will be different from that in the embedding process so that the embedded watermark cannot be correctly retrieved. Therefore, the embedded data is sensitive to the modifications made to the connectivity between vertices.

As for the mantissa truncation of vertex coordinate, which is stored as a single-precision floating-point number, if the truncation error is distributed within $(-T, T)$, then the errors introduced to the coordinates of the mesh centroid in Eq.(7) and the centroid of a vertex's neighboring vertices in Eq.(1) are also distributed within $(-T, T)$. The error introduced to $d'_i$ in Eq.(2) and $D$ in Eq.(8) will be both distributed within $(-2\sqrt{3}T, 2\sqrt{3}T)$. Based on Eq.(10), we know the error introduced to $\Delta$ is within $(-\frac{2\sqrt{3}T}{R}, \frac{2\sqrt{3}T}{R})$ so that Eq.(11) can be rewritten as

$$w'_i = \lfloor \frac{d'_i + \delta d}{\Delta + \delta_1} \rfloor \%2, \tag{12}$$

where $\delta d$ and $\delta_1$ are the change of $d_i'$ and $\Delta$ caused by the truncation, respectively. It can be seen the integer quotient $\lfloor \frac{d_i' + \delta d}{\Delta + \delta_1} \rfloor$ will be different from $\lfloor \frac{d_i'}{\Delta} \rfloor$ if $d_i' \% \Delta + \delta d - \lfloor d_i'/\Delta \rfloor \times \delta_1 \notin (0, \Delta)$. If Eq.(5) is used in the embedding process, $d_i' \% \Delta$ will be distributed within $(\epsilon, \Delta - \epsilon)$. As a result, the retrieved bit value $w_i'$ in Eq.(12) will be identical to $w_i$, i.e. $\lfloor d_i'/\Delta \rfloor \% 2$, if $|\delta d - \lfloor d_i'/\Delta \rfloor \times \delta_1| < \epsilon$. Since $\delta d \in (-2\sqrt{3}T, 2\sqrt{3}T)$ and $\delta_1 \in (-\frac{2\sqrt{3}T}{R}, \frac{2\sqrt{3}T}{R})$, the truncation of vertex coordinates is allowed if

$$T < \frac{\epsilon}{2\sqrt{3}(1 + \frac{\lfloor d_M'/\Delta \rfloor}{R})}, \tag{13}$$

where $d_M'$ is the greatest one among all the modified distance $\{d_1', d_2', \ldots, d_{m-1}'\}$. On the other side, truncation of vertex coordinates can be allowed by appropriately choosing the quantization step $\Delta$ if $\lfloor d_M'/\Delta \rfloor < (\frac{\epsilon}{2\sqrt{3}T} - 1)R$, or $\Delta > \frac{d_M'}{(\frac{\epsilon}{2\sqrt{3}T} - 1)R}$ since $\epsilon > 2\sqrt{3}T$ as indicated by Eq.(13). If the parameter $\epsilon$ in Eq.(5) is assigned proportional to the quantization step $\Delta$ (we take $\frac{\Delta}{6}$ for instance), the value of $\Delta$ should be chosen so that $\Delta > \frac{d_M'}{(\frac{\Delta}{12\sqrt{3}T} - 1)R}$, i.e.,

$$\Delta > 6\sqrt{3}T + \sqrt{108T^2 + \frac{12\sqrt{3}T d_M'}{R}}, \tag{14}$$

where the value of $d_M'$ and $R$ are obtained from the watermarked mesh. Otherwise, the embedded value will probably be altered.

For the geometrical modifications that take place on part of the vertices, we take for instance the case that one vertex is modified. The distance $d_i'$ from the modified vertex to its traversed neighbors will be changed by the modification as denoted by $d_i' + \delta d_i$ with $\delta d_i$ as the change. Suppose the quantization step $\Delta$ obtained from Eq.(10) is unchanged, the integer quotient $\lfloor \frac{d_i' + \delta d_i}{\Delta} \rfloor$ will be possibly changed if $|\delta d_i| > \epsilon$ given $d_i' \% \Delta \in (\epsilon, \Delta - \epsilon)$. For the untraversed neighbors of the modified vertex, i.e., those vertices regarding the modified vertex as their traversed neighbor, the distances from them to their traversed neighbors will also be changed by the modification so that the chance to detect the modification is increased. In summary, if one vertex is modified outside the allowed range, the data embedded by adjusting the positions of itself and its untraversed neighbors will probably be altered.

## 3   Experimental Results

We performed the proposed method on several mesh models as listed in Table 1, where the capacity of each mesh model is also given. Suppose the precision interval of vertex coordinates is $(-T, T)$, an appropriate quantization step $\Delta$ should be chosen as in Eq.(14) if $\frac{\Delta}{6}$ has been assigned to the parameter $\epsilon$ in Eq.(5). The runtime of the embedding and retrieval processes for the "teapot" model were only 0.750 and 0.875 seconds in a 2.66G Pentium 4 PC with 512MB RAM, while those for the "horse" model were 40.844 and 44.438 seconds, respectively.

**Table 1.** The mesh models used in the experiments

| Model | Meshes | Vertices | Polygons | Capacity(bits) |
|-------|--------|----------|----------|----------------|
| fish | 1 | 742 | 1408 | 741 |
| teapot | 5 | 1631 | 3080 | 1626 |
| dog | 48 | 7616 | 13176 | 7568 |
| wolf | 90 | 8176 | 13992 | 8086 |
| horse | 31 | 10316 | 18359 | 10285 |

### 3.1 Distortion of the Cover Mesh

In the experiments, the impact of the embedding process can be tuned by the quantization step $\Delta$ used. From Eq.(6), it can be seen that the adjustment of each vertex position is within the sphere with its original position as the centroid while $\Delta$ as the radius, since the change of the distance from a vertex to its traversed neighbors is bounded by $(-\Delta, \Delta)$. Upon the fact that the mesh topology has not been changed, the distance from the adjusted vertex to its former position is used to represent the distortion of the mesh content. In the experiments, if 0.01 was assigned to $\Delta$, the greatest error (i.e., the greatest distance among all the adjusted vertices) never exceeded 0.01, while the greatest error was below 0.001 if 0.001 had been assigned to $\Delta$, as shown in Fig. 1. The pictures rendered from the mesh models "teapot" and "horse" before and after the embedding process are shown in Fig. 2.

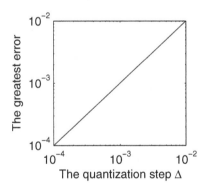

**Fig. 1.** The greatest error increases with the quantization step

### 3.2 Capacity

The proposed method is applicable to 3D polygonal meshes with arbitrary connectivity. Given $m$ vertices in the cover mesh, the capacity of our method will be $m - 1$ bits, tending to 1 bit/vertex when $m$ is sufficiently large. If a mesh model consists of $l$ separate meshes as in Table 1, the capacity will be $m - l$ bits since the first indexed vertex within each mesh is traversed without adjusting its position.

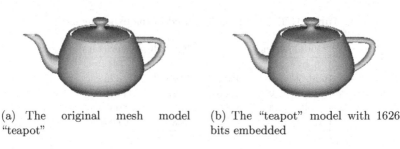

(a) The original mesh model "teapot"

(b) The "teapot" model with 1626 bits embedded

(c) The original mesh model "horse"

(d) The "horse" model with 10285 bits embedded

**Fig. 2.** 1626 and 10285 bits in total are hidden within the mesh model "teapot" and "horse", respectively, by choosing $1/10,000$ of the greatest distance $D_m$ from a vertex to the mesh centroid as the quantization step $\Delta$ and $\frac{\Delta}{6}$ as the parameter $\epsilon$

### 3.3 Security

The security of the proposed method relies on the secrecy of the key $K$, as well as the parameter $R$, which is used to calculate the quantization step $\Delta$ in the retrieval process. Given there are $m$ vertices and $p$ polygons in a polygonal mesh, the permutation of the vertex indices is $m!$. Without the secret key $K$, the mesh traversal must be performed $pm!$ times to guarantee the embedded data can be correctly retrieved, given the accurate quantization step $\Delta$. To make it hard to estimate the quantization step $\Delta$ from the set of modified distances, the parameter $\epsilon$ used in Eq.(5) should be assigned with a relatively small value, $\frac{\Delta}{6}$ for instance. Moreover, we define the embedding primitive over the neighborhood of a vertex so that resistance to substitution attacks is achieved, which makes it even harder to construct a counterfeit mesh with the same watermark.

### 3.4 Authentication of Polygonal Meshes

We try to apply the proposed method to authentication of polygonal meshes. To detect the illegal modifications made to the watermarked mesh and estimate its

**Table 2.** By assigning $1/100,000$ of the greatest distance from a vertex to the mesh centroid to the quantization step $\Delta$ and $\frac{\Delta}{6}$ to the parameter $\epsilon$, the $NC$ values are calculated from the extracted bit values and the original ones after the watermarked mesh have been processed by the following manipulations, respectively

| Meshes | RST transformations | Moving two vertices oppositely | Modifying one vertex position | Reducing one face | Truncating five LSBs | Truncating six LSBs |
|--------|--------|--------|--------|--------|--------|--------|
| fish | 1.0000 | 0.9932 | 0.9959 | 0.9757 | 1.0000 | 0.9838 |
| teapot | 1.0000 | 0.9963 | 0.9987 | 0.7915 | 1.0000 | 0.9907 |
| dog | 1.0000 | 0.9980 | 0.9984 | 0.5776 | 0.9988 | 0.9912 |
| wolf | 1.0000 | 0.9993 | 0.9997 | 0.6070 | 0.9991 | 0.9881 |
| horse | 1.0000 | 0.9997 | 0.9999 | 0.5402 | 0.9994 | 0.9860 |

strength, the retrieved watermark $W' = (w_i')_{i=1}^{N}$ is compared with the original one $W = (w_i)_{i=1}^{N}$ by defining a numerical value $NC$ over them

$$NC = \frac{1}{N} \sum_{i=1}^{N} I(w_i', w_i), \qquad (15)$$

with

$$I(w_i', w_i) = \begin{cases} 1 \text{ if } w_i' = w_i \\ 0 \text{ otherwise} \end{cases}. \qquad (16)$$

The value of $NC$ is expected to be less than 1 if the mesh content has been illegally modified.

The watermarked mesh model went through RST transformations, changing the positions of two vertices oppositely (respectively by adding the vectors $\{2\Delta, 2\Delta, 2\Delta\}$ and $\{-2\Delta, -2\Delta, -2\Delta\}$), modifying one vertex position by adding the vector $\{3\Delta, 3\Delta, 3\Delta\}$, reducing one face from the mesh, and truncating the least significant bits (LSB) of each vertex coordinate, respectively. By retrieving the embedded bit values from the processed mesh models and comparing them with the original ones by using Eq.(15), the resulting values of $NC$ listed in Table 2 indicated that the embedded data was robust against RST transformations and truncation of vertex coordinates to a certain degree, but sensitive to other modifications. It should be noted the allowed range of coordinate truncation could also be adjusted with the quantization step $\Delta$. If $1/10,000$ of $D_m$, which is defined as the greatest distance from a vertex to the mesh centroid, was assigned to $\Delta$, truncating of 8 least significant bits (LSB) of vertex coordinate was allowed for the "teapot" model. While $1/100,000$ of $D_m$ was assigned instead, only 5 LSBs of vertex coordinate could be truncated without changing the embedded data.

From the obtained $NC$ values, it can be seen the illegal modifications made to the watermarked mesh can be classified into severe and slight ones. Topological and severe geometrical modifications may lead the retrieved watermark to be dramatically different from the original one, while those geometrical modifications that have little impact on the quantization step $\Delta$ are possible to be localized by comparing the extracted values with the original ones. For a vertex where the two values do not match, its position or those of its previously traversed neighbors might have been changed. Normally, the number of the previously traversed neighbors of a vertex is very limited so that this type of modification can be localized. In our experiments, the watermarked mesh model "teapot" in Fig. 2(b) was tampered by modifying one vertex on its handle and the tampered mesh model is shown in Fig. 3(a). The illegal modification is detected by comparing the extracted watermark with the original one so as to find the region where the two values do not match, as shown in Fig. 3(b).

(a) The tampered mesh model "teapot"

(b) The mesh model with the tampered region detected

**Fig. 3.** The mesh model in Fig. 2(b) is tampered by modifying one vertex and the tampered region has been localized

## 4   Concluding Remarks and Future Works

A high-capacity data hiding method has been proposed for polygonal meshes by choosing the distance from a vertex to the centroid of its traversed neighbors as the embedding primitive. A new quantization method has been employed to embed a watermark by slightly modifying the embedding primitives. It is hard to estimate the quantization step from the modified primitives, while slight change of them can be allowed to a certain degree by reserving a margin around the quantization grid. The embedded data is robust against those content-preserving manipulations, such as RST transformations and truncation of vertex coordinates to a certain degree, but sensitive to malicious manipulations. The impact of embedding on the mesh content can be tuned by choosing an appropriate quantization step. In the future, we will further investigate on: (1) the information of the embedded data leaked from the watermarked mesh, if any; and (2) the attacks to the proposed method for authentication and secret message communication.

## Acknowledgment

The authors would like to sincerely thank the three anonymous reviewers for their valuable comments and insightful suggestions.

## References

1. Levoy, M., Pulli, K., Curless, B., Rusinkiewicz, S., Koller, D., Pereira, L., Ginzton, M., Anderson, S., Davis, J., Ginsberg, J., Shade, J., Fulk, D.: The Digital Michelangelo Project: 3D Scanning of Large Statues. In: Proc. ACM SIGGRAPH, pp. 131–144 (2000)
2. The protein data bank http://www.rcsb.org/pdb/
3. Petitcolas, F.A.P., Anderson, R.J., Kuhn, M.G.: Information hiding-A survey. Proc. of the IEEE, 87(7), 1062–1078 (1999)
4. Yeo, B.L., Yeung, M.M.: Watermarking 3-D objects for verification. IEEE Comput. Graph. Applicat. 36–45 (January/February 1999)
5. Lin, H.Y.S., Liao, H.Y.M., Lu, C.S., Lin, J.C.: Fragile Watermarking for Authenticating 3-D Polygonal Meshes. IEEE Transaction on Multimedia 7(6), 997–1006 (2005)
6. Benedens, O., Busch, C.: Toward blind detection of robust watermarks in polygonal models. Proc. EUROGRAPHICS Comput. Graph. Forum, 19, C199–C208 (2000)
7. Cayre, F., Macq, B.: Data hiding on 3-D triangle meshes. IEEE Trans. Signal Processing 51(4), 939–949 (2003)
8. Wu, H.T., Cheung, Y.M.: A Fragile Watermarking Scheme for 3D Meshes. In: Proc. ACM Multimedia & Security Workshop, pp. 117–123, New York (2005)
9. Benedens, O.: Geometry-based watermarking of 3-D models. IEEE Comput. Graph., Special Issue on Image Security, 46–55 (January/February 1999)
10. Praun, E., Hoppe, H., Finkelstein, A.: Robust mesh watermarking. In: Proc. ACM SIGGRAPH, pp. 69–76 (1999)
11. Ohbuchi, R., Masuda, H., Aono, M.: Watermarking Three-Dimensional Polygonal Models Through Geometric and Topological Modifications. IEEE J. Select. Areas Commun. 16, 551–560 (1998)
12. Ohbuchi, R., Takahashi, S., Miyasawa, T., Mukaiyama, A.: Watermarking 3-D polygonal meshes in the mesh spectral domain. In: Proc. Graphics Interface, pp. 9–17, Ottawa, ON, Canada (June 2001)
13. Date, H., Kanai, S., Kishinami, T.: Digital watermarking for 3-D polygonal model based on wavelet transform. In: Proc. ASME Des. Eng. Techn. Conf. 2006 (September 12-15, 1999)
14. Wagner, M.G.: Robust Watermarking of Polygonal Meshes. In: Proc. Geometric Modeling & Processing 2000, pp. 201–208, Hong Kong (April 2000)
15. Yin, K., Pan, Z., Shi, J., Zhang, D.: Robust mesh watermarking based on multiresolution processing. Computers & Graphics 25, 409–420 (2001)
16. Kalivas, A., Tefas, A., Pitas, I.: Watermarking of 3D Models using Principal Component Analysis. In: Proc. ICASSP, vol. 5, pp. 676–679 (2003)

17. Maret, Y., Ebrahimi, T.: Data Hiding on 3D Polygonal Meshes. In: Proc. ACM Multimedia & Security Workshop, pp. 68–74, Magdeburg, Germany (2004)
18. Uccheddu, F., Corsini, M., Barni, M.: Wavelet-based blind watermarking of 3d models. In: Proc. ACM Multimedia & Security Workshop, pp. 143–154, Magdeburg, Germany (2004)
19. Kalker, T.: Considerations on watermarking security. In: IEEE Int. Workshop on Multimedia Signal Processing, pp. 201–206, Cannes, France (October 2001)
20. The Web3D Consortium `http://www.vrml.org/`

# Steganography for Radio Amateurs— A DSSS Based Approach for Slow Scan Television

Andreas Westfeld*

Technische Universität Dresden
Institute for System Architecture
01062 Dresden, Germany
mailto:dl1dsx@inf.tu-dresden.de

**Abstract.** In 2005, Germany introduced a new Amateur Radio Ordinance prohibiting encrypted radio traffic at home. Crypto-bans can be circumvented using steganography. However, present steganographic methods are not eligible because the embedded message will not survive the usual distortions in a radio transmission. Robust as current watermarking methods are, they leave clearly detectable traces and have a smaller capacity.

This paper presents measures that improve the robustness of steganographic communication with respect to non-intentional, random channel errors and validates their effectiveness by simulation. For the scenario of a radio communication, we determine practicable parameters for least detectability under six different short wave conditions. The resulting method embeds messages with a length of up to 118 bytes in a narrow-band Slow Scan Television connection in Martin-M1 mode.

## 1 Requirements for Robust Steganography

Steganography is the art and science of invisible communication. Its aim is the transmission of information embedded invisibly into carrier data. Secure watermarking methods embed short messages protected against modifying attackers (robustness, watermarking security) while the existence of steganographically embedded information cannot be proven by a third party (indiscernibility, steganographic security).

The existence of steganographic methods is one of the main arguments against a crypto-ban, since steganography facilitates the confidential exchange of information like cryptography, but goes unnoticed and consequently cannot be effectively persecuted. Nevertheless, Germany expanded the regulation that international amateur communications should be "in plain language" [1] to domestic ones in its Amateur Radio Ordinance in 1998. The new German Amateur Radio Ordinance from 2005 [2] explicitly prohibits encrypted amateur communications

---

* DL1DSX

J. Camenisch et al. (Eds.): IH 2006, LNCS 4437, pp. 201–215, 2007.

in the operational framework: (§ 16) Amateur radio communication must not be encrypted to obscure the meaning thereof.[1]

In general, steganographic communication uses an error-free channel and messages are received unmodified. Digitised images reach the recipient virtually without errors when sent, e. g., as an e-mail attachment. The data link layer ensures a safe, i. e. mostly error-free, transmission. If every bit of the carrier medium is received straight from the source, then the recipient can extract a possibly embedded message without any problem. However, some modes (e. g., analogue voice radio, television) do without the data link layer, because the emerging errors have little influence on the quality and can be tolerated.

Without error correction, distortions are acceptable only in irrelevant places where they have the least influence on the carrier. However, typical steganographic methods prefer these locations for hiding payload. The hidden message would be most interfered with in error-prone channels. Therefore, robust embedding functions have to add redundancy and change only locations that are carefully selected regarding the proportion between unobtrusiveness and probability of error. This increases the risk of detection and permits a small payload only.

This paper presents measures that improve steganography in terms of robustness with respect to non-intentional, random channel errors as they occur in radio communications. Some watermarking methods are also robust against distortions in the time and frequency domains. Tachibana et al. introduced an algorithm that embeds a watermark by changing the power difference between the consecutive DFT frames [3]. It embeds 64 bits in a 30-second music sample. Compared to the proposed steganographic method this is a quarter of the payload in a host signal (carrier) occupying 50 times the bandwith. It is robust against radio transmission. However, it was not designed to be steganographically secure and the presence of a watermark is likely to be detected by calculating the statistics of the power difference without knowing the pseudo random pattern. Van der Veen et al. published an audio watermarking technology that survives air transmission on an acoustical path and many other robustness tests while being perceptionally transparent [4]. The algorithm of Kirovski and Malvar [5] embeds about 1 bit per second (half as much as the one in [3]) and is even more robust (against the Stirmark Benchmark [6]). In brief, there are watermarking methods that survive radio transmission, offer small capacities and achieve perceptual transparency, however, they are not steganographically secure.

Marvel et al. [7] developed a robust steganographic method for images based on spread spectrum modulation [8]. This technique enables the transmission of information below the noise or carrier signal level (signal to noise ratio below 0 dB). Likewise it is difficult to jam, as long as transmitter and receiver are synchronised. Therefore, successful attacks de-synchronise the modulated signal [9]. Messages embedded using the algorithm of Marvel et al. will not survive the time and frequency dispersion of the channel considered here.

---

[1] "Amateurfunkverkehr darf nicht zur Verschleierung des Inhalts verschlüsselt werden; ...".

Since it is almost impossible for an attacker to control the distortions in the time and frequency domains that a radio communication is exposed to we can allow for the additional requirement of steganography (undetectability) without restricting the typical capacity of watermarking.

The following Section 2 describes the model and simulation of high frequency (HF) propagation. Section 3 extends a known steganographic spread spectrum method stepwise by modules that decrease the error rate of the steganographic signal for radio communications. Sensible parameters are determined by simulation, which allow an error-free transmission. Some security concepts are discussed in Section 4, where the paper is also summarised.

## 2  HF Channel Simulation

Simulating the variable behaviour of the ionosphere not only allows faster bench testing in the lab during the development stage, but also the comparison under reproducible, standardised conditions. In this research a software implementation was employed, based on source codes of Johan Forrer, KC7WW[2]. We implemented it as an R package [10] named chansim that accommodates a wide range of simulated conditions, including those given in the Recommendation 520-1 of the CCIR[3] (good, moderate, poor, flutter-fading, see Table 1) [11]. The simulation model is an implementation of the Watterson Gaussian-scatter HF ionospheric channel model [12], which is the de facto standard for this kind of work [13].

Table 1. Preset parameters for channel simulation

| HF channel condition | Delay time | Doppler spread |
|---|---|---|
| Noise .............. | 0 ms | 0 Hz |
| Flat 1 ............. | 0 ms | 0.2 Hz |
| Flat 2 ............. | 0 ms | 1 Hz |
| CCIR good ........ | 0.5 ms | 0.1 Hz |
| CCIR moderate .... | 1 ms | 0.5 Hz |
| CCIR poor ........ | 2 ms | 1 Hz |
| CCIR flutter fading | 0.5 ms | 10 Hz |
| Extreme ........... | 2 ms | 5 Hz |

From a physical point of view, the HF channel is characterised as a multi-path time-varying environment that produces time and frequency dispersion [14]. The reason for the multitude of paths lies in the reflections of radio signals from

---

[2] These alphanumeric strings behind names are call signs of radio amateurs.

[3] Comité consultatif international pour la radio, which became the ITU-R (Radiocommunication Sector of the International Telecommunication Union) in 1992.

different layers in the ionosphere. In addition, multiple reflections can occur between the earth's surface and the ionosphere, giving rise to multi-hop propagation. Thus, the received signal can contain several echoes, separated in time by a matter of milliseconds (delay time). Doppler spread (frequency spread) occurs if the particular path lengths change due to a movement of the ionosphere with its specular nature.

For mid-latitude HF circuits, the amount of multi-path (delay time $\tau_i$) can range up to 6 ms and the fading rate (Doppler spread) can be as high as 5 Hz [15]. However, more typical values are 2 ms and 1 Hz, respectively, which are the basic parameters of the standardised CCIR "poor" HF channel.

One of the key contributions to HF channel modelling was a paper by Watterson et al. [12] in 1970. In this paper, a stationary model for the HF channel was proposed and experimentally validated with on-air measurements. Although HF channels are generally non-stationary, this model has been shown to be valid for sufficiently short times ($\approx$ 10 minutes) and for band-limited channels ($\approx$ 10 kHz). The Watterson Model views the HF channel as a transversal filter where the taps are complex and vary with time (see Figure 1). It produces phase and amplitude distortions in the signal.

The time-varying taps ($h_i$) are generated by filtering complex white Gaussian noise through filters whose frequency-domain power spectra have a Gaussian shape. The desired Doppler spread is controlled by the standard deviation of these power spectra.

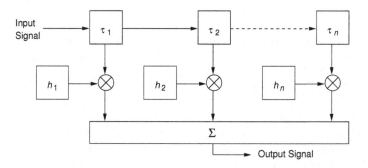

**Fig. 1.** Watterson HF channel model [12]

## 3   Design of the System

### 3.1   Slow Scan Television

Slow Scan Television (SSTV) has a relatively long transmission phase compared with voice radio. This increases the chance of a reasonable steganographic capacity despite the small bandwith of 3 kHz. SSTV is widespread among radio amateurs.

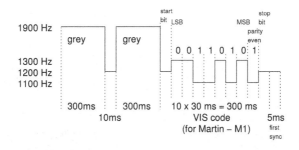

**Fig. 2.** VIS code to signal SSTV mode and start of an image[16]

An SSTV signal starts with a VIS[4] code that announces an image transmission and its mode. Its time–frequency diagram is shown in Figure 2. There exist about 30 different SSTV modes. Martin-M1 was developed by Martin H. Emmerson, G3OQD, and is one of the most commonly used.

The Martin-M1 mode encodes colour images with a resolution of $320 \times 256$ pixels. The image is sent row by row from top to bottom. For each row there is a synchronisation impulse followed by the intensity information for the green, blue, and red colour channel. These intensities are encoded as tones with frequencies in the range of $1400 \dots 2400\,\mathrm{Hz}$ (see Figure 3). A $1200\,\mathrm{Hz}$ tone serves as sync pulse. Altogether the SSTV signal lasts 1 minute and 55 seconds, possibly extended by the call sign of the sender in CW[5] (Morse code).

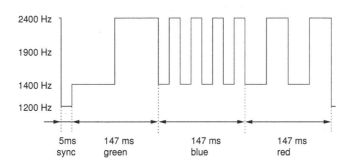

**Fig. 3.** One of 256 rows in Martin-M1 mode

We selected QSSTV [17] by Johan Maes, ON4QZ, as the most suitable open source SSTV software to base the implementation of our steganographic system on. Since most of the SSTV programs are closed source or obsolete implementations, there are no real alternatives.

---

[4] This name is inherited from weather fax: VIS=visible, IR=infrared.
[5] continuous wave.

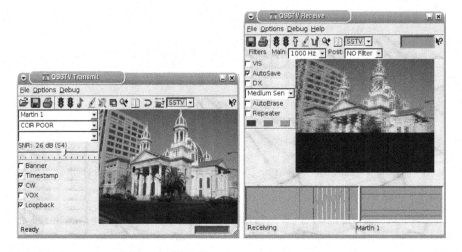

**Fig. 4.** Modified QSSTV with loopback HF channel simulator

We extended QSSTV with the already mentioned channel simulator by Johan Forrer, KC7WW. Figure 4 shows the graphical user interface with extra loopback option and settings for SNR (signal to noise ratio) and HF conditions. A simulated transmission lasts only a few seconds and is much faster than the 2 minutes for a real transmission. The Receive window in the figure is reconstructing the image from a simulated signal transmission (CCIR poor, SNR 26 dB).

The SSTV signal generated by QSSTV has a sampling rate of 8000 samples per second, offering sufficient resolution for the transmitted signal range 200 . . . 3000 Hz.

## 3.2   Steganographic SSTV System

This section describes the overall steganographic SSTV system (see Figure 5). Its components have three main goals: embedding, phase correction, and error correction.

First the message is made fault-tolerant by an error correcting code (ECC). The redundancy is added to compensate for the loss due to fading and atmospherics that cannot be prevented otherwise. However, an opponent cannot search for this redundancy because it is masked by the key derived spreading sequence, which acts like a stream cipher. The interleaver, which permutes the encoded message, prevents burst errors. The differential encoder enables a correct demodulation also for signals received with the wrong sign due to phase distortion. The resulting symbols are spread and their energy is distributed over a longer period of time. Pulse shaping with an RRC filter (root raised cosine) limits the bandwith of the spread signal, which is added with relatively low level to the SSTV signal ($-27 \ldots -11$ dB) and therefore difficult to detect. The sum of both signals is transmitted to the receiver. In our experimental environment the conditions of the HF channel are simulated in a reproducible way. For real use,

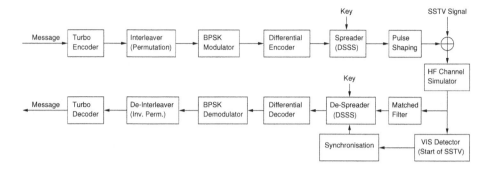

**Fig. 5.** Path of the steganographic signal in the steganographic SSTV system

the signal with its 8000 samples per second would be converted into an analogue audio signal by the sound card of the computer and then broadcast with an single side band (SSB) HF transmitter. The short-wave receiver of the remote station is connected to another sound card of a computer, which digitises the analogue signal and processes it further. The digitised signal can also be tapped from the output of the channel simulator of the experimental environment. It is an ordinary SSTV signal and therefore the image content can be demodulated as usual. The synchronisation information of the SSTV signal guarantees that the receiver also recognises the start of the steganographic signal. Before the steganographic signal is demodulated at the receiver side, a matched RRC filter must be applied to reduce the interference between the elements of the spreading sequence (chips). The de-spreader retrieves the energy of the particular binary symbols from the steganographic signal. It needs the same key that was used by the sender. The differential decoding corrects the signal in times when the signal was inverted due to phase distortions, and the de-interleaver coupled with the turbo decoder tries to correct the remaining errors in the signal. This allows the level of the received symbols act as a measure of reliability (soft decision decoding, see Section 3.7).

### 3.3 Pure Direct Sequence Spread Spectrum (DSSS)

DSSS converts the message to embed $m$ into an embedding sequence $s = mn$ by multiplication with a spreading sequence $n$ (see Figure 6). We use a long spreading sequence $n$, which is pseudo-randomly derived from the key. The elements of the spreading sequence are called *chips* and have a duration $T_c$. The symbol duration $T_s$ is a multiple of $T_c$. The embedding sequence $s$ is scaled by a gain factor $g$ (modulation degree) before it is added to the carrier signal $c$, resulting in the steganogram $c_s = c + gs$. The receiver extracts the message from the distorted signal $c'_s$ by integrating $c'_s n$ piecewise over the symbol duration $T_s$.[6]

---

[6] Figure 6 is simplified for clarity and the extraction is based on the distorted embedding sequence.

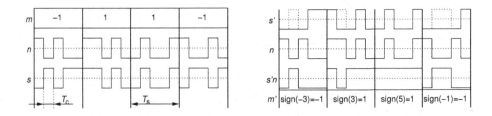

**Fig. 6.** DSSS modulation (left) and demodulation after distortion (right)

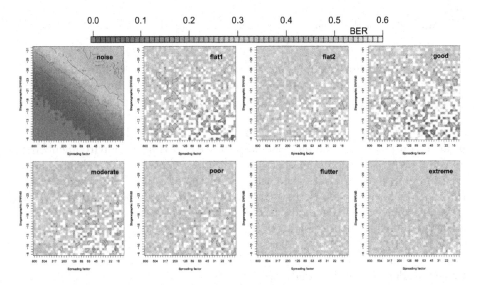

**Fig. 7.** Direct sequence spread spectrum (DSSS)

In the following first experiment, we tried different spreading factors with several steganographic SNR's and measured the resulting bit error rates (BER). This experiment was repeated for the eight HF conditions defined by the parameters of Table 1. Figure 7 shows the BER as a physical map. It plots the (logarithmically falling) spreading factor on one axis and the steganographic noise ratio (in decibel) on the other axis. The largest capacity is rightmost and the lowest detectability is upmost in the diagrams. Error-dominated regions (BER ≈ 50 %) are white, high error rates are brown, low error rates are green, and error-free areas are plotted in blue.

As expected, pure DSSS survives only the additive white Gaussian noise (AWGN) channel [7] (HF condition "noise"), which is a rather unlikely condition for a short wave transmission. The channel's SNR was set to 26 dB (S4). All other simulated conditions produce BERs around the mean 0.5 with varying standard deviations. This is due to the phase shift caused by a fading multi-path channel.

## 3.4  Differential Encoding of the Secret Message

The transmitted signal is complexly distorted, i.e., its phase is moving and its amplitude is Rayleigh distributed [18]. Since the radio amateur technology only receives the real part of the signal and therefore is not able to estimate the phase difference, the channel cannot be equalised. We use binary phase shift keying (BPSK), because other modulations like quadrature phase shift keying (QPSK) and quadrature amplitude modulation ($n$-QAM) assume a complex signal. The phase can adopt arbitrary values from 0 to 360°. This results in a bit error rate around 0.5. However, the relative change of the phase per symbol is small. The key to a successful transmission over a channel with (slowly) changing phase displacement is differential demodulation [19]. Figure 8 shows the demodulated sequence of 4000 impulses, which have been transmitted under "CCIR poor" conditions (correct reception has positive sign, erroneous reception negative sign). The grey curve represents the analogue signal intensity, the black one its sign.

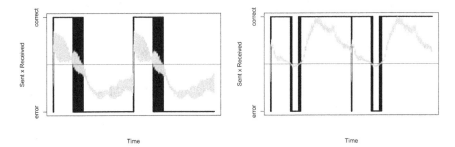

**Fig. 8.** Burst errors due to phase distortion (left) and improvement by differential demodulation (right)

One can convert the constantly wrong passages into a correct signal by differential encoding. This encoding ensures that the signal is not independently interpreted at a certain point in time, but based on its predecessor. Hence, the decoded signal is correct apart from the samples at destructive interference. A sequence of Boolean values $a$ (*true* encoded as $-1$ and *false* as 1) is converted into a differential encoded sequence $b$ and decoded again by the following rules:

$$b_k = \prod_{i=1}^{k} a_i = \begin{cases} k = 1: a_1 \\ k > 1: a_k \cdot b_{k-1} \end{cases} \qquad a_k = \begin{cases} k = 1: b_1 \\ k > 1: b_k \cdot b_{k-1} \end{cases}$$

Differential encoding results in a significantly lower error rate for all conditions with Doppler spread (see Figure 9). Only in the pure AWGN channel it increases the BER, because single errors have double effect after decoding. Error-free areas are not affected by differential encoding.

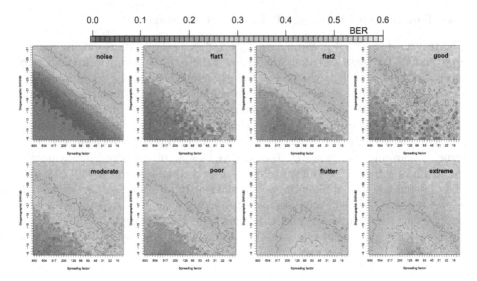

**Fig. 9.** Direct sequence spread spectrum (DSSS) with differential encoding

## 3.5   Error-Correcting Code for the Secret Message

To correct the loss due to fading, an error-correcting code (ECC) is used, which is based on an implementation of turbo codes for an OFDM sound modem (orthogonal frequency division multiplexing) [20]. This implementation permits code rates[7] in the range $\frac{1}{3}\ldots 1$. In the following experiments we worked with the smallest possible code rate of $\frac{1}{3}$. Unfortunately, no configuration was found that results in an error-free transmission for the conditions "flutter" and "extreme." One could try to reduce the code rate, however, most SSTV systems cannot even decode the image under such extreme conditions.

We estimated useful parameters for the least detectability from Figure 10. Table 2 shows parameters with best steganographic SNR for simulations that faultlessly transmitted three consecutive messages at the first go. These parameters are dependent on the channel conditions. Sensible parameters will be derived in measurements over the air that are currently prepared. The transmission with parameters off the table under a specific condition works the more reliably the less indented the northern shoreline of the error-free lake in the respective landscape appears. The steganographic SNR in the table is determined based on the undistorted signal, to which the attacker has no access.

We can see that the lowest error rate is not always expected for the largest spreading factor. The reason for this is the increased probability for a change of sign due to phase distortion in longer symbols. On the other hand, the gain from de-spreading is diminishing with shorter sequences (smaller spreading factors) and thus the interference between the embedded and the carrier signal is increasing.

---

[7] Ratio of the number of information bits to the number of bits in the code word.

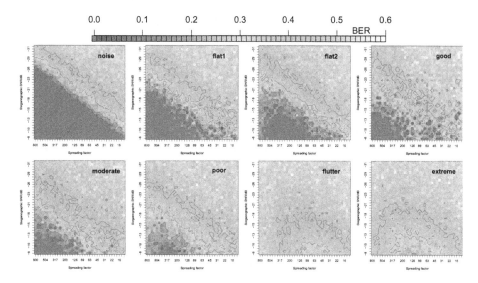

**Fig. 10.** Direct sequence spread spectrum (DSSS) with differential encoding and turbo code

### 3.6  Sender-Side Pulse Shaping and Matched Receive Filter

The spreading sequence consists of a sequence of square pulses with vertical transitions that occupy infinite bandwith. The Nyquist Criterion tells us that we cannot transmit square pulse shapes over a bandlimited channel [21]. An SSTV signal is limited to the frequency range 200 Hz . . . 3000 Hz. To reduce the loss, the signal is formed and restricted to the required spectrum by a pulse shaping root raised cosine (RRC) filter [22]. The impulse response $g(t)$ of the filter is defined as follows:

$$g(t) = \frac{4\alpha}{\pi\sqrt{T_c}} \frac{\cos\left(\frac{(1+\alpha)\pi t}{T_c}\right) + \frac{T_c}{4\alpha t}\sin\left(\frac{(1-\alpha)\pi t}{T_c}\right)}{1 - \left(\frac{4\alpha t}{T_c}\right)^2}$$

$$\lim_{t\to 0} g(t) = \frac{4\alpha + \pi(1-\alpha)}{\pi\sqrt{T_c}}$$

The RRC has a parameter $\alpha = 2f_u T_c - 1$ called roll-off factor. This can shift the upper cutoff frequency $f_u$ for the chip duration $T_c$ in certain limits. Since the amplitude of the RRC is decreasing on both sides it can be truncated below a certain threshold $\varepsilon$ and limited to a finite duration.

The spectrum for an RRC filter (roll-off factor $\alpha = \frac{1}{2}$, chip duration $T_c = 2$ sample points, 8000 Hz sampling rate) is shown in Figure 11 (left). The filter forms the signal before transmission and its upper cutoff frequency $f_u = 3000\,\text{Hz}$ adopts the signal bandwith to the channel.

**Table 2.** Parameters for SSTV steganography with least detectability

| HF channel condition | Spreading factor | Steganographic SNR | Capacity |
|---|---|---|---|
| Noise .............. | 800 | −27 dB | 46 bytes |
| Flat 1 ............. | 800 | −21 dB | 46 bytes |
| Flat 2 ............. | 320 | −16 dB | 118 bytes |
| CCIR good ........ | 640 | −15 dB | 58 bytes |
| CCIR moderate .... | 450 | −13 dB | 83 bytes |
| CCIR poor ........ | 320 | −11 dB | 118 bytes |
| CCIR flutter fading | — | — | 0 |
| Extreme ........... | — | — | 0 |

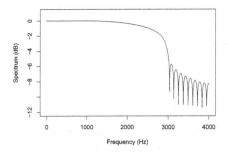 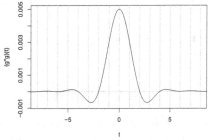

**Fig. 11.** Spectrum of a truncated RRC filter with $\alpha = \frac{1}{2}$ und $T_c = 2$ (left) and impulse response of a matched pair of RRC filters (right)

To fulfil the first Nyquist condition (zero inter-symbol interference), $T_c$ has to be the first root of the filter's impulse response. At the same time, the signal to noise ratio has to be maximised, which requires identical (matched) send and receive filters for real signals. The combination of two root raised cosine filters forms a raised cosine filter, which complies with this first Nyquist condition. Figure 11 (right) shows that for nonzero integers $k$ the impulse response of the combination fulfils $(g * g)(kT_c) = 0$. Consequently the signal does not interfere with neighbour chips at their sample points.

### 3.7    Soft Decision Decoding

Figure 12 shows the gain of pulse shaping (middle) compared with the modulation of square pulse shapes (left). We noticed a small increase from 18 to 22 error-free transmissions under CCIR poor conditions in our experiments. If not only the sign is considered in the decoding (=hard decision), but also the level of the received signal as a measure for its reliability (=soft decision), the number of error-free transmissions slightly increases again from 22 to 27.

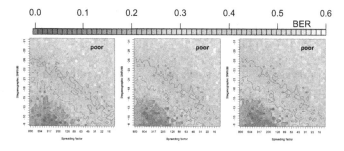

**Fig. 12.** Direct sequence spread spectrum (DSSS) with differential encoding and turbo code under CCIR-poor HF conditions with hard decision decoding (left), plus pulse shaping and matched filter (middle), and soft decision decoding (right)

## 4   Security Considerations and Conclusion

The simulations have shown that narrow-band radio links, as they are used by radio amateurs on short wave, can be used for the transmission of spread spectrum modulated embedded messages despite dynamic phase and frequency distortions on the channel. The physical limits of this scenario have been determined experimentally. Some ten thousand simulated radio communications have been compared to each other with different values for the parameters steganographic SNR and capacity under reproducible, standardised propagation conditions and in different system increments.

An attacker is facing the task to prove the existence of a steganographic message, i. e., to distinguish between messages with and without steganographic content. This distinction has to be made on the basis of the steganographic noise, which is either present or not. This noise ought to be separated from other available sources of noise: the noise that is already in the carrier-pattern, the noise of the transmitter, the ambient atmospheric noise, and the channel noise, i. e., the distortions, which the signal is exposed to on its way to the receiver.

An attacker can improve his or her situation by choosing a favourable geographical position, a more sensitive receiver, or an antenna with increased gain and a better directional receiving pattern. To decide the question of security we have to see if the advantage of the recipient, who knows the secret key used to spread the symbol energy over a longer period of time, is sufficient to protect from attackers under possibly better physical circumstances, who have to do without this knowledge. As the measurements have shown (cf. Section 3.5), there is an optimum for the spreading factor. This means that we cannot automatically decrease the capacity in favour of the steganographic SNR (by means of a larger spreading factor). The key advantage of using SSTV is its saving effect by providing synchronisation pulses. There is no need to add redundancy to the steganographic signal in order to synchronise sender and receiver. The existing synchronisation pulses are sufficient for this purpose. The time before the first row synchronisation pulse and after the end of the embedded message should be used for a smooth fade of the steganographic noise level since abrupt changes can be detected more easily.

One could try to derive a steganalytic method from the Twin Peaks attack on digital watermarks [23]. This attack relies on the duplication of peaks in the histogram when a spreading sequence $\{-d, +d\}^n$ is added. The success of this attack very much depends on the particular image, because the effect only appears in histograms with distinct peaks. In the SSTV scenario, an attacker cannot access the undistorted steganogram. We cannot preclude peaks in the histogram of SSTV signals, though they are polished on their way to the receiver. As the SSTV signal interferes with the steganographic signal, the attack becomes more difficult and therefore pure spreading sequences with exactly two peaks at $-d$ and $d$ have been analysed. After a simulated transmission, the distribution was—apart from the AWGN channel—always unimodal. A transmission with line of sight is similar to an AWGN channel but is still subject to fading (Rice fading) [18]. To what extent a line of sight attack is successful has to be researched in practice.

The security of the proposed system is hard to compare since robust steganography for radio links is a new territory and the absence of attacks impedes benchmarking the security within the simulation environment. The validation of the simulated results in practice is subject to future research.

## Acknowledgements

The author is grateful to Oliver Prätor for beneficial impulses and fruitful discussions as well as to the anonymous reviewers for their comments. The work on this paper was supported by the Air Force Office of Scientific Research, Air Force Material Command, USAF, under the research grant number FA8655-04-1-3036. The U. S. Government is authorised to reproduce and distribute reprints for Governmental purposes notwithstanding any copyright notation there on.

## References

1. International Telephone and Telegraph Consultative Committee (CCITT): Implementing order for the radio regulations (German designation: VO Funk) (1982)
2. German Federal Ministry of Economics and Labour: Ordinance concerning the Amateur Radio Act (German designation: AFuV) (2005) Online available at http://bundesrecht.juris.de/bundesrecht/afuv_2005/gesamt.pdf
3. Tachibana, R., Shimizu, S., Nakamura, T., Kobayashi, S.: An audio watermarking method robust against time- and frequency-fluctuation. In: Delp, E.J., Wong, P.W. (eds.) Security, Steganography and Watermarking of Multimedia Contents III (Proc. of SPIE), pp. 104–115. San Jose, CA (2001)
4. van der Veen, M., Bruekers, F., Haitsma, J., Klaker, T., Lemma, A.N., Oomen, W.: Robust multi-functional and high-quality audio watermarking technology. In: 110th Audio Engineering Society Convention. Volume Convention Paper 5345 (2001)

5. Kirovski, D., Malvar, H.S.: Spread-spectrum watermarking of audio signals. IEEE Trans. on Signal Processing 51, 1020–1033 (2003)

6. Steinebach, M., Petitcolas, F., Raynal, F., Dittmann, J., Fontaine, C., Seibel, S., Fates, N., Ferri, L.: StirMark benchmark: audio watermarking attacks. In: International Conference on Information Technology: Coding and Computing, pp.49–54 (2001)

7. Marvel, L.M., Boncelet, C.G., Retter, C.T.: Spread spectrum image steganography. IEEE Transactions on Image Processing 8, 1075–1083 (1999)

8. Pickholtz, R.L., Schilling, D.L., Milstein, L.B.: Theory of spread-spectrum communications—a tutorial. IEEE Transactions on Communications 30, 855–884 (1982)

9. Petitcolas, F.A.P., Anderson, R.J., Kuhn, M.G.: Attacks on copyright marking systems. In: Aucsmith, D. (ed.) IH 1998. LNCS, vol. 1525, pp. 219–239. Springer, Heidelberg (1998)

10. R Development Core Team: R: A language and environment for statistical computing. R Foundation for Statistical Computing, Vienna, Austria (2005) ISBN 3-900051-07-0. Online available at http://www.R-project.org

11. CCIR: Recommendation 520-1, Use of high frequency ionospheric channel simulators. Recommendations of the CCIR III, pp. 57–58 (1990)

12. Watterson, C.C., Juroshek, J.R., Bensema, W.D.: Experimental confirmation of an HF channel model. IEEE Transactions on Communication Technology 18, 792–803 (1970)

13. Forrer, J.B.: A low-cost HF channel simulator for testing and evaluating HF digital systems. In: Proceedings of the 18th ARRL and TAPR. Digital Communications Conference, Phoenix, Arizona (1999) http://www.tapr.org/pub_dcc18.html

14. Eleftheriou, E., Falconer, D.D.: Adaptive equalization techniques for HF channels. IEEE Journal on Selected Areas in Communications 5, 238–247 (1987)

15. Furman, W.N., Nieto, J.W.: Understanding HF channel simulator requirements in order to reduce HF modem performance measurement variability. In: Proceedings of HF01, the Nordic HF Conference, Fårö, Sweden (2001) Online available at http://www.nordichf.org/index.htm?forms/cdrom.htm\&2

16. Wumpus: Einige SSTV-Modi (1997) Online available at http://home.snafu.de/wumpus/sstvmod.htm

17. Maes, J.: QSSTV (2005) Online available at http://users.telenet.be/on4qz/qsstv/

18. Rappaport, T.S.: Wireless Communications: Principles and Practice. IEEE Press, Piscataway, NJ, USA (1996)

19. Couch II, L.W.: Digital and Analog Communication Systems. Prentice Hall, Upper Saddle River, NJ (2001)

20. Walma, M.: BCJR turbo code encoder/decoder (1998) Online available at http://cvs.berlios.de/cgi-bin/viewcvs.cgi/ofdm/soundmodem/newqpsk/turbo.c?rev=HEAD

21. Saucedo, R., Schiring, E.E.: Introduction to Continuous and Digital Control Systems. Macmillan, New York (1968)

22. Lee, E.A., Messerschmitt, D.G.: Digital Communications. Kluwer Academic Publishers, Boston (1994)

23. Maes, M.: Twin Peaks: The histogram attack to fixed depth image watermarks. In: Aucsmith, D. (ed.) IH 1998. LNCS, vol. 1525, pp. 290–305. Springer, Heidelberg (1998)

# Delayed and Controlled Failures in Tamper-Resistant Software

Gang Tan[1], Yuqun Chen[2], and Mariusz H. Jakubowski[2]

[1] Computer Science Department, Boston College
gtan@cs.bc.edu
[2] Microsoft Corporation
{yuqunc,mariuszj}@microsoft.com

**Abstract.** Tamper-resistant software (TRS) consists of two functional components: tamper detection and tamper response. Although both are equally critical to the effectiveness of a TRS system, past research has focused primarily on the former, while giving little thought to the latter. Not surprisingly, many successful breaks of commercial TRS systems found their first breaches at the relatively naïve tamper-response modules. In this paper, we describe a novel tamper-response system that evades hacker detection by introducing delayed, probabilistic failures in a program. This is accomplished by corrupting the program's internal state at well-chosen locations. Our tamper-response system smoothly blends in with the program and leaves no noticeable traces behind, making it very difficult for a hacker to detect its existence. The paper also presents empirical results to demonstrate the efficacy of our system.

## 1   Introduction

Software tampering continues to be a major threat to software vendors and consumers: Billions of dollars are lost every year to piracy[1]; tampered software, appearing legitimate to untrained consumers, also threatens their financial security and privacy. As the main countermeasure, the software industry has invested heavily in Tamper-Resistant Software (TRS) with varying degree of success. This paper focuses on a neglected aspect of tamper resistance, namely how the TRS should respond to tampering.

Software tampering is often conducted on a malicious host that is under a hacker's complete control: the hacker is free to monitor the hardware, as well as modify and observe the system software (i.e., OS). On current PC platform, without dedicated hardware support such as provided by NGSCB [6,17], TRS must rely on software obfuscation to evade detection and defeat hacking attempts [8,9,10,11,19]. Stealth, or the art of hiding code in the host program, is

---

[1] According to studies [1] by Business Software Alliance (BSA) and International Data Corporation (IDC), the retail value of pirated software globally is 29 billions, 33 billions, and 34 billions, in 2003, 2004, and 2005, respectively.

J. Camenisch et al. (Eds.): IH 2006, LNCS 4437, pp. 216–231, 2007.

the first and the *primary* defense that most TRS systems deploy against hackers. Ideally, the code pertaining to tamper resistance should be seamlessly intertwined with the host program's code, so that a hacker cannot discover its location(s) by either inspecting the program's code or monitoring its runtime behavior [7].

A TRS system consists of two functional components: *tamper detection* and *tamper response*; each can be made of multiple distinct modules. Both components are equally important to the effectiveness of a TRS system. In practice, however, most R&D work has gone into hiding the tamper-detection code, which verifies the host program's integrity [5,7,13]; surprisingly little has been done to improve the stealth of the tamper-response component. Since hackers tend to look for the weakest link to crack the defense perimeter of a TRS system, inadequate tamper-response mechanisms have often become the Achilles' heel of commercial TRS systems [4].

While some TRS systems can be effective if properly applied, software authors have often used only simple or default TRS features. For example, certain dongle- and CD-based copy protections perform just one or a few boolean checks, which may be easily patched out [14]. Thus, it is highly useful to automate the process of separating checks from responses.

In this paper, we describe a novel tamper-response system that evades hacker detection by introducing delayed, probabilistic failures in a program. The main technique is to corrupt certain parts of the host program's internal state at well-chosen locations so that the program either fails or exhibits degraded performance. One can also plug other failure-inducing techniques into our framework; some of them can be found in Section 6. Our tamper-response system smoothly blends in with the program and leaves no noticeable traces behind, making it very difficult for a hacker to detect its existence.

The rest of this paper is organized as follows. We describe some prior art and related work in Section 2. In Section 3, we introduce principles for effective tamper-resistant software. We describe our tamper-response system in Section 4. Implementation details and system evaluation are presented in Section 5. We discuss interesting extensions in Section 6, and conclude in Section 7.

## 2   Related Work

As informal advice, the idea of separating tamper detection from response has long been familiar to programmers of software-protection schemes [4]. The concept of "graceful degradation", or slow decay of a program's functionality after tamper detection, is a closely related technique, which has been widely reported to be used commercially [16]. Software authors typically have not revealed how specific implementations achieve these effects; in general, manual and application-specific techniques have been used. Our work provides systematic, automated methods of separating detection from response in general programs.

Commercial copy protection, licensing, and DRM systems have employed many unpublished techniques, which have been described by hackers on a large number of Internet sites and discussion boards. Such methods have often relied on "security by obscurity," which may be a valid tactic when only limited protection strength is desired or expected, as in the case of certain copy protections.

This work belongs to the general category of tamper-resistance, software obfuscation, and software watermarking. Representative examples in this category include runtime code encryption and decryption based on a visibility schedule [2]; taxonomies of generic obfuscating transformations and opaque predicates [9,10,11]; complication of pointer-aliasing and control-flow analysis [8,19]; and integrity verification of both static program code [5,13] and dynamic execution traces [7].

Theoretical treatment of obfuscation [3] has revealed that a general obfuscator cannot exist for arbitrary software under a specific model. This shows only the existence of certain contrived programs that cannot be obfuscated against a polynomial-time adversary, and thus does not necessarily block practical solutions. Furthermore, some forms of secret hiding, which include Unix-style password hashing, have been proven secure even in this framework [15,20]. An earlier, somewhat different model [12] showed that obfuscation is possible in the sense of randomizing memory accesses of certain programs, albeit at a performance cost impractical for typical applications.

## 3    Tamper-Resistant Software Model and Principles

Before describing our system, we first define a simple model of tamper-resistant software and lay out a set of principles to which an effective TRS system must adhere. In the following discussion, we consider a threat model with these participants: software vendors, legitimate users, and software pirates. *Software vendors* produce software, have the source code, and sell software in the form of executable code. *Legitimate users* and *software pirates* buy software (in the form of executable code) from the vendors. Software pirates try to tamper with the software to bypass its copyright-protection system.

In its simplest incarnation, a tamper-resistant software module resides in and protects another software module. The module being protected (or the *host module*) can be an application program, a library (either statically linked or dynamically loaded), an operating system or a device driver. In practice, multiple TRS modules are spread amongst several modules to create a complex web of defenses; in this paper, however, we concentrate on the simplified case of a single host module. This is to simplify the discussion without loss of generality.

The TRS module can be functionally decomposed into two components: tamper detection and tamper response. As the names imply, the former is responsible for detecting whether the host module, including the TRS module itself, has been (or is being) tampered with; the latter generates an appropriate response to either thwart such tampering or render the tampered host module unusable. More specifically,

**Detection.** We assume one or more detection-code instances exist in the host module. They communicate with the response code via *covert flags*: upon detecting tampering, the detection code sets one or more flags to inform the response module as opposed to calling the latter directly. A covert flag need not (and should not) be a normal boolean variable. It can take the form of a complex data structure, such as advocated by Collberg et al. [9,10,11].

Researchers have been putting a fair amount of effort into building detection systems. A *static checksum* based on either the static program code [5,13] or dynamic execution traces [7] of the code is computed and stored in a secret place. The detection system computes the new checksum when programs are running in malicious hosts, and check whether the new checksum is identical to the old one.

**Response.** When tampering is detected, an unusual event must happen to either stop the program from functioning (in the case of standalone applications) or informing the appropriate authority (in the case of network-centric applications). In this work, we restrict our attention to standalone applications in which a program failure is often a desirable event post tamper-detection.

We expect the TRS module to have multiple response code instances in place. Ideally they should be mutually independent so that uncovering of one does not easily lead to uncovering of others. In theory, the responses should be so crafted that the hacker cannot easily locate the code and disable it, nor backtrack to the detection code from it. However, in practice the detection mechanism can often be located by inspecting the code statically or back-tracing from the response that the tamper-resistant code generates.

We note that our work is about separating tamper response from detection, but not about choosing the detection sites in the first place. We assume that some list of detection locations is provided to our algorithm. For example, a programmer may choose such locations manually; alternately, a tool may generate a list of sites semi-randomly, possibly influenced by performance and security requirements, as well as by static and dynamic analysis. Related to the checking mechanisms themselves, such methods are beyond the scope of this paper.

### 3.1 Principles of Effective Tamper-Response Mechanisms

Let us first look at a naïve response system (an example also used by Collberg and Thomborson [10]) and see what kind of attacks adversaries can apply:

```
if tampered_with() then i=1/0
```

Upon detecting tampering, the above response code causes a divide-by-zero error and then the program stops. Since the program fails right at the place where detection happens, an adversary, with the ability to locate the failure point[2], can trivially trace back to the detection code and remove it. Alternatively, since divide-by-zero is an unusual operation, an adversary can statically scan the program to locate the detection code fragments and then remove it.

---

[2] A debugger is sufficient.

The naïve response reveals many information of the TRS module to an adversary. An ideal response system, in contrast, should not reveal information of the TRS module. Based on this guideline, we next propose a set of principles[3] for effective tamper-response mechanisms.

**Spatial separation.** Tamper response and the corresponding failure should be widely separated in space: While response is performed in one part of the program, its effect (failure) becomes only apparent in other parts. This way, even an adversary can identify the failure point, he cannot trace back to the response point.

One question is that what is a good metric for spatial separation. One metric is the number of function calls invoked between tamper response and program failure. By increasing the number of function calls, we hope that little trace has been left for an adversary to perform any analysis. In addition, the function where the response code resides is better not in the current call stack when the failure happens, because debuggers can give adversaries the information of the current call stack.

**Temporal separation.** If a response system can cause enough amount of delay before failure, it can effectively thwart the process of tampering. Imagine an attack whereby an adversary tries a number of tampering options. The adversary tries one option and starts to observe the program's behavior to see if the tampering works. Suppose our response system will not fail the program until after a large amount of time, say one day. Then only after one day, the poor adversary will discover that his trick is not working and he needs to spend another night to try another option. This is psychologically frustrating for the adversary and will certainly slow down the tampering process. The strategy of delayed failure is analogous to injecting extra delay between two consecutive password tries in a password protection system.

The metric for temporal separation is obviously the time or the number of instructions executed between response and failure.

**Stealth.** The code in a tamper-response system should blend in with the program being protected so that an automatic scanning tool will not identify the tamper-response code easily. A response system involving division-by-zero is definitely not a good idea.

Stealth is a highly context-sensitive quality. Response code that is stealthy in one program may not be so in another. Any metric for stealth has to be with respect to the context, or the program. One possible metric is the statistical similarity[4] between the program being protected and the response code.

---

[3] The principle of spatial/temporal separation has also been briefly discussed by Collberg and Thomborson [10].

[4] E.g., the percentage of each kind of machine instructions.

**Predictability.** A program that has been tampered with should eventually fail, with high probability. We also want to control when and where the failure (damage) can happen. A failure that happens during sensitive operations is probably undesirable.

In addition, any available obfuscation should be used to protect the tamper-detection and response code. Ideally, neither observation nor tampering should easily reveal patterns useful for determining where detection and response occur. In practice, both generic and application-specific obfuscation methods should be devised to maximize an attacker's workload.

## 4    System Description

We now describe a response mechanism we have built following the principles in Section 3.1. Our starting insight is that by corrupting a program's internal state, a response system can cause the program to fail. If we carefully choose which part of state to corrupt and when to corrupt, we may achieve the aforementioned spatial and temporal separation. This deliberate injection of "programming bugs" also satisfies our stealth principle because these bugs look just like normal programming bugs and are thus hard to pick out by static scanning.[5] Bugs due to programming errors are hard to locate. Some of these bugs cause delayed failure. As an example, an early system called HUW [18] appeared to run successfully, but crashed after about one hour. This was due to an elusive bug in its string handling module, which corrupted the system's global buffer. The data structures inside the corrupted buffer, however, were not used until about an hour later. Therefore, the system ran OK until the corrupted data structures were accessed.

As we can see from this example, corrupting programs' internal state might produce the effect of delayed failure. For clarity, we assume there are three kinds of sites: detection sites (where tamper detection happens), response sites (where corrupting the internal state happens), and failure sites (where failure happens). Response sites are also called corruption sites in our system. In the rest of this paper, for simplicity, we will identify detection sites with corruption sites. In practice, detection sites and corruption sites should be separated (and communicate via covert flags), and the techniques and implementation that we will introduce applies as well.

There are many ways to corrupt a program's internal state. Our system chooses the straightforward way: corrupt the program' own variables. By deliberately corrupting the program' variables, we hope to achieve the following results:

- Predictable failure of the program, due to the corruption of the program's internal state.

---

[5] If there is regularity in the type of bugs we introduce, an attacker may be able to employ static analysis to increase his/her likelihood of locating them.

- Stealthy response code, since the response code is just an ordinary variable assignment.
- Spatial and temporal separation, if we carefully choose when and where to corrupt the variables.

Not all variables are good candidates. Suppose the value of an integer variable ranges between 3 and 10. Then what would be the behavior of the program when the variable is changed to 100? Would the program fail? Where and when would it fail? We have to answer these questions to achieve some predictability in our response system. We suspect that for an arbitrary program variable, the result of any analysis is highly imprecise. However, one observation can be made about pointer variables, which are ubiquitous in C-style programs. If a pointer is corrupted by setting it to a NULL pointer or a value out of the program's address space, dereference of this pointer definitely crashes the program. Moreover, if the next dereference happens only after some time, we achieve the effect of delayed failure.

Corruption of local pointers (declared in a function body) is unlikely to achieve much delay. The corruption of local pointers has to happen locally, because their storage is in the run-time stack, Their values are also used locally, which means the corruption and usage would be very close if we had chosen to corrupt a local pointer.

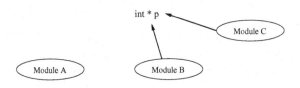

**Fig. 1.** Global pointers

For global pointers, the scenario is different and one example is depicted in Figure 1. Suppose there is a global pointer **p** which is used by modules B and C, but not touched by module A. If we choose to corrupt this pointer in module A, then the program will keep running until module A has finished and the program switches to module B or C. Based on this example, intuition is there that delayed failure can be achieved by corrupting a global pointer.

But what if the program has not many global pointers? Our solution is to perform transformations on the program to create new global pointers. One way to achieve this is to add a level of indirection to the existing global variables. The idea is illustrated by the example in Figure 2.

On the left of Figure 2 is the original program; the code after transformation is on the right. For the global variable **a**, we create a new pointer variable **p_a**, whose value is initialized to the address of **a**. Then we replace all uses, or some uses, of variable **a** by the dereference of the newly created pointer variable **p_a**.

Below are the benefits of the extra level of indirection to global variables:

```
int a;                          int a;
void f() {                      int *p_a = &a;
  a = 3;                        void f() {
}                                 *p_a = 3;
void main() {                   }
  f();                          void main() {
  printf(''a = %i\n'', a);        f();
}                                 printf(''a = %i\n'', *p_a);
                                }
```

**Fig. 2.** Example: Creating a layer of indirection to global pointers

- Any global variables can be used to create new pointers, alleviating the possible shortage of global pointers.
- The failure behavior of the new program is easily predictable. After p_a is corrupted, any subsequent use of the variable, p_a, would be a failure site.
- We can also control where the program fails. For example, if we do not want the program to fail inside the main function, we just do not replace a with p_a in main.

Note that the extra level of indirection to global variables does slow down the program because of the cost of extra dereferences. On the other hand, this performance hit is controllable since we can control how many uses of global variables are replaced by their pointer counterparts.

## 4.1  Choosing Corruption Sites

As we have explained, global pointer variables are the targets to corrupt in our system. The remaining question is where to corrupt those pointers? Since we could corrupt a global pointer anywhere in the program, the search space is the whole program.

To make our search algorithm scalable for large programs, we use functions as the basic search units instead of, say, statements. Based on this, we state the searching problem more rigorously. Corruption of global pointer variables can happen inside any function body; thus a function body is a possible *corruption site*. A *failure site* is a function where the program fails when the program reaches the function after pointer corruption. In our setting, failure sites correspond to those places where corrupted pointers are dereferenced. To find good corruption sites, we want to search for functions to embed pointer corruptions, to achieve wide spatial and temporal separation between corruption and failure.

First, we should make sure the function where corruption happens is not in the current call stack when the program fails. Otherwise, attacker could use a debugger to back-trace from the failure site to the corruption site. To avoid such attacks, we use a static-analysis tool called call graphs. Below is an example program and its call graph.

```
int a;
int *p_a = &a;
void g1();
void g2();
void h ();
void f() {
  g1(); g2();
  *p_a = 3;
}
void main() {
  f(); h();
}
```

In the example, the `main` function calls the `f` function; thus there is a directed edge from `main` to `f` in its call graph. Similarly, since `f` calls `g1` and `g2`, the call graph has the directed edges from `f` to `g1`, and from `f` to `g2`.

In the example program, suppose our system decides to corrupt the pointer variable `p_a`. Then the function `f` is a failure site since it dereferences `p_a`. Obviously, the corruption should not happen inside `f` because otherwise the program would fail in the function where the corruption happened. Furthermore, the `main` function should not be the corruption site since otherwise the `main` function would be in the current call stack when the program fails in the function `f`. In general, our system excludes all functions where the corrupted pointer variable is dereferenced; furthermore, it excludes all functions who in the call graph are ancestors of those functions where failure can happen. This heuristic guarantees that when the program fails the corruption site is not in the call stack.

Additionally, we want to achieve wide spatial and temporal separation between corruption and failure. We first present some experimental numbers, which show the spectrum of spatial and temporal separation. We conducted the experiment on a C program called Winboard. We picked 800 functions in Winboard, planted the corruption of a selected pointer variable into each function, and recorded the temporal and spatial separation between corruption and failure. Figure 3 shows the temporal separation, and Figure 4 shows the spatial separation. In both figures, the horizontal axis is the function ID where the corruption happens. In Figure 3, the vertical axis is the elapsing time between corruption and failure in microseconds. In the Figure 4, the vertical axis is the number of function calls happened between corruption and failure.

As we can see from the figures, the spread is over several orders of magnitude. The functions in the upper portion are the ones we want to search for. However, a static heuristic may be hard to succeed because essentially an estimate of time between two function calls is needed; we are not aware of any static-analysis techniques that can give us this information.

Our solution is to measure the average distance between two function calls in a dynamic function-call and time trace. This information estimates how far a function is from the nearest failure sites (functions that dereferences the pointer) in terms of both the number of function calls and time. Only functions that are

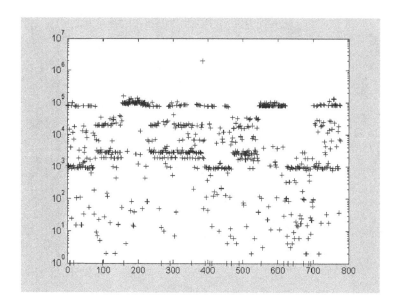

**Fig. 3.** Temporal separation between corruption and failure. The horizontal axis represents function IDs, and the vertical axis represents the elapsing time between corruption and failure in microseconds.

far from failure sites will be selected as corruption sites. We experimented this heuristic on the Winboard program and the results showed that those functions in the upper portion of Figure 3 and 4 are most likely to be selected. The shortcoming of this approach is that it depends on dynamic traces, which may be correlated to user inputs and other random events.

To make it more precise, we outline our algorithm for selecting good corruption sites in Figure 5. For a simple presentation, the algorithm processes a single C file, called example.c (Our implementation can process multiple files at once).

The algorithm takes three inputs. The first is the source file. The second is a function-distance matrix $T$, which tells distances between functions. The value $T[f_1, f_2]$ is the distance between functions $f_1$ and $f_2$. In our system, the matrix is computed from a typical dynamic trace of the program. The last input is a threshold parameter $\delta$ to dictate the minimal distance between corruption sites and failure sites.

For each global variable $g_i$, the algorithm first identifies those functions that use the value of $g_i$ (line 4). A function $f$ in this set is a failure site for $g_i$, because if we had created an indirect pointer to $g_i$, say $p_{g_i}$, and replaced the use of $g_i$ in $f$ by $*(p_{g_i})$, then the program would fail inside $f$ after $p_{g_i}$ had been corrupted. The algorithm then proceeds to rule out all functions that are ancestors of the failure sites in the call graph (line 6), so that when program fails, the function where corruption happens will not be in the call stack. Finally, the algorithm rules out those functions that are too close to failure sites (line 8 and 9).

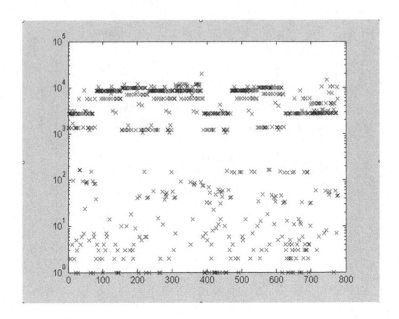

**Fig. 4.** Spatial separation between corruption and failure. The horizontal axis represents function IDs, and the vertical axis represents the number of function calls between corruption and failure.

## 5    Implementation and Evaluation

We have built a prototype system, which takes C programs as inputs and automatically inserts tamper-response code. The system identifies good global variables as target variables to corrupt when tampering is detected; it also selects good corruption sites according to the heuristics we explained in section 4.

The flow of our implemented system is depicted in Figure 6. In the figure and also in the following paragraphs, we use the Winboard program as the example application to explain our system. Winboard is a chess program written in C. It has totally 27,000 lines of C code, and contains 297 global variables, which are potential target variables to corrupt.

Winboard consists of a bunch of C files: `winboard.c`, `backend.c`, *etc.* In our system, these files are first fed into a `varusage` module. For each source file, the `varusage` module produces a `.use` file, which identifies places that global variables are used. Separate `.use` files are linked by the `uselink` module to produce the global `.use` file. Source C files are also fed into the `callgraph` module, which produces `.cg` files, or call graph files. Separate `.cg` files are linked together by the `cglink` to produce a global call graph.

We also run profiling tools on the program to produce a dynamic trace. The trace records the order of entering and exiting functions and also the corresponding timestamps. This trace is the input to the `trmatrix` module. The module measures the average distance between two functions in terms of both elapsing

**Input:**
      a) example.c, with global variables $g_1$, $g_2$, ..., $g_n$;
      b) Function-distance matrix T;
      c) $\delta$: Threshold for the distance between corruption and failure sites.
**Output:** The set of good corruption sites $C_i$, for each $g_i$.

1:  Compute the call graph $G$ of example.c
2: **for** each global variable $g_i$, $1 \leq i \leq n$ **do**
3:    $C_i \leftarrow$ the set of all functions in example.c
4:    Identify the set of functions where the value of $g_i$ is used, say $\{f_{i1}, \ldots, f_{im}\}$
5:    **for** each $f_{ij}$, $1 \leq j \leq m$ **do**
6:       Remove from $C_i$ all the ancestors of $f_{ij}$ in the call graph $G$.
7:       **for** each $f$ remaining in $C_i$ **do**
8:          **if** $T[f, f_{ij}] < \delta$ **then**
9:            remove $f$ from $C_i$
10:        **end if**
11:      **end for**
12:   **end for**
13:   Output $C_i$ for the global variable $g_i$
14: **end for**

**Fig. 5.** Algorithm for selecting good corruption sites

time and the number of function calls, records the information into a matrix, and writes the matrix into a `.tr` file.

At this point, we have `winboard.use` (recording where global variables are used), `winboard.cg` (the global call graph), and `winboard.tr` (the trace matrix). These files are inputs to the `delayedfailure` module. The module first computes the set of good corruption sites for each global variable, following the algorithm in Figure 5, and then randomly selects some global variables and good corruption sites. Finally, the `corrupt` module performs source-to-source transformation to first create a layer of indirection to selected global variables, and then plant the corruption of the newly-created pointers into selected corruption sites (on the condition that tampering is detected).

## 5.1 System Evaluation/Threat Analysis

Overall, our system protects software by making them exhibit the effect of delayed failure after tampering is detected. To remove our tamper-response code, the attacker has to trace back from the crash site to analyze what is corrupted and where the corruption happens. Since we corrupt pointer variables, the attacker essentially has to debug programs with elusive pointer-related bugs, which many programmers know can be extremely hard; the situation is actually worse for the attacker, because he has no source code. Next, we evaluate our system in more detail in terms of the principles we laid out in section 3.1.

**Spatial separation.** Our system can guarantee wide spatial separation between the corruption site and the failure site. We achieved the separation

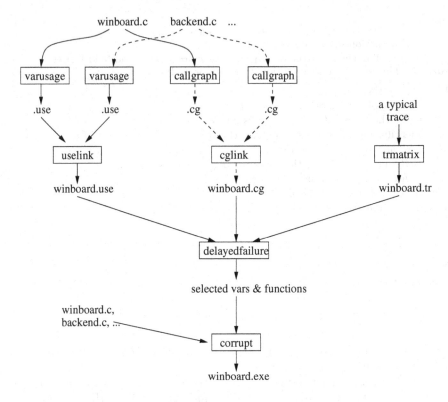

**Fig. 6.** System Implementation

on the order of $10^4$ functions calls in our experiment. With the help of call graphs, it can further guarantee that the corruption site will not be in the call stack when failure happens.

**Temporal separation.** Using the dynamic-trace approach, we achieved seconds of delay in our experiment, which is much better than immediate failure. Further delay can be achieved with the following techniques. First, our experiments were conducted by setting the pointer variable to NULL. Our system can be easily configured so that pointer corruption means adding random offsets to the pointer. In this case, the cumulative effect of several consecutive corruptions will most likely crash the program, and the delay will be boosted by this technique. Second, since we wanted automatic testing in our experiment, we avoided those functions which need human interaction to invoke, e.g., the functions that will be invoked only if certain buttons are clicked. User-behavior models can inform us of those functions that are called occasionally. For example, if we know that a certain function is called only once in an hour, then we can plant the corruption into that function to achieve long delay.

**Stealth.** Since our response system only manipulates pointers, it should be fairly stealthy in programs that have lots of pointer manipulations. For programs in which pointers are scarce, one possible attack for an adversary is to track the pointers of a program dynamically, identify the instructions that make pointers nonsensical, and then remove those instructions.

To counter this attack, our system should be combined with various types of obfuscation and integrity checks. For example, dynamic computation of global-variable pointers, including techniques such as temporary pointer corruption and runtime relocation of global data, should complicate attacks that track pointer usage via breakpoints or traces. We also embed multiple pointer corruptions, so that even one has been removed, others can still work. Finally, we are experimenting with the idea of corrupting data structures through pointers. In these kinds of corruption, pointer values always stay meaningful; only certain invariants of the data structure are destroyed.

**Predictability.** Our response system is predictable and controllable. Pointer dereferences after its corruption will surely fail the program. Any dereference becomes a failure site and we can control where failure happens.

# 6    Extensions

*Safe languages.* In safe, strongly typed languages such as C# and Java, pointers and global variables may be either unavailable or limited to atypical usage. While our pointer-corruption method does not have an immediate analogue in safe code, various other techniques can achieve similar results. In general, the main idea of separating tamper response from detection applies just as well to safe languages as to C/C++.

Below are some examples of delayed corruption possible via a safe language:

- Array out-of-bounds errors: Set up an array index to fall beyond the array's limits.
- Infinite loops: Change a variable in a loop-condition test to result in an infinite (or at least very time-consuming) loop.

Such techniques require implicit data-based links between the code at corruption and failure sites. While global variables in C/C++ serve to create such connections, proper object-oriented design stipulates object isolation and tightly controlled dataflow. Nonetheless, some object fields (e.g., public static members in C#) serve essentially as global variables. Some applications also use dedicated namespaces and classes that encapsulate global data, which can also substitute for true global variables.

To increase the number of opportunities for delayed responses, we can perform various semantically-equivalent code transformations that break object isolation, similar to how we create global pointer variables. As an example, we can convert a constant loop endpoint or API-function argument to a public static variable that can be modified to effect a tamper response. If a good response location contains no suitable code, we can inject new code that references such variables (e.g., a new loop or system-API call). Randomly generated and tightly integrated, such code should have no operational effects if tampering is not detected.

*Graceful degradation.* Some of the above techniques do not cause failures as predictably as pointer corruption. However, *graceful degradation* can be more stealthy and difficult to analyze than definite failures. Any particular response might not terminate the program, but if one or more checks continue to fail, the cumulative effect should eventually make the program unusable. Both the checks and responses can also be made probabilistic in terms of spatial/temporal separation and response action.

A program run could degrade its functioning via slowdown, high resource usage, and arbitrary incorrect operation (e.g., file corruption or graphics distortion). Such techniques may be generic and automated; for example, we can transform program loops to include conditions that take increasingly longer time to satisfy (e.g., via gradually incremented counters). While application-specific techniques require manual design and implementation, these could be quite effective (e.g., a game where the player's movements and aim become increasingly erratic [16]).

## 7    Conclusions

A tamper-resistant system consists of tamper detection and tamper response. Inadequate tamper response can become the weakest link of the whole system. In this paper, we have proposed a tamper-response mechanism that evades hacker removal by introducing delayed and controlled failures, accomplished by corrupting the program's internal state at well-chosen locations.

## Acknowledgment

We thank Stephen Adams and Manuvir Das for providing some static-analysis tools, and Matthew Cary for helpful conversations.

## References

1. Business Software Alliance and International Data Corporation. Annual BSA and IDC global software piracy study (2004-2006) http://www.bsa.org/globalstudy
2. Aucsmith, D.: Tamper resistant software: An implementation. In: First Information Hiding Workshop, pp. 317–333 (1996)
3. Barak, B., Goldreich, O., Impagliazzo, R., Rudich, S., Sahai, A., Vadhan, S., Yang, K.: On the (im)possibility of obfuscating programs. In: Kilian, J. (ed.) CRYPTO 2001. LNCS, vol. 2139, pp. 1–18. Springer, Heidelberg (2001)
4. Cerven, P.: Crackproof Your Software. No Starch Press, Inc. (2002)
5. Chang, H., Atallah, M.J.: Protecting software code by guards. In: Digital Rights Management Workshop, pp. 160–175 (2001)

6. Chen, Y., England, P., Peinado, M., Willman, B.: High assurance computing on open hardware architectures. Research Report MSR-TR-2003-20, Microsoft Research, Microsoft Corporation, Redmond, Washington, USA (March 2003)
7. Chen, Y., Venkatesan, R., Cary, M., Pang, R., Sinha, S., Jakubowski, M.H.: Oblivious hashing: A stealthy software integrity verification primitive. In: Information Hiding Workshop, pp. 400–414 (2002)
8. Chow, S., Gu, Y., Johnson, H., Zakharov, V.A.: An approach to the obfuscation of control-flow of sequential computer programs. In: Information Security, 4th International Conference, pp. 144–155 (2001)
9. Collberg, C., Thomborson, C., Low, D.: A taxonomy of obfuscating transformations. Technical Report 148, Department of Computer Science, University of Auckland (July 1997)
10. Collberg, C.S., Thomborson, C.D.: Watermarking, tamper-proofing, and obfuscation-tools for software protection. IEEE Trans. Software Eng. 28(8), 735–746 (2002)
11. Collberg, C.S., Thomborson, C.D., Low, D.: Manufacturing cheap, resilient, and stealthy opaque constructs. In: ACM Symposium on Principles of Programming Languages (POPL), pp. 184–196 (1998)
12. Goldreich, O., Ostrovsky, R.: Software protection and simulation on oblivious RAMs. Journal of the ACM 43(3), 431–473 (1996)
13. Horne, B., Matheson, L.R., Sheehan, C., Tarjan, R.E.: Dynamic self-checking techniques for improved tamper resistance. In: Digital Rights Management Workshop, pp. 141–159 (2001)
14. http://cdfreaks.com (2006)
15. Lynn, B., Prabhakaran, M., Sahai, A.: Positive results and techniques for obfuscation. In: Cachin, C., Camenisch, J.L. (eds.) EUROCRYPT 2004. LNCS, vol. 3027, pp. 20–39. Springer, Heidelberg (2004)
16. Macrovision. FADE, SafeDisc and SafeDVD copy protection (2002)
17. Peinado, M., Chen, Y., England, P., Manferdelli, J.: NGSCB: A trusted open system. In: Wang, H., Pieprzyk, J., Varadharajan, V. (eds.) ACISP 2004. LNCS, vol. 3108, pp. 86–97. Springer, Heidelberg (2004)
18. Pyle, I.C., McLatchie, R.C.F., Grandage, B.: A second-order bug with delayed effect. Software – Practice and Experience 1(3), 231–233 (1971)
19. Wang, C., Hill, J., Knight, J., Davidson, J.: Software tamper resistance: Obstructing static analysis of programs. Technical Report CS-2000-12, University of Virginia (December 2000)
20. Wee, H.: On obfuscating point functions. Cryptology ePrint Archive, Report 2005 /001 (2005) http://eprint.iacr.org/

# A Model for Self-Modifying Code*

Bertrand Anckaert, Matias Madou, and Koen De Bosschere

Ghent University, Electronics and Information Systems Department
Sint-Pietersnieuwstraat 41 9000 Ghent, Belgium
{banckaer,mmadou,kdb}@elis.UGent.be
http://www.elis.UGent.be/paris

**Abstract.** Self-modifying code is notoriously hard to understand and therefore very well suited to hide program internals. In this paper we introduce a program representation for this type of code: the state-enhanced control flow graph. It is shown how this program representation can be constructed, how it can be linearized into a binary program, and how it can be used to generate, analyze and transform self-modifying code.

## 1 Introduction

Self-modifying code has a long history of hiding the internals of a program. It was used to hide copy protection instructions in 1980s MS DOS based games. The floppy disk drive access instruction 'int 0x13' would not appear in the executable program's image but it would be written into the executable's memory image after the program started executing[1]. A number of publications in the academic literature indicate a renewed interest in the application of self-modifying code to prevent undesired reverse engineering [1,10,14].

While hiding the internals of a program can be used to protect the intellectual property contained within or protected by software, it can be applied for less righteous causes as well. Viruses, for example, try to hide their malicious intent through the use of self-modifying code [12].

Self-modifying code is very well suited for these applications as it is generally assumed to be one of the main problems in reverse engineering [3]. Because self-modifying code is so hard to understand, maintain and debug, it is rarely used nowadays. As a result, many analyses and tools make the assumption that code is not self-modifying, i.e., constant. Note that we distinguish self-modifying code from run-time generated code as used in, e.g., a Java Virtual Machine.

This is unfortunate as, in theory, there is nothing unusual about self-modifying code. After all, in the omnipresent model of the stored-program computer, which was anticipated as early as 1937 by Konrad Zuse, instructions and data are held in a single storage structure [22]. Because of this, code can be treated as data and can thus be read and written by the code itself.

---

* The authors would like to thank the Institute for the Promotion of Innovation by Science and Technology in Flanders (IWT) and the Fund for Scientific Research Flanders (FWO) for their financial support. This research is also partially supported by Ghent University and by the HiPEAC network.

[1] http://en.wikipedia.org/wiki/Self-modifying_code, May 5th 2006.

J. Camenisch et al. (Eds.): IH 2006, LNCS 4437, pp. 232–248, 2007.

If we want tools and analyses to work conservatively and accurately on self-modifying code, it is important to have a representation which allows one to easily reason about and transform that type of code. For traditional code, which neither reads nor writes itself, the control flow graph is such a representation. Its main benefit is that it represents a superset of all executions. As such, it allows analyses to reason about every possible run-time behavior of the program. Furthermore, it is well understood how a control flow graph can be constructed, how it can be transformed and how it can be linearized into an executable program. Until now, there was no analogous representation for self-modifying code. Existing approaches are often ad-hoc and usually resort to overly conservative assumptions: a region of self-modifying code is considered to be a black box about which little is known and to which no further changes can be made.

In this paper, we will discuss why the basic concept of the control flow graph is inadequate to deal with self-modifying code and introduce a number of extensions which can overcome this limitation. These extensions are: (i) a datastructure keeps track of the possible states of the program, (ii) an edge can be conditional on the state of the target memory locations, and (iii) an instruction uses the memory locations in which it resides.

We refer to a control flow graph augmented with these extensions as a state-enhanced control flow graph. These extensions ensure that we no longer have to artificially assume that code is constant. In fact, existing data analyses can now readily be applied on code, as desired in the model of the stored-program computer. Furthermore, we will discuss how the state-enhanced control flow graph allows for the transformation of self-modifying code and how it can be linearized into an executable program.

The remainder of this paper is structured as follows: Section 2 introduces the running example. Next, the extensions to the traditional control flow graph are introduced in Section 3. Section 4 provides algorithms to construct a state-enhanced control flow graph from a binary program and vice versa. Example analyses on and transformations of this program representation are the topic of Section 5. An experimental evaluation is given in Section 6. Related work is the topic of Section 7 and conclusions are drawn in Section 8.

## 2   The Running Example

For our example, we introduce a simple and limited instruction set which is loosely based on the 80x86. For the sake of brevity, the addresses and immediates are assumed to be 1 byte. It is summarized below:

| Assembly | Binary | Semantics |
|---|---|---|
| movb *value to* | 0xc6 *value to* | set byte at address *to* to value *value* |
| inc   *reg* | 0x40 *reg* | increment register *reg* |
| dec   *reg* | 0x48 *reg* | decrement register *reg* |
| push *reg* | 0xff *reg* | push register *reg* on the stack |
| jmp   *to* | 0x0c *to* | jump to absolute address *to* |

As a running example, we have chosen to hide one of the simplest operations. The linear disassembly of the obfuscated version is as follows:

| Address | Assembly | Binary |
|---------|----------|--------|
| 0x0 | movb 0xc    0x8 | c6 0c 08 |
| 0x3 | inc  %ebx | 40 01 |
| 0x5 | movb 0xc    0x5 | c6 0c 05 |
| 0x8 | inc  %edx | 40 03 |
| 0xa | push %ecx | ff 02 |
| 0xc | dec  %ebx | 48 01 |

If we would perform traditional CFG (Control Flow Graph) construction on this binary, we would obtain a single basic block as shown in Figure 1(a). If we step through the program however, we can observe that instruction A changes instruction D into instruction G, resulting in a new CFG as shown in part (b). Next instruction B is executed, followed by instruction C which changes itself into jump instruction H (c). Then, instruction G transfers control back to B after which H and F are executed. The only possible trace therefore is A,B,C,G,B,H,F. While not apparent at first sight, we can now see that these instructions could be replaced by a single instruction: inc %ebx.

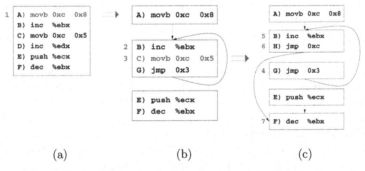

(a)                    (b)                    (c)

**Fig. 1.** Traditional CFG construction before execution (a), after the first write instruction A (b), and after the second write instruction C (c)

## 3   The State-Enhanced Control Flow Graph (SE-CFG)

CFGs have since long been used to discover the hierarchical flow of control and for data-flow analysis to determine global information about the manipulation of data [16]. They have proved to be a very useful representation enabling the analysis and transformation of code. Given the vast amount of research that has gone into the development of analyses on and transformations of this program representation, we are eager to reuse the knowledge resulting from this research.

## 3.1   A Control Flow Graph for Self-Modifying Code

One of the reasons a CFG is so useful is that it represents a superset of all the possible executions that may occur at run time. As a result, many analyses rely on this representation to reason about every possible behavior of the program. Unfortunately, traditional CFG construction algorithms fail in the presence of self-modifying code. If they are applied on our running example at different moments in time, we obtain the three CFGs shown in Figure 1. However, none of these CFGs allows for both a conservative and accurate analysis of the code.

We can illustrate this by applying unreachable code elimination on these CFGs. This simple analysis removes every basic block that cannot be reached from the entry block. If it is applied on Figure 1(a), then no code will be considered to be unreachable. This is not accurate as, e.g., instruction E is unreachable. If we apply it on Figure 1(b), instructions E and F are considered to be unreachable, while Figure 1(c) would yield G and E. However, both F and G are reachable. Therefore in this case, the result is not conservative.

We can however still maintain the formal definition of a CFG: a CFG is a directed graph $G(V, E)$ which consists of a set of vertices $V$, basic blocks, and a set of edges $E$, which indicate possible flow of control between basic blocks. A basic block is defined to be a sequence of instructions for which every instruction in a certain position dominates all those in later positions, and no other instruction executes between two instructions in the sequence.

The concept of an edge remains unchanged as well: a directed edge is drawn from basic block $a$ to basic block $b$ if we conservatively assume that control can flow from $a$ to $b$. The CFG for our running example is given in Figure 2.

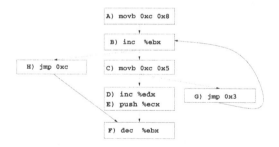

**Fig. 2.** The CFG of our running example (before optimization)

In essence, this CFG is a superposition of the different CFGs observed at different times. In the middle of Figure 2, we can easily detect the CFG of Figure 1(a). The CFG of Figure 1(b) can also be found: just mask away instruction D and H. Finally, the CFG of Figure 1(c) can be found by masking instruction C and D. We will postpone the discussion of the construction of this CFG given the binary representation of the program to Section 4. For now, note that, while this CFG does represent the one possible execution (A,B,C,G,B,H,F), it also represents additional executions that will never occur in practice. This will be optimized in Section 5.

## 3.2   Extension 1: Codebytes

The CFG in Figure 2 satisfies the basic property of a CFG: it represents a superset of all possible executions. As such it can readily be used to reason about a superset of all possible program executions. Unfortunately, this CFG does not yet have the same usability we have come to expect of a CFG.

One of the shortcomings is that it cannot easily be linearized into an executable program. There is no way to go from this CFG to the binary representation of Section 2, simply because it does not contain sufficient information.

For example, there are two fall-through paths out of block B. Note that we follow the convention that a dotted arrow represents a fall-through path, meaning that the two connected blocks need to be placed consecutively. Clearly, in a linear representation, only one of these successors can be placed after the increment instruction. Which one should we then choose?

To overcome this and other related problems, we will augment the CFG with a datastructure, called codebytes. This datastructure will allow us to reason about the different states of the program. Furthermore, it will indicate which instructions overlap and what the initial state of the program is.

In practice, there is one codebyte for every byte in the code segment. This codebyte represents the different states the byte can be in. By convention, the first of these states represents the initial state of that byte, i.e. the one that will end up in the binary representation of the program. For every instruction, there is a sequence of states representing its machine code. For our running example, this is illustrated in Figure 3. We can see that instruction A and C occupy three codebytes, while the others occupy two codebytes. A codebyte consists of one or more states. For example, codebyte $0x0$ has one state: $c6$ and codebyte $0x8$ has two states: $40$ and $0c$. We can also see that instruction H and C overlap as they have common codebytes. As the first state of codebyte $0x5$ is that of instruction C, and the other states are identical, instruction C will be in the binary image of the program, while instruction H will not.

Codebytes are not only useful for the representation of the static code section, but also for the representation of code that could be generated in dynamically allocated memory. A region of memory can be dynamically allocated and filled with bytes representing a piece of code which will be executed afterwards. The difference between a codebyte representing a byte in the static code section and a codebyte representing a byte that will be dynamically produced at run time is that it has no initial state because the byte will not end up in the binary representation of the program.

## 3.3   Extension 2: Codebyte Conditional Edges

We have repeatedly stressed the importance of having a superset of all possible executions. Actually, we are looking for the exact set of all possible executions,

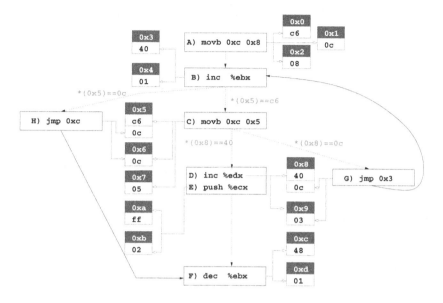

**Fig. 3.** The SE-CFG of our running example (before optimization)

not a superset. In practice, it is hard, if not impossible to find a finite representation of all possible executions and no others. The CFG is a compromise in the sense that it is capable of representing all possible executions, at the cost of representing executions that cannot occur in practice. Therefore, analyses on the CFG are conservative, but may be less accurate than optimal because they are safe for executions that can never occur.

A partial solution to this problem consists of transforming the analyses into path-sensitive variants. These analyses are an attempt to not take into account certain unexecutable paths. Clearly, for every block with multiple outgoing paths, only one will be taken at a given point in the execution. For constant code, the chosen path may depend upon a status flag (conditional jump), a value on the stack (return), the value of a register (indirect call or jump), .... However, once the target of the control transfer is known, it is also known which instruction will be executed next. For self-modifying code the target address alone does not determine the next instruction to be executed. The values of the target locations determine the instruction that will be executed as well. To take this into account, we introduce additional conditions on arrows. These conditions can be found on the arrows itself in Figure 3. As instruction B is not a control transfer instruction, control will flow to the instruction at the next address: $0x5$. For constant code, this would determine which instruction is executed next: there is at most one instruction at a given address. For self-modifying code, this is not necessarily the case. Depending on the state of the program, instruction B can be followed by instruction C ($*(0x5)==c6$) or instruction H ($*(0x5)==0c$).

### 3.4  Extension 3: Consumption of Codebyte Values

The third, and final extension is designed to model the fact that when an instruction is executed, the bytes representing that instruction are read by the CPU. Therefore, in our model, an instruction uses the codebytes it occupies. This will enable us to treat code as data in data-flow analyses. For example, if we want to apply liveness analysis on a codebyte, we have the traditional uses and definitions of that value: it is read or written by another instruction. For example, codebyte $0x8$ is defined by instruction A. On top of that, a codebyte is used when it is part of an instruction, *e.g.*, codebyte $0x8$ is used by instruction D and G. Note that this information can be deduced from the codebyte structure.

**Wrap-up.** The SE-CFG still contains a CFG and therefore, existing analyses which operate on a CFG can be readily applied to an SE-CFG. Furthermore, code can be treated exactly the same way as data: the initial values of the codebytes are written when the program is loaded, they can be read or written just as any other memory location and are also read when they are executed.

Note that in our model traditional code is just a special case of self-modifying code. The extensions can be omitted for traditional code as: (i) the code can easily be linearized since instructions do not overlap, (ii) the target locations of control transfers can only be in one state, and (iii) the result of data analyses on code are trivial as the code is constant.

Where possible, we will make the same simplifications. For example, we will only add constraints to arrows where necessary and limit them to the smallest number of states to discriminate between different successors.

## 4  Construction and Linearization of the SE-CFG

In this section, we discuss how an SE-CFG can be constructed from assembly code. Next, it is shown how the SE-CFG representation can be linearized.

### 4.1  SE-CFG Construction

Static SE-CFG construction is only possible when we can deduce sufficient information about the code. If we cannot detect the targets of indirect control transfers, we need to assume that they can go to every byte of the program. If we cannot detect information about the write instructions, we need to assume that any instruction can be at any position in the program. This would result in overly conservative assumptions, hindering analyses and transformations.

When looking at applications of information hiding, it is likely that attempts will have been made to hide this information. It is nevertheless useful to devise such an algorithm, because there are applications of self-modifying code outside the domain of information hiding which do not actively try to hide such information. Furthermore, reverse engineers often omit the requirement of proved conservativeness and revert to approximate, practically sound information. Finally, it could be used to extend dynamically obtained information over code not covered in observed executions. For programs which have not deliberately been obfuscated, linear disassembly works well. As a result, the disassembly phase can be separated from the flowgraph construction phase. However, when the code is intermixed with data in an unpredictable way, and especially when attempts have been made to thwart linear disassembly [13], it may produce wrong results. Kruegel *et al.*[11] introduce a new method to overcome most of the problems introduced by code obfuscation but the method is not useful when a program contains self-modifying code. To partially solve this problem, disassembly can be combined with the control flow information. Such an approach is recursive traversal. The extended recursive traversal algorithm which deals with self-modifying code is:

```
00: proc main()
01:    for ( addr = code.startAddr; addr ≤ code.endAddr; addr++)
02:        codebyte[addr].add(byte at address addr);
03:    while (change)
04:        MarkAllAddressesAsUnvisited();
05:        Recursive(code.entryPoint);
06: proc Recursive(addr)
07:    if (IsMarkedAsVisited(addr)) return;
08:    MarkAsVisited(addr);
09:    for each (Ins) — Ins can start at codebyte[addr]
10:        DisassembleIns(Ins);
11:        for each (v,w) — Ins can write v at codebyte w
12:            codebyte[w].add(v);
13:        for each (target) — control can flow to target after Ins
14:            Recursive(target);
```

Disassembly starts at the only instruction that will certainly be executed as represented in the binary: the entry point (line 5). When multiple instructions can start at a codebyte, all possible instructions are disassembled (line 9, codebyte $0x8$ in Figure 4(a)). When an instruction modifies the code, state(s) are added to the target codebyte(s) (line 11-12). This is illustrated in Figure 4(a): state $0c$ is added to codebyte $0x8$. Next, all possible successors are recursively disassembled (line 13-14). In our example, the main loop (line 3) will be executed three times, as the second instruction at codebyte $0x5$ will be missed in the first run. It will however be added in the second run. In the third run, there will be no further changes. The overall result is shown in Figure 4(b).

Once we have detected the instructions, the SE-CFG construction is straightforward: every instruction I is put into a separate basic block *basicblock$_I$*. If control can flow from instruction I to codebyte $c$, then for every instruction J that can start at $c$, we draw an edge *basicblock$_I$* → *basicblock$_J$*. Finally, basic blocks are merged into larger basic blocks where possible. The thus obtained SE-CFG for our running example is given in Figure 3. Note that it still contains instructions that cannot be executed and edges that cannot be followed. It is discussed in Section 5 how these can be pruned.

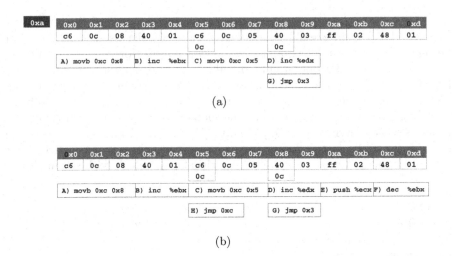

(a)

(b)

**Fig. 4.** Recursive Traversal Disassembly of Self-Modifying Code

## 4.2    SE-CFG Linearization

Traditional CFG linearization consists of concatenating all basic blocks that need to be placed consecutively in chains. The resulting chains can then be ordered arbitrarily, resulting in a list of instructions which can be assembled to obtain the desired program.

When dealing with self-modifying code, we cannot simply concatenate all basic blocks that need to be placed consecutively and write them out. One of the reasons is that this is impossible when dealing with multiple fall-through edges. Instead, we will create chains of codebytes. Two codebytes need to be concatenated if one of the following conditions holds: (i) $c$ and $d$ are successive codebytes belonging to an instruction, (ii) codebyte $c$ is the last codebyte of instruction I and codebyte $d$ is the first codebyte of instruction J and I and J are successive instructions in a basic block, and (iii) codebyte $c$ is the last codebyte byte of the last instruction in basic block $A$ and $d$ is the first codebyte of the first instruction in basic block $B$ and $A$ and $B$ need to be placed consecutively because of a fall-through path.

The resulting chains of codebytes can be concatenated in any order into a single chain. At this point, the final layout of the program has been determined, and all relocated values can be computed. Next, the initial states of the codebytes can be written out.

For example, in Figure 3, codebyte $0x0, 0x1$ and $0x2$ need to be concatenated because of condition (i), codebyte $0x9$ and $0xa$ because of condition (ii) and codebyte $0x4$ and $0x5$ because of condition (iii). When all conditions have been evaluated, we obtain a single chain. If we write out the first state of every codebyte in the resulting chain, we obtain the binary code listed in Section 2.

# 5   Analyses on and Transformations of the SE-CFG

In this section, we will demonstrate the usability of the SE-CFG representation by showing how it can be used for common analyses and transformations. We will illustrate how issues concerning self-modifying code can be mapped onto similar issues encountered with constant code in a number of situations.

Note that once the SE-CFG is constructed, the eventual layout of the code is irrelevant and will be determined by the serialization phase. Therefore, the addresses of codebytes are irrelevant in this phase. However, for the ease of reference, we will retain them in this paper. In practice, addresses are replaced by relocations.

## 5.1   Constant Propagation

The CFG of Figure 2 satisfies all requirements of a CFG: it is a superset of all possible executions. As this CFG is part of the SE-CFG in Figure 3, analyses which operate on a CFG can be reused without modifications. This includes constant propagation, liveness analysis, . . .

Because of the extensions, it is furthermore possible to apply existing data analyses on the code as well. This can be useful when reasoning about self-modifying code. A common question that arises when dealing with self-modifying code is: "What are the possible states of the program at this program point?". This question can be answered through traditional data analyses on the code-bytes, e.g., constant propagation.

If we would perform constant propagation on codebyte $0x8$ on the SE-CFG of Figure 3, we can see that codebyte $0x8$ it is set to 40 when the program is loaded. Subsequently, it is set to $0c$ by instruction A. Continuing the analysis, we learn that at program point C it can only contain the value $0c$. Therefore, the edge from instruction C to instruction D is unrealizable, since the condition *(0x8)==40 can never hold. The edge can therefore be removed.

## 5.2   Unreachable Code Elimination

Traditionally, unreachable code elimination operates by marking every basic block that is reachable from the entry node of the program. For self-modifying code, the approach is similar. For our running example, this would result in the elimination of basic blocks D and E. Note that the edge between C and D is assumed to have been removed by constant propagation.

Similarly, we can remove unreachable codebytes. A codebyte can be removed if it is not part of any reachable basic block and if it is not read by any instruction. This allows us to remove codebyte $0xa$ and $0xb$. While we have removed the inc %edx-instruction, its codebytes could not be removed, as they are connected through another instruction. Note that we now have a conservative and accurate unreachable code elimination.

## 5.3  Liveness Analysis

Another commonly asked question with self-modifying code is as follows: "Can I overwrite a piece of code?". Again, this is completely identical to the question whether you can overwrite a piece of data. You can overwrite a piece of the program if you can guarantee that the value will not be read later on by the program before it is overwritten. In our model, for self-modifying code, a value is read when (i) it is read by an instruction (standard), (ii) the flow of control can be determined by this value (extension 2), and (iii) the CPU will interpret it as (part of) an instruction (extension 3).

We could, for example, perform liveness analysis on codebyte $0x8$. This shows us that the value 40, which is written when the program is loaded, is a dead value: it is never read before it is written by instruction **A**. As a result, it can be removed and we could write the second state $0c$ immediately when the program is loaded. In our representation, this means making it the first state of codebyte $0x8$.

Subsequently, an analysis could point out that instruction **A** has now become an idempotent instruction: it writes a value that was already there. As a result, this instruction can be removed. We have now obtained the SE-CFG of Figure 5.

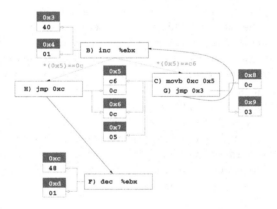

**Fig. 5.** The SE-CFG after partial optimization, before unrolling

## 5.4  Loop Unrolling

Subsequently, we could peel of one iteration of the loop to see if this would lead to additional optimizations. This results in the SE-CFG in Figure 6. Note that we had to double write operation **C**, as we should now write to both the original and the copy of the codebyte in order to be semantically equivalent.

## 5.5  Finishing Up

Similar to Section 5.1, we can now find out that the paths B' → H' and B → C are unrealizable. As a result, we no longer have a loop. Instruction **C**, **C2**, **G** and

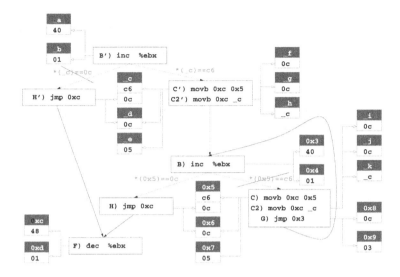

**Fig. 6.** The SE-CFG after unrolling

H' are unreachable. Applying the same optimization as in Section 5.3, we can remove the first state of codebyte 0x5 and instruction C'. The value written by C2' is never used and thus C2' can be removed. Through jump forwarding, we can remove instruction H. Finally, given that the decrement instruction performs exactly the opposite of the increment instruction, we now see that the code can be replaced by a single instruction: inc %ebx.

# 6   Evaluation

To evaluate the introduced concepts, we implemented a form of factorization through the use of self-modifying code. The goal however is not to shrink the binary, but to hide program internals. Therefore, we will also perform factorization if the cost is higher than the gain.

In the first phase, we split the code up in what we call *code snippets*. These code snippets are constructed as follows: if a basic block is not followed by a fall-through edge, the basic block itself makes up a code snippet. If basic block $a$ was followed by a fall-through edge $e$ to basic block $b$, a new basic block $c$ is created with a single instruction: a jump to $b$. The target of $e$ is then set to $c$. The combination of $a$ and $c$ is then called a code snippet.

A code snippet is thus a small piece of code that can be placed independently of the other code. It consists of at most two consecutive basic blocks. If there is a second basic block, this second basic block consists of a single jump instruction. The advantage of code snippets is that they can be transformed and placed independently. The downside is that their construction introduces a large number of jump instructions. This overhead is partially eliminated by performing jump forwarding and basic block merging at the end of the transformation.

Next, we perform what we call code snippet coalescing. Wherever possible with at most one modifier we let two code snippets overlap. Both code snippets are then replaced by at most one modifier and a jump instruction to the coalesced code snippet. On the 80x86, this means that code snippets are merged if they differ in at most 4 consecutive bytes.

As an example, consider the two code snippets in Figure 7(a). While these two code fragments seem to have little in common, their binary representation differs in only one byte. Therefore, they are eligible for code snippet coalescing. The result is shown in Figure 7(b). The codebytes of the modifier and jump instructions are not shown to save space. In this example, subsequent branch forwarding will eliminate one of the jumps. (Note that this example uses the actual 80x86 instruction set.)

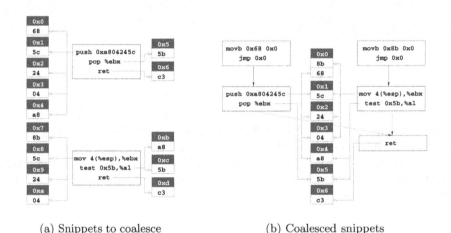

(a) Snippets to coalesce            (b) Coalesced snippets

**Fig. 7.** Example of coalescing code snippets

Intuitively, this makes the binary harder to understand for a number of reasons. Firstly, as overlapping code snippets are used within multiple contexts, the number of interpretations of that code snippet increases. It also becomes more difficult to distinguish functions as their boundaries have been blurred. And most importantly, the common difficulties encountered for self-modifying code have been introduced: the code is not constant and therefore, the static binary does not contain all the instructions that will be executed. Furthermore, multiple instructions will be executed at the same address, so there is no longer a one to one mapping between addresses and instructions.

To further obfuscate the program, we have added an additional transformation, called code snippet splitting. Whenever possible, two different versions are created for code snippets that were not yet protected by the previous transformation. This is often possible because of the redundancy of machine code and especially the 80x86 instruction set. Using an opaque predicate of the type $P^?$ [5] one of both versions is chosen at run time. Next, we merge both versions using code snippet coalescing.

The measurements have been performed a Linux system on a 2.8GHz Pentium IV on 10 C programs of the SPECint 2000 benchmark suite. The benchmarks have been compiled with gcc 3.3.2 and statically linked against uclibc 0.27. The library code has been obfuscated as well. We strongly recommend obfuscating library code as well as it otherwise serves as reference points about which the attacker knows everything and he can then continue to fill in the missing pieces in between two library calls, which allows him to focus on much smaller pieces of code. Furthermore, in the case of data obfuscation, escaping values would need to be turned back into the correct format before every library call, which would severely limit the scope of these obfuscating transformations.

As can be seen in the first row of Table 1, the small granularity of the code snippets and the relatively large overhead of the modifiers (7 byte for a one-byte modifier and 10 byte for a four-byte modifier) can cause a considerable increase in the code size of the program. The impact on the execution speed can be even higher. When all basic blocks are eligible for transformation, the slowdown is unacceptable for most real life applications. Therefore, we excluded hot code (based upon profile information collected from the train input sets) from consideration. The resulting slowdown on the reference input sets is given in the second row of Table 1. The third row indicates the percentage of the total number of original code snippets that is protected by code snippet coalescing. The fourth row the percentage that is protected by code snippet splitting.

**Table 1.** Increase in code size and execution speed; percentage of coalesced code snippets and split-coalesced code snippets

| Benchmarks | bzip2 | crafty | gap | gzip | mcf | parser | perlbmk | twolf | vortex | vpr |
|---|---|---|---|---|---|---|---|---|---|---|
| code bloat (%) | 114.51 | 100.95 | 111.8 | 123.17 | 121.38 | 151.63 | 106.63 | 100.19 | 142.01 | 102.2 |
| slowdown (%) | 27.47 | 128.82 | 71.47 | 15.71 | 0.5 | 116.37 | 300 | 36.38 | 274.42 | 21.16 |
| coalescing (%) | 22.98 | 18.14 | 26.18 | 22.66 | 21.79 | 22.02 | 27.67 | 19.6 | 22.07 | 21.55 |
| splitting (%) | 23.06 | 26.04 | 21.24 | 24.06 | 22.35 | 29.2 | 19.2 | 23.41 | 31.62 | 21.34 |

We have attached a dynamic instrumentation framework [15] to the resulting programs. When no modifications were made to the program other than to keep the program under control and to keep the internal datastructures consistent with the code, we experienced a slowdown of a factor 150 to 200. The bulk of this slowdown is due to the monitoring of the write instructions. These results show that the cost of self-modifying code is fairly high and that it is best avoided in code which will be frequently executed. On the other hand, the slowdown experienced by an attacker, who, e.g., wants to modify the program on the fly, can be much higher.

*The concepts described in this paper have been integrated into a link-time binary rewriter: Diablo. It can be downloaded from http://www.elis.ugent.be/diablo.*

# 7  Related Work

Some of the work on self-modifying code is situated in the domain of viruses, and therefore, not well documented. Because pattern matching is a common technique to detect viruses, some viruses contain an encrypted static image of the virus and code to decrypt it at run time [12]. As different keys are used in different generations, they can have many different static forms. This is a specific type of self-modifying code, which we call self-decryption.

Viruses which do not change during the execution of the virus, but which change in every new generation [20,19] are often referred to as self-modifying as well. We do not consider them to be self-modifying, however. Instead, we refer to this technique as mutation. An approach that could be used to detect viruses which change in every generation is proposed by Chistodorescu and Jha[2].

Protecting a program from being inspected trough the use of self-modifying code is also possible. When the architecture requires explicit cache flushing, a debugger could be fooled if it flushes the cache too early: it will execute the new instruction while the real execution will execute the old instruction untill a cache flush is forced. Vice versa, when cache flushing is done automatically as blocks of code are executed in an instrumentator, anti-debugging could be modifying the next instruction. The instrumentator will execute the old instruction while the real execution will execute the new instruction.

A technique similar to self-decryption can be used for program compaction. In this approach, described by Debray and Evans [6], infrequently executed portions of the code are compressed in the static image of the program and decompressed at run time when needed. This technique could be called self-extraction.

One of the earliest publications in academic literature on tamper-resistant software in general and self-modifying code in particular is due to Aucsmith [1]. The core of the discussed approach consists of integrity verification kernels, which are self-modifying, self-decrypting and installation unique and which verify each other and critical operations of the program.

Kanzaki *et al.* [10] scramble instructions in the static image of the program and restore them at run time. This restoration process is done through modifier instructions that are put along every possible execution path leading to the scrambled instructions. Once the restored instructions are executed, they are scrambled again. As only one instruction can be executed at a given memory location, there is still a one to one mapping between instructions and addresses.

Madou *et al.* [14] introduce a coarse-grained form of self-modifying code. Functions which are not frequently in the same working set are assigned to the same position in the binary. At this position, a template function is placed which contains the common pieces of both functions. Descriptions of the changes that need to be made to the template to obtain the original functions are stored in the binary image as well. At run time, a code editing engine uses these descriptions to create the desired function. As a result the one to one mapping between instructions and addresses is lost.

Dux *et al.* [8] discuss a time-based visualization of self-modifying code, the concept of which can be compared to that of Figure 1. While this visualization can clearly facilitate the understanding of self-modifying code, it does not represent a superset of all possible executions at any time. To the best of our knowledge, existing approaches use specific algorithms and do not use a generally usable representation as the one discussed in this paper.

Other research involves the use of self-modifying code for optimization [18] and the treatment of self-modifying code in dynamic binary translators like Crusoe [7] and Daisy [9].

There is a considerable body of work on code obfuscation in particular and code protection in general that focuses on techniques other than self-modifying code. We refer to other papers for an overview [4,17,21].

## 8 Conclusion

In this paper we have introduced a novel program representation for self-modifying code. We have shown how it enables the generation, accurate and conservative analysis, and transformation of self-modifying code. The evaluation illustrates that self-modifying code can significantly increase the effort an attacker needs to make, but that it should be avoided in frequently executed code.

## References

1. Aucsmith, D.: Tamper resistant software: an implementation. In: Anderson, R. (ed.) Information Hiding. LNCS, vol. 1174, pp. 317–333. Springer, Heidelberg (1996)
2. Christodorescu, M., Jha, S.: Static analysis of executables to detect malicious patterns. In: Proceedings of the 12th USENIX Security Symposium, pp. 169–186. USENIX Association (2003)
3. Cifuentes, C., Gough, K.: Decompilation of binary programs. Software - Practice & Experience 25(7), 811–829 (1995)
4. Collberg, C., Thomborson, C.: Watermarking, tamper-proofing, and obfuscation - tools for software protection. IEEE Transactions on Software Engineering 28(8), 735–746 (2002)
5. Collberg, C., Thomborson, C., Low, D.: Manufacturing cheap, resilient, and stealthy opaque constructs. In: Proc. of the 25th ACM SIGPLAN-SIGACT symposium on Principles of programming languages, pp. 184–196 (1998)
6. Debray, S., Evans, W.: Profile-guided code compression. In: Proc. of the ACM SIGPLAN Conference on Programming language design and implementation (2002)
7. Dehnert, J., Grant, B., Banning, J., Johnson, R., Kistler, T., Klaiber, A., Mattson, J.: The transmeta code morphing software: Using speculation, recovery, and adaptive retranslation to address real-life challenges (2003)
8. Dux, B., Iyer, A., Debray, S., Forrester, D., Kobourov, S.: Visualizing the behavior of dynamically modifiable code. In: Proc. of the 13th International Workshop on Program Comprehension, pp. 337–340 (2005)
9. Ebcioglu, K., Altman, E., Gschwind, M., Sathaye, S.: Dynamic binary translation and optimization. IEEE Transactions on Computers 50(6), 529–548 (2001)

10. Kanzaki, Y., Monden, A., Nakamura, M., Matsumoto, K.: Exploiting self-modification mechanism for program protection. In: Proc. of the 27th Annual International Computer Software and Applications Conference, pp. 170–181 (2003)
11. Kruegel, C., Robertson, W., Valeur, F., Vigna, G.: Static disassembly of obfuscated binaries. In: Proc. of the 13the USENIX Security Symposium (2004)
12. The Leprosy-B virus (1990) http://familycode.atspace.com/lep.txt
13. Linn, C., Debray, S.: Obfuscation of executable code to improve resistance to static disassembly. In: Proc. 10th. ACM Conference on Computer and Communications Security (CCS), pp. 290–299 (2003)
14. Madou, M., Anckaert, B., Moseley, P., Debray, S., De Sutter, B., De Bosschere, K.: Software protection through dynamic code mutation. In: Song, J., Kwon, T., Yung, M. (eds.) WISA 2005. LNCS, vol. 3786, pp. 194–206. Springer, Heidelberg (2006)
15. Maebe, J., Ronsse, M., De Bosschere, K.: DIOTA: Dynamic Instrumentation, Optimization and Transformation of Applications. In: Proc. Int. Conf. on Parallel Architectures and Compilation Techniques (2002)
16. Muchnick, S.: Advanced Compiler Design and Implementation. Morgan Kaufmann Publischers, Inc. San Francisco (1997)
17. Naumovich, G., Memon, N.: Preventing piracy, reverse engineering, and tampering. Computer 36(7), 64–71 (2003)
18. Pike, R., Locanthi, B., Reiser, J.: Hardware/software tradeoffs for bitmap graphics on the blit. Software - Practice & Experience 15(2), 131–151 (1985)
19. Szor, P.: The Art of Computer Virus Research and Defense. Addison-Wesley, London, UK (2005)
20. Szor, P., Ferrie, P.: Hunting for metamorphic (2001)
21. van Oorschot, P.C.: Revisiting software protection. In: Boyd, C., Mao, W. (eds.) ISC 2003. LNCS, vol. 2851, pp. 1–13. Springer, Heidelberg (2003)
22. Zuse, K.: Einführung in die allgemeine dyadik (1937)

# A Markov Process Based Approach
# to Effective Attacking JPEG Steganography

Yun Q. Shi, Chunhua Chen, and Wen Chen

New Jersey Institute of Technology
Newark, NJ, USA 07102
{shi,cc86}@njit.edu

**Abstract.** In this paper, a novel steganalysis scheme is presented to effectively detect the advanced JPEG steganography. For this purpose, we first choose to work on JPEG 2-D arrays formed from the magnitudes of quantized block DCT coefficients. Difference JPEG 2-D arrays along horizontal, vertical, and diagonal directions are then used to enhance changes caused by JPEG steganography. Markov process is applied to modeling these difference JPEG 2-D arrays so as to utilize the second order statistics for steganalysis. In addition to the utilization of difference JPEG 2-D arrays, a thresholding technique is developed to greatly reduce the dimensionality of transition probability matrices, i.e., the dimensionality of feature vectors, thus making the computational complexity of the proposed scheme manageable. The experimental works are presented to demonstrate that the proposed scheme has outperformed the existing steganalyzers in attacking OutGuess, F5, and MB1.

## 1 Introduction

Internet has become an important communication channel since the 90's of the last century, through which emails, speeches, images, and videos are easily transmitted and shared. With image steganography, covert communication through the Internet can also be conducted.

Steganography is the art and science of *invisible* communication, which is to conceal the very existence of hidden messages. Images have many attributes making themselves suitable for steganography. For instance, images can convey large payloads. Some steganographic method can accomplish a steganographic proportion exceeding 13% of the image file size [1]. Due to the non-stationarity of images, image steganography is hard to attack. Especially, the frequent interchange of digital images nowadays makes image steganography very promising.

Recently, research in the field of JPEG (Joint Photographic Experts Group) steganography has become active as JPEG images are used popularly. Many steganographic techniques operating on JPEG images have been published and become publicly available. Most of the techniques in this category modify the LSB (least significant bit) of the JPEG coefficients, which are the outcomes of block-wise two-dimensional (2-D) discrete Cosine transform (DCT) followed by quantization using JPEG quantization table.

J. Camenisch et al. (Eds.): IH 2006, LNCS 4437, pp. 249–264, 2007.
© Springer-Verlag Berlin Heidelberg 2007

In this paper we look at three modern and most advanced steganographic methods, i.e., OutGuess [2], F5 [1], and model-based steganography (MB) [3].

OutGuess constructs a universal steganographic framework, which embeds hidden data using the redundancy of cover images. For JPEG images, OutGuess preserves statistics of the JPEG coefficient histogram. Two measures are taken to reduce the change on cover images introduced by data embedding. Before embedding, OutGuess identifies the redundant JPEG coefficients which have least effect on the cover image and will be modified if necessary during data embedding. It also adjusts the untouched coefficients during the embedding procedure to preserve the original histogram of the JPEG coefficients after embedding.

F5 was developed from Jsteg, F3, and F4. F5 takes two main actions to increase the security against steganalysis attacks: straddling and matrix coding. Straddling scatters the message as uniformly as possible over the cover image to equalize the change density. With matrix embedding, F5 improves the embedding efficiency (the number of bits embedded per change of JPEG coefficients). Generally speaking, the smaller the embedding message size is, the larger the embedding efficiency of F5 is.

In general, the hidden data may be uncorrelated to the cover image, which is utilized by many steganalysis algorithms to attack the data hiding algorithms. MB embedding tries to make the embedded data correlated to the cover image. This is realized by splitting the cover image into two parts, modeling the parameter of the distribution of the second part given the first part, encoding the second part using the model and to-be-embedded message, and then combining the two parts to form the stego image. In embedding method MB1 ([3]), which operates on JPEG images, a modified generalized Cauchy distribution (MGCD) is used to model the JPEG mode histogram. The embedding procedure keeps the lower precision version of the JPEG mode histogram unchanged.

To attack steganography, some steganalysis schemes have been proposed. There are two categories, i.e., specific and universal steganalysis [4]. Specific steganalysis focuses on detecting some particular steganographic tool and has good performance on this steganographic tool if well designed. Universal steganalysis yet tries to steganalyze any steganographic tool, known or unknown in advance.

Farid proposed a universal steganalyzer based on image's high order statistics in [5]. Quadrature mirror filters are used to decompose the image into wavelet subbands and then the high order statistics are calculated for each high frequency subband. The second set of statistics is calculated for the errors in an optimal linear predictor of the coefficient magnitude. Both sets of statistical moments are used as features for steganalysis. It can achieve generally better detection rate than random guess for universal steganographic methods.

In [6], Shi et al presented a universal steganalysis system. The statistical moments of characteristic functions of the given image, its prediction-error image, and their discrete wavelet transform (DWT) subbands are selected as features. All of the low-low wavelet subbands are also used in their system. This steganalyzer can provide a better performance than [5] in general.

In [7], Fridrich proposed a set of distinguishing features aiming at detecting data embedded in JPEG images. The statistics of the original image are estimated by decompressing the JPEG image followed by cropping four rows and four columns on the boundary, and then recompressing the cropped image to JPEG format using the original but estimated quality factor (Q-factor). The author claimed that the obtained image has statistical properties very much similar to that of the cover image. Features for steganalysis are generated from the statistics of the given JPEG image and its estimated version. Designed specifically for detecting JPEG steganography, this scheme performs better than [5, 6] in attacking JPEG steganography [1, 2, and 3].

Recently, a specific steganalysis scheme detecting spread spectrum data hiding is proposed, in which the inter-pixel dependencies are used and a Markov chain model is adopted [8]. The empirical transition matrix of the given image with $256 \times 256 = 65,536$ elements for a grayscale image with a bit depth of 8 is formed. Obviously, these elements cannot be straightforwardly used as features. This paper selects several largest probabilities on the main diagonal together with their neighbors, and some randomly selected probabilities on the main diagonal as features. As a result, some information loss is inevitable due to the random fashion of feature selection. Furthermore, this method uses Markov chain only along horizontal direction, which cannot reflect the 2-D nature of images.

In this paper, a novel steganalysis scheme is presented to effectively detect the advanced JPEG steganography. First, we choose to work on JPEG 2-D arrays to formulate features for steganalysis. Difference JPEG 2-D arrays along horizontal, vertical, and diagonal directions are then used to generally enhance changes caused by JPEG steganography. Markov process is applied to modeling these difference JPEG 2-D arrays so as to utilize the second order statistics for steganalysis. In addition, a thresholding technique is developed to greatly reduce the dimensionality of the transition probability matrices, i.e., the dimensionality of feature vectors, thus making the computational complexity manageable. The experimental works are presented to demonstrate that the proposed scheme has outperformed the state-of-the-arts in attacking OutGuess, F5, and MB1.

The rest of this paper is organized as follows. The feature construction procedure is described in Section 2. In Section 3, support vector machine, the classifier used in our investigation, is introduced. Experimental results are given in Section 4. Next, some discussion is made in Section 5. In Section 6, we discuss our future research. Finally, conclusion is drawn in Section 7.

## 2    Feature Construction

In this paper, steganalysis is considered as a task of two-class pattern recognition. That is, a given test image needs to be classified as either a stego image (with hidden data) or a non-stego image (without hidden data). Therefore, feature construction is a key step in the steganalysis.

As mentioned in Section 1, modern steganorgraphic methods such as Out-Guess and MB have made great efforts to keep the changes on the histogram of

JPEG coefficients caused by data hiding as less as possible. Under these circumstances, we propose to use the second order statistics as features for steganalysis
to detect these JPEG steganographic methods.

In this section, we first define the JPEG 2-D array, followed by introducing the
difference JPEG 2-D array. We then propose to model the difference JPEG 2-D
array using Markov random process. According to the theory of random process,
the transition probability matrix can be used to characterize the Markov process.
Our proposed features are derived from the transition probability matrix. In
order to achieve an appropriate balance between steganalysis capability and
computational complexity, we use the so-called one-step transition probability
matrix in this work. In order to further reduce computational cost by reducing
the dimensionality of feature vectors, we resort to a thresholding technique.

### 2.1    JPEG 2-D Array

Generating features from the exact quantized BDCT domain to attack the
steganographic algorithms operating on JPEG images is natural and reasonable.
For this purpose, it is necessary to first study the property of JPEG coefficients.

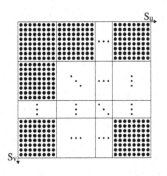

**Fig. 1.** A sketch of JPEG 2-D array

For a given image, consider the 2-D array consisting of all the JPEG coefficients which have been quantized with a JPEG quantization table and have not
been zig-zag scanned, run-length coded, and Huffman coded. That is, this 2-D
array has the same size as the given image with each $8 \times 8$ block filled up with the
corresponding quantized block DCT (BDCT) coefficients. Furthermore, we take
absolute value for each coefficient, resulting in a 2-D array as shown in Figure 1.
We call this resultant 2-D array as JPEG 2-D array in this paper. The features
proposed in this scheme are formed from the JPEG 2-D array.

The reason for taking absolute values is given below. Note that these JPEG
coefficients can be either positive, or negative, or zero. It is known that JPEG
coefficients have been decorrelated effectively. However, a JPEG coefficient is
still correlated to its within block neighbors. This correlation among neighbors
within a local block is called intra-block correlation [9]. It is also well-known

that the power of the 8×8 block of BDCT coefficients is highly concentrated in the DC (direct current) and low-frequency AC (alternative current) coefficients. The JPEG quantization, after which the majority of high-frequency BDCT AC coefficients may become zero, further enhances this disparity in power distribution among quantized BDCT coefficients. The general power distribution trend of JPEG coefficients in each block is non-increasing along the zig-zag scanning order of all of the JPEG coefficients in the block if we ignore some up-and-down of small magnitudes. This is consistent with the fact that the zig-zag scanning makes the use of run-length coding efficient [10]. Combining these observations, we can state that there exists correlation among the absolute values of JPEG coefficients along horizontal, vertical, and diagonal directions. This observation can be further justified by observing Figure 3 shown below. That is, the difference of the absolute values of two immediately (horizontally in Figure 3) neighboring JPEG coefficients are highly concentrated around 0, having a Laplacian-like distribution. The same is true along the vertical and diagonal directions.

In addition, the steganographic methods operating on the JPEG images do not touch the JPEG DC coefficients nor change the sign of the JPEG AC coefficients during data embedding [2, 3] (note that a coefficient with a non-zero magnitude changing to zero is not a sign change). Further discussion in this regard is made in Section 5.1, which shows that taking absolute value results in higher detection rates in general and lower computational complexity.

## 2.2  Difference JPEG 2-D Array

According to [6], the disturbance caused by the data embedding manifests itself more obviously in the prediction-error image than in the original test image. Hence, it is expected that the disturbance caused by the steganographic methods in JPEG images can be enlarged by observing the difference between an element and one of its neighbors in the JPEG 2-D array. For this purpose, we consider the following four difference JPEG 2-D arrays (difference 2-D arrays in short).

Denote the JPEG 2-D array generated from a given test image by $F(u,v)(u \in [0, S_u-1], v \in [0, S_v-1])$, where $S_u$ is the size of the JPEG 2-D array in horizontal direction and $S_v$ in vertical direction. Then as shown in Figure 2, the difference arrays are generated by the following formulae:

$$F_h(u,v) = F(u,v) - F(u+1,v), \tag{1}$$

$$F_v(u,v) = F(u,v) - F(u,v+1), \tag{2}$$

$$F_d(u,v) = F(u,v) - F(u+1,v+1), \tag{3}$$

$$F_m(u,v) = F(u+1,v) - F(u,v+1), \tag{4}$$

where $u \in [0, S_u-2]$, $v \in [0, S_v-2]$, and $F_h(u,v)$, $F_v(u,v)$, $F_d(u,v)$, and $F_m(u,v)$ denote the difference arrays in the horizontal, vertical, main diagonal, and minor diagonal directions, respectively.

In our experimental works reported in this paper, an image set consisting of 7,560 JPEG images with Q-factors ranging from 70 to 90 is used. The arithmetic

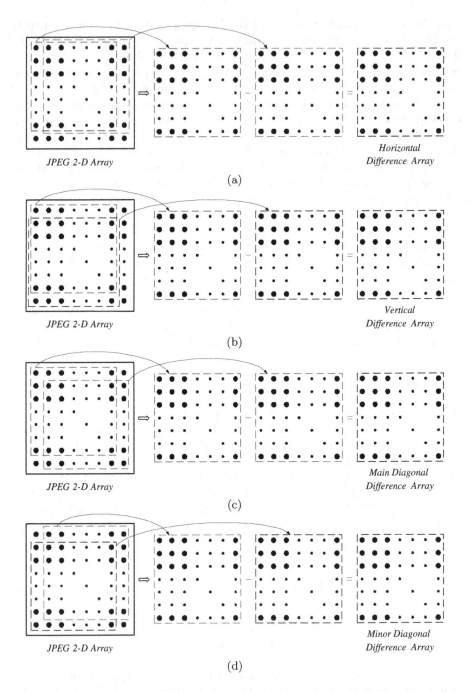

**Fig. 2.** The generation of four difference JPEG 2-D arrays. Parts (a), (b), (c), and (d) correspond to horizontal, vertical, main diagonal, and minor diagonal difference JPEG 2-D arrays, respectively

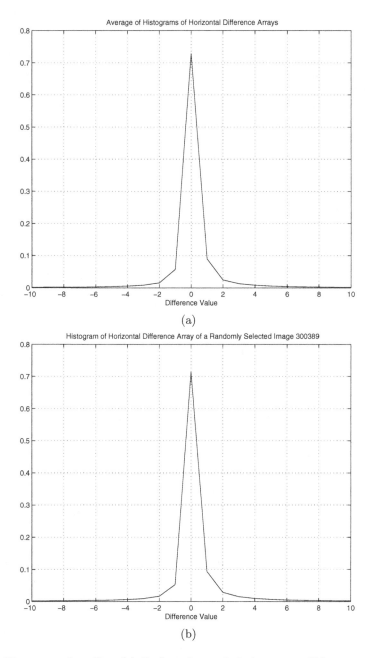

**Fig. 3.** Histogram plots. Part (a) displays the statistical average of histograms of horizontal difference arrays generated from the image set consisting of 7,560 JPEG images with quality factors ranging from 70 to 90. Part (b) corresponds to the histogram of horizontal difference array of a randomly selected image in the set.

average of the histograms of the horizontal difference 2-D arrays generated from this image set and the histogram of the horizontal difference 2-D array generated from a randomly selected image in the set are shown in Figure 3 (a) and (b), respectively. It is observed that the distribution of the elements of the difference 2-D arrays is Laplacian-like. Most of the difference values are close to zero. The values of mean and standard deviation of percentage number of elements of horizontal difference 2-D arrays for the image set falling into [-T, T] when T = 1, 2, 3, 4, 5, 6, and 7 are shown in Table 1. It is observed that more than 90% elements in the horizontal difference 2-D arrays fall into the interval [-3, 3]. Both Figure 3 and Table 1 support the claim of Laplacian-like distribution of the elements of the horizontal difference 2-D arrays. The same is true for the difference 2-D arrays along other three directions.

**Table 1.** Mean and standard deviation of percentage numbers of elements of horizontal difference JPEG 2-D arrays falling within [-T, T] for T = 1, 2, 3, 4, 5, 6, and 7

|  | [-1,1] | [-2,2] | [-3,3] | [-4,4](*) | [-5,5] | [-6,6] | [-7,7] |
|---|---|---|---|---|---|---|---|
| Mean | 84.72 | 88.58 | 90.66 | 91.99 | 92.92 | 93.60 | 94.12 |
| Standard deviation | 5.657 | 4.243 | 3.464 | 2.836 | 2.421 | 2.104 | 1.850 |

* 91.99% is the mean, meaning that on statistic average 91.99% of all elements of horizontal difference JPEG 2-D arrays generated from the image set fall into the range [-4, 4]. The standard deviation is 2.836%.

### 2.3   Transition Probability Matrix

As mentioned before, the modern steganographic methods such as OutGuess and MB have made great efforts to keep the changes on the histogram of JPEG coefficients as less as possible during data embedding. Therefore, we propose to use higher order statistics for steganalyzing the JPEG steganography. In this work the second order statistics are used in order not to increase the computational complexity dramatically.

We propose to model the above-defined difference JPEG 2-D arrays by using Markov random process. According to the theory of random process, the transition probability matrix can be used to characterize a Markov process. There are so-called one-step transition probability matrix and n-step transition probability matrix [11]. Roughly speaking, the former refers to the transition probabilities between two immediately neighboring elements in the difference 2-D array while the latter refers to the transition probabilities between two elements separated by (n-1) elements. In order to have a suitable balance between high steganalysis capability and manageable computational complexity, we only use the one-step transition probability matrix in this work, as shown in Figure 4.

In order to further reduce computational complexity, we resort to a thresholding technique. That is, we select a threshold value T, meaning that we only consider those elements in the difference JPEG 2-D arrays whose value falls into $\{-T, \cdots, -1, 0, 1, \cdots, T\}$. If an element's value is either larger than T or smaller

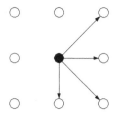

**Fig. 4.** The formation of the transition probability matrices

than -T, it will be represented by T or -T correspondingly. This procedure results in a transition probability matrix of dimensionality $(2T+1) \times (2T+1)$. The elements of these four matrices associated with the horizontal, vertical, main diagonal and minor diagonal difference 2-D arrays are given by

$$p\{F_h(u+1,v)=n|F_h(u,v)=m\}=\frac{\sum_{u,v}\delta(F_h(u,v)=m,F_h(u+1,v)=n)}{\sum_{u,v}\delta(F_h(u,v)=m)}, \quad (5)$$

$$p\{F_v(u,v+1)=n|F_v(u,v)=m\}=\frac{\sum_{u,v}\delta(F_v(u,v)=m,F_v(u,v+1)=n)}{\sum_{u,v}\delta(F_v(u,v)=m)}, \quad (6)$$

$$p\{F_d(u+1,v+1)=n|F_d(u,v)=m\}=\frac{\sum_{u,v}\delta(F_d(u,v)=m,F_d(u+1,v+1)=n)}{\sum_{u,v}\delta(F_d(u,v)=m)}, \quad (7)$$

$$p\{F_m(u,v+1)=n|F_m(u+1,v)=m\}=\frac{\sum_{u,v}\delta(F_m(u+1,v)=m,F_m(u,v+1)=n)}{\sum_{u,v}\delta(F_m(u+1,v)=m)}, \quad (8)$$

where $m,n \in \{-T,\cdots,0,\cdots,T\}$, the summation range for $u$ is from 0 to $S_u - 2$ and for $v$ from 0 to $S_v - 2$, and

$$\delta(A = m, B = n) = \begin{cases} 1 & \text{if } A = m \ \& \ B = n \\ 0 & \text{otherwise} \end{cases}. \quad (9)$$

In summary, we have $(2T+1) \times (2T+1)$ elements for each of these four transition probability matrices. In total, we have $(2T+1) \times (2T+1) \times 4$ elements. All of them are serving as features for steganalysis. In other words, we have $(2T+1) \times (2T+1) \times 4$-D feature vectors for steganaysis. It is clear that we should choose a proper $T$ value for good steganalysis capability with manageable computational complexity.

For this reason, in our experimental works, we set the threshold, $T$, equal to 4 according to our statistical study shown in Figure 3 and Table 1. Hence, if an element has an absolute value larger than 4, this element is reassigned a new absolute value 4 without sign change. The resultant transition probability matrix is of $9 \times 9$ for each of the four difference 2-D arrays. That is, $9 \times 9 = 81$ elements in each of these four transition probability matrices, or equivalently, we have $81 \times 4 = 324$ elements in total.

The feature construction procedure is summarized in Figure 5.

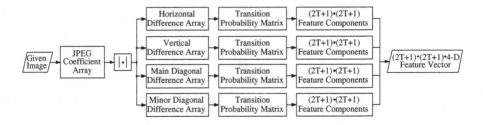

**Fig. 5.** The block diagram of the feature formation procedure

## 3  Support Vector Machine

The support vector machine (SVM) is a popularly used classifier for pattern recognition. In our experimental study, we find that it is easier to use than the neural network (NN) while its performance is comparable to that of NN.

SVM is based on the idea of hyperplane classifier. It uses Lagrangian multipliers to find the optimal separation hyperplane which distinguishes the positive pattern from the negative pattern. If the feature vectors are one-dimensional (1-D), the separation hyperplane reduces to a point on the number axis.

SVM can handle both linear separable and non-linear separable cases. Denote the training data pairs by $\{y_i, \omega_i\}, i = 1, \cdots, l$, where $y_i \in R^N$ is the feature vector, $N$ is the dimensionality of the feature vectors, and $\omega_i = \pm 1$ stands for positive/negative pattern class. In the steganalysis context, an image with hidden data (stego-image) is considered as a positive pattern while an image without hidden data is considered as a negative pattern. The linear support vector algorithm looks for a hyperplane $H : \boldsymbol{w}^T \boldsymbol{y} + b = 0$ and two hyperplanes $H_1 : \boldsymbol{w}^T \boldsymbol{y} + b = -1$ and $H_2 : \boldsymbol{w}^T \boldsymbol{y} + b = 1$ parallel to and with equal distances to $H$ on condition that there are no data points between $H_1$ and $H_2$ and the distance between $H_1$ and $H_2$ is maximized, where $\boldsymbol{w}$ and $b$ are parameters to be optimized. Once the SVM has been trained, the novel exemplar $\boldsymbol{z}$ from the testing data can be classified using $\boldsymbol{w}$ and $b$.

For non-linearly case, the learning machine maps the input feature vectors to a higher dimensional space where a linear hyperplane is located by using kernel function and there are three basic kernels: polynomial, radial basis function, and sigmoid. In our investigation, the polynomial kernel with degree 2 is used [12]. For more detailed information about SVM, readers please refer to [13].

## 4  Experiments and Results

### 4.1  Image Set

As mentioned in Section 2, an image set consisting of 7,560 JPEG images is used in our experimental work. Among these 7,560 images, 2,500 images were taken by members of our research group in different places at different time with different digital cameras; the other 5,060 images were downloaded from the Internet. Each image was cropped (central portion) to the dimension of either 768×512 or 512×768 in the JPEG coefficient domain without involving additional JPEG compression. Some sample images are given in Figure 6.

The images shown in Figure 6 are color images. In our experiments, the chrominance components are set to be zero while the luminance coefficients are untouched before data embedding.

**Fig. 6.** Some sample images used in this experimental work

## 4.2 Stego Images Generation

Our experiments focus on attacking the OutGuess, F5, and MB1 steganographic methods. The codes for these algorithms are publicly available [14, 15, and 16].

As mentioned before, there are quite a few zero coefficients in the JPEG 2-D array. Also, the number of zero coefficients per image varies from image to image. Therefore, the absolute embedding rate of each image also varies if we fix the message length. A reasonable way to define embedding rate is to consider a ratio between message length to non-zero elements in the JPEG 2-D array. The ratio is often measured in the unit of bpc, i.e., bits per non-zero JPEG AC coefficients. In our experiments, the considered embedding rates for OutGuess are 0.05, 0.1, and 0.2 bpc, respectively. The numbers of stego image generated are 7,498, 7,452, and 7,215, respectively. For F5 and MB1, we consider four embedding rates, 0.05, 0.1, 0.2, and 0.4 bpc. For each rate, we have 7,560 stego images. Note that we set step size to be two when implementing MB1. We deliberately ensure that the difference between a stego image and its corresponding cover image is only caused by data embedding in order to avoid the effect on steganalysis caused by JPEG double compression.

### 4.3    Experimental Results Obtained with SVM Polynomial Kernel

We randomly select 1/2 of the non-stego and stego image pairs to train the SVM classifier and the remaining 1/2 pairs to test the trained classifier. We use Farid's [4], Shi et al.'s [5], Fridrich's [6], and our proposed steganalyzers's features to detect OutGuess, F5, and MB1 the same way. The test results shown in Table 2 are the arithmetic average of 20 random experiments.

**Table 2.** Performance comparison using different methods (in the unit of %; TN stands for true negative rate, TP stands for true positive rate, and AR stands for accuracy)

|  | bpc | Farid's | | | Shi et al's | | | Fridrich's | | | Our Proposed | | |
|---|---|---|---|---|---|---|---|---|---|---|---|---|---|
|  |  | TN | TP | AR | TN | TP | AR | TN | TP | AR | TN | TP | AR |
| OutGuess | 0.05 | 59.0 | 57.6 | 58.3 | 55.6 | 58.5 | 57.0 | 49.8 | 75.4 | 62.6 | 87.6 | 90.1 | 88.9 |
| OutGuess | 0.1 | 70.0 | 63.5 | 66.8 | 61.4 | 66.3 | 63.9 | 68.9 | 83.3 | 76.1 | 94.6 | 96.5 | 95.5 |
| OutGuess | 0.2 | 81.9 | 75.3 | 78.6 | 72.4 | 77.5 | 75.0 | 90.0 | 93.6 | 91.8 | 97.2 | 98.3 | 97.8 |
| F5 | 0.05 | 55.6 | 45.9 | 50.8 | 57.9 | 45.0 | 51.5 | 46.1 | 61.0 | 53.6 | 58.6 | 57.0 | 57.8 |
| F5 | 0.1 | 55.5 | 48.4 | 52.0 | 54.6 | 54.6 | 54.6 | 58.4 | 63.3 | 60.8 | 68.1 | 70.2 | 69.1 |
| F5 | 0.2 | 55.7 | 55.3 | 55.5 | 59.5 | 63.3 | 61.4 | 77.4 | 77.2 | 77.3 | 85.8 | 88.3 | 87.0 |
| F5 | 0.4 | 62.7 | 65.0 | 63.9 | 71.5 | 77.1 | 74.3 | 92.6 | 93.0 | 92.8 | 95.9 | 97.6 | 96.8 |
| MB1 | 0.05 | 48.5 | 53.2 | 50.8 | 57.0 | 49.2 | 53.1 | 39.7 | 66.9 | 53.3 | 79.4 | 82.0 | 80.7 |
| MB1 | 0.1 | 51.9 | 52.3 | 52.1 | 57.6 | 56.6 | 57.1 | 45.6 | 70.1 | 57.9 | 91.2 | 93.3 | 92.3 |
| MB1 | 0.2 | 52.3 | 56.7 | 54.5 | 63.2 | 66.7 | 65.0 | 58.3 | 77.5 | 67.9 | 96.7 | 97.8 | 97.3 |
| MB1 | 0.4 | 55.3 | 63.6 | 59.4 | 74.2 | 80.0 | 77.1 | 82.9 | 86.8 | 84.8 | 98.8 | 99.4 | 99.1 |

It is observed that our proposed steganalyzer outperforms the prior-arts by a significant margin. The detection rate for F5 at the same embedding rate is lower than that of MB1. This will be discussed in the next section.

### 4.4    Experimental Results with Features from One Direction at a Time

We also implement experiment with reduced dimensionality of feature vectors in order to examine the contributions made by features along different directions. Hence, we use features from only one direction at a time. The results shown in Table 3 are the arithmetic average of 20 random experiments.

**Table 3.** Detection rates with reduced feature space (in the unit of %)

| | bpc | Horizontal | | | Vertical | | | Main Diagonal | | | Minor Diagonal | | |
|---|---|---|---|---|---|---|---|---|---|---|---|---|---|
| | | TN | TP | AR | TN | TP | AR | TN | TP | AR | TN | TP | AR |
| OutGuess | 0.05 | 77.7 | 82.6 | 80.1 | 78.9 | 83.1 | 81.0 | 75.9 | 79.0 | 77.5 | 73.8 | 77.4 | 75.6 |
| OutGuess | 0.1 | 89.1 | 95.0 | 92.0 | 90.5 | 95.4 | 93.0 | 88.8 | 93.1 | 90.9 | 86.6 | 92.3 | 89.4 |
| OutGuess | 0.2 | 95.4 | 98.3 | 96.8 | 95.8 | 98.2 | 97.0 | 95.3 | 97.9 | 96.6 | 93.8 | 97.5 | 95.6 |
| F5 | 0.05 | 55.8 | 53.7 | 54.7 | 56.7 | 52.4 | 54.6 | 51.6 | 56.3 | 54.0 | 51.3 | 52.9 | 52.1 |
| F5 | 0.1 | 61.6 | 62.3 | 62.0 | 61.7 | 62.3 | 62.0 | 57.4 | 62.8 | 60.1 | 54.2 | 56.9 | 55.5 |
| F5 | 0.2 | 75.0 | 79.8 | 77.4 | 75.8 | 80.2 | 78.0 | 71.8 | 76.2 | 74.0 | 61.4 | 65.7 | 63.6 |
| F5 | 0.4 | 91.5 | 95.6 | 93.5 | 91.3 | 95.7 | 93.5 | 89.1 | 92.5 | 90.8 | 77.4 | 82.7 | 80.1 |
| MB1 | 0.05 | 69.9 | 72.4 | 71.1 | 70.6 | 72.8 | 71.7 | 67.6 | 69.6 | 68.6 | 66.1 | 67.4 | 66.7 |
| MB1 | 0.1 | 82.5 | 87.9 | 85.2 | 83.7 | 87.7 | 85.7 | 81.2 | 84.4 | 82.8 | 78.1 | 82.5 | 80.3 |
| MB1 | 0.2 | 92.5 | 96.4 | 94.4 | 94.1 | 96.8 | 95.5 | 92.8 | 95.6 | 94.2 | 90.1 | 93.9 | 92.0 |
| MB1 | 0.4 | 97.6 | 98.9 | 98.2 | 98.2 | 99.4 | 98.8 | 97.9 | 99.1 | 98.5 | 96.5 | 98.7 | 97.6 |

It is observed that the contributions made from the horizontal and vertical directions are more than that from the diagonal directions. Furthermore, the contribution made from the main diagonal is larger than that from the minor diagonal direction. Comparing Table 2 and Table 3, we can observe that combining four directions has enhanced the performance in attacking JPEG steganography.

# 5  Discussion

Some further discussions are made in this section.

## 5.1  Taking Absolute Value in Forming JPEG 2-D Arrays: Advantages

In Section 2, we have indicated that the magnitudes (i.e., absolute values) of the neighboring JPEG coefficients are correlated to each other and the known JPEG steganographic algorithms do not change the signs of coefficients. These motivated us to take absolute values of the JPEG coefficients in forming JPEG 2-D array. Now we continue this discussion.

We shall show that if we do not take absolute value, the performance of the steganalysis will deteriorate and the computational complexity will increase.

Let's consider the formulation of JPEG 2-D array without taking absolute value. While forming difference 2-D array, the dynamic range will obviously increase. Hence, a larger threshold T is needed. Assume that we set up a new threshold 8, thus resulting in four transition probability matrices of $17 \times 17$ each. The resultant feature dimensionality will be $17 \times 17 \times 4 = 1,156$, which raises the computational cost significantly. Table 4 provides a performance comparison between using 324-D feature vectors (T=4) and using 1,156-D feature vectors (T=8) for attacking the MB1 with an embedding rate 0.2 bpc. Our experiments indicate that this trend of performance reduction also holds for other embedding

**Table 4.** Performance comparison: with vs without taking absolute value (in the unit of %)

| | bpc | with | | | without | | |
|---|---|---|---|---|---|---|---|
| | | TN | TP | AR | TN | TP | AR |
| MB1 | 0.2 | 96.7 | 97.8 | 97.3 | 93.9 | 94.2 | 94.1 |

rates, and for OutGuess and F5 as well. This concludes that taking absolute value gives better performance and lower computational complexity.

## 5.2   Detection Rates for F5

Taking a close look at Table 2, one can observe that the detection rates achieved by our proposed steganalyzer for MB1 are higher than that for F5 at the same embedding rates. It appears contradicting to what reported in [7, 17]. In what follows we discuss this issue from two different points of view.

One is from a theoretical analysis. We can show that a steganographic method, which either keeps a non-zero JPEG AC coefficient unchanged or reduces its magnitude by one in order to embed one bit (F5 belongs to this category), will have a relatively larger probability to keep the elements in the difference JPEG 2-D array unchanged after data embedding than another steganographic method, which either keeps a non-zero JPEG AC coefficient unchanged, or increases or decreases its magnitude by one in order to embed one bit (MB1 belongs to this category). A simple case is described as follows. When two neighboring non-zero JPEG AC coefficients are positive and differ by an odd number, if these two coefficients have to be changed, with MB1 embedding and embedding step size of two, the corresponding element in the difference JPEG 2-D array will change, while this element will not change with F5 embedding.

Another point of view is from an experimental investigation, which is based on the 7,560 images used in our experimental works. The mean values of embedding efficiency (defined in Section 1) of MB1 and F5 at four different data embedding rates, i.e., 0.05, 0.1, 0.2, and 0.4 bpc are obtained and listed in Table 5. From these statistics, one can see that at lower rates such as 0.05 bpc and 0.1 bpc, F5 changes fewer JPEG coefficients than MB1 does. That is, with matrix coding, F5 gains higher embedding efficiency at shorter message length. The opposite is true at the higher rates such as 0.2 bpc and 0.4 bpc. These statistics reveal some inside information, which can partially explain the phenomenon. Further investigation in this regard is needed, which is our future work.

## 6   Future Work

The future works are as follows:

(1) The proposed scheme uses features with dimensionality 324, or, 81 for each of the four directions. Due to its simple mechanism, the feature generation

**Table 5.** The mean values of embedding efficiency

| | bpc | | | |
|---|---|---|---|---|
| | 0.05 | 0.1 | 0.2 | 0.4 |
| F5 | 2.8695 | 2.4586 | 2.0606 | 1.7484 |
| MB1 | 2.1141 | 2.1139 | 2.1142 | 2.1141 |

procedure takes quite short time. Generally speaking, the feature extraction process takes less time than that by [7]. Nevertheless, larger feature vectors need more training samples. How to reduce the feature size is one of our future tasks.

(2) By taking difference between the magnitudes of a coefficient and its immediate neighbors, we mainly utilize the intra-block correlation. How to make more use of the inter-block correlation should be taken into consideration.

(3) We use a thresholding technique, which reduces computational complexity while keeps the steganalysis effective. Further research to find the relationship between the quality factor of JPEG image and the threshold is needed.

## 7    Conclusion

We have presented an effective steganalysis scheme in this paper, which outperforms the state-of-the-arts in detecting the modern steganographic methods for JPEG images: OutGuess, F5, and MB1. The success can be attributed to the following measures taken in this new scheme.

(1) Taking absolute value in forming JPEG 2-D arrays not only helps raise steganalysis capability but also helps reduce computational complexity.

(2) Difference JPEG 2-D arrays along horizontal, vertical, diagonal, and minor diagonal directions have effectively catch changes caused by data embedding.

(3) Thresholding technique applied to handling transition probability matrices has reduced dimensionality of feature vectors to a manageable extent.

(4) Through using Markov process to model difference JPEG 2-D arrays and using all of elements of transition probability matrices as features, the second order statistics have been used in this proposed steganalyzer.

## Acknowledgement

Authors appreciate Dr. Dekun Zou for his helpful technical discussion and support. We also thank the reviewers for their constructive review comments.

## References

1. Westfeld, A.: F5 a steganographic algorithm: high capacity despite better steganalysis. In: 4th International Workshop on Information Hiding, Pittsburgh, PA, USA (2001)
2. Provos, N.: Defending against statistical steganalysis. In: 10th USENIX Security Symposium, Washington DC, USA (2001)

3. Sallee, P.: Model-based methods for steganography and steganalysis. International Journal of Image and Graphics 5(1), 167–190 (2005)
4. Kharrazi, M., Sencar, H.T., Memon, N.: Image steganography: concepts and practice, Lecture Note Series, Institute for Mathematical Sciences, National University of Singapore (2004)
5. Farid, H.: Detecting hidden messages using higher-order statistical models. In: International Conference on Image Processing, Rochester, NY, USA (2002)
6. Shi, Y.Q., Xuan, G., Zou, D., Gao, J., Yang, C., Zhang, Z., Chai, P., Chen, W., Chen, C.: Steganalysis based on moments of characteristic functions using wavelet decomposition, prediction-error image, and neural network. In: International Conference on Multimedia and Expo, Amsterdam, Netherlands (2005)
7. Fridrich, J.: Feature-based steganalysis for JPEG images and its implications for future design of steganographic schemes. In: 6th International Workshop on Information Hiding, Toronto, ON, Canada (2004)
8. Sullivan, K., Madhow, U., Chandrasekaran, S., Manjunath, B.S.: Steganalysis of spread spectrum data hiding exploiting cover memory, the International Society for Optical Engineering, Electronic Imaging, San Jose, CA, USA (2005)
9. Tu, C., Tran, T.D.: Context-based entropy coding of block transform coefficients for image compression. IEEE Transactions on Image Processing 11(11), 1271–1283 (2002)
10. Shi, Y.Q., Sun, H.: Image and Video Compression for Multimedia Engineering: Fundamentals, Algorithms, and Standards, CRC press (1999)
11. Leon-Garcia, A.: Probability and random processes for electrical engineering, 2nd edn. Addison-Wesley, London, UK (1994)
12. Chang, C.C., Lin, C.J.: LIBSVM: a library for support vector machines (2001) http://www.csie.ntu.edu.tw/~cjlin/libsvm
13. Burges, C.J.C.: A tutorial on support vector machines for pattern recognition. Data Mining and Knowledge Discovery 2(2), 121–167 (1998)
14. http://www.outguess.org/
15. http://wwwrn.inf.tu-dresden.de/~westfeld/f5.html
16. http://redwood.ucdavis.edu/phil/papers/iwdw03.htm
17. Kharrazi, M., Sencar, H.T., Memon, N.D.: Benchmarking steganographic and steganalysis techniques, Security, Steganography, and Watermarking of Multimedia Contents 2005, San Jose, CA, USA (2005)

# Batch Steganography and Pooled Steganalysis

Andrew D. Ker

Oxford University Computing Laboratory, Parks Road, Oxford OX1 3QD, England
adk@comlab.ox.ac.uk

**Abstract.** Conventional steganalysis aims to separate cover objects from stego objects, working on each object individually. In this paper we investigate some methods for pooling steganalysis evidence, so as to obtain more reliable detection of steganography in large sets of objects, and the dual problem of hiding information securely when spreading across a batch of covers. The results are rather surprising: in many situations, a steganographer should *not* spread the embedding across all covers, and the secure capacity increases only as the square root of the number of objects. We validate the theoretical results, which are rather general, by testing a particular type of image steganography. The experiments involve tens of millions of repeated steganalytic attacks and show that pooled steganalysis can give very reliable detection of even tiny proportionate payloads.

## 1 Introduction

The classic definition of *steganography* involves an actor (Steganographer) aiming to communicate with a passive conspirator over an insecure channel, and an eavesdropper (or Warden) monitoring the channel. The Steganographer hides his communication inside some other medium by taking a seemingly-innocent *cover object* and making changes, hopefully imperceptible to the Warden, which convey the secret information to the recipient. The Warden's aim is not to decode the hidden information but merely to deduce its presence. This is *steganalysis*: the creation of hypothesis tests which can distinguish cover objects from so-called stego objects in which a payload has been embedded. Such language assumes that each cover object is treated in isolation by both the embedder and the eavesdropper, and in the literature the focus is almost exclusively on single cover objects (usually individual digital images, but also sometimes audio files, movies, or more unusual digital objects). In this paper we begin to ask about large groups of cover objects, and how the methods for both embedding into, and steganalysis of, individual pieces can be applied to the groups as a whole.

There are two good reasons for doing so. First, we contend that practical applications of steganalysis inevitably will involve multiple objects: the Warden will surely have intercepted more than one communication from the Steganographer, and the Steganographer will surely have access to more than one cover. Second, even given state-of-the-art steganalysis and weak steganography, very high reliability steganalysis (in which false positive rates are as low as, say,

J. Camenisch et al. (Eds.): IH 2006, LNCS 4437, pp. 265–281, 2007.

$10^{-5}$) is simply not possible with the small amount of evidence obtained from a single cover (except for deeply flawed steganography which leaves a particular signature, or perhaps enormous objects such as entire digital movies).

In this paper we assume that an imperfect method of statistical steganalysis already exists for individual cover objects, and investigate how the set of detection statistics computed over a group can be combined by the Warden into an overall detector for steganography for the whole group. This gives information on the opposite problem, where the Steganographer has to decide how best to spread secret information amongst a batch of covers. The answers to this latter question, at least for some of the pooled detectors suggested here, are rather surprising. There seems to be little literature on this problem: Trivedi [1] has used sequential hypothesis tests to repeat steganalysis, but only in the context of locating a hidden message embedded sequentially within a single image.

In Sect. 2 we formulate more precisely the competing aims of *batch steganography* and *pooled steganalysis*. In this work, which only scratches the surface of what appears to be a complex topic, we allow certain assumptions (which are not implausible) about the steganalysis methods for individual objects which we aim to combine; they are discussed in Sect. 2. In Sect. 3 we suggest three possible pooling strategies for the Warden, analysing them for performance and deriving the Steganographer's best tactic to avoid detection. In Sect. 4 we move away from the abstract nature of the first part of the paper, and focus on Least Significant Bit Replacement in digital images, a well-studied problem; for this embedding method, and a popular detection algorithm, we perform millions of simulations to benchmark the strategies of Sect. 3, confirming the theoretical results. Briefly, we return to our assumptions about steganalysis response – there is a sting in the tail here. Finally, Section 5 suggests avenues for further work.

## 2     Problem Formulation

The scenario we have in mind, which motivates this paper, is the following. Suppose that a criminal wishes to hide information on his computer, deniably, using steganography. He already has a large number of innocent cover pictures on his hard disk. To be quite sure of hiding his secret information well, he might split it into many small pieces and hide a little in each of a selection of the pictures, believing that this is more secure than the alternative of filling a smaller number of images to maximum capacity.

When the authorities impound his computer, they are faced with a dilemma: how do they know which pictures to examine? Even possessing state-of-the-art steganalysis, they still observe fairly large false positive rates, and so if they test every picture on his computer they will inevitably turn up a lot of positive diagnoses – even if he is not a steganographer at all. They must run their statistical detector on every picture individually, and then find some way to combine the detection statistics into an overall "pooled" steganalysis for the presence of data, possibly spread across all the images.

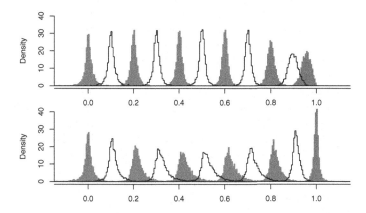

**Fig. 1.** Histograms of detector response; two detectors for LSB Replacement in digital images, calculated on each of 3000 never-compressed grayscale bitmap images with embedding at $p = 0, 0.1, \ldots, 1$. Above, "Sample Pairs" detector. Below, "WS" detector.

## 2.1 The Shift Hypothesis and Other Assumptions

In this work we will assume that the Warden already possesses a *quantitative* detector for whatever type of steganography the Steganographer is using, an estimator for the length of hidden message in an individual stego object as a proportion of the maximum. We will call this *the component detector*. We assume that it suffers from random errors due to properties of the cover objects, or the hidden messages. The Warden aims to detect steganography in a set of objects by combining the *component statistics* – the values of the component detector on each object in the set.

We write $\psi_p$ for the density function of the component estimator, when proportion $p$ of the maximum is embedded in a cover object; we expect that it is unbiased i.e. $\int x \psi_p(x)\,\mathrm{d}x \approx p$ if the detector is any good. In this analysis we go further, assuming what we call the *shift hypothesis*. This is that

$$\psi_p(x) = \psi_0(x - p),$$

i.e. the distribution of the detector response only depends on $p$ in the form of a shift, so that the (additive) estimation error is independent of the true value. Our primary reason is to reduce the analyses of pooled steganalysis to tractable problems. Since in this case all $\psi_p$ are determined by $p$ and $\psi_0$ we write $\psi$ for $\psi_0$, and $\Psi$ for the corresponding cumulative distribution function.

Before we continue, we ask whether the shift hypothesis is plausible. In Fig. 1 we display histograms for two particular quantitative steganalysis methods for the detection of LSB Replacement in digital images (the Sample Pairs (SPA) detector of [2] and the detector now known as WS from [3]). These histograms are the observed detector response for a set of 3000 images, with the experiments repeated at 10 embedding rates. We see that the shift hypothesis holds approximately for the SPA detector, for embedding rates of less than 0.8, but there is both a shape change and a negative bias for higher rates[1]. For the WS detector, the shift hypothesis seems less apt, but for medium values of $p$ there is still evidence of a constant distributional shape. We view these histograms as evidence that we should be able to develop detectors which are not far away from satisfying the shift hypothesis.

Finally, although we try to keep the first part of this paper abstract, we may need some assumptions about the functional form of $\psi$ itself. We will certainly want that $\psi$ is symmetric about 0. In a detailed analysis of the response of detectors for LSB Replacement in images [4], we found that the Student $t$-family provides a good model, up to a scaling constant. The density function is

$$f(x; \lambda, \nu) = \frac{\Gamma(\frac{\nu+1}{2})}{\lambda\sqrt{\nu\pi}\Gamma(\frac{\nu}{2})}\left(1 + \frac{x^2}{\lambda^2\nu}\right)^{-\frac{\nu+1}{2}}$$

where $\lambda > 0$ is the scale factor and $\nu > 0$ the *degrees of freedom* parameter. An advantage of this family is that it can model a wide range of unimodal symmetric distributions, including the cases of finite and infinite variance, and it seems to have uses in all types of steganalysis. When $\nu = 1$ it is the Cauchy distribution, when $\nu \leq 2$ it has infinite variance, but as $\nu \to \infty$ it tends to the Gaussian.

When we need to make assumptions about the shape of $\psi$, therefore, we will suppose that it is a $t$-density. We have found that quantitative LSB detectors are often well-modelled by $t$-distributions with approximately 2 degrees of freedom (numbers both above and below 2 are observed, depending on the type of detector and also the type of cover, indicating that finite variance is a possibility but cannot be guaranteed) and a scale factor of the order of 0.01. These will be useful figures for the generation of some synthetic data in Subsect. 3.3.

## 2.2   Batch Steganography and Pooled Steganalysis

We now pose precisely the problem of *batch steganography*. Given a number of cover objects $N$, the Steganographer hides data in $rN$ of them, using proportionate capacity $p$ of each, and leaves the other covers alone. We assume that a) the number of cover objects is fixed, b) all cover objects have the same capacity, c) the Steganographer has no control over the objects themselves, and chooses which to embed in at random. We also assume that the Steganographer wants to embed a fixed total amount of secret data, $BNC$, where $C$ is the capacity of each cover object and $B < 1$ is the proportionate *bandwidth*. He therefore must ensure that $rp = B$. The conditions $r \leq 1$ (he cannot embed in more objects than are present) and $p \leq 1$ (each object has a maximal capacity) give the dual conditions $p \geq B$ and $r \geq B$. (We assume that $B < 1/N$ so that $r$ as low as $B$ is a meaningful option.) Within this range, he can vary $r$ or $p$ and should do so to try to minimize the chance of overall detection.

---

[1] In fact we believe that the SPA detector can be corrected to remove the negative bias at high embedding rates, but that is not our current topic of study.

The Warden's task is *pooled steganalysis*: given the $N$ objects treated by the Steganographer, the Warden's aim is to detect whether any steganography at all has been performed. That is, to perform the hypothesis test

$$H_0 : r = 0$$
$$H_1 : p, r > 0 \tag{1}$$

with best reliability. We *do not* assume that the Warden wants to estimate the values of $r$ and $p$, or $B$, or tries to determine which of the objects do contain steganography, although these are certainly secondary aims for future study.

We assume that the Warden applies a component steganalysis method satisfying the assumptions of the previous subsection. Then its density function, on a randomly selected object output by the Steganographer, is

$$f(x) = (1 - r)\psi(x) + r\psi(x - p).$$

This is a *mixture model*, of a simple kind. Finite mixtures are quite well-studied, although there is much more literature on Gaussian mixtures than mixtures of longer-tailed distributions we expect from steganalysis. For a good survey, see [5].

Finally, we emphasise that we are assuming that the number of cover objects $N$ is fixed from the start, and known to both the Steganographer and Warden. In practice, it seems likely that the Steganographer will gain access to new covers over time, and that in some cases (such as network monitoring) the Warden will obtain more evidence over time. This suggests the study of *sequential* embedding and tests. We reserve this topic for future work; the theory of sequential hypothesis tests is rather different from that of standard tests of finite samples, and we believe that the practice of sequential steganography and steganalysis may be rather different from the fixed-size batch problems studied here.

### 2.3   Performance Metric

We choose the following as a measure of performance, for the Warden's task of pooled steganalysis. Fix a detection threshold so that the overall false negative rate (the probability of type-II error for (1)) is 50%; then measure the false positive rate (the probability of type-I error), which we will denote $p_f$.

This is a rather unusual measure, but suitable for two reasons. Firstly, it allows for tractable analysis (many other measures of performance do not). Second, we have found it to be a good summary of the performance of detectors in general. Although it might be preferable to plot a full *Receiver Operating Characteristics* (ROC) curve, this results in too much information to display concisely. And in almost all cases the ROC curve takes the form of a sudden jump from a very low detection rate of almost 0% to a high detection rate well above 50%, as the false positives increase past a certain point. Therefore the most important information is to be found in the location of that jump, which is well-measured by the false positive rate when the false negative rate is 50%.

While the false negative rate is a measure of a Steganographer's chance to evade detection, the false positive rate shows *how certain* the Warden is that they have caught the right person: fundamental from the latter's point of view.

## 3    Possible Strategies for Warden

We examine three strategies which the Warden might use to detect batch steganography, given a component detector satisfying the assumptions of Subsect. 2.1. Of course there are other possible pooling strategies, but we have included a range of methods: simple nonparametric tests for median, the average component statistic, and a more sophisticated method based on a generalized maximum likelihood ratio test.

At the end of the section we summarise by asking the following questions of each detection strategy. Given a bandwidth $B$, how can the Steganographer best avoid detection, by trading $p$ against $r$? In the Steganographer's best case, how does the false positive rate for the Warden depend on $N$ and $B$ (assuming a threshold set for 50% false negatives)? And what must be the relationship between $N$ and $B$, if the error rate is to be held constant?

### 3.1    Count Positive Observations (Sign Test)

The first method for pooled steganalysis is the simplest: the Warden should simply count the number of positive values produced by the component estimator, which we will denote by the random variable $\#P$. If there is steganography in some of the objects, we expect that $\#P > \frac{1}{2}N$. This is simply the traditional *sign test* for whether the median of a distribution, from which we have a sample, is greater than zero. It has the advantage of being nonparametric: its distribution under the null hypothesis does not depend on $\psi$, being $\#P \sim \text{Bi}(N, \frac{1}{2})$.

Under the alternative hypothesis, $\#P \sim \text{Bi}\big((1-r)N, \frac{1}{2}\big) + \text{Bi}\big(rN, \Psi(p)\big)^2$ of which the median is $(1-r)N\frac{1}{2} + rN\Psi(p) = \frac{1}{2}N + rN(\Psi(p) - \frac{1}{2})$. Making the Gaussian approximation to the binomial distribution (valid for even moderately large values of $N$) the probability of false positive for the Warden when the false negative rate is 50% and the Steganographer's bandwidth is $B$, is therefore

$$p_f = 1 - \Phi\left(2\sqrt{N}B\big(\tfrac{\Psi(p)-\frac{1}{2}}{p}\big)\right).\tag{2}$$

where $\Phi$ is the normal distribution function. Let us consider the Steganographer's best strategy. He wants to maximize the false positive probability, and therefore to minimize $\frac{\Psi(p)-\frac{1}{2}}{p}$. Provided that $\psi$ is a nonincreasing function on $[0, \infty)$, this is achieved by maximizing $p$. Therefore the Steganographer will choose $p = 1$ and $r = B$, hiding maximal amounts of data in as few cover objects as possible. The makes intuitive sense, because the sign test is no more sensitive to large positive detection values than small positive values.

In Sect. 4 we will additionally test the more powerful nonparametric test known as the *Wilcoxon signed rank test*. Here the component values are ranked by absolute value, and the test statistic used is the sum of the ranks of the

---

[2] This sum of distributions notation indicates the *independent* sum of random variables.

positive observations. For reasons of space we do not attempt to analyse the behaviour of this statistic. One might expect superior performance to the sign test, given parallel results in standard hypothesis testing, but we shall see that the improvement is not very substantial in this application.

## 3.2   Average Detection Statistic

The main weakness of the sign test is that it ignores all information except the sign of each observation. An alternative method without this drawback, and seemingly a simple one, is to take the component statistics and compute their mean: $\bar{X} = \frac{1}{N}\sum X_i$ where $X_i$ is the component detector response for object $i$ of the batch. It is immediate that $\text{median}(\bar{X}) \approx \mathbf{E}[\bar{X}] = rp$ if the expectation exists at all and, given the shift hypothesis, the distributional shape of $\bar{X}$ does not depend on $r$ or $p$. Therefore, the Steganographer has no reason to select any particular value of $r$ and $p$, as long as they multiply to his bandwidth constraint $B$.

The complexity here is in computing the distribution of $\bar{X}$ under the null hypothesis. If the distribution density $\psi$ has thin enough tails, the variance of the $X_i$ is finite and the Central Limit Theorem applies. However, we have already noted that in practice the variance of the detector response may be infinite. Thankfully, there is a generalized from of the Central Limit Theorem, which is presented in detail in [6], from which we extract the following result:

**Lemma 1.** *Suppose that all $X_i$ are independent and identically distributed, and the tail index of $X_i$ is $\nu > 1$, i.e. $P(|X_i| > x) \sim cx^{-\nu}$ as $x \to \infty$, for some constant $c$. Then $\mathbf{E}[X_i]$ exists and*

*(i) if $1 < \nu < 2$ then $\bar{X} \xrightarrow{d} \mathbf{E}[X_i] + kN^{\frac{1}{\nu}-1}Z$ where $Z$ has a standardized Symmetric Stable distribution with index of stability $\nu$, and $k$ is a constant (depending on the dispersion of the $X_i$, and $\nu$).*

*(ii) if $\nu > 2$ then $\bar{X} \xrightarrow{d} \mathbf{E}[X_i] + kN^{-\frac{1}{2}}Z$ where $Z$ has a standard Normal distribution, and $k$ is a constant (depending on the variance of the $X_i$).*

There is a more complex case when $\nu$ is exactly 2, but we will not concern ourselves with it because it is unlikely that the tail index will be precisely 2. Note that the $t$-distribution with $\nu$ degrees of freedom has tail index $\nu$.

The median value of $\bar{X}$ under the null hypothesis is approximately $B$. Therefore

$$p_f = \begin{cases} 1 - \Phi(N^{\frac{1}{2}}B/k), & \text{if } \nu > 2 \\ 1 - F_\nu(N^{1-\frac{1}{\nu}}B/k), & \text{if } 1 < \nu < 2. \end{cases} \tag{3}$$

where $F_\nu$ is the distribution function for the Symmetric Stable distribution with stability index $\nu$ and $k$ is some constant. As long as $\nu > 1$, evidence does accumulate, but the rate at which this happens, as $N$ increases, depends critically on whether $\nu$ is greater, or less, than 2.

### 3.3   Generalized Likelihood Ratio Test

A general and powerful tool for hypothesis testing is the likelihood ratio test. In the case of two simple hypotheses this takes the form of the quotient of the likelihood of observations given the null and alternative hypothesis (and, according to the Neyman-Pearson Lemma, is the optimal test); when one or both of the hypotheses is composite we use the generalized likelihood ratio test instead. The statistic is computed as $\ell = \log\left(\frac{L(X_1,\ldots,X_n;\hat{\theta}_1)}{L(X_1,\ldots,X_n;\hat{\theta}_0)}\right)$ where $L$ is the likelihood function, $\hat{\theta}_0$ denotes the maximum likelihood estimator (MLE) for unknown parameter(s) $\theta$ when constrained by the null hypothesis, and $\hat{\theta}_1$ the MLEs when constrained by the alternative hypothesis. The test rejects the null hypothesis for large values of $\ell$.

We apply the test to the problem of pooled steganalysis as follows. Suppose that the component response $\psi$ is known. Then we can compute

$$\ell = \log\left(\frac{L(X_1,\ldots,X_N;\hat{r},\hat{p})}{L(X_1,\ldots,X_N;r=0,p=0)}\right) \tag{4}$$

where $L$ is the likelihood function for the mixture pdf $f(x) = (1-r)\psi(x) + r\psi(x-p)$ and $\hat{r}$ and $\hat{p}$ are MLEs for $r$ and $p$ given the observations.

The test is powerful, but there are two pitfalls here. The first is that it is not so easy to compute MLEs for $r$ and $p$. In the case of mixture distributions when $\psi$ is nontrivial the maximization problem admits no closed form solutions, and the likelihood function contains more than one local maximum. Therefore we are forced to use numerical optimization techniques, and it is quite possible to find the wrong local maximum and hence to mis-estimate $r$ and $p$. This is true whether one uses standard numerical methods to maximize $L(X_1,\ldots,X_N;r,p)$, or whether specialised techniques such as *Expectation Maximization* are applied. See [7] for some discussion of this problem. Our solution is the computationally-expensive one of using a coarse grid search to find good starting values for $r$ and $p$, and then using a standard iterative optimization procedure [8] to hone the answer (while accepting that this leaves the possibility of convergence to the wrong root, but with low probability).

The second pitfall is more subtle. It is commonly stated that the log-likelihood ratio statistic $\ell$ has a particular asymptotic null distribution: up to a scaling factor, the $\chi^2$ distribution with $\dim(\theta_1) - \dim(\theta_0)$ degrees of freedom. This is Wilks' Theorem [9], but we have omitted a vital hypothesis – we require some regularity conditions of the likelihood function *and that the null hypothesis be contained within the interior of the alternative hypothesis*. In the case of the hypothesis test (1) this is not so: the null hypothesis is on the boundary of the alternative.

Nonetheless, there is some recent work which generalizes Wilks' Theorem and shows that the conclusions often remain true, perhaps with modified scaling constants or degrees of freedom parameter, even when some of the hypotheses are violated (see e.g. [10]). Alternatively, there are scoring methods which modify the likelihood ratio statistic into one with a known null distributions [11]. Rather

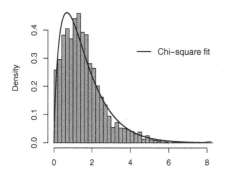 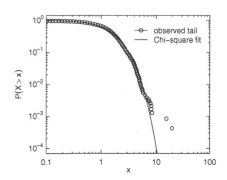

**Fig. 2.** Histogram and logarithmic tail plot of observed log-likelihood ratio statistic. 2500 samples of $N = 500$ observations were generated from a $t$-distribution ($\nu = 2$, $\lambda = 0.01$) and fitted to a scaled $\chi^2$ distribution.

than be diverted into a discussion of this issue, we generated 2500 samples of $N = 500$ synthetic data points from a $t$-distribution (using $\nu = 2$ and $\lambda = 0.01$ so as to be a good model for steganalysis statistics) and compared the distribution of $\ell$, from (4), with the $\chi^2$ family. We found that a scale factor of 0.45 and degrees of freedom 3.45 were the best fit (this df parameter is higher than predicted by Wilks' Theorem), which is displayed in Fig. 2. There is a good match and it appears that a modified form of Wilks' Theorem is still approximately valid.

We now examine the likelihood ratio under the alternative hypothesis.

**Lemma 2.** *Let $\psi$ be any probability density, assumed known, such that*
  *a) $\psi$ is symmetric about 0,*
  *b) $\frac{\psi(x+p)-\psi(x)}{p\psi(x)}$ is bounded for $x \in \mathbb{R}$ and $p \in [0, 1]$,*
  *c) $\int \frac{\psi(x+p)^2-\psi(x)^2}{p^2\psi(x)}\,\mathrm{d}x$ is an increasing function of $p$, for $p \in [0, 1]$,*
*along with the usual regularity conditions sufficient for MLEs of the mixture parameters $r$ and $p$ to be consistent. Then, in the limit as $N \to \infty$, and for sufficiently small $B$, the Steganographer's best strategy to evade detection by the generalized likelihood ratio test is to take $p = B$ ($r = 1$), in which case the expectation of the generalized log-likelihood ratio statistic is asymptotically*

$$\mathbf{E}[\ell] \sim \frac{NB^2}{2}\int \frac{\psi'(x)^2}{\psi(x)} + \psi''(x)\,\mathrm{d}x \;+\; NO(B^3) \tag{5}$$

The proof may be found in the Appendix. Conditions a) and b) are quite easy to check, but c) is more difficult to establish. However they all seem to hold for common density functions $\psi$, including the $t$-distribution pdf with zero location parameter and $\nu > 1$[3].

---

[3] To match exactly our performance metric we should be considering the *median* of the statistic under the alternative hypothesis, rather than the *mean* as here. However the former is much harder to examine, and commonly in generalized likelihood ratio tests the mean and median differ only by a small constant.

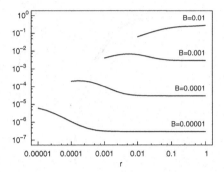 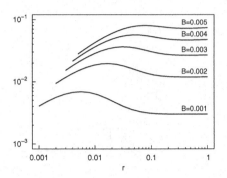

**Fig. 3.** Expected value of log-likelihood ratio statistic ($y$-$axis$) according to (7) without the scaling factor $N$, plotted against $r$ ($x$-$axis$). Some different values of $B$ are displayed.

Finally, in the case of a $t$-distribution with $\nu$ degrees of freedom and scale factor $\lambda$, we have

$$\frac{NB^2}{2} \int \frac{\psi'(x)^2}{\psi(x)} + \psi''(x)\,\mathrm{d}x = \frac{NB^2}{2\lambda^2}\frac{\nu+1}{\nu+3}. \tag{6}$$

This indicates that the parameter $\nu$ is not vitally important to the accuracy of the likelihood ratio detector (as a function of $\nu$, for $\nu$ around 2, (6) varies rather slowly and $\nu = 2$ is not a critical value).

Now the statement of Lemma 2 is not ideal in that it only informs the Steganographer what to do in the limiting case of small $B$. On further examination, it seems that the best strategy is exactly the reverse – $p = 1$ and $r = B$ – for $B$ above a certain point and then switches to the proven optimal method for $B$ below. Using the pdf of a $t$-distribution with 2 degrees of freedom and scale factor 0.01 we plot numerically-computed values of (7) (which, in the Appendix, is shown to be the asymptotic expectation of $\ell$ even when $B$ is not small), without the scaling factor $N$, in Fig. 3. On the left we see how the magnitude of $B$ influences the choice of $r$: for small $B$ there is a definite disadvantage to the Steganographer in using small values of $r$, because detection becomes easier. On the right we examine more closely the values of $B$ around which the best strategy switches from $r = 1$ to $p = 1$. We observe that there is no internal minimum on any of the displayed curves, so that the best strategy is switches directly from one extreme (spread the payload as thinly as possible for small $B$) to the other (concentrate the payload in as few covers as possible for large $B$).

Finally, we can also apply a generalized likelihood ratio test when the distribution $\psi$ has unknown parameters, forming MLEs for the unknowns in the usual way. This may be a useful application, because the distribution parameters of the steganalysis error distribution may well depend on the source of covers, of which the Warden might be unaware. But the theory of Lemma 2 does not apply directly in this case and we will not consider it further in this paper.

### 3.4   Summary of Warden's Strategies

For the sign test, and the likelihood ratio test for large bandwidths, we see that the Steganographer's best strategy is to take $p=1$ and $r=B$, concentrating all the payload in as few covers as possible. We find this result rather counterintuitive, as there is a natural inclination to spread hidden data thinly.

The total amount of data hidden by the Steganographer is proportional to $BN$. Consider equations (2), (3), and (5). To fix the risk of detection, we must have $B \propto N^{-\frac{1}{2}}$ (sign or likelihood ratio test, or average if $\nu > 2$) or $B \propto N^{-1+\frac{1}{\nu}}$ (average if $\nu < 2$). Therefore the "capacity" (of the undetectable kind) for the Steganographer appears to grow as $N^{\frac{1}{2}}$ or $N^{\frac{1}{\nu}}$ – not proportionately to $N$.

We can compare the false positive rates of the tests by looking at the tail probabilities for the Normal, Symmetric Stable, and $\chi^2$ distributions. It can be shown that, as long as $\nu > 2$, the false positive rate is of the form $p_f \sim a(NB^2)^b \exp(-cNB^2)$ for each of the three tests, where $a$, $b$ and $c$ are constants. The parameter $c$ is most important to the shape here with larger $c$ meaning that evidence is gained more quickly as $N$ increases. For the sign test, $c$ is no larger than 2. For the average and likelihood ratio tests, it is generally much larger, being inversely proportional to the square of the dispersion of $\psi$.

Although the results for the other tests are not changed when $\nu < 2$, in this case the discrimination of the average statistic increases only as a power law, with $p_f \sim aN^{1-\nu}B^{-\nu}$. Ensuring that steganalysis detectors have finite variance appears to be important. However we emphasise that there is no sudden discontinuity at $\nu = 2$. When $\nu$ is slightly above 2, the standard Central Limit Theorem applies but convergence to the asymptotic distribution is extremely slow. The key for the steganalyst is to keep the tails of the component steganalysis estimator as light as possible.

## 4   Case Study: LSB Replacement in Images

We now move away from the abstract setting and select a particular type of cover object, steganographic embedding, and component steganalysis. We choose LSB Replacement in bitmap grayscale images, because this problem is extremely well-studied and also because it is a poor enough form of steganography for fairly good component steganalysis methods to be known. There are many to choose from, and we have selected the one known as *Sample Pairs Analysis* (SPA) [2]. It was not selected because it is the best – there are now newer methods such as [12] which are more sensitive – but because it shares the advantages of computational simplicity (highly desirable given the scale of our experiments) with an approximate validation of the shift hypothesis (see Fig. 1).

We aim to benchmark the pooled steganalysis methods of Sect. 3. Because we want to consider large samples (up to $N = 4000$) we need a particularly large corpus of cover images, a random selection of which is presented to the Steganographer for each trial. Also, to keep as closely as possible to the shift hypothesis and the other assumptions of Sect. 2, we want all the images to be the same size and of similar "character" (each image should have macroscopic characteristics which indicate similar sensitivity to steganography). We used a set of 14000 images, selected for size and image quality out of 20000 on a stock photo CD[4]. The images selected were all $640 \times 416$ pixels and had been stored as colour JPEG images (at quality factor 58), later converted to grayscale. This is probably representative of the type of images which a Steganographer can gain access to in large quantity: big, never-compressed images are more scarce.

The distribution of the SPA estimator, when no data is hidden in these images, is well modelled by a $t$-distribution with $\nu = 1.61$ and $\lambda = 0.00956$ (and we will use these values to compute approximate likelihoods for benchmarking the pooling method of Subsect. 3.3). These values indicate that, even with maximal embedding, for single images there will be a false positive rate of approximately $2 \times 10^{-4}$ when the false negative rate is 50%. For more reliable detection, or for smaller bandwidths, the Warden has no option but to gather multiple images as evidence and apply pooled steganalysis.

## 4.1   Empirical Performance

The majority of our experiments were performed with the following parameters: $B \in \{0.01, 0.003, 0.001\}$ and three out of $N \in \{10, 100, 1000, 4000\}$, depending on $B$. This covers the interesting range of possibilities, as detection moves from easy to very difficult.

For each $N$ we took 10000 samples of $N$ detection statistics when $p = 0$ and then fitted the data according to the theoretical models[5]: Normal distributions for the sign and signed rank statistics, Symmetric Stable distributions for the average statistic, and scaled $\chi^2$ distributions for the likelihood ratio statistic. The fits were good, and the fitted parameters were in the expected range.

For each $B$, up to 11 different pairs of $r$ and $p$ were chosen, subject to $1 \geq r \geq 1/N, B$ and $rp = B$. Repeating 1000 times, $N$ covers were picked at random (for technical reasons it is necessary to sample *with replacement*) and random data embedded at rate $p$ in $Nr$ of these. Values of the SPA estimator were computed for all $N$ objects, and combined using each of the pooling methods described in Sect. 3. The false positive rate, at which detection rates are 50%, was computed for each statistic at each value of $r$.

In total, therefore, the results shown here come from tens of millions of steganography and steganalysis computations. Figure 4 shows the results. We see that for small $N$ or $B$ none of the methods gives reliable detection. Once detection becomes possible, observe that the sign and signed rank tests very effectively punish the Steganographer if he uses a high value of $r$, but otherwise they are poor performers. The averaging method is generally superior for the values of

---

[4] "20,000 photos", published in 2002 by Focus Multimedia Ltd, Staffordshire, UK. http://www.focusmm.co.uk.

[5] Although we would prefer to avoid fitting a distribution which might not be exact, we can only draw conclusions about false positive rates less than $1/S$, where $S$ is the number of repeated simulations, by doing so.

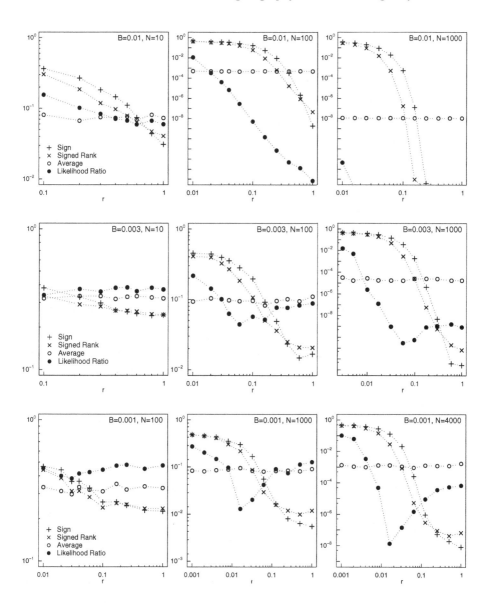

**Fig. 4.** The false positive detection rate (*y-axis*) when the false negative rate is 50%, for varying $r$ (*x-axis*) with $p = B/r$, of pooled steganalysis using the SPA detector on grayscale images. Four pooling methods are evaluated, the null distributions being fitted to the theoretically-predicted shapes based on 10000 simulations, and the medians of the alternative distributions computed from 1000 simulations for each $r$. From top to bottom, the bandwidths of the embedding are $B = 0.01$, $B = 0.003$, $B = 0.001$. Increasing values of $N$, from left to right. The pooled detectors have no discrimination power for $(B, N) = (0.003, 10)$ or $(0.001, 100)$ and poor reliability for $(0.01, 10)$, $(0.003, 100)$, $(0.001, 1000)$, but then reliability increases rapidly with $N$.

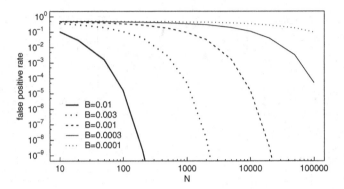

**Fig. 5.** False positive rate ($y$-axis) when false negative rate is 50%, for varying sample sizes $N$ ($x$-axis), observed in 1000 experiments when data is embedded at $p = 1$, $r = B$

$N$ and $B$ tested here, but given sufficiently large values of $N$ it looks possible that the likelihood ratio test will become the better test (some other results, not displayed, emphatically confirm this). Also, the average method cannot punish the Steganographer for using a suboptimal embedding strategy.

We observe that concentrating the steganography is the best strategy against the likelihood ratio test, but that for the smallest value of $B$ tested a second peak is forming near $r = 1$. If we had been able to test lower $B$ we would expect to see the results of Lemma 2, with $r = 1$ (spreading the payload thinly across all covers) the least detectable embedding method. But we cannot test lower $B$ without substantially increasing $N$ (else there is no detection power), and we cannot do this because of the size of the corpus of images from which we sample.

Finally, focussing only on the averaging pooling method, we tested a larger range of $B$ and $N$ in Fig. 5. Because performance of the average detector does not depend on $r$, we can pick only a single value of $r$ and plot the false positive rate as $N$ varies. This indicates that, once $N$ passes a point where detection takes place with reasonable reliability, false positive rates drop extremely fast with a few extra observations.

## 4.2   Assumptions Revisited

We also tested pooled steganalysis performance with alternative types of cover image, and noticed a possible problem. Of the assumptions of Sect. 2, the simplest and apparently mildest is that the steganalysis detector response is symmetric about zero, hence unbiased. Indeed, for the 14000 cover images we tested in Sect. 4, this is fairly accurate: the observed bias was 0.00018. However in certain other types of cover, for example colour never-compressed images, it is common to observe a systematic and significant bias of as much as 0.005 or higher. Whether an artifact of the SPA method or the covers themselves is irrelevant; the effect is to destroy the reliability of the pooled detectors, flooding them with false positives for any large value of $N$. This must be so, because a systematic bias of $b$ is indistinguishable from a batch Steganographer's behaviour with $p = b$ and $r = 1$.

If we train the detector first on covers of the right type (effectively removing the bias) then the problem goes away. The difficulty is that the bias varies, depending on the source of covers (and the problem is not limited to the SPA component detector). We see two options for dealing with this difficult issue. On one hand, we could set a maximum bias which we believe is "possible" in natural images, and alter detection thresholds for all the pooled detectors by, for example, subtracting this value before diagnosis. Of course, this reduces their performance and makes it impossible to detect small bandwidths. The alternative is to modify the likelihood ratio test to include a location parameter in both null and alternative hypotheses (possibly constrained). This will detect a Steganographer using small $r$, as distinct clusters are observed, but not $r = 1$.

In previous work we, and other authors, have not considered a small detector bias (say as small as 0.001) to be significant. For pooled steganalysis, where small bandwidths are in principle detectable given large enough $N$, removing the bias becomes the best way to improve pooled performance.

## 5    Conclusions and Directions for Further Research

We have motivated and defined the problems of batch steganography and pooled steganalysis, presenting a menu of techniques for the latter and examining the implications for the former. The pooled steganalysis methods have been benchmarked for a particular type of steganography, with results in line with the theoretical predictions.

The conclusion, that in many cases the Steganographer should cluster the embedding in a small number of cover objects, seems rather counterintuitive. We emphasise that it cannot apply to *every* type of pooling algorithm. For example, the number of observations greater than 1 is quite sensitive to embedding at $p = 1$, although worthless for other batch parameters. There are many other possible pooling algorithms, and some advanced techniques based on mixture modelling, which should be the first priority for further study. In this work we have deliberately avoided methods which are parametric for the Warden – for example the pooling method of counting observations greater than some threshold $T$ – because this leads to a game theoretical setup which can be intractable.

We have only modelled the simplest type of batch steganography. In future work we should consider allowing the Steganographer to vary the amount of data embedded in each object (this results in a larger mixture), and to deal with objects of varying capacity. We must also consider other pooling strategies; we did test, briefly, a pooled detector which simply stitches together $N$ images and applies one steganalysis method to the entire montage, but omitted it from this paper because the performance is similar but a little inferior to the average method. More information on the individual steganalysis response, as it depends on object size and other object parameters, will be needed here. Finally, we would like to prove a general result on how steganographic capacity increases with $N$.

Given the assumptions we made in this paper, including all covers being the same size, there is an additional possibility we have not explored. If we may assume that all, or most, of the steganography is performed using *the same secret key*, this may imply that the same pixels in each cover would be used for steganography (depending on the embedding method). If so, there could be an amplification of the statistical traces, which we might exploit.

More speculatively, consider whether these results give information about adaptivity and steganography in individual images. If it is optimal to cluster data amongst a set of objects, it is not implausible to suggest also clustering stego noise within each single object, although the analogy is not perfect.

## Acknowledgements

The author is a Royal Society University Research Fellow.

## References

1. Trivedi, S., Chandramouli, R.: Active steganalysis of sequential steganography. In: Delp III, E.J., Wong, P.W. (eds.): Security and Watermarking of Multimedia Contents V. vol. 5020 of Proc. SPIE, pp. 123–130 (2003)
2. Dumitrescu, S., Wu, X., Wang, Z.: Detection of LSB steganography via sample pair analysis. In: Petitcolas, F.A.P. (ed.) IH 2002. LNCS, vol. 2578, pp. 355–372. Springer, Heidelberg (2003)
3. Fridrich, J., Goljan, M.: On estimation of secret message length in LSB steganography in spatial domain. In: Delp III, E.J., Wong, P.W. (eds.): Security, Steganography, and Watermarking of Multimedia Contents VI. vol. 5306 of Proc. SPIE, pp. 23–34 (2004)
4. Böhme, R., Ker, A.: A two-factor error model for quantitative steganalysis. In: Delp III, E.J., Wong, P.W. (eds.): Security, Steganography and Watermarking of Multimedia Contents VIII. vol. 6072 of Proc. SPIE, pp. 59–74 (2006)
5. Everitt, B., Hand, D.: Finite Mixture Distributions. Chapman and Hall, Sydney, Australia (1981)
6. Gnedenko, B., Kolmogorov, A.: Limit Distributions for Sums of Independent Random Variables. Addison-Wesley, London, UK (1954)
7. Marin, J., Mengersen, K., Robert, C.: Bayesian modelling and inference on mixtures of distributions. In: Dey, D., Rao, C. (eds.) Handbook of Statistics, vol. 25, Elsevier, Amsterdam (2006)
8. Byrd, R., Lu, P., Nocedal, J., Zhu, C.: A limited memory algorithm for bound constrained optimization. SIAM J. Scientific Computing 16, 1190–1208 (1995)
9. Wilks, S.: The large-sample distribution of the likelihood ratio for testing composite hypotheses. Ann. Mathematical Statistics 9, 60–62 (1938)
10. Fan, J., Zhang, C., Zhang, J.: Generalized likelihood ratio statistics and Wilks phenomenon. Annals of Statistics 29, 153–193 (2001)
11. Pilla, R., Loader, C., Taylor, C.: New technique for finding needles in haystacks: Geometric approach to distinguishing between a new source and random fluctuations. Phys. Review Letters, vol. 95 (2005)
12. Ker, A.: A general framework for the structural steganalysis of LSB replacement. In: Barni, M., Herrera-Joancomartí, J., Katzenbeisser, S., Pérez-González, F. (eds.) IH 2005. LNCS, vol. 3727, pp. 296–311. Springer, Heidelberg (2005)

## Appendix: Proof of Lemma 2

Let $L$ be the likelihood function, and $\hat{r}$ and $\hat{p}$ the MLEs for $r$ and $p$ given the observations. The log-likelihood ratio statistic is

$$\ell = \log\left(\frac{L(X_1, \ldots, X_n; \hat{r}, \hat{p})}{L(X_1, \ldots, X_n; 0, 0)}\right) = \sum \log\left(\left(\frac{(1-\hat{r})\psi(X_i) + \hat{r}\psi(X_i - p)}{\psi(X_i)}\right)\right)$$

$$= \sum \log\left(1 + \hat{r}\left(\frac{\psi(X_i - \hat{p}) - \psi(X_i)}{\psi(X_i)}\right)\right)$$

Let $Y_i$ be independent random variables with pdf $\psi$. We know that $(1-r)N$ of the $X_i$ are distributed as $Y_i$, and the others as $Y_i + p$, and all are independent. We may also assume, as $N$ grows large, that $\hat{r} \sim r$ and $\hat{p} \sim p$ (by consistency of the MLEs). Therefore we have

$$\mathbf{E}[\ell] \sim \mathbf{E}\left[\overbrace{\sum \log\left(1 + r\left(\frac{\psi(Y_i) - \psi(Y_i + p)}{\psi(Y_i + p)}\right)\right)}^{\substack{rN \\ \text{terms}}} + \overbrace{\sum \log\left(1 + r\left(\frac{\psi(Y_i - p) - \psi(Y_i)}{\psi(Y_i)}\right)\right)}^{\substack{(1-r)N \\ \text{terms}}}\right]$$

$$= N\int r \log\left(1 + r\left(\frac{\psi(y) - \psi(y+p)}{\psi(y+p)}\right)\right)\psi(y)\,dy$$

$$+ N\int (1-r) \log\left(1 + r\left(\frac{\psi(y-p) - \psi(y)}{\psi(y)}\right)\right)\psi(y)\,dy$$

$$= N\int \left(\log\left(1 + \frac{B}{p}\left(\frac{\psi(x+p)}{\psi(x)} - 1\right)\right)\right)\left(1 + \frac{B}{p}\left(\frac{\psi(x+p)}{\psi(x)} - 1\right)\right)\psi(x)\,dx. \qquad (7)$$

(In the last step substituting $x = -y - p$ in the first integral, and $x = -y$ in the second, making use of condition a), that $\psi(x) = \psi(-x)$, and writing $r = \frac{B}{p}$.)

Condition b) allows us to use the Taylor expansion $\log(1+z) \sim z - \frac{z^2}{2} + O(z^3)$ in the knowledge that, here, $z$ is of order $B$: given sufficiently small $B$ and neglecting terms of order $B^3$, we have

$$\mathbf{E}[\ell] \sim N\int \left(\frac{B}{p}\left(\frac{\psi(x+p)}{\psi(x)} - 1\right)\right)\left(1 - \frac{1}{2}\frac{B}{p}\left(\frac{\psi(x+p)}{\psi(x)} - 1\right)\right)\left(1 + \frac{B}{p}\left(\frac{\psi(x+p)}{\psi(x)} - 1\right)\right)\psi(x)\,dx.$$

Parts of this integral can be removed, using the fact that $\int \psi(y)\,dy = 1$, leaving

$$\mathbf{E}[\ell] \sim \frac{NB^2}{2}\int \frac{\psi(x+p)^2 - \psi(x)^2}{p^2\psi(x)}\,dx.$$

The Steganographer wants to minimize $\mathbf{E}[\ell]$, to reduce his chance of detection. By condition c) this integral is an increasing function of $p$, so the Steganographer should minimize $p$, taking $r = 1$ and $p = B$. Given that $B$ is small, we may now use a Taylor expansion for $\psi$. We need the first three terms:

$$\mathbf{E}[\ell] \sim \frac{N}{2}\int \frac{\left(\psi(x) + B\psi'(x) + \frac{B^2}{2}\psi''(x) + O(B^3)\right)^2 - \psi(x)^2}{\psi(x)}\,dx.$$

The constant terms (in $B$) cancel, the term in $B$ is zero ($\psi'$ is an odd function), and the term in $B^2$ is $\frac{\psi'(x)^2}{\psi(x)} + \psi''(x)$. This leads to the stated result.

# On Steganographic Embedding Efficiency

Jessica Fridrich[1], Petr Lisoněk[2], and David Soukal[1]

[1] Binghamton University, Binghamton, NY 13902–6000
[2] Simon Fraser University, Burnaby, Britsh Columbia, V5A 1S6, Canada
{fridrich,dsoukal1}@binghamton.edu, plisonek@cecm.sfu.ca

**Abstract.** In this paper, we study embedding efficiency, which is an important attribute of steganographic schemes directly influencing their security. It is defined as the expected number of embedded random message bits per one embedding change. Constraining ourselves to embedding realized using linear covering codes (so called matrix embedding), we show that the quantity that determines embedding efficiency is not the covering radius but the average distance to code. We demonstrate that for linear codes of fixed block length and dimension, the highest embedding efficiency (the smallest average distance to code) is not necessarily achieved using codes with the smallest covering radius. Nevertheless, we prove that with increasing code length and fixed rate (i.e., fixed relative message length), the relative average distance to code and the relative covering radius coincide. Finally, we describe several specific examples of $q$-ary linear codes with $q$ matched to the embedding operation and experimentally demonstrate the improvement in steganographic security when incorporating the coding methods to digital image steganography.

## 1   Introduction

Steganography is the art of undetectable communication. It was originally formalized by Simmons [1] as the prisoners' problem. Alice and Bob are prisoners in separate cells who want to develop an escape plan. Their communication is monitored by a warden. Alice and Bob resort to steganography and hide the details of the escape plot in cover objects, such as digital images, by slightly modifying them. Their goal is to not raise the warden's suspicion. In the simplest case, the warden is passive in that he just observes the traffic without modifying the messages in any way.

The main requirement of any steganographic technique is *undetectability*—the warden should not be able to distinguish between *cover* and *stego objects* (cover embedded with data) with success better than random guessing. A formal definition of steganographic security was given by Cachin [2]. The detectability of data hidden in a stego object is influenced by many factors, such as the choice of the cover object, the selection rule used to identify individual elements of the cover that could be modified during embedding, the type of embedding operation that modifies the cover elements, and the number of embedding changes (directly related to the secret message length). Assuming two embedding methods share the same source of cover objects, the same selection rule and embedding operation,

J. Camenisch et al. (Eds.): IH 2006, LNCS 4437, pp. 282–296, 2007.

the one that introduces fewer embedding changes will be less detectable as it decreases the chance that any statistics used by the warden will be sufficiently disturbed to mount a successful steganalysis attack. The expected number of random message bits embedded per one embedding change is called *embedding efficiency*. This concept has been introduced by Westfeld [3] and has since been accepted as an important attribute of steganographic schemes [4,5].

In 1998, Crandall [6] and Bierbrauer [7, page 195–197] showed that embedding efficiency of steganographic schemes can be improved by applying covering codes to the embedding process. This fact has been later independently rediscovered by van Dijk et al. [8] and Galland et al. [9]. In particular, a linear code can be used to construct an embedding scheme[1] whose embedding capacity is the code redundancy, while the covering radius corresponds to the maximal number of embedding changes necessary for embedding any message.

In this paper, we first show that the *expected* number of embedding changes, which is directly related to the concept of embedding efficiency as used in current steganographic literature, corresponds to the *average distance to code* rather than the covering radius. Moreover, we show that in the class of linear codes of fixed length and dimension the highest embedding efficiency may not always be attained for a code with the smallest covering radius. However, with increasing code length and fixed rate (i.e., fixed relative message length), the relative covering radius and the relative distance to code asymptotically coincide.

In Section 2, we review selected known facts about embedding schemes realized using $q$-ary linear codes and state bounds on embedding efficiency. In Section 3, we study the properties of the average distance to code. Examples of specific coding schemes that can substantially improve the embedding efficiency of steganographic schemes are given in Section 4, where we experimentally demonstrate the benefit of using the proposed coding techniques for steganography. The paper is concluded in Section 5.

# 2   Covering Codes in Steganography

In this section, we briefly review some known results about steganographic schemes and covering codes including bounds on achievable embedding efficiency. We do so for a rather general definition of an embedding scheme in which message symbols from some finite field (rather than bits) are embedded at each pixel. The reason for this more general approach will become clear in Section 4 when we discuss the importance of ternary codes for steganography. Throughout the text, boldface symbols stand for vectors or matrices and the calligraphic font is used for sets. Italicized text highlights definitions of new concepts.

We will assume that the *cover image* $\mathbf{X}$ is an element of $\mathcal{G}^n$, where $\mathcal{G}$ is the set of all possible pixel values. For example, in steganography using 8-bit grayscale digital images, $\mathcal{G}$ is the set of all integers in the range $[0, 255]$ and $n$ is the number of pixels. Data embedding consists of modifying the values of selected pixels so

---

[1] In steganographic literature, such embedding schemes realized using linear codes are called *matrix embedding* [6,3,10].

that the modified (stego) image $\mathbf{Y}$ conveys the desired secret message. The impact of embedding is captured by a *distortion metric* $D : \mathcal{G}^n \times \mathcal{G}^n \to [0, \infty)$.

We further assume that there is a *symbol-assignment function* $s : \mathcal{G} \to \mathbb{F}_q$ that assigns an element of a finite field[2] $\mathbb{F}_q$ to each possible pixel value. The most common symbol-assignment function used in steganography is the least significant bit (LSB) of pixel values

$$s(i) = i \bmod 2. \tag{1}$$

Examples of other symbol-assignment functions are given in Section 4.

Writing the pixels of image $\mathbf{X}$ as a one-dimensional vector, its vector of symbols $s(\mathbf{X}) = \mathbf{x} \in \mathbb{F}_q^n$ is obtained by applying $s$ to each element. Everywhere in this paper, we measure the impact of embedding in the symbol space $\mathbb{F}_q^n$ using the Hamming distance $d : \mathbb{F}_q^n \times \mathbb{F}_q^n \to \{0, 1, \ldots, n\}$ between the corresponding symbol vectors, which is the number of embedding changes

$$D(\mathbf{X}, \mathbf{Y}) = d(s(\mathbf{X}), s(\mathbf{Y})) \text{ for all } \mathbf{X}, \mathbf{Y} \in \mathcal{G}^n. \tag{2}$$

Let $\mathcal{M}$ be the set of all messages that can be communicated. An *embedding scheme* with a distortion bound $R$ is a pair of embedding and extraction functions *Emb* and *Ext*,

$$Emb : \mathbb{F}_q^n \times \mathcal{M} \to \mathbb{F}_q^n \text{ and } Ext : \mathbb{F}_q^n \to \mathcal{M}, \tag{3}$$

$$d(\mathbf{x}, Emb(\mathbf{x}, \mathbf{m})) \leq R \text{ for all } \mathbf{m} \in \mathcal{M} \text{ and all } \mathbf{x} \in \mathbb{F}_q^n, \tag{4}$$

such that for all messages $\mathbf{m} \in \mathcal{M}$ and all $\mathbf{x} \in \mathbb{F}_q^n$, $Ext(Emb(\mathbf{x}, \mathbf{m})) = \mathbf{m}$. In other words, (3) means that we can embed any message from $\mathcal{M}$ in any $\mathbf{x}$ and (4) states that we can do it by imposing at most $R$ changes.

The value $h = \log_2 |\mathcal{M}|$ is called the *embedding capacity* of the scheme (in bits) and $\alpha = h/n$ the relative embedding capacity (or relative payload). We have an obvious upper bound

$$|\mathcal{M}| \leq q^n \text{ or } \alpha \leq \log_2 q. \tag{5}$$

We further define $\underline{e} = \frac{h}{R}$ as the *lower embedding efficiency* and $e = \frac{h}{R_a}$ as the embedding efficiency, where $R_a$ is the expected number of changes over uniformly distributed cover objects $\mathbf{x} \in \mathbb{F}_q^n$ and messages $\mathbf{m} \in \mathcal{M}$. Note that since $R$ is the upper bound on the number of embedding changes, for any embedding scheme $\underline{e} \leq e$.

We next review some known facts about embedding schemes and covering codes and state a bound on embedding efficiency. More details and proofs can be found in [9,12,13]. Throughout this article, we will use some standard concepts and results from Coding Theory that can be found for example in [11]. Unless stated otherwise, all codes considered in this article are linear codes, and we use the notation "$[n, k, d]$ code" for a $k$-dimensional linear code with block length

---

[2] Here, $q$ is a prime power. For background on finite fields, see for example Chapters 3 and 4 in [11].

$n$ and minimal distance $d$. If the minimal distance $d$ is not important for our considerations, we may omit it and only speak of an $[n, k]$ code. We note that the covering radius $R$ of a $q$-ary code $\mathcal{C}$ is defined as

$$R = \max_{\mathbf{x} \in \mathbb{F}_q^n} d(\mathbf{x}, \mathcal{C}), \tag{6}$$

where $d(\mathbf{x}, \mathcal{C}) = \min_{\mathbf{c} \in \mathcal{C}} d(\mathbf{x}, \mathbf{c})$ is the distance between $\mathbf{x}$ and the code $\mathcal{C}$. An $R$-covering of $\mathbb{F}_q^n$ is any subset $\mathcal{C}$ of $\mathbb{F}_q^n$ such that $\bigcup_{\mathbf{x} \in \mathcal{C}} \mathcal{B}(\mathbf{x}, R) = \mathbb{F}_q^n$, where $\mathcal{B}(\mathbf{x}, R)$ is the ball with center $\mathbf{x}$ and radius $R$.

We now state and prove the matrix embedding theorem. It gives a recipe how to use an $[n, k]$ code to communicate $n - k$ symbols using at most $R$ changes in $n$ pixels. Examples of specific matrix embedding schemes for binary and ternary codes are given in Section 4.

**Theorem 1.** *(Matrix embedding) Let $\mathcal{C}$ be an $[n, k]$ code with a parity check matrix $\mathbf{H}$ and covering radius $R$. The embedding scheme below can communicate $n - k$ symbols in $n$ pixels with pixel symbols $\mathbf{x}$ using at most $R$ changes:*

$$Emb(\mathbf{x}, \mathbf{m}) = \mathbf{x} + \mathbf{e}_L = \mathbf{y},$$
$$Ext(\mathbf{y}) = \mathbf{Hy},$$

*where $\mathbf{m} \in \mathbb{F}_q^{n-k}$ is a sequence of $n - k$ message symbols and $\mathbf{e}_L$ is a coset leader of the coset $\mathcal{C}(\mathbf{m} - \mathbf{Hx})$ for the syndrome $\mathbf{m} - \mathbf{Hx}$.*

*Proof.* Since $\mathcal{C}$ has covering radius $R$, we know that $d(\mathbf{x}, \mathbf{y}) = w(\mathbf{e}_L) \leq R$, which proves that the embedding scheme has (a tight) distortion bound $R$. To prove that $Ext(Emb(\mathbf{x}, \mathbf{m})) = \mathbf{m}$, note that $Ext(Emb(\mathbf{x}, \mathbf{m})) = \mathbf{Hy} = \mathbf{Hx} + \mathbf{He}_L = \mathbf{Hx} + \mathbf{m} - \mathbf{Hx} = \mathbf{m}$.

Because there are $\sum_{i=0}^{R} \binom{n}{i}(q-1)^i$ ways in which one can make up to $R$ changes in $n$ pixels, we have

$$h = \log_2 |\mathcal{M}| \leq \log_2 \sum_{i=0}^{R} \binom{n}{i}(q - 1)^i = \log_2 V_q(n, R) \leq n H_q(R/n), \tag{7}$$

where $V_q(n, R)$ is the volume of a ball of radius $R$ in $\mathbb{F}_q^n$ and $H_q(x) = -x \log_2 x - (1 - x) \log_2(1 - x) + x \log_2(q - 1)$ is the $q$-ary entropy function[3]. Inequality (7) also gives us an upper bound on the lower embedding efficiency $\underline{e} = \frac{h}{R}$ for a given relative payload $\alpha = \frac{h}{n}$:

$$H_q^{-1}(\alpha) \leq \frac{R}{n} \implies \underline{e} = \frac{h}{R} = \alpha \cdot \frac{n}{R} \leq \frac{\alpha}{H_q^{-1}(\alpha)}, \tag{8}$$

---

[3] We note that this definition of $q$-ary entropy function is slightly different from how this concept is usually defined in the literature. The difference is the multiplicative factor $\log_2 q$. This is because we define the relative payload $\alpha$ in *bits* per pixel, which is more common in steganography, rather than in $q$-ary *symbols* per pixel.

where $H_q^{-1}(\alpha) \in [0, (q-1)/q]$. We note that this upper bound on $\underline{e}$ is asymptotically achievable using linear codes because the relative redundancy $(n-k)/n = h/n$ of almost all random $[n, k]$ codes asymptotically achieves $H_q(R/n)$ for a fixed $R/n < (q-1)/q$ and $n \to \infty$ (see, e.g., Theorem 12.3.5 in [14] for the binary case). Thus, there exist embedding schemes based on linear codes whose lower embedding efficiency is asymptotically optimal.

## 3   Average Distance to Code

From the Matrix Embedding Theorem 1, for fixed block length $n$ and embedding capacity $n-k$, the highest lower embedding efficiency is achieved using an $[n, k]$ code with the smallest covering radius $R$. However, as argued in the Introduction, steganographers are more interested in the embedding efficiency and thus the average number of embedding changes. In this section, we first show that this concept is related to the average distance to code and then we demonstrate that a code with the smallest average distance to code does not have to have the smallest covering radius.

For an embedding scheme from Theorem 1, the expected number of embedding changes for messages uniformly distributed in $\mathbb{F}_q^{n-k}$ is equal to the average weight of all coset leaders of $\mathcal{C}$. It is reasonable to assume that the messages are drawn uniformly at random from $\mathbb{F}_q^{n-k}$ since typically they will be encrypted before embedding. We now show that the expected number of embedding changes is equal to the average distance to the code defined as

$$R_a = \frac{1}{q^n} \sum_{\mathbf{x} \in \mathbb{F}_q^n} d(\mathbf{x}, \mathcal{C}). \tag{9}$$

Because any two words $\mathbf{x}, \mathbf{y}$ from the same coset $\mathcal{C}_i$ have the same distance from $\mathcal{C}$: $d(\mathbf{x}, \mathcal{C}) = d(\mathbf{y}, \mathcal{C}) = w(\mathbf{e}_i)$, the weight of a coset leader of $\mathcal{C}_i$, we have

$$R_a = \frac{1}{q^n} \sum_{\mathbf{x} \in \mathbb{F}_q^n} d(\mathbf{x}, \mathcal{C}) = \frac{1}{q^n} \sum_{i=1}^{q^{n-k}} \sum_{\mathbf{x} \in \mathcal{C}_i} d(\mathbf{x}, \mathcal{C}) = \frac{1}{q^n} \sum_{i=1}^{q^{n-k}} q^k w(\mathbf{e}_i) = \frac{1}{q^{n-k}} \sum_{i=1}^{q^{n-k}} w(\mathbf{e}_i),$$

which is the average number of embedding changes for messages uniformly chosen from $\mathbb{F}_q^{n-k}$.

The remaining results in this section are formulated for binary codes. We first study codes of small dimension $k = 1, 2$ because such codes allow calculating the average distance to code analytically. Moreover, matrix embedding with codes of small dimension was recently proposed as a means to improve steganographic security when embedding large payloads close to the embedding capacity [13].

**Theorem 2.** *For a binary $[n, 1]$ code*

$$R_a \geq \frac{n}{2}\left(1 - 2^{-n+1}\binom{n-1}{\lceil \frac{n-1}{2} \rceil}\right). \tag{10}$$

*Proof.* Consider the matrix $\mathbf{H} = [\mathbf{I}, \mathbf{1}]$, where $\mathbf{I}$ is the $(n-1) \times (n-1)$ identity matrix and $\mathbf{1}$ is the column of $n-1$ ones. It is easy to see that for $i \leq \lfloor (n-1)/2 \rfloor$ all $\binom{n}{i}$ possible sums of $i$ columns of $\mathbf{H}$ produce all syndromes of weight $i$ and $n-i$. Thus, for $n$ odd, $R_a = 2^{-n+1} \sum_{i=1}^{(n-1)/2} i\binom{n}{i}$ and no other code can have a smaller $R_a$. For $n$ even, we need to include $\binom{n-1}{\lceil (n-1)/2 \rceil}$ sums of $\lceil (n-1)/2 \rceil$ columns of the identity matrix $\mathbf{I}$. Thus, $R_a = 2^{-n+1} \sum_{i=1}^{\lfloor (n-1)/2 \rfloor} i\binom{n}{i} + \lceil (n-1)/2 \rceil \binom{n-1}{\lceil (n-1)/2 \rceil}$ and, again, no code can have a smaller $R_a$. Both expressions simplify to the right hand side of (10) after simple algebra. Note that the proof also shows that the inequality (10) is tight.

To present the analogue of Theorem 2 for 2-dimensional codes, we first need to introduce some notation. For an $[n, 2]$ code $\mathcal{C}$ with basis $\{\mathbf{x}, \mathbf{y}\}$, let us define $\psi(\mathcal{C})$ to be the multiset (set with possibly repeated elements) $\{\alpha, \beta, \gamma\}$, where

$$\alpha = |\{i : x_i = y_i = 1\}|, \ \beta = |\{i : x_i = 1, y_i = 0\}|, \ \gamma = |\{i : x_i = 0, y_i = 1\}|.$$

Notice that the mapping $\psi$ is well defined, that is, $\psi(\mathcal{C})$ is independent of the choice of a basis for $\mathcal{C}$.

**Theorem 3.** *Let $n$ be fixed, $n \geq 4$, and let $\mathcal{C}$ be a binary $[n, 2]$ code. Then $\mathcal{C}$ achieves the minimum average distance to code among all binary $[n, 2]$ codes if and only if no coordinate of $\mathcal{C}$ is identically zero, and $\psi(\mathcal{C})$ is in one of the following forms:*

$$\{\alpha, \alpha, \alpha+1\}, \{\alpha, \alpha+1, \alpha+3\}, \{\alpha, \alpha+1, \alpha+2\}, \{\alpha, \alpha+3, \alpha+3\}, \{\alpha, \alpha+1, \alpha+1\}.$$

It is quite interesting to note that the most symmetric $[3\alpha, 2]$ codes $\mathcal{C}$ defined by $\psi(\mathcal{C}) = \{\alpha, \alpha, \alpha\}$ are *never* optimal unless $\alpha = 1$. This theorem is taken from [15].

To show that a code minimizing the average distance to code among all $[n, k]$ codes with given $n, k$ does not need to minimize the covering radius in this class, we now present the following example.

Let $\mathbf{M}$ be the $4 \times 15$ binary matrix whose columns are all nonzero vectors from $\mathbb{F}_2^4$. Let $\mathbf{M}'$ be a matrix obtained from $\mathbf{M}$ by deleting a single column. Let $\mathcal{C}$ be the $[14, 4]$ code generated by $\mathbf{M}'$. The average distance to $\mathcal{C}$ is $3548/2^{10}$. We have proved by an exhaustive classification of all $[14, 4]$ binary codes up to isomorphism that, for any $[14, 4]$ code $\mathcal{C}'$ not isomorphic to $\mathcal{C}$, the average distance to $\mathcal{C}'$ is at least $3602/2^{10}$, which is at least 1.5% more than that of $\mathcal{C}$. Since the maximum weight of $\mathcal{C}$ is 8, the distance of the all-one vector from $\mathcal{C}$ is 6. However, there are $[14, 4]$ codes with covering radius 5 (see Table 7.1 on page 193 in [14]) and thus $\mathcal{C}$ does not minimize the covering radius among all $[14, 4]$ codes.

Even though the average distance to code and the covering radius are two different values that are not necessarily optimized by the same code, we prove that in the binary case these two concepts asymptotically coincide with increasing length of the code and fixed rate. Let us suppose that we are embedding relative payload $\alpha$, $0 \leq \alpha \leq 1$, in an $n$-element cover object. Thus, the message consists of $\alpha n$ bits and the code that realizes the embedding is a binary $[n, (1 - \alpha)n]$ code[4]. The following theorem states that for almost all such codes the *relative covering radius* $\rho = R/n$ and the *relative distance to code* $\rho_a = R_a/n$ converge with $n \to \infty$.

**Theorem 4.** *For any $0 < \alpha < 1$ and any $\epsilon > 0$, the fraction of all binary $[n, (1 - \alpha)n]$ codes for which $|\rho - \rho_a| \leq \epsilon$ tends to 1 as $n$ goes to infinity.*

The proof of this theorem is in the appendix. We note that this result implies that the bound (8) is also an asymptotic bound on the embedding efficiency $e$

$$e \lesssim \frac{\alpha}{H^{-1}(\alpha)}. \tag{11}$$

## 4 Practical Embedding Schemes

In this section, we first explain the reasons for constructing steganographic schemes using $q$-ary codes with $q$ matched to the embedding operation and then we give several examples of codes suitable for practical applications. Finally, we demonstrate how the codes improve steganographic security of $\pm 1$ embedding in the spatial domain.

Let us start with the simple LSB embedding paradigm frequently employed in steganographic schemes for images, audio, and other digital media objects. To be specific, we assume that the cover is a grayscale digital image and we also assume that the sender can use all pixels for embedding, i.e., the embedding is not constrained to any selection channel [5]. The message bits are embedded as LSBs of pixels along a pseudo-random path determined by a secret stego key. The recipient reads the message from LSBs of pixels obtained by scanning the image in the same pseudo-random order as during embedding.

LSB flipping is a very unnatural operation that is quite detectable by modern steganalytic tools (see [16] and references therein). The fundamental reason for this is the special character of the LSB flipping operation that pairs up grayscale values $2i$ and $2i + 1$ for $i = 0, \ldots, 127$. In other words, during embedding the value $2i$ is either left unchanged or changed to $2i + 1$. In particular, it is never changed to $2i - 1$. All reliable LSB detectors rely on this fact in some way or another.

An obvious and quite simple countermeasure is to make the embedding operation symmetrical and allow changes in both directions for all pixel values (with the obvious exception of the boundary values 0 and 255). For example, to modify the LSB of the grayscale value $i$ of a given pixel, the embedder may flip a coin and with probability $1/2$ increase the value of $i$ by one and with probability $1/2$ decrease its value by one. Note that this process introduces the same distortion

---

[4] Statements involving the quantity $\alpha n$ hold whenever this value is an integer, and are void otherwise.

to the image as LSB embedding. This type of embedding is known as $\pm 1$ embedding [17,18] or LSB matching [19,20]. In this paper, we will call this method *binary $\pm 1$ embedding*.

The embedding efficiency of LSB embedding and binary $\pm 1$ embedding is the same and equal to 2—assuming we are embedding a random bit-stream with uniform distribution of 0's and 1's, we embed 1 bit by making a change with probability $1/2$. However, in the case of $\pm 1$ embedding, we have three possibilities for each pixel—either leave it unchanged or modify by $\pm 1$. Obviously, we can use the following symbol-assignment function

$$t = s(i) = i \bmod 3 \tag{12}$$

and embed a *ternary* symbol $t \in \{0, 1, 2\} = \mathbb{F}_3$ in each pixel. We call this method *ternary $\pm 1$ embedding*.

Assuming the embedded stream of ternary symbols is random with uniform distribution on $\mathbb{F}_3^n$, the probability that the pixel value $i$ will stay unchanged, be modified by 1, or $-1$ is the same and equal to $1/3$. Thus, we make a change with probability $2/3$ and embed $\log_2 3$ bits. The embedding efficiency is thus $\log_2 3/(\frac{2}{3}) \doteq 2.3774$. This is already larger than the embedding efficiency of binary $\pm 1$ embedding. We can do, obviously, much better because we can now embed up to $\log_2 3$ bits per pixel (bpp) and thus the relative payload $\alpha$ shortens by the same factor. This means that we can further increase the embedding efficiency by applying matrix embedding with ternary codes.

## 4.1 Examples of Good Covering Codes

Probably the simplest case of matrix embedding is based on $q$-ary $[\frac{q^m-1}{q-1}, \frac{q^m-1}{q-1} - m, 3]$ Hamming codes, which are perfect codes with minimum distance 3 and covering radius $R = 1$. Since there are $q^{n-m}$ codewords whose distance to code is 0 and $q^n - q^{n-m}$ words $\mathbf{x} \in \mathbb{F}_q^n$ whose distance to code is 1, the average distance to code is $R_a = (q^n - q^{n-m})/q^n = 1 - q^{-m}$. Using Theorem 1, we can embed $m$ $q$-ary symbols in $\frac{q^m-1}{q-1}$ pixels using at most one change. In other words, we can embed a relative payload $\alpha = m\frac{q-1}{q^m-1} \log_2 q$ bpp with lower embedding efficiency $\underline{e} = m \log_2 q$ and embedding efficiency $e = m \log_2 q/(1 - q^{-m})$.

Note that for $q = 2$, $m = 1$, and the symbol-assignment function (1), we obtain the classical LSB embedding. With increasing $m$, the payload $\alpha$ decreases while the embedding efficiency increases. The binary Hamming code was used for the first time in the JPEG steganographic algorithm F5 [3].

In Figure 1, we show the upper bound (8) on embedding efficiency for $q = 2, 3, 4$ as a function of relative payload $\alpha$ (in bpp). The embedding efficiency of binary and ternary Hamming codes for different values of $m$ is shown with "+" and "×" signs, respectively. Note that the curves start at the point $\alpha = \log_2 q$, $e = \frac{q}{q-1} \log_2 q$, which corresponds to embedding at the largest relative payload of $\log_2 q$ bpp. We also want to point out the benefit of using $q$-ary codes for a fixed relative payload $\alpha$. For example, for $\alpha = 1$, the ternary $\pm 1$ embedding can theoretically achieve embedding efficiency $e \simeq 4.4$, which is significantly

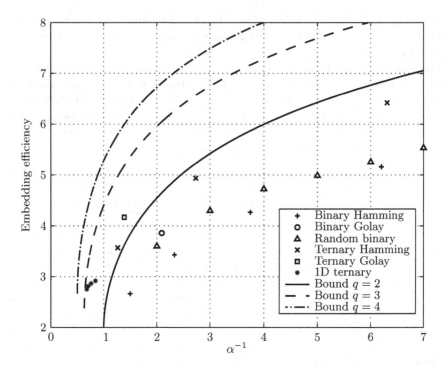

**Fig. 1.** Embedding efficiency of various $q$-ary codes with the upper bound (8) for $q = 2, 3, 4$

higher than 2—the maximal efficiency of LSB embedding at this relative message length.

The remaining non-trivial perfect codes, the binary $[23, 12, 7]$ Golay code and the ternary $[11, 6, 5]_3$ Golay code, also provide very good performance (see Figure 1). The average distance to the binary Golay code is $R_a = \frac{1}{2^{23}}(1 \cdot \binom{23}{1} + 2 \cdot \binom{23}{2}) + 3 \cdot \binom{23}{3})) \cdot 2^{12} \doteq 2.8525$, which gives $e = 11/R_a \doteq 3.8562$ at relative payload $\alpha = 11/23 \doteq 0.4783$. The average distance to the ternary Golay code is $R_a = \frac{1}{3^{11}}(1 \cdot \binom{11}{1} \cdot 2 + 2 \cdot \binom{11}{2} \cdot 4) \cdot 3^6 \doteq 1.9012$, giving $e = 5\log_2 3/R_a \doteq 4.1683$ at relative payload $\alpha = 5\log_2 3/11 \doteq 0.7204$.

For large payloads close to $\log_2 3$ bpp, the following simple one-dimensional ternary code can greatly improve embedding efficiency. Let $\mathcal{C}$ be the ternary $[n, 1]$ code (1-dimensional subspace of $\mathbb{F}_3^n$) spanned by the all-one vector. Suppose that we use matrix embedding defined by the code $\mathcal{C}$, and that the embedding of ternary symbols into the grayscale image is realized using the $\pm 1$ embedding as explained earlier in this section. If we denote the number of 0's, 1's and 2's in an arbitrary vector of $\mathbb{F}_3^n$ by $a$, $b$ and $c$, respectively, then the average distance to $\mathcal{C}$ can be computed as

$$R_a = \frac{1}{3^n}\sum(n - \max\{a, b, c\})\binom{n}{a}\binom{n-a}{b}, \tag{13}$$

where the sum extends over all triples $(a, b, c)$ of non-negative integers such that $a + b + c = n$. For the matrix embedding part, we can use the ternary matrix $\mathbf{H} = [\mathbf{I}, \mathbf{u}]$ where $\mathbf{I}$ is the $(n-1) \times (n-1)$ identity matrix and $\mathbf{u}$ is the column vector of 2's. The number of bits embedded per $n$ pixels is $\log_2 3^{n-1}$, which gives relative payload $\alpha = \frac{n-1}{n} \log_2 3$. The points $[\alpha, R_a]$ are shown in Figure 1 as "$\star$" signs. For example, we can embed 1.188 bpp with embedding efficiency of almost 3 bits per change.

Binary matrix embedding schemes for large payloads were discussed in [13]. The authors proposed a class of random linear codes of small dimension and codes derived from simplex codes.

Finally, as shown in [5] random linear codes in $\mathbb{F}_2^n$ with small codimension can also be used to construct computationally tractable embedding schemes with improved embedding efficiency (the triangle signs in Figure 1 correspond to codes with codimension $n - k = 19$). In this case, due to the small code codimension the coding can be done using efficient search techniques. Note that these random linear codes outperform binary Hamming codes. Another advantage of this approach is that we obtain a parametrized family of codes rather than a few instances of individual coding schemes, which greatly simplifies implementation.

## 4.2   Experiments

Even though it is clear that increased embedding efficiency should improve steganographic security, it would be useful to obtain a quantitative statement for a specific embedding scheme applied to real images. We evaluate the steganographic security using the current state-of-the-art blind feature-based classifier [21] on 2500 cover images obtained with 22 different digital cameras. The images include a mixture of indoor and outdoor shots taken under varying light conditions with and without flash, landscapes, and closeups. All images were taken in the raw (uncompressed) format, converted to grayscale and cropped to their central $1000 \times 1000$ region. We chose a database of raw images intentionally because previously JPEG compressed images should not be used for spatial domain steganography [22].

For our tests, we used three methods: (1) uncoded binary $\pm 1$ embedding, (2) binary $\pm 1$ embedding with binary Hamming codes, and (3) ternary $\pm 1$ embedding with ternary Hamming codes. Note that in order to embed a message of relative length $\alpha$ bpp, we need to choose the parameter $m$ of the Hamming code so that $(m + 1)\frac{q-1}{q^{m+1}-1} \log_2 q < \alpha \leq m\frac{q-1}{q^m-1} \log_2 q$. Obviously, we are most efficient when $\alpha$ is close to $m\frac{q-1}{q^m-1} \log_2 q$. Thus, we chose the payloads for our tests in such a manner so that $\alpha$ is close to the upper bound for both binary and ternary codes.

We ran the following experiment for each payload and each embedding technique. Half of the images from the database were chosen as cover images and the other half were embedded using the corresponding method and payload. Then, using the blind classifier [21] we calculated the Receiver Operating Characteristic curve (ROC) as a measure of separability between the clusters of features of cover and stego images. To obtain a numerical characteristic of the performance of the detector, we used two quantities that are frequently used in current steganalysis literature—false alarms (cover images incorrectly detected as stego) at stego image detection accuracy 50% and 80%. Table 1 shows both numerical characteristics for the three embedding methods and two relative payloads. The parameters for payloads $\alpha_1$ and $\alpha_2$ were $m = 2$ and 3, respectively, for both binary and ternary Hamming codes.

**Table 1.** False alarms at 50% and 80% stego image detection for three embedding methods and two relative payloads

|                   | $\alpha_1 = 0.666$ | | $\alpha_2 = 0.365$ bpp | |
| ----------------- | ----- | ----- | ----- | ----- |
| Embedding method  | FA50% | FA80% | FA50% | FA80% |
| Uncoded binary    | 1.3%  | 15%   | 3.9%  | 21%   |
| Binary Hamming    | 2.5%  | 19%   | 8.1%  | 29%   |
| Ternary Hamming   | 3.9%  | 21%   | 12.7% | 38%   |

The results in Table 1 demonstrate that methods that use matrix embedding can be detected less reliably than the uncoded method. For example, for relative payload $\alpha_1 = 0.666$ bpp applying a ternary Hamming code *triples* the false alarm rate when compared to the uncoded binary $\pm1$ embedding.

We close this section with some general considerations about the limitations of the applicability of matrix embedding to steganography. It is not clear what improvement in embedding efficiency can be expected from using $q$-ary codes with $q > 3$ because in this case the act of embedding will have to start making changes with amplitude more than 1. It is an open and little researched area in steganography whether it is beneficial to decrease the number of embedding changes by allowing embedding changes of higher amplitude. In other words, it is not clear whether it is better to make more changes of low amplitude or fewer changes with larger amplitude. The answer to this question likely depends on other properties of the steganographic scheme, such as placement of embedding changes, the type of embedding operation, and the cover object. Recent studies [17] suggest that with increasing amplitude of embedding changes, the detection of steganography becomes more reliable quite rapidly. Because the improvement in embedding efficiency becomes increasingly smaller with increasing $q$ (see Figure 1), it is not likely that incorporating $q$-ary codes for $q > 3$ would improve steganographic security.

Also, not all steganographic algorithms can benefit from ternary encoding. For example, in the F5 algorithm for JPEG images [3], the absolute value of quantized DCT coefficients is always decreased when necessary to change the LSB. If changes in both directions were allowed in F5, severe artifacts would be introduced in the histogram. Thus, the embedding operation in F5 does not allow applying ternary codes. Another example is Perturbed Quantization [23]. In this case, the direction of embedding changes is determined by side-information provided by a high resolution version of the cover object to minimize the combined distortion due to quantization and embedding. The character of the embedding operation here is also inherently binary.

## 5  Conclusions

Matrix embedding using linear codes (syndrome coding) is a general approach to improving embedding efficiency of steganographic schemes. The covering radius of the code corresponds to the maximal number of embedding changes needed to embed any message. Steganographers, however, are more interested in the average number of embedding changes rather than the worst case. In fact, the concept of embedding efficiency—the average number of bits embedded per embedding change—has been frequently used in steganography to compare and evaluate performance of steganographic schemes.

In this paper, we showed that the embedding efficiency is determined by the average distance to code rather than the covering radius. Thus, designers of steganographic systems should minimize the average distance to code rather than the covering radius. We demonstrated on an example that, within the class of linear codes of fixed dimension and length, the code with the minimal average distance to code does not have to have the smallest covering radius. However, with increasing code length and fixed rate, we proved that the average distance to code and the covering radius coincide.

In the second part of this paper, we demonstrated that embedding efficiency can be dramatically improved using $q$-ary codes with $q$ matched to the steganographic embedding operation. We also briefly studied specific coding methods that can be used to realize embedding schemes in practice. In particular, we compared the performance of binary and ternary Hamming codes. Additionally, we proposed a simple one-dimensional ternary code suitable for improving embedding efficiency when embedding large payloads.

An important open problem is how to find families of binary or ternary codes with efficient coding procedures with embedding efficiency close to the theoretical bound. The recently proposed computationally efficient quantizers based on sparse generator matrices [24] look especially relevant to this problem. Alternatively, we plan to investigate random ternary linear codes and development of computationally efficient algorithms similar to those reported in [5].

## Acknowledgements

The work on this paper was supported by Air Force Research Laboratory, Air Force Material Command, USAF, under the research grants number FA8750-04-1-0112 and F30602-02-2-0093. Research of Petr Lisoněk was partially supported by the Natural Sciences and Engineering Research Council of Canada (NSERC).

The U.S. Government is authorized to reproduce and distribute reprints for Governmental purposes notwithstanding any copyright notation there on. The views and conclusions contained herein are those of the authors and should not be interpreted as necessarily representing the official policies, either expressed or implied, of Air Force Research Laboratory, or the U.S. Government. The authors would like to thank Miroslav Goljan for providing the steganalysis results.

# References

1. Simmons, G.J: The prisoners' problem and the subliminal channel. In: McCurley, K.S., Ziegler, C.D. (eds.) Advances in Cryptology, pp. 51-67.Plenum Press, NewYork (1999)
2. Cachin, C.: An information-theoretic model for steganography. In: Aucsmith, D. (ed.) IH 1998. LNCS, vol. 1525, pp. 306–318. Springer, Heidelberg (1998)
3. Westfeld, A.: High capacity despite better steganalysis F5—a steganographic algorithm. In: Moskowitz, I.S. (ed.) Information Hiding. LNCS, vol. 2137, pp. 289–302. Springer, Heidelberg (2001)
4. Sallee, P.: Model-based methods for steganography and steganalysis. International Journal of Image Graphics 5, 167–190 (2005)
5. Fridrich, J., Goljan, M., Soukal, D.: Steganography via codes for memory with defective cells. In: 43rd Conference on Coding, Communication, and Control, September 28–30, 2005 (2005)
6. Crandall, R.: Some notes on steganography. Steganography Mailing List (1998) available from http://os.inf.tu-dresden.de/~westfeld/crandall.pdf
7. Bierbrauer, J.: Introduction to Coding Theory. Chapman & Hall/CRC (2004)
8. van Dijk, M., Willems, F.: Embedding information in grayscale images. In: Proceedings of the 22nd Symposium on Information and Communication Theory in the Benelux, Enschede, The Netherlands, May 15–16, 2001, pp. 147–154 (2001)
9. Galand, F., Kabatiansky, G.: Information hiding by coverings. In: Proceedings ITW 2003, Paris, France, 2003, pp. 151–154 (2003)
10. Fridrich, J., Goljan, M., Soukal, D.: Wet paper codes with improved embedding efficiency. IEEE Transactions on Information Security and Forensics 1, 102–110 (2006)
11. Williams, F.J.M., Sloane, N.J.: The Theory of Error-Correcting Codes. North-Holland, Amsterdam (1977)
12. Bierbrauer, J.: On crandall's problem. Personal Communication (1998) available from http://www.ws.binghamton.edu/fridrich/covcodes.pdf
13. Fridrich, J., Soukal, D.: Matrix embedding for large payloads. In: Delp, E., Wong, P.W. (eds.) Proceedings SPIE Electronic Imaging, Security, Steganography, and Watermarking of Multimedia Contents VIII, San Jose, CA, 2006, pp. W1–W15 (2006)
14. Cohen, G.D., Honkala, I., Litsyn, S., Lobstein, A.: Covering Codes. Elsevier, North-Holland Mathematical Library, vol. 54 (1997)
15. Khatirinejad, M., Lisoněk, P.: Linear codes for high payload steganography. In: AAECC-16, Las Vegas, Nevada, February 20–24, 2006 (2006)
16. Ker, A.: A general framework for structural analysis of LSB replacement. In: Barni, M., Herrera-Joancomartí, J., Katzenbeisser, S., Pérez-González, F. (eds.) IH 2005. LNCS, vol. 3727, pp. 296–311. Springer, Heidelberg (2005)
17. Soukal, D., Fridrich, J., Goljan, M.: Maximum likelihood estimation of secret message length embedded using PMK steganography in spatial domain. In: Delp, E., Wong, P.W. (eds.) Proceedings SPIE, Electronic Imaging, Security, Steganography, and Watermarking of Multimedia Contents VII, San Jose, CA, January 16–20, 2005, vol. 5681, pp. 595–606 (2005)

18. Wong, P.W., Chen, H., Tang, Z.: On steganalysis of plus-minus one embedding in continuous-tone images. In: Delp, E., Wong, P.W. (eds.) Proceedings SPIE, Electronic Imaging, Security, Steganography, and Watermarking of Multimedia Contents VII, San Jose, CA, January 16–20, 2005, vol. 5681, pp. 643–652 (2005)
19. Ker, A.: Resampling and the detection of LSB matching in color bitmaps. In: Delp, E., Wong, P.W. (eds.) Proceedings SPIE, Electronic Imaging, Security, Steganography, and Watermarking of Multimedia Contents VII, San Jose, CA, January 16–20, 2005, vol. 5681, pp. 1–15 (2005)
20. Ker, A.D.: Steganalysis of LSB matching in grayscale images. IEEE Signal Processing Letters 12, 441–444 (2005)
21. Goljan, M., Fridrich, J., Holotyak, T.: New blind steganalysis and its implications. In: Delp, E., Wong, P.W. (eds.) Proceedings SPIE, Electronic Imaging, Security, Steganography, and Watermarking of Multimedia Contents VIII, San Jose, CA, January 16–19, 2006, vol. 6072, pp. 1–13 (2006)
22. Fridrich, J., Goljan, M., Du, R.: Steganalysis based on JPEG compatibility. In: Tescher, A.G. (ed.) Special Session on Theoretical and Practical Issues in Digital Watermarking and Data Hiding, SPIE Multimedia Systems and Applications IV, Denver, CO, August 20–24, 2001, vol. 4518, pp. 275–280 (2001)
23. Fridrich, J., Goljan, M., Soukal, D.: Perturbed quantization steganography using wet paper codes. In: Dittman, J., Fridrich, J. (eds.) Proceedings ACM Multimedia and Security Workshop, Magdeburg, Germany, September 20-21, 2004, pp. 4–15. ACM Press, New York (2004)
24. Wainwright, M.J., Maneva, E.: Lossy source encoding via message-passing and decimation over generalized codewords of LDGM codes. In: Proceedings of the International Symposium on Information Theory, Adelaide, Australia 2005 (2005)

# A    Proof of Theorem 4

Before we give a proof of the theorem, we formulate two auxiliary lemmas ($H(x)$ is the binary entropy function).

**Lemma 1.** *For any $0 \leq \rho < 1/2$ there exists an integer sequence $k_n$ with*

$$k_n/n \leq 1 - H(\rho) + f(n),$$

*where $f(n) \in O(n^{-1} \log n)$, such that the fraction of all binary $[n, k_n]$ codes that are $\lfloor \rho n \rfloor$-coverings tends to 1.*

*Proof.* This lemma is proved in [14, page 325] (Theorem 12.3.5).

**Lemma 2.** *For any $H^{-1}(\alpha) < \rho < 1/2$, the fraction of all binary $[n, (1 - \alpha)n]$ codes with covering radius at most $\lfloor \rho n \rfloor$ tends to 1 as $n \to \infty$.*

*Proof.* Let us denote $\rho^\star = H^{-1}(\alpha)$. Because $1 - H(\rho) < 1 - H(\rho^\star)$ and $f(n) \to 0$ as $n$ goes to infinity, there exists $n_0$ such that for any $n > n_0$,

$$1 - H(\rho) + f(n) \leq 1 - H(\rho^\star) = 1 - \alpha.$$

Applying Lemma 1 to $\rho$, we obtain an integer sequence $k_n$ for which

$$k_n/n \leq 1 - H(\rho) + f(n) \leq 1 - H(\rho^\star) = 1 - \alpha,$$

for $n > n_0$. Thus, $k_n \leq (1 - \alpha)n$ and the fraction of all $[n, k_n]$ codes whose covering radius is at most $\lfloor \rho n \rfloor$ tends to one. However the same is true for at least the same fraction of $[n, (1 - \alpha)n]$ codes as well. This is so because for any two codes $C_1 \subset C_2$, $C_1$ an $[n, k_1]$ code with covering radius $R_1$ and $C_2$ an $[n, k_2]$ code with covering radius $R_2$, we have $R_2 \leq R_1$.

*Proof of Theorem 4.* Let $\rho^\star = H^{-1}(\alpha)$ and let $C$ be an $[n, (1 - \alpha)n]$ code. From (7) applied to $C$ (note that $h = \alpha n$), we have for its relative covering radius $\rho$, $\rho^\star = H^{-1}(\alpha) \leq R/n = \rho$. On the other hand, from Lemma 2 it follows that $\rho \leq \rho^\star + \epsilon$ for all $n > n_0$, for a fraction of all $[n, (1 - \alpha)n]$ codes that goes to 1 as $n \to \infty$.

The average distance to such codes is $R_a = \frac{1}{2^{\alpha n}} \sum_{l=0}^{\rho n} l c_l$, where $c_l$ is the number of coset leaders of weight $l$. Because $\rho_a \leq \rho$, we need a lower bound on $\rho_a$. Writing

$$R_a = \frac{1}{2^{\alpha n}} \sum_{l=0}^{\lfloor (\rho^\star - \epsilon)n \rfloor} l c_l + \frac{1}{2^{\alpha n}} \sum_{l=\lfloor (\rho^\star - \epsilon)n \rfloor + 1}^{\rho n} l c_l, \tag{14}$$

we will find a lower bound on the second sum. To do so, we first derive an upper bound on $c_l$ for $l$ satisfying $l < (\rho^\star - \epsilon)n$. We start with

$$c_l \leq \binom{n}{l} \leq 2^{nH(l/n)}. \tag{15}$$

The second inequality follows from Lemma 2.4.2 in [14] and holds for any $l < n/2$ for sufficiently large $n$ (e.g., $n > n_1$). Using the fact that $H(x)$ is increasing on $[0, 1/2]$, from Taylor expansion of $H(x)$ at $\rho^\star$,

$$2^{nH(l/n)} \leq 2^{nH(\rho^\star - \epsilon)} = 2^{n(\alpha - \epsilon H'(\xi))}, \tag{16}$$

where $\rho^\star - \epsilon < \xi < \rho^\star$. Finally, because $H'$ is decreasing on the same interval,

$$c_l \leq 2^{\alpha n} 2^{-n\epsilon H'(\xi)} < 2^{\alpha n} 2^{-n\epsilon H'(\rho^\star)}, \tag{17}$$

for any $l < (\rho^\star - \epsilon)n$.

We now obtain a lower bound for $R_a$. Writing $l_0 = \lfloor (\rho^\star - \epsilon)n \rfloor$, from (14)

$$R_a \geq \sum_{l=l_0+1}^{\rho n} \frac{l c_l}{2^{\alpha n}} \geq (\rho^\star - \epsilon)n \sum_{l=l_0+1}^{\rho n} \frac{c_l}{2^{\alpha n}} = (\rho^\star - \epsilon)n \left( 1 - \sum_{l=0}^{l_0} \frac{c_l}{2^{\alpha n}} \right)$$

because $\sum_{l=0}^{R} c_l = 2^{\alpha n}$. Using (17)

$$R_a \geq (\rho^\star - \epsilon)n \left( 1 - (\rho^\star - \epsilon)n \cdot 2^{-n\epsilon H'(\rho^\star)} \right) = (\rho^\star - \epsilon)n(1 - \delta(n)), \tag{18}$$

where $\delta(n) \to 0$ exponentially fast with $n \to \infty$. Combining this result with $\rho_a \leq \rho \leq \rho^\star + \epsilon$, we obtain the following bounds for the average distance to code in terms of the relative quantities (for $n > \max(n_0, n_1)$)

$$(\rho^\star - \epsilon)(1 - \delta(n)) \leq \rho_a \leq \rho \leq \rho^\star + \epsilon, \tag{19}$$

which proves the claim because $\epsilon > 0$ was arbitrary and $\delta(n) \to 0$ for $n \to \infty$.

# Bandwidth Optimal Steganography Secure Against Adaptive Chosen Stegotext Attacks

Tri Van Le[1] and Kaoru Kurosawa[2]

[1] Department of Computer Science
Florida State University
Tallahassee, Florida 32306-4530, USA
levan@cs.fsu.edu
[2] Department of Computer and Information Sciences
Ibaraki University 4-12-1
Nakanarusawa, Hitachi, Ibaraki 316-8511, Japan
kurosawa@cis.ibaraki.ac.jp

**Abstract.** We provide construction of steganographic schemes secure against adaptive chosen stegotext attacks. Our constructions achieve embedding rate equals to the Shannon entropy bound on steganographic channel capacity. Further the covertext distribution can be given as either an integrable probability function or as a random covertext sampler. We also introduce steganographic codes that are of interests in constructing other steganographic protocols such as steganographic secret sharing or steganographic distributed computations.

**Keywords:** bandwidth, information hiding, steganography, adaptive chosen stegotext attack.

## 1 Introduction

*Definition.* The *Prisoner's Problem* introduced by G.J. Simmons [14] and generalized by R. Anderson [1] can be stated informally as follows: Two prisoners, Alice and Bob, want to communicate to each other their secret escape plan under the surveillance of a warden, Wendy. In order to pass Wendy's censorship, Alice and Bob have to keep their communications as innocent as possible so that they will not be banned by Wendy.

*Motivation.* A fundamental question to steganography is what are the limits of provably secure steganography? We answer this question constructively and positively by constructing provably secure schemes with extremely low overhead. We prove that our schemes are secure and essentially optimal. For covertext distributions that support high bandwidth (e.g. thousands of bits per cover), our schemes achieve this bandwidth (Section 5) and are several orders of magnitude better than all previously known secure schemes.

Our schemes are very flexible in that they can work with either an integrable probability function or a random covertext sampler. Their security can be chosen

J. Camenisch et al. (Eds.): IH 2006, LNCS 4437, pp. 297–313, 2007.

in the information theoretic setting or in the computational complexity theoretic setting and are proved in the corresponding setting. In the information theoretic setting, we show matching bounds for both cases of probability function and covertext sampler. In the computational complexity theoretic setting, matching bound is proved only for the most general case of random covertext sampler. Our results show that a probability model of the covertext distribution is sufficient for practical secure steganography, regardless of the security setting.

*Discussion.* We solve the steganographic problem in a novel way. At the heart of our solution are uniquely decodable variable length coding schemes $\Gamma$, called $\mathcal{P}$-codes, with source alphabet $\Sigma$ and destination alphabet $C$ such that: if $x \in \Sigma^\infty$ is chosen uniformly randomly then $\Gamma(x) \in C^\infty$ distributes according to $\mathcal{P}$, where $\mathcal{P}$ is a given distribution over sequences of covertexts.

Note that such a coding scheme is quite related to homophonic coding schemes [7], which are uniquely decodable variable length coding scheme $\Gamma'$ with source alphabet $C$ and destination alphabet $\Sigma$ such that: if $c \in C^*$ is chosen randomly according to distribution $\mathcal{P}$ then $\Gamma'(c) \in \Sigma^*$ is a sequence of independent and uniformly random bits.

Of course, one can hope that such a homophonic coding scheme $\Gamma'$ will give rise to a uniquely decodable $\mathcal{P}$-code $\Gamma$. However, this is not necessarily true because $\Gamma'$ can map one-to-many, as in the case of [7]. Therefore by exchanging the encoding and decoding operations in $\Gamma'$, we will obtain a non-uniquely decodable $\mathcal{P}$-coding scheme $\Gamma''$, which is not what we need.

To construct these $\mathcal{P}$-codes, we generalize an idea of Ross Anderson [1] where one can use a perfect compression scheme on the covertexts to obtain a perfectly secure steganographic scheme. Nevertheless, in practice one can never obtain a perfect encryption scheme, so we have to build our $\mathcal{P}$-coding schemes based on the idea of arithmetic coding. The result is a coding scheme that has near optimal information rate, no decoding error and provable security.

*Related work.* Previously, the Prisoner's Problem was considered in the secret key setting by: Cachin [3], Mittelholzer [11], Moulin and Sullivan [12], Zollner et.al. [16] in the unconditional security model; and Katzenbeisser and Petitcolas [10], Hopper et.al. [8], Reyzin and Russell [13] in the conditional security model. In this article, we consider the problem in the *public key* setting. In this setting, Craver [4] and Anderson[1] proposed several general directions to solve the problem. Katzenbeisser and Petitcolas [10] gave a formal model. Hopper and Ahn [9] constructed proven secure schemes, and then modified it in [15] to remove the dependence on unbiased functions [3]. Michael Backes and Christian Cachin [2] have been able to improve efficiency of Hopper and Ahn's scheme by some factor. Nevertheless all the approaches outlined above have very high overhead and extremely low bit rate [3,8,9,13,2]. In some cases, the bit rate is less than a hundredth of a bit per cover.

*Organization.* The paper is organized as follows: we describe the model in Section 2, our new primitive $\mathcal{P}$-codes in Section 3, show constructions of public key steganographic schemes and their security proofs in Section 4, and give a rate calculation for our schemes in Section 5. We conclude in Section 6.

# 2 Definitions

## 2.1 Channel

Let $C$ be a finite *message space*. A *channel* $\mathcal{P}$ is a probability distribution over the space $C^\infty$ of infinite message sequences $\{(c_1, c_2, \dots) \mid c_i \in C, i \in \mathbb{N}\}$. The communication channel $\mathcal{P}$ may be *stateful*. This means that: for all $n > 0$, $c_n$ might depend probabilistically on $c_1, \dots, c_{n-1}$. When individual messages are used to embed hiddentexts, they are called covertexts. Therefore $C$ is also called the covertext space. Denote $C^*$ the space of all finite message sequences $\{(c_1, \dots, c_l) \mid l \in \mathbb{N}, c_i \in C, 1 \leq i \leq l\}$. If $h \in C^*$ is a prefix of $s \in C^\infty$, that is $s_i = h_i$ for all $1 \leq i < \ell(h)$, then we write $h \sqsubset s$. The expression $s \in_{\mathcal{P}} C^\infty$ means that $s$ is chosen randomly from $C^\infty$ according to distribution $\mathcal{P}$. Denote $\mathcal{P}(c) = \Pr[c \sqsubset s \mid s \in_{\mathcal{P}} C^\infty]$ for all $c \in C^*$.

*Sampler.* A *sampler* $S$ for the channel $\mathcal{P}$ is a sampling oracle such that upon a query $h \in C^*$, $S$ randomly outputs a message $c_i \in C$ according to the marginal probability distribution $\mathcal{P}_h$:

$$\mathcal{P}_h(c_i) = \Pr[(h\|c_i) \sqsubset s \mid h \sqsubset s \; \wedge \; s \in_{\mathcal{P}} C^\infty],$$

where $h\|c_i$ is the concatenation of $h$ and $c_i$. In general, we define $\mathcal{P}_h(c) = \Pr[(h\|c) \sqsubset s \mid h \sqsubset s \; \wedge \; s \in_{\mathcal{P}} C^\infty]$ for all $h \in C^*$ and $c \in C^* \cup C^\infty$. The expression $s = S(h)$ means $s$ is the result of querying $S(h)$. Since $S$ responses randomly, each individual query may have a different result. Finally, $x \in_R X$ means $x$ is chosen uniformly randomly from the set $X$. Finite message sequences can always be included in $\mathcal{P}$ by appending copies of a special *null* symbol to get infinite sequences.

*Assumption.* From now on, we assume that $\mathcal{P}$ is a channel over message space $C$, and that a corresponding sampler $S$ is given. The channel $\mathcal{P}$ represents the probability distribution of an innocent communication channel; the sampler $S$ generates covertexts according to $\mathcal{P}$. Our objective is to construct steganographic systems whose stegotext distributions are indistinguishable from $\mathcal{P}$. We also assume that the query $h$ given to sampler $S$ is always the history of messages communicated between Alice and Bob.

## 2.2 Steganographic Systems

A public key *steganographic system* is specified by a pair of key spaces $\mathcal{K}_e \times \mathcal{K}_d$, and three randomized algorithms, `Setup`, `Embed`, `Extract`, that works as follows:

- Setup: takes a security parameter $k$ as input, and returns system parameters params and a pair of keys $(e, d) \in \mathcal{K}_e \times \mathcal{K}_d$. Among other things, the system parameters params include a short description of a finite hiddentext space $\mathcal{M}$.
- Embed: takes as input a public key $e \in \mathcal{K}_e$, a hiddentext $m \in \mathcal{M}$, and returns a stegotext $s \in C$. The algorithm may query the sampler $S$.
- Extract: takes as input a secret key $d \in \mathcal{K}_d$, a stegotext $s \in C$, and returns either the symbol $\perp$ on failure, or a hiddentext $m \in \mathcal{M}$.

As usual, we require that $\texttt{Extract}(d, \cdot)$ reverses the action of $\texttt{Embed}(e, \cdot)$.

## 2.3   Adaptive Chosen Stegotext Attacks

The task of warden Wendy is to distinguish two cases: whether the communications between the prisoners are innocent, or contain hiddentexts. In order to detect hiddentexts, Wendy is allowed to mount chosen stegotext attacks, which are plausible in practice when Wendy has oracle access to the extraction machine and would like to detect who uses this machine to communicate steganographically.

Chosen stegotext attacks on steganographic systems are parallel to chosen ciphertext attacks on encryption systems. The only difference is in the purposes of the two attacks. In the first attack, the objective is to detect the existence of hidden messages or hiddentexts. In the second attack, the objective is to discover partial information about the content of the secret messages. Our definition of *chosen stegotext security* reflects this difference:

- In an indistinguishability under (adaptive) chosen ciphertext attack (IND-CCA), the challenger randomly chooses one of the two plaintexts submitted by the adversary and encrypts it. An encryption scheme is secure against this attack if an adversary cannot tell which plaintext was encrypted.
- In a hiding under (adaptive) chosen stegotext attack (HID-CSA), the challenger randomly flips a coin, and depending on the result decides to encrypt the submitted hiddentext or to randomly sample a cover message. A steganographic scheme is secure against this attack if an adversary cannot tell stegotexts from covertexts.

While the hiding objective of steganographic systems is substantially different from the semantic security objective of encryption systems, we shall show later that HID-CSA security implies IND-CCA.

Formally, we say that a steganographic system is secure against an adaptive chosen stegotext attack if no polynomial time adversary $\mathcal{W}$ has non-negligible advantages against the challenger in the following game:

- Setup: The challenger takes a security parameter $k$ and runs Setup algorithm. It gives the resulting system parameters params and public key $e$ to the adversary, and keeps the secret key $d$ to itself.

- Phase 1: The adversary issues $j$ queries $c_1, \ldots, c_j$ where each query $c_i$ is a covertext in $\mathcal{C}$. The challenger responds to each query $c_i$ by running Extract algorithm with input secret key $d$ and message $c_i$, then sending the corresponding result of $\texttt{Extract}(d, c_i)$ back to the adversary. The queries may be chosen adaptively by the adversary.
- Challenge: The adversary stops Phase 1 when it desires, and sends a hiddentext $m \in \mathcal{M}$ to the challenger. The challenger then picks a random bit $b \in \{0, 1\}$ and does the following:
  - If $b = 0$, the challenger queries $S$ for a covertext $s$, and sends $s = S(h)$ back to the adversary.
  - If $b = 1$, the challenger runs the Embed algorithm on public key $e$ and plaintext $m$, and sends the resulting stegotext $s = \texttt{Embed}(e, m)$ back to the adversary.
- Phase 2: The adversary makes additional queries $c_{j+1}, \ldots, c_q$ where each query $c_i \neq c$ is a covertext in $\mathcal{C}$. The challenger responds as in Phase 1.
- Guess: The adversary outputs a guess $b' \in \{0, 1\}$. The adversary wins the game if $b' = b$.

Such an adversary $\mathcal{W}$ is called an HID-CSA attacker. We define the adversary $\mathcal{W}$'s advantage in attacking the system as $|\Pr[b' = b] - \frac{1}{2}|$ where the probability is over the random coin tosses of both the challenger and the adversary.

We remind the reader that a standard IND-CCA attacker would play a different game, where at the challenge step:

- Challenge: The adversary sends a pair of plaintexts $m_0, m_1 \in \mathcal{M}$ upon which it wishes to be challenged to the challenger. The challenger then picks a random bit $b \in \{0, 1\}$, runs the encryption algorithm on public key $e$ and plaintext $m_b$, and sends the resulting ciphertext $c = \texttt{Encrypt}(e, m_b)$ back to the adversary.

We note that a HID-CHA game is a restriction of the HID-CSA game where the adversary makes $q = 0$ queries.

As in IND-CCA game against an encryption system, we also define an IND-CCA game against a steganographic system. The definition is exactly the same, except with necessary changes of names: the Encrypt and Decrypt algorithms are replaced by the Embed and Extract algorithms; and the terms plaintext and ciphertext are replaced by the terms hiddentext and stegotext, respectively. Similarly, a steganographic system is called IND-CCA secure if every polynomial time adversary $\mathcal{W}$ has negligible advantages in an IND-CCA game against the steganographic system.

## 3   Construction of $\mathcal{P}$-Codes

A uniquely decodable coding scheme $\Gamma$ is a pair consisting of a probabilistic encoding algorithm $\Gamma_e$ and a deterministic decoding algorithm $\Gamma_d$ such that $\forall m \in dom(\Gamma_e) : \Gamma_d(\Gamma_e(m)) = m$. In this article, we are interested in coding schemes whose source alphabet is binary, $\Sigma = \{0, 1\}$.

**Definition 1.** *Let $\mathcal{P}$ be a channel with message space $C$. A $\mathcal{P}$-code, or a $\mathcal{P}$-coding scheme, is a uniquely decodable coding scheme $\Gamma$ whose encoding function $\Gamma_e : \Sigma^* \rightarrow C^*$ satisfies:*

$$\epsilon(n) = \sum_{c \in \Gamma_e(\Sigma^n)} \left| \Pr\left[ \Gamma_e(x) = c \mid x \in_R \Sigma^n \right] - \mathcal{P}(c) \right|$$

*is a negligible function in $n$. In other words, the distribution of $\Gamma_e(x)$ is statistically indistinguishable from $\mathcal{P}$ when $x$ is chosen uniformly randomly. The function*

$$e(n) = \frac{1}{n} \sum_{c \in \Gamma_e(\Sigma^n)} \mathcal{P}(c) H_{\mathcal{P}}(c)$$

*is called the expansion rate of the encoding, where $H_{\mathcal{P}}(c) = -\log \mathcal{P}(c)$.*

In this definition, $e(n)$ is $\frac{1}{n}$ the Shannon entropy of covertexts used in encoding of binary strings of length $n$. Ideally, we would have used $\Pr\left[\Gamma_e(x) = c \mid x \in_R \Sigma^n\right]$ instead of $\mathcal{P}(c)$. However, the two distributions are statistically indistinguishable so this makes no real difference. For ideal encoding scheme, $e(n)$ should be 1. We will now construct encoding scheme that has $e(n)$ approaches 1 as $n$ grows.

Let $\mathcal{P}$ be a channel with sampler $S$. We assume here that $\mathcal{P}_h$ is polynomially sampleable[1] This is equivalent to saying that $S$ is an efficient algorithm that given a sequence of covertexts $h = (c_1, \ldots, c_n)$ and a uniform random string $r \in_R \{0,1\}^{R_n}$, $S$ outputs a covertext $c_{n+1} = S(h, r) \in C$ accordingly to probability distribution $\mathcal{P}_h$. Nevertheless, we assume less that the output of $S$ to be statistically close to $\mathcal{P}_h$. In the case of computational security, we would relax this condition to only require that the output distribution of $S$ is computationally indistinguishable from $\mathcal{P}_h$.

We use algorithm $S$ to construct a $\mathcal{P}$-coding scheme $\Gamma$. For $x = (x_1, \ldots, x_n) \in \Sigma^n$, denote $\bar{x}$ the non-negative integer number whose binary representation is $x$. For $0 \le a \le 2^n$, denote $\underline{a} = (a_1, \ldots, a_n)$ the binary representation of integer number $a$. In the following, let $t$ be an integer parameter, $h_0$ is the history of all previous communicated messages between Alice and Bob. Further let us assume that the distribution $\mathcal{P}_h$ has minimum entropy bounded from below by a constant $\xi > 0$. Let $G$ be a cryptographically secure pseudo-random generator. Let $G[k]$ be the next $k$ bits extracted from $G$. See Figure 1 and Figure 2 for illustrations of the encoding and decoding operations.

$\Gamma_1$-*Encode.* **Input:** $z \in_R \{0,1\}^{R_n}$, $x = (x_1, \ldots, x_n) \in \Sigma^n$.
        **Output:** $c = (c_1, \ldots, c_l) \in C^*$.

1. let $a = 0, b = 2^{n+k}, h = \epsilon$.
2. let $z$ be the seed to initialize $G$.
3. let $f \leftarrow G[k]$ and $x_f = x \| f$.

---

[1] Theoretically, allowing $\mathcal{P}_h$ to be non-polynomially sampleable would allow hard problems to be solvable.

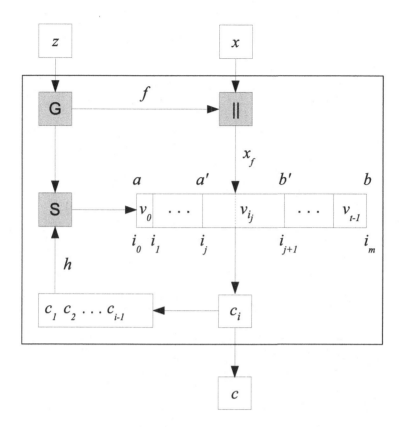

**Fig. 1.** Encode algorithm

4. **while** $\lceil a/2^k \rceil < \lfloor b/2^k \rfloor$ **do**
   (a) **let** $v_i \leftarrow S(h_0 \| h, G)$ for $0 \le i < t$.
   (b) Order the $v_i$'s in some fixed increasing order:
      $$v_0 = \cdots = v_{i_1-1} < v_{i_1} = \cdots = v_{i_2-1} < \cdots < v_{i_{m-1}} = \cdots = v_{t-1},$$
      where $0 = i_0 < i_1 < \cdots < i_m = t$.
   (c) **let** $0 \le j \le m-1$ be the unique $j$ such that
      $$i_j \le \lfloor (\overline{x}_f - a)t/(b-a) \rfloor < i_{j+1}.$$
   (d) **let** $a' = a + (b-a)i_j/t$, $b' = a + (b-a)i_{j+1}/t$.
   (e) **let** $(a,b) = (a',b')$.
   (f) **let** $h = h \| v_{i_j}$.
5. Output $c = h$.

Everyone who is familiar with information theory will immediately realize that the above encoding resembles to the arithmetic decoding of number $\overline{x}_f$. Indeed, the sequence $c$ is a proper prefix of decoded $\overline{x}_f$.

   Each time the sender outputs a covertext $v_{i_j}$, the receiver will obtain some information about the message $x$, i.e. the receiver is able to narrow the range

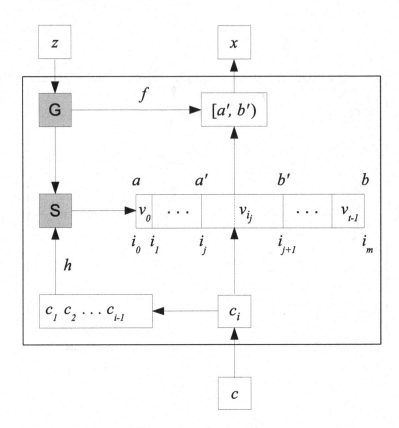

**Fig. 2.** Decode algorithm

$[a, b]$ containing $\overline{x}_f$. The sender stops sending more covertexts until the receiver can completely determine the original value $x$, i.e. when the range $[a, b]$ is less than $2^k$. Thus the decoding operation for the $\mathcal{P}$-coding scheme $\Gamma$ follows.

$\Gamma_1$-*Decode.* **Input:** $z \in_R \{0, 1\}^{R_n}$, $c = (c_1, \ldots, c_l) \in C^*$.
               **Output:** $x = (x_1, \ldots, x_n) \in \Sigma^n$.

1. **let** $a = 0, b = 2^{n+k}, h = \epsilon$.
2. **let** $z$ be the seed to initialize $G$.
3. **let** $f \leftarrow G[k]$.
4. **for** *step* **from 1 to** $l$ **do**
   - (a) **let** $v_i \leftarrow S(h_0 \| h, G)$ for $0 \leq i \leq t - 1$.
   - (b) Order the $v_i$'s in some fixed increasing order:
     $$v_0 = \cdots = v_{i_1-1} < v_{i_1} = \cdots = v_{i_2-1} < \cdots < v_{i_{m-1}} = \cdots = v_{t-1},$$
     where $0 = i_0 < i_1 < \cdots < i_m = t$.
   - (c) **let** $0 \leq j \leq m - 1$ be the unique $j$ such that $v_{i_j} = c_{step}$.
   - (d) **let** $a' = a + (b - a)i_j/t$, $b' = a + (b - a)i_{j+1}/t$.
   - (e) **let** $(a, b) = (a', b')$.
   - (f) **let** $h = h|v_{i_j}$.

5. **if** $f \geq (a \mod 2^k)$ **then** $y = \lfloor a/2^k \rfloor$ **else** $y = \lfloor b/2^k \rfloor$.
6. Output $x = y$.

If $x$ is chosen uniformly randomly from $\Sigma^n$ then the correctness of our $\mathcal{P}$-coding scheme $\Gamma$ is established through the following theorem.

**Theorem 1.** $\Gamma_1$ *described above is a $\mathcal{P}$-code.*

*Proof.* First, the values of $i_0, \ldots, i_t, j, a', b', h, a, b, f$ in the encoding are the same as in the decoding. Further, due to our choice of $j$, $\bar{x} \in [a, b)$ is true not only before the iterations, but also after each iteration. Therefore at the end of the encoding, we obtain $\bar{x} = \lfloor a2^{-k} \rfloor$ or $\bar{x} = \lfloor b2^{-k} \rfloor$. Note that the range $[a, b)$ only determines $x_f$ up to two possible consecutive values of $x$. Together with $f$, we can uniquely determine $x$ since only one value $x_f$ falls into the range. Therefore $\Gamma_1$ is uniquely decodable. Next, we will prove that it is also a $\mathcal{P}$-code.

Indeed, let us assume temporarily that $a, b$ were real numbers. Note that the covertexts $c_0^*, \ldots, c_{t-1}^*$ are generated independently of $x$, so $i_0, \ldots, i_t$ are also independent of $x$. By simple induction we can see that after each iteration, the conditional probability distribution of $\bar{x}_f$ given the history $h = c_1 \| \ldots \| c_{step}$, is uniformly random over integers in the range $[a, b)$. However, in our algorithms the numbers $a, b$ are represented as integers using rounding. So the conditional distribution of $\bar{x}$ at the end of each iteration except the last one is not uniformly random, but anyway at most $4/(b - a) \leq 2^{2-k}$ from uniformly random due to rounding, and due to the fact that $b - a \geq 2^k$. Since $2^{2-k}$ is negligible, and our encoding operations are polynomial time, they can not distinguish a truly uniformly random $\bar{x}_f$ from a statistically-negligible different one. So for our analysis, we can safely assume that $\bar{x}_f$ is indeed uniformly random in the range $[a, b)$ at the *beginning* of each iteration, including the last one.

Then at the beginning of each iteration *step*, conditioned on the previous history $h = c_0 \| \ldots \| c_{step-1}$, $u = \lfloor (\bar{x} - a)t/(b - a) \rfloor$ is a uniformly random variable on the range $[0, t-1]$, thus $u$ is probabilistically independent of $c_0^*, \ldots, c_{t-1}^*$. Since $c_0^*, \ldots, c_{t-1}^*$ are identically distributed, $c_u$ must also be distributed identically. Further, by definition, $i_j \leq k < i_{j+1}$, so $c_u = c_{i_j}^* = c_{step}$. Hence $c_{step}$ distributes identically as each of $c_0^*, \ldots, c_{t-1}^*$ does. By definition of $S$, this distribution is $\mathcal{P}_{h_0 \| h}$, i.e. $c$ distributes accordingly to $\mathcal{P}_{h_0}$. Since $x$ is not truly uniformly random but rather statistically indistinguishable from uniformly random, we conclude that the output $c$ of the encoding operation is statistically indistinguishable from $\mathcal{P}_{h_0}$. Therefore, by definition, our coding scheme is indeed a $\mathcal{P}$-code.     $\square$

Our coding scheme has a small overhead rate of $\frac{1}{n} \lceil \frac{k}{\log_2 \frac{1}{\rho}} \rceil = O(\frac{k}{n})$. However, this overhead goes to 0 when $n > k^{1+\epsilon}$ as $n \to \infty$ and $\epsilon > 0$. Therefore our encoding is essentially optimal (see Section 5).

Note that in the case that $m = 0$, the encoding/decoding operations still work correctly, i.e. there are no errors. In such case, the range $[a, b)$ does not change: the encoding will output $c_0^*$ without actually embedding any hidden information, while the decoding operation will read $c_0^*$ without actually extracting any hidden information. This happens more often when the entropy of the cover distribution is very near zero. However, from now on we will assume that our distribution $\mathcal{P}_h$

will have minimal entropy bounded from below by a fixed constant $1 > \rho > 0$, i.e. $\forall h \in C^*, c \in C : \mathcal{P}_h(c) < \rho$. Then with overwhelming probability of at least $1 - |C|\rho^t$, we will have $m > 0$.

# 4   Construction of Public Key Steganographic Systems

Our purpose in this section is to construct steganographic systems based on the $\mathcal{P}$-coding scheme $\Gamma$. Using the notations from Sections 2 and 3, our construction is the following. Here, $h$ denotes the history of previously communicated messages, $h_0$ refers to the value of $h$ at the start of embed and extract operations.

## 4.1   Public Key Steganographic Systems

We use the idea of Diffie-Hellman key exchange to obtain an efficient public key steganographic scheme. Denote $H_\mathcal{P}(c) = -\log_2(\mathcal{P}(c))$ the entropy of $c \in C^*$ according to the covertext distribution $\mathcal{P}$. We assume that there exists a constant $0 < \rho < 1$ such that:

$$\forall h \in C^*, \forall c \in C : \mathcal{P}_h(c) < \rho.$$

In other words, $\mathcal{P}_h$ has its minimum entropy bounded from below by a positive constant $(-\log_2(\rho))$. Furthermore, let $D = (\texttt{Setup},\texttt{Sign},\texttt{Verify})$ be a secure digital signature scheme.

$S_1$-*Setup.* Call D-Setup to generate a key pair $(k_{sig}, k_{ver})$. The system parameter is a generator $g$ of a cyclic group $<g>$, whose decisional Diffie-Hellman problem is hard and whose order is a prime number $p$. Let $(g, g^a, k_{ver})$ be the public key of sender Alice, and $(g, g^b, k'_{ver})$ be the public key of receiver Bob. Let $F(X, Y)$ be a public cryptographically secure family of pseudo-random functions, indexed by variable $X \in <g>$. Let $k$ be the security parameter, $n = O(poly(k))$ and $U$ be a true random generator. The embedding and extracting operations are as follows (also refer to Figure 3.)

$S_1$-*Embed.* **Input:** $m \in \{0,1\}^n$, $a \in \mathbb{Z}_p$, $g^b \in \mathbb{Z}_p$.
$\qquad\qquad$ **Output:** $c \in C^*$.

1. Let $h_0 = \epsilon$.
2. **for** $i$ **from** 1 **to** $\lceil \frac{k}{\log_2 \frac{1}{\rho}} \rceil$ **do** $h_0 \leftarrow h_0 \| S(h_0, U)$.
3. **let** $r\|z = F((g^b)^a, h_0)$.
4. **let** $m' = m\|\texttt{Sign}(k_{sig}, m)$.
5. **let** $c' = \Gamma_e(z, r \oplus m')$.
6. Output $c = h_0\|c'$.

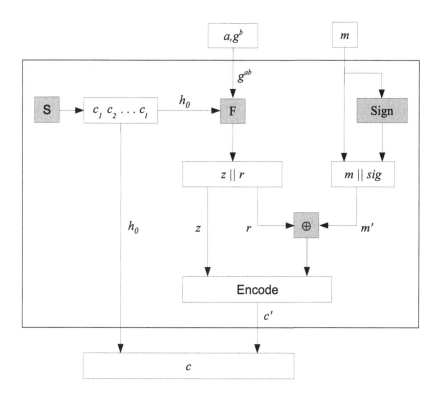

**Fig. 3.** Embed algorithm

$S_1$-$\mathit{Extract}$. **Input:** $c \in C^*$, $b \in \mathcal{Z}_p$, $g^a \in \mathcal{Z}_p$. **Output:** $m \in \{0,1\}^n$.

1. Let $c = h_0 \| c'$ such that $|h_0| = \lceil \frac{k}{\log_2 \frac{1}{\rho}} \rceil$.
2. **let** $r\|z = F((g^a)^b, h_0)$.
3. **let** $m' = \Gamma_d(z, c') \oplus r$.
4. **if** $c' \neq \Gamma_e(z, r \oplus m')$ **then** return $\perp$.
5. Parse $m' = m\|\mathtt{Sign}(k_{sig}, m)$.
6. **if** $\mathtt{Verify}(k_{ver}, m') \neq success$ **then** return $\perp$.
7. Output $m$.

**Theorem 2.** *The steganographic scheme $S_1$ is CHA-secure.*

*Proof.* By definition of the family $F$ and the hardness of the Diffie-Hellman problem over $<g>$, we obtain that $g^{ab}$, and therefore $r$, is computationally indistinguishable from uniformly random. Thus, by definition of our $\mathcal{P}$-code, $c$ is computationally indistinguishable from $\mathcal{P}$.

Further, since $H_\mathcal{P}(h_0) \geq k$, with overwhelming probability $h_0$ is different each time we embed. Therefore even when the embedding oracle is queried repeatedly, $r$ still appears to the attacker as independently and uniformly random. Therefore

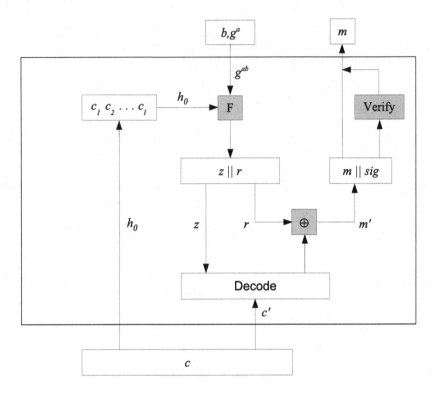

**Fig. 4.** Extract algorithm

in the attacker's view the ciphertexts obtained by him in the warm up step are independent of of the challenged ciphertext, i.e. they are useless for the attack. That means our scheme is CHA-secure.

**Theorem 3.** *The steganographic scheme $S_1$ is CSA-secure.*

*Proof.* Since signature scheme $D$ is unforgeable and that a pair of plaintext $m$ and history $h_0$ uniquely determines the stegotext, an active adversary cannot construct a different valid stegotext sequence with the same $m$ and $h_0$. Therefore with overwhelming probability, all queries made to the extraction oracle will return $\perp$ at step 4 of the extraction algorithm. Therefore an active adversary, having access to decryption oracle of another sender, obtains no more advantage than a passive one does. Since $S_1$ is already CHA-secure, we obtain that our scheme is CSA-secure.

This shows that with overwhelming probability, a CSA-attack against $S_1$ can be reduced to a CHA-attack against $S_1$ by returning $\perp$ to all decryption queries (the receiver has the public key of the sender to check for stegotext validity.)

*Expansion Rate.* The expansion rate of this scheme equals to the rate of the underlying $\mathcal{P}$-code plus the overhead in sending $h_0$ and a signature. Nevertheless, the overhead of $h_0$ and the signature, which is $O(\lceil \frac{k}{\log_2(\frac{1}{\rho})} \rceil)$, only depends on the security parameter $k$. Thus it diminishes when we choose $n$ large enough so that $k = o(n)$, say $n = k \log(k)$. Therefore the expansion rate of our steganographic system is essentially that of the $\mathcal{P}$-code.

## 4.2  Private Key Steganographic Systems

Let $G$ be a cryptographically secure pseudo-random generator, and $k$ be a shared secret key. In the setup step, $k$ is given as seed to $G$. The state of $G$ is kept between calls to $G$. This state is usually not much more than the space for a counter, which is quite small.

$S_2$-Embed. **Input:** $m \in \Sigma^n$.
         **Output:** $c \in C^*$.

1. **let** $r\|z = G(k)$.
2. **let** $m' = m\|\texttt{Sign}(k_{sig}, m)$.
3. Output $c = \Gamma_e(z, r \oplus m)$.

$S_2$-Extract. **Input:** $c \in C^*$.
           **Output:** $m \in \Sigma^n$.

1. **let** $r\|z = G(k)$.
2. **let** $m' = \Gamma_e(z, r \oplus m)$.
3. Parse $m' = m\|\texttt{Sign}(k_{sig}, m)$.
4. **if** $\texttt{Verify}(k_{ver}, m') \neq success$ **then** return $\perp$.
5. Output $m$.

**Theorem 4.** *The steganographic scheme $S_2$ is CHA-secure.*

*Proof.* The proof is straight-forward: $z$ and $r \oplus m$ is computationally indistinguishable from uniformly random, so by the property of $\Gamma_e$, the output covertext sequence $c = \Gamma_e(z, r \oplus m)$ is computationally indistinguishable from $\mathcal{P}$. Further, each time the embedding operation is performed, the pseudo-random generator $G$ changes its internal state, so its output $z, r$ are independent of each others in the attacker's view. Consequently, the values of $z, r \oplus m$, and so do the values of $c = \Gamma_e(z, r \oplus m)$, are probabilistically independent of each others to the attacker. This means that the ciphertexts obtained by the attacker in the warm up step do not help him in the guessing step in anyway. Therefore our scheme is secure against chosen hiddentexts attack.

**Proposition 1.** *The steganographic scheme $S_2$ is CSA-secure.*

*Expansion Rate.* It is clear that the expansion rate of this scheme is the same as the expansion rate of the $\mathcal{P}$-code. Additionally, both sides must maintain the status of the generator $G$. However, this status is very small. Note that our scheme $S_2$ is a somewhat more efficient than $S_1$ because it does not have to send the preamble $h_0$. In the next section, we will see that they are both asymptotically optimal.

## 5 Essentially Optimal Rates

In this section we consider applications of our schemes in two cases: distribution $\mathcal{P}$ is given explicitly by a cumulative distribution function $F$, and is given implicitly by a black-box sampler $S$. In both cases, we show that the achieved information rate is essentially optimal.

### 5.1 Cumulative Distribution Function

We show here that in case we have additionally a cumulative distribution function $F$ of the given distribution, then the construction can be much more efficient. First, let us define what a cumulative distribution function is, and then how to use this additional information to construct $\mathcal{P}$-coding schemes.

Let the message space $C$ be ordered in some strict total order '$<$' so that $\xi_0 < \xi_1 < \dots$ is a sorted sequence of all covertexts. A *cumulative distribution function* (CDF) for the channel $\mathcal{P}$ is a family of functions $F_h : C \to [0,1]$ such that $F_h(\xi) = \sum_{\xi' < \xi} \mathcal{P}_h(\xi')$ for all $h \in C^*$ and $\xi \in C$. We modify our $\mathcal{P}$-code slightly so that it can use the additional information available effectively.

$\Gamma_2$-*Encode.* **Input:** $z \in \{0,1\}^k$, $x = (x_1, \dots, x_n) \in \Sigma^n$.
         **Output:** $c = (c_1, \dots, c_l) \in C^*$.

1. **let** $a = 0, b = 2^{n+k}, h = \epsilon$.
2. **while** $\lceil a/2^k \rceil < \lfloor b/2^k \rfloor$ **do**
   (a) **define** $i_j = tF_{h_0 \| h}(\xi_j)$ for all $j \geq 0$.
   (b) **let** $x_z = x \| z$.
   (c) **let** $j$ be the unique integer such that
   $$i_j \leq \lfloor (\overline{x}_z - a)t/(b-a) \rfloor < i_{j+1}.$$
   (d) **let** $a' = a + (b-a)i_j/t, b' = a + (b-a)i_{j+1}/t$.
   (e) **let** $(a,b) = (a', b')$.
   (f) **let** $h = h | \xi_{i_j}$.
3. Output $c = h$.

The only difference here is that instead of using $S$ to generate $v_i$ ($0 \leq i \leq t-1$) and then deduce $i_j$ ($0 \leq j \leq m-1$), we use $\xi_0, \xi_1, \dots \in C$ directly and let $i_j = tF_{h_0 \| h}(\xi_j)$ for $j = 0, 1, \dots$. Note that the sorted sequence $\xi_0, \xi_1, \dots$ of all covertexts can either be given explicitly, or be given by a function $\xi : \mathbb{N} \to C$. In the either case, the determination of $j$ in step $2(b)$ can be done by binary searching, thus allows large covertext space $C$ to be used.

$\Gamma_2$-*Decode.* **Input:** $z \in \{0,1\}^k$, $c = (c_1, \dots, c_l) \in C^*$.
         **Output:** $x = (x_1, \dots, x_n) \in \Sigma^n$.

1. **let** $a = 0, b = 2^{n+k}, h = \epsilon$.

2. **for** $i$ **from** 1 **to** $|c|$ **do**
   (a) **let** $i_j = tF_{h_0\|h}(\xi_j)$.
   (b) **let** $i_j$ be the unique integer such that $\xi_{i_j} = c_i$.
   (c) **let** $a' = a + (b-a)i_j/t$, $b' = a + (b-a)i_{j+1}/t$.
   (d) **let** $(a,b) = (a',b')$.
   (e) **let** $h = h|\xi_{i_j}$.
3. **if** $\bar{z} \geq (a \mod 2^k)$ **then** $y = \lfloor a/2^k \rfloor$ **else** $y = \lfloor b/2^k \rfloor$.
4. Output $x = y$.

**Theorem 5.** *The coding scheme described above is a $\mathcal{P}$-code.*

*Proof.* The proof is the same, word by word, as in proof of Theorem 1, with only necessary changes of $v_i$ and $i_j$ as noted above.

**Theorem 6.** *The expansion rate $e(n)$ is bounded from above by $1 + \frac{1}{n}\log_2(|C|)$.*

*Proof.* At each iteration $i$, the range $[a,b]$ is reduced in size by a factor of $(b' - a')/(b-a) = (i_{j+1} - i_j)/t = F_h(\xi_{j+1}) - F_h(\xi_j) = \mathcal{P}_h(\xi_{i_j}) = \mathcal{P}_h(c_i)$. Further, before the last iteration $b - a \geq 2^k$, so we get:

$$\mathcal{P}(c_1\|\dots\|c_{l-1}) = \prod_{i=1}^{l-1}\mathcal{P}_{c_1\|\dots\|c_{i-1}}(c_i) \geq \frac{2^k}{2^{n+k}} = 2^{-n}.$$

This means $H_\mathcal{P}(c_1\|\dots\|c_{l-1}) \leq n$. Summing over all $x \in \Sigma^n$ we get:

$$\sum_{c\in\Gamma_e(\Sigma^n)} \mathcal{P}(c)H_P(c) \leq n + \log_2(|C|).$$

This shows that the expansion rate $e(n)$ is bounded above by:

$$e(n) = \frac{1}{n}\sum_{c\in\Gamma_e(\Sigma^n)} \mathcal{P}(c)H_P(c) \leq 1 + \frac{\log_2(|C|)}{n}.$$

Since $\log_2(|C|)$ is a constant, we obtain that $e(n) \to 1$ when $n \to \infty$.

## 5.2   General Case

In this case, we know nothing about the distribution $\mathcal{P}_h$, except a given black box sampler $S$. We give a proof showing that our scheme is optimal.

**Theorem 7.** *The $\mathcal{P}$-code defined in Section 3 is essentially optimal.*

*Proof.* First, note that any steganographic scheme defined over channel $\mathcal{P}$ is indeed a $\mathcal{P}$-coding scheme. Second, the expansion rate of our steganographic schemes is essentially the expansion rate of the underlying $\mathcal{P}$-code. Hence it is enough to show that our $\mathcal{P}$-code $\Gamma_1$ is optimal.

Let $\Gamma'$ be any $\mathcal{P}$-coding scheme that works generically like $\Gamma$, i.e. $\Gamma'$ works on any black box $S$ whose output has minimal entropy bounded from below (e.g. by

$\xi$). Let $t$ be the number of oracle calls to $S$ by $\Gamma'$, and let $c^* = (c_0^*, \ldots, c_{t-1}^*)$ be the corresponding results. Then $\Gamma'$ can only return one of the covers $c_0^*, \ldots, c_{t-1}^*$ as its next stegotext to be sent to the receiver.

Indeed, let us assume otherwise that this is not the case. Consider a sampler $S'$ that output covertexts including a long random string signed with a secure digital signature. Apply $\Gamma'$ to $S'$. If $\Gamma'$ outputs anything that is not in the list of covers returned by $S'$, the output of $\Gamma'$ will not contain a valid signature. Such invalid covers is immediately detectable by a polynomial time signature verification algorithm. Therefore the output of $\Gamma'$ is distinguishable from the output of $S'$. This contradicts with our assumption that $\Gamma'$ is a $\mathcal{P}$-code. Since $\Gamma'$ cannot tell whether the output of $S$ contains some sort of a digital signature or not, we conclude that $\Gamma'$ must always output one of the $c_i^*$'s as its output.

We consider two cases. First if the entropy of $\mathcal{P}_h$ is at least $(1 + \epsilon) \log_2(t)$ for some fixed constant $\epsilon > 0$, then from the method of types (cf. [3,5,6]), we know that the $c_i^*$'s are distinct with overwhelming probability. Therefore $\Gamma_1$ achieves rate of $\log_2(t)$ bits per symbol. However, we know from previous paragraph that $\Gamma'$ has its rate bounded by $\log_2(t)$. Hence in this case, $\Gamma'$ does not do better than $\Gamma_1$.

In the second case, the entropy of $\mathcal{P}_h$ is at most $\log_2(t)$. In this case, method of types(cf. [3,5,6]) tell us that for any fixed constant $\delta > 0$ and large enough $t$, with overwhelming probability: the sample entropy calculated from the frequency vector of the sample $(c_0^*, \ldots, c_{t-1}^*)$ is at least $(1 - \delta)H(\mathcal{P}_h)$. In this case our encoding $\Gamma_1$ achieves at least $(1 - \delta)H(\mathcal{P}_h)$ bits per symbol. Moreover the rate of the encoding $\Gamma'$ must be bounded from above by $(1 + \delta)H(\mathcal{P}_h)$, otherwise the output of $\Gamma'$ will be distinguishable from $\mathcal{P}_h$ with overwhelming probability by simply estimating the entropies of the two distributions [5,6].

We conclude that for all $\delta > 0$, our encoding $\Gamma_1$'s rate is within $(1 - \delta)$ fraction of the best possible rate minus some negligible factor, i.e. $\Gamma_1$ is essentially optimal. $\qquad\square$

Note that our proof works in computational security setting but the same argument would also work in information theoretic setting by replacing digital signature with message authentication code.

## 6    Conclusions

We have shown in this article:

- Introduction and construction of $\mathcal{P}$-codes, and their applications.
- Efficient general construction of public key steganographic schemes secure against chosen hiddentext attacks using public key exchange assuming no special conditions.
- Efficient general construction of private key steganographic schemes secure against chosen hiddentext attacks assuming the existence of a pseudo-random generator.

Our constructions are essentially optimal in many cases, and they are general constructions, producing no errors in extraction. Nevertheless, our solutions do not come for free: they require polynomially sampleable cover distributions. The question of efficient steganography on cover distributions without such a probability model is left open.

# References

1. Anderson, R.J., Petitcolas, F.A.P.: On the limits of steganography. IEEE Journal of Selected Areas in Communications 16(4), 474–481 (1998)
2. Backes, M., Cachin, C.: Public key steganography with active attacks. Technical report, IACR ePrint Archive 2003/231 (2003)
3. Cachin, C.: An information-theoretic model for steganography. In: Aucsmith, D. (ed.) IH 1998. LNCS, vol. 1525, pp. 306–318. Springer, Heidelberg (1998)
4. Craver, S.: On public-key steganography in the presence of an active warden. In: Aucsmith, D. (ed.) IH 1998. LNCS, vol. 1525, pp. 14–17. Springer, Heidelberg (1998)
5. Csiszar. The method of types. IEEETIT: IEEE Transactions on Information Theory, 44 (1998)
6. Csiszar, I., Korner, J.: Information theory: Coding Theory for Discrete Memoryless Systems. Academic Press, NewYork (1981)
7. Gurther, G.: A universal algorithm for homophonic coding. In: Günther, C.G. (ed.) EUROCRYPT 1988. LNCS, vol. 330, Springer, Heidelberg (1988)
8. Hopper, N., Langford, J., von Ahn, L.: Provably secure steganography. In: Yung, M. (ed.) CRYPTO 2002. LNCS, vol. 2442, Springer, Heidelberg (2002)
9. Hopper, N., von Ahn, L.: Public key steganography. In: Crypto 2003 (submitted)
10. Katzenbeisser, S., Petitcolas, F.: On defining security in steganographic systems (2002)
11. Mittelholzer,: An information-theoretic approach to steganography and watermarking. In: Pfitzmann, A. (ed.) IH 1999. LNCS, vol. 1768, Springer, Heidelberg (2000)
12. Moulin, P., O'Sullivan, J.: Information-theoretic analysis of information hiding (1999)
13. Reyzin, L., Russell, S.: More efficient provably secure steganography. Technical report, IACR ePrint Archive 2003/093 (2003)
14. Simmons, G.J.: The prisoner's problem and the subliminal channel. In: Chaum, D. (ed.) Advances in Cryptology: Proceedings of Crypto '83,New York, USA, 1984, pp. 51–70. Plenum Publishing, New York, USA (1984)
15. von Ahn, L., Hopper, N.: Public key steganography. In: Eurocrypt 2004 (submitted)
16. Zollner, J., Federrath, H., Klimant, H., Pfitzmann, A., Piotraschke, R., Westfeld, A., Wicke, G., Wolf, G.: Modeling the security of steganographic systems. In: Information Hiding, pp. 344–354 (1998)

# Modified Matrix Encoding Technique for Minimal Distortion Steganography

Younhee Kim, Zoran Duric, and Dana Richards

George Mason University, Fairfax, VA 22030, USA
{ykim9,zduric,richards}@cs.gmu.edu

**Abstract.** It is well known that all information hiding methods that modify the least significant bits introduce distortions into the cover objects. Those distortions have been utilized by steganalysis algorithms to detect that the objects had been modified. It has been proposed that only coefficients whose modification does not introduce large distortions should be used for embedding. In this paper we propose an efficient algorithm for information hiding in the LSBs of JPEG coefficients. Our algorithm uses modified matrix encoding to choose the coefficients whose modifications introduce minimal embedding distortion. We derive the expected value of the embedding distortion as a function of the message length and the probability distribution of the JPEG quantization errors of cover images. Our experiments show close agreement between the theoretical prediction and the actual embedding distortion. Our algorithm can be used for both steganography and fragile watermarking as well as in other applications in which it is necessary to keep the distortion as low as possible.

## 1 Introduction

The goal of digital steganography is to modify a digital object (cover) to encode and conceal a sequence of bits (message) to facilitate covert communication. The goal of steganalysis is to detect (and possibly prevent) such communication. Often, the cover media correspond to graphics files. Graphics files are the typical choice because of their ubiquitous presence in digital society, but any medium that contains a substantial amount of perceptually insignificant data can be used.

Most steganographic methods operate in two steps. First, a cover object is analyzed and the perceptually insignificant bits are identified. It is assumed that changing these bits will not make observable changes to the cover. Second, the identified bits are replaced by the message bits to create an altered cover object. In this paper, cover object is an image in either bitmap or compressed JPEG [13] formats. The perceptually insignificant bits usually correspond to the LSBs in the image representation: in bitmap images these bits correspond to a subset of the LSBs of the image pixels or the LSBs of the color palette entries, in JPEG images they correspond to a subset of LSBs of the JPEG coefficients. Our work applies to both image representations, but our empirical studies have only

J. Camenisch et al. (Eds.): IH 2006, LNCS 4437, pp. 314–327, 2007.

used the JPEG coefficients. Although, the LSBs of JPEG coefficients are usually considered perceptually insignificant modifying some of these bits can produce significant (but imperceptible) distortions of the original image. In this paper we propose an algorithm that embeds a message into the LSBs of a JPEG image. Our algorithm uses modified matrix-coding technique to minimize the distortion of the stego image relative to the clean (non-stego) image.

The paper is organized as follows. In Sec. 2 we briefly review the relevant prior work in the field. In Sec. 3 we provide technical background for our work including the basic facts about JPEG compression and the matrix coding. In Sec. 4 we describe our method and sketch the theoretical analysis of our method. In Sec. 5 we present some experimental results. Finally, in Sec. 6 we present the concluding remarks.

## 2    Literature Survey

Digital steganography is a relatively new research field [12]. Detailed survey of early algorithms and software for steganography and steganalysis can be found in [12,11,19].

The first quantitative technique for steganalysis was designed by Westfeld and Pfitzmann [17]. They exploited the fact that many steganographic techniques change the frequencies of pairs of values (pairs of colors, gray levels, or JPEG coefficients) during a message embedding process. Their method was shown to be effective in detecting messages hidden by several steganographic techniques. This research prompted interest in both improving statistical detection techniques [5,8] as well as building new steganographic methods that would be difficult to detect by statistical methods [15,18,16,9].

Various attempts have been made to make steganographic content difficult to detect including reducing their capacity or payload and spreading the message across the whole carrier. Anderson and Petitcolas [1] suggested using the parity of bit groups to encode zeroes and ones; large groups of pixels could be used to encode a single bit, the bits that need to be changed could be chosen in a way that would make detection hard.

Provos [15] designed a steganographic method *OutGuess* that spreads a message over a JPEG file; the unused coefficients are adjusted to make the coefficient histogram of the modified file as similar as possible to the histogram of the original image. Fridrich [6] recently developed method for successful breaking of this algorithm. The method exploits the fact that *blockiness* is strongly correlated with the embedding rate. Outguess increases the number of changed bits, which increases *blockiness* between DCT blocks.

Fridrich et al. [5,7,8] reported several techniques for detecting steganographic content in images. If a message is inserted into the LSBs of an image, some features of the image change in a manner that depends on the message size. A possible shortcoming of these methods is that they depend on empirical observations about the feature values of clean—i.e., unmodified—images. However, the authors have demonstrated very promising results on their data sets.

Westfeld [18] designed a steganographic algorithm $F5$ that uses matrix coding to minimize the modifications of the LSBs. His method first discovers the number of available bits and then spreads the message bits over the whole file. To reduce detectability $F5$ decrements the coefficient value to change bits unlike previous algorithms (e.g. OutGuess [15]) that use bit complement to change bits. Fridrich [5] developed a method that successfully breaks this algorithm. The method exploits the fact that modification of the JPEG coefficients by $F5$ increases the number of zero-valued coefficients. Sallee [16] developed a hiding method that preserves distributions of individual JPEG coefficients. On the sender's side the method estimates the distributions of the AC coefficients in JPEG images from the distribution of the most significant bits (MSBs) of the coefficients. The estimated distribution is used by an *entropy decoder* to encode compressed and encrypted messages into the LSBs of the coefficients. On the receiver's side the same distribution is estimated from the MSBs of the coefficients and the message is extracted from the LSBs of the coefficients by an *entropy encoder*. As Böhme and Westfeld [2] observed the fact that the distribution of the JPEG coefficients closely matches the distribution of the MSBs can be used to detect messages hidden by this method.

Fridrich et al. [9] have proposed an information hiding method that guarantees low distortion rates of stego objects. The method makes use of the JPEG quantization errors by computing all rounding errors of the JPEG coefficients. Note that for some coefficients the rounding error is $0.5 \pm \epsilon$. These coefficients can be rounded either down or up without a noticeable difference and they are considered changeable. The algorithm uses a random key to generate a binary matrix $D$ that is known to both the sender and the receiver. To embed a $q$-bit messages the sender solves a system of $q$ linear equations in $GF(2)$.

There are two ways to guarantee that a solution exists. First, the embedding rates can be very low. Second, the authors proposed to use double quantization to guarantee that there is a sufficient number of changeable coefficients. Recently, Kim et al. [20] have described a parity-coding based hiding algorithm that minimizes distortion error by utilizing the rounding errors in JPEG quantization. Given a block of JPEG coefficients the algorithm modifies the coefficients that introduce the smallest additional distortion relative to the rounding step in JPEG quantization. The theoretical analysis accurately predicting embedding distortion was presented. In this paper we describe an algorithm based on a modified matrix-coding technique that minimizes added distortion while keeping the embedding rates at least as high as those obtained by $F5$ [18]. In addition to minimizing distortion our algorithm does not change the distribution of JPEG coefficients significantly. Therefore, we believe that for reasonable (i.e. not full-capacity) rates no existing technique can be used to detect stego content hidden by our method.

# 3   Technical Background

## 3.1   Information Hiding System

The goal of information hiding is to convey a message secretly and imperceptibly to people except a specific receiver. Generally, it modifies a cover object to embed the message. We define the cover object as a vector $C$ and the message as $M$. $M$ is embedded in $C$ by modifying $C$ into $S$, which is called a stego object.

$$M = (m_1, m_2, \ldots, m_k).$$
$$C = (c_1, c_2, \ldots, c_l).$$
$$S = (s_1, s_2, \ldots, s_l).$$

An information hiding algorithm is a pair of functions **f** and **g** such that

$$S = \mathbf{f}(C, M), \quad M = \mathbf{g}(S). \tag{1}$$

## 3.2   JPEG Image Format

We assume that the cover object is an image file in JPEG format. JPEG is a widely used image format because its size is relatively small. JPEG image formatting removes some image details to obtain considerable saving of storage space without much loss of image quality. The savings are based on the fact that humans are more sensitive to changes in lower spatial frequencies than in the higher ones. At the encoder side each channel is divided into $8 \times 8$ blocks and transformed using the two-dimensional Discrete Cosine Transform (DCT). Let $f(i, j)$, $i, j = 0, \ldots, N-1$ be an $N \times N$ image block in any of the channels and let $F(u, v)$, $u, v = 0, \ldots, N-1$ be its DCT transform. See [10] for the mathematical specifics.

The coefficient $F(0, 0)$ is the DC coefficient and all others are called AC coefficients. JPEG uses a quantization and rounding formula,

$$F'(u, v) = \frac{F(u, v)}{Q(u, v)}, \tag{2}$$

$$F''(u, v) = Round(F'(u, v)). \tag{3}$$

to obtain integer-valued coefficients $F''(u, v)$, where $Q(u, v)$ is a quantization table [10]. The process results in a quantization rounding error:

$$\delta(u, v) = F''(u, v)Q(u, v) - F(u, v). \tag{4}$$

## 3.3   Information Hiding in JPEG Coefficients

Information hiding into JPEG image adds more distortion beside the JPEG compression rounding errors (see Eq. (4)).

Define $C'$ and $C''$ to be two vectors of DCT coefficients before and after the rounding, respectively (see Eq. (3)). The rounding error is given by $r_i = c''_i - c'_i$.

$$C' = (c'_1, c'_2, \ldots, c'_l).$$
$$C'' = Round(C') = (c''_1, c''_2, \ldots, c''_l).$$
$$R = C'' - C' = (r_1, r_2, \ldots, r_l).$$

A message M is to be embedded into $C'$, and the message embedded set is $S$. In prior work, the cover object $C$ is typically $C''$, but in this paper, $C$ will be $C'$. We modify $C''$ to create an $S$ such that the LSBs of S are equal to the message bits. To accomplish this, we will add or subtract one from the coefficients in $C''$. Our embedding method depends on rounding error, $r_i$. If the coefficient, $c''_i$, was rounded up, we will subtract one from the coefficient; if it was rounded down, we will add one. However, when $c''_i = \pm 1$, we will make $s_i = \pm 2$ to avoid creating additional zero-valued coefficients.

We denote $LSB(c''_i)$ as $x_i$. If $x_i = m_i$, then $s_i = c''_i$. If $x_i \neq m_i$, then,

$$s_i = \begin{cases} -2, & \text{if } r_i \leq 0 \ \& \ c''_i = -1 \\ Round(c'_i) + 1, & \text{if } r_i \leq 0 \ \& \ c''_i \neq -1 \\ 2, & \text{if } r_i > 0 \ \& \ c''_i = 1 \\ Round(c'_i) - 1, & \text{if } r_i > 0 \ \& \ c''_i = 1. \end{cases} \tag{5}$$

The distortion, $d_i$, is given by

$$d_i = |s_i - c'_i|. \tag{6}$$

In terms of rounding error, $r_i$, the distortion is given by

$$d_i = \begin{cases} 1 + |r_i|, & \text{if } c''_i r_i > 0 \ \& \ c''_i = \pm 1 \\ 1 - |r_i|, & \text{otherwise .} \end{cases}$$

Finally, the additional distortion $e_i$ caused by changing any single bit $c''_i$ is given by

$$e_i = \begin{cases} 1, & \text{if } c''_i r_i > 0 \ \& \ c''_i = \pm 1 \\ 1 - 2|r_i|, & \text{otherwise .} \end{cases} \tag{7}$$

A goal in information hiding is to design embedding functions such that $D = \sum_{i=1}^{l} d_i$ is minimal. Since $r_i$s are already given, minimizing $D$ is equivalent to minimizing $E = \sum_{i=1}^{l} e_i$.

## 3.4   Matrix Coding

Matrix coding was proposed by Crandall [4] to improve the embedding efficiency by decreasing the number of required bit changes. Westfeld [18] proposed $F5$, a steganographic algorithm which implemented the matrix coding. Matrix coding uses as cover data the set of LSBs of quantized DCT coefficients after rounding. The notation $(1, n, k)$, where $n = 2^k - 1$. denotes embedding $k$ message bits into an $n$ bit sized block by changing only one bit of it The embedding process divides

$C$, into blocks of length $n$ and message data, $M$, into blocks of length $k$. To embed $i^{\text{th}}$ message block, $\{m_{k(i-1)+1}, \ldots, m_{ki}\}$, a cover data block $\{c_{n(i-1)+1}, \ldots, c_{ni}\}$ is used. Let us define $MB$ and $CB$ as a message block and cover block.

The advantage of matrix coding is that we change only one bit to embed several bits. A function $b$ needs to be defined:

$$b(CB) = \bigoplus_{j=1}^{n} (cb_j) \cdot j. \tag{8}$$

To calculate the position, $\alpha$, of the bit that needs to be changed, we calculate

$$\alpha = MB \oplus b(CB). \tag{9}$$

If $\alpha \neq 0$, the $\alpha^{\text{th}}$ bit in the block of $CB$ should be flipped, 1 to 0 or 0 to 1. The modified block is then given by

$$SB = \begin{cases} CB, & \text{if } \alpha = 0. \\ cb_1, \ldots, \neg cb_\alpha, \ldots, cb_n & \text{if } \alpha \neq 0. \end{cases} \tag{10}$$

On the decoder's side, $k$ message bits are obtained from an $n$ bit sized cover data by computing the following:

$$MB = b(SB). \tag{11}$$

## 4 Modified Matrix Encoding

$F5$ [18] used $(1, n, k)$ codes to embed $k$-bits into an $n$-bits LSB block. Because of that, in each block a bit that needs to be changed is given by (9). We propose to use $(t, n, k)$, $t \geq 1$ coding to increase the number of possible bit-change choices in each block. We describe our approach for $t = 2$. We call our method modified matrix encoding (MME).

### 4.1 Embedding Algorithm

For $t = 2$, we find pairs of numbers $(\beta, \gamma)$ such that $\beta \oplus \gamma = \alpha$. Note that for any $\alpha$, there are $\frac{n-1}{2}$ such pairs which can be enumerated easily. If we use the embedding technique described in Sec. 3.3 for each cover block, $CB$ of length $n$, we are given coefficients $(c'_1, \ldots, c'_n), (c''_1, \ldots, c''_n)$, the rounding errors $(r_1, \ldots, r_n)$, and the message block $MB$ of length $k$. We compute $\alpha$ using (9) and the pairs $(\beta_1, \gamma_1), \ldots, (\beta_{\frac{n-1}{2}}, \gamma_{\frac{n-1}{2}})$ such that $\beta_i \oplus \gamma_i = \alpha$, $i = 1, \ldots, \frac{n-1}{2}$.

Given $r_\alpha$, the embedding error, $e_0$ is given by (7), i.e. $e_0 = 1 - 2|r_\alpha|$. For each of the pairs $(\beta_i, \gamma_i)$, the embedding error is given by one of four cases:

$$e_i = \begin{cases} 2, & \text{if } c''_{\beta_i} r_{\beta_i} > 0 \ \& \ c''_{\gamma_i} r_{\gamma_i} > 0 \ \& \ c''_{\beta_i} = \pm 1 \ \& \ c''_{\gamma_i} \pm 1 \\ 2 - 2|r_{\gamma_i}|, & \text{if } c''_{\beta_i} r_{\beta_i} > 0 \ \& \ c''_{\beta_i} = \pm 1 \ \& \ c''_{\gamma_i} \neq \pm 1 \\ 2 - 2|r_{\beta_i}|, & \text{if } c''_{\gamma_i} r_{\gamma_i} > 0 \ \& \ c''_{\gamma_i} = \pm 1 \ \& \ c''_{\beta_i} \neq \pm 1 \\ 2 - 2(|r_{\beta_i}| + |r_{\gamma_i}|), & \text{otherwise.} \end{cases} \tag{12}$$

In order to decide how to create $SB$, we find

$$\mu = \min_j\{e_j\}, \ 0 \le j \le \frac{n-1}{2}.$$

Given $\mu$, we compute $SB$ by

$$SB = \begin{cases} CB, & \text{if } \alpha = 0 \\ cb_1, \ldots, \neg cb_\alpha, \ldots, cb_n, & \text{if } \mu = e_0 \\ cb_1, \ldots, \neg cb_{\beta_i}, \ldots, \neg cb_{\gamma_i}, \ldots, cb_n, & \text{if } \mu = e_i, i = 1, \ldots, \frac{n-1}{2}. \end{cases} \tag{13}$$

## 4.2   Embedding Distortion of MME

We have assumed that each $r_i$ is i.i.d. random variable and that their probability density $f_r(x)$ is known. Probability distribution for $y = |r|$ is given by

$$F_y(x) = \int_{-x}^{x} f_r(x)dx, \quad x \in [0, 0.5].$$

Probability density for $z = |r_1| + |r_2|$ is given by

$$f_z(x) = f_y(x) \bigotimes f_y(x), \quad z \in [0, 1],$$

where $\bigotimes$ stands for convolution. Probability distribution, $F_z(x)$ is given by

$$F_z(x) = \int_0^z f_z(x)dx, \quad z \in [0, 1].$$

Probability distribution for $\nu = 1 - 2y$ is given by

$$F_\nu(x) = 1 - F_y(\frac{1-x}{2}), \quad \nu \in [0, 1].$$

Probability distribution for $\omega = 2 - 2z$ is given by

$$F_\omega(x) = 1 - F_z(2 - x), \quad \omega \in [0, 2].$$

To estimate the probability distribution of the embedding distortion due to embedding for $(1, n, k)$ matrix codes, we use the order statistics [14]. As the first approximation, we only consider the case when all embedding errors are $e_i \le 1$.

Given the probability distribution $F_\nu(x)$ and $F_\omega(x)$, the distribution of $\mu$ is given by

$$F_\mu = 1 - (1 - F_\nu(x)) \times (1 - F_\omega(x))^{\frac{n-1}{2}}.$$

The expected value $E[\mu]$ is given by

$$E[\mu] = \int_0^\infty x dF_\mu(x).$$

More accurate analysis takes into account the fact that some of the additional embedding error distribution will be different from those have presented here. That analysis will be presented elsewhere.

Since changes occur in $\frac{n}{n+1}$ cases in any blocks, the expected embedding error per bit is given by

$$E[\|E\|_1] = E[\mu] \times \frac{n}{n+1}.$$

## 5  Results

We have implemented our modified matrix encoding algorithm in Java. In this section we demonstrate the operation of our method on several images. Figure 1 shows the test images, which are color JPEG images. Rounding error histograms are also shown in Fig. 1; we estimate the rounding-error distributions by normalizing the histograms.

**Fig. 1.** Left column: armadillo image. Right column: tiger image. Top row: test images. Bottom row: rounding error histograms of the nonzero AC jpeg coefficients. The histogram is normalized to estimate a probability density of rounding errors.

The algorithm modifies a publicly available implementation of the JPEG image compression algorithm. After computing the DCT, all non-zero AC coefficients are marked for possible embedding and collected to form $C''$; the corresponding rounding errors form $R$. The implementation follows the algorithm described in Sec. 4.1. Our algorithm uses modified matrix encoding to choose the coefficients whose modifications introduce the minimal embedding distortion.

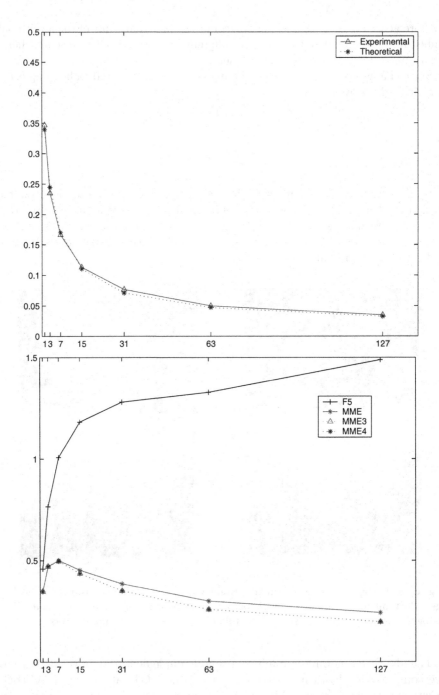

**Fig. 2.** Embedding error analysis for the armadillo image (left image in Fig. 1). Top row: Embedding error for various block sizes, n. Bottom row: Embedding error per changed coefficient for F5, MME, MME3, and MME4.

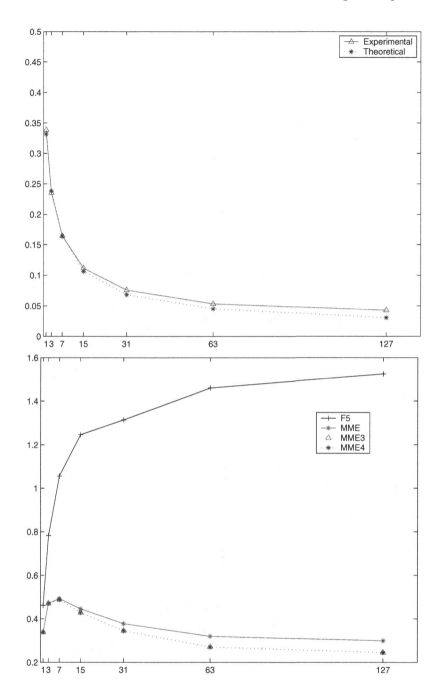

**Fig. 3.** Embedding error analysis for the tiger image (right image in Fig. 1). Top row: Embedding error for various block sizes, n. Bottom row: Embedding error per the changed coefficient for F5, MME, MME3, and MME4.

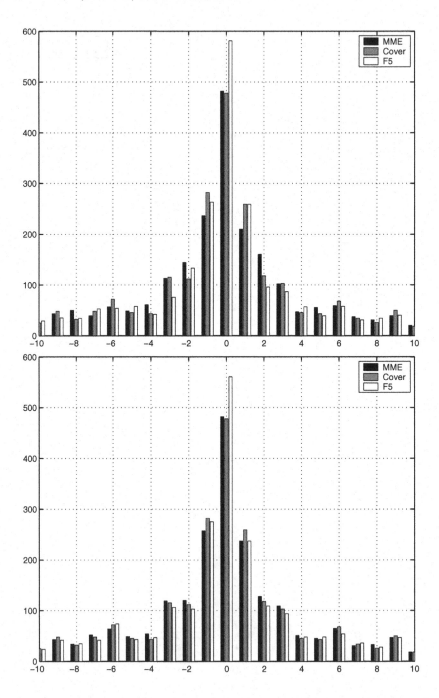

**Fig. 4.** Comparison of histograms of JPEG coefficient (1, 2) for the armadillo image (left image in Fig. 1). The figure plots histograms for MME stego, F5 stego, and cover images. Top row: (1, 3, 2) code. Bottom row: (1, 7, 3) code.

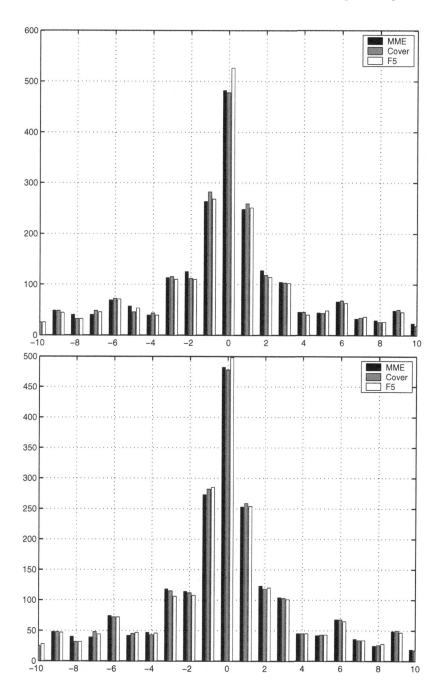

**Fig. 5.** Comparison of histograms of JPEG coefficient (1, 2) for the armadillo image (left image in Fig. 1). The figure plots histograms for MME stego, F5 stego, and cover images. Top row: (1, 15, 4) code. Bottom row: (1, 31, 5) code.

All tests was accomplished with 6 different block-size encode; $(1, 2^{k-1}, k)$, $k = 2, \ldots, 7$. Top rows of the Fig. 2 and Fig. 3 plot the comparison of the predicted embedding error to the real experimental embedding error, and they show close agreement between the theoretical prediction and the actual embedding distortion. Bottom rows show the embedding errors per the changed bit in *F5*, *MME* and the extended versions of *MME*, MME3 and MME4, that modify up to 3 and 4 bits per block, respectively.

Figure 4 and Fig. 5, the histograms of coefficient $(1, 2)$ JPEG coefficients are shown with the various block sizes, from $(1, 3, 2)$ code to $(1, 31, 5)$ code. Notice that our algorithm doesn't change the number of zero while F5 algorithm does. With block size becoming larger, the MME stego histogram becomes very close to the cover image histogram.

# 6   Conclusions

In this paper we propose an efficient information hiding algorithm that embeds message in the least significant bits of JPEG coefficients of images. Our algorithm uses a modified matrix encoding technique that embeds information by modifying the coefficients in such a way that the introduced distortion is minimized. We derive the expected value of the introduced distortion as a function of the message length and the probability distribution of the JPEG quantization errors of cover images. We have implemented our method in Java and performed the extensive experiments with it. The experiments have shown that our theoretical predictions agree closely with the actual introduced distortions.

# References

1. Anderson, R.J., Petitcolas, F.: On the limits of steganography. IEEE Journal on Selected Areas in Communications 16, 474–481 (1998)
2. Böhme, R., Westfeld, A.: Exploiting preserved statistics for steganalysis. In: Fridrich, J. (ed.) IH 2004. LNCS, vol. 3200, pp. 82–96. Springer, Heidelberg (2004)
3. Cachin, C.: An information-theoretic model for steganography. In: Aucsmith, D. (ed.) IH 1998. LNCS, vol. 1525, pp. 306–318. Springer, Heidelberg (1998)
4. Crandall, R.: Some Notes on Steganography. Posted on Steganography Mailing List (1998) http://os.inf.tu-dresden.de/ westfeld/crandall.pdf
5. Fridrich, J.: Feature-based steganalysis for JPEG images and its implications for future design of steganographic schemes. In: Proc. 6th Information Hiding Workshop, Toronto, Canada, 2004 (2004)
6. Fridrich, J., Goljan, M., Hogea, D.: Attacking the OutGuess. In: Proc. ACM Workshop Multimedia and Security 2002. ACM Press, New York, NY (2002)
7. Fridrich, J., Goljan, M., Du. R.: Detecting Steganography LSB in color and grayscale images. IEEE Multimedia Magazine, 22–28 (October 2001)
8. Fridrich, J., Goljan, M., Hogea, D.: Steganalysis of JPEG images: Breaking the F5 algorithm. In: Petitcolas, F.A.P. (ed.) IH 2002. LNCS, vol. 2578, pp. 310–323. Springer, Heidelberg (2003)

9. Fridrich, J., Goljan, M., Soukal, D.: Perturbed quantization steganography with wet paper codes. In: Proc. ACM Multimedia Workshop, Magdeburg, Germany (2004)

10. Gonzales, R.C., Woods, R.E.: Digital Image Processing. Addison-Wesley, London, UK (2002)

11. Johnson, N., Duric, Z., Jajodia, S.: Information Hiding: Steganography and Watermarking — Attacks and Countermeasures. Kluwer Academic Publishers, Boston (2000)

12. Katzenbeisser, S., Petitcolas, F.A.P. (eds.): Information Hiding: Techniques for Steganography and Digital Watermarking. Artech House, Norwood, MA (2000)

13. Joint Photographic Experts Group.
http://www.jpeg.org/public/jpeghomepage.htm

14. Paopoulis, A.: Probability, Random Variables, and Stochastic Processes. McGraw-Hill, Boston, MA (1991)

15. Provos, N.: Defending against statistical steganalysis. In: Proc. 10th USENIX Security Symposium, 2001 pp. 323–325 (2001)

16. Sallee, P.: Model-based steganography. In: Kalker, T., Cox, I., Ro, Y.M. (eds.) IWDW 2003. LNCS, vol. 2939, pp. 154–167. Springer, Heidelberg (2004)

17. Westfeld, A., Pfitzmann, A.: Attacks on steganographic systems. In: Pfitzmann, A. (ed.) IH 1999. LNCS, vol. 1768, pp. 61–75. Springer, Heidelberg (2000)

18. Westfeld, A.: F5—a steganographic algorithm: High capacity despite better steganalysis. In: Moskowitz, I.S. (ed.) Information Hiding. LNCS, vol. 2137, pp. 289–302. Springer, Heidelberg (2001)

19. Wayner, P.: Disappearing Cryptography, 2nd edn. Morgan Kaufmann, San Francisco (2002)

20. Kim, Y., Duric, Z., Richards, D.: Limited Distortion in LSB Steganography. In: Proc. SPIE Electronic Image, 2006 (2006)

# Statistically Secure Anti-Collusion Code Design for Median Attack Robustness for Practical Fingerprinting

Jae-Min Seol and Seong-Whan Kim

Department of Computer Science,
University of Seoul, Jeon-Nong-Dong, Seoul, Korea
seoleda@gmail.com, swkim7@uos.ac.kr

**Abstract.** Digital fingerprinting is a technique to prevent customers from redistributing multimedia contents illegally. Main attack for fingerprinting is the collusion attack, where multiple users collude by creating an average or median of their individual fingerprinted copies, and escape identification. Previous research such as ACC (anti-collusion code) cannot support large number of users, and also vulnerable to LCCA (linear combination collusion attack). We present a practical SACC (scalable ACC) scheme to generate codebooks for supporting large number of users; and angular decoding scheme to be robust on LCCA. We implemented the SACC codebook using a Gaussian distributed random variable for various attack robustness, and the fingerprint embedding using human visual system based watermarking scheme. We experimented with standard test images for collusion detection performance, and it shows good collusion detection performance over average, median attacks. For LCCA collusion attack on SACC, our angular decoding scheme identifies the correct colluder set under various WNR (watermark to noise ratio).

**Keyword:** fingerprinting, ACC, LCCA, BIBD, angular decoding.

## 1 Introduction

A digital watermark or watermark is an invisible mark inserted in digital media, and fingerprinting uses digital watermark to determine originators of unauthorized/pirated copies. Multiple users may collude and collectively escape identification by creating an average or median of their individually watermarked copies. An early work on designing collusion-resistant binary fingerprint codes for generic data was based on marking assumption, which states that undetectable marks cannot be arbitrarily changed without rendering the object useless [1]. However, multimedia data have very different characteristics from generic data, and we can embed different marks or fingerprints in overall images, which biased strict marking assumption. Trappe et al presented the design of collusion-resistant fingerprints using code modulation. They proposed a (k-1) collusion-resistant fingerprints scheme, which is based on (v, k, 1) balanced incomplete block design (BIBD) [2]. The resulting (k-1) resilient ACC code vectors are v-dimensional, and can represent $n = (v^2 -v) / (k^2 -k)$ users with these v basis vectors. However, recent research shows that LCCA (linear combination

J. Camenisch et al. (Eds.): IH 2006, LNCS 4437, pp. 328–342, 2007.

collusion attack) can successfully make collusion for ACC based fingerprinting schemes [6]. Also, ACC which derived form BIBD cannot provide flexible coding parameters for practical fingerprinting use.

We present a scalable ACC fingerprinting design scheme, which extends ACC for large number of user support. We extend the ACC (anti-collusion code) scheme using a Gaussian distributed random variable for average and medium attack robustness. We also present an improved detection scheme using the angular decoding scheme to be robust on LCCA. We evaluate our scheme with standard test images, and show good collusion detection performance over average, median, and linear combination collusion attacks.

# 2  Related Works

An early work on designing collusion-resistant binary fingerprint codes was presented by Boneh and Shaw in 1995 [3], which primarily considered the problem of fingerprinting generic data that satisfy an underlying principle referred to as the marking assumption. The marking assumption states that undetectable marks cannot be arbitrarily changed without rendering the object useless; however, it is considered possible for the colluding set to change a detectable mark to any state (collusion framework). Under the collusion framework, Boneh and Shaw show that it is not possible to design totally c-secure codes, which are fingerprint codes that are capable of tracing at least one colluder out of a coalition of at most c colluders. Instead, they used hierarchical design and randomization techniques to construct c-secure codes that are able to capture one colluder out of a coalition of up to c colluders with high probability. Fingerprint codes (e.g. c-secure codes) for generic data was intended for objects that satisfy the marking assumption, multimedia data have very different characteristics from generic data, and a few fundamental aspects of the marking assumption may not always hold when fingerprinting multimedia data. For example, different marks or fingerprints can be embedded in overall images through spread spectrum techniques, thereby it makes impossible for attackers to manipulate individual marks at will.

Min Wu presented the design of collusion-resistant fingerprints based on anti-collusion code (ACC) [2]. It has the property that the bits shared between code vectors uniquely identify groups of colluding users. ACC codes have the property that the composition of any subset of K or fewer code vectors is unique. This property allows for the identification of up to K colluders. It has been shown that binary-valued ACC can be constructed using balanced incomplete block design (BIBD) [4]. The definition of $(v, k, \lambda)$ BIBD code is a set of k-element subsets (blocks) of a v-element set $\chi$, such that each pair of elements of $\chi$ occur together in exactly $\lambda$ blocks. The $(v, k, \lambda)$ BIBD has a total of $n = (v^2 - v)/(k^2 - k)$ blocks, and we can represent $(v, k, \lambda)$ BIBD code using an v x n incidence matrix M, where M(i, j) is set to 1 when the i-th element belongs to the j-th block, and set to 0 otherwise. The corresponding $(k - 1)$-resilient ACC code vectors are assigned as the bit complements (finally represented using -1 and 1 for the 0 and 1, respectively) of the columns of the incidence matrix of a (v, k, 1) BIBD. The resulting (k-1) resilient ACC code vectors are v-dimensional, and can represent n = $(v^2 - v) / (k^2 - k)$ users with these v basis vectors. This anti-collusion code can be used with code modulation to construct a family of fingerprints with the ability to identify colluders. The fingerprint signal $w_j$ for the $j^{th}$ user is constructed using a linear combination of a total of v orthogonal basis signals $\{u_i\}$, multiplied by the coefficients $\{b_{ij}\}$, representing the fingerprint codes from $\{\pm 1\}$ as shown in Equation(1).

$$\mathbf{w}_j = \sum_{i=1}^{v} c_{ij}\mathbf{u}_i. \tag{1}$$

To embed fingerprinted signal into still images, we use the Equation(2) where $\mathbf{y}_j$ is $j^{th}$ user's fingerprinted image, $\mathbf{x}$ is a host image, and $\alpha$ is scaling factor.

$$\mathbf{y}_j = \mathbf{x} + \alpha\mathbf{w}_j \tag{2}$$

To determine who are colluders, Trappe et al used the v dimensional collusion detection vector ($\hat{\mathbf{T}}$) as shown in Equation(3), which is correlation between $\mathbf{w}_j$ and $\{u_i\}$. The $\hat{\mathbf{T}}$ vector is converted to binary valued vector ($\hat{\mathbf{T}}_b$) using a predefined threshold value, which determines detection performance. If the '1' position between $\hat{\mathbf{T}}_b$ and all $\mathbf{c}_j$ ($j^{th}$ user's signature) matches, we can decide that $j^{th}$ user is suspected to be a traitor.

$$\hat{\mathbf{T}} = \{t_1, t_2, \cdots, t_v\} = \frac{\mathbf{w}_j \cdot \{\mathbf{u}_1, \mathbf{u}_2, \cdots, \mathbf{u}_v\}}{\sqrt{|\mathbf{w}_j|^2 \times |\mathbf{u}_i|^2}} \tag{3}$$

This collusion detection procedure (hard detection) is suggested in [2] with other two detection strategies (adaptive sorting approach, sequential algorithm), however, they did not consider any detection strategies for the linear combination collusion attack [2]. The linear collusion attack is generalized by the following Equation(4), where $\mathbf{z}$ denotes additive noise and $\varphi$ is the colluder set. If $j^{th}$ user does not participate in collusion ($j \notin \varphi$), the coefficient of $j^{th}$ user will be zero ($\beta_j = 0$).There are two constraints: (1) $\sum_{j=1}^{n} \beta_j = 1$ (not to decrease quality of image) and (2) if $j^{th}$ and $k^{th}$ users participate in collusion, $|\beta_j| \approx |\beta_k|$ (to equalize the probability of captured) [5].

$$\hat{\mathbf{y}} = \sum_{j=1}^{n} \beta_j \mathbf{y}_j + \mathbf{z} = \sum_{j=1}^{n} \beta_j \mathbf{x} + \sum_{j=1}^{n} \beta_j \mathbf{w}_j + \mathbf{z} = \mathbf{x} + \hat{\mathbf{w}} + \mathbf{z} \tag{4}$$

The average attack shown in Equation (5) and linear combinational collusion attack (LCCA) shown in Equation (6) is a special case of linear collusion attack.

$$\hat{\mathbf{w}} = \sum_{j \in \varphi} \frac{1}{k} \mathbf{w}_j, \quad where \ |\varphi| = k \qquad (5)$$

$$\hat{\mathbf{w}} = \sum_{j \in \varphi_1} (-1) \cdot \mathbf{w}_j + \sum_{k \in \varphi_2} (+1) \cdot \mathbf{w}_k, \qquad where \ |\varphi_2| - |\varphi_1| = 1 \qquad (6)$$

The anti-collusion code is reported to be resilient to average attack, but not to LCCA [6]. For example, if $1^{st}$, $4^{th}$ and $8^{th}$ users, whose fingerprint code are derived from (16, 4, 1)-BIBD collude, they will make pirated copy to $\hat{\mathbf{w}} = (\mathbf{w}_1 + \mathbf{w}_4 + \mathbf{w}_8)/3$ by average attack. The correlation with basis $\{\mathbf{u}_{i.}\}$ makes $\hat{\mathbf{T}}$ vectors as $\{-1/3, -1/3 \ 1/3 \ 1/3, 1 \ 1 \ 1/3 \ 1, 1/3 \ 1 \ 1/3 \ 1/3, 1/3 \ 1 \ 1/3 \ 1\}$. and is converted to $\{0 \ 0 \ 0 \ 0, 1 \ 1 \ 0 \ 1, 0 \ 1 \ 0 \ 0, 0 \ 1 \ 0 \ 1\}$. Finally, Comparing it with $\mathbf{C}$, the location of '1' uniquely identifies user 1, 4 and 8 are colluders. However, attackers can make their fingerprint using LCCA ($\hat{\mathbf{w}} = -\mathbf{w}_1 + \mathbf{w}_4 + \mathbf{w}_8$), and the correlation with basis $\{\mathbf{u}_{i.}\}$ make $\hat{\mathbf{T}}$ vector as $\{1 \ 1 \ 3 \ 3, 1 \ 1 \ -1 \ 1, -1 \ 1 \ -1 \ -1, -1 \ 1 \ -1 \ 1\}$ and the binary values are $\{1 \ 1 \ 1 \ 1, 1 \ 1 \ 0 \ 1, 0 \ 1 \ 0 \ 0, 0 \ 1 \ 0 \ 1\}$. In this case, the location of 1 gives no more clues to attackers (failure to collusion detection).

## 3 Scalable and Robust Fingerprint Scheme

In our scheme, we construct each user's fingerprint as the composition of ACC and a Gaussian distributed random signal (lambda). Lambda means the random signal. The dimension of code vectors (M) can be increased to fit the size of fingerprinting users. For fingerprint generation, we select one mark from M marks. The selected mark will be one of ACC, and the other marks will be lambda. For example, when the fingerprint ID is f(2,3), it means that we embed ACC #3 code in second mark, and Lambda on the other marks. Finally, the code is repeated R times and permuted. Like Boneh's scheme, the permutation sequence is unique to all users, but unknown to attackers. It also prevents interleaving collusion attack.

We embed fingerprint block by block basis, and we should select M times R suitable blocks to hide fingerprint signals as shown in Equation(7). We exploited human visual sensitivity using noise visibility function [10]. Each selected blocks are added by anti-collusion code or lambda code. Lambda code is generated using Gaussian distributed random sequence.

$$y_k = \begin{cases} x_k + (1-NVF)w_j, & w_j = \sum_{i=1}^{v} c_{ij}\mathbf{u}_{i.}, \quad k=1, \cdots, M \times R \\ x_k + (1-NVF)\lambda, & \lambda \sim N(0,\sigma^2) \end{cases} \qquad (7)$$

To make scalable-ACC robust median attack, we should have lambda signal, which is similar to ACC signal and the variance of lambda is important factor; the Figure 1 shows the ACC and lambda signal. When the variance of lambda signal gets small, colluders can easily classify ACC signal and lambda signal. The easy way to classify signal is taking the median value of pixels. As shown the Figure 1(b), the line graph shows effect of taking median values, dashed line means ACC signal, dotted lines are lambda signal whose variance is small, and solid line represent their median values. The solid line does not have any ACC signal. Though, if the variance of lambda gets larger than ACC signals, by taking maximum or minimum values, colluders also can escape identification. From the experimentation, we heuristically set the variance of lambda to be 16 (which is equal to v parameter of BIBD code design) when we use (16, 4, 1)-BIBD code. However, lambda signal can degrade the detection precision. To achieve detection performance and median attack robustness, all signals are repeated.

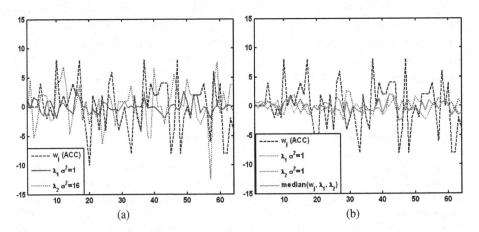

(a)                                    (b)

**Fig. 1.** Comparison of $w_j$ and $\lambda$ value for block size = 64: (a): ACC modulated signal $w_j$, and two lambda signals with different variance $\lambda_1$ ( $\sigma^2 = 1$ ) $\lambda_2$ ( $\sigma^2 = 16$ ), (b) ACC modulated signal $w_j$, two small variance lambda signals $\lambda_1$ ( $\sigma^2 = 1$ ) $\lambda_2$ ( $\sigma^2 = 1$ ), median ( $w_j, \lambda_1, \lambda_2$ ) signals

For fingerprint extraction, we used non-blind scheme. For each block, we compute Equation (8) and $f_k$ s are inversely permuted.

$$f_k = \frac{y_k - x_k}{1 - NVF} \qquad (8)$$

To detect colluder, we used the code matrix $\hat{\mathbf{T}}$ in Equation (9), and the $\hat{t}_{m,i}$ means $m^{th}$ mark's averaged correlation of $i^{th}$ basis. The v-dimensional column vectors of T represent each mark. If the signals $f_k$ are averaged, the variance of lambda will be decreased.

$$\hat{t}_{m,i} = \frac{1}{R}\sum_{k=1}^{R}\frac{f_{k+R(m-1)}\cdot \mathbf{u_i}}{\sqrt{|\mathbf{u_i}|^2}}, \ where \ m=1\cdots M, \ i=1\cdots v \qquad (9)$$

If there is no collusion, we can get either ACC or lambda, not both after extracting signals from each block ($f_k$). When collusion occurs, the signals will be mixed form of ACC and lambda (linear combination of ACC and lambda). However collusion occurs, the result will be complicated. But, we can use the fact that the statistics of ACC and lambda are very different. the $\hat{t}_{m,i}$ will be zero if it comes from $\lambda$ because the random signal and basis are uncorrelated. To differentiate ACC modulated signal $w_j$ and $\lambda$, we compute the score function as shown in Equation (10) for each mark. If the score is small for a mark, we do not consider the mark for colluder identification because the mark is mixed signal of $\lambda$. We focus on the high scored mark $\hat{m}$ for colluder identification.

$$Score_m = -\sqrt{\sum_{i=1}^{v}t_{mi}^2}\cdot \log[P(\tau_m \mid \mu=0)]$$
$$\hat{m} = \arg\max_{m=1\cdots M}(score_m) \qquad (10)$$

Equation (12) is composed of $\hat{t}_{m,i}$'s power and p-value. We compute $\hat{t}_{m,i}$'s power using $\sqrt{\sum_{i=1}^{v}t_{mi}^2}$, and compute the p-value $P(\tau_m \mid \mu=0)$, which is the probability of $\hat{t}_{m,i}$'being derived from $\lambda$, using the Equation(11).

$$P(\tau_m \mid \mu=0) = 2\int_{\tau_m}^{\infty}\frac{\Gamma[(r+1)/2]}{\sqrt{\pi r}\Gamma[r/2]}(1+w^2/r)^{-(r+1)/2}dw,$$
$$where \ r=v\text{-}1, \ \tau_m = \frac{\bar{t}_m - 0}{S/\sqrt{v}}, \ \bar{t}_m = \frac{1}{v}\sum_{i=1}^{v}t_{mi}, \ S = \frac{1}{v-1}\sum_{i=1}^{v}(t_{mi}-\bar{t})^2 \qquad (11)$$

When the power is higher and $P(\tau_m \mid \mu=0)$ is closer to zero, the score function gets higher than others. This score function comes from the basic idea of entropy function. After we compute scores for each mark, we inspect the highest scored mark. The mark should have more evidence of colluder than low scored marks. When the mark is linear combination lambda, we assume that the mean of column vector has student T distribution with v-1 degree.

Without collusion attack, population of lambda is known. However, collusion occurs, the population will be changed, and the number of colluders is not known. For instance, if we average two lambda signals whose variance is sigma, the result will be sigma/2. However the 2 is not known to detector. But we can compute an unbiased estimator of the variance of lambda. For statistical perspective, when the variance is not known, hypothesis test on mean uses t-test with student's T distribution.

For the highest scored mark, we use our angular decoding scheme which use singular property of (v, k, 1)-BIBD. Colluders can use LCCA, where they combine their fingerprint in various ways and some users can escape identification. For example, three colluders have fingerprints $w_1\lambda\lambda$, $w_2\lambda\lambda$ and $\lambda w_3\lambda$, and they combine their fingerprints such as $\hat{f}_1 = w_1\lambda\lambda + w_2\lambda\lambda - \lambda w_3\lambda$ or $\hat{f}_2 = -w_1\lambda\lambda + w_2\lambda\lambda + \lambda w_3\lambda$. In the case of $\hat{f}_1$, the extracted signals (three marks) are $< w_1 + w_2 - \lambda, \lambda + \lambda - w_3, \lambda + \lambda - \lambda >$, and we can capture 1[st] and 2[nd] users from mark 1, however, we cannot capture 3rd user from mark 2. Even worse, innocent users can be under suspicion. In the case of $\hat{f}_2$, we can only capture 3rd user in mark 2, and no way for 1st and 2nd user. In this section, we present angular decoding scheme to capture LCCA colluders.

The direct sequence spreading makes collusion into linear combination of each user's fingerprint code. Mathematically, it says $\mathbf{T} = \beta_1\mathbf{c}_{.1} + \beta_2\mathbf{c}_{.2} + \cdots + \beta_n\mathbf{c}_{.n} = \mathbf{C}\boldsymbol{\beta}$ For example, if 1[st] and 3[rd] users are collude by averaging, the solution of $\boldsymbol{\beta}$ will be $\{1/2, 0, 1/2, 0, \cdots, 0\}$ But it is hard to estimate $\boldsymbol{\beta}$ from $\hat{\mathbf{T}}$ which is modeled as $\hat{\mathbf{T}} = \mathbf{C}\boldsymbol{\beta} + \mathbf{d}$, where $\mathbf{T}, \mathbf{d} \in R^{v\times 1}$, $\mathbf{C} \in \{-1,1\}^{v\times n}$ and $\boldsymbol{\beta} \in R^{n\times 1}$. $\mathbf{d}$ is the processing error and noise, that can be observed at $\hat{\mathbf{T}}$. To estimate $\boldsymbol{\beta}$, we compute Equation(12): [7, 8].

$$\min_{\boldsymbol{\beta} \in R^{n\times 1}} \left\| \hat{\mathbf{T}} - \mathbf{C}\boldsymbol{\beta} \right\|^2 \tag{12}$$

Equation (12) is called least square problem and finding exact solution is NP-hard [7]. If the $\boldsymbol{\beta}$'s domain is finite, we can use sphere decoding to solve Equation (12) [8], LCCA (linear combination collusion attack) does not give change for finite domain, However we can use the singular property of (v,k,1)-BIBD, the angles between any of two user's fingerprinting code ($\mathbf{c}_{.i}, \mathbf{c}_{.j}$   $i \neq j$) are computed as Theorem 1.

**Lemma 1.** Let $\mathbf{C}_i$ as i[th] block from (v, k, 1)-BIBD, which represents i[th] user's finger print code, and let $\mathbf{C}_j$ as j[th] block from (v, k, 1)-BIBD, which represents j[th] user's fingerprint code. For any i and j, any two blocks ($\mathbf{C}_i$ and $\mathbf{C}_j$) will share at most one element. Mathematically, $n(\mathbf{C}_i \cap \mathbf{C}_j) = 0 \ or \ 1$.

**Proof.** It can be derived from definition of BIBD easily. Because each pair of element of $\chi$ determines only one block, the element of intersection between arbitrary two bl ocks cannot exceed two [2].

**Theorem 1.** The angle $a_{jk}$ between arbitrary two users (j[th] user and k[th] user) ' fingerpr int codes are

$$a_{jk} = \cos^{-1}\left(\sum_{i=1}^{v} c_{ij} c_{ik} \middle/ \left(\sqrt{\sum_{i=1}^{v} c_{ij}^2} \cdot \sqrt{\sum_{i=1}^{v} c_{ik}^2}\right)\right)$$

$$= \cos^{-1}\left(1 - \frac{4(k-1)}{v}\right) \text{ or } \cos^{-1}\left(1 - \frac{4k}{v}\right)$$

**Proof.** The norm of $j^{th}$ user's fingerprint code ($\sqrt{\sum_{i=1}^{v} c_{ij}^2}$) is $\sqrt{v}$ by the definition of (v, k, 1)-BIBD. The norm of $k^{th}$ user's fingerprint code ($\sqrt{\sum_{i=1}^{v} c_{ik}^2}$) is $\sqrt{v}$ by the definition of (v, k, 1)-BIBD. We can compute $\sum_{i=1}^{v} c_{ij} \cdot c_{ik}$ by comparing the sign of each element. If $i^{th}$ elements of j-th and k-th user have same sign, the multiplication of the two elements will be 1. Otherwise -1 ($\because$ Domain of C is $\{-1,1\}$). Therefore, $\sum_{i=1}^{v} c_{ij} \cdot c_{ik} = \#$ of $same-sign$ $elements$ (S) $-$ $\#$ of $different-sign$ $elements$ (D). The number of different-sign elements D is $n(\mathbf{C}_j \cup \mathbf{C}_k) - n(\mathbf{C}_j \cap \mathbf{C}_k)$, and the number of same-sign elements S is $v - D = v - [n(\mathbf{C}_j \cup \mathbf{C}_k) - n(\mathbf{C}_j \cap \mathbf{C}_k)]$. Using Lemma 1, we can simplify the D and S as follows.

$$D = n(\mathbf{C}_i \cup \mathbf{C}_j) - n(\mathbf{C}_i \cap \mathbf{C}_j) = n(\mathbf{C}_i) + n(\mathbf{C}_j) - 2n(\mathbf{C}_i \cap \mathbf{C}_j)$$

$$= 2(k - n(\mathbf{C}_i \cap \mathbf{C}_j)) = 2(k-1) \text{ or } 2k$$

$$S = v - D = v - 2(k-1) \text{ or } v - 2k$$

$$\therefore \sum_{i=1}^{v} c_{ij} c_{ik} = v - 2(k-1) - 2(k-1) \text{ or } v - 2k - 2k$$

$$= v - 4(k-1) \text{ or } v - 4k$$

$$a_{jk} = \cos^{-1}\left(1 - \frac{4(k-1)}{v}\right) \text{ or } \cos^{-1}\left(1 - \frac{4k}{v}\right)$$

To identify colluder, we compute the angles between $\hat{\mathbf{T}}$ and each user's fingerprint codes ($\mathbf{c}_{.j}$) using Equation(13). If $j^{th}$ user participates in collusion, the angle $a_{jt}$ between $j^{th}$ user's fingerprint code and $\hat{\mathbf{T}}$ is closer to 0 or $\pi$.

$$a_{jt} = \cos^{-1}\left(\sum_{i=1}^{v} t_i \cdot c_{ij} \middle/ \sqrt{\sum_{i=1}^{v} t_i^2 \cdot \sum_{i=1}^{v} c_{ij}^2}\right) \tag{13}$$

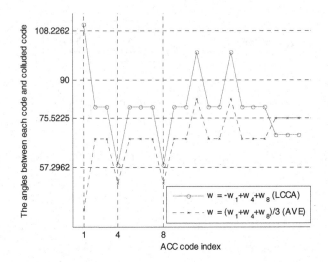

**Fig. 2.** The angles between $\hat{T}$ and $c_{\cdot j}$ after average attack and LCCA

Figure 2 shows the result of Equation (13) which computes the angles between $\hat{T}$ and $c_{\cdot j}$ , after $1^{st}$ $4^{th}$ and $8^{th}$ users collude using average attack($\hat{w} = (w_1 + w_4 + w_8)/3$) and LCCA ($\hat{w} = -w_1 + w_4 + w_8$ ).In this case, we can suspect $1^{st}$, $4^{th}$ and $8^{th}$ users after an average attack and $4^{th}$ and $8^{th}$ users after LCCA.

## 4   Analysis and Experimental Results

We experimented with the standard test images, and Figure. 3 shows test images and their enlarged fingerprints. To generate fingerprint signal we used (16, 4, 1)-BIBD and the Hadamard matrix whose size is 4096 (64x64) for orthogonal basis. We used $\lambda \sim N(0,4^2)$ for $\lambda$ signal and we chose $\sigma^2$ as 16.0 experimentally to tradeoff between median attack robustness and false positive error rate. After fingerprint embedding, the average PSNR is over 42 dB with good subjective quality.

We tested our scalable fingerprinting code for various collusion attacks (average, median, min, max, min-max, modified negative, randomized negatives and LCCA) for the test images. Average collusion is widely used collusion attack [13], because it is efficient to attack fingerprints, and also it makes better image quality after collusion (usually it increases 4-5 dB). Figure 4 shows a collusion example, when five colluders make pirated copies from their fingerprinted copies. It shows original image, five fingerprinted images, and colluded images after average, median, and LCCA. As shown in Figure 4, the average and median attacks make better image quality after collusion; however, LCCA spoils the quality of colluded image. There are many ways for collusion in LCCA, and we use $\hat{f} = -w_1 \lambda\lambda\lambda\lambda\lambda\lambda - \lambda\lambda w_4 \lambda\lambda\lambda\lambda + w_2 \lambda\lambda\lambda\lambda\lambda\lambda$ $+ \lambda\lambda w_5 \lambda\lambda\lambda\lambda + \lambda\lambda\lambda\lambda w_7 \lambda\lambda\lambda$ for our LCCA collusion.

Figure 5 shows the fingerprint detection result (T vectors) after average and median attack, respectively. The score results recommend that we should suspect highest scored mark #1. Next, we need to investigate $1^{st}$ column of T matrix in detail. With detailed investigation, $1^{st}$ and $2^{nd}$ ACC codes are extracted from mark 1. After average and median attack, angular decoding scheme and hard decision scheme can correctly trace colluders.

**Fig. 3.** Fingerprinted images, and their fingerprints (Enlarged) The number of Marks (M) =8, Repetition factor (R) =2, Block size = 64x64, (top) Baboon (PSNR: 38.86 dB), (second) Lena (PSNR: 42.84 dB), (third) Boat (PSNR: 41.25 dB), (bottom) F16 (PSNR: 42.46 dB)

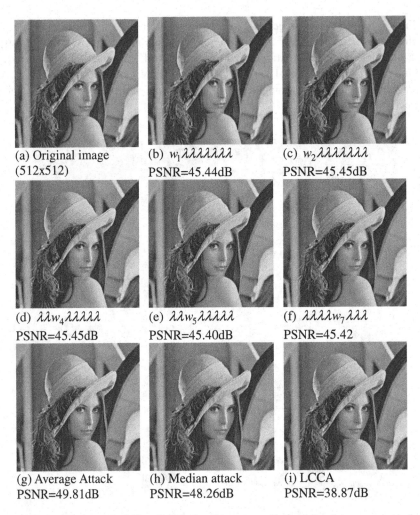

(a) Original image
(512x512)

(b) $w_1 \lambda\lambda\lambda\lambda\lambda\lambda\lambda$
PSNR=45.44dB

(c) $w_2 \lambda\lambda\lambda\lambda\lambda\lambda\lambda$
PSNR=45.45dB

(d) $\lambda\lambda w_4 \lambda\lambda\lambda\lambda\lambda$
PSNR=45.45dB

(e) $\lambda\lambda w_5 \lambda\lambda\lambda\lambda\lambda$
PSNR=45.40dB

(f) $\lambda\lambda\lambda\lambda w_7 \lambda\lambda\lambda$
PSNR=45.42

(g) Average Attack
PSNR=49.81dB

(h) Median attack
PSNR=48.26dB

(i) LCCA
PSNR=38.87dB

**Fig. 4.** (a) original image, (b-f) five fingerprinted images, collusion after (g) average attack (h) median attack, and (i) LCCA. (Repetition factor = 2, number of marks = 8).

Figure 6 shows the fingerprint detection result (T vectors) after linear combination collusion attack. After the attack, the mark #3 gets highest score, we can suspect the users in mark 3 and angular decoding scheme traces correct colluder ACC #4 in mark 3, but hard decision capture the innocent colluders. The reason why innocent users are captured is the fingerprint copy of user whose signal is acc #4 in mark 4, is negatively summed and its signal is reversed. In summary, angular decoding scheme can detect LCCA, average, and median attack.

To evaluate our angular decoding scheme without scalability, we generated 20 user's fingerprint signal, and performs average collusion, median collusion, and linear combination collusion for randomly chosen 3 users. We added white Gaussian

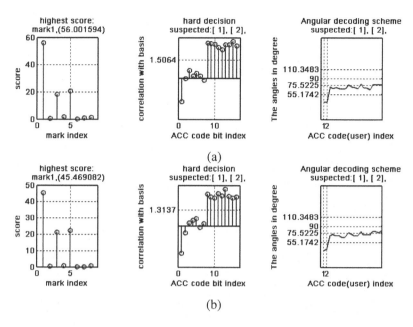

**Fig. 5.** Angular decoding scheme and hard detection result: (a) after average attack shown in Figure 4 (g), (b) after median attack shown in Figure 4 (h)

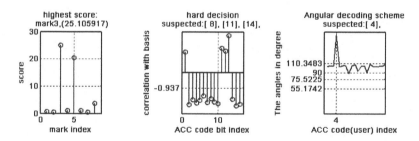

**Fig. 6.** Angular decoding scheme and hard detection result after linear combination collusion attack shown in Figure 4 (i)

random noise according to WNR (watermark to noise ratio), which is $WNR = 20\log_{10}\left(\left\|\mathbf{w}_j\right\| / \left\|\mathbf{d}\right\|\right)$ . In this experiment, we do not apply scalable fingerprinting scheme and we only use simple anti-collusion code to compare detection performance.

Figure 7 shows that angular decoding scheme is superior to hard detection for all attacks. Although attackers collude using the LCCA, colluders can not escape identification with angular decoding strategy. The fraction of captured means the at least one colluder is captured. ( $D \neq \varnothing, D \subset R$ , where D: detected colluders set and R: real colluders set).

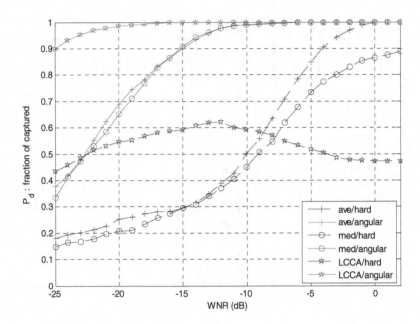

**Fig. 7.** The performance compared with hard decoding and angular decoding using (16, 4, 1)-BIBD and 256 dimension basis

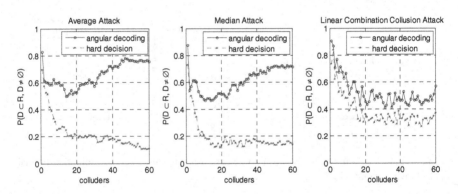

**Fig. 8.** Randomly select k users as colluders from total 160 users and compare the result with 200 iterations, after collusion, 3x3 median filter applied to remove noise and fingerprint

Figure 8 shows the collusion performance of scalable anti-collusion code. The horizontal line represents the number of colluders. We randomly select colluders, and perform collusion, and detection. After detection, we compare detection result and previously selected colluders. When, the detected colluders are subset of real colluders, we considered it as success, which means that at least one colluder is captured, and there are no innocent users. Y-axis represents success ratio, and, the solid line shows the angular decoding scheme and the dotted line represents hard decision. It shows that the performance of angular decoding scheme is better then hard decision scheme, under various collusion attack cases. After the LCCA, the angular decoding scheme shows better performance than hard decision scheme.

## 5  Conclusions

In this paper, we presented a scalable ACC fingerprinting scheme, which covers large number of fingerprint codes and angular decoding scheme robust to LCCA An ACC (anti-collusion code) is hard to support large number of users (To support large users, the length of basis must be long. The longer basis is hard to hide and handle) and does not consider linear combination collusion attack We constructed the scalable fingerprint by spreading BIBD codes over M×R (M: number of marks; R: repetition factor) image blocks. To improve the detection performance, we repeated embedding the same fingerprints over R image blocks. To increase the robustness over average and median attack, we designed a scalable ACC scheme using a Gaussian distributed random variable. We evaluated our fingerprints on standard test images, and showed good collusion detection performance over average and median collusion attacks and moderate performance over LCCA. An angular decoding scheme makes ACC not vulnerable to LCCA. Although the scalability scheme makes collusion more complex and decreases detection performance of angular decoding scheme; it can easily control the supported max users. And with block embedding, the fingerprint signals can be embedded in motion vectors in video codec.

## References

1. 1 Yacobi, Y.: Improved Boneh-Shaw Content Fingerprinting. In: Proc. CTRSA 2001, pp. 378–391 (2001)
2. Trappe, W., Wu, M., Wangm, Z.J., Liu, K.J.R.: Anti-Collusion Fingerprinting for Multimedia. IEEE Trans. Signal Proc. 51, 1069–1087 (2003)
3. Boneh, D., Shaw, J.: Collusion-Secure Fingerprinting for Digital Data. IEEE Trans. Inform. Theory 44, 1897–1905 (1998)
4. Colbourn, C.J., Dinitz, J.H.: The CRC Handbook of Combinatorial Design. CRC Press, Boca Raton, FL (1996)
5. Kundur, D., Karthik, K.: Video Fingerprinting and Encryption Principles for Digital Rights Management. IEEE Proc. 92, 918–932 (2004)
6. Wu., Y.: Linear Combination Collusion Attacks and its Application on an Anti-Collusion Fingerprinting. IEEE Conf. on Acoustics, Speech, and Signal Processing 51, 1069–1087 (2005)
7. Hassibi, B., Vikalo, H.: On the Sphere Decoding Algorithm I. Expected Complexity. IEEE trans. on signal processing 53, 2806–2818 (2005)
8. Li., Z., Trappe, W.: Collusion-Resistant Fingerprinting from WBE sequence Sets. IEEE Conf. on communications 2, 1336–1340 (2005)
9. Voloshynovskiy, S., Herrige, A., Baumgaertner, N., Pun, T.: A Stochastic Approach to Content Adaptive Digital Image Watermarking. In: 3rd Int. Workshop on Information Hiding. LNCS, vol. 1768, pp. 211–236. Springer, Heidelberg (1999)

10. Watson, A.B., Borthwick, R., Taylor, M.: Image Quality and Entropy Masking. In: SPIE Conf. Human Vision, Visual Processing, and Digital Display VI (1997)
11. Kim, S.W., Suthaharan, S., Lee, H.K., Rao, K.R.: An Image Watermarking Scheme using Visual Model and BN Distribution. IEE Elect. Letter, 35(3) (February 1999)
12. Walpole, R.E., Myers, R.H., Myers, S.L.: Probability and Statistics for Engineers and Scientists, 6/e. Prentice-Hall, Englewood Cliffs (1998)
13. Zhao, H., Wu, M., Wang, J., Ray Liu, K.J.: Nonlinear Collusion Attacks on Independent Fingerprints for Multimedia. ICASSP 5, 664–667 (2003)

# A Collusion-Resistant Video Watermarking Scheme

Amir Houmansadr[1] and Shahrokh Ghaemmaghami[2]

[1] Electrical Engineering Department, Sharif University of Technology, Tehran, Iran
houmansadr@mehr.sharif.edu
[2] Electronics Research Center, Sharif University of Technology, Tehran, Iran
ghaemmag@sharif.edu

**Abstract.** A video watermarking scheme is proposed in this paper using the concept of the secret sharing scheme. The owner's mark is split into twin shares, where the shares are inserted into the video frames in the spatial domain in a simple manner. The detection algorithm uses a linear function applied to the twin shares to reconstruct the secret. This makes the watermarked video sequence robust against pirate attacks, such as frame averaging and frame swapping. Due to the compatibility of the exploited secret sharing scheme to geometrical distortions, the watermarking system is also robust to this kind of processing schemes. On account of insertion of various marks into different frames, which are linearly related, the watermarked sequence is robust to collusion attack that is a major concern in the field of video watermarking.

## 1   Introduction

Illegal copying and distribution of digital media has made the owner's rights to be more and more frequently violated. Traditional solutions for copyright protection, such as encryption, can no longer protect digital contents by themselves. Sooner or later, encrypted media have to be revealed for the aim of consumer's usage that may be the malicious one. At the end of $20^{th}$ century, digital watermarking was introduced as a complementary solution to protection of digital media ownership.

In copyright protection applications, a digital watermark is an invisible mark that is inserted into a digital media such as audio, image, or video, which is used to identify illegal distributions of copyright protected digital media and also law-breaking customers. A digital watermark should have certain features to achieve desired functionalities in this case. The embedded mark is to be robust enough against various watermarking attacks, while keeping the perceived quality of the host image unchanged (the imperceptibility requirement). Watermarking attacks consist of deliberate attacks made maliciously to remove or change the mark sequence by lawbreakers and unintentional attacks caused as a result of different kinds of coding and compression made to the digital media prior to transmission and/or storage and also errors occurred during the transmission of the media through networks.

J. Camenisch et al. (Eds.): IH 2006, LNCS 4437, pp. 343–354, 2007.

Video contents can be mentioned as the most valuable digital media, which are increasingly used illegally, resulting in a huge damage to filmmaking industry. Video watermarking is utilized for different video applications such as copyright protection, fingerprinting, broadcast monitoring, copy protection, and so on [1]. Distinct challenges have arisen in this field, as compared to image watermarking. Because of the more possibilities to perform the collusion attack on video streams, it is a main concern in designing video watermarking systems. Collusion refers to using some watermarked data that is utilized for the aim of watermark removal.

The main goal of this paper is to design a watermarking scheme for video sequences which is robust to collusion attack. In Sect. 2, the main concept of secret sharing is introduced. Sect. 3 describes the proposed insertion and detection watermarking schemes based on the mentioned secret sharing scheme. The collusion attack, in the proposed scheme, is analyzed in Sect. 4 and simulation results are presented in Sect. 5. Finally, the paper is concluded in Sect. 6.

## 2    Visual Secret Sharing

A secret sharing scheme shares a secret into a number of shares so that the cooperation of a predetermined group of shareholders reveals the secret, while the secret reconstruction is impossible to any unauthorized set of shareholders. *Naor et al.* in [2] proposed a 2-dimentional secret sharing scheme which is known as visual secret sharing (VSS). Since we are using this scheme in the proposed watermarking scheme in this paper, VSS scheme is described in this section.

VSS scheme shares a binary-valued image, which is known as secret image, into two double-sized images so that reconstruction of the secret image from these twin images can be done only if both of them are available. So, a VSS system is composed of the following components:

- Secret image: a digital image composed of $M \times N$ white and black pixels, whose anonymity is the goal of the system;

- VSS sharing scheme: derives two share-images from a secret image in a pseudo-random manner;

- Share-images: digital images composed of $2M \times 2N$ white and black pixels, that are driven from the secret image in a pseudo-random manner. Two share-images are produced in every run of the VSS sharing scheme, known as twin share-images. Different runs of the VSS scheme generates different share-images, and each of these share-images reveals no information about the secret image unless its twin, i.e. the share-image generated in the same run of the VSS sharing scheme, is available;

-VSS reconstruction scheme: retrieves the secret image from every corresponding couple of share-images, i.e. twin share-images. VSS reconstruction scheme is lossless if share-images have not been distorted in any way.

According to the VSS sharing scheme, each pixel in the secret image is split into two $2 \times 2$ blocks of pixels, which are chosen form the blocks shown in Fig. 1.

This leads to two double-sized share-images for every secret image. For the aim of sharing a white pixel from the secret image, two corresponding share blocks within the twin share-images are chosen the same. In other words, one of the six blocks in Fig. 1 is selected for both of the share-images. On the other hand, if we aim to share a black pixel from the secret image, different blocks from the same type of blocks are chosen, e.g. two different horizontal share blocks. Therefore there is 6 alternatives to share either a black or a white pixel and there are $6^{M \times N}$ solutions for the problem of sharing an $M \times N$ pixels binary-valued secret image. Fig. 2 illustrates the twin share-images corresponding to the shown secret image.

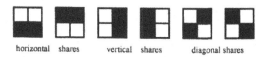

horizontal   shares        vertical   shares        diagonal shares

**Fig. 1.** Different blocks which are used to share a pixel in the secret image

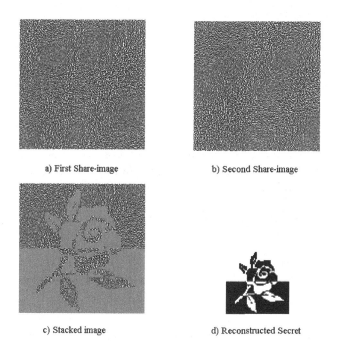

a) First Share-image            b) Second Share-image

c) Stacked image            d) Reconstructed Secret

**Fig. 2.** Different blocks which are used to share a pixel in the secret image

Different mechanisms can be devised for the aim of reconstructing an $M \times N$ pixels secret image, $S$, from one of its twin share-images, $SH1$, and $SH2$. Fig. 3 shows the scheme of a simple system which we propose to be used as the VSS reconstruction scheme in this paper.

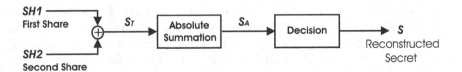

**Fig. 3.** Block diagram of the proposed VSS reconstruction scheme

First, twin share-images are added together to generate $S_T$, which we call it the stacked-image. This is because addition of twin share-images resembles printing them on two transparent sheets and then stacking them together. By allocating +1 and -1 values to white and black pixels respectively in the share-images, pixels of $S_T$ will have one of the +2, -2, or 0 values. Recalling the VSS sharing scheme mentioned above, if $S_T$ is divided into non-overlapping blocks of $2 \times 2$ pixels, each block corresponding to a white pixel of the secret image have two +2 and two -2 values, while every block corresponding to a black pixel have four 0 values. So, by applying an absolute summation over every block of $S_T$ as in (2), we can decide whether the block represents a white or a black pixel in the secret image. This is done as below:

$$S(x,y) = \begin{cases} +1 & if \quad S_A(x,y) = 8 \\ -1 & if \quad S_A(x,y) = 0 \end{cases}, \tag{1}$$

where:

$$S_A(x,y) = \sum_{m=0}^{1} \sum_{n=0}^{1} |S_T(2x-m, 2y-n)| \quad x = 1..M, y = 1..N . \tag{2}$$

The proposed reconstruction scheme acts as a lossless reverse function for the mentioned VSS sharing scheme. As we will see in the next section, share-images are inserted as digital watermarks into video frames. In a watermarking system, it is expected that the inserted marks get distorted because of different losses due to the noisy channel, watermark extraction scheme, and so on. As a result, we modify the mentioned reconstruction scheme to be used in the proposed watermarking scheme efficiently:

$$S(x,y) = \begin{cases} +1 & if \quad S_A(x,y) > 4 \\ -1 & if \quad S_A(x,y) \leq 4 \end{cases}. \tag{3}$$

## 3   The Proposed Watermarking Scheme

In the proposed watermarking scheme watermark, $W$, is a sequence of $M \times N$ bits (+1 and -1 values), where every frame of the video sequence is $2M$ by $2N$ pixels in size. The video stream is first divided into several successive GOPs (Group Of Pictures) with the length of $L$, where $L$ is an even number, e.g. 12. Considering the $M \times N$ bits watermark sequence as an $M$ by $N$ pixels image, for the $i$-th GOP , i.e. $F_{i,j}$, $j=1...L$, the VSS scheme is performed $L/2$ times to split the watermark image, $W$, into $L$ sub-watermarks, i.e. $W_{i,j}$, $j=1...L$ (two sub-watermarks are produced in every run of the VSS scheme). These sub-watermarks are inserted into the frames of the corresponding GOP as:

$$F_{i,j}^W = F_{i,j} + JND_{i,j}.Per_j(\{W_{i,j}|j=1..L\}), \quad i=1..Num \ , \tag{4}$$

where $F_{i,j}^W$ is the $j$-th frame of the $i$-th GOP in the watermarked video sequence, $JND_{i,j}$ is the weighting coefficient corresponding to $F_{i,j}$, $Num$ is the number of GOPs in the video sequence, and $Per(.)$ applies a permutation to the sub-watermarks of the $i$-th GOP by changing their order of appearance. As a simple permutation function, modular permutation can be used as:

$$Per_j(\{W_{i,j}|j=1..L\}) = W_{i,m}, \quad m = mod(p.j, L) + 1 \ . \tag{5}$$

$mod(x,y)$ is the modular residue of $x$ with respect to $y$. Mathematically, if $p$ is an integer number which is prime relative to $L$, the original video frames and the permuted video frames are related through a one-to-one relationship.

Choosing the $JND_{i,j}$ coefficients equal to a constant number leads to a simple and fast watermarking scheme, while a more robust watermarked video stream would be achieved, if the coefficients are adopted to the video frames as cited in the next section.

Fig. 4 shows the block diagram of the watermark extraction scheme. First, a noise estimator block is performed on the received possibly watermarked video sequence. Since the embedded sub-watermarks are noise-like, this leads to an efficient estimation of them as in (6). To design a noise estimator, different approaches have been suggested in the literature [3,4,5]. Our simulations show that using a simple FFT (Fast Fourier Transform) filter provides a fast and effective estimation of the inserted sub-watermarks. Fig. 5 shows the basic structure of the utilized FFT filter. The two-dimensional FFT transform of the video frame, $IM$, is passed through a masking stage which drops its low-frequency components and then an inverse two-dimensional FFT transform is performed.

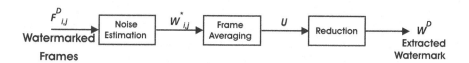

**Fig. 4.** Block diagram of the watermark extraction scheme

**Fig. 5.** Block diagram of the FFT filtering

$$W_{i,j}^* \approx W_{i,j} = \frac{1}{JND_{i,j}}(F_{i,j}^W - F_{i,j}), \quad i = 1..Num, j = 1..L . \tag{6}$$

After noise estimation, $W_{i,j}^*$ is an appropriate estimation of the inserted sub-watermark $W_{i,j}$. To retrieve the original watermark, $W$, from the sequence of estimated sub-watermarks, $W^*$ sequence is passed from two more blocks. First, an average is computed over the frames of the resulting video sequence as:

$$U = \frac{2}{Num.L} \sum_{i=1}^{Num} \sum_{j=1}^{L} W_{i,j}^* . \tag{7}$$

The resulting $2M \times 2N$ pixels image, $U$, is then passed from a reduction function which returns the $M \times N$ pixels extracted watermark as:

$$W^D(x,y) = \begin{cases} +1 & if \quad R(x,y) > 4 \\ -1 & elsewhere \end{cases}, \tag{8}$$

where $W_D(x,y)$ is the $(x,y)$-th pixel of the extracted watermark and $R(x,y)$ is defined as:

$$R(x,y) = \sum_{i=0}^{1} \sum_{j=0}^{1} |U(2x-i, 2y-j)|, \quad 1 \le x \le M, \quad 1 \le y \le N . \tag{9}$$

Finally, a normalized correlation is evaluated between $W_D$ and the watermark sequence, $W$, as:

$$\rho = \frac{\sum\limits_{x=1}^{M} \sum\limits_{y=1}^{N} W^D(x,y).W(x,y)}{\sqrt{\sum\limits_{x=1}^{M} \sum\limits_{y=1}^{N} W^D(x,y). \sum\limits_{x=1}^{M} \sum\limits_{y=1}^{N} W(x,y)}} . \tag{10}$$

This correlation is compared by a threshold value, $TH$, to decide if the watermark $W$ exists in the video sequence received.

The main idea behind the definition of reduction function is the structure cited for VSS reconstruction scheme in the previous section. In fact, passing average of the frames, $U$, through the reduction function is equivalent to applying the mentioned reconstruction function to the twin share-images and then returning the average value.

## 4   Collusion Analyses

Collusion refers to a set of users who merge their knowledge to have access to the unwatermarked contents. Collusion can be performed in two different manners. In collusion type-I the same watermark is embedded into different data, which can be estimated by a linear combination and removed from the watermarked contents. On the other hand, collusion type-II refers to the case where different watermarks are embedded into different copies of the same data. In this case colluders can obtain the unwatermarked data by a simple linear combination of different copies, e.g. averaging. This is because averaging different watermarks generally converges toward zero.

There are also two different approaches to implementation of collusion attack in the case of video watermarking. Inter-videos collusion refers to a number of users who have different videos containing the same watermark, or the same videos with different embedded watermarks, where collusions type-I and II could be applied respectively. Inter-videos collusion is the same as what have been considered for still images, so the solutions can be borrowed from the literature. For instance, inserting a Trusted Third Party in the watermarking system, which produces and encrypts hash of the host data, is proposed to prevent collusion type-I. Also, traditional countermeasures exist for collusion type-II which are based on the projective geometry or the theory of combinational designs [1].

In the case of video watermarking, there is another kind of collusion which is a video-specific origin. Intra-video collusion is the main threat to video watermarking, because a watermarked video alone is enough to remove the watermark. Inserting the same watermark in each frame, which is the baseline of many video watermarking schemes, makes collusion type-I feasible exploiting frames of the video sequence as watermarked images. On the other hand, by inserting different watermarks into different frames, collusion type-II can be implemented in static scenes, since there are similar frames with different watermarks. Intra-video collusion is considered in this research which is investigated in the proposed watermarking scheme in the following sections.

### 4.1 Linear Collusion

For a set of watermarked frames $F_k^W = F_k + \beta_k W_k$, $k=1,..,(Num.L)$, and their corresponding raw video frames, $F_k$ , the linear collusion attack is made as:

$$\overline{X} = \sum_{k=1}^{L} \beta_k F_k^W = \sum_{k=1}^{L} \beta_k F_k + \sum_{k=1}^{L} \beta_k \alpha_k W_k^* \ , \tag{11}$$

where $W_k^*$ is the possibly distorted watermark sequence, and $\beta_k$ is a weighting coefficient. $\overline{X}$ gives an optimal MSE (Mean Squared Error) estimate of the watermark or the host signal in the case of collusions type-I or type-II, respectively [6].

In the proposed watermarking scheme, different sub-watermarks are inserted into different frames. As a result, collusion type-I is entirely infeasible. In fact, collusion type-I needs some video frames containing the same watermark to be estimated by some linear combination such as frame averaging. Even if the original watermark, $W$, is estimated by attacker in some way, it can not be used to produce the unwatermarked video sequence; this is because what is inserted into video frames is not the original watermark, $W$, itself but sub-watermarks, $W_{i,j}$, which has been obtained from it in a pseudo-random manner during different runs of the VSS scheme. So, we just have to investigate collusion type-II on the proposed scheme.

The main idea in this research to defeat collusion is to insert different sub-watermarks into video frames so that a linear combination of them results in the main watermark sequence. As we mentioned in Sect. 3, the watermark is extracted by performing a linear combination on the video frames, i.e. averaging (see (7) and (8)).

Collusion type-II, e.g. averaging, is performed by modifying a number of successive frames in still regions of the watermarked video sequence, $F_i^W$, $i=1,..,k$, as:

$$\overline{F_i^W} = \tfrac{1}{k} \sum_{j=1}^{k} F_j^W = \tfrac{1}{k} \sum_{j=1}^{k} F_j + \tfrac{1}{k} \sum_{j=1}^{k} JND_j W_j^*$$
$$\approx F_i + \tfrac{1}{k} \sum_{j=1}^{k} JND_j W_j^* \tag{12}$$

where the second line of the above equation is valid in still regions of video sequence. So, evaluating $U$ from (6), (7), and (12) is as follows:

$$U = \tfrac{2}{Num.L} \sum_{i=1}^{Num} \sum_{j=1}^{L} W_{i,j}^* = \tfrac{2}{Num.L} \sum_{p=1}^{Num.L} W_p^*$$
$$= \tfrac{2}{Num.L} \sum_{p=1}^{k} W_p^* + \tfrac{2}{Num.L} \sum_{p=k+1}^{Num.L} W_p^* \tag{13}$$
$$= \tfrac{2}{Num.L} \sum_{p=1}^{k} \tfrac{1}{JND_p} \tfrac{1}{k} \sum_{j=1}^{k} JND_j W_j^* + \tfrac{2}{Num.L} \sum_{p=k+1}^{Num.L} W_p^*$$

Even if the $JND$ coefficients are not constant, they are very similar in still regions, because they depend on the host frames. So, $U$ is evaluated as:

$$U = \tfrac{2}{Num.L} \sum_{p=1}^{k} \tfrac{1}{k} \sum_{j=1}^{k} W_j^* + \tfrac{2}{Num.L} \sum_{p=k+1}^{Num.L} W_p^*$$
$$= \tfrac{2}{Num.L} \sum_{j=1}^{k} W_j^* + \tfrac{2}{Num.L} \sum_{p=k+1}^{Num.L} W_p^* \tag{14}$$
$$= \tfrac{2}{Num.L} \sum_{j=1}^{Num.L} W_j^*$$

which is the same as (7). So, linear collusion has no effect on the detection process of the proposed scheme.

We simulated the collusion type-II on *hawk3* video sequence which was watermarked using the proposed scheme. As mentioned earlier, watermark detection in the proposed scheme is performed by evaluating a normalized correlation and comparing it by an appropriate detection threshold. Choosing this threshold is a tradeoff between minimizing wrong rejection and wrong confirmation of the watermark. This threshold should be chosen in respect to the average True to False detection Ratio (TFR) which is opted to 0.15 in our simulations. A watermarking attack to be effective should decrease the correlation coefficient below this detection threshold, making the watermark signal undetectable. So, we investigated the effect of collusion on the watermarked video by surveying the amount of decrement enforced to the correlation coefficient. The mentioned video sequence has also been watermarked by CDMA scheme proposed by *Mobasseri* [7], which is a well-known similar video watermarking scheme, and the effect of collusion type-II on two schemes has been compared. To make a fair judgment, both watermarked sequences have the same watermark energy. Fig. 6 illustrates the effect of collusion type-II on the watermarked sequences versus number of frames exploited in performing the collusion attack. Simulations show that CDMA scheme is clearly vulnerable to collusion attack and the watermark is undetectable as the number of colluded frames increases. In contrary, the proposed scheme which is fundamentally similar to CDMA scheme shows a great amount of robustness to this kind of attack. As the number of colluded frames grows, detection coefficient in the proposed scheme varies around a fixed value near the correlation coefficient of the collusion-free detection.

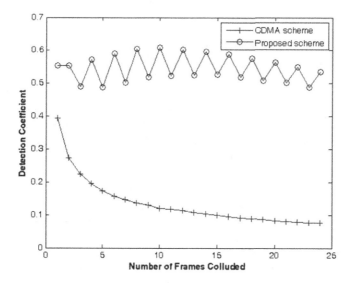

**Fig. 6.** Block diagram of the FFT (Detection coefficient vs. number of frames used for making collusion type-II for proposed scheme and CDMA watermarking scheme. Watermarks have the same energy in two schemes.

As it can be seen, simulation results are in conformity with mathematical analysis presented earlier regarding robustness of the proposed watermarking scheme against collusion attack. The alternating behavior of the proposed scheme in Fig. 6 is due to the fact that for odd number of frames one of the frames missing its twin frame acts as noise which reduces the system functionality; this effect decreases as the number of colluded frames increases.

## 4.2    Generalized Collusion

Even if the collusion is not linear, the watermark can be extracted efficiently. As described in the previous section, collusion type-I is infeasible due to inserting different watermarks into different frames. So, we just have to investigate collusion type-II.

As mentioned previously, collusion type-II is performed over the still regions. So, we propose to use only moving objects of video frames in evaluating $U$ from (7) because colluders cannot change the sub-watermarks in these regions. As described in Sect. 3, corresponding shares of the watermark are inserted in the frames belonging to the same GOP. It is supposed that there are common moving areas in the frames belonging to a GOP, so a part of the main watermark can be extracted by superimposing the moving parts of every twin sub-watermark.

According to visual models, human eye decreases its sensitivity in high entropy regions, i.e. moving areas in the video sequences. So, by evaluating $JND$ coefficients in an adaptive manner as in [8], the system robustness to collusion and other attacks will be elevated.

## 5    Other Attacks

We simulated the proposed watermarking scheme using *Matlab7* software. A constant value of 3 is chosen for $JND$ coefficients, which preserves the quality of watermarked sequences according to subjective experiments. Using adaptive $JND$ values leads to a more robust watermarking system at the expense of more computational complexity. According to mathematical analysis and simulations presented in the previous section, linear collusion makes an ignorable difference to the extracted watermark. Also, other watermarking attacks have been considered in the proposed scheme.

We applied different geometric distortions to the watermarked sequence to see how the detection response alters. In the case of video watermarking, the attacker has to perform the same geometric distortion on all of the frames to keep the continuity of the video sequence. By performing spatial synchronization prior to detection, output of the detection algorithm following various amounts of frame cropping, frame rotating, and changing the Aspect Ratio (AR) showed a high resilience against such distortions. As discussed in Sect. 3, decision on the watermark existence is made by evaluating a correlation coefficient. Tables 1 to 3 show the decrement of this correlation coefficient after performing frame cropping, frame rotating, and changing the AR of the watermarked video sequence, respectively. This high resistance to geometric attacks is due to the VSS compatibility with this kind of distortions which is further discussed in [9].

Also, the proposed scheme has brilliant robustness against some common pirate attacks. Changing the video bit rate, which is usually performed by a linear combination of frames, has little effect on the correlation coefficient. Because detection scheme is independent from the order of frames, frame swapping makes

**Table 1.** Decrement of $\rho$ after frame cropping

| Cropping Percentage | 10 | 20 | 30 | 40 | 50 |
|---|---|---|---|---|---|
| Decrement of $\rho$ (%) | 3 | 5 | 3 | 6 | 4 |

**Table 2.** Decrement of $\rho$ after frame rotating

| Rotation Angle (*degrees*) | 5 | 10 | 15 | 20 | 25 |
|---|---|---|---|---|---|
| Decrement of $\rho$ (%) | 7 | 6 | 8 | 12 | 15 |

**Table 3.** Changing the AR of 240*360 pixels watermarked frames

| New Size (*pixels*) | $240 * 180$ | $240 * 90$ | $480 * 360$ |
|---|---|---|---|
| Decrement of $\rho$ (%) | 21 | 18 | 23 |

nothing to the extracted watermark. Also, frame dropping makes little changes to the extracted watermark, which is evaluated by averaging a pool of share-images.

Finally, temporal synchronization, which is crucial in the detection stage of many video watermarking schemes, is not needed in the proposed scheme because detection is independent from the order of frames.

As expected from its simple structure, the used VSS scheme is very fast. This leads the proposed watermarking system to be implemented in real-time using *Matlab7* software.

# 6  Conclusions

In this paper, we have proposed a novel video watermarking scheme, based on the concept of visual secret sharing. It is shown that the watermarked video sequence is robust to linear collusion and, by performing a more complex detection scheme, i.e. using moving areas, the watermark can be extracted in the presence of any kind of collusion. This robustness is based on the fact that the embedded watermark can be extracted by a linear combination between different share-images, i.e. sub-watermarks, which are inserted into different frames of the watermarked sequence. This linear combination also makes the watermarking system robust to pirate attacks, such as frame dropping, frame swapping, and changing the rate of video frames. No temporal synchronization is needed for the aim of watermark extraction due to this linear combination. Also the watermarked sequence is robust to geometrical distortions, which is due to compatibility of the VSS scheme with this kind of distortions. The proposed watermarking system is fast and is implemented in real-time.

# References

1. Doer, G., Dugelay, J.L.: A guide tour of video watermarking. In: Signal processing: Image communications, vol. 18, pp. 263–282. Elsevier Science, North-Holland, Amsterdam (2003)
2. Naor, M., Shamir, A.: Visual cryptography. In: De Santis, A. (ed.) EUROCRYPT 1994. LNCS, vol. 950, pp. 1–12. Springer, Heidelberg (1995)
3. Voloshynovskiy, S., Herrigel, A.N.B., Pun, T.: A stochastic approach to content adaptive digital image watermarking. In: Pfitzmann, A. (ed.) IH 1999. LNCS, vol. 1768, pp. 212–236. Springer, Heidelberg (2000)
4. Perona, P., Malik, J.: Scale-space and edge detection using anisotropic diffusion. IEEE Transactions on Pattern Analysis and Machine Intelligence 12(7), 629–639 (1990)
5. Torkamani-Azar, F., Tait, K.E.: Image recovery using the anisotropic diffusion equation. IEEE Trans. on Image Processing 5(11), 1573–1578 (1996)
6. Su, K., Kundur, D., Hatzinakos, D.: A novel approach to collusion-resistance video watermarking. In: Proceedings of SPIE Security of Watermarking of Multimedia contents IV. San Jose, CA, pp. 491–502 (2002)
7. Mobasseri, B.G.: Exploring CDMA for watermarking of digital video. In: Proceedings of the SPIE 3657, pp. 96–102 (1999)
8. Podilchuk, C.I., Zeng, W.: Image-adaptive watermarking using visual models. IEEE Journal on selected areas in communications 16(4), 525–539 (1998)
9. Houmansadr, A., Ghaemmaghami, S.: A digital image watermarking scheme based on the visual cryptography. In: Proc. 3rd Int'l Symposium on Telecommunications, pp. 843–848 (2005)

# An Elliptic Curve
# Backdoor Algorithm for RSASSA

Adam Young[1] and Moti Yung[2]

[1] Cryptovirology Labs
aly@cryptovirology.com
[2] RSA Labs and Columbia University
moti@cs.columbia.edu

**Abstract.** We present the first (1,2)-SETUP algorithm for the RSA digital signature scheme with appendix. A SETUP algorithm $C'$ is an algorithmic modification of algorithm $C$ that (1) contains an asymmetric backdoor that can only be used by the designer, even if the backdoor algorithm is fully public, and (2) ensures that the public outputs of $C$ and $C'$ are computationally indistinguishable under black-box queries. The SETUP is presented in RSASSA-PSS and it transmits the RSA private key within two w.l.o.g consecutive digital signatures. This problem has been solved for DSA and other discrete-log based digital signature algorithms, but not RSA. We therefore solve a long-standing problem in kleptography.

## 1 Introduction

There has been a lot of research into designing backdoors into key generation algorithms, encryption algorithms, key exchanges, and digital signature schemes. Such backdoors are dual-edged in nature. When deployed by an honest key recovery agent, they can be used to enable an organization to have timely access to private keys. However, when deployed by dishonest recovery agents, they can be used to surreptitiously access private information.

In this paper we continue the line of research that seeks to design asymmetric backdoors in digital signing algorithms. More specifically, we present the first high-bandwidth asymmetric backdoor for the RSASSA-PSS digital signature scheme that is defined in PKCS #1 [21]. An asymmetric backdoor is a covert backdoor that can only be utilized by the designer that deploys it, even when the entire backdoor algorithm is made public. RSASSA-PSS is based on the RSA signature algorithm [23], except that it is probabilistic and incorporates a nonce in each digital signature that is output. RSASSA has a formal proof of security and it appears in [4,5].

The backdoor that we present is non-trivial since the subliminal channel in RSASSA is rather small. For example, when SHA-1 [11,12] is used and the salt length is 20 bytes, the subliminal channel is also 20 bytes (the channel is the salt). The RSA function is a deterministic permutation and it is therefore challenging

J. Camenisch et al. (Eds.): IH 2006, LNCS 4437, pp. 355–374, 2007.

to conduct subliminal communication using RSA after the RSA key pair has already been generated.

Previous work on designing a backdoor into RSA key generation includes Anderson's construction [2]. Later the notion of an asymmetric backdoor (that can only be used by the designer even when the device is fully reverse-engineered and all "secrets" are learned) was introduced [26,27]. Related work includes [9]. It is worth pointing out that efforts have primarily focused on designing backdoors in RSA key generation as opposed to RSA signing.

The notion of (1,2)-leakage bandwidth in kleptographic attacks was put forth in [27]. A $(m, n)$-leakage scheme is an asymmetric backdoor (SETUP mechanism) that leaks $m$ keys/secret messages over $n$ keys/messages that are output by the cryptographic device $(m \leq n)$. A (1,2)-leakage scheme was presented in DSA [28] that leaks the signing private key over the course of two w.l.o.g consecutive DSA signatures. Other work includes [29] that presents a method for transmitting a 20-bit asymmetrically encrypted message covertly over a single RSASSA-PSS signature. However, no RSA digital signature backdoors to date achieve anywhere near the capacity of what we achieve, namely, the secure (asymmetric) and subliminal transmission of the RSA private key over two RSA signatures. Work that is related to this includes a study of subliminal-freeness in the nonce-devoid version of RSA-PSS [6].

The significance of our high-bandwidth backdoor in RSA signing is as follows. Our backdoor algorithm makes it possible to generate an RSA key pair normally (i.e., no backdoor involved), load it into a smartcard, and then leak the RSA private key securely and subliminally through two RSA signatures. This is not possible in any of the previous RSA backdoor designs (this includes key generation backdoors and backdoors in RSA signing algorithms).

Our backdoor exploits in a constructive and forward-engineering fashion the recent cryptanalysis of both MD5 and SHA-1 [24,25]. In short, we argue that the collapse of these primitives is a boon for *information hiding* since the traditional security parameter of $k = 1024$ for RSA *has stayed the same* yet the range of hash functions that are deemed secure has increased significantly (i.e., the move from SHA-1 to SHA-224 and higher). The backdoor we present exploits this shift in the size of contemporary security constants. Just how this shift is exploited is covered in Section 8.

## 2   Definition of a (1,2)-SETUP

The notion of a secretly embedded trapdoor with universal protection (SETUP) was put forth in [26]. In short, a SETUP is an algorithmic modification made to cryptosystem $C$ to derive cryptosystem $C'$ that leaks secret key bits to the cryptosystem designer. A SETUP has the properties that: (1) even if the entire implementation of $C'$ becomes public, the backdoor can still only be used by the designer, and (2) the public outputs of $C$ and $C'$ are polynomially indistinguishable under black-box queries. The exclusive use of the backdoor by the designer applies to previously output values of the black-box and also values that are output by the black-box in the future (forward security).

This paradigm has been used to construct robust backdoors in RSA key generation [26,29]. It has also been used to construct robust backdoors in discrete-logarithm based digital signature schemes such as DSA and ElGamal [28]. A SETUP in a signature scheme that has $(1,2)$-leakage bandwidth leaks the signing private key over the course of 2 w.l.o.g. consecutive digital signatures that are output by $C'$. The underlying idea is that the cryptographic black-box conducts a covert Diffie-Hellman key exchange [10] with the designer using the public outputs of the device and the shared secret is subsequently used to securely transmit private information. In this paper we present a SETUP for RSASSA-PSS that has $(1,2)$-leakage bandwidth (so it is a $(1,2)$-SETUP).

We now present a working definition of a secure SETUP for RSASSA. The definition is adapted from [29]. The model involves a designer, an eavesdropper, and an inquirer. The designer builds a black-box RSASSA signing device $A$ that contains the SETUP and a black-box $B$ that conducts normal (i.e., no backdoor) RSASSA signing. Signatures are verified using the public RSA exponent $e$ and the signer's public modulus $n$. A message is signed using $(n,d)$ where $d$ is the private RSA exponent corresponding to $n$. The designer is given access to the signatures that are generated and the goal of the designer is to obtain the RSA private signing key of a user of $A$.

We define security using two-player games. Prior to the start of the games, the eavesdropper and inquirer are given access to the SETUP algorithm and the normal RSASSA signature algorithm. However, once the games start they are not given access to the internals of $A$ nor $B$—they are tamper-resistant black-boxes. It is assumed that the eavesdropper and inquirer are probabilistic poly-time algorithms.

**Game 1.** Select $T \in_R \{A, B\}$ and let the inquirer have oracle access to $T$. The inquirer wins if he correctly determines whether or not $T = A$ with non-negligible advantage and fails otherwise.

**Property 1.** (computational indistinguishability) The inquirer fails Game 1.

**Game 2:** The eavesdropper may query the signing oracle $A$ using any set of messages. The eavesdropper receives the resulting signatures computed using $((n, e), d)$. He wins if he can use $A$ to compute $e^{\text{th}}$ roots mod $n$ with non-negligible probability and fails otherwise.

**Property 2.** (confidentiality) The eavesdropper fails Game 2.

**Property 3.** (completeness) Let $S_1, S_2$ be signatures on messages $M_1, M_2$, respectively, generated using $((n, e), d)$ in device $A$. The designer computes $p$ with overwhelming probability given $(n = pq, e), M_1, S_1, M_2, S_2$ and possibly other (private) auxiliary information.

**Property 4.** (uniformity) The SETUP is the same in every black-box device $A$ that is manufactured.

Property 4 implies that there are no unique identifier strings in the SETUP device. This permits distribution in a compiled program (which may be code-signed) in which all instances of the program are identical without diminishing security. Also, this makes it simpler to manufacture the SETUP in hardware and software.

**Definition 1.** *If a backdoor RSASSA signature algorithm satisfies properties 1, 2, 3, and 4 then it is a (1,2)-SETUP algorithm.*

The use of a twisted pair of curves is central to our design. Related work includes [20] that shows how to use a twist over binary curves to implement a space efficient public key stegosystem. Twists over elliptic curves is a well-studied area [16,17,18].

For typical elliptic curves used in cryptography, only about half of $\mathbb{F}_q$ corresponds to the $x$-coordinates on the given curve. By using two curves where one is the twist of the other, it is possible to implement a trapdoor one-way permutation from $\mathbb{F}_q$ onto itself. Twists have been used to implement trapdoor one-way permutations that have the conjectured property that inverting the function is exponentially hard [18].

# 3   Background on RSASSA-PSS

## 3.1   RSASSA Signing

We believe that this section covers enough of PKCS #1 to clearly present our backdoor algorithm. The reader is referred to [21] for details not covered here.

The function Hash can be MD5, SHA-1, SHA-224, SHA-256, etc. $hLen$ denotes the length in octets of the hash function output. I2OSP is an Integer-to-Octet-String primitive and OS2IP is an Octet-String-to-Integer primitive. MGF1 is a mask generation function (MGF) that is based on Hash. Let $A \parallel B$ denote the string that results from concatenating string $A$ with string $B$.

MGF1($mgfSeed, maskLen$):
Input: octet string $mgfSeed$ from which $mask$ is generated
$\qquad maskLen \geq 2^{32} * hLen$, intended length in octets of $mask$
Output: an octet string $mask$ of length $maskLen$
1. if ($maskLen > 2^{32} * hLen$) then output "mask too long" and halt
2. let $T$ be the empty octet string
3. for $counter = 0$ to ($\lceil maskLen/hLen \rceil - 1$) do:
4. $\qquad C = \text{I2OSP}(counter, 4)$
5. $\qquad T = T \parallel \text{Hash}(mgfSeed \parallel C)$
6. output the leading $maskLen$ octets of $T$ as the octet string $mask$

$sLen$ is the length in octets of the salt. For ease of exposition, the version of EMSA-PSS-ENCODE below is tailored to the case that $sLen \neq 0$. Appendix A.2.3 of [21] states that the default value of $sLen$ is the octet length of the hash value. The function MGF can be instantiated using MGF1. Let $A \oplus B$ denote the string that results from applying the bitwise exclusive-or operation on bit strings $A$ and $B$.

EMSA-PSS-ENCODE($M, emBits$):

Input: message $M$ to be encoded. $M$ is an octet string
$emBits \geq 8 * hLen + 8 * sLen + 9$, maximum possible bit length of the integer output by OS2IP($EM$)

Output: octet string $EM$ that is the encoding of $M$

1. if ((length of $M$) > (input limitation for Hash($\cdot$))) then
   output "message too long" and halt
2. let $mHash = \text{Hash}(M)$ and set $emLen = \lceil emBits/8 \rceil$
3. if ($emLen < hLen + sLen + 2$) then output "encoding error" and halt
4. generate a random octet string $salt$ of length $sLen$
5. let $M' = (0x)00\ 00\ 00\ 00\ 00\ 00\ 00\ 00\ \|\ mHash\ \|\ salt$
6. let $H = \text{Hash}(M')$
7. generate octet $PS$ that is ($emLen - sLen - hLen - 2$) octets of 0x00
8. let $DB = PS\ \|\ 0x01\ \|\ salt$
9. let $dbMask = \text{MGF}(H, emLen - hLen - 1)$
10. let $maskedDB = DB \oplus dbMask$
11. set the leftmost ($8 * emLen - emBits$) bits of the leftmost octet in $maskedDB$ to 0
12. output $EM = maskedDB\ \|\ H\ \|\ 0xbc$

Note that the input limitation for SHA-1 is $2^{61} - 1$ octets.

Step 4 chooses $salt$ uniformly at random. It is well-known that these bits constitute a subliminal channel since they are recoverable by everyone in Step 12 of EMSA-PSS-VERIFY that is described below [14]. This channel is made possible due to the fact that RSASSA is a probabilistic algorithm. This channel is utilized in this paper.

Let $modBits$ be the length in bits of the RSA modulus $n$. The RSASSA-PSS-SIGN($K, M$) function signs octet $M$ using the RSA private key $K$. This function operates as follows. First, $EM = \text{EMSA-PSS-ENCODE}(M, modBits - 1)$ is computed and signing continues only if no error message is printed out. The octet $EM$ is then converted to an integer using $m = \text{OS2IP}(EM)$. This integer is signed using an efficient version of the Chinese Remainder Theorem by computing $s = \text{RSASP1}(K, m)$. Finally, the resulting RSA signature integer $s$ is converted to a length $k$ octet using $S = \text{I2OSP}(s, k)$.

### 3.2  RSASSA Signature Verification

The function RSAVP1($(n, e), s$) outputs an error if $s$ is not between 0 and $n - 1$. When $s$ is in this range it returns $s^e \bmod n$.

EMSA-PSS-VERIFY($M, EM, emBits$):

Input: message $M$ to be verified, possible encoding $EM$ of
$M$, and maximum bit length $emBits$ of OS2IP($EM$)

Output: message stating "consistent" or "inconsistent"

1. if ((length of $M$) > (input limitation for Hash($\cdot$))) then
    output "inconsistent" and halt
2. let $mHash = \text{Hash}(M)$
3. if ($emLen < hLen + sLen + 2$) then output "inconsistent" and halt
4. if ((rightmost octet of $EM$) $\neq$ 0xbc) then output "inconsistent" and halt
5. let $maskedDB$ be the leftmost ($emLen - hLen - 1$) octets of $EM$ and
    let $H$ be the next $hLen$ octets
6. if the leftmost ($8 * emLen - emBits$) bits of the leftmost octet in
    $maskedDB$ are not all equal to 0 then output "inconsistent" and halt
7. let $dbMask = \text{MGF}(H, emLen - hLen - 1)$
8. let $DB = maskedDB \oplus dbMask$
9. set the leftmost ($8 * emLen - emBits$) bits of the leftmost octet in $DB$ to 0
10. if the ($emLen - hLen - sLen - 2$) leftmost octets of $DB$ are not 0x00 then
     output "inconsistent" and halt
11. if ((octet at position $emLen - hLen - sLen - 1$ of DB) $\neq$ 0x01) then
     output "inconsistent" and halt
12. let $salt$ be the last $sLen$ octets of $DB$
13. let $M' = (0x)00\ 00\ 00\ 00\ 00\ 00\ 00\ 00\ \|\ mHash\ \|\ salt$
14. let $H' = \text{Hash}(M')$
15. if ($H = H'$) then output "consistent" else output "inconsistent"

The function RSASSA-PSS-VERIFY is used to verify the signature $S$.

RSASSA-PSS-VERIFY$((n, e), M, S)$:
Input: public key $(n, e)$, signature $S$ on message $M$
Output: message indicating valid/invalid signature

1. if ((length of $S$) $\neq k$ octets) then output "invalid signature" and halt
2. $s = \text{OS2IP}(S)$
3. set $m = \text{RSAVP1}((n, e), s)$, halt with "invalid signature" on error
4. set $EM = \text{I2OSP}(m, emLen)$, halt with "invalid signature" on error
5. $result = \text{EMSA-PSS-VERIFY}(M, EM, modBits - 1)$
6. if ($result = $ "consistent") then output "valid signature" else
    output "invalid signature"

## 4    Background on Twists over GF($p$)

We use uppercase to denote a point on an elliptic curve and lowercase to denote
scalar multipliers. When $x$ is a scalar, $xG$ denotes the operation of adding $G$
to itself $x$ times. Kaliski [16,17,18] studied and applied twists using the general
class of elliptic curves over GF($p$). Let $E_{a,b}(\mathbb{F}_p)$ denote the elliptic curve $y^2 = x^3 + ax + b$ over the finite field $\mathbb{F}_p$. Also, let $\#E_{a,b}(\mathbb{F}_p)$ denote the number of
points on the curve $E_{a,b}(\mathbb{F}_p)$. Let $E_{a,b}$ be shorthand for $E_{a,b}(\mathbb{F}_p)$. The value $k$
is the length in bits of the prime number $p$.

We give important definitions, lemmas, and background on twists over GF($p$)
in Appendix A. We will now give functions that permit us to do embeddings

using bit strings that are fixed in length. The input point $P$ to function Encode originates on curve $c \in \{0, 1\}$. The algorithms $X_T$, $X_{T,even}^{-1}$, and $X_{T,odd}^{-1}$ are given in Appendix A.

Encode($T_{a,b,\beta}(\mathbb{F}_p), P, c$):
1. let $t_s$ be the binary string representing $t = X_T[T_{a,b,\beta}(\mathbb{F}_p)](P, c)$
2. if $|t_s| > k + 1$ then output $0^k$ and halt
3. output $P_s = 0^{k+1-|t_s|} \ || \ t_s$

For the primes we use in this paper, step 2 will never output $0^k$. Algorithm Decode outputs $(P, c)$ where the point $P$ resides on curve $c \in \{0, 1\}$.

Decode($T_{a,b,\beta}(\mathbb{F}_p), P_s$):
1. let $ysgn$ be the least significant bit of $P_s$
2. if $(ysgn = 0)$ then output $(P, c) = X_{T,even}^{-1}[T_{a,b,\beta}(\mathbb{F}_p)](P_s)$ and halt
3. output $(P, c) = X_{T,odd}^{-1}[T_{a,b,\beta}(\mathbb{F}_p)](P_s)$

Appendix A gives details on the following fact.

**Fact 1:** Let $T_{a,b,\beta}(\mathbb{F}_p)$ be a twisted pair. Encode is a polynomial time computable, probabilistic polynomial time invertible mapping between the set of points on the twisted pair $T_{a,b,\beta}(\mathbb{F}_p)$ and all $(k+1)$-bit strings corresponding to the integers in the set $\{0, ..., 2p + 1\}$ (padded with leading zeros as necessary). The inverse function of Encode is Decode.

The following is Definition 6.4 from Kaliski [17].

**Definition 2.** A **twisted instance** of parameter $k$ consists of $T_{a,b,\beta}(\mathbb{F}_p)$ which is a twisted pair of parameter $k$, generating pairs $(G_1, G_2)$ and $(G_1', G_2')$ for, respectively, the curves $E_{a,b}(\mathbb{F}_p)$ and $E_{a\beta^2, b\beta^3}(\mathbb{F}_p)$ contained in the twisted pair, a point $P$ in the twisted pair, and $c \in \{0, 1\}$ that denotes the curve that $P$ was chosen from.

## 5    RSASSA SETUP Algorithm

Let $n = pq$ be the RSA public modulus of the signer. The idea is to conduct an elliptic curve DH key exchange between the designer of the black-box signing algorithm and the black-box itself and then use the shared secret to compromise $p$. The designer plants his ECDH public keys $(Y, Y')$ in the black-box, where each key is for a curve in the twisted pair.

The backdoor works as follows (this explanation glosses over details). For every even numbered signing operation, the device chooses a DH key exchange value to serve as the RSASSA random salt. This is chosen to be on one of the curves in the twisted pair in such a way that the key exchange value is (nearly) a uniformly random bit string. In the odd numbered invocation that follows, the RSASSA salt is chosen to be a random pad XORed with the upper order bits of the RSA prime $p$. The pad is the output of a random function with the DH shared secret (resulting from the key exchange in the previous even numbered invocation) being passed into it.

The designer recovers the random salts from the signatures (everyone can do this). This reveals the DH key exchange value that the device chose. Using the ECDH private keys $(x, x')$ corresponding to $(Y, Y')$ the designer recovers the DH shared secret. Only the designer can do this and hence it is an *asymmetric* backdoor. By using the random function and applying the bitwise exclusive-or operation, the designer recovers the upper order bits of $p$. The designer then uses Coppersmith's factoring algorithm to recover all of $p$. This explanation fails to account for certain portions of the backdoor algorithm and is intended only to convey the general idea.

We utilize a twist over $GF(p)$ in this paper. We remark that the backdoor can also be constructed using twisted binary curves. Binary curves are used for information hiding in [20,29]. Curves over $GF(p)$ have some advantages. The bit length of $p$ can be fine-tuned. For $GF(2^m)$ it is advised that $m$ be prime to avoid the GHS attack [13]. This inhibits the ability to use compressed points of certain bit lengths. In our opinion, twists over $GF(p)$ make our reduction arguments simpler. While using twists over $GF(p)$ in other work we realized that this approach would improve the proofs in this paper.

## 5.1    Building Blocks for RSASSA SETUP

Let $n$ be the RSA modulus used to verify signatures. For concreteness we describe a backdoor where $|n|/4$ is the bit length of the output of the underlying hash function (see Subsection 5.2). We choose the length of $p$ to satisfy $|p| + 1 = |n|/4$. For example, we can take $|n| = 1024$ and use SHA-256 as the underlying hash function. In this case we make the elliptic curve parameter $p$ satisfy $|p| = k = 255$ (this $p$ is not to be confused with the RSA prime $p$). This value permits an encoded point to be $k + 1 = 256$ bits in length. We consider other configurations of the attack in Section 8.

For the key exchange we require that the prime $p = 2^k - \delta$ where the value $\delta$ is randomly chosen satisfying $2\sqrt{2^k} < \delta < 4\sqrt{2^k}$ until a prime $p$ of this form is found. The key exchange relies on the ECDDH assumption. We greatly simplify the exchange and corresponding proof by requiring that $E_{a,b}$ and $E_{a',b'}$ have prime order. So, $r = \#E_{a,b}(\mathbb{F}_p)$ is prime and $r' = \#E_{a',b'}(\mathbb{F}_p)$ is prime. From Section 4 it follows that $r + r' = 2p + 2$. w.l.o.g. we assume that $r < r'$. The bounds on $\delta$ ensure that $2r' < 2^{k+1}$ (shown using the Hasse Interval). The backdoor utilizes the predicate $\texttt{SelCurv}(1^k)$ that outputs 0 with probability $r/(2p + 2)$ and 1 with probability $r'/(2p + 2)$.

Let $G_1$ be a base point on $E_{a,b}$ having order $r$ and $G'_1$ be a base point on $E_{a',b'}$ having order $r'$. Since the group structure is $(r, 1)$ for $E_{a,b}$ and $(r', 1)$ for $E_{a',b'}$ we take $G_2$ to be the point at infinity $O$ for $E_{a,b}$ and $G'_2$ to be the point at infinity $O'$ for $E_{a',b'}$.

It is required that $G_1$ and $E_{a,b}$ provide a secure setting for the elliptic curve Decision Diffie-Hellman problem (ECDDH). The same holds for $G_1'$ and $E_{a',b'}$. It is well-known that for certain elliptic curves, DDH is tractable [15].

The recovery agent chooses $x$ randomly such that $0 < x < r$ and chooses $x'$ randomly such that $0 < x' < r'$. He computes $(Y, Y') = (xG_1, x'G_1')$.

GenDHExchangeValues():
1. compute $u = \mathtt{SelCurv}(1^k)$
2. if $(u = 0)$ then
3.     choose $w \in_R [1, r-1]$
4.     set $(s_{pub}, s_{priv}) = (\mathtt{Encode}(T_{a,b,\beta}(\mathbb{F}_p), wG_1, u), \mathtt{Encode}(T_{a,b,\beta}(\mathbb{F}_p), wY, u)$
5. else
6.     choose $w \in_R [1, r'-1]$
7.     set $(s_{pub}, s_{priv}) = (\mathtt{Encode}(T_{a,b,\beta}(\mathbb{F}_p), wG_1', u), \mathtt{Encode}(T_{a,b,\beta}(\mathbb{F}_p), wY', u)$
8. output $(s_{pub}, s_{priv})$

Observe that $s_{pub}$ is an encoded point that is selected uniformly at random from $T_{a,b,\beta}(\mathbb{F}_p)$. Fact 2: Due to the special form of $p$, GenDHExchangeValues produces encoded points $s_{pub}$ that are statisitically indistinguishable from random $(k+1)$-bit strings. Fact 2 is straightforward to show. It forms the basis for Property 1.

RecSecret($s_{pub}, x, x'$):
Input: $(k+1)$-bit string $s_{pub}$ and EC private keys $x, x'$
Output: $(k+1)$-bit string $s_{priv}$
1. compute $(U, u) = \mathtt{Decode}(T_{a,b,\beta}(\mathbb{F}_p), s_{pub})$
2. if $(u = 0)$ then compute $P = xU$ else compute $P = x'U$
3. output $s_{priv} = \mathtt{Encode}(T_{a,b,\beta}(\mathbb{F}_p), P, u)$

Coppersmith showed that if the $|n|/4$ most significant bits of $p$ are known then $n = pq$ can be efficiently factored [8]. Following [9,29], we use this cryptanalytic method to factor $n$. Let $(p, w) = \mathrm{DCAlg}(n, v)$ denote the execution of Don Coppersmith's algorithm. Here $v$ is the upper half of the bits of $p$. The Boolean $w$ is set to 1 if $p \mid n$ and it is set to 0 otherwise. $w$ is therefore an error code that is returned by DCAlg. Let $\mathcal{S} \doteq \mathcal{W}$ denote that $\mathcal{S}$ is defined to be $\mathcal{W}$.

$$\mathcal{S}_\pi \doteq \{s || c : P \in E_{a,b}, s = \mathtt{Encode}(T_{a,b,\beta}(\mathbb{F}_p), P, 0), c \in \{0,1\}\}$$
$$\mathcal{S}_{\pi'} \doteq \{s || c : P \in E_{a',b'}, s = \mathtt{Encode}(T_{a,b,\beta}(\mathbb{F}_p), P, 1), c \in \{0,1\}\}$$
$$\mathcal{T}_\pi \doteq \text{a random subset of } \{0,1\}^{k+1} \text{ having cardinality } 2r$$
$$\mathcal{T}_{\pi'} \doteq \text{a random subset of } \{0,1\}^{k+1} \text{ having cardinality } 2r'$$

Define $\pi : \mathcal{S}_\pi \to \mathcal{T}_\pi$ to be a random bijection. Define $\pi' : \mathcal{S}_{\pi'} \to \mathcal{T}_{\pi'}$ to be a random bijection. Note that for $\pi$ and $\pi'$, the symbols in the domain differ from the symbols in the range (so they are not permutations). Both $\pi$ and $\pi'$ are idealizations and so we are working in a model similar to the random oracle model [3]. Define $\pi_0 : \mathcal{S}_\pi \bigcup \mathcal{S}_{\pi'} \to \mathcal{T}_\pi \bigcup \mathcal{T}_{\pi'}$ as follows. If the $k+1$ uppermost bits of the argument $s$ to $\pi_0$ is an encoded point on $E_{a,b}$ then output $\pi(s)$ else output $\pi'(s)$.

## 5.2   The RSASSA Backdoor

Let $n = pq$ be the public RSA modulus of the user where $|p| = |q|$. The private signing key is supplied to the signing algorithm, so $p$ is available to the EMSA-PSS-ENCODE function. The Boolean $\alpha$ is stored in non-volatile memory and is initially 0. The variable $s_{priv}$ is stored in non-volatile memory and is initially $0^{k+1}$. The Boolean $\alpha$ permits the signing algorithm to alternate between transmitting a key exchange value and transmitting the encryption of the upper order bits of $p$. Non-volatile memory is needed in black-boxes that are powered down between signing operations.

EMSA-PSS-ENCODE-BACKDOOR($M, emBits$):
Input: message $M$ to be encoded. $M$ is an octet string
$\qquad emBits \geq 8 * hLen + 8 * sLen + 9$, maximum possible bit length of the
$\qquad\qquad$ integer output by OS2IP($EM$)
Output: octet string $EM$ that is the encoding of $M$
1. if ((length of $M$) > (input limitation for Hash($\cdot$))) then
$\qquad$ output "message too long" and halt
2. let $mHash = \text{Hash}(M)$ and set $emLen = \lceil emBits/8 \rceil$
3. if ($emLen < hLen + sLen + 2$) then output "encoding error" and halt
4. if ($\alpha = 0$) then
5. $\qquad$ compute $(salt, s_{priv}) = (s_{pub}, s_{priv}) = \text{GenDHExchangeValues}()$
6. else
7. $\qquad$ let $ptext$ be the $|p|/2$ uppermost bits of the RSA prime $p$
8. $\qquad$ choose $c \in_R \{0, 1\}$ and set $pad = \pi_0(s_{priv}\|c)$
9. $\qquad$ set $salt = (pad \oplus ptext)$, and zeroize $s_{priv}$
10. set $\alpha = \alpha \oplus 1$
11. let $M' = (0\text{x})00\ 00\ 00\ 00\ 00\ 00\ 00\ 00\ \|\ mHash\ \|\ salt$
12. let $H = \text{Hash}(M')$
13. generate octet $PS$ that is ($emLen - sLen - hLen - 2$) octets of 0x00
14. let $DB = PS\ \|\ 0\text{x}01\ \|\ salt$
15. let $dbMask = \text{MGF}(H, emLen - hLen - 1)$
16. let $maskedDB = DB \oplus dbMask$
17. set the leftmost ($8 * emLen - emBits$) bits of the leftmost octet
$\qquad$ in $maskedDB$ to 0
18. output $EM = maskedDB\ \|\ H\ \|\ 0\text{xbc}$

This algorithm generates and stores the DH shared secret $s_{priv}$ in every even invocation and uses $s_{priv}$ in every odd invocation to transmit the upper half of $p$. Let $SIGS_1$ be shorthand for EMSA-PSS-ENCODE-BACKDOOR.

## 5.3   RSASSA SETUP Key Recovery

The key recovery agent obtains the RSA public key $(n, e)$ corresponding to the RSA private key $d$ of the user. The following algorithm permits $n$ to be factored.

RSASSA-PSS-RECOVER$((n, e), M_1, S_1, M_2, S_2, x, x')$:

Input:  public key $(n, e)$, signed messages $(M_1, S_1), (M_2, S_2)$
         computed using $(n, d)$, EC private keys $(x, x')$

Output: prime $p \mid n$ or "failure"

1. if $S_1$ is not a valid RSA signature on $M_1$ then halt with "failure"
2. if $S_2$ is not a valid RSA signature on $M_2$ then halt with "failure"
3. let $EM_i$ be the encoding of $M_i$ for $i = 1, 2$
4. let $salt_i$ be the salt as recovered in line 12 of
         EMSA-PSS-VERIFY$(M_i, EM_i, |n| - 1)$ for $i = 1, 2$
5. set $s_{pub} = salt_1$
6. if $s_{pub}$ is not an encoded point on $T_{a,b,\beta}(\mathbb{F}_p)$ then halt with "failure"
7. set $s_{priv} = \mathsf{RecSecret}(s_{pub}, x, x')$
8. set $pad_1 = \pi_0(s_{priv}\|0)$ and $pad_2 = \pi_0(s_{priv}\|1)$
9. set $ptext_1 = salt_2 \oplus pad_1$ and set $ptext_2 = salt_2 \oplus pad_2$
10. compute $(p, w) = \mathrm{DCAlg}(n, ptext_1)$
11. if $(w = 1)$ then output $p$ and halt
12. compute $(p, w) = \mathrm{DCAlg}(n, ptext_2)$
13. if $(w = 1)$ then output $p$ else output "failure"

# 6    The Twisted DDH Problem (TDDH)

The proof of security uses a decision problem that is equivalent to ECDDH. Let $IG_1$ be an instance generator that on input $k$ (in unary) generates the tuple $(T_{a,b,\beta}(\mathbb{F}_p), G_1, G_2, G_1', G_2')$.

**Definition 3.** *A TDDH algorithm $A_1$ for $\tau = (T_{a,b,\beta}(\mathbb{F}_p), G_1, G_2, G_1', G_2')$ is a probabilistic polynomial time (in $k$) algorithm satisfying, for some fixed $\alpha > 0$ and sufficiently large $k$:*

$$|\Pr[A_1(\tau, (aG_1, bG_1, abG_1), (a'G_1', b'G_1', a'b'G_1')) = 1\,] -$$
$$\Pr[A_1(\tau, (aG_1, bG_1, cG_1), (a'G_1', b'G_1', c'G_1')) = 1\,]| > \tfrac{1}{k^\alpha}$$

*The probability is over the random choice of $\tau$ according to the distribution induced by $IG_1(k)$, the random choice[1] of $a, b, c \in \{1, 2, ..., r - 1\}$, the random choice of $a', b', c' \in \{1, 2, ..., r' - 1\}$, and the bits used by $A_1$.*

The TDDH assumption is that no such $A_1$ exists. It is simple to construct an algorithm that solves TDDH given an oracle that solves ECDDH. The other direction is non-trivial to prove and we prove it in Appendix B.

**Theorem 1.** *ECDDH is computationally equivalent to TDDH.*

# 7    Security

In the following lemmas it is understood that when we say that two algorithms are indistinguishable we mean that the probability ensembles corresponding to

---

[1] These $a$ and $b$ are not to be confused with the Weierstrass coefficients.

their outputs are (comp./stat.) indistinguishable. Let $SIGS_4$ be shorthand for EMSA-PSS-ENCODE. Define $SIGS_3$ to be as follows: (1) in every even invocation $SIGS_3$ operates the same as $SIGS_4$ except that $SIGS_3$ computes $\sigma = \text{SelCurv}(1^k)$ and if $\sigma = 0$ then the salt (which is $salt_1$) is a random encoded point on $E_{a,b}$ and if $\sigma = 1$ then the salt is a random encoded point on $E_{a',b'}$, and (2) $SIGS_3$ operates the same as $SIGS_4$ in every odd invocation. The following lemma can be shown.

**Lemma 1.** *$SIGS_3$ is statistically indistinguishable from $SIGS_4$.*

Define $SIGS_2$ to be the same as $SIGS_3$ with the following exception. The variable $\sigma$ from the even invocation is stored in non-volatile memory. $SIGS_2$ operates as follows in every odd invocation. The bit $c \in_R \{0,1\}$ is chosen. If $\sigma = 0$ then $s_r$ is an encoded point chosen randomly from $E_{a,b}$. If $\sigma = 1$ then $s_r$ is an encoded point chosen randomly from $E_{a',b'}$. For the odd invocations $SIGS_2$ sets $salt_2 = salt = \pi_0(s_r\|c)$. Lemma 2 is proven in Appendix C.

**Lemma 2.** *(random oracle model) $SIGS_2$ is statistically indistinguishable from $SIGS_3$.*

In the remaining proofs, $M_1$ and $M_2$ can be any two messages. Let $\gamma$ be the tuple $(G_1, Y, G'_1, Y', T_{a,b,\beta}(\mathbb{F}_p))$. We now review the DDH randomization method from [7] adjusted for the case of elliptic curves. Let $(E_{a,b}, G_1, X, Y, Z)$ be an ECDDH problem instance over $\tau = (E_{a,b}, G_1)$. Algorithm $f_\tau$ chooses scalars $u_1, u_2, v$ randomly satisfying $0 < u_1, u_2, v < r$. $f_\tau$ returns $(X_2, Y_2, Z_2)$ that is computed as follows.

$$f_\tau(X, Y, Z) = (X_2, Y_2, Z_2) = (vX + u_1 G_1, Y + u_2 G_1, vZ + u_1 Y + vu_2 X + u_1 u_2 G_1)$$

This randomization method has the following property. If the input triple is a DH triple then the output is a random DH triple. If the input triple is not a DH triple then the output is a random 3-tuple. A random 3-tuple is not a DH triple with a probability that is overwhelming (in $k$). Similarly, we define $f_{\tau'}$ to be this randomization algorithm for the other curve in the twist. So, the parameters are specified by $\tau' = (E_{a',b'}, G'_1)$.

**Lemma 3.** *(random oracle model) If TDDH is hard then $SIGS_1$ is computationally indistinguishable from $SIGS_2$.*

*Proof.* We show that the contrapositive holds. Suppose that there exists a distinguisher $D$ that distinguishes signatures computed using $SIGS_1$ from signatures computed using $SIGS_2$ with non-negligible advantage. We will show how to use $D$ to solve TDDH.

$TM_1(X_1, Y_1, Z_1, X'_1, Y'_1, Z'_1)$:
Input: $(X_1, Y_1, Z_1, X'_1, Y'_1, Z'_1)$ is a TDDH problem instance over $T_{a,b,\beta}(\mathbb{F}_p)$
1. compute $(X_2, Y_2, Z_2) = f_\tau(X_1, Y_1, Z_1)$ and $(X'_2, Y'_2, Z'_2) = f_{\tau'}(X'_1, Y'_1, Z'_1)$
2. compute $\sigma = \text{SelCurv}(1^k)$ and choose $c \in_R \{0,1\}$

3. if $\sigma = 0$ then
4.     set $Y = X_2$ and set $salt_1 = s_{pub} = \text{Encode}(T_{a,b,\beta}(\mathbb{F}_p), Y_2, 0)$
5.     set $s_{priv} = \text{Encode}(T_{a,b,\beta}(\mathbb{F}_p), Z_2, 0)$ and set $pad = \pi_0(s_{priv}||c)$
6. else
7.     set $Y' = X_2'$ and set $salt_1 = s_{pub} = \text{Encode}(T_{a,b,\beta}(\mathbb{F}_p), Y_2', 1)$
8.     set $s_{priv} = \text{Encode}(T_{a,b,\beta}(\mathbb{F}_p), Z_2', 1)$ and set $pad = \pi_0(s_{priv}||c)$
9. generate RSA primes $(p, q)$ randomly (based on exponent $e$)
10. let $ptext$ be the $|p|/2$ uppermost bits of the RSA prime $p$
11. set $salt_2 = pad \oplus ptext$
12. construct signature $S_i$ on $M_i$ using $salt_i$ in RSASSA-PSS for $i = 1, 2$
13. output $D(p, q, e, M_1, S_1, M_2, S_2, \gamma)$

$TM_2(X_1, Y_1, X_1', Y_1')$:
Input: $(X_1, Y_1)$ is a ECDH problem instance over $E_{a,b}$ using base $G_1$
       $(X_1', Y_1')$ is a ECDH problem instance over $E_{a',b'}$ using base $G_1'$
1. choose $e_1, e_2 \in_R \{1, 2, 3, ..., r-1\}$ and compute $X_2 = e_1 X_1$ and $Y_2 = e_2 Y_1$
2. choose $e_1', e_2' \in_R \{1, 2, 3, ..., r'-1\}$ and compute $X_2' = e_1' X_1'$ and $Y_2' = e_2' Y_1'$
3. compute $\sigma = \text{SelCurv}(1^k)$ and choose $c \in_R \{0, 1\}$
4. if $\sigma = 0$ then
5.     set $Y = X_2$ and set $salt_1 = s_{pub} = \text{Encode}(T_{a,b,\beta}(\mathbb{F}_p), Y_2, 0)$
6.     choose $Z_2 \in_R E_{a,b}$ and set $s_{priv} = \text{Encode}(T_{a,b,\beta}(\mathbb{F}_p), Z_2, 0)$
7. else
8.     set $Y' = X_2'$ and set $salt_1 = s_{pub} = \text{Encode}(T_{a,b,\beta}(\mathbb{F}_p), Y_2', 1)$
9.     choose $Z_2' \in_R E_{a',b'}$ and set $s_{priv} = \text{Encode}(T_{a,b,\beta}(\mathbb{F}_p), Z_2', 1)$
10. generate RSA primes $(p, q)$ randomly (based on exponent $e$)
11. let $ptext$ be the $|p|/2$ uppermost bits of the RSA prime $p$
12. let $pad = \pi_0(s_{priv}||c)$ and set $salt_2 = pad \oplus ptext$
13. construct signature $S_i$ on $M_i$ using $salt_i$ in RSASSA-PSS for $i = 1, 2$
14. step through the operation of $D(p, q, e, M_1, S_1, M_2, S_2, \gamma)$ and
    store the $k+1$ uppermost bits of each argument to $\pi_0$ in list $L$
15. when $D$ terminates, select $u_s$ uniformly at random from $L$ but
    if $L$ is empty then halt with "failure"
16. if $u_s$ is not an encoded point on $T_{a,b,\beta}(\mathbb{F}_p)$ then halt with "failure"
17. compute $(U, u) = \text{Decode}(T_{a,b,\beta}(\mathbb{F}_p), u_s)$
18. if $(u = 0)$ then output $(e_1 e_2)^{-1} U$ else output $(e_1' e_2')^{-1} U$

Let $\psi$ be the event that $D$ supplies the encoded ECDH shared secret corresponding $(X_2, Y_2)$ or $(X_2', Y_2')$ to $\pi_0$. If $\psi$ occurs with negligible probability then $TM_1$ solves TDDH. Since $D$ is a poly-time algorithm, $L$ is poly-bounded. So, if $\psi$ occurs with non-negligible probability then $TM_2$ solves ECDH for the problem instance $(X_1, Y_1)$ or $(X_1', Y_1')$. This implies the solution to TDDH.     ◇

**Fact 1.** Let $D_k^1$, $D_k^2$, and $D_k^3$ be probability ensembles with common security parameter $k$. It is well-known that if $D_k^1$ and $D_k^2$ are computationally indistinguishable and $D_k^2$ and $D_k^3$ are computationally indistinguishable, then $D_k^1$ and $D_k^3$ are computationally indistinguishable (see Lecture 7, [19]).

By combining Lemmas 1, 2, 3, Theorem 1, and Fact 1 we have shown the following theorem and corollary to the theorem.

**Theorem 2.** *(random oracle model) If TDDH is hard then $SIGS_1$ is computationally indistinguishable from $SIGS_4$.*

**Corollary 1.** *(random oracle model) If ECDDH is hard then Property 1 holds.*

**Claim 2.** (random oracle model) If RSASSA-PSS is secure and ECDH is hard then confidentiality (Property 2) holds.

We prove this by showing that the contrapositive holds. Suppose that there exists an algorithm $A$ that outputs $\sqrt[e]{c} \bmod n$ (where $c \in_R \mathbb{Z}_n^*$) with non-negligible probability on input $((n, e), c)$, the signed message pairs $(M_1, S_1)$ and $(M_2, S_2)$, and $\gamma$. Here $S_i$ is a signature on $M_i$ for $i = 1, 2$ computed using EMSA-PSS-ENCODE-BACKDOOR. $S_1$ and $S_2$ are computed using the private key corresponding to $(n, e)$. $A$ succeeds for backdoor signatures over both curves, or signatures over $E_{a,b}$, or signatures over $E_{a',b'}$. w.l.o.g., suppose $A$ succeeds with non-negligible probability for backdoor signatures computed using $E_{a,b}$.

Suppose that we are given a pair of points $(X_1, Y_1)$ over $E_{a,b}$ and our goal is to learn the corresponding ECDH secret using base $G_1$. Suppose also that we are given $(n, e)$, the message/signature pairs $(M_1, S_1)$, $(M_2, S_2)$, and $c$ and our goal is to learn $\sqrt[e]{c} \bmod n$. Our reduction algorithms permit at least one of these goals to be achieved.

$TM_1(M_1, S_1, M_2, S_2, c, n, e)$:
1. randomly generate ECDH key parameters $(G_1, Y, G_1', Y')$
2. recover $salt_1$ from $S_1$ and set $s_{pub} = salt_1$
3. if $s_{pub}$ is not an encoded point on $E_{a,b}$ then halt with "failure"
4. compute $u = A(M_1, S_1, M_2, S_2, c, n, e, \gamma)$
5. if $u \notin \mathbb{Z}_n^*$ then (output "failure") else output $u$

$TM_2(X_1, Y_1)$:
1. choose $e_1, e_2 \in_R \{1, 2, 3, ..., r - 1\}$ and compute $X_2 = e_1 X_1$ and $Y_2 = e_2 Y_1$
2. choose $Y'$ to be a random point on $E_{a',b'}$
3. generate RSA primes $(p, q)$ randomly (based on exponent $e$)
4. compute $n = pq$
5. set $Y = X_2$ and set $salt_1 = s_{pub} = \text{Encode}(T_{a,b,\beta}(\mathbb{F}_p), Y_2, 0)$
6. choose $Z_2$ to be a random point on $E_{a,b}$ and choose $w \in_R \{0, 1\}$
7. set $s_{priv} = \text{Encode}(T_{a,b,\beta}(\mathbb{F}_p), Z_2, 0)$
8. let $ptext$ be the $|p|/2$ uppermost bits of the RSA prime $p$
9. let $pad = \pi_0(s_{priv} \| w)$ and set $salt_2 = pad \oplus ptext$
10. construct signature $S_i$ on $M_i$ using $salt_i$ in RSASSA-PSS for $i = 1, 2$
11. choose $c \in_R \mathbb{Z}_n^*$
12. step through the operation of $A(M_1, S_1, M_2, S_2, c, n, e, \gamma)$ and store the $k + 1$ uppermost bits of each argument to $\pi_0$ in list $L$
13. when $A$ terminates, select $u_s$ uniformly at random from $L$ but

if $L$ is empty then halt with "failure"
14. if $u_s$ is not an encoded point on $T_{a,b,\beta}(\mathbb{F}_p)$ then halt with "failure"
15. compute $(U, u) = \mathtt{Decode}(T_{a,b,\beta}(\mathbb{F}_p), u_s)$
16. if $u = 1$ then (output "failure") else output $(e_1 e_2)^{-1} U$

For step 3 in $TM_1$ it is reasonable to assume access to signed messages that do not cause this failure. Let $\psi$ be the event that $A$ supplies the encoded DH shared secret corresponding to $Y$ and $s_{pub}$ as the uppermost $k + 1$ bits of an argument to $\pi_0$. If $\psi$ occurs with negligible probability then $TM_1$ breaks RSASSA-PSS (since $TM_1$ outputs $\sqrt[e]{c}$ with non-negligible probability). If $\psi$ occurs with non-negligible probability then $TM_2$ solves ECDH.                    ◇

Properties 3 and 4 are straightforward to show. We have shown the following.

**Theorem 3.** *(random oracle model) If EC Decision Diffie-Hellman is hard and RSASSA-PSS is secure then algorithm EMSA-PSS-ENCODE-BACKDOOR and algorithm RSASSA-PSS-RECOVER form a (1,2)-SETUP for RSASSA-PSS.*

# 8   Other Configurations and Practical Use

Our backdoor is attractive due to the recent migration towards the larger SHA algorithms. The limiting factor in achieving a (1,2)-leakage bandwidth SETUP is Coppersmith's algorithm that requires the upper half of $p$. With SHA-1 and $|n| = 1024$, the subliminal channel is *too small*. The range of SHA-256 matches the number of bits of $p$ needed by Coppersmith's algorithm for $|n| = 1024$.

Consider the configuration Hash = SHA-224 and $|n| = 1024$. In this case we can adjust the backdoor attack and use $k = 223$. $2^{32}$ is a small number, so it is straightforward to adjust the algorithm to exhaustively test all possible values for the missing 32 bits of the RSA prime $p$ in the loop in RSASSA-PSS-RECOVER.

Another straightforward configuration is Hash = SHA-512 and $|n| = 2048$. In this configuration $k = 511$ can be used. We have therefore shown the backdoor algorithm to work with 3 configurations of RSASSA-PSS.

In practice we may instantiate $\pi$ using a hash function (e.g., SHA-512) with the output truncated to $k + 1$ bits. Our application does not require a poly-time inversion function $\pi^{-1}$. This instantiation is clearly not a bijection. Heuristically, $\pi$ will appear to all efficient algorithms like a bijection since collisions will be hard to find. This is similar to replacing a random oracle (function) with a cryptographic hash function. The same applies to $\pi'$.

# 9   Conclusion

We presented the first (1,2)-SETUP for the RSA digital signature scheme with appendix. In particular, our construction works when PKCS #1 signatures are configured for 1024-bit moduli using the hash functions SHA-224 or SHA-256 and also for 2048-bit moduli when the hash function is SHA-512. We leave open the issue of extending this backdoor algorithm to other configurations.

# References

1. Adleman, L.M., Manders, K., Miller, G.: On Taking Roots in Finite Fields. IEEE Foundations of Computer Science—FOCS '77, 175–177 (1977)
2. Anderson, R.J.: A Practical RSA Trapdoor. Elec. Letters, 29(11) (1993)
3. Bellare, M., Rogaway, P.: Random oracles are practical: A paradigm for designing efficient protocols. In: 1st Annual ACM CCCS, pp. 62–73 (1993)
4. Bellare, M., Rogaway, P.: The Exact Security of Digital Signatures—How to Sign with RSA and Rabin. In: Maurer, U.M. (ed.) EUROCRYPT 1996. LNCS, vol. 1070, pp. 399–416. Springer, Heidelberg (1996)
5. Bellare, M., Rogaway, P.: PSS: Provably Secure Encoding Method for Digital Signatures. IEEE P1363 working group August 1998 (submission)
6. Bohli, J.M., Steinwandt, R.: On Subliminal Channels in Deterministic Signature Schemes. In: Park, C.-s., Chee, S. (eds.) ICISC 2004. LNCS, vol. 3506, pp. 182–194. Springer, Heidelberg (2005)
7. Boneh, D.: The Decision Diffie-Hellman Problem. In: Third Algorithmic Number Theory Symposium, pp. 48–63 (1998)
8. Coppersmith, D.: Finding a small root of a bivariate integer equation; Factoring with high bits known. In: Maurer, U.M. (ed.) EUROCRYPT 1996. LNCS, vol. 1070, pp. 178–189. Springer, Heidelberg (1996)
9. Crépeau, C., Slakmon, A.: Simple Backdoors for RSA Key Generation. In: Joye, M. (ed.) CT-RSA 2003. LNCS, vol. 2612, pp. 403–416. Springer, Heidelberg (2003)
10. Diffie, W., Hellman, M.: New Directions in Cryptography. IEEE Transactions on Information Theory IT-22(6), 644–654 (1976)
11. NIST. Announcing Draft FIPS 180-2, Secure Hash Standard, and RFC. Federal Register, vol. 66(104), p. 29287 (2001)
12. NIST. Announcing Approval of FIPS 180-2, Secure Hash Standard; a Revision of FIPS 180-2. Federal Register, vol. 67(165), pp. 54785–54787 (2002)
13. Gaudry, P., Hess, F., Smart, N.: Constructive and Destructive Facets of Weil Descent on Elliptic Curves. Journal of Cryptology 15(1), 19–46 (2002)
14. IEEE P1363 working group. IEEE P1363a D10: Standard Specifications for Public Key Cryptography: Additional Techniques (November 1, 2001) Available from http://grouper.ieee.org/groups/1363/
15. Joux, A., Nguyen, K.: Separating DDH from CDH in Cryptographic Groups. Journal of Cryptology 16(4), 239–247 (2003)
16. Kaliski, B.S.: A Pseudo-Random Bit Generator Based on Elliptic Logarithms. In: Odlyzko, A.M. (ed.) CRYPTO 1986. LNCS, vol. 263, pp. 84–103. Springer, Heidelberg (1987)
17. Kaliski, B.S.: Elliptic Curves and Cryptography: A Pseudorandom Bit Generator and Other Tools. PhD Thesis, MIT (February 1988)
18. Kaliski, B.S.: One-Way Permutations on Elliptic Curves. Journal of Cryptology 3(3), 187–199 (1991)
19. Luby, M.: Pseudorandomness and Cryptographic Applications. Princeton Computer Science Notes (1996)
20. Möller, B.: A Public-Key Encryption Scheme with Pseudo-Random Ciphertexts. In: Samarati, P., Ryan, P.Y A., Gollmann, D., Molva, R. (eds.) ESORICS 2004. LNCS, vol. 3193, pp. 335–351. Springer, Heidelberg (2004)
21. PKCS #1 v2.1: RSA Cryptography Standard. RSA Labs (June 14, 2002)
22. Rabin, M.: Probabilistic Algorithms in Finite Fields. SIAM Journal on Computing 9, 273–280 (1980)

23. Rivest, R., Shamir, A., Adleman, L.: A Method for Obtaining Digital Signatures and Public-Key Cryptosystems. CACM 21(2), 120–126 (1978)
24. Wang, X., Yu, H.: How to Break MD5 and Other Hash Functions. In: Cramer, R.J.F. (ed.) EUROCRYPT 2005. LNCS, vol. 3494, pp. 19–35. Springer, Heidelberg (2005)
25. Wang, X., Ying, Y., Yu, H.: Finding Collisions in the Full SHA-1. In: Shoup, V. (ed.) CRYPTO 2005. LNCS, vol. 3621, pp. 17–36. Springer, Heidelberg (2005)
26. Young, A., Yung, M.: The Dark Side of Black-Box Cryptography, or: Should we trust Capstone? In: Koblitz, N. (ed.) CRYPTO 1996. LNCS, vol. 1109, pp. 89–103. Springer, Heidelberg (1996)
27. Young, A., Yung, M.: Kleptography: Using Cryptography Against Cryptography. In: Fumy, W. (ed.) EUROCRYPT 1997. LNCS, vol. 1233, pp. 62–74. Springer, Heidelberg (1997)
28. Young, A., Yung, M.: The Prevalence of Kleptographic Attacks on Discrete-Log Based Cryptosystems. In: Kaliski Jr., B.S. (ed.) CRYPTO 1997. LNCS, vol. 1294, pp. 264–276. Springer, Heidelberg (1997)
29. Young, A., Yung, M.: A Space Efficient Backdoor in RSA and its Applications. In: Preneel, B., Tavares, S. (eds.) SAC 2005. LNCS, vol. 3897, pp. 128–143. Springer, Heidelberg (2006)

# A    Twists over GF($p$)

Every finite commutative group $A$ satisfies a unique isomorphism of the form $A \cong (\mathbb{Z}/n_1\mathbb{Z}) \times ... \times (\mathbb{Z}/n_r\mathbb{Z})$ where $n_{i+1}$ divides $n_i$ for $1 \leq i < r$ and $n_r > 1$. The integer $r$ is called the *rank* of the group $A$, and the $r$-tuple $(n_1, ..., n_r)$ is called the *group structure*. Below we give Definition 4.1 from [17] and Lemma 6.5 and Definition 6.1 from [17].

**Definition 4.** *Let $A$ be a commutative group, and let $(n_1, ..., n_r)$ represent the structure of the group. A **generating tuple** for the group $A$ is an ordered tuple $(G_1, ..., G_r) \in A^r$ for which every element $X \in A$ can be written uniquely as $X = a_1 G_1 + ... + a_r G_r$ where $0 \leq a_i < n_i$.*

**Lemma 4.** *Let $\beta \neq 0$ be a quadratic nonresidue in the field $\mathbb{F}_p$ and let $E_{a,b}(\mathbb{F}_p)$ be an elliptic curve. Then for every value $x$, letting $y = \sqrt{x^3 + ax + b}$:*

1. *If $y$ is a quadratic residue, then the points $(x, \pm y)$ are on the curve $E_{a,b}(\mathbb{F}_p)$.*
2. *If $y$ is a quadratic nonresidue, then the points $(\beta x, \pm\sqrt{\beta^3 y})$ are on the curve $E_{a\beta^2, b\beta^3}(\mathbb{F}_p)$.*
3. *If $y = 0$, then the point $(x, 0)$ is on the curve $E_{a,b}(\mathbb{F}_p)$ and the point $(\beta x, 0)$ is on the curve $E_{a\beta^2, b\beta^3}(\mathbb{F}_p)$.*

A corollary to this lemma is that the number of points on the two curves is $2p + 2$, two points for each value of $x$ and two identity elements.

**Definition 5.** *Let $E_{a,b}(\mathbb{F}_p)$ be an elliptic curve of parameter $k$ and let $\beta$ be a quadratic nonresidue modulo $p$. A twisted pair $T_{a,b,\beta}(\mathbb{F}_p)$ of parameter $k$ is the union [sic][2] of the elliptic curves $E_{a,b}(\mathbb{F}_p)$ and $E_{a\beta^2, b\beta^3}(\mathbb{F}_p)$.*

---

[2] It is perhaps more accurate to say "collection" instead of "union" since Kaliski's small example in Table 6.1 has $(0, 0)$ appearing twice in $T_{5,0,3}(\mathbb{F}_7)$. He confirms this by noting the possibility that the twisted pair may be a multiset.

A twisted pair may be a multiset, since the curves $E_{a,b}(\mathbb{F}_p)$ and $E_{a\beta^2,b\beta^3}(\mathbb{F}_p)$ may intersect. Kaliski uses the symbol $'$ (prime) to differentiate points originating from the two curves. In other words, he uses $P$ to denote a point from $E_{a,b}$ and $P'$ to denote a point from $E_{a',b'} = E_{a\beta^2,b\beta^3}$. Kaliski uses twists in his provably secure pseudorandom bit generator (PRBG). The presence or absence of the $'$ in the input to Kaliski's generator is really a parameter by itself. To clarify things we add a Boolean parameter to indicate which curve $P$ was selected from instead of appending $'$ to $P$. We let $c = 0$ denote that $P$ is a point chosen from $E_{a,b}$ and we let $c = 1$ denote that $P$ is a point chosen from $E_{a',b'}$. Also, in general for these curves there are two values of $y$ for each value of $x$.

Define $sgn : \mathbb{F}_p \to \{0,1\}$ to be 0 if $(p-1)/2 \geq y > 0$ and 1 otherwise. The function $X_T[T_{a,b,\beta}(\mathbb{F}_p)](P,i)$ is defined as,

$$X_T[T_{a,b,\beta}(\mathbb{F}_p)](P,i) = \begin{cases} 2x + sgn(y) & \text{if } P = (x,y), \, y \neq 0, \, i = 0 \\ 2x/\beta + sgn(y) & \text{if } P = (x,y), \, y \neq 0, \, i = 1 \\ 2x & \text{if } P = (x,0), \, i = 0 \\ 2x/\beta + 1 & \text{if } P = (x,0), \, i = 1 \\ 2p & \text{if } P = O, \, i = 0 \\ 2p + 1 & \text{if } P = O, \, i = 1 \end{cases}$$

**Lemma 5.** *Let $T_{a,b,\beta}(\mathbb{F}_p)$ be a twisted pair. The function $X_T[T_{a,b,\beta}(\mathbb{F}_p)](P,i)$ is a polynomial time computable, probabilistic polynomial time invertible mapping between the set of points on the twisted pair $T_{a,b,\beta}(\mathbb{F}_p)$ and the set $\{0, ..., 2p+1\}$.*

The above Lemma is Lemma 6.6 from [17]. The proof of this lemma defines the inverse function, broken down for the case that the input is even or odd. The probabilistic polynomial time algorithm to compute square roots is used [22,1] that can be assumed to return the principal square root (the one whose sign is 0). Define $w = x^3 + ax + b$ for $x \neq p$.

$$X_{T,even}^{-1}[T_{a,b,\beta}(\mathbb{F}_p)](2x) = \begin{cases} ((x, \sqrt{w}), 0) & \text{if } w \text{ is a quadratic residue} \\ ((\beta x, \sqrt{\beta^3 w}), 1) & \text{if } w \text{ is a quadratic nonresidue} \\ ((x,0),0) & \text{if } w = 0 \\ (O,0) & \text{if } x = p \end{cases}$$

$$X_{T,odd}^{-1}[T_{a,b,\beta}(\mathbb{F}_p)](2x+1) = \begin{cases} ((x, -\sqrt{w}), 0) & \text{if } w \text{ is a quadratic residue} \\ ((\beta x, -\sqrt{\beta^3 w}), 1) & \text{if } w \text{ is a quadratic nonresidue} \\ ((x,0),1) & \text{if } w = 0 \\ (O,1) & \text{if } x = p \end{cases}$$

## B    The TDDH Problem

In this appendix we show that if ECDDH is hard then TDDH is hard. The functions $f_\tau$ and $f_{\tau'}$ are defined in Section 7.

*Proof.* Suppose there exists a probabilistic polynomial time distinguisher $D$ that solves TDDH. Let $t = (X, Y, Z)$ be an ECDDH problem instance over $(E_{a,b}, G_1)$ and let $t' = (X', Y', Z')$ be an ECDDH problem instance over $(E_{a',b'}, G'_1)$. We will show that algorithm $M_0$ solves ECDDH over $(E_{a,b}, G_1)$ or algorithm $M_1$ solves ECDDH over $(E_{a',b'}, G'_1)$.

$M_0(E_{a,b}, G_1, X, Y, Z)$:
1. set $\tau = (E_{a,b}, G_1)$ and compute $u = f_\tau(X, Y, Z)$
2. generate a random 3-tuple $u'$ over $(E_{a',b'}, G'_1)$ and output $d = D(\tau, u, u')$

$M_1(E_{a',b'}, G'_1, X', Y', Z')$:
1. set $\tau' = (E_{a',b'}, G'_1)$ and compute $u' = f_{\tau'}(X', Y', Z')$
2. generate a random DH triple $u$ over $(E_{a,b}, G_1)$ and output $d = D(\tau, u, u')$

Let $S_{0,DH}$ be the set of all DH triples over $(E_{a,b}, G_1)$ and let $S_{1,DH}$ be the set of all DH triples over $(E_{a',b'}, G'_1)$. Let $S_{0,T}$ be the set of all 3-tuples over $(E_{a,b}, G_1)$ and let $S_{1,T}$ be the set of all 3-tuples over $(E_{a',b'}, G'_1)$. Without loss of generality we may suppose that the TDDH distinguisher $D$ outputs 1 with non-negligible advantage $\delta_1$ in $k$ when both 3-tuples are DH triples and 0 with non-negligible advantage $\delta_0$ in $k$ when both 3-tuples are random 3-tuples.

Consider the case that $v_0 \in_R S_{0,DH}$ and $v_1 \in_R S_{1,T}$. There are 3 cases:

**Case 1:** Consider the case that $D(\tau, v_0, v_1)$ outputs 0 with advantage $\gamma$ that is negligible in $k$ (so it outputs 1 with negligible advantage on this input). Consider algorithm $M_0$. Algorithm $M_0$ generates $u'$ to be a random 3-tuple over $(E_{a',b'}, G'_1)$. Suppose that $t$ is a DH triple. Then by $f_\tau$, $u$ is a random DH triple. So, in this case 0 is output with probability $1/2 + \gamma(k)$. Suppose that $t$ is a non-DH triple. Then by $f_\tau$, $u$ is a random 3-tuple. So, 0 is output with probability $1/2 + \delta_0(k)$. Therefore, $M_0$ solves ECDDH over $(E_{a,b}, G_1)$. There is a polynomial time observable difference in behavior here. By amplifying and applying Chernoff Bounds $M_0$ can be used to construct a Perfect-ECDDH distinguisher.

**Case 2:** Consider the case that $D(\tau, v_0, v_1)$ outputs 0 with probability $1/2 - \delta_2(k)$ and 1 with probability $1/2 + \delta_2(k)$ where $\delta_2$ is non-negligible. Consider algorithm $M_0$. Algorithm $M_0$ generates $u'$ to be a random 3-tuple over $(E_{a',b'}, G'_1)$. Suppose that $t$ is a DH triple. Then by $f_\tau$, $u$ is a random DH triple. So, in this case 1 is output with probability $1/2 + \delta_2(k)$. Suppose that $t$ is a non-DH triple. Then by $f_\tau$, $u$ is a random 3-tuple. So, 0 is output with probability $1/2 + \delta_0(k)$. Therefore, $M_0$ solves ECDDH over $(E_{a,b}, G_1)$.

**Case 3:** Consider the case that $D(\tau, v_0, v_1)$ outputs 0 with probability $1/2 + \delta_3(k)$ and 1 with probability $1/2 - \delta_3(k)$ where $\delta_3$ is non-negligible. Consider algorithm $M_1$. Algorithm $M_1$ generates $u$ to be a random DH triple over $(E_{a,b}, G_1)$. Suppose that $t'$ is a DH triple. Then by $f_{\tau'}$, $u'$ is a random DH triple. So, in this case 1 is output with probability $1/2 + \delta_1(k)$. Suppose that $t'$ is a non-DH triple. Then by $f_{\tau'}$, $u'$ is a random 3-tuple. So, 0 is output with probability $1/2 + \delta_3(k)$. Therefore, $M_1$ solves ECDDH over $(E_{a',b'}, G'_1)$.

Either $M_0$ or $M_1$ solves ECDDH. So, the contrapositive holds.    ◇

## C   Statistical Indistinguishability Proof

We now review the definition of statistical distance (Lecture 7, [19]). Let $\mathcal{D}_k$ : $\{0,1\}^k$ and $\mathcal{E}_k$ : $\{0,1\}^k$ be distributions. Also, let $X \in_{\mathcal{D}_k} \{0,1\}^k$ and $Y \in_{\mathcal{E}_k} \{0,1\}^k$.

**Definition 6.** *The **statistical distance** between $\mathcal{D}_k$ and $\mathcal{E}_k$ is,*

$$\text{dist}(\mathcal{D}_k, \mathcal{E}_k) = \frac{1}{2} \cdot \sum_{z \in \{0,1\}^k} |\Pr_X [X = z] - \Pr_Y [Y = z]| \qquad (1)$$

Define $\mathcal{S}_e$ to be all $(k+1)$-bit strings that are encoded points on $T_{a,b,\beta}(\mathbb{F}_p)$. Define $\mathcal{S}$ to be $\mathcal{S}_e \times \{0,1\}^{k+1}$. Let $\mathcal{X}$ denote the probability ensemble corresponding to the salts $(salt_1, salt_2)$ output by $SIGS_2$. Let $\mathcal{Y}$ denote the probability ensemble corresponding to the salts $(salt_1, salt_2)$ output by $SIGS_3$. The distance between $\mathcal{X}$ and $\mathcal{Y}$ is,

$$\text{dist}(\mathcal{X}, \mathcal{Y}) = \frac{1}{2} \cdot \sum_{(z_1, z_2) \in \mathcal{S}} |\Pr_X [X = (z_1, z_2)] - \Pr_Y [Y = (z_1, z_2)]| \qquad (2)$$

**Lemma 6.** *The statistical distance between $\mathcal{X}$ and $\mathcal{Y}$ is negligible in $k$.*

*Proof.* We break the statistical distance sum into 4 terms $t_{i,j}$ for $i, j \in \{0,1\}$. Here $i = 0 \Leftrightarrow z_1$ is an encoded point on $E_{a,b}$. Also, $j = 0 \Leftrightarrow (i = 0$ and $z_2 \in \mathcal{T}_\pi)$ or $(i = 1$ and $z_2 \in \mathcal{T}_{\pi'})$. The statistical distance is $\frac{1}{2}(t_{0,0} + t_{0,1} + t_{1,0} + t_{1,1})$. Recall that $p = 2^k - \delta$. The terms are:

$$t_{0,0} = r(2r)|\frac{1}{2p+2}\frac{1}{2r} - \frac{1}{2p+2}\frac{1}{2^{k+1}}| = \frac{r^2}{2p+2}|\frac{1}{r} - \frac{1}{2^k}| = \frac{r(2^k - r)}{(2p+2)2^k}$$

$$t_{0,1} = r(2^{k+1} - 2r)|\frac{1}{2p+2} * 0 - \frac{1}{2p+2}\frac{1}{2^{k+1}}| = \frac{r(2^k - r)}{(2p+2)2^k}$$

$$t_{1,0} = r'(2r')|\frac{1}{2p+2}\frac{1}{2r'} - \frac{1}{2p+2}\frac{1}{2^{k+1}}| = \frac{r'^2}{2p+2}|\frac{1}{r'} - \frac{1}{2^k}| = \frac{r'(2^k - r')}{(2p+2)2^k}$$

$$t_{1,1} = r'(2^{k+1} - 2r')|\frac{1}{2p+2} * 0 - \frac{1}{2p+2}\frac{1}{2^{k+1}}| = \frac{r'(2^k - r')}{(2p+2)2^k}$$

Every term is negligible in $k$. So, the statistical distance is negligible in $k$. ⋄

# A Subliminal-Free Variant of ECDSA

Jens-Matthias Bohli[1], María Isabel González Vasco[2], and Rainer Steinwandt[3]

[1] Institut für Algorithmen und Kognitive Systeme, Universität Karlsruhe,
76128 Karlsruhe, Germany
bohli@ira.uka.de

[2] Departamento de Matemática Aplicada, Universidad Rey Juan Carlos, c/ Tulipán,
s/n, 28933 Madrid, Spain
mariaisabel.vasco@urjc.es

[3] Center for Cryptology and Information Security, Dept. of Mathematical Sciences,
Florida Atlantic University, 777 Glades Road, Boca Raton, FL 33431, USA
rsteinwa@fau.edu

**Abstract.** A mode of operation of the Elliptic Curve Digital Signature Algorithm (ECDSA) is presented which provably excludes subliminal communication through ECDSA signatures. For this, the notion of a signature scheme that is *subliminal-free with proof* is introduced which can be seen as generalizing *subliminal-free signatures* and being intermediate to the established concepts of *invariant* and *unique signatures*.

Motivated by the proposed use of ECDSA for signing passports, our focus is not on proving the mere existence of a subliminal-free ECDSA mode of operation, but on demonstrating its practical potential. The proposed construction relies on the availability of a party acting as warden and on a reasonably-sized non-interactive proof of subliminal-freeness. For instance, in the passport scenario, the passport holder plays the role of the warden, and we show that a suitable combination of the pseudo random function of Naor and Reingold with bit commitments and non-interactive zero-knowledge proofs can be used for accomplishing the required proof of subliminal-freeness with acceptable efficiency.

**Keywords:** subliminal communication, digital signature, ECDSA.

## 1 Introduction

It is a well-known phenomenon that cryptographic schemes can also be used for purposes or in a way they have not been designed for (cf., for instance, [DGB87, Des88a, Des88b, YY04]). One well-explored example of this is the use of *subliminal channels* in signature schemes: Subliminal channels in signature schemes were introduced by Simmons in [Sim84] as a solution to the prisoner's problem: two prisoners are allowed to exchange signed messages, but their communication is monitored by a warden. The prisoners want to exchange a secret message unnoticeable to the warden and hide the message in a signature of a "harmless" cover message. In contrast, the warden is interested in implementing a subliminal-free signature scheme that prevents any subliminal communication.

J. Camenisch et al. (Eds.): IH 2006, LNCS 4437, pp. 375–387, 2007.
© Springer-Verlag Berlin Heidelberg 2007

Of course, this scenario does not address the use of steganographic techniques for embedding information, and is mainly of interest if the signer has no or only limited control over the messages to be signed.

However, already developing a general formalization of subliminal communication is quite an ambitious goal. In the context of interactive zero-knowledge proofs for languages, a formalization of subliminal-freeness has been put forward by Burmester et al. in [BDI+99]. For the specific case of subliminal communication through digital signatures such a formalization has been proposed in [BS05]. Specifically, [BS05] provides a definition of a (non-interactive) *subliminal-free signature scheme* and proves the well-established RSA-PSS scheme to be subliminal-free in this sense (if being used in deterministic mode along with a precautious key generation).

However, for the common family of Digital Signature Algorithm (DSA)-like signatures no subliminal-free variant is known[Sim94]. Simmons [Sim93] gives an interactive signing procedure between the signer and the warden for generating DSA    signatures,    but    as    pointed    out    by    Desmedt    in [Des96], this scheme contains a subliminal channel, if the signer can reject some protocol runs and start anew. While the warden in an interactive protocol could take some precautions against this, it makes a transformation into a non-interactive signing procedure where the signer uses a pseudo random generator to simulate the warden's input impossible—the signer can reject the signing process privately and unnoticeably.

A cryptographic primitive that turns out to be closely related to subliminal-free signature schemes is known as *invariant signature schemes* [GO93]. A special type of *invariant signature schemes* are *unique signature schemes*, defined by [Lys02] as those schemes for which only one valid signature is provided for each message and verification key. Unique signature schemes are subliminal-free in the sense of [BS05], but in most scenarios where subliminal channels matter, signatures do not need to be unique w.r.t. the verification, as long as the warden is convinced that the signing algorithm has been used "in a unique manner". We will refer to signatures, where the warden can be convinced of such uniqueness, as *subliminal-free with proof* and show that they lie between invariant and unique signatures.

Within our new framework a subliminal-free usage of ECDSA is possible in the following sense: If the proof delivered along with the signature is correct, the warden can be sure that the signature does not contain suspicious information (and delete the proof). Note that we do not care about subliminal information embedded in the proof: We aim at preventing communication between signer and verifier through signatures, not at preventing communication between signer and warden. A scenario where the availability of a warden is quite natural is in the context of digitally signed passports: e.g., Germany considers using ECDSA for signing passports [Bun05]. Thus, one may ask whether it is possible to produce ECDSA signatures where the owner of a passport (who is taking the role of the warden here) can be sure that the signature contains no subliminal compromising information.

Motivated by application scenarios like this, we are not interested in solutions that rely on an interactive verification protocol for checking subliminal-freeness or that require a modification of ECDSA signatures: We want the obtained signatures to be well-formed ECDSA signatures, but along with a (message, signature)-pair we allow a proof to be delivered that can be verified off-line. In the context of passports, this proof could then be checked by the card holder to be sure that no subliminal message has been embedded into the ECDSA signature on her passport. As shown below, already with a non-optimized implementation, ECDSA affords proofs with a size of less than 8 MB. Thus, for a setting like this implementing ECDSA subliminal-free with proof can be considered as practical.

## 2    Basic Definitions

Let us first recall the standard definition of a signature scheme:

**Definition 1.** *A* signature scheme *$S = (\mathsf{Gen}, \mathsf{Sig}, \mathsf{Ver})$ is a triple of algorithms, where*

- $\mathsf{Gen}$ *is a probabilistic polynomial time (ppt) algorithm that takes the security parameter $l$ as input and returns a pair of public and private keys $(pk, sk)$.*
- $\mathsf{Sig}$ *is a ppt algorithm that takes a message $m$ and the private key $sk$ as input and produces a valid signature $\sigma$ for $m$ under $sk$.*
- $\mathsf{Ver}$ *is a deterministic polynomial time algorithm that takes a message $m$, a signature $\sigma$ and the public verification key $pk$ as input and returns* valid *if $\sigma$ is a valid signature for $m$ w. r. t. $pk$, and* invalid *otherwise.*

For accepted relaxations of the above definition, as well as for an in-depth discussion of standard security notions for signature schemes see [Gol04, Chapter 6].

In [GO93] Goldwasser and Ostrovsky defined *invariant signature schemes* and proved their equivalence to non-interactive zero-knowledge proofs in the common random string model. In an invariant signature scheme additionally a deterministic polynomial-time computable function $\mathsf{Inv}$ exists such that $\mathsf{Inv}(\sigma)$ is identical for all legal signatures $\sigma$ of a message $m$. Moreover, $\mathsf{Inv}(\sigma)$ is hard to distinguish from a truly random string if only the public key $pk$ and the message $m$ are known.

A similar concept is a *unique signature scheme*, where only one signature for each message exists.

**Definition 2.** *([Lys02]) A* unique signature scheme *is a signature scheme where no values $pk$, $m$, $\sigma_1$, $\sigma_2$ exist such that*

$$\sigma_1 \neq \sigma_2 \text{ and } \mathsf{Ver}(m, \sigma_1, pk) = \mathsf{Ver}(m, \sigma_2, pk) = \mathsf{valid}.$$

If the algorithm $\mathsf{Sig}$ is transformed to satisfy the pseudorandomness property, this turns out to be a special case of invariant signature schemes.

As for unique signature schemes there is exactly one valid signature for any given message-public key pair, it is impossible to hide a single bit of information in a valid signature and one can easily prove them to be subliminal-free in the sense of [BS05]. Though, in invariant signature schemes and unique signature schemes the uniqueness is absolute, while in the definition of subliminal-free in [BS05] the uniqueness holds only with overwhelming probability for polynomial-time algorithms. In the following we have respective analogs of invariant and unique signatures in mind.

*Signature schemes that are subliminal-free with proof.* However, for most scenarios it is not necessary to impose uniqueness in this sense, as long as it can be proven that Sig was used in a unique way. If there is one distinguished entity who is absolved from being a subliminal receiver—the warden— this entity can check the proofs and stop or accuse a dishonest signer. The subsequent definition tries to formalize this intuitive notion of a signature scheme that is subliminal-free with proof.

**Definition 3.** *A* subliminal-free with proof *signature scheme is a quintuple of algorithms* $S = (\mathsf{Gen}, \mathsf{SFGen}, \mathsf{Sig}, \mathsf{Ver}, \mathsf{Chk})$, *where*

- Gen *and* Ver *are probabilistic and deterministic polynomial time algorithms for key generation and signature verification, respectively, as in Definition 1.*
- SFGen *is a ppt algorithm that takes pk and sk as input and generates the information ci that the warden needs for checking the signature computation.*
- Sig *is a ppt algorithm that takes a message m and the private key sk as input and produces a valid signature $\sigma$ for m under pk and a proof t.*
- Chk *is a deterministic polynomial time algorithm that takes a message m, a signature $\sigma$, a public key pk, the checking information ci and a proof t as input, and returns* true *if* $\mathsf{Ver}(m, \sigma, pk) = $ valid *and* $(\sigma, t)$ *is a valid output of* $\mathsf{Sig}(m, sk)$.

*Moreover, for any ppt algorithm $\mathcal{A}$ taking the security parameter $k$ as input, the probability of giving as output values $pk, sk, ci, m, \sigma_1, \sigma_2, t_1, t_2$ such that $(pk, sk), ci$ are computationally indistinguishable from the output of* Gen *respectively* SFGen,*

$$\sigma_1 \neq \sigma_2 \quad and \quad \mathsf{Chk}(m, \sigma_1, pk, ci, t_1) = \mathsf{Chk}(m, \sigma_2, pk, ci, t_2) = \text{true}$$

*is negligible in the security parameter $l$.*

*Remark 1.* It has to be proven that the subliminal-free with proof signature scheme maintains the security of the original scheme. I.e., the forger's probability is still negligible if the checking information $ci$ is given as an additional input and the signing oracle outputs a signature $\sigma$ along with a proof $t$.

*Remark 2.* With this definition a subliminal-free signature with proof, $(\sigma, t)$ is an invariant signature with respect to the verification via the Chk algorithm. The invariant function $\mathsf{Inv}((\sigma, t))$ is to be chosen as a random extractor as given in [MRV99] for the unique part $\sigma$ of a signature $(\sigma, t)$. The signature can be seen as a unique signature insofar, as the part $\sigma$ that is unique with respect to Chk is in itself a signature with respect to the verification algorithm Ver.

Thus, if a warden (e.g., the owner of a passport) accepts a signature $\sigma$ only, if it comes along with a valid proof $t$, then she can be sure that not a single bit of subliminal information has been embedded into $\sigma$. In this sense, subliminal-free with proof signature schemes implement subliminal-freeness as defined in [BS05]. Clearly, any unique signature scheme (like RSA-PSS in a deterministic mode as considered in [BS05]) is subliminal-free with proof. However, a subliminal-free with proof signature scheme may well allow for several different valid signatures $\sigma$ for a message $m$ and a public key $pk$, as long as, except with negligible probability, only one of these signatures is accepted by the check algorithm Chk. Specifically, for a subliminal-free with proof signature scheme we do not impose that an invariant value can be extracted from all valid signatures for a pair $(m, pk)$ (as is the case for invariant signatures).

# 3   Making ECDSA Subliminal-Free with Proof

For the sake of convenience, let us quickly recapitulate the basic setup of the ECDSA signature scheme (see, e.g., [ISO02] for details). Basically, ECDSA builds on a publicly known finite field $\mathbb{F}_p$, an elliptic curve $E(\mathbb{F}_p)$ over $\mathbb{F}_p$ where $q_{ec} | \#E(\mathbb{F}_p)$ with $q_{ec}$ prime, and a point $G \in E(\mathbb{F}_p)$ of order $q_{ec}$. Choosing the elliptic curve with $q_{ec}^2 \nmid \#E(\mathbb{F}_p)$ ensures that every point $P \in E(\mathbb{F}_p)$ of order $q_{ec}$ is a multiple of the generator $G$ and a malicious signer willing to communicate subliminally cannot deviate from the scheme by a faked key generation.

**Private key:** The signer holds a random $d \in \{1, \ldots, q_{ec} - 1\}$ as her private key.
**Public key:** The multiple $P := d \cdot G$ is made public.
**Signature generation:** The signature of a message $m \in \{0, 1\}^*$ is a pair $(r, s)$
  such that
  - $r = \pi(k \cdot G) \bmod q_{ec}$ with a random $k \in_R \{1, \ldots, q_{ec} - 1\}$, and
  - $s = k^{-1}(dr + \mathfrak{h}(m)) \bmod q_{ec}$.

  Here, $\mathfrak{h}(\cdot)$ is a collision-free hash function and $\pi(\cdot)$ a *conversion function* transforming the representation of the $x$-coordinate of a point on $E(\mathbb{F}_p)$ to an integer.
**Signature verification:** A signature $(r, s)$ for $m \in \{0, 1\}^*$ is accepted if and only if $r = \pi((s^{-1}\mathfrak{h}(m) \bmod q_{ec}) \cdot G + (s^{-1}r \bmod q_{ec}) \cdot P) \bmod q_{ec}$ holds.

## 3.1   A Deterministic ECDSA Mode of Operation

The first step towards an ECDSA that is subliminal-free with proof is a deterministic mode of operation for ECDSA. Basically, a deterministic ECDSA variant can be obtained by replacing the random choice of $k$ in the signing algorithm with the output of a pseudo random function applied to a known input value. However, determinism alone is not enough to exclude subliminal communication (see [BS05]). Additionally, the warden has to be able to verify the correct deterministic construction of a signature — a proof has to be given. We have to ensure that

- the value $k$ computed in this way remains secret and
- the correct computation and use of $k$ is verifiable (offline and efficiently).

The first condition is needed to maintain security—disclosure of $k$ would reveal the private key $d$. The second one allows to establish the desired proof for subliminal-freeness—if it cannot be checked that the signer used the algorithm honestly, a subliminal channel can be used (cf. [BS05]).

Moreover, the first condition rules out the possibility of using a verifiable pseudo random function, that would allow to verify the correct generation of the pseudo randomness, provided the generated randomness (here $k$) is public. Therefore, we use for our construction an efficient pseudo random function by Naor and Reingold building on a Decision Diffie Hellman (DDH) assumption [NR04] and give a zero-knowledge proof that does not leak any information (at the price of some idealized assumptions).

**Naor and Reingold's pseudo random function.** The pseudo random function from [NR04] is parameterized by two prime numbers $p_1$, $q_1 \mid p_1 - 1$, an element $g_1 \in \mathbb{Z}_{p_1}^*$ of order $q_1$ and $n+1$ random elements $a = a_0, \ldots, a_n \in \mathbb{Z}_{q_1}$. Then the one-way output of the pseudo random function for input $x = x_1 \ldots x_n \in \{0,1\}^n$ is

$$f_{p_1,q_1,g_1,a}(x) = g_1^{a_0 \prod_{x_i=1} a_i}.$$

This value is pseudo random in the cyclic group of order $q_1$ generated by $g_1$.

For our purposes $x$ will be computed by applying a collision-resistant hash function $\mathfrak{h}(m)$ with $n$-bit output to the message $m$ that is to be signed. Moreover, as the output of $f_{p_1,q_1,g_1,a}$ will have to serve as $k$-value in ECDSA we have to pass from a pseudo random element in the group generated by $g_1$ to an equally distributed random value in $\mathbb{Z}_{q_{ec}}$ as needed in the signature generation. For this, we can apply a universal hash function to $f_{p_1,q_1,g_1,a}$'s output. The following variant of the left over hash lemma [ILL89, IZ89, Sti02] guarantees then an almost equal distribution in $\mathbb{Z}_{q_{ec}}$.

**Lemma 1.** *With the above notation, let $X$ be a subset of $\mathbb{Z}_{p_1}$ of cardinality $|X| \geq q_1$. Moreover, let $e > 0$ and denote by $\mathcal{H}$ an almost universal family of hash functions mapping $\mathbb{Z}_{p_1}$ to $\mathbb{Z}_{q_{ec}}$, where $\log q_{ec} = \log q_1 - 2e$. Then the distribution $(\mathfrak{h}, \mathfrak{h}(x))$ is quasi-random within $2^{-e}$, where $\mathfrak{h} \in_R \mathcal{H}$ and $x \in_R X$ are chosen independently and uniformly at random.*

*Proof.* The proof of this lemma is analogous to [IZ89] and hence omitted here. □

As pseudo-random function we will use the following function from [IZ89]

$$\mathfrak{h}_{a,b} : \mathbb{Z}_{p_1} \longrightarrow \mathbb{Z}_{q_{ec}}$$
$$y \longmapsto a \cdot y + b \bmod p_1 \bmod q_{ec}.$$

Let us outline a deterministic variant of ECDSA by replacing the random choice of $k$ in the signing algorithm with the output of Naor-Reingold's function.

**Initialization phase:** Given the usual ECDSA parameters $E(\mathbb{F}_p)$ and a point $G \in E(\mathbb{F}_p)$ of order $q_{ec}$, the algorithm SFGen, on input $sk$ and $pk$, outputs the following values:

- Primes $p_1$ and $q_1$ with $q_1|(p_1 - 1)$—for the proof we will require that $q_1$ is close to a power of 2 to allow for exact range proofs.
- (Truly) random values $\boldsymbol{a} = a_0, \ldots, a_n \in \mathbb{Z}_{q_1}$ needed for the pseudo random function of Naor and Reingold.
- Elements $a$ and $b$ chosen uniformly at random from $\mathbb{Z}_{p_1}$ (which determine a universal hash function).
- A set of system parameters determining the proof constructed in the next section, which we will denote by PROOF.

The string $ci := (p_1, q_1, a, b, \text{PROOF})$ is sent to the warden (that is, all parameters constructed above except $\boldsymbol{a}$). For parties that only have to verify signatures, the signatures will look like ECDSA signatures and no additional parameters are needed.

**Signature generation:** The signature of a message $m \in \{0, 1\}^*$ is a pair $(r, s)$ computed as follows:

- The hashed message $\mathfrak{h}(m)$ is given as input to the Naor-Reingold function to compute

$$k = a \cdot g^{a_0 \prod_{x_i=1} a_i} + b \quad \bmod p_1 \bmod q_{ec}(\text{with } x = \mathfrak{h}(m)).$$

- A proof for the correct computation of $k$ is constructed and sent to the warden. This proof is ideally a (non-interactive) zero-knowledge proof.
- $r = \pi(k \cdot G) \bmod q_{ec}$
- $s = k^{-1}(dr + \mathfrak{h}(m)) \bmod q_{ec}$.

Here, $\mathfrak{h}(\cdot)$ is a collision-free hash function and $\pi(\cdot)$ a *conversion function* transforming the representation of the $x$-coordinate of a point on $E(\mathbb{F}_p)$ to an integer. As usual the signature is $(r, s)$.

**Proof verification:** The warden can check with the signature $(r, s)$ and the proof, if indeed the value

$$k = a \cdot g^{a_0 \prod_{x_i=1} a_i} + b \quad \bmod p_1 \bmod q_{ec}(\text{with } x = \mathfrak{h}(m))$$

was used.

**Proposition 1.** *Provided ECDSA is secure, then the deterministic variant of ECDSA is also secure.*

*Proof.* Our scheme basically differs from "standard" ECDSA in three aspects:

(i) the way $k$ is obtained,
(ii) the fact that a forger can make use of the value $ci$

(iii) the fact that a forger can make use of the proof $t$ which is provided together with each signature.

Concerning (i), as we have only modified the way the value $k$ is generated by Sig, it suffices to check this new generation still yields a *sufficiently* unpredictable $k$ (see [Vau03] for a survey on security proofs of DSA and ECDSA). The pseudo random function guarantees that $k$ is indistinguishable from a random group element and from the fact that the family $\mathcal{H} = \{\mathfrak{h}_{a,b} | a, b \in \mathbb{Z}_{p_1}, a \neq 0\}$ is almost universal, (see, for instance, [CW79]) and the output of Naor and Reingold's random function is always indistinguishable from independent of the parameters $a$ and $b$. Thus, the output of the random function is indistinguishable from random even under adversarial choice of $m$.

Let us now argue why knowledge of the proofs $t$ or the checking information $ci$ gives no advantage to a forger: on one hand, $t$ is a ZK proof of the correctnes of $k$, so obviously is giving an adversary no advantage. Moreover, the amount of "compromised" information contained in $ci$ is negligible if the commitment scheme used to construct PROOF is robust enough.

Therefore, an adversary trying to forge our ECDSA variant is in no better situation than one facing the standard ECDSA scheme.     □

In summary, building on Naor and Reingold's pseudo random function, we can basically achieve a deterministic variant of ECDSA, and we are left with the task of implementing the proof in a verifiable manner without compromising the secrecy of $k$.

## 3.2   Building Blocks for the Proof

*Commitment scheme.* To implement the required non-interactive proof, we use a commitment scheme as in [CM99, Ped92]: Given are two primes $p, q$ with $q | p - 1$. To commit to elements of a subgroup of $\mathbb{Z}_q$ this commitment scheme builds on elements $g, h \in \mathbb{Z}_p^*$ that generate the same subgroup of size $q$ such that $\log_g h$ is unknown. The commitment to $u \in \mathbb{Z}_q$ is

$$BC_{g,h}(u) = g^u h^v$$

for a random $v \in \mathbb{Z}_q$. As shown in [Ped92], this commitment scheme is perfectly hiding, and breaking the binding property is as hard as computing discrete logarithms to the base $g$ or $h$.

We want to prove that in the signing process $k$ has indeed been computed as

$$k = a \cdot g^{a_0 \prod_{x_i = 1} a_i} + b \quad \mod p_1 \mod q_{ec}(\text{with } x = \mathfrak{h}(m))$$

*without revealing* $k$. As $\mathfrak{h}(m)$ must be considered as public, we will not reveal the values $a_0, \dots, a_n$, either, but only commitments to them. Given these commitments, we construct a commitment $BC(k)$ and prove that $k$ is indeed the output of the pseudo random function.

*Basic zero-knowledge proofs.* We use non-interactive zero-knowledge proofs for modular arithmetic as given in [CM99, FO97] and proofs of the range of committed values as specified in [Bou00]. We also adopt the notation for proofs of knowledge from [CM99]. To obtain non-interactive proofs we can replace the verifier's choices with pseudo-randomness in the Common Random String or the Random Oracle model [BSMP91]. As we commit to values from a cyclic group and always choose a group of suitable size and change the group if necessary, we do not have to carry out a modulo reduction. More specifically, the main building blocks for our zero-knowledge proof of correct usage are:

- proving knowledge of a discrete logarithm denoted by $PK\{(x) : g^x\}$
- proving knowledge of a committed value denoted by $PK\{(x, \alpha) : g^x h^\alpha\}$
- proving equality of committed values denoted by $PK\{(x, \alpha, \beta) : g^x h^\alpha \wedge g^x h^\beta\}$
- addition of values committed to denoted by
  $PK\{(x, y, z, \alpha, \beta, \gamma) : g^x h^\alpha \wedge g^y h^\beta \wedge g^z h^\gamma \wedge z = x + y\}$
- multiplication of values committed to denoted by
  $PK\{(x, y, z, \alpha, \beta, \gamma) : g^x h^\alpha \wedge g^y h^\beta \wedge g^z h^\gamma \wedge z = x \cdot y\}$
- exponentiation of values committed to denoted by
  $PK\{(x, y, z, \alpha, \beta, \gamma) : g^x h^\alpha \wedge g^y h^\beta \wedge g^z h^\gamma \wedge z = x^y\}$
- proving the range $[r_{min}, r_{max}]$ of a committed value denoted by
  $PK\{(x, \alpha) : g^x h^\alpha \wedge r_{min} \leq x \leq r_{max}\}$

*Proving equality of committed values.* We will introduce a way to prove in zero-knowledge equality of committed values for commitments in cyclic groups of different prime order $q_1$ and $q_2$. Therefore these groups need to be embedded in a cyclic group of order $q_0$ with subgroups of order $q_1$ and $q_2$ generated by $\{g_0, h_0\}$. Generators for the subgroups are then $g_1 = g_0^{q_2}$ and $g_2 = g_0^{q_1}$, analogously, we set $h_1 := h_0^{q_2}$ and $h_2 := h_0^{q_1}$.

Then one readily checks that for two given commitments $BC_{g_1, h_1}(x) = g_1^x h_1^{v_1}$ and $BC_{g_2, h_2}(x) = g_2^x h_2^{v_2}$ the following procedure allows $\mathcal{P}$ to convince $\mathcal{V}$ that both are commitments on the same value $x < \min(q_1, q_2)$.

1. $\mathcal{P}$ computes $v_0 := \mathrm{CRT}^{-1}(v_1, v_2)$, where $\mathrm{CRT}^{-1}$ denotes the inverse isomorphism of the Chinese remainder theorem.
2. $\mathcal{P}$ sends the commitment $BC_{g_0, h_0}(x) = g_0^x h_0^{v_0}$ to $\mathcal{V}$.
3. $\mathcal{P}$ proves $x < \min(q_1, q_2)$ for the commitment $BC_{g_0, h_0}(x)$. As there is no exact proof of a range for commitments in prime order groups a suitable method has to be chosen in each case. We will explicitly state which methods we use in our proof.
4. $\mathcal{V}$ checks $BC_{g_0, h_0}(x)^{q_2} = BC_{g_1, h_1}(x)$ and $BC_{g_2, h_2}(x) = BC_{g, h}(x)^{q_1}$.

## 3.3 Construction of the Proof

For the commitments a further prime $p_0$ with $q_1 p_1 q_{ec} | (p_0 - 1)$ is computed and generators $g_0, h_0 \in \mathbb{Z}_{p_0}^*$ of order $q_1 p_1 q_{ec}$ are selected. The generators $g_1 = g_0^{p_1 q_{ec}}$, $g_2 = g_0^{q_1 q_{ec}}$ and $h_{ec} = g_0^{q_1 p_1}$ are selected. Moreover, commitments $BC(a_0), \ldots,$ $BC(a_n)$ to the secret random values $\boldsymbol{a} = a_0, \ldots, a_n \in \mathbb{Z}_{q_1}$ needed for the pseudo random function of Naor and Reingold are computed. For the proof we will need the additional parameters

$$\mathsf{PROOF} = (p_0, g_0, h_0, g_1, g_2, h_{ec}, BC(a_0), \ldots, BC(a_n)).$$

The zero-knowledge proof that the randomness used for signing the message $m$ is

$$k = \left(ag^{a_0 \prod_{x_i=1} a_i} + b \bmod p_1\right) \bmod q_{ec}$$

with $x = \mathfrak{h}(m)$, is constructed in the following extension to the signing algorithm:

1. Compute a commitment $BC_{g_1,h_1}(\pi)$ to the product $\pi = a_0 \prod_{x_i=1} a_i \bmod q_1$ and a non-interactive proof

$$PK\{(a_0, \ldots, a_n, \pi, v_0, \ldots, v_{n+1}) : g_1^{a_0} h_1^{v_0} \wedge \cdots \wedge g_1^{a_n} h_1^{v_n} \wedge$$
$$g_1^{\pi} h_1^{v_{n+1}} \wedge \pi = a_0 \prod_{x_i=1} a_i \bmod q_1\}.$$

2. Construct a commitment $BC_{g_2,h_2}(\pi)$ and a non-interactive proof for the values committed to in $BC_{g_1,h_1}(\pi)$ and $BC_{g_2,h_2}(\pi)$ being equal

$$PK\{(\pi, v_1, v_2) : g_1^{\pi} h_1^{v_1} \wedge g_2^{\pi} h_2^{v_2}\}.$$

Since the groups were chosen accordingly and $q_1$ is close to a power of 2 this is possible using the range proof via the bit expansion. Namely, we compute commitments $BC_{g_0,h_0}(b_i)$ for $0 \le i \le \lfloor \log_2(q_1)\rceil$ to the bits $b_i$ of $\pi$ and prove $b_i \in \{0, 1\}$ as well as $\sum_{i=0}^{\lfloor \log_2(q_1)\rceil} b_i 2^i = \pi$.

3. Compute $g^{\pi} \bmod p_1$ and commit to that value $BC_{g_2,h_2}(g^{\pi})$ and prove along the square-and-multiply algorithm

$$PK\{(\pi, x, v_1, v_2) : g_2^{\pi} h_2^{v_1} \wedge g_2^{x} h_2^{v_2} \wedge x = g^{\pi}\}.$$

We can reuse the bit representation of $\pi$ from Step 2 to prove the exponentiation along the square-and-multiply algorithm as done in [CM99].

4. Compute $k = (a \cdot g^{\pi} + b) \bmod p_1 \bmod q_{ec}$ and a commitment $BC_{g_2,h_2}(k)$ to $k$. Prove

$$PK\{(\pi, k, v_1, v_2) : g_2^{(g^{\pi})} h_2^{v_1} \wedge g_2^{k} h_2^{v_2} \wedge k = a \cdot (g^{\pi}) + b - \alpha \cdot q_{ec} \wedge 0 \le k < 3q_{ec}\}.$$

For this we use the range proof going back to [BCDvdG88]. This proof is exact enough as executing the proof $x < q_{ec}$ assures $x < 3q_{ec} < p_1$ what indeed is enough for the change of the group in the next step.

5. Compute a commitment $BC_{g_{ec},h_{ec}}(k)$ and prove the equivalence with

$$PK\{(k, v_1, v_2) : g_2^{h} h_2^{v_1} \wedge g_{ec}^{k} h_{ec}^{v_2}\}.$$

The range proof given in the last step is sufficient for this step. So, no additional proof via the bit representation is needed here.

6. Prove that $k$ was indeed used for the signature $(r, s)$. Another commitment $BC_{G,H}(k) = kG + v_1 H$ in the elliptic curve $E(\mathbb{F}_p)$ is computed. There, $G$ is the generator used in the signing algorithm, and $H$ is another generator for the group generated by $G$ such that $\log_G H$ is unknown. For the zero-knowledge proof

$$PK\{(k, v_1, v_2) : kG + v_1 H \wedge g_{ec}^k h_{ec}^{v_2}\}$$

the standard protocol can be can be used since the two groups have the same order. Proving the knowledge of the respective discrete logarithms of the factors $kG$ and $v_1 H$ convinces the verifier that the discrete logarithm of $kG$ is indeed the value committed to in $BC_{G,H}(k)$. Given $kG$ it is easy to verify $r = \pi(kG) \bmod p$.

**Proposition 2.** *The deterministic variant of ECDSA is subliminal-free with proof.*

*Proof.* This is now immediately clear as the non-interactive zero-knowledge proof allows to check that the signature was indeed computed as the unique signature from the deterministic signing function.    □

*Size of the zero-knowledge proof.* To show that giving such a proof to the warden for each signature can be practical, we give a rough estimate of the space needed for the zero-knowledge proof.

For the choice of parameters we aim at achieving high security as it is used in electronic passports. For the bitlength of the parameters we assume $q_{ec}$ to be a 256 bit prime, $q_1$ a 356 bit prime and $p_1$ a 3,072 bit prime to keep the high security from ECDSA. For the commitments $p_0$ will then at least be a 3,685 bit prime. Similarly the output length of the hash function for the input of the pseudo random function should be 256 bits.

For simplicity we assume now a bit commitment to have 4 kbit and assume also the group sizes to be of 4 kbit. Proofs of knowledge of a committed value and equivalence of committed values take roughly 16 kbit. Proofs for addition and multiplication can be built from the basic proofs and will both take 64 kbit. We review now the steps of the algorithm:

1. One bit commitment and 256 multiplications sum up to $16,400$ kbit.
2. In this step we need to prove $\log_2(q_{ec}) + 1$ bit commitments and $\log_2(q_{ec}) + 1$ multiplication and additions. Together with proofs of equivalence and knowledge of commitments this sums up to roughly $37,000$ kbit.
3. The square-and-multiply algorithm takes $2 \cdot 3,072$ multiplications. The proof size of this step will sum up to $6,144$ kbit.
4. This step takes one bit commitment and two operations for 144 kbit. However, the range proof needs to be repeated and will sum up to $\approx 1,000$ kbit.
5. The new commitment and the equivalence will take 32 kbit.
6. The last step takes no essential space as just elliptic curve elements have to be given.

All together the size of the proof is less than $60,500$ kbit, i.e., less than 8 MB.

# 4  Conclusion

We have presented a new notion for signature schemes: being *subliminal-free with proof*. Besides relating this concept to subliminal-free, invariant and unique signatures, we showed that ECDSA can be used in a mode that is subliminal-free with proof and has reasonable proof sizes in a scenario with high security needs. It remains an open question if an operation mode of ECDSA allowing for unique signatures (without proof) can be found. Also, it seems interesting to explore possibilities of efficient adaptations of our approach to other signature schemes.

# References

[BCDvdG88]  Brickell, E.F., Chaum, D., Damgård, I.B., van de Graaf, J.: Gradual and verifiable release of a secret. In: Pomerance, C. (ed.) CRYPTO 1987. LNCS, vol. 293, pp. 156–166. Springer, Heidelberg (1988)

[BDI+99]  Burmester, M., Desmedt, Y., Itoh, T., Sakurai, K., Shizuya, H.: Divertible and Subliminal-Free Zero-Knowledge Proofs for Languages. Journal of Cryptology 12(3), 197–223 (1999)

[Bou00]  Boudot, F.: Efficient Proofs that a Committed Number Lies in an Interval. In: Preneel, B. (ed.) EUROCRYPT 2000. LNCS, vol. 1807, pp. 431–444. Springer, Heidelberg (2000)

[BS05]  Jens-Matthias, B., Steinwandt, R.: On Subliminal Channels in Deterministic Signature Schemes. In: Park, C., Chee, S. (eds.) ICISC 2004. LNCS, vol. 3506, pp. 182–194. Springer, Heidelberg (2005)

[BSMP91]  Blum, M., De Santis, A., Micali, S., Persiano, G.: Noninteractive Zero-Knowledge. SIAM Journal on Computing 20, 1084–1118 (1991)

[Bun05]  Bundesamt für Sicherheit in der Informationstechnik. Digitale Sicherheitsmerkmale im elektronischen Reisepass (2005) At the time of writing available at
http://www.bsi.de/fachthem/epass/Sicherheitsmerkmale.pdf

[CM99]  Camenisch, J., Michels, M.: Proving in Zero-Knowledge that a Number Is the Product of Two Safe Primes. In: Stern, J. (ed.) EUROCRYPT 1999. LNCS, vol. 1592, pp. 107–122. Springer, Heidelberg (1999)

[CW79]  Carter, L., Wegman, M.N.: Universal Classes of Hash Functions. Journal of Computer and System Sciences 18(2), 143–154 (1979)

[Des88a]  Desmedt, Y.: Abuses in Cryptography and How to Fight Them. In: Goldwasser, S. (ed.) CRYPTO 1988. LNCS, vol. 403, pp. 375–389. Springer, Heidelberg (1990)

[Des88b]  Desmedt, Y.: Subliminal-Free Authentication and Signature (Extended Abstract). In: Günther, C.G. (ed.) EUROCRYPT 1988. LNCS, vol. 330, pp. 23–33. Springer, Heidelberg (1988)

[Des96]  Desmedt, Y.: Simmons' Protocol is Not Free of Subliminal Channels. In: Proceedings 9th IEEE Computer Security Foundations Workshop, pp. 170–175. IEEE Computer Society Press, Los Alamitos, CA, USA (1996)

[DGB87]  Desmedt, Y., Goutier, C., Bengio, S.: Special Uses and Abuses of the Fiat-Shamir Passport Protocol. In: Pomerance, C. (ed.) CRYPTO 1987. LNCS, vol. 293, pp. 21–39. Springer, Heidelberg (1988)

[FO97]      Fujisaki, E., Okamoto, T.: Statistical Zero Knowledge Protocols to Prove Modular Polynomial Relations. In: Kaliski Jr., B.S. (ed.) CRYPTO 1997. LNCS, vol. 1294, pp. 16–30. Springer, Heidelberg (1997)

[GO93]      Goldwasser, S., Ostrovsky, R.: Invariant Signatures and Non-interactive Zero-Knowledge Proofs Are Equivalent. In: Brickell, E.F. (ed.) CRYPTO 1992. LNCS, vol. 740, Springer, Heidelberg (1993)

[Gol04]     Goldreich, O.: Foundations of Cryptography, Volume II. Cambridge University Press, Cambridge (2004)

[ILL89]     Impagliazzo, R., Levin, L.A., Luby, M.: Pseudo-random generation from one-way functions. In: Proceedings of the twenty-first annual ACM symposium on Theory of computing, pp. 12–24. ACM Press, New York, NY, USA (1989)

[ISO02]     ISO/IEC 15946-2: Information technology – Security techniques – Cryptographic techniques based on elliptic curves – Part 1: Digital Signatures (2002)

[IZ89]      Impagliazzo, R., Zuckerman, D.: How to recycle random bits. In: 30th Annual Symposium on Foundations of Computer Science, pp. 248–253. IEEE, New York (1989)

[Lys02]     Lysyanskaya, A.: Unique Signatures and Verifiable Random Functions from the DH-DDH Separation. In: Yung, M. (ed.) CRYPTO 2002. LNCS, vol. 2442, pp. 597–612. Springer, Heidelberg (2002)

[MRV99]     Micali, S., Rabin, M., Vadhan, S.: Verifiable Random Functions. In: Proceedings of the 40th Annual Symposium on the Foundations of Computer Science, pp. 120–130. IEEE, New York (1999)

[NR04]      Naor, M., Reingold, O.: Number-Theoretic Constructions of Efficient Pseudo-Random Functions. Journal of the ACM 51(2), 231–262 (2004)

[Ped92]     Pedersen, T.P.: Non-interactive and Information-Theoretic Secure Verifiable Secret Sharing. In: Feigenbaum, J. (ed.) CRYPTO 1991. LNCS, vol. 576, pp. 129–140. Springer, Heidelberg (1992)

[Sim84]     Simmons, G.J.: The Prisoners' Problem and the Subliminal Channel. In: Advances in Cryptology – CRYPTO '83, pp. 51–67. Plenum Press, New York and London (1984)

[Sim93]     Simmons, G.J.: An Introduction to the Mathematics of Trust in Security Protocols. In: Proceedings of the Computer Security Foundations Workshop VI, pp. 121–127. IEEE Computer Society Press, Los Alamitos, CA, USA (1993)

[Sim94]     Gustavus, J.: Subliminal Communication Is Easy Using the DSA. In: Helleseth, T. (ed.) EUROCRYPT 1993. LNCS, vol. 765, pp. 218–232. Springer, Heidelberg (1994)

[Sti02]     Stinson, D.R.: Universal hash families and the leftover hash lemma, and applications to cryptography and computing. Journal of Combinatorial Mathematics and Combinatorial Computing 42, 3–31 (2002)

[Vau03]     Vaudenay, S.: The Security of DSA and ECDSA. In: Desmedt, Y.G. (ed.) PKC 2003. LNCS, vol. 2567, pp. 309–323. Springer, Heidelberg (2002)

[YY04]      Young, A., Yung, M.: Malicious Cryptography: Exposing Cryptovirology. Wiley Publishing (2004)

# Author Index

# Lecture Notes in Computer Science

Sublibrary 4: Security and Cryptology

Vol. 4107: G. Di Crescenzo, A. Rubin (Eds.), Financial Cryptography and Data Security. XI, 327 pages. 2006.

Vol. 4083: S. Fischer-Hübner, S. Furnell, C. Lambrinoudakis (Eds.), Trust and Privacy in Digital Business. XIII, 243 pages. 2006.

Vol. 4064: R. Büschkes, P. Laskov (Eds.), Detection of Intrusions and Malware & Vulnerability Assessment. X, 195 pages. 2006.

Vol. 4058: L.M. Batten, R. Safavi-Naini (Eds.), Information Security and Privacy. XII, 446 pages. 2006.

Vol. 4047: M.J.B. Robshaw (Ed.), Fast Software Encryption. XI, 434 pages. 2006.

Vol. 4043: A.S. Atzeni, A. Lioy (Eds.), Public Key Infrastructure. XI, 261 pages. 2006.

Vol. 4004: S. Vaudenay (Ed.), Advances in Cryptology - EUROCRYPT 2006. XIV, 613 pages. 2006.

Vol. 3995: G. Müller (Ed.), Emerging Trends in Information and Communication Security. XX, 524 pages. 2006.

Vol. 3989: J. Zhou, M. Yung, F. Bao (Eds.), Applied Cryptography and Network Security. XIV, 488 pages. 2006.

Vol. 3969: Ø. Ytrehus (Ed.), Coding and Cryptography. XI, 443 pages. 2006.

Vol. 3958: M. Yung, Y. Dodis, A. Kiayias, T.G. Malkin (Eds.), Public Key Cryptography - PKC 2006. XIV, 543 pages. 2006.

Vol. 3957: B. Christianson, B. Crispo, J.A. Malcolm, M. Roe (Eds.), Security Protocols. IX, 325 pages. 2006.

Vol. 3956: G. Barthe, B. Grégoire, M. Huisman, J.-L. Lanet (Eds.), Construction and Analysis of Safe, Secure, and Interoperable Smart Devices. IX, 175 pages. 2006.

Vol. 3935: D.H. Won, S. Kim (Eds.), Information Security and Cryptology - ICISC 2005. XIV, 458 pages. 2006.

Vol. 3934: J.A. Clark, R.F. Paige, F.A.C. Polack, P.J. Brooke (Eds.), Security in Pervasive Computing. X, 243 pages. 2006.

Vol. 3928: J. Domingo-Ferrer, J. Posegga, D. Schreckling (Eds.), Smart Card Research and Advanced Applications. XI, 359 pages. 2006.

Vol. 3919: R. Safavi-Naini, M. Yung (Eds.), Digital Rights Management. XI, 357 pages. 2006.

Vol. 3903: K. Chen, R. Deng, X. Lai, J. Zhou (Eds.), Information Security Practice and Experience. XIV, 392 pages. 2006.

Vol. 3897: B. Preneel, S. Tavares (Eds.), Selected Areas in Cryptography. XI, 371 pages. 2006.

Vol. 3876: S. Halevi, T. Rabin (Eds.), Theory of Cryptography. XI, 617 pages. 2006.

Vol. 3866: T. Dimitrakos, F. Martinelli, P.Y A Ryan, S. Schneider (Eds.), Formal Aspects in Security and Trust. X, 259 pages. 2006.

Vol. 3860: D. Pointcheval (Ed.), Topics in Cryptology – CT-RSA 2006. XI, 365 pages. 2006.

Vol. 3858: A. Valdes, D. Zamboni (Eds.), Recent Advances in Intrusion Detection. X, 351 pages. 2006.

Vol. 3856: G. Danezis, D. Martin (Eds.), Privacy Enhancing Technologies. VIII, 273 pages. 2006.

Vol. 3786: J.-S. Song, T. Kwon, M. Yung (Eds.), Information Security Applications. XI, 378 pages. 2006.

Vol. 3108: H. Wang, J. Pieprzyk, V. Varadharajan (Eds.), Information Security and Privacy. XII, 494 pages. 2004.

Vol. 2951: M. Naor (Ed.), Theory of Cryptography. XI, 523 pages. 2004.

Vol. 2742: R.N. Wright (Ed.), Financial Cryptography. VIII, 321 pages. 2003.